Fodor's

MOROCCO

5th Edition

Fodor's Travel Publications New York, Toronto, London, Sydney, Auckland
www.fodors.com

FODOR'S MOROCCO

Editor: Douglas Stallings

Editorial Contributors: Rachel Blech, Patricia Gorman, Simona Schneider, Ian Thomas, Victoria Tang

Production Editor: Carolyn Roth
Maps & Illustrations: David Lindroth, Mark Stroud, *cartographers;* Bob Blake, Rebecca Baer, *map editors;* William Wu, *information graphics*
Design: Fabrizio La Rocca, *creative director*; Guido Caroti, *art director*; Tina Malaney, Nora Rosansky, Chie Ushio, *designers*; Melanie Marin, *associate director of photography*
Cover Photo: (Hand painted ceramic at Serghini-Poterie de Fes, Aïn Nokbi, outside Fez) J.D. Dallet/age fotostock
Production Manager: Angela McLean

COPYRIGHT

5th Edition

ISBN 978–0–307–92832–0

ISSN 1527–4829

SPECIAL SALES

This book is available at special discounts for bulk purchases for sales promotions or premiums. Special editions, including personalized covers, excerpts of existing books, and corporate imprints, can be created in large quantities for special needs. For more information, write to Special Markets/Premium Sales, 1745 Broadway, MD 3-1, New York, NY 10019, or e-mail specialmarkets@randomhouse.com.

AN IMPORTANT TIP & AN INVITATION

Although all prices, opening times, and other details in this book are based on information supplied to us at press time, changes occur all the time in the travel world, and Fodor's cannot accept responsibility for facts that become outdated or for inadvertent errors or omissions. So **always confirm information when it matters,** especially if you're making a detour to visit a specific place. Your experiences—positive and negative—matter to us. If we have missed or misstated something, **please write to us.** Share your opinion instantly through our online feedback center at fodors.com/contact-us.

PRINTED IN COLOMBIA

10 9 8 7 6 5 4 3 2 1

CONTENTS

MAPS

ABOUT THIS BOOK

Our Ratings

At Fodor's, we spend considerable time choosing the best places in a destination so you don't have to. By default, anything we recommend in this book is worth visiting. But some sights, properties, and experiences are so great that we've recognized them with additional accolades. Orange **Fodor's Choice** stars indicate our top recommendations; black stars highlight places we deem **Highly Recommended;** and **Best Bets** call attention to top properties in various categories. Disagree with any of our choices? Care to nominate a new place? Visit our feedback center at *www.fodors.com/feedback.*

Hotels

Hotels have private bath, phone, TV, and air-conditioning, and do not offer meals unless we specify that in the review. We always list facilities but not whether you'll be charged an extra fee to use them.

For expanded hotel reviews, visit **Fodors.com**

Restaurants

Unless we state otherwise, restaurants are open for lunch and dinner daily. We mention dress only when there's a specific requirement and reservations only when they're essential or not accepted—it's always best to book ahead.

Credit Cards

We assume that restaurants and hotels accept credit cards. If not, we'll note it in the review.

Budget Well

Hotel and restaurant price categories from **¢** to **$$$$** are defined in the opening pages of the respective chapters. For attractions, we always give standard adult admission fees; reductions are usually available for children, students, and senior citizens.

Listings

- ★ Fodor's Choice
- ★ Highly recommended
- ✉ Physical address
- Directions or Map coordinates
- Mailing address
- ☎ Telephone
- Fax
- On the Web
- E-mail
- Admission fee
- Open/closed times
- Metro stations
- No credit cards

Hotels & Restaurants

- Hotel
- Number of rooms
- Facilities
- Meal plans
- ✕ Restaurant
- Reservations
- Dress code
- Smoking

Outdoors

- Golf
- Camping

Other

- Family-friendly
- ⇨ See also
- Branch address
- Take note

Experience Morocco

WHAT'S WHERE

Numbers refer to chapters.

2 Tangier and the Mediterranean. Many of Morocco's most dramatic social and economic contrasts are immediately and painfully evident in Tangier and vicinity. Both the mountain stronghold at Chefchaouen and the coastal city of Tetouan are also worth visiting.

3 Northern Atlantic Coast. Morocco's economic capital, Casablanca, and political capital, Rabat, are the country's most Europeanized cities. Meanwhile, the Atlantic beaches offer miles and miles of wild surf, sand, and sea.

4 Fez and the Middle Atlas. The alternating Arab-Islamic and Berber chapters in Morocco's history are most evident in the imperial cities of Fez and Meknès. Side trips to the Roman ruins at Volubilis and the holy town of Moulay Idriss are also musts, while the Middle Atlas is an underrated mountain range of great natural beauty.

5 Marrakesh. Marrakesh is the turning point between Morocco's north and south, Arab and Berber, big city and small town. If you can see only one city in Morocco, make it Marrakesh.

6 The High Atlas. Although parts of the High Atlas can be mobbed with hikers at certain

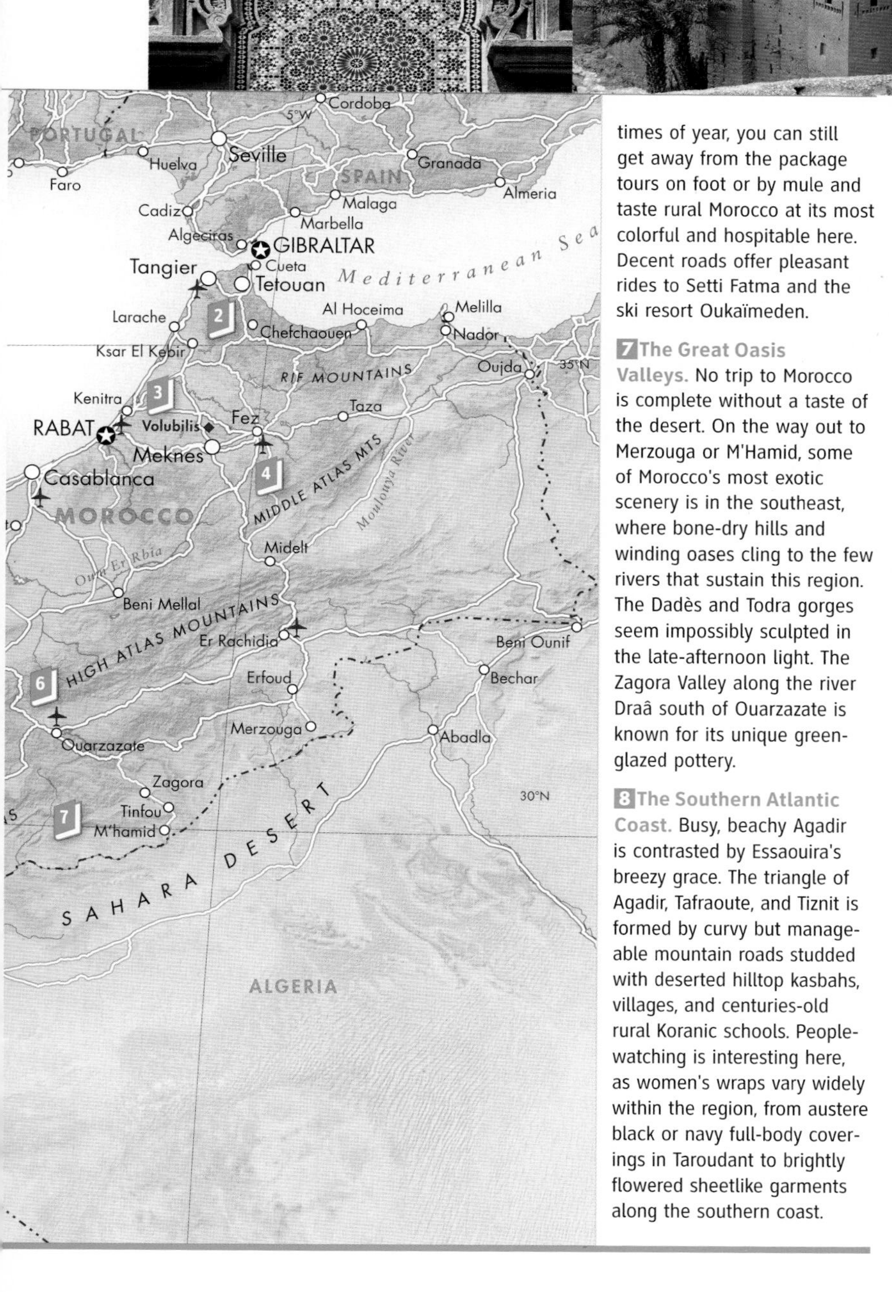

times of year, you can still get away from the package tours on foot or by mule and taste rural Morocco at its most colorful and hospitable here. Decent roads offer pleasant rides to Setti Fatma and the ski resort Oukaïmeden.

7 The Great Oasis Valleys. No trip to Morocco is complete without a taste of the desert. On the way out to Merzouga or M'Hamid, some of Morocco's most exotic scenery is in the southeast, where bone-dry hills and winding oases cling to the few rivers that sustain this region. The Dadès and Todra gorges seem impossibly sculpted in the late-afternoon light. The Zagora Valley along the river Draâ south of Ouarzazate is known for its unique green-glazed pottery.

8 The Southern Atlantic Coast. Busy, beachy Agadir is contrasted by Essaouira's breezy grace. The triangle of Agadir, Tafraoute, and Tiznit is formed by curvy but manageable mountain roads studded with deserted hilltop kasbahs, villages, and centuries-old rural Koranic schools. People-watching is interesting here, as women's wraps vary widely within the region, from austere black or navy full-body coverings in Taroudant to brightly flowered sheetlike garments along the southern coast.

QUINTESSENTIAL MOROCCO

Mint Tea

When in Morocco, it's a good idea to make friends with mint tea. This sweet and aromatic brew is the national drink, offered for, with, and following breakfast, lunch, and dinner. It's served as an icebreaker for anything from rug selling in the Meknès souk to matchmaking at the Imilchil marriage market. Dubbed "Moroccan (or Berber) whiskey," *thé à la menthe* is Chinese green tea brewed with a handful of mint leaves and liberally loaded up with sugar. Introduced to Morocco only in the mid-19th century when blockaded British merchants unloaded ample quantities of tea at major ports, the tradition has now become such a symbol of Moroccan hospitality that not drinking three small glasses of tea when your host or business contact offers it to you is nearly a declaration of hostilities. Generally ordered by the pot and poured from on high in order to release the aromas and aerate the beverage, mint tea is recommended in cold weather or in sweltering heat as a tonic, a mild stimulant, and a digestive.

Music

Music is integral to daily and ritual life in Morocco, both for enjoyment and as a form of social commentary. It emanates from homes, stores, markets, and public squares everywhere you go. Joujouka music is perhaps the best known, but every region has its own distinct sound. In the Rif you'll hear men singing poetry accompanied by guitar and high-pitched women's choruses; in Casablanca, *rai* (opinion) music, born of social protest, keeps young men company on the streets; cobblers in the Meknès medina may work to the sounds of violin-based Andalusian classical music or the more-folksy Arabic *melhoun*, sung poetry; and you know you've reached the south when you hear the banjo of the roving storytelling *rawais* in Marrakesh. Gnaoua music

For a sense of Moroccan culture, a good start would be to embrace some of the ongoing rituals of daily life. These are a few highlights—customs and sites you can experience with relative ease.

is best known for its use in trance rituals, but it has become popular street entertainment; the performer's brass *qaraqa* hand cymbals and cowrie shell–adorned hat betray the music's sub-Saharan origins. Seek out live music at public squares such as Marrakesh's Djemaâ el-Fna, or attend a festival, a regional *moussem* (pilgrimage festival), or even a rural market to see the performances locals enjoy.

Markets

Moroccan markets, souks, and bazaars buzz with life. Every town and city in Morocco revolves, in one way or another, around its market, and beginning your exploration at the hub of urban life is one of the best ways to start a crash course in wherever you find yourself. The chromatically riotous displays of fruit and vegetables are eye-bogglingly rich and as geometrically complex as the most intricate aspects of Islamic architecture and design. Fez el-Bali is virtually all market, with the exception of the craftsmen and artisans preparing their wares for market. Fez's henna souk is famous for its intimate ambience and archaic elegance. Marrakesh's central market stretching out behind Djemaâ el-Fna square could take a lifetime to explore. The Meknès market next to Place el-Hedim is smaller but loaded with everything from sturdy earthenware tagines to a wide selection of Moroccan spices and fish fresh from the Atlantic. Casablanca's Marché Central in the heart of the city is one of the most picturesque and least Europeanized parts of an otherwise unremarkable urban sprawl. Essaouira's crafts and produce market shares this light and cheerful town's easygoing atmosphere, and shopping there becomes a true pleasure rather than a grim battle over haggling leverage.

MOROCCO TOP ATTRACTIONS

Ben Youssef Medersa, Marrakesh

(A) The Saadian sultan Abdallah el-Ghallib rebuilt this 9th-century madrassa as the largest Koranic school to rival Fassi imams' madrassa in Fez. The visual impact is evident in the expansive main courtyard and exquisite tile mosaics. It's one of the best-preserved historic sites in Marrakesh.

Cascades d'Ouzoud, Central High Atlas Mountains

(B) Some 40 miles southwest of Bin el-Ouidane, the majestic succession of waterfalls plunging into the canyon of Wadi el-Abid 330 feet below is a natural wonder not to be missed.

Djemaâ el-Fna and Souks, Marrakesh

Haggle for handmade rugs, leather, silver, and pottery still crafted in ancient artisanal workshops. Feast on succulent lamb kebabs, chicken tagine, pigeon pastilla, and vegetable couscous. Sip mint tea. Wend your way through the narrow labyrinth of medina passages and squares. This must-do experience will thrill, entertain, and sometimes overwhelm even the most seasoned traveler.

Erg Chebbi and Erg Chigaga Sand Dunes, near Merzouga

(C) For a once-in-a-lifetime experience, escape into the world of the Berber nomads and explore these windswept Saharan dunes stretching 19 miles and rising to a maximum height of 820 feet.

Essaouira, the Fortified Coastal Town

(D) The rough Atlantic waves pounding against the rocky shoreline add drama to this romantic fortressed fishing village that has been designated a World Heritage Site. Stroll along the cannon-lined *sqalas* (sea bastions) toward the ramparts that lead to the picturesque port and medina.

Fez el-Bali (Old City), Fez

(E) Step into a time warp as you enter this 9th-century medina, the world's most active medieval city. With culturally important fondouks, riads, medersas, mosques, and palaces dating back 1,000 years, it's no surprise the Fez el-Bali with its 9,500 alleyways remains a UNESCO World Heritage Site.

Hassan II Mosque, Casablanca

(F) One of the largest mosques in the world covers almost a million square feet and can hold some 25,000 people. Two-thirds of the building is built over the sea, where the minaret's light beacon shines 20 miles towards Mecca. It ranks as the country's most exceptional representation of Moroccan artistry for its ornate carved stucco, *zellij* tilework (a type of mosaic), and onyx and marble details.

Koutoubia Minaret, Marrakesh

(G) Rising 300 feet, the iconic carved stone-and-green-tile tower is the architectural centerpiece of the Almohad dynasty. One of the largest mosques of the Western Muslim world, the Koutoubia is off-limits to non-Muslims; its minaret, however, is used by everyone as the orientation point by which other city sites are located and captures the collective ear when the imam delivers the daily call to prayer.

Valley of the Kasbahs, near Ouarzazate

(H) Secret gorges. Breathtaking canyons. Spectacular rock formations. In the High Atlas, the stunning Dades Valley is a mystical region dotted with palm trees and sandstone kasbahs that rise from the barren landscape. To start the magical journey, head to the Aït Ben Haddou, a World Heritage Site featured in blockbuster films and only a short excursion from the oasis town of Ouarzazate.

TOP EXPERIENCES

Trek the mountains of the High Atlas.

For spectacular vistas and fresh air, the High Atlas is a perfect getaway from the hustle and bustle of urban Morocco. Hiking North Africa's tallest peak, Djebel Toubkal, rising to nearly 14,000 feet, is only a two-day climb best done in late summer. Guides can lead amateur hikers through rural Berber villages and rocky paths less strenuous but equally rewarding. Head to the Ourika Valley for a variety of outdoor adventure—it's a justifiably popular region to hang-glide, ski, or ride mules to hidden waterfalls and tranquil hilltop gardens.

Bargain for babouches in the leather tanneries of Fez.

With the stench of animal skins curing in the hot sun and sounds of workmen laboring in the rainbow of dye vats beneath rows of open terraces, there is no better place to contribute to the artisanal cooperatives if you want to buy beautifully handmade leather house slippers, bags, belts, jackets, and poufs. Negotiating in one of the many shops claiming to be the best producer of leather goods guarantees a memorable experience as you haggle dirhams while sniffing a complimentary bunch of mint leaves to offset the strong acidic smell of natural curing ingredients in the medina air.

Dine on kebabs and harira from a street-market grill.

The intoxicating aromas of freshly grilled skewers of meat and simmering spicy soup in *qissarias* (open markets) and roadside stands tantalize even the most cautious traveler. Follow the rising smoke from burners and indulge in local cuisine ranging from beef brochettes and merguez sausages to fried calamari and whole fish caught fresh from the Atlantic and seared to perfection. For the more adventurous gourmand, snail soup and sheep's brains can be sampled. Sop it all up with freshly baked *kesra* (flatbread).

People-watch on the Djemaâ el-Fna in Marrakesh.

From morning to night, the historic square at the center of the medina guarantees to entertain and provide a glimpse into local living and the unusual. Surrounded by colorful dried fruit and juice carts scattered near terraced cafés and rows of shops brimming with activity, the carnival-like atmosphere of snake charmers, fortunetellers, monkey handlers, musicians, and costumed water sellers adds to the exotic flavor of what was once the principal meeting point for tradesmen and regional farmers, as well as gruesome site for public criminal beheadings in ancient times.

Appreciate Koranic scholarship in a historic medersa.

A quiet spot in front of the central marble ablutions pool is the perfect place to view masterpieces of Islamic architecture. Look for intricate zellij tilework along arched corridors, ornate wood carvings in domed ceilings, sculpted stone friezes bearing symbolic Arabic calligraphy, and beautifully detailed stained-glass windows in prayer halls and reflection rooms of these culturally rich buildings.

Savor the scents and sights of a food souk.

Weave through the labyrinth of open and covered streets to discover a feast for the senses. The indoor food souk of Meknès is a must. Along coastal towns, discover fish markets by the harbor. In rural villages, look for carts peddling freshly picked apricots and dates. From pyramids of marinated olives and preserved lemons to

bulging sacks of finely milled grains and multicolored spices and nuts, the food souks reflect the wide range of aromatic ingredients used in traditional Moroccan cuisine. Follow your nose to sweet rosewater and honey-laden pastries flavored with cinnamon, saffron, and almonds.

Listen and learn at a local festival.

One of the best ways to experience the rich heritage is to participate in a local event. Head to Kelaa-des-Mgouna in the Dadès Valley in May; home to the country's largest rose water distillery plant, this small oasis village celebrates the flower harvest each spring. In early June, enjoy the chants, lyricism, and intellectual fervor of international musicians, Sufi scholars, and social activists at the World Sacred Music Festival in Fez. In late June, the traditions of Gnaoua music, a blend of African, Berber and African song and dance, are celebrated in the seaside resort village of Essaouira. Experience the Imilchil Berber marriage feast in autumn. In December, the Marrakech International Film Festival is the hottest spot for international celebrity sightings. The all-important Eid al-Fitr (Feast of the Fast Breaking) best showcases Moroccan tradition with three days of joyous celebration at the end of Ramadan.

Pamper yourself in a hammam.

Getting scrubbed and steamed at a local hammam can do wonders for the weary. Whether you choose a communal public bath or private room in an upscale riad, this traditional therapy of brisk exfoliation and bathing using natural cleansers has promoted physical and mental hygiene and restoration for centuries. Public hammams are clean and inexpensive. Le Royal Mansour and the Angasa Spa in Marrakesh are exceptionally luxurious spots to experience this unique cultural ritual.

Relax in a riad.

Forgo the standard setting of a modern hotel chain, and opt for a room with character in the heart of the medina. Former private homes, multistoried riads have been restored to their original beauty and authenticity, furnished with antiques and local crafts, and outfitted with latest technology for those who want to stay connected. Many are family owned and operated, providing guests with personalized service, generous breakfasts, and spacious accommodations overlooking lush inner courtyard gardens. More luxurious riads have full-scale spas, panoramic terrace bars, swimming pools, and world-class restaurants.

Soothe the eyes in the blue-washed town of Chefchaouen.

Founded in the 15th century by Spanish exiles, the village of Chefchaouen tucked in the foothills of the Rif Mountains, is widely considered to be one of Morocco's most picturesque places. Relax beneath verdant shade trees on the cobblestoned Plaza Uta el-Hamman. Wander the steep Andalusian passageways, where buildings bathed in cobalt and indigo hues blend with terracotta-tiled roofs, pink-scarved women, violet blossoms, and ochre-and-poppy red wool carpets to create an incredibly vibrant canvas of color.

Ride a camel to the dunes of the Sahara.

For an unforgettable adventure, mount a dromedary to experience the undulating orange dunes and abandoned kasbahs of the desert, a magical region immortalized in film and fiction. Select an overnight tour to stay in a Bedouin tent in the Erg Chebbi or Erg Chigaga desert wilderness.

IF YOU LIKE

Beaches

With coasts on both the Mediterranean Sea and the Atlantic Ocean, Morocco has hundreds of miles of sandy beaches, many of them little developed. Dangerous currents and national-park preservation explain why some beaches are unused, but gems abound. Surfing the Atlantic beaches has become popular, and surfing schools are increasingly easy to find along the beaches between Rabat and Essaouira. The port towns of Essaouira, Sidi Ifni, Asilah, and Al Hoceima make peaceful, low-key coastal getaways. Those familiar with Tunisia's topless beaches may be struck by the modesty that reigns on Moroccan public beaches, where picnicking local families spend their holidays.

- **Agadir.** Agadir is a major destination for the high-density European package-tour tanning crowd. For families looking for safe beaches and bathing with plenty of activities for the young, this is the spot.

- **Oualidia.** With a first-class beach often compared to those of the French Riviera, and a surfing and windsurfing scene as hot as any in Europe, this is an important beach destination just 90 minutes southeast of Casablanca.

- **Plage Robinson.** Just west of Tangier, this much-visited beach offers sun and sand, the Caves of Hercules where mythology has Hercules resting up after separating Africa from Europe, and a lively café and restaurant scene.

- **Sidi Ifni and Essaouira.** Well off the beaten beach paths, Sidi Ifni and Essaouira offer, respectively, burgundy rock formations and some of the strongest windsurfing breezes in all of Africa.

People-Watching

Morocco is a visual spectacle in every sense, and the human fauna are beyond a doubt the runaway stars of the show. French painters such as Delacroix and Matisse and the great Spanish colorist Marià Fortuny all found the souks, fondouks, and street scenes of Marrakesh, Fez, and Tangier irresistible. Today's visitors to this eye-popping North African brouhaha are well advised to simply pull up a chair and take in some of the most exotic natural street theater in the world.

- **Djemaâ el-Fna, Marrakesh.** This cacophonous market square is unlike anything else on earth. Settle into a rooftop café for an unobstructed view of the acrobats, storytellers, musicians, dancers, fortune-tellers, juice carts, and general organized chaos.

- **Fez el-Bali.** The to-and-fro pulsing of Fez's medina makes it the perfect place to watch Moroccans doing what Moroccans do. Great spots include the cafés around Bab Boujeloud and Bab Fteuh, though the latter is much less amenable to travelers.

- **Place Moulay Hassan, Essaouira.** Locals, temporary locals, and fishermen are all welcome to linger in this laid-back plaza, watching the world go by from an outdoor café. Try a cup of *louiza*—warm milk with fresh verbena leaves.

- **Grand Socco, Tangier.** Every conceivable manifestation of Old Testament–looking humanity seems to have found its way to Tangier's Grand Socco from the Rif Mountains and the interior. A stroll down Rue de la Liberté into the food souk will put you in the middle of it all.

The Outdoors

A range of spectacular landscapes has made Morocco a major destination for rugged outdoor sporting challenges and adventure travel. Much of Morocco's natural beauty lies in its mountains, where the famous Berber hospitality can make hiking an unforgettable experience. You can arrange most outdoor excursions yourself or with the help of tourist offices and hotels in the larger cities. Rock climbing is possible in the Todra and Dadès gorges and the mountains outside Chefchaouen. Oukaïmeden has facilities for skiing, and a few other long, liftless runs await the more athletic. Golf is available in Rabat, Casablanca, Marrakesh, and Agadir. Several High Atlas rivers are suitable for fishing.

■ **High Atlas.** People come from around the world to trek in these mountains, drawn by the rugged scenery, bracing air, and rural Berber (Imazighen) culture. Hiking is easily combined with mule riding, trout fishing, and vertiginous alpine drives.

■ **Merzouga dunes.** Southeast of Erfoud, beyond Morocco's great oasis valleys, these waves of sand mark the beginning of the Sahara. Brilliantly orange in the late-afternoon sun, they can be gloriously desolate at sunrise.

■ **Palm groves and villages, Tafraoute.** A striking tropical contrast to the barren Anti-Atlas Mountains and the agricultural plains farther north, the oases are scattered with massive, pink cement houses built by wealthy urban merchants native to this area.

Architecture

Refined Islamic architecture graces the imperial cities of Fez, Meknès, Marrakesh, and Rabat. Mosques and *medersas* (schools of Koranic studies) dating from the Middle Ages, as well as 19th-century palaces, are decorated with colorful geometric tiles, bands of Koranic verses in marble or plaster, stalactite crevices, and carved wooden ceilings. The *mellahs* built by Morocco's Jews with glassed-in balconies contrast with the Islamic emphasis on turning inward. French colonial architecture prevails in the Art Deco and neo-Mauresque streets of Casablanca's Quartier des Habous. Outside these strongholds of Arab influence are the *pisé* (rammed earth) kasbahs in the Ouarzazate–Er-Rachidia region, where structures built with local mud and clay range from deep pink to burgundy to shades of brown.

■ **Aït-Benhaddou, near Ouarzazate.** Strewn across a hillside, the red-pisé towers of this village fortress resemble a melting sand castle. Crenellated and topped with blocky towers, it's one of the most sumptuous sights in the Atlas Mountains.

■ **La Bahia Palace, Marrakesh.** Built as a harem's residence, and interspersed with cypress-filled courtyards, La Bahia has the key Moroccan architectural elements—light, symmetry, decoration, and water.

■ **Bou Inania medersa, Fez.** The most celebrated of the Kairaouine University's 14th-century residential colleges, Bou Inania has a roof of green tile, a ceiling of carved cedar, stalactites of white marble, and ribbons of Arabic inscription.

FLAVORS OF MOROCCO

Morocco's first inhabitants, the Berbers, left their mark on the country's cuisine with staple dishes like tagines and couscous. New spices, nuts, dried fruits, and the common combination of sweet and sour tastes (such as a lamb tagine containing prunes), arrived with the Arab invasion. Olives and citrus fruits can be traced to the Moors. The Ottoman Empire can be thanked for introducing barbecue (kebabs) to Morocco. The French, although their colonization period was quite short, left behind a tradition of cafés, pastries, and wine.

Drinks

Mint tea is at the very heart of not only Moroccan cuisine but of the culture itself. Whether in cosmopolitan Casablanca or a rural Berber village in the Atlas Mountains, there is one universal truth: *até* will be served. Recipes vary from region to region—and even from family to family—but all contain a mix of green tea, fresh mint leaves, and sugar. **Coffee** is served black (*café noir*), with a little milk (*café crème*), or half milk/half coffee (*nuss nuss* in the Morocan dialect). **Orange juice,** freshly squeezed, is abundantly available in cafés and restaurants.

Bread

Bread is truly the cornerstone of a traditional Moroccan meal, eaten at every meal (except with couscous) and also as a snack with mint tea. Due to bread's cultural and religious significance, it is never thrown away. Families put their leftover bread aside, either for the poor or to feed their animals.

Bread in Morocco comes in many shapes and sizes. The most common is a simple round, somewhat thick, white bread. Depending on the region, this same bread can be found in a whole-wheat form. In the countryside, breads vary from village to village. *Batbout,* a soft, pitalike bread is often sold in bakeries stuffed with *kefta* (seasoned ground meat) and hard-boiled egg slices. *Hacha,* another type, is a pan-fried semolina bread.

Seasonings

Several notable spices and herbs are common in Moroccan cuisine: cumin, paprika, garlic, salt, pepper, ginger, cinnamon, coriander, saffron, turmeric, sesame seeds, fresh parsley, cilantro, *harissa* (red chili pepper and garlic paste), olive oil, and olives. Preserved lemons are another key ingredient in many tagine recipes and some salads.

Breakfast

Breakfast in Morocco means mint tea or coffee, freshly squeezed orange juice, bread (often topped with olive oil and/or honey), and omelets with *khlea* (preserved dried meat). Two delightful Moroccan breakfast treats are *raif* (also call *msemn* in certain regions), a mix between a crepe and flat pastry, made with intricately layered dough, which is then fried; and *baghir,* a pancakelike delicacy that is not flipped and has many tiny bubbles on the top side, due to the yeast. Both can be topped with honey or jam.

Moroccan Salads

Moroccan salads may be either raw or cooked. The most typical raw Moroccan salad (often called *salade marocaine*) is made of finely diced tomatoes, onions, garlic, parsley, and salt and then topped with olive oil. Cooked salads, such as *zaalouk* and *bakoula* combine different vegetables and spices, all cooked together and served either cold or hot.

Tagines

A tagine is both the name for the stew served in most Moroccan homes for lunch and dinner and the name of the traditional clay pot with a tall, cone-shaped lid in which it is generally cooked. Moroccan tagines use chicken, beef, or lamb as the base along with a variety of other ingredients. Vegetables can include carrots, peas, green beans, along with chickpeas, olives, apricots, prunes, and nuts. Typical tagines include chicken and preserved lemon; lentils with meat and prunes; chicken and almonds; and kefta and egg.

Couscous

Couscous is probably the most famous Moroccan dish, combining tiny little balls of steamed wheat pasta with a meat and vegetable stew that is poured on top. The meat base for the stew can be chicken, beef, or lamb and the vegetables usually include a combination of turnip, carrot, sweet potato, pumpkin, and zucchini with chickpeas and raisins sprinkled throughout. Couscous is typically a Friday lunch meal but can be served at other occasions as well.

Barbecue

In Morocco, eating establishments can basically be divided into two categories: the typical sit-down restaurant and what appears at first glance to be a questionable, seedy grill shop. Don't dismiss the grill option out of hand—they usually offer tasty, high-quality meat, at reasonable prices. Customers either buy their meat on premises or at a butcher shop next door. A nominal fee will be charged by the grill shop for grilling the meat. The shop also typically offers a menu with salads, grilled tomatoes and onions, french fries, and beverages to go along with the kabobs.

Pastilla

Pastilla is an elaborate meat pie combining sweet and salty flavors. Traditionally filled with pigeon, it is often prepared with shredded chicken. The meat is slow-cooked with spices and then combined with crisp, thin layers of a phyllolike dough; the mixture includes cinnamon and ground almonds. Pastilla is reserved for special occasions due to the complexity of its preparation. It can also be pre-ordered in some pastry shops.

Vegetarians

Since meat is expensive and considered a luxury for many Moroccans, the idea of vegetarianism is foreign to the culture. Vegetarians, when eating out, should hesitate when ordering a meatless tagine, since in all likelihood the stock was prepared with meat. Salads, breads, cheeses, and eggs offer more reliable alternatives.

Dessert

After a meal, Moroccan desserts are often limited to fresh seasonal fruit. Many types of Moroccan pastries and cookies exist, almost always made with almond paste. These pastries are often reserved for special occasions or are served to guests with afternoon tea. One common pastry is *kaab el-ghzal* ("gazelle's horns"), which is filled with almond paste and topped with sugar.

Prohibited Items

Both pork and alcohol are forbidden by Islam. Pork is difficult to find in the country except in larger cities with upscale markets and hotels catering to foreigners. However, alcohol is drunk (discreetly) by men all over the country and sold openly in hotels catering to foreigners. Both beer and wine are produced domestically.

KIDS AND FAMILIES

Traveling in Morocco with children is really great fun—especially since Moroccans adore kids—so you will find that the locals warm to you and greet you with more enthusiasm than the average tourist. However, at the same time you can expect a few practical challenges along the way.

Choosing a Place to Stay

Choosing the right place depends largely on the age of your brood, the type of holiday you want, the regions you wish to visit, and your budget.

For a beach-based holiday with on-site kid's activities, then a modern resort destination like Agadir is ideal. Here there is **Club Med** or **ClubHotel Riu Tikida Dunas**. Further up the coast, the beach at Essaouira offers lots of water sports, and **Sofitel** has a private beach and a pool. There is a pretty coastal lagoon resort at Oualidia too—popular with Moroccan vacationers—and hotel **La Sultana Oualidia** is luxurious.

For rural-based activity holidays and trekking, most places are fairly simple mountain *gites* (self-catering apartments or homes), *auberges* (hostels), and *maisons d'hôtes* (essentially bed-and-breakfasts based in private homes). For top-notch deluxe accommodation accessible by road try **Kasbah Tamadot** in Asni near Mt. Toubkal National Park, or **La Pause Marrakech**, a deluxe desert-style camp near Marrakesh with outdoor activities including donkey and camel rides. The **Xaluca** group of hotels also have family-friendly five-star hotels convenient for hiking trips to the Dadès Gorge and for trips to the Sahara desert in Erfoud and Merzouga.

Cities such as Fez, Meknès, and Marrakesh have the widest variety of accommodations. Although a traditional Moroccan riad or riad-style boutique hotel offers atmosphere in the old medinas, it may be a less attractive option for families with younger kids. You may prefer a more modern hotel, but realize that not all hotels have elevators, even newer ones. If you don't fancy a hotel in the new town and a riad doesn't suit you, then consider renting a villa or apartment, some of which can provide maid, cook, and babysitting services.

Top Experiences for Families

Morocco does not have many ready-made attractions such as zoos and theme parks, but if you like spectacular natural beauty, then your family will be well served.

Sahara Desert. You can see the desert by foot, by camel, or by four-wheel-drive vehicle; you can also crest the dunes on a camel for only an hour, or take a day trek through an oasis. You can also pack off for several days deep into the Sahara with a nomad guide. Visit Erg Chebbi or Erg Chegaga to climb the highest sand dunes in Morocco, and then glide down on a sand-board. Many hotels have their own desert camps, and there are countless agencies in Marrakesh, Ouarzazate, Zagora, Merzouga, and M'Hamid who can fix you up.

Water Sports and Beaches. Agadir has a large concentration of all-inclusive resorts, though few people would go all the way to Morocco for a beach vacation. Families with older children and teenagers should check out the coast between Sidi Ifni and Essaouira for some of the best spots for **kite-surfing, windsurfing,** and **surf schools.** In Marrakesh, **Oasiria** offers two pools and waterslides, gardens and restaurant for hungry kids and parents.

Mountain Trips. Mule trekking or hiking in the **High Atlas Mountains** near Mt. Toubkal is easily achievable for younger children, while toddlers can hop up in front of mom

or dad on a mule. Families with younger kids can stay in one place and take day hikes; if you have older children, you can travel with a guide, staying in simple mountain gites as you pass through neighboring valleys or even attempt the summit. In the foothills of the High Atlas Mountains near Marrakesh, **Terres d'Amanar** is an outdoor activity center offering archery, climbing, zip lines, and crafts workshops. Near the **Dadès Gorge,** with the help of a local guide, you can visit nomad families living in caves and old salt mines.

Film Studios. The **Atlas Film Studios** in Ouarzazate makes for an interesting visit if you're heading south. You can walk through some of the film sets used in major movies such as *Kundun, Kingdom of Heaven,* and *The Mummy.*

Markets and Bazaars. The ancient medieval medinas of Fez and Marrakesh are full of exotic delights—the intricate architecture of imperial palaces and mosques, the colorful chaos of the souks, the intoxicating smell of sizzling street food, and the maze of alleyways where tourists, shoppers, and traders intertwine. In Marrakesh, the bustling main square, **Place Djemaâ el-Fna,** will fascinate children and adults alike with its daily cornucopia of musicians, snake charmers, henna artists, storytellers, and acrobats. At night, it is transformed into the biggest outdoor barbecue in the world.

History. Explore one of Morocco's most famous historic sights, the ruined Roman city of **Volubilis** near Meknès, and the **Rabat Archaeological Museum,** which houses many of the relics from this site. In the Valley of a Thousand Kasbahs, along the Draâ and Dadès valleys, go to see especially the kasbahs of **Telouet, Aït Benhaddou,** and **Taourirt.** The museum at **Ksar Tissergate** near Zagora is also well worth visiting.

Wildlife. Walk in the beautiful cedar forests near **Azrou** and visit an 800-year-old tree as Barbary apes swoop overhead.

Classes. Learning to shop for vegetables in the souks and cook your own tagine is a great family activity. Cooking classes at **Souk Cuisine** in Marrakesh and **Café Clock** in Fez are good starting points.

Practical Considerations

Baby care. There are almost no public baby-changing facilities anywhere in Morocco. You can buy disposable diapers in city chain supermarkets such as Aswak Assalam, Marjane, and Acima. In rural areas you may struggle to find them, so stock up if touring. The same goes for baby formula, though any café or restaurant will be happy to boil water for you for mixing. Breast-feeding should be done discreetly and away from public view.

Traveling with smaller kids. Most car-rental agencies and tourist transport providers will be able to supply a child seat (but check in advance). In taxis and buses there is rarely even a seat belt. If a child is small enough to sit on your lap, he or she will usually travel for free on buses and taxis.

Walking. Sidewalks are rare, or else they are broken and narrow, which can make pushing a stroller difficult. It's easier to hook up a baby knapsack or carry small children.

Sun care. Children are very prone to sunburn, dehydration, and sunstroke, so always have plenty of drinking water, strong sunscreen, sunhats, and T-shirts for covering up.

WHAT'S NEW

Strides in Transportation

Morocco's transportation infrastructure is growing significantly. New highways connect many major cities, making it easier for travelers to get from one place to another. Traveling by road between Casablanca and Marrakesh, Tangier, or Agadir is now easy, reliable, and quick. Morocco's first tramway is up and running in Rabat, connecting the country's capital to its sister city, Salé, and helping ease congestion between and within the two cities. Casablanca is also constructing a tramway.

Women's Rights

In 2004, Morocco made sweeping reforms to its family law code, the Moudawana, creating one of the most progressive family codes in the Arab world. The new Moudawana gives women significantly more rights and protections. The new legislation gives women the right to request a divorce, increases the legal age to marry from 15 to 18, severely restricts polygamy, and gives women rights to shared custody and child support. As with any significant legal reform, the practical and societal changes that accompany legislative change take time, but can already be seen and felt in the day-to-day lives of Moroccan women.

Luxury and Boutique Accommodations

While Morocco has offered travelers luxury accommodation options for many decades—La Mamounia in Marrakesh and Michlifen in Ifrane, for example—in recent years, there has been a significant increase in top-end hotels and spas. The Mazagan Beach Resort, a five-star hotel with 500 rooms just south of Casablanca on the coast, boasts a top-notch golf course, no fewer than 11 restaurants, a casino, a fantastic spa, and spectacular beaches. For those looking for a bit more intimacy, La Sultana, ideally situated on Oulidia's breathtaking lagoon, is an ideal choice. With only 11 rooms, the hotel offers pampering and the tranquillity of one of Morocco's most beautiful beaches. Boutique accommodations in riads (traditional Moroccan houses or palaces with an interior garden) are available in every major city and provide a great alternative to hotel accommodations. Each riad is unique, combining the traditional, original architecture of the building with the individual taste of the owners.

Music Festivals

Morocco's music festivals are growing every year in terms of size, quality, and recognition.

Rabat's Mawazine Rhythms of the World Festival (mid-May) attracts many internationally renowned artists, but its lineup also includes talented unknown artists from all five continents.

The Essaouira Gnaoua Festival (late June) focuses on Gnaoua music, which utilizes drums and other instruments and combines African rhythms with Islamic rituals, elevating the performers into a trancelike state.

The Fez Festival of Sacred Music (early June) is dedicated to the city's strong connection to knowledge, art, and spirituality.

During the Casablanca Festival (mid-July) the city's streets come alive with concerts, dance, and other events.

For jazz enthusiasts, a few options include Casablanca's Jazzablanca in April, Tangier's TANJAzz festival in September, and the Fez Jazz Festival in October.

FAQS

Is Morocco safe?

Despite recent political unrest, Morocco continues to be a safe and popular tourist destination for international travelers. Throughout the country, modern tourist facilities and transportation are widely available. Though pickpockets can be problematic in bustling public areas, souks, and beaches, violent crime is relatively rare in Morocco. Female visitors, especially those traveling alone, may face irritating harassment from vendors or unwanted attention from local men; though this attention is rarely dangerous, it's best to avoid eye contact, ignore the pestering, and walk away briskly as you would anywhere in the world. Travel to remote regions of the country poses no particular safety risks; however, it's best to travel with a qualified guide. Unfortunately, at this writing, the potential for terrorist violence—particularly against U.S. interests and citizens—remains elevated.

Is the water safe to drink?

Though Moroccan tap water is relatively safe, tourists should still drink bottled or boiled water and avoid drinking from public fountains. Resist the temptation to add ice to room-temperature beverages. Brushing your teeth with tap water is usually okay.

How conservatively should I dress?

In larger cities, Morocco continues to be at a crossroad between traditional and modern culture, but still tolerant of foreign influences. As a visitor, it's best to respect the locals with proper attire. Men should wear short- or long-sleeved shirts with long pants. Women should always cover their legs and shoulders. Very short skirts, shorts, and tank tops will offend Moroccans, especially in smaller villages. Beachwear is strictly for the beach or private pools.

Do I need to speak Arabic?

Basic knowledge of Arabic and French phrases will get you far since these are Morocco's official languages. Many locals speak Moroccan Arabic dialect with rural Berber roots, with English heard more often in shops, hotels, and restaurants in larger towns.

Is it possible to drink wine, beer, or alcohol here?

Although alcohol is forbidden by Islam, it is readily available in restaurants, bars, and hotels classified with three stars or more. Supermarkets also sell wine and spirits to foreigners with proper identification, except during the holy days of Ramadan.

How much should I tip?

Tipping between 10% and 15% is customary. Keep on hand small bills and coins for attendants, taxi drivers, and servers. Guides expect about 100 DH per each hour hired. If someone helps you find your way back to your hotel, a tip of 10 DH should be offered.

Can I use my cell phone and laptop in Morocco?

As long as international roaming is enabled on your quad-band GSM mobile phone, you should be able to make and receive calls, though you may pay a hefty surcharge for this service; data roaming is particularly expensive. If you want to use a Moroccan prepaid SIM card, ask your service provider to unlock your phone. Laptops work with a European French plug adapter. Wi-Fi is widely available, especially in hotels and cafés.

RECOMMENDED TOUR OPERATORS

Tour operators tend to fall into two major groups: those organized in advance—most often these days via the Internet—and those engaged on the ground. Morocco's infrastructure has improved in recent years, making traveling around the country by train or even by car easier. But there are two areas where it may be more helpful to have a local guide, even if you don't choose to do a fully guided trip to Morocco. Despite some development in rural Morocco's infrastructure, the High Atlas remains relatively undiscovered: hence its unspoiled charm. In order to reap the rewards of such an area, suitable transport (whether organized in advance or upon arrival in the region) and an experienced driver are keys to a successful trip. The same can be said for the desert, where arranging for camels or four-wheel-drive transportation and tented camps can best be done with a well-connected local guide.

For both the High Atlas and Sahara regions, local guides are easily found in Marrakesh or (for the High Atlas) in the small hill stations, most notably Imlil. A homegrown guide will personalize your traveling experience, often suggesting unknown restaurants and small riads or organizing (with your permission) a visit to their own home. The plus side here is the authentic cultural experience; the downside may be a lack of reliability, possibly poor vehicle maintenance, and basic English. All the good hotels in Marrakesh can make these arrangements, even with little prior notice. Prices can vary greatly, but you should expect to pay around $150 a day for a vehicle and driver/guide (and you should tip around $10 per day). If recruiting locally, you will be expected to pay in dirhams (in cash) rather than by credit card. If you are making these arrangements in advance, check how experienced a tour operator or guide is. The reader forums on Fodors.com can be a useful source of feedback and control.

You tend to get what you pay for in Morocco, and almost anything is possible, with operators capable of arranging all manner of tours. High-end travel, for example, might include air-conditioned luxury transport, five-star accommodations, spa treatments, and lavish meals. Another option might be experience-based: with quad biking, ballooning, cookery courses, a trip to a local *moussem* (festival), or skiing in Oukaïmeden. Very popular these days are ecotours, which typically offer stays in unspoiled Berber hamlets or eco-lodges, visits to local cooperatives, such as the salt pans and potteries, and showers under breathtaking waterfalls.

Luxury Tours

Abercrombie and Kent. Pioneers for years in the luxury travel market, this hugely respected outfitter offers a number of tailor-made, high-end packages to Morocco. ☎ *800/554–7016* 🌐 *www.abercrombiekent.com.*

Kensington Tours. The inspiration of intrepid explorer and Royal Geographic Society Fellow Jeff Willner, the company vows to delve deeper into the real Morocco without compromising on comfort or quality. Trips are devised to ensure more personal discovery than the typical package tour. ☎ *888/903–2001* 🌐 *www.kensingtontours.com.*

Experiential Tours

Blue Men of Morocco. This American-owned company was formed to organize ecotours of Morocco. Founder Elena Hall lives in Spain and puts together itineraries for travelers wishing to engage in low-impact voyages, such as simple Sahara

stays and camel excursions. Guides are locally recruited, and many of the profits are funneled back into local communities. ☎ *(34) 952–463–387 in Spain* 🌐 *www.bluemenofmorocco.com.*

Overseas Adventure Travel. This small-group tour operator, which offers a fairly comprehensive two-week tour of Morocco, is especially popular with older travelers. ☎ *800/493–6824 toll-free in the U.S.* 🌐 *www.oattravel.com.*

Wild Fontiers. This South Africa–based operator has an impressive 30-years' experience in the supply of high-standard and exciting tours. The owner-run operator has strong links with many African countries, dating back to the days when travel to these areas was fraught with complications and, sometimes, danger. ☎ *(27) 11/888–4037 in Johannesburg* 🌐 *africanadrenalin.com.*

Xaluca Tours. This company based in the Middle Atlas offers an impressive list of life-changing experiences in tour-form including desert treks along nomad trails by camel and 4x4. ☎ *0535/57–84–50 in Morocco* 🌐 *www.xaluca.com.*

High Atlas Tours

Discover Ltd UK. A company with one foothold in the United Kingdom and the other in the snowcapped mountains of the High Atlas, this outfit excels in team-bonding retreats, field trips, and independent travel. Ask to visit a revolutionary Berber girl's boarding school, which is making it possible for youngsters from isolated communities to gain an education. ☎ *(44)1883–744392 in the UK.* 🌐 *www.discover.ltd.uk.*

Moroccan Mountain Guides. This team of young, passionate Berber and Spanish guides specializes in the High Atlas. The crew is adept at finding hotels with a family atmosphere and offering cultural tours in remoter areas. There's a strong slant to ecotours, including, mountain biking, Toubkal ascents, and bivouacs. English, Spanish, French, Arabic, and Berber speakers are available. ☎ *(212) 0657/71–10–53 in Morocco* 🌐 *www.moroccomountainguides.co.uk.*

Riad Cascades. Perched above these impressive waterfalls, Riad Cascades boosts one of the High Atlas's most experienced guides. Muloud does not waste much time on small talk, but 40 years of experience means he is better equipped than any other to trek with travelers to isolated villages around the falls, most notably on the trail of the elusive native Barbary apes. ✉ *Riad Cascades, Ouzoud* ☎ *(212) 0523/42–91–73 in Morocco* 🌐 *www.ouzoud.com.*

Fodorites Say They Love

Around Morocco, Lahcen Boujouija: "Our guide, Lahcen Boujouija, was absolutely wonderful and made our trip something special. He felt a responsibility to make sure our trip was perfect from start to finish. We went to Morocco as strangers and left the country knowing that we had made a lifelong friend in Lahcen."—rayner. ☎ *(212) 0661/09–47–95 in Morocco* 🌐 *www.aroundmorocco.com.*

Mad About Morocco, Mark Willenbrock: "Fantastic guide and more than fairly priced."—jersey1977. ☎ *(212) 0676/46–85–53 in Morocco* 🌐 *www.madaboutmorocco.com.*

Rough Tours: "They were very reasonably priced. 4x4 good condition. Very good holiday. Camel trekking in the Sahara and off-roading."—Mandoza. ☎ *(212) 0617/20–33–78 in Morocco* 🌐 *roughtours.com.*

RENTING A RIAD

Only once you have ventured forth into the ancient higgledy-piggledy medinas of Fez, Meknès, Marrakesh, or Essaouira will you find a truly authentic Moroccan riad, and even then you could still walk past it, blissfully unaware.

What is a riad?

These beautiful, cloistered dwellings are usually tucked away discreetly behind heavy wooden doors set into high, featureless walls on blind alleys, called *derbs*. Traditional riad-style houses were (and still are) the domain of wealthier families and pass down from one generation to the next. They contain many of the same decorative and structural elements as their more palatial counterparts, including hand-cut, colorful tiles (zellij), silky tadelakt walls of finely pressed and waxed plaster, painted cedar-wood ceilings, arched colonnades, living rooms on the ground floor, and sleeping quarters on the upper floors. At the center of a riad is an ornamental garden with central fountain or water feature and rooms that peer inward through windows of either wrought iron or wooden latticework.

In more recent times, with changing fashions and the development of modern *nouvelle villes* by colonial rulers, many Moroccans relinquished their old houses for more comfortable dwellings with 20th-century sanitation and modern household amenities. However, the faded charm and beauty of these traditional structures have captured the imagination of foreign investors, who often snap them up as holiday retreats; many have been restored lovingly to their former glory with sumptuous attention to detail and the addition of state-of-the art facilities. Now, hundreds of riads offer boutique accommodations in Morocco's older cities, usually with about three to six bedrooms over two levels.

Why rent a riad?

Renting a riad in one of Morocco's medieval towns is a superb alternative to the often-charmless option of larger hotels in the modern districts. Most riads are rented on a per-room, per-night basis, and public areas are shared with other tourists. However, nearly all riads will offer their entire accommodation at a reduced rate for exclusive rental if booked far enough in advance (perhaps six months to one year ahead). For large families and groups of friends, taking on an entire riad gives an authentic and colorful taste of traditional Moroccan life. Noise easily carries in a riad, due to its enclosed nature, so renting the entire premises gives more freedom to party well after bedtime.

What is included?

Riads that operate year-round as guesthouses will have an on-site manager who will attend to daily housekeeping and security and who will perform concierge services. Of course, some people want complete privacy, so ask if the manager will be on duty during the time of your stay. Quoted prices usually include daily cleaning, breakfast, bed linen and towels, use of Wi-Fi, satellite TV, a DVD player, hair dryers, and access to the kitchen for cooking your own meals. Ask at the time of booking if there's an extra charge for electricity or firewood. Additional meals, private transport, guides, and special activities or excursions can normally be arranged for an additional cost.

How much does it cost?

Riads come in all sizes and differing levels of luxury, so prices can range anywhere from 300 DH to 3,000 DH per room per night. A midrange, well-equipped and stylishly furnished riad will cost approximately 700 to 1000 DH per night per room; for a typical riad with four bedrooms, you can expect to pay around 2,500 DH to 3,5000 DH per night, including a reduction for stays of more than one night. For deluxe riads or villas in the outlying Palmery area of Marrakesh, the sky is the limit for nightly rental prices.

What about location?

Riads are usually tucked away into side streets just wide enough for a donkey cart and buzzing mopeds. Check how far the riad is from the main tourist areas and souks. Check whether the neighborhood is safe and well lit and whether there is a taxi stand or parking lot within easy walking distance. Moroccan medinas can be hazardous after dark because sidewalks are poorly maintained, and tourists can get hassled by beggars.

How many rooms/beds do you need?

Riad bedrooms are often narrow, so double beds are most common. Ask in advance if you need twin-bedded rooms. Also ask if extra single beds or cribs can be added to rooms should you require them.

Do you need a pool?

Most riads will have some kind of water feature within the patio or perhaps on the roof terrace; however, a "pool" is usually little more than a plunge pool. If you want to be able to swim, you might prefer a hotel. Or you could really splurge by renting a private pavilion within the grounds of a villa in the Palmery area of Marrakesh.

What time of year are you visiting?

Moroccan winters can be bitterly cold and wet, so check that rooms are heated and that cost of heating is included. If there are open fires, ask who will supply the firewood and set the fire for you. By contrast, the summers can be ferociously hot, so check that there is air-conditioning and that it is included in the rental price.

How old are the members of your party?

Most riads have three levels, with access to most of the upper bedrooms via narrow and winding tiled staircases. If you have small children or if members of your party have restricted mobility, a riad may not be the best alternative for you. Also, be sure to check with the owner to ensure that a riad even allows children to stay there.

How do you find a riad to rent?

A simple Internet search will turn up dozens of riads, and if you are booking far ahead then you should be able to rent a full riad. If you do not speak French, search for a riad with English-speaking management—one simple indicator is if the Web site is written in good English. Good sources for privately owned riads that can be rented directly from the owner include 🌐 *www.ownersdirect.co.uk* and 🌐 *www.vacationrentalpeople.com*. There are also agencies such as 🌐 *www.riadsmorocco.com*, which represent various properties. Finally, for the top end of the market, companies such as 🌐 *www.boutiquesouk.com* and 🌐 *www.fesmedina.com* that can organize a premier property with full concierge service throughout your stay.

BOOKS AND MOVIES

One of the best ways to get into the spirit of a trip to any country is to read about it or watch a film set there. Here are some mood-setting recommendations.

RECOMMENDED READING

Books on Morocco written by foreign authors abound and provide a great way to learn about the country's culture and traditions before you travel there.

Paul Bowles

The late American expatriate writer, who lived for many years in Tangier, is among the most well known. Although Bowles's most famous novel, *The Sheltering Sky,* purports to take place in Algeria, the tale of a doomed triangle of young Americans adrift in North Africa is quintessentially Moroccan in both tone and content. *The Spider's House* is a superb historical novel and portrait of Fez at the end of the French protectorate. The most comprehensive collection of Bowles's short stories is the *Collected Stories of Paul Bowles 1939–76. Days: A Journal,* is a series of musings and accounts of daily events that Bowles effortlessly (or so it seems) elevates to the level of artistic essays. All of Bowles's nonfiction is notable, but *Their Heads Are Green and Their Hands Are Blue* is the most revealing and informative on Morocco.

Writings by Jane Auer Bowles, Paul's wife, are no less interesting than her husband's. A Tangier resident from the 1940s until her 1973 death in a Spanish mental institution, Auer Bowles's *Everything Is Nice: Collected Stories* is a flawless portrait of expatriate life in Morocco.

Tahir Shah

A recent addition to the Moroccan expatriate artist community is the Anglo-Afghan travel writer Tahir Shah. In 2003, he packed up his cushy life in London, moved to Morocco with his wife and young children, and bought a crumbling mansion in the middle of a Casablanca slum. *The Caliph's House* humorously depicts Shah's yearlong restoration of Dar Khalifa, including his struggle to rid the house of jinns, magical spirits that haunt unoccupied houses. Shah's account of living in a jinn-infested house offers an outsider's inside perspective of Moroccan culture. Another of Shah's Morocco-based novels, *In Arabian Nights,* looks at how stories and the art of storytelling are used to transmit information, education, and values from one generation to the next in Morocco and the Arab world in general.

Travel Literature

Highlights include *The Voices of Marrakesh,* by Elias Canetti; *Tangier: City of the Dream,* by Iain Finlayson; and *A Year in Marrakesh,* by Peter Mayne. Among turn-of-the-20th-century accounts, French novelist Pierre Loti's *Au Maroc* is a classic. Charles de Foucauld, a French nobleman, army officer, and missionary, chronicled his time in Morocco in his book *Reconnaissance au Maroc.* For more historical and ethnographical accounts, find Edith Wharton's 1920 *In Morocco*; Antoine de Saint-Exupéry's *Wind, Sand and Stars*; and Walter Harris's 1921 *Morocco That Was. Zohra's Ladder & Other Moroccan Tales,* by Pamela Windo, is a collection of stories that took place during the author's seven years living in Morocco; Windo depicts both the stunning landscapes of the country and the genuine connections she made with the people. The book makes a good companion to a guidebook when travelling to Morocco. And although it's really a work of history, *Lords of the Atlas: The Rise and Fall of the House of Glaoua*

1893–1956 by Gavin Maxwell, is the quintessential tale of a Moroccan dynasty that built some of most important and iconic kasbahs in the High Atlas; although out of print in the United States, the British edition can be ordered online.

Food

Paula Wolfert's *Couscous and Other Good Food from Morocco* is excellent for its fabulous recipes as well as its photographs and background on the Moroccan social context. Kitty Morse, born in Casablanca to a French mother and British father, is the author of five cookbooks on the cuisine of Morocco and North Africa, including *Cooking at the Kasbah: Recipes from my Moroccan Kitchen* and *The Scent of Orange Blossoms. Clock Book: Recipes from a Modern Moroccan Kitchen,* by food critic and travel writer Tara Stevens, provides new twists on traditional Moroccan dishes.

Current Events

Written by a former correspondent to the *New York Times,* Marvine Howe's *Morocco: The Islamist Awakening and Other Challenges* describes Morocco's development during the late King Hassan II's reign, as well as the present King Mohammed VI's attempts to move the country away from autocracy to democracy.

FILMS

More and more often, films from Moroccan directors are both entertaining and shed light on Moroccan culture, but they may be difficult to find on DVD.

À la recherche du mari de ma femme (*Looking for My Wife's Husband*) is the light-hearted semiautobiographical 1995 film (in French) by director Mohamed Abderrahmen Tazi. It tells the story of Hadj and his three wives, each woman from a different generation, and the difficulties when he kicks one of his wives out.

Marock, a 2005 film (in French) by female director Laila Marrakchi, was highly controversial, exploring the romantic relationship between two teenagers, one Muslim and one Jewish. In addition to the interreligious theme, the movie allows viewers to see the contrast between rich and poor—how the worlds of the rich and poor meet continuously yet stay forever separate.

Of the many Western films set in Morocco, no doubt the most famous is the 1942 classic *Casablanca.*

Hideous Kinky, the 1998 adaptation of the novel by the same name, tells the story of an adventurous young mother who moves to Marrakesh in the 1960s.

The Sheltering Sky, Bernando Bertolucci's 1990 interpretation of Paul Bowles's 1949 novel, is a dark, romantic comedy with stunning images of North Africa.

One story line in Alejandro González Iñárritu's 2006 *Babel,* featuring Brad Pitt and Cate Blanchett, takes place in the High Atlas Mountains.

Morocco has a vibrant film studio, and a great many films that do not take place in Morocco were nonetheless shot there, most notably *Othello, Lawrence of Arabia, The Last Temptation of Christ, Kundun, Gladiator, Black Hawk Down, Alexander, Body of Lies, Green Zone, The Bourne Ultimatum,* and *Hanna.*

GREAT ITINERARIES

THE IMPERIAL CITIES: THE CLASSIC TOUR OF MOROCCO

For longer stays in Morocco, you can tailor your tour around more exhaustive exploring of regions and more adventurous diversions, but if you have limited time, focus on the major experiences and sights. This weeklong holiday gives you enough time to sample the best of Morocco. Remember to add a day for getting there plus a day to get back (a direct flight from New York to Casablanca takes approximately eight hours), and pace yourself to see the most important places.

Day 1: Arrival in Casablanca

Flights generally arrive in Casablanca in the early morning. Casa doesn't have that many sights, so once you drop your bags at your hotel, you should head out to explore; a few hours should do the trick. As your starting point, visit the **Hassan II Mosque** and the Mohammed V Square in the **Habous Quarter** designed in French colonial–Art Deco style. You're going to be exhausted after a transatlantic flight, so spend your first night in Casablanca; however, if you want to make an early start in the morning, you can travel one hour along the coast to Rabat.

Day 2: Rabat

Explore the capital city of Rabat. The best sites in the city are the **Hassan Tower** and **Mohammed V Mausoleum, Chellah Gardens and Necropolis,** and **Oudayas Kasbah** overlooking the Atlantic Ocean. In the late afternoon, drive to Meknès, where you'll spend the night.

Day 3: Meknès & Volubilis

Begin your tour by passing the **Bab Mansour** and visiting the holy **Tomb of Moulay Ismail,** which is open to non-Muslims. Walk towards the lively Place el-Hedim, which leads towards the medina. Tour the open bazaars of the medina streets. Enjoy an inexpensive classic Moroccan lunch. Near the row of pottery stands, visit the food souk. The **Museum of Moroccan Art** in the 19th-century Dar Jamai palace and **Heri el-Souaini** (Royal Granaries) are recommended stops. By afternoon, drive 30 minutes to the ancient Roman archeological ruins of **Volubilis.** When you approach, the Triumphal Arch rises in the open field. Count on 90 minutes for a thorough visit. The Tangier Gate, House of Orpheus, House of Columns, and House of Ephebus are must-sees. You can spend the night at Volubilis or head back to Meknès.

Days 4 and 5: Fez

Try to arrive in Fez as early as possible so you can spend two full days exploring everything the **Fez el-Bali, Fez el-Djedid,** and **Ville Nouvelle** have to offer—medieval monuments, artisan workshops, public squares, ancient tombs, cultural museums, chaotic souks, atmospheric cafés, and palatial gardens. The blue-tiled gate of **Bab Boujeloud** is the gateway to the main alley of Talaa Kebira. The most important sites include the **Bou Inania medersa, Attarine madrassa, Moulay Idriss zaouia,** and **Karaouine Mosque and University** (the latter generally considered the oldest academic institution in the world). Visit the restored **Nejjarine fondouk** for the best examples of woodworking craftsmanship. Watch the full fabrication process of the leather tanneries from a rooftop terrace. Shop for the famous blue-and-white Fassi pottery. If time permits, see the arts and crafts (including a must-see collection of astrolabes) at the **Dar Batha Museum** housed in a beautiful 19th century Hispano-Moorish palace. Discover the area of the **Royal**

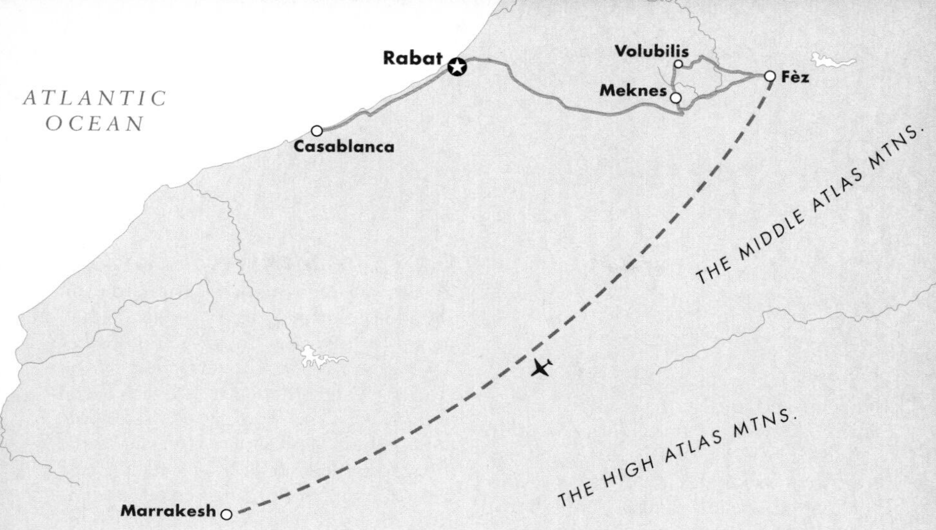

Palace (*Dar el-Makhzen*) that leads to the active mellah quarter beyond the Fez el-Djedid. Watch the sunset over the entire medina from the **Merenid tombs** or **Musée des Armes** atop the hills of the Borj Nord or from the **Borj Sud,** south of the walled city. Indulge in an authentic Fassi dinner in a riad courtyard. Spend two nights here.

Days 6 and 7: Marrakesh

The quickest way to travel the 398-km (242-mi) distance between Fez and Marrakesh is by plane; if you plan well, you can be in Marrakesh by midmorning. After dropping your bags at your hotel, hit the ground running. The best place to start is the famed **Djemaâ el-Fna,** the perfect gateway into the labyrinth of medina streets filled with hundreds of souks, including the **Souk des Teinturiers** for leather, **Souk Addadine** for metalwork, and **Souk Zarbia,** the main carpet market. The **Ali Ben Youssef Medersa, Dar Si Saïd** museum, **Palais Bahia,** and **Koutabia Mosque** are important sites (though non-Muslims cannot enter the mosque). Walk south of the Palais Bahia to explore the bustling streets of the mellah, the former Jewish quarter and largest in Morocco. In the evening, splurge on a Moroccan feast, or head to the open grills back on the busy main square. On your second day in Marrakesh, take a *petit taxi* for a relaxing promenade through the **Ville Nouvelle** and lush **Majorelle Gardens and Museum,** where you can do some bird-watching and see an extraordinary collection of Islamic ceramics, textiles, jewelry, and art. After, head back towards the medina and visit the **Saadian Tombs,** which date back to the late 16th century, for one of the country's finest representations of Islamic architecture. Plan a relaxing hammam treatment to rejuvenate after a week of touring.

TIPS

- The only mosque in Morocco that non-Muslims can enter is the Hassan II Mosque in Casablanca. Visits are allowed only between prayer times (with official on-site guides) at 10 am, 11 am, and 2 pm.
- During Ramadan, check for special hours; while many sites are open on holy days, some local restaurants and cafés close for the day or entire month.
- Make your visit more special. Plan a visit around an annual outdoor venue, such as the World Sacred Music Festival held in Fez or the Marrakesh Popular Arts Festival hosting traditional musicians and dancers from all over Morocco.

GREAT ITINERARIES

COASTAL AND INLAND OASES: THE SOUTHERN TOUR

For those who want to escape the bustling medinas and touristy feel of the imperial cities, the Southern Atlantic coastline is the perfect alternative to experience Morocco, with miles of deserted beaches, enchanting seaside villages, and colorful exotic landscapes to enrich the mind and spirit. The scenery is stunning and varied with rocky wilderness, vast seascapes, and fertile plains. Much of the area (except for Agadir) remains pristine and gets relatively few visitors. Swim, surf, sunbathe, bird-watch, and breathe in fresh ocean air. Laid-back towns, surfer havens, coastal resorts, and unexpected oases offer a holistic way to learn about local culture, food, language and history.

Day 1: Marrakesh

Fly directly to Marrakesh Menara International Airport. Rent a car in the airport terminal, and check in to a hotel in Guéliz. Take a taxi to enjoy a delectable Moroccan dinner and experience the exotic activity of the **Djemaâ el-Fna,** the city's main square. Don't miss the city's excellent nightlife with live street entertainment, local clubs, bars, and theater performances showcasing the fusion of Berber, Arab, African, and Andalusian influences in music and dance.

Day 2: Essaouira

Rise early to drive west towards the relaxing, picturesque port city of Essaouira. After you check in to your hotel, take a walking tour of the harbor and town of whitewashed houses. Have lunch near the shore. Don't miss the fresh charcoal-grilled sardines and shrimp in seaside food stalls. The town is a hub for contemporary Moroccan artists—check out **art galleries** showcasing Gnaoua expressionism. Shop the colorful pedestrian-only medina streets for ceramics, thuya wood, leather *babouches* (leather slippers), and woven fabrics. Watch the sunset on the ocean horizon atop the ramparts of the **kasbah.** For the best panoramic view, access the fortress at **Skala de la Ville,** the cliff-side sea bastion lined with brass cannons. Dine on fresh local seafood at a casual open grill or in one of many restaurants along the shore.

Day 3: Agadir

Head south to Agadir, stopping off for magnificent sea views on undisturbed sand dunes of Morocco's most beautiful beaches. **Sidi Kaouki, Tafelney, Bhibeh,** and **Moulay Bouzerktoun** are the most-well-known beaches to sunbathe and dip your toes into the Atlantic waters. **Taghazoute** attracts windsurfers and offers brisk ocean breezes. When you finally arrive in Agadir, visit the **kasbah** and **fish stalls** by the harbor. Enjoy dinner and one night here.

Day 4: Tiznit

Continue your journey to Tiznit, famous for its silver and wool blankets. Stay one night in Tiznit to experience local Berber living and hit its wonderful market, especially if you are looking for jewelry.

Day 5: Tafroute

On day five, discover the natural beauty of the Anti-Atlas region, passing palm groves, almond orchards, rocky landscapes, fertile valleys, and fortified towns. You'll pass through the small villages **Igherm** and **Oumesmat** before enjoying the exotic beauty of Tafraoute. Explore the **Amen Valley** region, then return to town in the late afternoon. Spend the night at the Hotel Kerdous, overlooking a dramatic valley on the road to Tiznit.

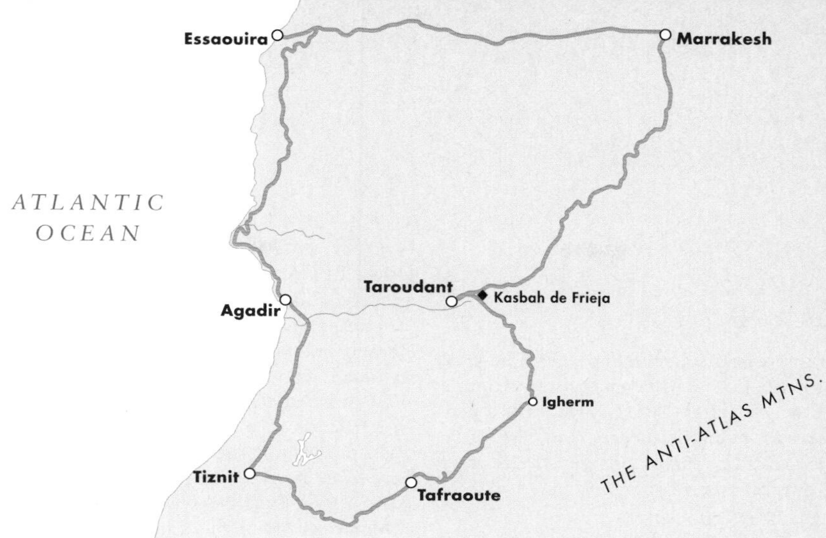

Day 6: Taroudant

Take a relaxing drive towards Taroudant. The atmosphere is very low-key. Walk around the open markets and historic ramparts. The red ochre-walled city is well-known for handcrafted silver items and aromatic spices. There are two main souks in the village. In the medina, don't miss the jeweler's souk, fish market, kasbah, and pretty gardens. Listen for Tashelheit, the Berber dialect of the southern Souss region. On Sundays, locals from surrounding areas sell produce, livestock, and all sorts of wares near the main gate. A short loop drive east, about 10 km from Taroudant, will take you through the fertile Souss valley plains and barren terrain leading towards the ruins of the Kasbah de Frieja. Spend the night in Taroudant.

Day 7: Return to Marrakesh

Count on a few hours to return to your starting point. If you plan to depart on the same day, head straight to the Menara airport. If you decide to stay one more evening, head back to the famed Djemaâ el-Fna, and shop for last-minute souvenirs in the **Souk des Teinturiers** for leather, **Souk Addadine** for metalwork, and **Souk Zarbia** for carpets. The **Ali Ben Youssef Medersa, Dar Si Saïd** museum, **Palais Bahia,** and **Saadien Tombs** are important sites. If time and energy permit, walk south of the Palais Bahia to explore the bustling streets of the mellah, the largest former Jewish quarter in Morocco. As another option, book a hamman treatment in your hotel for a final hedonistic treat.

TIPS

■ Go off the beaten track—head to coastal destinations of Oualidia and Mirleft, a small village fast becoming a trendy spot for surfers and sun-worshippers.

■ For an outdoor adventure, arrange a horse ride on the beach or rent ATVs through several stables and quad-trek companies.

■ To avoid serious problems, buy and carry a supply of bottled water to beat the heat on beaches and while walking through villages and open terrain of the Anti-Atlas. Bring sunscreen. Both are difficult to find on the road.

■ Carry an Arabic phrase book. English is not widely spoken in rural regions.

GREAT ITINERARIES

QUINTESSENTIAL MOROCCO: THE GRAND TOUR

In two weeks you can experience most of Morocco: coastal havens on the Atlantic coast, the High Atlas Mountains, pre-Saharan palmeries, Berber and Moorish architecture, rural hillside towns, and exquisite imperial cities.

Days 1 and 2: Tangier, Tetouan, and Chefchaouen

The best way to enjoy Tangier is by taking a walking tour along the beachfront. Enter the medina and see the **Grand Mosque** and large market at the **Grand Socco.** Head to the north side of the mosque to enter the beautiful **Mendoubia Gardens** before meandering the smaller alleyways to reach the **Petit Socco.** From here, reach the 15th-century **kasbah** and sultanate palace of **Dar el-Kakhzen,** which houses the **Museum of Moroccan Arts** and **Museum of Antiquities.** Visit the historic **American Legation Cultural Center and Museum** commemorating the first diplomatic relations between the United States and Morocco. Enjoy a leisurely dinner by the water. On day two, pick up a rental car and drive southeast through the Rif Mountains to visit the Berber village of **Tetouan**, the historic town dating from the 8th century that has been designated a UNESCO World Heritage Site. Continue onto the stunning blue-washed hillside city of **Chefchaouen**; stay in Casa Perleta in the old medina district of Bab Souk and explore on foot.

Day 3: Meknès and Volubilis

Start early on day three. Drive through **Ouazzane** en route to Fez, stopping off at the Roman ruins of **Volubilis.** Spend at least 90 minutes walking the grounds. The Tangier Gate, Diana and the Bathing Nymphs mosaic, House of Orpheus, House of Columns, and House of Ephebus are must-sees. Then continue onto Meknès, arriving by midday. Pass the **Bab Mansour** and visiting the holy **Tomb of Moulay Ismail,** which is open to non-Muslims. Walk toward the lively Place el-Hedim, which leads into the medina. Tour the open bazaars of the medina streets and have some lunch. Near the row of pottery stands, visit the food souk. The **Museum of Moroccan Art** in the 19th-century Dar Jamai palace and **Heri el-Souaini** (Royal Granaries) are recommended stops. Late in the afternoon, get back in the car and continue to Fez, arriving by nightfall, and splurge on a sumptuous Fassi meal.

Days 4 and 5: Fez and the Middle/High Atlas

Spend day four and the morning of day five exploring the Fez **medina,** absorbing the view from one of many rooftop terraces overlooking this ancient labyrinth or atop the hill of the **Musée des Armes** for an incredible panorama of the whole city. Tour the Fez el-Bali and Fez el-Djedid. Don't miss the blue-tiled gate of **Bab Boujeloud, Bou Inania medersa, Attarine madrassa, Moulay Idriss zaouia, Nejjarine fondouk,** and **Karaouine Mosque and University**. Visit the tanneries to find leather bargains, and explore the souks for famous blue-and-white Fassi pottery and carved thuya wood. On the afternoon of day five head south through olive groves and small villages before reaching the indigenous macaques playing in their natural habitat of the serene **Azrou Cedar Forest** en route to **Erfoud,** where you can spend the night.

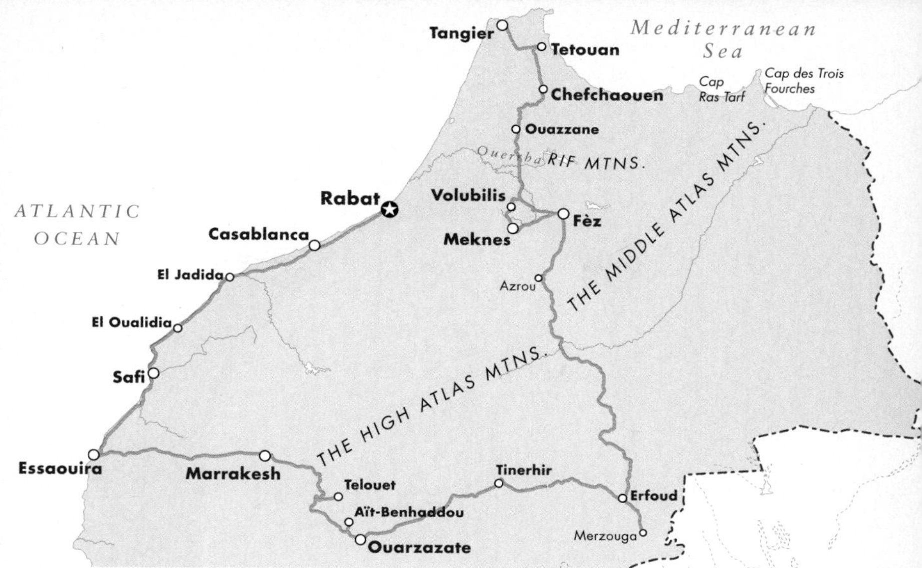

Days 6 and 7: Merzouga Dunes and Ouarzazate

Rise very early on day six to catch the sunrise over the **Merzouga dunes,** and then get on the road to **Tinerhir.** Visit the spectacular **Todra Gorge** and stay overnight in this pastoral region. On day seven explore the rugged landscape on the **kasbah** route in the Dadès Valley, passing stunning cliffs and canyons on the road to **Ouarzazate.** Treat yourself for a night at the luxurious La Berbère Palace, where the movie stars stay when they're in town for a location shoot.

Days 8–11: Marrakesh and Essaouira

Devote day eight to drive the Tizi-n-Tichka Pass to Marrakesh, stopping off at the *ksour* (fortified villages) of **Aït-Benhaddou** and **Telouet.** Settle into a Marrakesh hotel by nightfall, and spend day nine and 10 storming the medina, architectural monuments, and **Djemaâ el-Fna.** On day 11, escape the crowds and head west to the calm coastal town of **Essaouira** for a relaxing afternoon and evening by the Atlantic shores.

Days 12–14: Safi, Casablanca, and Rabat

Day 12 can take you north along the coast to **El Oualidia,** where you may want to have some of the famous oysters, then on to the Portuguese port town of **El Jadida.** Spend the night here or in Casablanca. On day 13, check out the stunning ocean-side **Hassan II Mosque** in Casablanca before heading up to Rabat for your last day. Wander through Rabat's **Rue des Consuls** for last-minute purchases on your way to the 12th-century **Kasbah des Oudayas,** savoring your final taste of imperial Morocco. Casablanca is about an hour by train.

TIPS

- If you'd rather stick mainly to the four imperial cities, take the train instead of a rental car. It's inexpensive, reliable, and fast.
- A car is the best and sometimes only way to reach Morocco's mountainous area, small coastal villages, and rural regions that are often paved with rough dirt roads.
- If you're driving, avoid driving at night. Roads are not well lit, if at all.
- Consider an adventure tour like camel riding in the Sahara, white-water rafting on the Ahansel River, or hot-air ballooning over the Ourika Valley.
- Avoid faux guides and unlicensed tour drivers.

THE DYNASTIES OF MOROCCO

For centuries, Morocco, whose essence lies in a culturally rich mosaic of Arabic, European, and African influences, has lured and intrigued foreigners. With a complex and tumultuous history dating back more than 5,000 years, Morocco today is as unique and exotic as the diverse ethnic civilizations that have shaped everything here from language, music, art, and architecture to politics, education, and the economy. *by Victoria Tang*

At the crossroads between East and West, Africa and Europe, Morocco has attracted invading conquerors seeking a strategic foothold in fertile valleys, desert oases, and coveted coastal outposts on the Atlantic and Mediterranean. Excavations from the 12th century BC show the remains of Phoenician settlements in ancient times. It was not until the 7th century, when Arabian crusaders introduced Islam, that the Moroccan political landscape became more spectacular, often extreme, with radical religious reformers founding Muslim kingdoms in the midst of Christian encroachments and nomadic Berber tribal rule. Rural Berber tribes engaged in lawless conflict, battling it out with bloody family feuds in the harsh Sahara and unforgiving cliffs of the Atlas mountains. Successive invasions by Arab, French, and Spanish civilizations ensued, but the indigenous Berbers survived, remaining an integral component of today's Morocco. European colonization ultimately gave way to Morocco's independent state and a centralized constitutional government, still ruled today by sultan monarchs, descended from the Alaouite Dynasty.

(left) Casablanca's Hassan II Mosque (top) Tomb of Moulay Ismail, Méknes

1200 BC	800 BC	400 BC	0
Phoenicians begin trading salt from Morocco	Phoenicians settle in Lixus		

(left) A mosaic in the Roman ruins at Volubilis (above) an aerial view of the city of Moulay Idriss (right) a Roman coin excavated near Essaouira, on Morocco's Atlantic coast

1200 BC – AD 700

Predynastic Morocco

As Phoenician trading settlements expanded along the Mediterranean, the Romans also began to spread west through North Africa, declaring Volubilis its capital, whose ruins stand outside of Meknès. Along Morocco's coasts, Portuguese incursions left ramparts surrounding Essaouira and El Jadida. The first Arab invasions occurred circa AD 682, collapsing the Roman Empire. The indigenous Imazighen Berbers embraced Islamic conquests, paving the way for the emergence of dynastic kingdoms.

- Lixus (⇨ Ch2)
- Volubilis (⇨ Ch4)
- Essaouira (⇨ Ch8)

788 – 1000

Idrissid Dynasty

Under the regime of Oqba Ibn Nafi, Arabs spread the religion of Islam and its holy language, Arabic, both of which took hold (to varying degrees) throughout Morocco. In 788, exiled from Baghdad, Moulay Idriss I established the first Islamic and Arab dynasty that lasted almost 200 years. He set out to transform the village of Fez into the principal city of western Morocco. In 807, Idriss II, his son, founded Fez el-Bali (literally, Fez the Old) as the new intellectual capital in the Fez River's fertile basin—the Oued Fez, also known as Oued el-Yawahir, the River of Pearls. Attracted by its importance, Andalusian and Tunisian Muslims arrived and established one of the most significant places of learning during its time—the Kairaouine University. The Fez medina is divided into two quarters on either side of the Fez River. The Andalusian Quarter originally housed refugees from Moorish Spain, who had begun to flee the *Reconquista* (the Christian re-conquest of Spain); the Kairaouine Quarter originally housed refugees from the Kairaouine. By the 10th and 11th centuries, the Bedouin tribe known as the Benu Hilal descended upon rural regions, destroying farmlands and villages.

- Kairaouine University (Fez, ⇨ Ch4)
- Moulay Idriss Mausoleum (Fez, ⇨ Ch4)

(top left) Aït Ben Hadou, a ksar near Ouarzazate (near right) the entrance gates to Chellah, Rabat (far right) the towering minaret for the Koutoubia Mosque in Marrakesh

1060–1150 Almoravid Dynasty

From the south, one of the major Berber tribes emerged to create the Almoravid Dynasty, which led conquests to control desert trade routes to the north. By 1062, the Almoravids controlled what is now Morocco, Western Sahara, and Mauritania. Youssef ibh Tashfin established Marrakesh as his capital, building fortressed walls and underground irrigation channels, and conquered Tiemcen—what is today Algeria. He eventually extended his kingdom north into Spain by 1090.

- Ben Youssef Medersa (Marrakesh, ⇨ Ch5)
- Aït Benhaddou (⇨ Ch7)

1150–1248 Almohad Dynasty

The Almohad Dynasty, started by radical reformer Ibn Toumert (the Torch) in the High Atlas village of Tinmal, gave rise to an empire stretching across Spain, Tunisia, and Algeria. The Almohads built the current capital of Rabat and its famous landmarks, Marrakesh's iconic Koutoubia mosque, and the Giraldi Tower in Seville. After 100 years of rule, the Almohad empire collapsed because of civil warfare, causing Berbers to return to local tribes.

- Koutoubia Mosque (Marrakesh, ⇨ Ch5)
- Hassan Tower (Rabat, ⇨ Ch3)

1248–1465 The Merinid Dynasty

The nomadic Ben Merin Berber tribe from the Sahara established the Merinid Dynasty, pushing westward into northeastern Morocco and ousting the Almohads, who were once their masters. As Merinid tribesmen waged holy wars, they seized control of the Fez el-Jdid, constructing numerous Islamic mosques and madrassas (colleges). Jewish and Muslim refugees arrived fleeing the Spanish Inquisition, while invasions from Portugal and Spain captured coastal cities.

- Bou Inania (Fez, ⇨ Ch4)
- Chella necropolis (Rabat, ⇨ Ch3)

(far left) Asilah, a city in northern Morocco (near left) the Saadian Tombs in the Marrakesh medina (above) the fortified walls of Taroudant

1465 – 1554 The Wattisid Dynasty

Facing mounting territorial occupation by the Portuguese in what are now Tangier, Essaouira, and Agadir, the Merinids lost control to the Wattisids, who recruited high-ranking Muslim chiefs (viziers) to assume powers of the sultanate. The Wattisids reigned between 1472 and 1554 from Fez, relinquishing rule because of Moorish conquests on the Moroccan side of the Straits of Gibraltar. By 1492, Muslims had lost control of Spain and sought refuge back in the Maghreb.

- Dar el Makhzen (Fez, ⇨ Ch4)
- Asilah (⇨ Ch2)

1554 – 1669 The Saadian Dynasty

As the first Arab kingdom since the Idrissids, the Saadian Dynasty drove out the Christians. Lacking any loyalty to Berber tribes, they also proclaimed their superiority as direct descendants of the prophet Mohammed. The Saadi family originally settled in the Drâa Valley near Zagora in the 12th century and later in the Sous near Taroudant, which became the Saadian capital until they declared Marrakesh their sultanate in 1524. The greatest of the eleven Saadian sultans, Ahmed el Mansour, reigned for more than 25 years, building ties with England's monarchy as well as Spain. He commanded an army to conquer the West African Songhai empire and led a gold rush on the Niger River. His impact on Morocco as "The Victorious" ended when he died in 1603, leaving his vast kingdom to his sons, who continued to reign for the next 60 years in both Marrakesh and Souss but failed to keep order and peace. General anarchy swept the country as Jewish and Muslim refugees from Catholic Spain arrived on chaotic shores while bands of pirates (the notorious Barbary pirates) sailed from Rabat and Salé.

- Saadian Tombs (Marrakesh, ⇨ Ch5)
- Taroudannt (⇨ Ch8)
- Salé (⇨ Ch3)

Moulay Rashid captures Marrakesh from Saadiens

Morocco signs a treaty with Spain

Morocco becomes a French protectorate

Moroccan independence

1700 | 1800 | 1900 | 2000

(far left) Moulay Ismail, who united and liberated Morocco from European powers in 1672 (near left) the gardens of the Museum of Moroccan Arts, Fez (bottom right) Tangier's waterfront promenade

1669–1894 The Alaouite Dynasty

The Alaouite Dynasty, founded by Moulay Rashid, captured Marrakesh in 1669. By 1672, the ruler Moulay Ismail seized Meknès, launching years of brutal holy wars while effectively liberating the country from European powers and laying the foundation for European trade relations. In 1767, Morocco signed a peace treaty with Spain and a trading agreement with France. In 1787, a U.S. peace treaty was signed. But the 19th century saw losses of territory to France.

- Moulay Ismail Mausoleum (Meknès, ⇨ Ch4)
- Dar Batha Museum (Fez, ⇨ Ch4)

1906–1956 European Conquest

By 1906, the majority of Africa was under European rule. Moulay el Hassan was the last of the pre-colonial sultans. After his son Abd el Aziz took over, Morocco, though still independent, was on the verge of bankruptcy after years of borrowing from European powers, in particular France. The Treaty of Fez in 1912 distributed Morocco's regions between Spain and (mostly) France, declaring the country as a French protectorate with Rabat as its capital. It was during this time that the Glaoui, who controlled one of the High Atlas passes from their kasbah at Telouet, became allies with the French. Uprisings took place in the 1920s, and by the 1930s and 1940s, violent protests across the country heightened as the independence movement of the Istiqulal Party gained strength in Fez. Writers including Paul Bowles settled in Tangier, an international zone since 1923, and began an artistic counter-culture there. By 1955, the situation had reached a boiling point; France granted Morocco independence in 1956.

- El Bahia Palace (Marrakesh, ⇨ Ch5)
- Glaoui Kasbah (Telouet, ⇨ Ch6)
- Tangier (⇨ Ch2)

(above) The Mohammed V Mausoleum, Rabat (right) Agadir's popular beachfront

1956 - 1961 Return of the Alaouite Dynasty

In 1956, Mohammed V returned from exile to regain the Moroccan throne. The Glaoui-French alliance was broken, and the Glaoui Dynasty went into an immediate decline. When Mohammed V died unexpectedly in 1961, his son, Hassan II, inherited the responsibility to continue social and political reforms, building up the country and maintaining his position as the country's spiritual leader. Hassan II was instrumental during the 1970s and 1980s in developing foreign relations between North Africa and the world.

■ Mohammed V Mausoleum (Rabat)

1961 - 1987 A New Morocco

The ascension of King Hassan II reflected the dynamic yet insecure spirit of a country in transition. Radical left-wing supporters emerged as serious threats to the monarchy. The Socialist Union of Popular Forces campaigned for radical reforms, a view shared by newly-independent Algeria, which briefly engaged in a territorial war with Morocco over disputed frontiers. Militants tried but failed to assassinate King Hassan II five times between 1963 and 1977. Rioting leftists took to the streets in violent protest against what they considered autocratic, absolute rule. At the same time, beach resorts were being built in Agadir in the 1970s and early 1980s, creating an influx of European beach-goers.

The desolate Western Sahara region in the deep south became one of Africa's most controversial and longest-running territorial conflicts beginning with the Green March of 1975, when Morocco exerted its control over the territory. The area remained a powder keg for explosive behavior throughout the 1980s, as stakes remain high to own the area's valuable natural resources, including phosphate deposits, fish reserves, and oil.

■ Agadir (⇨ Ch8)

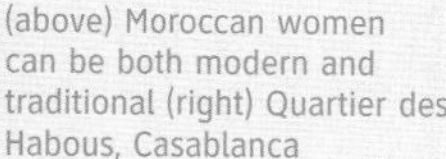

(above) Moroccan women can be both modern and traditional (right) Quartier des Habous, Casablanca

1987 – 1999 The Progressive Years

Morocco granted more local control and even elected a house of representatives. Infrastructure began to improve. The Casablanca Stock Exchange installed an electronic trading system in the early 1990s. A busy film economy, which had begun in the early 1960s, began to develop in Ouarzazate. With the death of King Hassan II in 1999, his son, Mohammed Ben al Hassan, was immediately enthroned as Mohammed VI at the age of 36 in a peaceful transition.

- Atlas Studios (Ouarzazate, ⇨ Ch7)
- Hassan II Mosque (Casablanca, ⇨ Ch3)

1999 – 2011 Modern Morocco

When King Mohammed VI married engineer Salma Bennani in 2002, she became the first wife of a Moroccan ruler to be publicly acknowledged and given a royal title. Women's rights have since improved. The minimum age for matrimony has risen to 18, and women have more freedom of choice in marriage and divorce. Women have also won seats in parliamentary elections. Terrorist bombings in 2003 and 2011 have raised fears of radical Islamic extremists, but King Mohammed VI has tried to expand constitutional reforms to create more freedom and limit the powers of the monarchy. The government continues to improve daily living conditions, and expand and improve the country's infrastructure, including roads, rails, and utilities, which are much improved from even the early years of the 21st century. Morocco has sought membership in the European Union, but the stalemate in Western Sahara remains unresolved, something that has hindered the region's stability and prosperity. However, the country continues to modernize, with King Mohammed VI promising even more comprehensive constitutional reform in the face of increasingly widespread protests demanding change. Still, Morocco continues to remain a major draw tor international tourists.

WHEN TO GO

The best times to go to Morocco are spring and fall, specifically March, April, and October. Spring may be ideal—the sky is a beautiful deep blue, washed clear by the winter rain, and wildflowers blanket the landscape. Winter is the best time to see the desert and most of the south; summer is the best time to explore the High Atlas. If you like a hot sun, come in July, August, or early September. The months between late September and December are pleasant, with cool evenings. January, February, and March are changeable and can sometimes be chilly or rainy.

The Atlantic and Mediterranean coastal resorts are crowded during summer school vacation. It's best to see the coast another time; June is still warm, and the beaches are much less crowded.

Ramadan is not usually a huge impediment to travel by non-Muslims. However, during this monthlong fast all cafés and nearly all restaurants are closed during the day, and the pace of work is reduced. The dates for Ramadan vary annually. Ramadan lasts for 29 or 30 days.

Climate

Morocco enjoys a Mediterranean climate. Inland temperatures are high in summer—sometimes in excess of 40°C (104°F)—and cool in winter. The coastal regions have a more temperate climate, warmer in winter and less brutally hot in summer. Rain falls mainly in winter, from October through March, often with more in November and March. Northern Morocco, especially the Rif Mountains, gets more rain than the south.

At right are average daily maximum and minimum temperatures for Marrakesh and Rabat, a comparison of which reveals the tempering effects of the ocean on coastal destinations. Climate varies widely throughout Morocco, so consult the appropriate chapters for details on each region you'll be visiting.

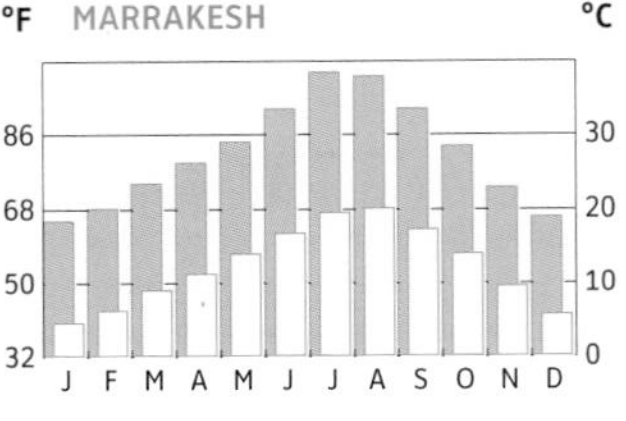

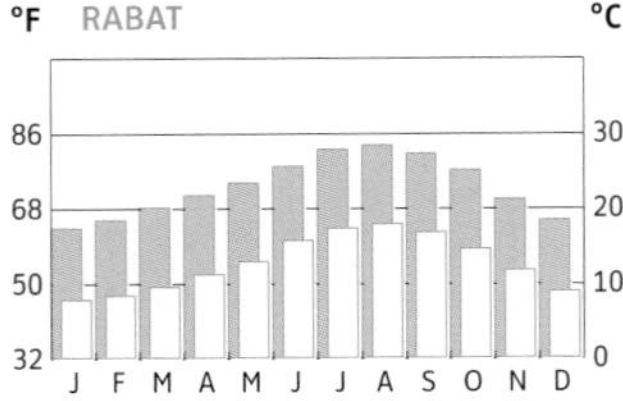

Tangier and the Mediterranean

WORD OF MOUTH

"[W]e enjoyed an extra day [in Chefchaouen] to get away from the center area that gets a lot of tourists. Towards the west side of town is a climbing series of steps that wanders in areas that are very nontouristy. Very different from the other cities on your itinerary as well."

—Clifton

WELCOME TO TANGIER AND THE MEDITERRANEAN

TOP REASONS TO GO

★ **Tangier:** This city charms many newcomers with its eye-popping views, calm breezes, its internationalism, and its friendly inhabitants who are always curious to know more about the outside world.

★ **The Rif Mountains:** Running parallel to the Mediterranean coast for 200 km (180 mi), this is the highest range in the north and offers some of the best scenery and trekking in Morocco.

★ **Tetouan:** Overlooking the verdant Martil Valley, Tetouan is famous for its Hispano-Moorish architecture and medina.

★ **Chefchaouen:** This charming blue-and-white mountain stronghold is one of Morocco's through-the-looking-glass fantasy spots, and is especially popular with nature lovers.

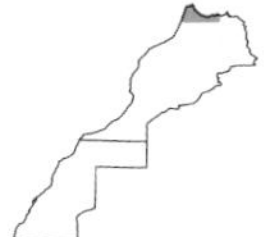

1 Tangier. The sights, sounds, and aromas of Morocco are never better highlighted than in this tumultuous collision of Rifi Berber, Arabic, and European cultures. The city conveniently and uniquely offers within its small borders lively souks, laid-back cafés and bars, access to both the Atlantic and the Mediterranean, and a natural pine forest with a large biological plant diversity.

2 The Ceuta Peninsula. With its lighthouse marking the meeting place of Atlantic and Mediterranean waters, the Ceuta Peninsula leads on to glorious beaches and modern resort towns. Tetouan's curiously Spanish medina is just one of the highlights.

3 Chefchaouen and the Rif. A mountain stronghold and sanctuary only opened to Christian visitors in the 20th century, Chefchaouen has since become a favorite of Moroccophiles. The dry mountain air, the cool blue medina, and the colorful display of local arts and crafts make Chefchaouen an indispensable destination.

GETTING ORIENTED

Tangier's strategic location on the Strait of Gibraltar has made it a cosmopolitan city, sought after by countless empires including the Phoenicians, Visigoths, Arabs, British, Portuguese, French, and Spanish. Tangier has traces of each empire visible in its architecture, culture, and lore. The Atlantic and Mediterranean coastlines support a rich commercial and private fishery—with rocky coastal outcroppings where local anglers cast lines from long poles. The Rif valleys and plateaus, extremely fertile thanks to the region's reliable annual rainfall—typically two weeks straight in late November and mid-April—yield some of the country's finest agricultural products, including olives, wheat, barley, and honey.

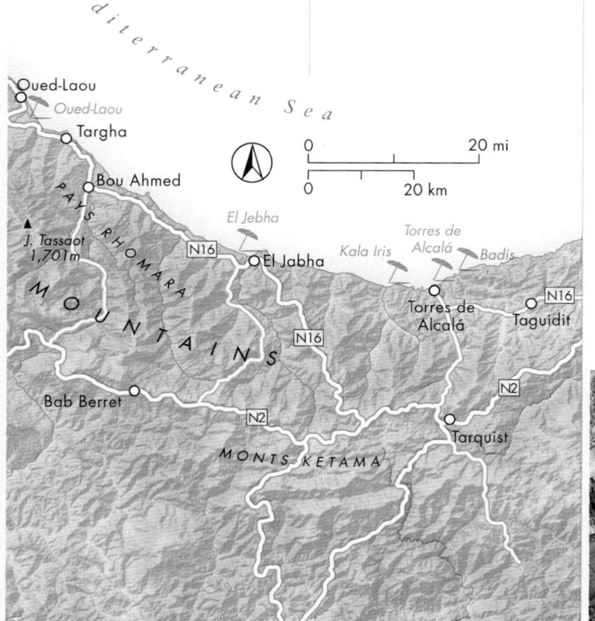

MOROCCAN WRITERS

Morocco has a rich literary tradition. Marrakesh's Koutoubia Mosque, the city's largest, derives its name from the Arabic word for librarian. Dating to the 12th century, it served not only as an important place of worship but also as a library and the world's first marketplace for manuscripts.

(above) Koutoubia Mosque, Marrakesh (opposite page, bottom) Tahar Ben Jelloun (opposite page, top) Siham Benchekroun

Moroccans have been writing about the world since the 14th century, when the *Rihla* (*The Journey*) recounted the story of the Moroccan Islamic scholar Ibn Battuta, who traveled an astounding 75,000 miles over 30 years. More recently, Morocco has served as an oasis for foreign writers looking for inspiration in this magical country. By the 20th century, when dramatic political changes inspired a new generation of Moroccan writers, much of the writing turned inward. Contemporary Moroccan authors address a remarkably diverse range of topics, including such controversial subjects impacting Moroccan society as gender roles, discrimination, poverty, and class division, by writers who create their works in Arabic, French, Berber, and even English.

EXPATS IN MOROCCO

During the 1950s and '60s, Morocco served as a literary sanctuary for many foreign writers, including William S. Burroughs, Paul Bowles, Brion Gysin, Jack Kerouac, Allen Ginsberg, and Tennessee Williams. They took refuge, to varying degrees, in Morocco, particularly in Tangier. Bowles, perhaps the most famous among them, lived in Morocco for more than 50 years.

Five of the brightest lights of Moroccan letters can be discovered in translation (though sometimes only in import editions).

DRISS CHRAÏBI

Novelist, radio producer, and commentator Driss Chraïbi writes novels that address themes of colonialism, the clash between cultures, and the treatment of women within Muslim society. Many of his works are semiautobiographical. His works include *Le Passé Simple* (*The Simple Past*), *Les Boucs* (*The Butts*), *La Civilisation, Ma Mère* (*Mother Comes of Age*), and his autobiography *Vu, Lu, Entendu* (*Seen, Read, Heard*).

ABDELKEBIR KHATIBI

A playwright, novelist, literary critic, and scholar, Abdelkebir Khatibi often incorporated political and social issues into his novels during his most productive periods, the 1960s and '70s. His novels include *La Mémoire Tatouée* (*Tattooed Memory*), *Amour Bilingue* (*Bilingual Love*) and *La Blessure du Nom Propre* (*The Wound Under Its Own Name*).

TAHAR BEN JELLOUN

Born in 1944 to a Fez shopkeeper, Tahar Ben Jelloun is considered one of North Africa's most successful authors. Both a poet and novelist, he has received international acclaim for his works, which provide an insight into Moroccan culture on a variety of controversial themes such as gender identity, sexuality, and male domination within the society. Novels include *The Sand Child*, *Harrouda*, *Racism Expliqué à Ma Fille* (*Racism Explained to My Daughter*), and *La Nuit Sacrée* (*The Sacred Night*).

SIHAM BENCHEKROUN

A doctor, journalist, and writer, Siham Benchekroun is known as much in the West for her pioneering work in medical journalism as for her novels and poetry, which often focus on the lives of Moroccan women. They include the novels *Oser Vivre* (*Dare to Live*) and *Chama*, as well as *À toi* (*For You*), a compilation of poems. Though available in French, none of her books have been translated into English.

RITA EL KHAYAT

Anthropologist, psychologist, and feminist scholar, Rita El Khayat has written more than 30 books focusing predominately on psychiatry and anthropology. She was a moving force in the late 1990s in Morocco's movement to modernize the country's family law code. In 2008, she was nominated for the Nobel Peace Prize. *Open Correspondence*, published in 2010, is a compilation of enlightening correspondence between El Khayat and Abdelkebir Khatabi.

Updated by Simona Schneider

Nestled between the Mediterranean Sea and the backbone of the Rif Mountains are figurative golden gates through which many travelers enter Morocco. Though not associated with the *maroc typique* of deserts and oases, this northern region holds all the *Arabian Nights* allure that many people associate with the country—as well as an energy unparalleled in the rest of Morocco. The ancient cities of Tangier and Tetouan offer a glimpse of evolving urban Morocco with their Arab-inspired sophistication, European dress and languages, palm-lined boulevards, and extensive infrastructure for travelers. Here the vast majority of the population is under 25, and the streets are full of children until late in the evening, especially in the summer months. Tangier is in sharp contrast to the villages and small towns along the Rif Mountains routes, where regional dress and a traditional, agricultural way of life persist. As you travel farther east, the language shifts from Arabic to Rifi Berber (Tarifit), spotted with Spanish and French.

PLANNING

WHEN TO GO

The region has a temperate, coastal climate throughout the year, though the bone-chilling winter weather can catch unprepared tourists off guard. Inland, the Rif Mountains see rain in winter and spring, and the high peaks are often snowcapped through April. Springtime, particularly the month of May, is the region's finest season, with hundreds of varieties of wildflowers in full bloom. Though swimming weather by most standards starts in June, the traditional high season is from late July to the end of August. During this time prices are higher, rooms hard to find, beaches very busy, roads crowded, and the sun intense.

GETTING HERE AND AROUND

BY AIR

Several airlines now fly directly to Tangier, but you'll have to hit the ground with other sorts of transportation to see the region.

BY BOAT AND FERRY

Many travelers arrive in Tangier by boat from Europe. Tangier's port has a new passenger-only terminal, and all commercial activity has moved to the Tanger-Med complex further on the Mediterranean coast closer to Ceuta.

BY BUS

CTM buses offer intercity transportation.

BY CAR

Renting a car in Tangier to explore the region is possible and manageable (though automatics are still very scarce), as is hiring local drivers (and their cars) for varying lengths of time through local travel agencies. The latter may work best for those looking to explore the region immediately surrounding Tangier. Construction of the train line can be seen from most major routes around Tangier, including the entire coastal highway from Tangier to Al Hoceima.

BY TAXI

Grands taxis (taxis that travel fixed routes indicated by their parking stations and leave only when full, meaning with six people) are good ways to get from point to point. They travel between cities as well as on fixed routes within Tangier. To avoid a squeeze or unpredictable delay, offer to pay for more than one spot.

BY TRAIN

Trains connect Tangier with Casablanca and Rabat, where you can connect to points south, but most of the destinations in the immediate region are not served. A major overhaul, which includes high-speed train service between Tangier and Casablanca, is planned for completion in 2015, and construction and demolition toward this end are visible throughout Tangier. If you're driving in the north, keep a lookout for frequent detour signs.

GUIDES AND TOURS

In the port area there are still plenty of fake guides wanting to show you around. Simply walk quickly past these unsolicited assistants, pretend you know exactly where you're going, and show no sign that you're bewildered (not to mention astonished) by this sudden onslaught of new friends passionately interested in your welfare. Most licensed guides sport a badge and work for tour companies.

RESTAURANTS

As much of a mosaic as the region itself, northern Moroccan cuisine combines influences from several other cultures with added spices and native ingredients—and notably features Spanish tapas (*sans* ham, though there is a cured turkey variety that is mischievously called *jambon de dinde,* or "ham of turkey"). Tapas are one way to roll here, as you can eat a filling meal for free with the purchase of a few beers at many of the bars. Tagines are made with particular flair in the north, where olives and spices are local. The abundance of fresh seafood makes it a natural choice in coastal areas. Fresh grilled sardines, shrimp, and calamari are standard fare here, as are larger more-gourmet Mediterranean catches such as *pageot* (red sea bream), swordfish, sole, *St. Pierre* (John Dory), and *dorado* (sea bream). The catch of the day is often displayed in windows making it an easy to point-and-eat option.

HOTELS

Accommodations in the north range from opulent to downright spare, with everything in between. You'll have a range of options in most areas. Hotels in Tangier can be on a par with those of Europe, but the farther you venture off the beaten path, the farther you might feel from Tangier's five-star welcome. Particularly in some of the smaller cities east of Chefchaouen and Tetouan, hotels lack the amenities to call themselves top-tier. Look a bit closer, though—what they lack in luxury these hotels often make up in charm, character, and, most of all, location.

In Tangier and Tetouan, advance reservations are a must if you want decent accommodations. Note that prices rise in July and August, and that if you'll be staying anywhere other than a five-star hotel you may want to inquire in advance (quite seriously) about the state of the hotel's credit-card machine.

WHAT IT COSTS IN DIRHAMS

	¢	$	$$	$$$	$$$$
Restaurants	under 50 DH	50 DH–100 DH	101 DH–150 DH	151 DH–200 DH	over 200 DH
Hotels	under 250 DH	250 DH–500 DH	501 DH–1,000 DH	1,001 DH–1,500 DH	over 1,500 DH

Restaurant prices are per person for a main course at dinner. Hotel prices are for a high-season standard double room, excluding service and tax.

TANGIER

15 km (9 mi) across Strait of Gibraltar from Algeciras, Spain; 350 km (220 mi) north of Casablanca; 278 km (172 mi) north of Rabat.

Giddy from the rush provided by crossing the Strait of Gibraltar from the European continent to Africa, first-time visitors may find the Tangier port such a rude awakening that they fail to see the beauty of the place. Mobs of faux guides and bona fide hustlers greet the arriving ferries hungry for greenhorns to fleece in any way they can. Once you hit your stride and start going places with confidence, Tangier has a charm that this raucous undercurrent only enhances: crumbling kasbah walls, intimate corners in the serpentine medina, piles of bougainvillea, French balconies, Spanish cafés, and other remnants of times gone by.

Grab a seat at a sidewalk café and you'll begin to see how dramatically the urban brouhaha is set against the backdrop of the turquoise Mediterranean. Tangier is a melting pot—a place where it's not uncommon to see sophisticated Moroccans sharing sidewalks with rural Rifi Berbers wrapped in traditional striped *mehndis* (brightly striped blankets women wear tied around their waists) and eccentric expatriates, as well as the new generation of fashion-conscious teenagers. This is also Hercules' city, and recently rudimentary graffiti tags in the empty lots have sported this name; musclemen advertise fitness clubs and burgeoning gymnasts and acrobats, many of whom then join the world's foremost circuses and shows, can be spotted practicing on the beaches and in the parks.

GETTING HERE AND AROUND

BY AIR

Tangier's Boukhalef Airport, 15 km (9 mi) from the city center, is linked by taxis and buses to the Grand Socco (Nos. 17 and 70). Several airlines fly to Tangier through European gateways, including Air Arabia (from Paris-CDG), EasyJet (from Madrid and Paris-CDG), Iberia (from Madrid), Royal Air Maroc (from several European gateways), and Ryanair (from Paris-Beauvais, Brussels, and Madrid). However, only a handful of companies (Air Arabia, Iberia, and Royal Air Maroc) have local offices).

Contacts **Air Arabia** ☎ *0802/00–08–03 toll-free in Morocco* 🌐 *www.airarabia.com.* **Iberia** ☎ *0539/39–31–56 in Tangier* 🌐 *www.iberia.com.* **Royal Air Maroc** ☎ *0539/37–46–31 in Tangier.*

BY BOAT AND FERRY

There are many options for ferrying across the Strait of Gibraltar (20 to 30 mi) from Spain, but it's better to leave from Tarifa rather than Algeciras. The former port, a kite-surfer's paradise, is more pleasant than the latter, which is primarily a commercial port, and ferries from Tarifa are generally cleaner and swifter.

FRS, a Spanish company, runs a 30-minute ferry between Tangier and Tarifa (450 DH passenger, 1,200 DH car) and 70-min between Tangier and Algeciras (420 DH passenger, 1080 DH car). Trasmediterranea and Comarit offer one-hour hydrofoil trips from Algeciras along with other ferry options. Southern Ferries Ltd., a British company whose headquarters is in London, offers a car ferry with cabin accommodations from Sète in southern France, a 36-hour journey. Infrequent ferries connect Tangier and Gibraltar.

Make sure you get on a ferry going to Tangier, and not to the new Tanger-Med passenger port two hours away along the coast. Passenger-only hydrofoils are your best bet, since multi-use ferries often get delayed if they don't have enough freight to merit the run. Also, be aware that no company can guarantee a smooth ride on a choppy day, and ferries sometimes even turn around in exceptional circumstances.

Contacts **Comarit Ferry** ☎ *34/956–657–462 in Algeciras, Spain, 0539/32–00–32 in Tangier* 🌐 *www.comarit.com.* **FRS** ✉ *Port of Tangier* ☎ *0539/94–26–12* 🌐 *www.frs.es.* **Port Tanger-Med** ☎ *0801/00–50–60 toll-free in Morocco, 0539/33–71–55 from outside Morocco* 🌐 *www.tmsa.ma.* **Southern Ferries Ltd** ☎ *0844/815–7785 in the UK* 🌐 *www.southernferries.co.uk.* **Trasmediterránia** ☎ *902/45–46–45 in Spain* 🌐 *www.trasmediterranea.es.*

BY BUS

CTM is the region's main and only recommended bus company. It runs several buses daily between Tangier, Tetouan, Chefchaouen, Al Hoceima, Nador, and many other cities. The company even has an overnight 10-hour bus to Marrakesh.

Contacts **CTM Tangier** ✉ *Av. Louis Van Beethoven at Gare Routière* ☎ *0539/32–03–83 local, 0522/54–10–10 countrywide* 🌐 *www.ctm.ma.*

BY CAR

If you want to rent a car to explore this region of Morocco on your own time, there are major car-rental companies operating in Tangier.

Contacts **Avis** ✉ *54, bd. Pasteur* ☎ *0539/93–46–46.* **Europcar/InterRent** ✉ *87, bd. Mohammed V* ☎ *0539/94–19–38.* **Hertz** ✉ *36, bd. Mohammed V* ☎ *0539/32–21–65.*

BY TAXI

In the new part of the city, abundant *petits taxis* are the safest and most efficient way to get around. Petits taxis have a meter, so make sure to insist that the driver turns it on. You can wave one down by indicating the general direction you wish to travel. If the driver is going your way, he'll stop. For longer distances, or if you are among a group of four or more, you'll need the larger *grand taxi*. A 10-minute petit taxi ride should cost about 8 to 10 DH; in a grand taxi (by yourself), the same journey would be about 30 DH. At night the fare increases by half. From the port and airport, the price should be 20 to 30 DH and 100 to 150 DH, respectively, and depending if it's day or night. Make sure to agree on a price before making yourself comfortable to avoid an uncomfortable situation later.

BY TRAIN

The only northern city served by ONCF, the Moroccan rail service, is Tangier. Tangier Ville station is 3 km (2 mi) west of town. At this writing, nine daily trains connect Tangier with Casablanca, a journey of six hours. Three daily trains get you to Fez in four to five hours, and an overnight train gets you to Marrakesh in 10½ hours, though in the middle of the day it can be 8½ hours. First-class sleeping accommodations are highly recommended.

Train Contacts **Office National des Chemins de Fer** (*ONCF*). ☎ *0890/20–30–40* 🌐 *www.oncf.ma.*

TIMING AND PRECAUTIONS

Tangier has become a much safer place since it became the favorite, prodigal son of the current king, who recognized its potential to be a great tourist destination and subsequently increased police presence. Using common sense when exploring by day and staying out of dark alleys at night will help keep you out of harm's way. When in doubt about walking through dimly lighted areas, take a taxi. The medina in Tangier can be dangerous at night. Tangerines are known as late sleepers, so don't be surprised that the streets are usually empty and stores shut until 10 am.

VISITOR INFORMATION

Tangier's Tourist Information center is open daily and can usually supply information about local events as well as brochures and some rudimentary maps, but if you need or want a good city map, you'll have to buy one.

Visitor Information **National Tourism Office** ✉ *29, bd. Pasteur* ☎ *0539/94–80–50.*

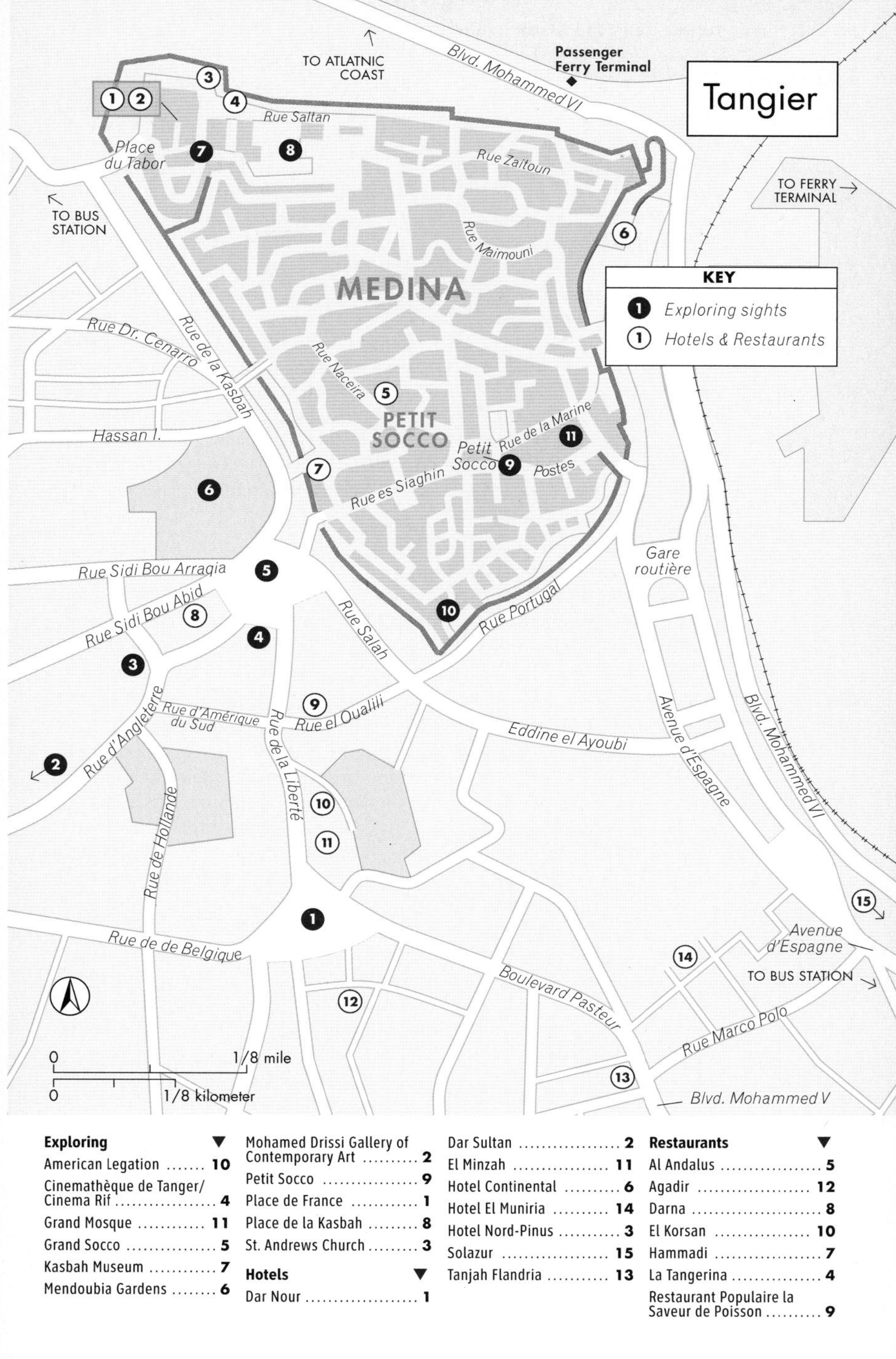
Tangier
KEY
Exploring sights
Hotels & Restaurants
TO ATLATNIC COAST
Passenger Ferry Terminal
Blvd. Mohammed VI
TO FERRY TERMINAL
TO BUS STATION
Place du Tabor
Rue Saltan
Rue Zaitoun
Rue Maimouni
MEDINA
Rue Naceira
PETIT SOCCO
Petit Socco
Rue de la Marine
Postes
Rue es Siaghin
Rue Dr. Cenarro
Rue de la Kasbah
Hassan I.
Rue Sidi Bou Arraqia
Rue Sidi Bou Abid
Rue Salah
Rue Portugal
Gare routière
Rue d'Amérique du Sud
Rue de la Liberté
Rue el Oualili
Eddine el Ayoubi
Avenue d'Espagne
Blvd. Mohammed VI
Rue d'Angleterre
Rue de Hollande
Rue de de Belgique
Boulevard Pasteur
Avenue d'Espagne
TO BUS STATION
Rue Marco Polo
Blvd. Mohammed V
0 1/8 mile
0 1/8 kilometer
Exploring
American Legation 10
Cinemathèque de Tanger/ Cinema Rif 4
Grand Mosque 11
Grand Socco 5
Kasbah Museum 7
Mendoubia Gardens 6
Mohamed Drissi Gallery of Contemporary Art 2
Petit Socco 9
Place de France 1
Place de la Kasbah 8
St. Andrews Church 3
Hotels
Dar Nour 1
Dar Sultan 2
El Minzah 11
Hotel Continental 6
Hotel El Muniria 14
Hotel Nord-Pinus 3
Solazur 15
Tanjah Flandria 13
Restaurants
Al Andalus 5
Agadir 12
Darna 8
El Korsan 10
Hammadi 7
La Tangerina 4
Restaurant Populaire la Saveur de Poisson 9

EXPLORING

MEDINA

TOP ATTRACTIONS

American Legation. Preserved today as an American Historic Landmark, this property was given to the United States by the Moroccan sultan in 1821. The museum has an impressive collection of paintings, ethonographic portraits, maps, and not-to-be-missed miniature depictions of famous battles from the Forbes Museum's collection. There's also a Paul Bowles room with a new audio archive recently remastered by the Library of Congress. Displays showcase Tangier's history, including handwritten correspondence between the sultan and George Washington, and a letter home from a panicked ambassador receiving a now-extinct Barbary lion gift as a sign of goodwill and friendship toward the "Sultans of America." The museum hosts a regular lending library, which has a small but interesting collection of English-language books. ✉ *8, Zankat d'Amérique, Medina* ☎ *0539/93–53–17* 🌐 *www.legation.org* ⏲ *Weekdays 10–1 and 3–5; and by appointment.*

Cinema Rif. This bustling cinema and cultural center, the Cinémathèque de Tanger, housed in a renovated 1938 theater, offers retrospective screenings and cutting-edge films in its two theaters. Old Spanish film flyers dazzle from under the glass at the café, where there is a full menu of curious, ciné-inspired cocktails. Wi-Fi is also on hand. The colorful, comfy chairs spill out onto the Grand Socco. ✉ *Grand Socco-Place du 9 Avril, Medina* ☎ *0539/93–46–83* 🌐 *www.cinemathequedetanger.com.*

Kasbah. Sprawling across the ancient medina's highest point, Tangier's kasbah can be blinding at midday as the infamous Mediterranean sun bounces off the pristine white walls, but the narrow streets give ample shade and breeze later in the afternoon, and it is a pleasant place to spend some time. Modified since the Roman era, its impressive wall is a relic of the Portuguese in the 16th century. During early Arab rule it was the traditional residence of the sultan and his harem. The kasbah has always been shared by Moroccans and foreign residents alike—and particularly in the International Zone era. It is also the site of some of the best hotels in the city. The kasbah square is the site of snake tamers for tourists (imported from Marrakesh), and also the iconic Bab el-Bhar, a literal hole in the wall that offers a glorious view of the Atlantic and Spain (only 20 mi away), alternately advancing and receding with the currents of the strait. There is also Bab el-As'aa (Door of the Rod), a beautiful worn zellij gate that used to be the site of punishments, and Bab Haha, which must speak for itself. You can reach the kasbah by passing through Bab el-Fahs (checkpoint Gate in Arabic) into the medina from the Grand Socco and climbing Rue d'Italie and entering through the kasbah gate, Bab el-Kasbah, at the top or by winding up the medina's Rue des Chrétiens to the kasbah area. ✉ *Medina.*

Petit Socco. Tennessee Williams based his play *Camino Real* on the square—and it is indeed dramatic, with the cast of characters that are passing through at any time of day. It has a theatrical range of seating, which is split among the three main cafés—parterre (Tingis), orchestra (Centrale), or balcony (Fuentes). The Fuentes used to be the German

A fishing trawler returns to Tangier's harbor after a long day at sea.

post office in the International Zone period—supposedly the most reliable one before the Germans got kicked out during WWII. It's a great place to take a break before plunging back into the souks that surround it or let gravity take you down past the Grand Mosque to the viewing platform looking out onto the port. ✉ *Medina.*

WORTH NOTING

Grand Mosque. You can't miss the striking green-and-white-tile minaret of Tangier's Grand Mosque. Built in 1685 (on the site of a destroyed European-built church) by Moulay Ismail, the mosque was a tribute to and celebration of Morocco's return to Arab control. Although its entrances are blocked from view by wooden screens and entrance is strictly forbidden to non-Muslims, its bold colors make it one of the most recognizable of the medina's attractions. It's worth a look as you wander through the medina. ✉ *Between Rue de la Marine and Rue des Postes, on Rue Siaghine, Medina.*

Kasbah Museum. Constructed by the 17th-century sultan Moulay Ismail, this was the kasbah's palace. The sultan's former apartments now house an interesting Moroccan-art museum, with mosaic floors, carpets, traditional Fez furniture, jewelry, ceramics, leather, daggers, illuminated manuscripts, textiles, and historic, finely crafted examples of carved and painted cedar ceilings. The marble columns in the courtyard were taken from the ancient Roman city of Volubilis. Don't miss the mosaic *Voyage of Venus* or the life-size Carthaginian tomb. Exit the palace via the former treasury of Moulay Ismail, the Bit el-Mal; look for the giant knobby wooden boxes that once held gold and precious gems. ✉ *Pl. de la Kasbah, Medina* ☎ *0539/93–20–97* 🎟 *10 DH* ⏲ *Wed.–Mon. 9–4.*

Tangier's Grand Socco is a popular destination both day and night.

VILLE NOUVELLE

TOP ATTRACTIONS

Fodor's Choice ★ **Grand Socco.** Tangier's chief market area in times past, the Grand Socco (a combination of French and Spanish meaning "great souk")—and otherwise Place du 9 Avril, which corresponds to the date of a famous speech made by King Mohammed V on the occasion of independence—now serves as a local transportation hub. Bab el-Fahs, the main door to the medina, stands at the bottom. As late as the 1940s, when the new city was just beginning, the door was locked at night to seal off outsiders, thus its name, literally "Inspection Gate." One main attraction here is the recently restored movie theater, the Cinema Rif, which displays photographs and old movie posters highlighting Tangier's glamorous past. Head up some steps to the right of the cinema, and you'll find a babouche market, or for a good view, take a break at Passengers de Tangers, a rooftop restaurant/café on the far side of the Grand Socco from the cinema. ✉ *At bottom of Rue de la Liberté, just south of Mendoubia Gardens, Ville Nouvelle.*

Mendoubia Gardens. Adjacent to the Grand Socco, this former residence of the Mendoub—the sultan's representative on the governing commission during the international years—is now a park with palm tree–lined paths that is popular with families on weekends. To the right of the entrance is a large banyan tree that locals claim is more than 800 years old. The park also used to be a large European cemetery, and several markers still bear witness. ✉ *Rue Bouarrakia at Rue d'Italie, Ville Nouvelle.*

Place de France. Famous for its café scene in the first half of the 20th century, Place de France is one of Tangier's main squares and is named for the French Consulate that takes up one corner behind a large billboard alternately advertising real estate and the king. The square fills up after about 6 pm for a nightly promenade. Next to it is the humorously named **Wall of the Lazies,** a viewing platform where three canons still stand pointed at Spain. Here kids climb the canons, errant balloon and roasted-nut sellers keep you happy and sated, and photographers offer to take your picture. Yes, you too could become lazy here for a good moment, especially at sunset. ✉ *Ville Nouvelle.*

WORTH NOTING

Mohamed Drissi Gallery of Contemporary Art. Located in the stately former British Consulate building built in 1890 and surrounded by a lovely garden, this gallery, run by the country's ministry of culture, shows mostly traveling exhibitions. ✉ *52, rue d'Angleterre* ☎ *0539/94–99–72* ⏲ *Wed.–Mon. 9–1 and 2–6.*

St. Andrew's Church. This Anglican church built in 1894 is one of the purest vestiges of Tangier's international days. The architecture and interior are both Moorish in flavor (the Lord's Prayer is inscribed in Arabic above the altar), while the cemetery hosts expats from the International Zone period. The priest comes from Gibraltar on Sunday for services. The graveyard holds the tombs of legendary journalist Walter Harris and eccentric Tangier memoirist David Herbert. ✉ *50, rue d'Angleterre, Ville Nouvelle* ☎ *039/93–46–33* ⏲ *Mon.–Sat. 9:30–12:30 and 2–6; Sun. services 8:30, 9:30, and 11.*

WHERE TO EAT

Tangier's cuisine has notable Moroccan, Spanish, and French influences, and a new crop of restaurants are successfully blending all three. Often the most delicious dishes are the simplest, such as freshly caught grilled fish with a touch of garlic. There are also the traditional dishes like tagine, couscous, or *baissara,* a bean soup. In the Ville Nouvelle there are a plethora of opulent choices in old palaces. In the medina, the restaurants are intimate and often associated with lodgings.

MEDINA

¢ SEAFOOD ✕ **Al Andalus.** This no-frills restaurant specializes in a variety of fresh seafood—including sole, swordfish, shrimp, and dorado—expertly grilled or fried with a side of fries or rice and the option of a refreshing tomato sauce. The kitchen also prepares delicious and cheap Spanish-style *tortillas* (hearty omelets with deep-fried potatoes). One of the few good options for a late meal, they usually stay open until at least 1 am. ✉ *7, rue de Commerce, Medina* ☎ *No phone* ▭ *No credit cards* ⏲ *No lunch.*

$$$ MOROCCAN ✕ **El Korsan.** One of Tangier's most reliable restaurants, El Korsan is located in the peerless Minzah hotel. The kitchen serves traditional Moroccan cuisine in the most sumptuous manner possible. Specialties include succulent *mechoui* (roasted lamb or mutton), slow-cooked tagines, and couscous. The food is excellent, the staff is attentive, and the decor is classically Moroccan, with soaring arches and handicrafts.

Andalusian music is performed nightly. ✉ *Hotel el Minzah, 85, rue de la Liberté, Medina* ☎ *0539/93–58–85.*

$ MOROCCAN ★ ✕ **Hammadi.** Decorated in an over-the-top Moroccan style, with banquettes covered with sumptuous pillows and rich brocades, Hammadi is not to be missed. With a live band playing traditional Andalusian music and several nightly shows, it is anything but dull. The place is definitely touristy, but it also has a charm. Try the house pastilla, chicken tagine, or *kefta* (beef patties). ✉ *2, rue de la Kasbah, Medina* ☎ *0539/93–45–14.*

$$$ SEAFOOD ★ ✕ **Hotel Nord-Pinus.** Boasting an unforgettably romantic ambience, this world-class restaurant serves traditional Moroccan dishes with a creative twist. Along with dishes like chicken-and-raisin tagine, there's a splendid array of vegetarian dishes such as the eggplant caviar. Almost as delicious as the food is the windowed balcony overlooking the sea. Call around 11 am for the menu of the day. ✉ *11, rue Riad Sultan, Medina* ☎ *0661/22–81–40* 🌐 *www.nord-pinus-tanger.com* ✍ *Reservations essential.*

VILLE NOUVELLE

$ MOROCCAN ★ ✕ **Agadir.** This cozy restaurant offers an expansive menu of traditional Moroccan cuisine, with a number of delicious tagines (try the lamb and prune, or chicken with vegetables). The harrira soup makes a good starter. There's also plenty of Continental fare; both wine and beer are available. Retro warm colors make this simple room seem romantic and relaxed; it's a great place to go after a long day of sightseeing, but not if you're starving. Expect a bit of a wait, as the waiter is also the chef. ✉ *Rue Prince Heritier, Ville Nouvelle* ☎ *0668/82–76–96* 💳 *No credit cards* ⏲ *Closed Wed. No lunch.*

¢ MOROCCAN ★ ✕ **Darna.** Located in an old British prison, the women's section of this multidimensional nonprofit vocational training center, whose name means "Our House," prepares scrumptious home-style lunches. The restaurant is a favorite of Tangier's expat community, not least for its sun-drenched patio and remarkably vivacious fig tree growing out from cheerful tiles. Traditional couscous is served on Friday and should not be missed. Check out the textile shop or the bath products and jewelry after a delicious lemon tart or chocolate mousse dessert. Darna also offers a four-handed massage in the beauty salon. ✉ *Rue Jules Cot, off Pl. du 9 Avril, Ville Nouvelle* ☎ *0539/94–70–65* 🌐 *www.darnamaroc.org* ⏲ *No dinner. No lunch Sun.*

$$$ SEAFOOD ★ ✕ **Saveurs de Poisson.** The owner of this restaurant doesn't hesitate to say the food here is extraordinary—in fact, he claims it has magical healing powers. Mohammed Belhadj, a colorful Tangier character obsessed with Popeye, the restaurant's mascot, likes to explain the salutary effect of each recipe. The menu and the price are fixed, so there's no choice; just sit down and be prepared for four courses served in large tagines to be shared by the table. The main course is always the catch of the day, which is served grilled and as kebabs—it's usually St. Pierre, dorado, or sole. The meal is followed by a dessert of roasted pine nuts with strawberries (in season) covered in local honey. You'll be served special fruit juice based on prune juice and infused with flowers, cloves, and other secret ingredients, and a souvenir earthenware mug is usually part of

the price. Not recommended for those with stomachs sensitive to spices. ✉ *2, Escalier Waller (on the steps down from the El Minzah Hotel), Ville Nouvelle* ☎ *0539/33–63–26* ▭ *No credit cards* ⊙ *Closed Fri. No lunch.*

WHERE TO STAY

Whether the style is sparse modernism or over-the-top opulence, Tangier is all about leisure and luxury, sometimes with a vintage or old-world feel. Add Morocco's famous hospitality and Tangier's plethora of gorgeous views and you have an unforgettable experience.

For expanded hotel reviews, visit Fodors.com.

MEDINA

$$ ★ **Dar Nour and Le Salon Bleu.** In the center of the old medina and boasting a 360-degree view over the city, the Atlantic, the Strait of Gibraltar, the Bay of Tangier, and Spain, this "House of Light" is partly built right on the kasbah's western ramparts. **Pros:** personal attention; cozy atmosphere. **Cons:** as with everywhere in the kasbah, you must climb up before you can come down again. ✉ *20, rue Gourna, Medina* ☎ *0662/11–27–24, 0654/32–76–18* 🌐 *www.darnour.com* *9 rooms* *In-room: no a/c. In-hotel: restaurant* 🍽 *Breakfast.*

$$ **Dar Sultan.** The chaotic harmony of every style of carpet known make this the exotic abode you'd expect in the kasbah. **Pros:** in the heart of the medina; romantic atmosphere. **Cons:** a bit hard to find. ✉ *49, rue Touila, La Kasbah, Medina* ☎ *0539/33–60–61* 🌐 *www.darsultan.com* *6 rooms* *In-room: no a/c, Internet* 🍽 *Breakfast.*

$$ **Hotel Continental.** Morocco's very first hotel was built in 1865 in the Victorian style—appropriately since Victoria's son Alfred was the first official guest. **Pros:** great views; excellent location; good value. **Cons:** not all rooms are air-conditioned; some renovated rooms are impersonal. ✉ *36, Dar Baroud, Medina* ☎ *0539/93–10–24* 🌐 *www.continental-tanger.com* *66 rooms* *In-room: a/c, Wi-Fi. In-hotel: restaurant, parking* 🍽 *Breakfast.*

$$ ★ **La Tangerina.** Across from the outer wall of the kasbah, this four-story hotel is minimally decorated in a Sahara-safari style with large palms among other plants, black-and-white checkered floors, and beautiful carpets. **Pros:** beautiful setting; stunning views from balcony. **Cons:** many rooms give onto the center of the house only, though it is usually quite serene. ✉ *19, Riad Sultan, Medina* ☎ *0539/94–77–31* 🌐 *www.latangerina.com* *10 rooms* *In-room: no a/c, Wi-Fi. In-hotel: gym, spa* 🍽 *Breakfast.*

VILLE NOUVELLE

$$$$ **El Minzah.** Tangier's top hotel was built in 1930 by the English Lord Bute. **Pros:** great service; excellent facilities. **Cons:** on the expensive side. ✉ *85, rue de la Liberté, Ville Nouvelle* ☎ *0539/93–58–85, 0539/33–34–44* 🌐 *www.elminzah.com* *125 rooms, 15 suites* *In-room: a/c, Wi-Fi. In-hotel: restaurant, bar, pool, gym, spa, laundry facilities, business center, parking, some pets allowed* 🍽 *Breakfast.*

$$$ ★ **Tanjah Flandria.** On Ville Nouvelle's main thoroughfare, this modern, jet-set chic hotel has a rooftop pool, a pleasant, atmospheric lounge-bar with bay views. **Pros:** recently renovated; central location for beach and

This elaborately tiled room is in the Hotel Continental.

medina; friendly staff. **Cons:** international decor unspecific to Tangier. ✉ *6, bd. Mohammed V, off Bd. Pasteur, Ville Nouvelle* ☎ *0539/93–32–79* *146 rooms, 4 suites* *In-room: a/c, Internet, Wi-Fi. In-hotel: restaurant, bar, pool, gym, spa, laundry facilities, business center, parking* *Breakfast.*

NIGHTLIFE

Tangier's nightlife begins with the early-evening promenade and café hour, from about 6 to 9, when the streets teem with locals and expats alike. In summer many beachfront cafés are full well into the night. Late dining is another mainstay of Tangerine nightlife, with many restaurants open past 10 pm—rare in Morocco and, along with tapas, another example of Spanish influence in the region.

Cafés and writers seem inextricably linked, whether the substance sought is caffeine, hops, absinthe, or worse. Tangier café life is especially vibrant. Most patrons are men, as women tend to go to the salons de thé. Some men do all their business out of cafés, whether it be real estate, hustling, or philosophizing.

Discos, of which there is no shortage in Tangier, begin to fill around 11 and thump well into the morning. Beware of girls that look like they're just out with a group of friends—very few women go out to bars here unless they are working.

2

MEDINA

CAFÉS

Café Centrale. Ringside seating at the greatest show on Earth can be had at Café Centrale, which sits on the Petit Socco. A good place to catch your breath with a *panaché orange* (orange-flavor fruit shake) and a *croque-monsieur* (grilled cheese sandwich) or a full meal of succulent lamb chops as you watch the strange cast of characters wander past. ✉ *Petit Socco, Medina* ☎ *No phone.*

Les Fils du Detroit. Andalusian musicians hold jam sessions every night around 5 or 6 in closet-sized Les Fils du Detroit. Sometimes your presence is enough to get the band going. You'll pay just the price of a tea, but it's nice to leave a tip for the musicians. ✉ *Pl. du Méchouar, off Pl. de la Kasbah, Medina.*

Gran Café de Paris. With its tufted brown leather seats, impeccable service, mirrors galore, and a wall covered with fading photographs of Volubilis and wood carvings of astrological creatures, Gran Café de Paris will make you feel like you're back in the 1950s with Burroughs (he wrote here), or in *The Bourne Ultimatum* (it was filmed here as well as on the rooftops of Tangier). This is a perfect place to watch the *paseo* (evening stroll) on the boulevard or the Wall of the Lazies. Have an orange juice or a Nescafé with milk (café au lait). ✉ *Pl. de France, Medina* ☎ *No phone.*

VILLE NOUVELLE

BARS

Number One Bar. This renovated apartment with pink walls and an impressive collection of memorabilia from the last 20-odd years gives you the feeling that you are behind the scenes of the myth. Karim, the bar's owner, has great taste in blues and jazz and has lived in America for ten years. The low-lit outpost occupies the building on the corner across from the Rembrandt hotel, where Boulevard Pasteur ends. Though the tapas are a bit pricey, an adjoining restaurant is also a decent option for dinner. ✉ *1, bd. Mohammed V, Ville Nouvelle.*

Les Passagers de Tanger. This restaurant-bar is remarkable for its wonderful view over the Grand Socco and for its theme nights with dancing. The outdoor patio is pleasant day or night and inside is plain, with sepia-tone snapshots of modern Tangerines lining the walls. You can come here if you're craving otherwise illicit Serrano ham, but expect to pay a price to sate your hunger. For a snack, try the red and black olive tapenade that resembles caviar. ✉ *4, pl. du 9 Avril, on the Grand Socco, 3rd fl., Ville Nouvelle.*

Tanger Inn. A best late-night libation at the Tanger Inn is the opportunity for literary nostalgia. Knowing that your bar stool may have supported the likes of William Burroughs, Allen Ginsberg, Jack Kerouac, Paul Bowles, Jean Genet, Tennessee Williams, or Federico García Lorca always adds a dash of erudition to your cocktail. Approaching from Boulevard Mohammed V with a friend is advisable, as the area can be sketchy by night. On weekends the place is unmanageably packed with young locals and is anything but smoke-free. ✉ *El Muniria, 1, rue Magellan, Ville Nouvelle.*

CAFÉS

Café Hafa. Café Hafa west of the kasbah overlooking the Strait of Gibraltar and set up on seven levels plunging toward the sea, this laid-back cliff café has been the favorite sunset-watching haunt of all Tangier glitterati. Waiters impressively deliver 16 steaming and sticky cups of tea at a time despite swarms of bees that seem not to sting very often. People will test if you've been to Tangier by whether or not you have been here. Eggs and traditional pea soup (baissara) are also available. ✉ *Av. Mohammed Tazi, Ville Nouvelle* ☎ *No phone.*

DANCE CLUBS

Chellah Beach Club. Especially lively on summer nights and highly recommended, Chellah Beach Club is tucked among the clubs along the strip on Tangier Bay. Dine or have drinks accompanied by a Copacabana-style lively jazz band that has the dance floor swinging from 9 until the crowd disperses. There is also a popular open-mike night Monday from 9 to 11 pm that attracts all kinds of local talent. ✉ *Av. Mohammed VI, Ville Nouvelle* ☎ *0539/32–50–68.*

Morocco Palace. Morocco Palace is an energetic dance hall with a live band. The singers' vocals can be jarring—the flat tones come out of *sheikhates* (female Arabic vocalists from Morocco) traditions. The star lotar player, who accompanies belly-dancing shows, is a truly amazing musician and plays three sets a night, at 11 pm, 1 am, and 3 am. ✉ *11, av. du Prince de Moulay Abdellah, Ville Nouvelle* ☎ *0539/93–86–14.*

MARSHAN

BARS

Cabaña. Though it's just beyond center city, Cabaña feels as if you've stepped onto Gilligan's Island. You'll be greeted by monkeys and tropical fragrances at this cliff-side bar and restaurant. Enter a campground, pass monkeys and banana tree groves, and head to the platform with two restaurants, a pool (open 10 am–6 pm), and a patio for dancing. Tell the taxi driver to take you to "Camping Miramonte" in Marshan. ✉ *Camping Miramonte, Marshan* ⏲ *Open until 1 am.*

SHOPPING

Tangier can be an intense place to shop; proprietors are accustomed to inflicting their hard sell on overwhelmed day-trippers from Spain. Ville Nouvelle boutiques offer standard Moroccan items, such as carpets, brass, leather, ceramics, and clothing at higher—but fixed—prices. The more unusual and creative high-quality items, however, are mostly in the specialty shops throughout the medina. Don't be afraid to stop at small, unnamed stores, as these often stock real off-the-beaten-path treasures.

ANTIQUES

Boutique Majid. One of the finest antiques shops in Morocco, Boutique Majid has a wide collection of antique textiles, silks, rich embroideries, rugs, and Berber jewelry (often silver with coral and amber), as well as wooden boxes, household items, copper, and brass collected from all over Africa on yearly scouting trips. Prices are high, but the quality is indisputable. As master showman and proprietor Abdelmajid says,

"It's an investment!" He ships internationally. ✉ *66, rue des Chrétiens, Medina* ☎ *0539/93–88–92* 🌐 *www.boutiquemajid.com.*

Galerie Tindouf. Galerie Tindouf, across from the Hotel Minzah, is a pricey antiques shop specializing in clothing, home furnishings, and period pieces from old Tangier. The owners also run the Bazaar Tindouf, right down the street, which sells modern Moroccan crafts in ceramics, wood, iron, brass, and silver, plus embroidery and rugs. The staff here won't give you the hard sell and has a large inventory of older rugs. ✉ *72, rue de la Liberté, Ville Nouvelle* ☎ *0539/93–86–00.*

CRAFTS

Boutique Marouaini. The simple Boutique Marouaini sells ceramics, wood, rugs, clothing, and metalware, as well as paintings by local artists at very reasonable prices. ✉ *65, rue des Chrétiens, Medina* ☎ *0539/33–60–67.*

Coin de l'Art Berbère. The extensive collection of rugs at Coin de l'Art Berbère includes samples from the Middle and High Atlas regions, made by Saharan and southern Berber tribes. Check out the collection of doors, locks, windows, and boxes from southern Morocco and the Sahara. You'll need to bargain here. ✉ *53, rue des Chrétiens, Medina* ☎ *0539/93–80–94.*

Dar D'Art. This "house of art" showcases local artists all year round in a plethora of media and styles, but mostly nonorientalist paintings. Ask to be shown the stock, as well, for the gallery artists. The owner, Choukri, is charming and knowledgeable about the small but strong art scene in Tangier and Morocco. ✉ *6, rue Khalid Matran, Ville Nouvelle* ☎ *0539/37–57–07, 0661/19–73–31* 🌐 *www.dardart.com* ⏲ *10–1 and 3–7 or by appointment.*

Ensemble Artisanal. The fixed-price, government-regulated Ensemble Artisanal offers handicrafts from all over Morocco. The store is a little pricey, but it's a good place to develop an eye for quality items and their market prices before you hit the medina shops. You can also custom emboss or cover bound books in leather. ✉ *Rue de Belgique at Rue Ensallah, 3 blocks west of Pl. de la France, Ville Nouvelle* ☎ *0539/93–78–41.*

Fondoq Shejrah. This weaving cooperative is housed on the second floor of an old stable and inn whose name translates to "tree hotel" and overlooks what used to be the large courtyard where visitors parked horses. Weavers and their looms are tightly packed into nooks that are also shops, with walls lined in naturally dyed blankets, throws, curtains, linens, thick wool djellebahs and synthetic silk scarves all hot off the looms. As the cooperative is unmarked from the outside, it is best if a local shows you the portal that leads into the complex, which is below Restaurant Saveur de Poisson, the Waller steps, and the chicken coop alley. ✉ *Rue el-Oualili, below and to the right of Escalier Waller and Rue de la Liberté, Ville Nouvelle* ☎ *No phone.*

OUTDOOR ACTIVITIES

New activities are popping up all the time—everything from quad riding to jet skiing to golf. There are also nature walks that take in the diverse fauna of the region. Though the majority of these are in French, more and more are offered in English.

GOLF

Golf, the favorite sport of the late King Hassan II, has spread throughout Morocco.

Royal Golf de Tanger. The 18-hole Royal Golf de Tanger, founded in 1914, is one of two premier courses in the north and is located 3 km (1.8 mi) outside of the city center. The course measures 6,605 yards and is par 70. The greens fee is 400 DH for 18 holes and 50 DH for practice. ✉ *Rte. Boubana Tanger* ☎ *0539/93–89–25* 🌐 *royalgolftanger.com.*

SAILING

Tanger Nautique. The company offers wakeboarding and waterskiing, fishing trips with all the equipment included, or simply a half day on the water. This is a fun way to discover Tangier's bay and the wilder strait and make unforgettable memories. Fishing is 3000 DH for a half day for up to six people. The company also offers wakeboarding further out on the Mediterranean coast. ✉ *Port de Tanger, Yacht Club* ☎ *0539/94–16–70, 0649/93–67–74* 🌐 *tanger-nautique.com.*

THE CEUTA PENINSULA

The Ceuta Peninsula offers such splendid views and gentle breezes that it is difficult not to recommend it if you have the time and curiosity to spend a day there. The N16 coast road east from Tangier hugs the edge of the Strait of Gibraltar all the way to the Djebel Musa promontory.

CAP SPARTEL

16 km (10 mi) west of Tangier.

Minutes from Tangier is the jutting Cap Spartel, the African continent's extreme northwest corner. Known to Romans as Ampelusium ("cape of the vines"), this fertile area sits high above the rocky coast. A shady, tree-lined road leads up to the summit, where a large lighthouse has wonderful sweeping views out over the Mediterranean at the very point where it meets the Atlantic; ask the kindly gatekeeper to show you around.

Cap Spartel's beaches vary widely from wide inlets to long stretches of sand. Ashakar is a public beach with three parts: the first is level with the road while the following two, more highly recommended, are accessed by descending steep steps down cliffs and sometimes flowering dunes. It becomes the currently abandoned Robinson Beach, still on the strait, and then turns the corner at the Mirage Hotel onto the long Atlantic coast. There are lifeguards on duty and straw umbrellas for rent.

Cap Spartel's lighthouse looks out over the Mediterranean.

GETTING HERE AND AROUND

Cap Spartel is most easily reached by grand taxi from Tangier.

EXPLORING

Caves of Hercules. Five kilometers (3 mi) south of the cape are the so-called Caves of Hercules, a popular and harmless tourist attraction tied to the region's relationship with the mythical hero, who was said to rest here after his famous labors. Inhabited in prehistoric times, the caves were used more recently to cut millstones, hence the hundreds of round indentations on their walls and ceiling otherwise attributed to Hercules' clawing fingers. The caves are known for their windowlike opening in the shape of the African continent, through which the surf comes crashing into the lagoon and lower cave. Here you can buy souvenirs and have a camel ride in the parking lot. *10 DH* *Daily 9–1 and 3–6.*

NEED A BREAK?

Above and to the right of the entrance to the Caves of Hercules, follow the tiled wall down to a path leading to a small, unnamed platform café. Run by Abdelkader, this tiny café is the prime spot from which to view the caves from the outside. Its small wicker seats are ideal places to take in the stunning Atlantic views and to look down at local fishermen trying their luck on the rocks below while bold divers jump from the cliff. The café also offers a hidden secret. The small gray door near the kitchen opens into a two-story dining room inside Abdelkader's own personal cave; he will serve up one of his wonderful tagines while the surf's sound echoes off the cool cave walls. It's a one-of-a-kind place.

Rmilet Park. Halfway to Cap Spartel, Rmilet is a park popular with local families on weekends. It has shady pine, mimosa, and eucalyptus groves, as well as acrobats, ponies, drum circles, and humble kebab huts at the end of the path in a parking lot with incredible views. Here, too, you can see the abandoned house of Ion Perdicarus and imagine his kidnapping by the Rifi bandit El Raissouni, with whom he later became friends. It's a great stop-off or day trip for a few hours with the family. The café across from the main entrance offers yet another stunning and unusual view of Tangier.

WHERE TO EAT AND STAY

$$$$ **Hotel Mirage.** Located above the Caves of Hercules, this modern resort has traditional touches, a local art gallery, and an appropriately stunning 180-degree view of the horizon. **Pros:** great service; excellent facilities; peaceful setting. **Cons:** 20-minute drive or taxi ride from the city. ✉ *Grotte de Hercules, Rte. de Cap Spartel* ☎ *0539/33–33–31* 🌐 *www.lemirage-tanger.com* *25 bungalows* *In-room: a/c, Wi-Fi. In-hotel: restaurant, bar, pool, spa, beach, laundry facilities, business center, parking* *Closed mid-Nov.–Feb.* *Multiple meal plans.*

ASILAH

40 km (25 mi) southwest of Tangier.

Known as one of the country's most artistic communities, the sleepy fishing village of Asilah hosts a two-week festival every year in August in which artists from all over the world are invited to paint murals on the city's walls and exhibit. Asilah was conquered by the Portuguese in 1471, and its Old Town retains a Portuguese feel. Las Cuevas beach is a nice beach for basking in the sun.

GETTING HERE AND AROUND

Asilah can be reached from Tangier by either a grand taxi or a CTM bus, which leaves from Tangier's central bus station.

WHERE TO EAT AND STAY

$ SPANISH **Casa Garcia.** People flock to this unassuming seafood restaurant for no-nonsense fresh fish and langoustines (a large Mediterranean prawn). You can be sure you're being served the catch of the day. Unlike its neighbors, this place serves alcohol. Weekend afternoons can be a difficult time to find a table, as whole families join tables banquet-style. ✉ *51, rue Moulay Hassan Ben el-Mehdi* ☎ *0539/41–74–65* *No credit cards.*

$ MOROCCAN **Oceano Casa Pépé.** Reliable and friendly, this small restaurant is located outside Bab el-Kasaba, the Old Town's main gate. The anchovy appetizer is not to be missed, and neither is the paella. The selection of tapas makes this place popular with groups. ✉ *Rte. de Rabat* ☎ *0539/41–73–95* *No credit cards.*

$ PIZZA **Yali's Restaurant.** This unassuming pizzeria among a strip of similar restaurants along the old medina wall stands out for the unbeatable freshness of its fare, which is best at lunchtime. Specialties include a pleasantly spiced and salted catch-of-the-day served with the traditional fresh pureed tomato dip. Crispy pizzas are especially good for the kids.

There's an exceedingly good-natured staff. ✉ *Av. Hassan II, in the Town Center* ☎ *No phone* ▭ *No credit cards.*

$$ **Al Alba.** Offering impeccably neat and tidy traditional-style rooms, this hotel gestures at cloud and sky with its blue stained-glass skylights and patios. **Pros:** staff is helpful; offers full board upon request. **Con:** not in the medina proper. ✉ *35, lot. Nakhil* ☎ *0539/41–69–23* 🌐 *www.asilahalalba.com* *7 rooms, 3 suites* *In-room: a/c, Internet, Wi-Fi. In-hotel: restaurant* *Multiple meal plans.*

$$ **Dar Manara.** Renting a room here really means that you have the whole house and its various atmospheres to explore and enjoy, complete with a festive Moroccan tent on the rooftop. **Pros:** in the heart of the medina. **Cons:** small; book ahead. ✉ *23, M'Jimaa St.* ☎ *0539/41–69–64* 🌐 *www.asilah-darmanara.com* *5 rooms* *In-room: no a/c, Wi-Fi. In-hotel: restaurant* ▭ *No credit cards* *Breakfast.*

LARACHE

80 km (50 mi) southwest of Tangier.

Known primarily for its proximity to the ruins of the ancient town of Lixus, Larache is worth a stop for a stroll along the Balcon Atlantico, a seaside promenade that runs along the rocky shore. There are numerous cafés on the promenade where you can enjoy a fruit drink. Another enjoyable walk is to French writer Jean Genet's grave in the Catholic Cemetery just south of the medina. It's near the Muslim graveyard, which boasts decorative tile graves and dramatic views.

Larache's sleepy plaza feels like Spain all over again. Many of the people in this town grew up speaking Spanish as their first language and even attending Spanish Catholic schools—a few nuns still live here. Visible from afar, the 16th-century Geubibat Fort sits atop the highest cliff in Larache. The mouth of the snaking Loukos River is the fabled site of the Garden of Hesperides where Hercules picked his golden apples.

GETTING HERE AND AROUND

Larache can be reached from Tangier by either a grand taxi or a CTM bus, which leaves from Tangier's central bus station.

EXPLORING

Lixus BC. You may have heard of Volubilis, Morocco's most famous Roman ruins in Meknès. On the Loukkos River, Lixus BC is a lesser-known but no-less-impressive site just 45 minutes away from Tangier. The main attractions are an amphitheater, a column-lined road, a mosaic of the sea god—half man, half crab—and the religious center of the town, high on the hill, which retains the foundations for the places of worship of each civilization to have settled there. The hill held great importance to a series of seafaring civilizations, starting with the Phoenicians in the 7th century until the time of the Arabs. The guides at the entrance are official and informative. They are paid by the government to do their job but appreciate a tip. *Free* *Daily 9–6.*

WHERE TO STAY

For expanded hotel reviews, visit Fodors.com.

$ ★ **La Maison Haute.** Located in the kasbah, and offering great rooftop views of the city and ocean, this little gem of a hotel is hidden behind an unassuming exterior. **Pros:** friendly staff; great location. **Cons:** steep steps; not all rooms have bathrooms. ✉ *6, Derb Ben Thami* ☎ *065/34–48–88* 🌐 *lamaisonhaute.free.fr* *7 rooms* *Breakfast.*

CEUTA

94 km (58 mi) northeast of Tangier.

When it was incorporated into Spanish rule in 1580, Ceuta was one of the finest cities in northern Morocco. Thriving under its Arab conquerors, the city was extolled in 14th-century documents for its busy harbors, fine educational institutions, ornate mosques, and sprawling villas. Smelling prosperity, the Portuguese seized Ceuta in 1415; the city passed to Spain when Portugal itself became part of Spain in 1580, and it remains under Spanish rule today. The town's Arabic name "Sebta" comes from the Latin *septum* from *sepir* ("to enclose").

Ceuta's strategic position on the Strait of Gibraltar explains its ongoing use as a Spanish military town (many of the large buildings around the city are military properties). There has been little contestation by Morocco to claim the small peninsula, despite a small incident in 2002. This can be explained by a desire not to lose Spanish support for Moroccan rule over the Western Sahara but also to maintain steady relations with Spain in general. Walls built by the Portuguese surround the city and are, together with the ramparts, impressive testimony to the town's historic importance on European–Near Eastern trade routes.

Now serving mainly as a port of entry or departure between Spain and Morocco, Ceuta has scant attractions for travelers, though the mere existence of this Hispano-African hybrid that has successively belonged to Phoenicians, Carthaginians, Romans, Vandals, Byzantines, Arabs, Portuguese, and Spaniards is staggering. If you're short on time, you might give it a miss, as the town is a bit sleepy, especially during siesta time. The most interesting sights are in the upper city, away from the port's bustle.

GETTING HERE AND AROUND

Ceuta can be reached from Tangier by either a grand taxi or a CTM bus, which leaves from Tangier's central bus station.

Ceuta has ferry service to and from the Spanish port of Algeciras (1½ hours; 360 DH per passenger, approximately 800 DH per car). If you're driving, the N2 and N16 connect Tangier, Ceuta, Tetouan, and the beaches.

Crossing into Ceuta from Morocco involves a roughly 30-minute process of having your passport stamped and being shuffled through several checkpoints. A taxi from the border to downtown Ceuta costs about €7. Note that euros are the standard currency here, with dirhams accepted only in some establishments. Cash machines are available downtown; try the Banco de España (Place de España). Large hotels will also change money for their guests, but you'll get a better rate if you just use an

ATM. When calling Ceuta from Morocco or from overseas, use the country code for Spain (34).

Visitor Information Ceuta Tourist Information ✉ *s/n Baluarte de los Mallorquines, C/Edrissis, Spain* ☎ *0856/20–05–60 C/Edrissis, 0956/50–62–75 Estación Marítima* 🌐 *www.ceuta.es.*

ESSENTIALS

EXPLORING

Castillo del Desnarigado. Located just under Ceuta's lighthouse, and named for a flat-nosed Berber pirate who made the cove his home in the 1417 after escaping from an Algerian mining prison, the fort was built here in the 19th century and now houses a military museum showcasing the evolution of weapons from the 16th to 19th centuries. You can look out across Ceuta's port and, on clear days, drink in a stunning view of Gibraltar from the ramparts. ✉ *Carretera Del Hacho* ☎ *956/51–40–66 in Spain* 🎫 *Free* ⏲ *Mon.–Fri. 9:30–1; Sat. 11–1:30.*

Foso de San Felipe. St. Philip's Moat was built in 1530 by Portuguese crusaders to strengthen the town's fortifications. Crossing the moat gives you grand views of the ramparts, including their inner walls and structures. ✉ *Calle del la Independencia.*

Plaza de África. A lovely Andalusian-style space, the plaza is the heart of the old city. Check out the Plaza de África's noteworthy **war memorial,** honoring those who took part in the Spanish invasion of Morocco in 1859. Flanking the main plaza is a pair of impressive churches, both built on the sites of former mosques. To the north is the church of **Nuestra Señora de África** (Our Lady of Africa), an ornate baroque structure much frequented by Ceutíes (residents of Ceuta) looking for peace and quiet. On the southern end of Plaza de África, look for the city's **cathedral.** Constructed in an 18th-century baroque style—much like Nuestra Señora de África—it is larger and lushly ornate. ✉ *Plaza de África.*

WHERE TO EAT

Much like Ceuta itself, the city's cuisine is a hybrid of Spanish and Moroccan influences. With the Mediterranean at its doorstep, Ceuta's culinary expertise lies in seafood. From shrimp sautéed in a spicy pepper sauce to creamy baked whitefish dishes and enormous grilled sardines to Spanish-style cold anchovy, garlic, and olive-oil tapas, Ceutan seafood is a pleasure not to be missed. Moroccan influences show up in the form of couscous, as well as sweet-salty combinations such as prunes with roast lamb. A favorite pastime here is eating Serrano ham and drinking wine (both totally impossible just a few minutes away).

$$$ SEAFOOD ✕ **El Club Nautico C.A.S.** Modest on the inside, but offering a nice view and a waterfront location, this port restaurant's a catch for its daily offerings of fresh seafood. Enter through an aging revolving door and be pleasantly surprised. Be careful; Ceuta port has two yacht clubs, and while this restaurant is very good, the other is quite bad. ✉ *Muelle Deportivo* ☎ *956/51–37–53.*

$ SPANISH ✕ **La Esquinita Iberica.** For an inexpensive and pleasurable snack, head to this no-nonsense tapas bar near La Plaza Nuestra Señora de África, where the treats come with your drink. Try the *insalata russo* (a Spanish

CLOSE UP

Morocco's Mediterranean Beaches

The one constant across northern Morocco is outstanding beaches. From crowded city beaches to miles of empty space, from fine sand to high cliffs, you'll find whatever combination of leisure, civilization, and scenery you have in mind on these shores.

On the far-northern Atlantic coast west of Tangier, Robinson Beach offers several uninterrupted miles of fine sand and good waves ideal for families and surfers alike. Like its counterpart at Tarifa across the Strait of Gibraltar, there is generally a lot of wind buffeting the strand at Robinson, making it also ideal for windsurfing. This is the last beach on the Atlantic Ocean before its waters merge with those of the Mediterranean Sea at Cap Spartel, so the winds and current can be tricky. Staying close to shore is recommended.

The northern Mediterranean beaches, centered on Cap Malabata, between Tangier and Ceuta, are some of the region's finest. Their water is classic Mediterranean turquoise, and secluded spots are easy to come by.

The road from Ceuta south to Martil passes more than 32 km (20 mi) of modern beach resorts that offer a wide array of sports and activities. These good, if somewhat touristy, family beaches are heavily populated in summer, the North African answer to Spain's Costa del Sol.

Farther east, the road from Tetouan to Al Hoceima offers sweeping views along the Mediterranean coast. The water is calm here, and the beaches, usually empty, range from slightly pebbly to golden and sandy. The tiny fishing villages of Oued Laou, Torres de Alcalá, and Kalah Iris make good afternoon stops for lunch and a swim on the way east.

The area around Al Hoceima has some of the north's finest Mediterranean beaches. Quemado Beach, a busy urban strip in Al Hoceima proper, is a cove tucked between large hills, with fine sand and crystalline water—during a simple swim you can see coral and schools of fish below. There are plenty of beaches to explore just outside, for instance Tala Youssef, just west of Al Hoceima, is where the king summers.

Farther east, the beaches beyond Nador such as Kariet Arkmane, Ras Kebdana, and Saïdia are lonelier and less well equipped for family activities but excellent for communing with nature, your traveling companions, and the sun, sea, and sand.

---

take on the Russian Salade Olivier), a Spanish tortilla (like a mix between an omelet and potato pancake) or some pure Serrano ham with bread. ✉ *4, Calle Jaudenes* ☎ *0956/51-61–04 in Spain.*

$$$ SPANISH ✕ **Parador la Muralla Ceuta Restaurant.** Generally considered Ceuta's best restaurant, this charming dining room with exposed beams, tropical plants serves classic Andalusian dishes such as seafood paella, stuffed shrimp, shellfish in sauce, and creative daily specials. Dramatic lighting is provided by Andalusian lanterns hanging from the high ceiling in a romantic constellation, while the tables are a bit musty. Reservations are advised. ✉ *Gran Hotel Parador–La Muralla, 15, pl. de África* ☎ *956/51–49–40 in Spain.*

WHERE TO STAY

For expanded hotel reviews, visit Fodors.com.

$$$ **Gran Hotel Parador–La Muralla.** An aging monument—but still one of your best options in Ceuta—La Muralla is conveniently located on the main square, with views of the well-maintained garden, changeable sea, or the plaza itself. **Pros:** central location; good restaurant, relaxing. **Cons:** rooms can be stuffy; service is slow. ✉ *15, pl. Ntra. Sra. de África* ☎ *956/51–49–40 in Spain* 🌐 *www.parador.es* *77 rooms, 29 suites* *In-room: a/c. In-hotel: restaurant, bar, pool, parking* *No meals.*

$$$ **TRYP Ceuta.** On a busy street in Ceuta's commercial center, the TRYP offers comfort and amenities within walking distance of the main sights. **Pros:** good location close to the port and heliport; modern building renovated in 2003. **Cons:** stuffy rooms; details sometimes shabby; service not always attentive. ✉ *3, av. Alcalde Sánchez Prados* ☎ *956/51–12–00 in Spain, 888/956–3542 toll-free in the U.S.* 🌐 *www.solmelia.com* *121 rooms* *In-room: a/c, Wi-Fi. In-hotel: restaurant, bar, pool, gym, business center, parking* *No meals.*

SPORTS AND THE OUTDOORS

Kayak Aventura. You can take a water-borne tour around Ceuta's fortifications, enter the moats and canals of El Foso (literally *moat* or *trench*) by day, or you can tour the glowing and ancient walls by night. The company also offers excursions to the natural cliffs, pools, and beaches around the peninsula, all in single or double kayaks. Opt to snorkel if you like, or more hearty souls can venture all the way to La Isla Perejil. Regularly scheduled guided nightly excursions leave at 7 pm and cost a mere €10. Otherwise, call ahead and reserve any time of day for an excursion suitable for adults or children. ✉ *Playa de la Ribera* ☎ *0676/27–80–86 in Morocco* 🌐 *ceutakayak.com.*

SAILING

El Puerto Deportivo. El Puerto Deportivo can advise on sailboat charters or windsurfing equipment rental. ✉ *Puerto de Ceuta* ☎ *956/51–37–53 in Spain.*

SCUBA DIVING

Ceuta-Sub. Ceuta-Sub gives classes and runs dives in select locations around the peninsula. ✉ *Club Santo Ángel, Carretera de San Amaro* ☎ *0669/28–80–00 in Morocco.*

EN ROUTE

Winding south out of Ceuta, back into Morocco, the N13 follows the coast toward Martil. The road gives you easy access to a string of well-developed beach resorts that combine modern amenities with gorgeous Mediterranean beaches and northern Moroccan charm.

RESTINGA-SMIR

18 km (11 mi) south of Ceuta, 42 km (26 mi) east of Tangier.

Until recently Restinga-Smir was a small fishing village. Development has come quickly: it's now one of the region's priciest summering spots, rimmed by a long, uninterrupted beach. Its beaches are yellow sand and protected from wind. An amusement park, Smir, has roller coasters for kids; outfitters in the port area offer other diversions such as windsurfing, horseback riding, miniature golf, tennis, and camping, all of which your hotel can arrange. Marina Smir is lined with shops, cafés, and small restaurants geared toward tourists and affluent locals. Most upscale restaurants are in the hotels, but the seafood places on the marina are all good bets, grilling up the catch of the day in a pleasant outdoor atmosphere.

GETTING HERE AND AROUND

Restinga-Smir can be reached from Tangier by either a grand taxi or a CTM bus; however, you must take a bus or taxi to Tetouan and then change once in Tetouan.

WHERE TO STAY

For expanded hotel reviews, visit Fodors.com.

$$$ **Barcelo Marina Smir Thalasso Spa.** Right on the beach, this luxurious hotel provides every comfort. **Pros:** on a beautiful coast; close to Ceuta and Tetouan; great views of the Rif Mountains. **Cons:** impersonal vibe; no shuttle to the towns. ✉ *Rte. de Sebta* ☎ *0539/97–12–34, 800/337–2356 in the U.S.* 🌐 *www.barcelomarinasmir.com* *110 rooms, 9 suites* *In-room: a/c. In-hotel: restaurant, bar, pool, tennis court, gym, spa, beach, water sports, laundry facilities, business center, parking, some pets allowed* *Breakfast.*

KABILA

20 km (12 mi) south of Ceuta, 114 km (71 mi) east of Tangier.

Kabila is quite literally a tourist village—a sprawling complex complete with hotel, villas, a helpful staff, a shopping center, and a marina with restaurants. The beaches—the majority of which are reserved for resort guests—are spotless (if a bit grainier than those farther north and south). Well-kept grounds and plenty of flowers keep the area green. Think California, with Moroccan food and decor. To arrange sailing and other outdoor activities, call Hotel Kabila.

GETTING HERE AND AROUND

Kabila can be reached from Tangier by either a grand taxi or a CTM bus; however, you must take a bus or taxi to Tetouan and then change once in Tetouan.

WHERE TO STAY

For expanded hotel reviews, visit Fodors.com.

$$$$ **Hotel Kabila.** No expense was spared in creating this full-blown tourist resort, which has rooms furnished with a distinctively Rifi Berber flair, featuring regional handicrafts, and with their own patios (or, on upper floors, balconies). **Pros:** exotic experience; plenty of activities. **Cons:** outdated main building; garden a bit overgrown; service spotty. ✉ *Rte. de Ceuta, Km 20* ☎ *0539/66–60–13* 🌐 *www.kabilahotel.com* *92 rooms, 4 suites* *In-room: no a/c. In-hotel: restaurant, bar, golf course, pool, tennis court, gym, spa, beach, water sports, parking, some pets allowed* *Breakfast.*

Tetouan was the capital of the part of Morocco controlled by Spain in the first half of the 20th century.

TETOUAN

40 km (24 mi) south of Ceuta, 57 km (35 mi) southeast of Tangier on the N2.

Andalusian flavor mingles with the strong Rifi Berber and traditional Arab identities of the majority of the populace to make Tetouan a uniquely Moroccan fusion of sights, sounds, and social mores. Tetouan's medina, which was classed as a World Heritage Site by UNESCO in 1997, remains basically untouched by tourism and retains its quotidian life and authenticity. The name Tetouan itself comes from the Tarifit (Rifi) Berber word for "the springs," to which the city owes its numerous fountains and gardens.

Nestled in a valley between the Mediterranean Sea and the Rif Mountains' backbone, the city of Tetouan was founded in the 3rd century BC by Berbers, who called it Tamuda. Romans destroyed the city in the 1st century AD and built their own in its place, the ruins of which you can still see on the town's edge. The Merenids built a city in the 13th century, which flourished for a century and was then destroyed by Spanish forces, which ruled intermittently from the 14th to the 17th century. The medina and kasbah that you see today were built in the 15th and 16th centuries and improved upon thereafter: Moulay Ismail took Tetouan back in the 17th century, and the city traded with the Spanish throughout the 18th. Tetouan's proximity to Spain, and especially to the enclave of Ceuta, kept its Moroccan population in close contact with the Spanish throughout the 20th century. As the capital of the Spanish protectorate from 1913 to 1956, Tetouan harbored Spanish religious orders that set up schools here and established trading links between

Tetouan, Ceuta, and mainland Spain. Their presence infused the city with Spanish architecture and culture. Peek into the vintage cinemas you see along the way, such as the Spanish-built Teatro Espagnol just off of Place Feddane, for a hint at the opulence of a bygone era. At this writing, a museum of contemporary art is under construction and was expected to open in late 2011.

GETTING HERE AND AROUND

Tetouan's small Aéroport de Sania R'Mel, 5 km (3 mi) outside town, has domestic flights to Rabat, Casablanca, and Al Hoceima. CTM is the region's main bus company and runs several buses daily between Tangier, Tetouan, Chefchaouen, Al Hoceima, and Nador. If you're driving yourself, the N2 and N16 connect Tangier, Ceuta, Tetouan, and the beaches.

Bus Contacts **CTM Tetouan** ✉ *Av. Hassan II* ☎ *0539/96–16–88* 🌐 *www.ctm.co.ma.*

VISITOR INFORMATION

Contacts **Tetouan Tourism Office** ✉ *30, bd. Mohammed V* ☎ *0539/96–19–15.*

EXPLORING

TOP ATTRACTIONS

Medina. Tetouan's medina is one of Morocco's most active and interesting, and includes a rectilinear Jewish quarter, "the Mellah," as well as exceptional 19th-century Spanish architecture from the period of the protectorate. Note the constantly flowing fountains, such as the one in the corner of Souk el-Fouki; they are supplied by underground springs that have never failed and have never been explained. Crafts, secondhand clothing, food, and housewares markets are scattered through the medina in charming little squares such as Souk el-Houts el-Kadim (the old fish market) and L'Wusaa. Kharrazin is where animal hides are hung to dry in the sun, and through a door to the north you'll find *debbagh*, or the traditional leather treatment baths. Tetouan's medina is fairly straightforward, so don't hesitate to deviate from the main path and explore; it's hard to get lost. There are also plenty of chances for refreshment. ✉ *Rue Terrafin at Bab er-Rouah.*

Place Feddane (*Mechouar Saaid*). If you follow the pedestrian Boulevard Mohammed V past Spanish houses with wrought-iron balconies and tilework, you will eventually flow into Place Feddane, the open square near the Royal Palace, unusually located in the very center city and a central gathering place in the evening. On the east side look up to see Dar Tair (the "House of the Bird"), an old Spanish apartment building crowned with a majestic bronze statue of a man fighting an eagle. The square is also the entrance point to Bab er-Rouah, the historical covered market on the north side, the Mellah and M'sala on the East and south, and Rue Zawiya, where you'll find a few nice eating options. ✉ *East end of Bd. Mohammed V.*

Place Moulay Mehdi. A leisurely stroll through Tetouan begins most naturally in the Place Moulay Mehdi, a large plaza ringed with cafés, a post office, and the Spanish Eglise Nuestra Señora de Las Victorias aglow with strings of lights in the evening. It is often the site of outdoor concerts and evening snack vendors and strollers. ✉ *Bd. Mohammed V at Bd. al-Moukaouama (Bd. of the Resistance).*

WORTH NOTING

Archaeological Museum. West of Place Feddane, this three-room museum holds a large collection of Roman mosaics and statuettes, coins, bronzes, and pottery found at various sites in northern Morocco such as Lixus and Cotta, as well as pictures of the archaeological site of Tamuda (recalling Stonehenge), where Anteus is fabled to have been buried after his battle with Hercules. The garden paths are rimmed with Jewish tombstones marked with pre-Columbian motifs brought back from South America and elaborate calligraphic Muslim tombstones. ✉ *2, rue Ben H'sain* ☎ *0539/96–48–43* 🎟 *10 DH* ⏲ *Mon.–Sat. 10–6.*

Dar San'aa (*School of Arts and Crafts*). Located across from Bab al-Okla, this living museum founded by the monarchy is considered the premier school in Morocco for the creation and preservation of traditional Andalusian-, Berber-, and Arab-influenced crafts and interior design since 1919. The school has resided in its current, architecturally significant Moorish-Andalusian home since 1928. The architectural splendor includes a colonnade inscribed with Kufic inscriptions, stained-glass details, and a green-tiled exterior in the style of Fez. There's no shop inside, but on the other hand you can hone your skills for the souks without being hassled. ✉ *Bab el-Oukla, Dar San'aa* ☎ *0539/97–27– 21* ⏲ *Mon.–Fri. 8–4:30.*

Ethnographic Museum of Tetouan. Transformed into a museum in 1948, the Ethnographic Museum is housed in the former fortress of the sultan Moulay Abderrahman, built around 1830 and surrounded by an Andalusian garden. The museum has a wonderful collection of traditional Moroccan costumes, jewelry, embroidery, weapons, musical instruments, and other handcrafted objects. The most elaborate displays are of the accoutrements of Tetouani wedding ceremonies, which are among the most elaborate of Moroccan wedding attires and mixed with Jewish traditions. ✉ *Av. Skala Bab el-Oukla* ☎ *0539/97–05–05* 🎟 *10 DH* ⏲ *Weekdays 9–noon and 2:30–5:30.*

WHERE TO EAT

While Tetouan's visitors formerly ate most of their meals in their lodgings, in recent years the town has seen an expanding number of good restaurants; though a fair percentage of them are foreign owned, they retain the local charm. Otherwise, street delicacies are best here. Local specialties are found especially in the *mellah*, the old Jewish quarter, for example at the corner of Rue al-Quds, are not to be missed. You may wish to sample *z'az'a* (a shake), flan *beldi* (meaning it is made with fresh country milk and eggs), and a pastry soaked in honey called *aslia*.

$ MOROCCAN ✕ **Restaurant Palace Bouhlal.** This palatial house was built in the 19th century and has colorful, finely painted floral doors and zellij columns. The traditional menu includes a sampling of Moroccan dishes including harira, couscous, kebabs, mint tea, and dessert. Be aware that the place is often used for tour groups and weddings. ✉ *48, Jamaa Kebir* ☎ *0670/85–95–63* ✍ *Reservations essential* 💳 *No credit cards.*

¢ MOROCCAN **Restaurant Restinga.** Look closely at the south facade of this pedestrian street lined with stores, and you'll see a small arch that leads into a simple courtyard with a large white ficus tree as its centerpiece. This is Restaurant Restinga. Try one of the traditional tagines with lamb or chicken or the platter of fried fish "Friture de poisson," which usually includes sole, *merlan* (whiting), calamari, *rouget* (red mullet), and shrimp. Dining is available inside or in the breezy courtyard. Service is friendly, and beer and wine are available. The restauarant also serves complimentary tapas with each order of alcohol. ✉ *21, bd. Mohammed V* ☎ *0539/96–35–76* ▭ *No credit cards.*

¢ CAFÉ **La TouRouge.** Located in the wall of the old medina next to Ryad al Ocha and overlooking Moulay Rachid Garden (otherwise known as "lovers' garden" with its large rock face), this small, hip café offers an umbrella-shaded patio, good espresso, and sandwiches; it often hosts informal concerts. This is a nice place for a break from the winding, narrow streets of M'sala in the outer Medina. ✉ *9, rue al-Hafa, next to Riad el-Ocha, Medina* ☎ *0539/71–31–32* ▭ *No credit cards.*

WHERE TO STAY

For expanded hotel reviews, visit Fodors.com.

$$ **Blanco Riad.** Renovated and opened by Spanish owners in 2009, this beautiful, crisp, upscale riad once served as the Spanish Consulate. **Pros:** peaceful atmosphere. **Cons:** must reserve ahead for the restaurant; pricey. ✉ *25, rue Zawiya* ☎ *0539/70–42–02* 🌐 *www.blancoriad.com* *8 rooms* *In-room: a/c, Internet. In-hotel: restaurant, laundry facilities* *Breakfast.*

$$ ★ **Hotel and Restaurant El Reducto.** Friendly, quadrilingual hosts Ruth and Brahim bring enthusiasm and warmth to this new hotel and restaurant, making it one of the best options in Tetouan. **Pros:** nice staff. **Cons:** the busy restaurant in the courtyard can make rooms noisy until late at night. ✉ *38, (Mechwar) Essaid Zanqat Zawya Kadiriya* ☎ *0539/96–81–20* 🌐 *www.riadtetouan.com* *7 rooms* *In-room: a/c, Wi-Fi. In-hotel: restaurant* *Breakfast.*

$ **Hotel Panorama.** Unreproachably clean, this new budget hotel boasts views of the mountains (either Jbel Ghorghiz and Jbel Derssa) across the valley from Tetouan from several of the rooms. **Pros:** clean; nice staff. **Cons:** on the outskirts of the new city; very basic hotel. ✉ *Av. Moulay el-Abbas* ☎ *0539/96–49–70* 🌐 *www.panoramavista.com* *63 rooms* *In-room: a/c* ▭ *No credit cards* *No meals.*

SHOPPING

The most interesting shopping is found in the medina where *mendils*, the bright, multicolored cloth used by farmers from the Rif for all-purpose protection from the elements, are made and sold in a little square northeast of Bab er-Rouah. Wood and leather are other artisanal products to look for in the medina.

Ensemble Artisanal. Ensemble Artisanal is a government-sponsored crafts center where rug weavers, leather workers, woodworkers, and jewelry designers manufacture and sell their wares. Prices are not negotiable here, but the value is excellent, especially if you factor in saved haggling time. ✉ *Av. Hassan I* ☎ *0539/99–20–85* ⏲ *Daily 8:30–6:30.*

CHEFCHAOUEN AND THE RIF

The trip south from Tetouan to Chefchaouen takes you through fertile valleys where locals sell produce along the road, sheep graze in golden sunshine, and the pace of life slows remarkably from that of the regions just to the north. The route from Chefchaouen to Al Hoceima winds through the Rif, northern Morocco's highest mountains.

CHEFCHAOUEN

64 km (38 mi) south of Tetouan, 98 km (61 mi) southeast of Tangier.

★ Nestled high in the gray Rif Mountains, Chefchaouen, known as the "Blue City," is built on a hillside, and is a world apart from its larger, Spanish-style neighbors. The pace of life here seems somehow in tune with the abundant natural springs, wildflowers, and low-lying clouds in the surrounding mountainsides. From Rifi Berbers dressed in earth-tone wool *djellabas* (long, hooded robes) and sweaters (ideal for cold, wet Rif winters) to the signature blue-washed houses lining its narrow streets, Chefchaouen has managed to maintain its singular identity.

Founded in 1471 by Moulay Ali ben Rachid as a mountain base camp for launching attacks against the Portuguese at Ceuta, Chefchaouen, historically off-limits to Christians, had been visited by only three Europeans when Spanish troops arrived in 1920. Vicomte Charles de Foucauld—French military officer, explorer, and missionary—managed to make it inside the walls disguised as a rabbi in 1883. In 1889 British journalist Walter Harris, intrigued by the thought of a city closed to Westerners a mere 97 km (60 mi) from Tangier, used a similar strategy to gain access to Chefchaouen while researching his book *Land of an African Sultan*. The third visitor, American William Summers, less lucky, was caught and poisoned in 1892.

Chefchaouen's isolationism had increased with the arrival of Muslims expelled from Spain at the end of the 15th century and again at the start of the 17th. Jews expelled from Spain with the Muslims chose various shades of blue for the facades of their houses (according to one theory, as more effective against flies), while the Muslim houses remained green or mauve. When the Spanish arrived in 1920 they were stunned to find Chefchaouen's Sephardic Jews speaking and writing a medieval Spanish that had been extinct in Spain for four centuries. The medina has been walled since its earliest days, and is still off-limits to cars.

Somehow, even the burgeoning souvenir shops don't make much of a dent in the town's mystique. Chaouen, as it's sometimes called, is an ideal place to wander through a tiny medina, walk up into the looming mountains above the valley, and sip mint tea in an open square. No other place in Morocco (unless a maritime version, Essaouira, could be said to rival it) has Chefchaouen's otherworldly, bohemian appeal—a place that ranks as a consistent favorite among travelers to the region. The Alegria Festival (🌐 *www.alegriafestival.com*), usually held in mid-July (though the date changes), brings together talented artists and musicians from Spain and Morocco.

GETTING HERE AND AROUND

CTM is the region's main and only recommended bus company, with several buses daily between Tangier, Tetouan, Chefchaouen, Al Hoceima, and Nador.

Bus Contacts CTM ☎ *0539/98–76–69* 🌐 *www.ctm.co.ma.*

VISITOR INFORMATION

Visitor Information Chefchaouen Tourist Information ✉ *Pl. de Mohammed V* ☎ *No phone.*

> **DRIVING IN THE RIF**
>
> If you decide to continue from Chefchaouen, remember that driving at night can be dangerous in the Rif, where a false roadblock of stones can lead to robberies or forcible purchase of *kif* (hashish). Especially around Ketama, never accept invitations to private village ceremonies or even a mint tea, as this is usually a setup of some kind: someone slips a package of kif into your car and then the police are suddenly interested in searching your vehicle. Remember that kif, though prevalent, is still illegal, and punishments for drug crime harsh.

EXPLORING

OFF THE BEATEN PATH

Akshour Waterfall and God's Bridge. Two waterfalls and a natural bridge both located a short walk from the village of Akshour, a 40-minute drive from Chefchaouen toward Oued Laou on the coast, are the highlights of any trip into the heart of the Rif Mountains. The path to the first waterfall is an easy 45-minute walk. From there, you have the option of continuing on a five-to-six-hour round-trip hike to a second, much larger waterfall. On the other side of the river, you can either head up on a very steep path to the so-called God's Bridge itself, a natural bridge, or follow the canyon to a view from below. Be prepared to wade a little if the water is high. Small bungalow cafés offering vegetable tagines and mint tea sprinkle the path, as do wildflowers and small wildlife. ✉ *Akshour.*

Talassemtane National Park. Established in 1989, Talassemtane National Park is just outside Chefchaouen's city walls. The 145,000-acre expanse boasts a Mediterranean ecosystem that hosts a unique variety of Moroccan pine as well as more than 239 plant species, many of which are endangered, such as the black pine and the Atlas cedar. There are short day hikes, and more ambitious hikes along a large loop trail. ✉ *3, rue Machichi* ☎ *039/98–72–67.*

WHERE TO EAT

¢ MOROCCAN

Café Kasbah. Located just across from the 500-year-plus fondouk (horse stable hotel), this unassuming restaurant is itself a renovated old fondouk. Away from the chaos of the main plaza, it has intimate booths offering a much welcome egress from the hot sun. Starry-night colored tiles on fantastic iron chairs add to the magic of the colorful surroundings. It's open continually from 7 am to midnight. ✉ *Pl. Uta el-Hammam* ☎ *0539/88–33–97* ▭ *No credit cards.*

$ MOROCCAN

Casa Aladdin. This three-story riad has two terraces and is decorated with more experimental mixed-media approaches to the standard blue street scenes than you can shake a stick at. The main dishes can be hit or miss (tagines are the best bet), but the bird's-eye views over the main square are unique, and the fresh dairy products on the reasonably priced prix-fixe menu are local and scrumptious: the goat cheese salad

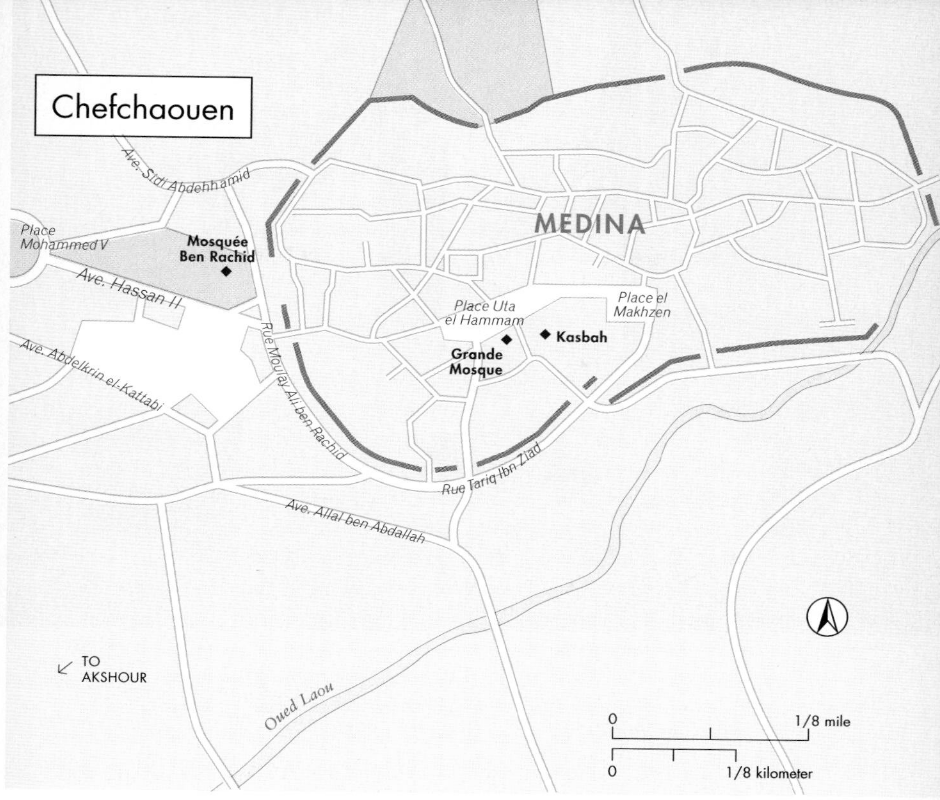

appetizer and the fresh yogurt and cinnamon dessert are both highly recommended. And it's open late. ✉ *Pl. Uta el-Hammam, 17, rue Targui* ☎ *0539/98–90–71* ▭ *No credit cards.*

WHERE TO STAY

For expanded hotel reviews, visit Fodors.com.

$ **Caiat Lounge Refuge.** An excellent base camp from which to explore the Rif, this eco-friendly oasis in the mountains is more than bare-bones—a plateau of cute houses across from a dramatic valley. *Taghzoute, Jemaa el-Oued, Km. 12 on road between Chefchaouen and Oued Laou, Asmetan* ☎ *0539/70–77–51* 🌐 *www.caiat.com* *5 houses, 7 rooms* *In-room: no a/c. In-hotel: restaurant, parking* *Multiple meal plans.*

$$ ★ **Casa Hassan-Dar Baibou.** Renowned throughout Morocco, this 350-year-old family home houses an excellent restaurant with a handful of guest rooms. **Pros:** friendly atmosphere; a real bargain. **Cons:** need to reserve far ahead in high season. ✉ *22, rue Targui* ☎ *0539/98–61–53* 🌐 *www.casahassan.com* *24 rooms* *In-room: a/c. In-hotel: restaurant* *Some meals.*

$ ★ **Hotel Dar Mounir.** This sleek and chic B&B opened in 2003 and was designed by a local painter Al-Haoulani, whose paintings also decorate the walls. **Pros:** great staff and interior design. **Cons:** neighborhood can be noisy at night, but this is true of most places in the medina. ✉ *Pl.*

Chefchaouen is known as the "blue city" for its blue-washed walls.

Uta el-Hammam, Kadi Alami Hay Souika ☎ *0539/98–82–53* 🌐 *www.hotel-darmounir.com* *11 rooms* *In-room: a/c, Wi-Fi. In-hotel: restaurant* *Breakfast.*

$ **Hotel Parador.** Ideally situated on the medina's edge, the simple and plain Hotel Parador was originally built in the 1920s as the Spanish governor's house. **Pros:** comfortable rooms; friendly atmosphere, parking. **Cons:** little of the charm of the old city. ✉ *Pl.el-Mahkzen* ☎ *0539/98–63–24* 🌐 *www.hotel-parador.com* *34 rooms, 4 suites* *In-room: a/c, Wi-Fi. In-hotel: restaurant, bar, pool, parking* *Breakfast.*

SHOPPING

Chefchaouen is one of the north's best places to shop for quality traditional crafts. Wool items and leather goods are the main local export: look in small medina stores for thick blankets, rugs, bags, and shoes.

Abdellah Alami. Abdellah Alami sells nothing but bronze products, made by a family of bronze workers who produce some of this region's finest handmade plates, bowls, and trays. Prices are reasonable, and the selection is vast. ✉ *257, Onsar Rasselma* ☎ *0539/98–73–03.*

Artisanal Chefchaouen. This small cooperative workshop produces beautiful, inexpensive hand-painted wood boxes, shelves, birdcages, chests, and mirrors of extremely high quality. ✉ *Pl. el-Makhzen, in parking lot of Hotel Parador* ☎ *No phone.*

Casa Marbella/Coin de l'Artisanat. Accredited by the Moroccan Ministry of Industry and Artisanal Commerce, Casa Marbella/Coin de l'Artisanat creates some of the country's finest zellij work, as well as metalwork, pottery, silver filigree, and bronze. Traditional henna application is also available for women. Prices are reasonable, and orders can be shipped via airmail around the world. (Retain all receipts and the store's contact information if you choose to ship directly.) ✉ *40, rue Grandade Hay Andalouss* ☎ *0539/98–71–20.*

AL HOCEIMA

215 km (133 mi) east of Chefchaouen.

Surrounded on three sides by the Rif Mountains' foothills and rimmed on the fourth by turquoise Mediterranean waters, Al Hoceima is striking. From its perch in rolling hills, the town looks directly down on a stunning bay. It isn't nearly as developed as Tangier and Tetouan, but its natural sights and exquisite coastline make it the perfect place to relax for a day or two.

Established by the Spanish in 1925 as Villa Sanjuro, Al Hoceima was built as a stronghold against Rifi Berber rebellions. Al Hoceima is now a proudly Berber place, and Berber flags and signs are becoming more and more prominent. The king recognized *Tamazight*—a general term that encompasses six different Berber dialects, four of which are in use by Morocco's Berber population—as Morocco's second official language, alongside Arabic. Tarifit, Rifi Berber, is spoken by about 4 million people in the Rif, sometimes exclusively of any other language, though there are many Spanish words in the dialect.

Al Hoceima's Spanish architecture and atmosphere remain visible. The finest Spanish edifice is the beautifully tiled **Collège Espagnol** (Spanish College) at the end of Boulevard Mohammed V. The Old Town is centered on the pretty, Art Deco **Place du Rif.** There are few sights here, but you can wander the town's markets, kick back at a café, and just enjoy the relative quietude. In the Ville Nouvelle, the cliff-top **Place Mohammed VI,** just above the main beach, is the focal point of the evening *paseo* (promenade) and has a fun sidewalk punctuated by fountains. Festivals and citywide events are held here in the summer months, when many expatriate Al Hoceimans residing in Europe return home on vacation.

GETTING HERE AND AROUND

Al Hoceima's Aéroport Côte du Rif, 17 km (11 mi) southeast of town, offers daily flights on Royal Air Maroc to Tangier, Tetouan, Casablanca, and Rabat, as well as weekly flights to Europe. Compagnie de Transports Marocains is the region's main and only recommended bus company. It runs several buses daily between Tangier, Tetouan, Chefchaouen, Al Hoceima, and Nador. If you're driving yourself, the N2 cuts east toward Al Hoceima, Nador, and Melilla. The coastal road from Tetouan may soon be the best way to get here, but at the time of this writing, it was entirely torn up and under construction.

Bus Contacts CTM ✉ *46, pl. Rif* ☎ *039/98–22–73* 🌐 *www.ctm.co.ma.*

VISITOR INFORMATION

Contacts Al Hoceima Tourism Office ✉ *Rue Al Hamra, Calabonita* ☎ *0539/98–11–85.*

EXPLORING

The real reasons to come to Al Hoceima are the beaches. The main city beach, **Plage Quemado,** sits in a natural bay formed by mountains on each side. The water is crystal clear, perfect for snorkeling and scuba diving, and you can rent equipment from a very obvious stall on the beach. (However, be warned that the quality of the equipment is hit-or-miss. Be sure to check the equipment carefully before use, and if you're an inexperienced diver, you should take a pass.) Near Quemado Beach is Al Hoceima's port, where several restaurants cook up wonderful seafood. The coastline outside of town is equally scenic; the beach at **Asfiha** (1 km (0.5 mi) west of the city, stretches around the bay with miles of uninterrupted fine ash-colored sand. It is a popular family resort and usually very crowded in summer, with many beachside bungalow-cafés in which to hide from the sun and have tea or lunch. The beach is very much worth a trip, for from here you can see the tiny Spanish rock fortress **Peñon de Alhuceimas**, meaning "Lavendar Rock." **Souani Beach** is a nice small bay backed by pine forest, a perfect place for a picnic.

WHERE TO EAT

$ SEAFOOD **Club Nautique.** Fresh, simply grilled fish and other seafood reign supreme here, along with several resort-style bars placed strategically around the two terraces and captain's cabin–style interior; there is a large selection of Moroccan wines on offer, with Gerrouane being a good bet. The house salads are well prepared and can be made to suit the size of your party. The views of the bay and local fishing boats from the outdoor tables are stunning. ✉ *Port d'Al Hoceima* ☎ *0539/98–14–61* ▭ *No credit cards.*

WHERE TO STAY

For expanded hotel reviews, visit Fodors.com.

$$$$ **Chafarina's Beach.** This tourist complex 4 km (2 mi) north of Al Hoceima and overlooking Bouskour (the king's favorite public beach in the area) offers kitschy Romanesque decadence in the communal areas with beautiful sweeping views over the Mediterranean, aquatic and sports activities, and a splendid dining hall. **Pros:** lively in summer; plenty of activities. **Cons:** can be deserted in the off-season. ✉ *Tala Youssef, Plage Bouskour* ☎ *0539/84–16–01* *30 suites* *In-room: a/c, kitchen, Wi-Fi. In-hotel: restaurant, bar, beach* *Breakfast.*

$$ **Hotel Amir Plage.** In a cove of its own between the brand-new Kalah Bonita bus station and the Place du Rif, this hotel sits directly on its beach. **Pros:** on the water; very private; reasonable prices. **Cons:** down a steep driveway; small beach can be crowded in peak season. ✉ *Plage du Matadero* ☎ *0539/98–32–90* *22 rooms 10 suites* *In-room: a/c, Wi-Fi. In-hotel: restaurant, beach, water sports* *Breakfast.*

$$$ **Suites Hotel Mohammed V.** Al Hoceima's grand old hotel has sleek, chic, remodeled rooms (albeit in a sanatorium style) and bungalows, which were under renovation at this writing. **Pros:** away from the hubbub; near the beach. **Cons:** rooms a bit utilitarian. ✉ *Pl. de la Marche Verte* ☎ *0539/98–22–33* ⊕ *suiteshotelmohammedv.ma* *30 suites* *In-room: a/c, Wi-Fi. In-hotel: restaurant, bar, pool, gym, beach, parking* *Breakfast.*

The Northern Atlantic Coast

WORD OF MOUTH

"I thought Rabat was a pleasant, low-key introduction to Morocco, and definitely worth two full days (three nights)."

—thursdaysd

WELCOME TO THE NORTHERN ATLANTIC COAST

TOP REASONS TO GO

★ **Rabat's Kasbah des Oudayas:** Rabat's medieval Kasbah des Oudayas is worth exploring. The mosque, the Oudayas Gardens, and the Oudayas Museum overlook the mouth of the Oued Bou Regreg river and the city of Salé beyond.

★ **Casablanca's Tour Hassan II:** Second only in scope to the mosque at Mecca, this modern extravaganza makes elaborate use of traditional Moroccan craftsmanship.

★ **Colonial France's southern Riviera:** The alpine colony at Ifrane and Casablanca's Quartier des Habous in Casablanca and La Corniche all managed to bring parts of France to North Africa.

★ **Casablanca's southern beaches:** For a refreshing ramble along a largely unspoiled coastline with not much more going on than surfable waves crashing in from the Atlantic, the beaches between Casablanca and El Oualidia are some of the world's best.

1 Rabat. Visitors are enticed by the beautiful tranquillity of Rabat, with its Moorish gardens bordered by charming cafés. They marvel at the Hassan Tower, which has overlooked the city for eight centuries, and the Mohammed V Mausoleum. The Musée Archéologique houses the country's most extensive collection of archaeological artifacts. Golf fanatics may play at the Royal Golf Dar Es-Salam, while beach lovers will enjoy the shore south of Rabat.

2 Excursions from Rabat. Bird lovers should consider a day at Lake Sidi Bourhaba, near Mehdiya Plage, known for its nearly 200 species of birds. For those captivated by Morocco's medinas, the nearby city of Salé feels entirely different from Rabat, and shoppers will enjoy Salé's pottery shops. Moulay Bousselham has a breathtaking lagoon and is a great place to unwind in front of the sea.

3 Casablanca. With its spacious avenues of contemporary and Hispano-Moorish structures, Art Deco architecture, public fountains, and spacious shoreline, Casablanca appeals to Western visitors. Modern structures amid a mosque shooting its laser beams to Mecca underscore Casablanca's eclectic spirit. An appealing blend of East and West, it successfully balances history and innovation.

4 Excursions from Casablanca. Dar Bouazza, an eclectic fishing village and resort town, has great beaches and nice oceanfront restaurants. Azemmour has a whitewashed medina and artsy atmosphere. El Jadida was built by the Portuguese and feels quite different from other Moroccan cities as well as offering more restaurant and lodging options.

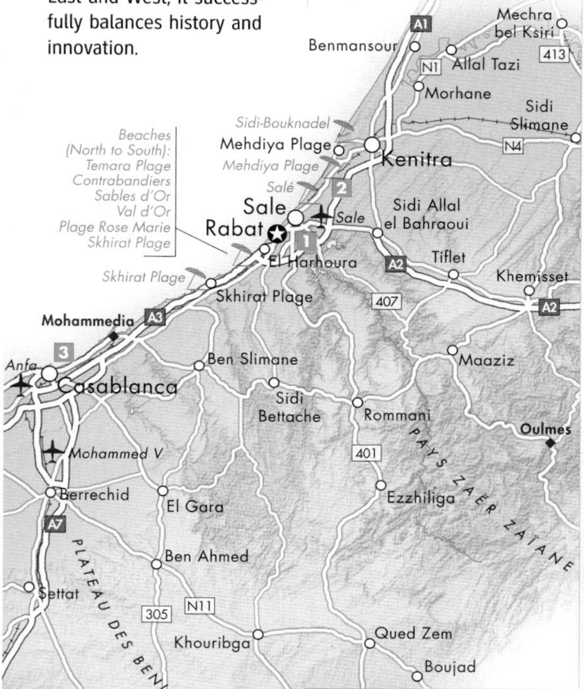

Beaches (North to South):
Temara Plage
Contrabandiers
Sables d'Or
Val d'Or
Plage Rose Marie
Skhirat Plage

A1
Benmansour
Mechra bel Ksiri
413
N1
Allal Tazi
Morhane
Sidi Slimane
Sidi-Bouknadel
Mehdiya Plage
Kenitra
N4
Mehdiya Plage
Salé
2
Sale
Sale
Rabat
Sidi Allal el Bahraoui
1
El Harhoura
A2
Tiflet
Khemisset
Skhirat Plage
Skhirat Plage
407
A2
Mohammedia
A3
3
Anfa
Casablanca
Ben Slimane
Maaziz
Sidi Bettache
Rommani
Oulmes
Mohammed V
401
PAYS ZAËR ZAÏANE
Berrechid
El Gara
Ezzhiliga
A7
Ben Ahmed
PLATEAU DES BENI MESKINE
Settat
305
N11
Khouribga
Qued Zem
Boujad
308
El Borouj

GETTING ORIENTED

Driving from the north to Rabat works well if you're coming from Tangier or Tetouan; the other (Casablanca to El Oualidia) leads nicely into a trip farther south, to Essaouira, Marrakesh, or the Atlas Mountains. Either way you'll absorb plenty of coastal scenery. If you're flying into Casablanca but can't spend much time in this region, you may want to go straight to Rabat, as it's only an hour and a half from the airport by car or train and is richer in traditional sights.

THE ROMANS IN MOROCCO

(above) A Roman mosaic at the ruins at Volubilis (opposite page, bottom) several columns that remain standing from the basilica (opposite page, top) the triumphal arch, which was restored in 1932

Rome's influence in the Maghreb was geographically limited, but for 300 years it was of strategic importance and a source of vast wealth for the empire. The breathtaking archaeological remains, especially at Volubilis, point to Rome's commitment to the region.

By the 3rd century BC, Carthage (modern-day Tunis) had caught the attention of Rome, who eyed it with a desire that epitomized the empire's insatiable appetite for expansion. A trio of Punic Wars, spanning 100 years, caused Rome to fear for its future. However, Carthaginian potency waned with the death of Hannibal, and in 146 BC, after a three-year siege, Carthage was finally crushed. Rome annexed North Africa and now controlled the Mediterranean. The region was divided among various client kings, headed by the Numidian prince Jugurtha. When he attempted to unify the kingdoms in revolt, Rome had no choice but to act. In 106 BC, after a six-year war, Jugurtha was dead and Rome's grip on North Africa left unchallenged—at least for another 60 years that is.

VOLUBILIS

Volubilis was home to Juba II and his son Ptolemy. Under this cultured duo, the city blossomed and continued to thrive well after Rome's departure in the 3rd century AD. After a millennium of constant occupation, the city was plundered for its stone in the 17th century by Moulay Ismail, but what remains is simply stunning—one reason the ruins were named a UNESCO World Heritage Site.

Following Julius Caesar's march on Rome in 49 BC, Republican resistance had been growing and nowhere more rapidly than in North Africa. Caesar arrived there in 47 BC with 30,000 men. One year later, at Thapsus (in present-day Tunisia), his outnumbered legions soundly defeated the armies of King Juba of Numidia (in present-day Algeria) and Republican forces led by Scipio. Over the following months, resistance was crushed throughout North Africa, and Rome's grip on the Maghreb became tighter than ever.

Despite his father's allegiances, Juba II was installed as the client king of Numidia and later Mauretania. Juba had been educated in Rome and was a sophisticated and respected monarch. While living in Volubilis with his wife Cleopatra Selene (daughter of Antony and Cleopatra), he wrote many geographical and historical works. It was under his rule that the city flourished and became a showcase for palatial architecture as well as a center for commerce.

Juba II was of Berber descent and co-ruled with his son Ptolemy, nurturing their comfortable relationship with Rome, even asking for (and receiving) military assistance in crushing a violent Berber rebellion in AD 24.

In AD 40, all of that was to change with the arrival of the notoriously unstable Caligula who, in a fit of jealousy, had Ptolemy murdered and then declared an end to Berber autonomy. Unsurprisingly, the province rose up in a bloody revolt that was eventually put down by emperor Claudius.

Claudius divided the province into Mauretania Caesariensis (West Algeria) and Mauretania Tingitana (Morocco) whose capital was Tingis, present-day Tangier. Rome developed existing towns rather than starting new settlements, and Volubilis in particular benefited. It exported vast quantities of olive oil and wheat to Rome, eventually supplying fully two-thirds of that city's food. There was also a healthy trade in wild animals for slaughter in the Coliseum; it is thought that in the course of two centuries the lion, bear, and elephant populations in the province were reduced to nothing.

In 285 Rome called a halt to its ambitions in Africa and left the region after 300 years of almost undisputed occupancy. A small garrison remained, and Morocco remained part of the Roman empire until the 5th century AD.

Roman influence in the Maghreb was confined to the northwest of the country and stopped just north of Rabat. Although relatively brief and limited, the Roman presence has left Morocco architectural remains to rival any in North Africa.

Updated by Patricia Gorman

The Atlantic breakers roll in all along Morocco's North Atlantic coast, contrasting markedly with the placid waters of Morocco's Mediterranean coast. From here, the ocean stretches due west to the United States. Much of this coast is lined with sandy beaches, and dotted with simple white *koubbas,* the buildings that house a Muslim saint's tomb.

This region contains Rabat, the political capital of the kingdom, and, less than 100 km (62 mi) to the southwest, Casablanca, the undisputed commercial capital. Morocco's main industrial and commercial axis stretches from Casablanca to Kenitra. Rich strata of history are piled here. A simple unmarked cave on the coast near Rabat is thought to be one of the first sites ever inhabited by humans. Rabat and its twin city Salé have some of the most important historical sights in the country. Rabat has monuments from successive Arab dynasties. The modern city of Casablanca was developed by the French from 1912 to independence.

Yet despite the historical riches, Rabat, Casablanca, and indeed the rest of this region are somewhat removed from the pressures of the larger tourist centers—Marrakesh, Fez, and Agadir. Quite apart from the gentle climate, you'll generally find yourself—unlike in, say, Fez—free to wander around unmolested. This part of Morocco treats travelers gently.

PLANNING

WHEN TO GO

Try to avoid this region in July, August, and the first half of September unless you only plan to visit Rabat and Casablanca. Corresponding to Morocco's school vacation, the coastal resorts are extremely crowded in summer, hotels are packed, and prices are much higher. Moreover, huge numbers of Moroccans working in Europe return in July and August. In April, May, June, and October, the weather is delightful—easily warm enough to enjoy the beaches—and most resorts are pleasantly empty. If you don't need to swim or sunbathe, you can sightsee from November through March (and even then the weather can be quite warm). The relatively cold period lasts from around early December through the end of January; temperatures on the coast can plunge to 4°C–6°C (39°F–43°F).

GETTING HERE AND AROUND

BY AIR

The only major airport in this region of Morocco is Casablanca's Mohammed V International Airport, which is located about 25 km (16 mi) south of the city. It's the most common international gateway for Americans traveling to Morocco. Many airlines fly directly from Middle Eastern and European cities, as well as those in the United States and Canada. Casablanca, Rabat, and other destinations in the region can be easily reached via the numerous train, shuttle, or taxi services located outside the arrivals terminal.

BY BUS

You can reach some outlying destinations by bus if you don't wish to drive, but the trips can be less than comfortable and long.

BY CAR

If your stay in this region is limited to Casablanca and Rabat, you won't need a car at all. If, however, your aim is to relax in small coastal towns like Moulay Bousselham and El Oualidia, a car is far more useful than the slow and complicated public transportation to those places.

BY TRAIN

There is excellent nonstop train service almost hourly between Casablanca and Rabat (even more frequently at the beginning and end of the day). This is the best way to move between the cities. You can travel onward to Tangier, Fez, Meknès, Marrakesh, and a few other destinations by train. This can be a comfortable and reasonably priced way to travel in Morocco.

SAFETY

Official guides in Morocco are identified by large, brass badges. Be wary of the numerous unofficial guides, generally young men, who will offer to find you a hotel, take you on a tour of the city, or, in some cases, find hashish or "kif" for you. Some will falsely claim to be students who merely wish to practice their English. To avoid these hustlers, you should appear confident and aware of where you are going. If you feel bullied or harassed, do not hesitate to summon police. As in any large city, pickpockets exist, and you should be alert and aware of your surroundings while walking around the city.

RESTAURANTS

Morocco's northern Atlantic coast is its center of seafood par excellence. Along the entire North Atlantic coast the menus are remarkably similar: *salades (salads), crevettes* (prawns), *friture de poisson* (fried fish and octopus), *calamar* (squid), and various kinds of fish. *Fruits de mer* are always shellfish and prawns, not fish. In addition to seafood, Casablanca and Rabat offer many types of international cuisine—Italian and other Mediterranean restaurants, as well as Asian and even American eateries—and, of course, traditional Moroccan fare and French cuisine. Although it's tempting to think you can find good Moroccan restaurants anywhere, the best ones on this stretch of the coast are really limited to Casablanca and Rabat. (Moroccans eat Moroccan cuisine in the home, so when they dine out, they tend to want something more unusual.)

HOTELS

It's always a good idea to book ahead in this part of the country, as Rabat and Casablanca fill up with business travelers, and the beach resorts are packed in summer months. Casablanca has branches of the familiar international business hotels, and most business hotels in both Casablanca and Rabat will discount their published rates by applying corporate rates at the drop of a company's name. In the smaller coastal resorts you'll typically find midrange sea-view hotels with pools, but increasingly these towns also offer smaller, more personalized, bed-and-breakfast—type lodgings.

WHAT IT COSTS IN DIRHAMS

	¢	$	$$	$$$	$$$$
Restaurants	under 40 DH	40 DH–80 DH	81 DH–120 DH	121 DH–160 DH	over 160 DH
Hotels	under 400 DH	400 DH–900 DH	901 DH–1,500 DH	1,501 DH–2,000 DH	over 2,000 DH

Restaurant prices are per person for a main course at dinner. Hotel prices are for a high-season standard double room, excluding service and tax.

FESTIVALS

Le Festival de Casablanca, a citywide arts event, attracts international visitors every July. L'Boulevard, which takes place in May, is an annual competition among local and foreign artists and is popular with the younger crowd. Rabat's Mawazine festival, also in May, has achieved international recognition, bringing high-quality performers to Morocco.

RABAT

40 km (25 mi) southwest of Kenitra, 91 km (57 mi) northeast of Casablanca.

Rabat is an excellent place to get acquainted with Morocco, as it has a medina and an array of historical sites and museums, yet exerts significantly less of the pressure that most foreign travelers experience in a place like Fez. You'll generally find yourself free to wander and browse without being hassled to buy local wares or engage a guide. As a diplomatic center, Rabat has a large community of foreign residents. Attractive and well kept, with several gardens, it's arguably Morocco's most pleasant and easygoing city.

Rabat was founded in the 12th century as a fortified town—now the Kasbah des Oudayas—on a rocky outcrop overlooking the River Bou Regreg by Abd al-Mu'min of the Almohad dynasty. Abd al-Mu'min's grandson, Yaqoub al-Mansour, extended the city to encompass the present-day medina, surrounded it with ramparts (some of which still stand), and erected a mosque, from which the unfinished Hassan Tower protrudes as Rabat's principal landmark. Chellah, a neighboring Roman town now within Rabat, was developed as a necropolis in the 13th century.

In the early 17th century Rabat itself was revived with the arrival of the Muslims, who populated the present-day medina upon their expulsion from Spain. Over the course of the 17th century the Kasbah des Oudayas grew notorious for its pirates, and an independent republic of the Bou Regreg was established, based in the kasbah; the piracy continued when the republic was integrated into the Alaouite kingdom and lasted until the 19th century. Rabat was named the administrative capital of the country at the beginning of the French protectorate in 1912, and it remained the capital of the Alaouite kingdom when independence was restored in 1956.

The city has grown considerably over the last 20 years, and today it has many important districts outside the kasbah, the medina, and the original French Ville Nouvelle. These include L'Océan, the seaside area that was once Spanish and Portuguese (during the French protectorate); Hassan, the environs of the Hassan tower; Agdal, a fashionable residential and business district; Ryad, an upscale residential district; and Souissi, an affluent enclave of wealthy folks and diplomats. Take a ride in a taxi or your own car around the various neighborhoods to get a real understanding of the city as a whole.

GETTING HERE AND AROUND

BY AIR

For international visitors, Rabat is best reached via Casablanca's Mohammed V International Airport. Rabat-Salé Airport, which has only domestic flights, is 10 km (6 mi) northeast of the capital. Train service from Casablanca's airport into Rabat is reliable and frequent.

BY BUS

The bus station in Rabat is on the outskirts of the city in a neighborhood known as Kamara; from there you can take a taxi or a city bus into town.

Bus Information **CTM** ✉ *Av. Hassan II, Kamara* ☎ *0537/28–14–78* 🌐 *www.ctm.co.ma.*

BY CAR

You won't want (or need) a car if you are only visiting Rabat and Casablanca, but if you want to explore further, one may be helpful. Major international agencies do have rental outlets in Rabat or at the domestic airport.

Rental Cars **Avis** ✉ *7, rue Abou Faris el-Marini* ☎ *0537/72–18–18* 🌐 *www.avis.com.* **Budget** ✉ *Rabat-Salé Airport* ☎ *0675/38–60–54* 🌐 *www.budget.com.* **Hertz** ✉ *Rabat-Salé Airport* ☎ *0537/70–73–66* 🌐 *www.hertz.com.*

BY TAXI

Rabat's *petits taxis,* which are blue, can get you easily from point A to point B, and you'll find them just about everywhere in town. A typical metered fare will cost you about 15 to 20 DH (after 9 pm there is a 50% supplement to the metered price).

BY TRAIN

Rabat has two train stations: Rabat-Agdal, on the outskirts of town toward Casablanca, and Rabat-Ville, closer to most hotels and attractions. Rabat is three hours by train from Meknès, four hours from Fez, and four hours from Marrakesh. All these trains also call at Casablanca. In addition, there are overnight trains from Rabat to Oujda, and three direct trains daily to Tangier, which also have bus connections from an intermediate stop (just before Asilah) to Tetouan. Casablanca's new tramway costs 7 DH per ride and is an excellent way to get around the city.

Train Contacts **Office National des Chemins de Fer** ✉ *8 bis, rue Abderrahmane el-Ghafiki* ☎ *0890/20–30–40* 🌐 *www.oncf.org.ma.*

GUIDES AND TOURS

Guided tours of several cities in this region are best reserved in your home country. Generally speaking, you can't buy a place on a local guided tour upon arrival the way you can in many other countries. For customized tours, try Select Travel & Event in Casablanca, which serves all of Morocco, or Atlas Voyages in Rabat.

Tour Information **Atlas Voyages** ☎ *0802/00–20–20* 🌐 *www.atlasvoyages.com.* **Select Travel & Event** ✉ *24, bd. Rachidi, Casablanca* ☎ *0522/47–59–00.*

TIMING AND PRECAUTIONS

Rabat is considered one of the safest, least harried cities in Morocco. Travelers can generally expect minimal harassment from vendors and fake tour guides. Nonetheless, streets can be somewhat desolate after sundown, so visitors should use taxis then.

EXPLORING

TOP ATTRACTIONS

Archaeological Museum. Opened in 1931, the Musée Archéologique holds prehistoric, Roman, and Islamic-period artifacts discovered throughout the country. The emphasis is on Roman pieces, including many inscribed tablets; the Chellah and Volubilis sites are particularly well represented, and there's an ample collection of Roman bronze items. Also on display is a plaster cast of the early human remains found at Harhoura Beach, on the coast south of the city. ✉ *23, rue Al Brihi, Ministères* ☎ *0537/70–19–19* 🌐 *www.minculture.gov.ma* 🎟 *10 DH* ⏲ *Wed.–Mon. 9–11:30 and 2:30–5:30.*

Fodor's Choice ★ **Chellah.** Chellah was an independent city before Rabat ever existed. It dates from the 7th or 8th century BC, when it was probably Phoenician. You'll see the remains of the subsequent Roman city, Sala Colonia, on your left as you walk down the path. Though these remnants are limited to broken stone foundations and column bases, descriptive markers point to the likely location of the forum, baths, and market. Sultan Abu Saïd and his son Abu al-Hassan, of the Merenid dynasty, were responsible for the ramparts, the entrance gate, and the majestic portals. The Merenids used Chellah as a spiritual retreat, and at quiet times the *baraka* (blessing) of the place is still tangible.

The entrance to the Merenid sanctuary is at the bottom of the path, just past some tombs. To the right is a pool with eels in it, which is said to produce miracles—women are known to toss eggs to the eels for fertility. The ruins of the mosque are just inside the sanctuary: beautiful

DID YOU KNOW?

Chellah is far older than Rabat, but the magnificent ramparts and entry gate were built by the Merenid sultan Abu Al Hassan in the mid-14th century.

Rabat
Oued Bou Regreg
MELLAH
MEDINA
CENTRE VILLE
Av. Al Marsa
R. des Consuls
Bab El Mellah
Av. Moulay Ismail
Av. Al Alaouine
R. Abdelmoumen
R. Al Mouwahidine
R. Al Marinyine
Av. Chellah
R. Mekka
Bb. el Alou
Rue Bouktoun
R. Souika
Bd. Hassan II
Parc du Triangle de Vue
R. Sidi Fatah
Av. Mohammed V (El Gzah)
Bab Bouiba
R. Patrice Lumumba
R. Al Mourabatine
Pl. Achouhada
R. Mansour Addahbi
Av. Abou Inan
R. Allal ben Abdellah
Bd. Mohammed V
Av. Al Mouqawama
Av. Jazirat Al Arab
Bab Al Had
R. Soekarno
Av. Ibn Toumert
Gare Rabat Ville
Djemaa Sunna
Av. Moukhtar Gazoulit
Av. Abdelkrim Al Khattabi
R. Loubnane
Rue Sénégal
Bd. Al Maghrib al Arabi
Bd. Hassan II
Av. Jean Jaurès
Av. Pasteur
R. Descartes
Pl. Italia
Av. Mali
R. Abdelwahed Al Marrakchi
R. Abou Chouaib
Adoukkali
Bab Rouah
Pl. Russia
R. Qadi Ayad
Av. Al Ghazali
Av. Tonkin
Av. Madagascar
Av. Al Muqawama
Bd. Annasr (Av. de la Victoire)
Stade Olympique
Av. Ibn Khaldoune
Av. Ibn Hazm
R. Oqba
R. Al Baftani
Jardin d'Essais
Bab Tamesna
Pl. Ibn Al Widane
Av. Mohamed Zerktouni
Av. Sidi Mohamed ben Abdellah
R. Ibn Hajar
R. Al Achaari
Bab Marrakech
R. Innaouen
TO AGDAL
1
2
3
4
7
9
10
11
12
17

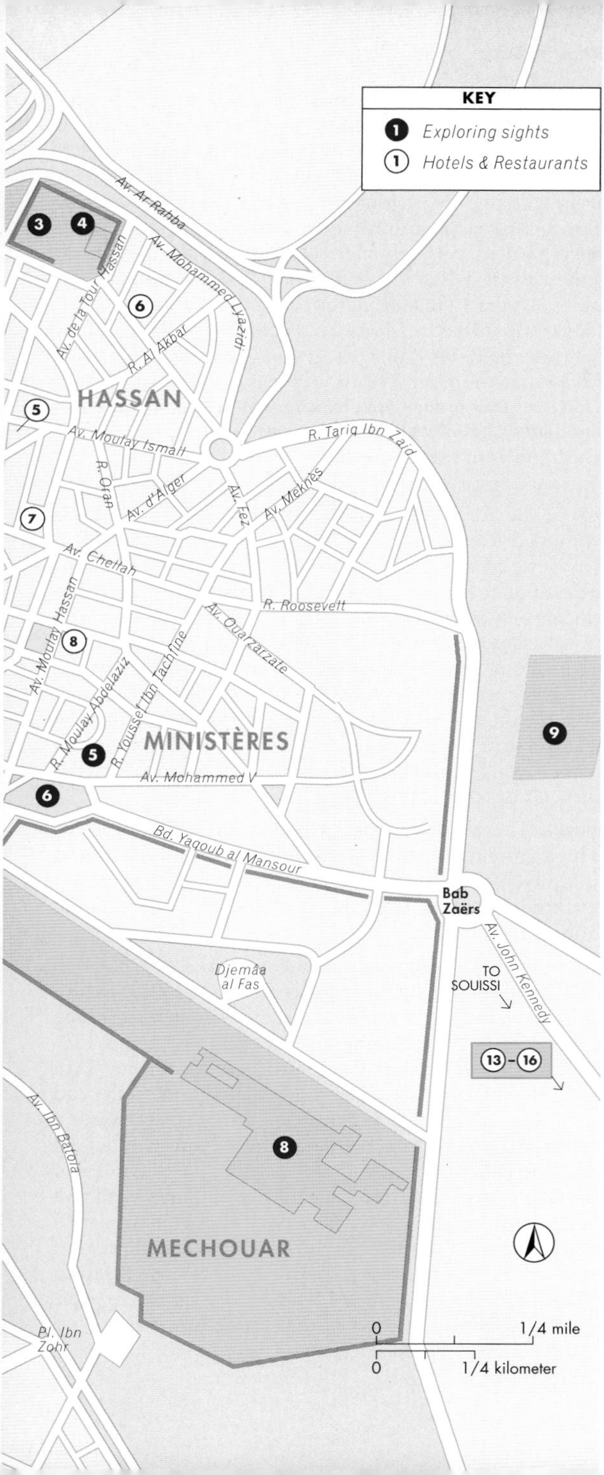

KEY
Exploring sights
Hotels & Restaurants
Av. Ar Rahba
Av. Mohammed Lyazidi
Av. de la Tour Hassan
R. Al Akbar
HASSAN
Av. Moulay Ismail
R. Tariq Ibn Zaid
R. Oran
Av. d'Alger
Av. Fez
Av. Meknès
Av. Chellah
R. Roosevelt
Av. Ouarzazate
Av. Moulay Hassan
R. Moulay Abdelaziz
R. Youssef Ibn Tachfine
MINISTÈRES
Av. Mohammed V
Bd. Yaqoub al Mansour
Bab Zaërs
Av. John Kennedy
TO SOUISSI
Djemâa al Fas
Av. Ibn Batoria
MECHOUAR
Pl. Ibn Zohr
0
1/4 mile
0
1/4 kilometer

Exploring ▼

Hotels ▼

Restaurants ▼

arches and the *mihrab* (prayer niche). Storks nest on the impressive minaret. On the far side of the mosque is a beautiful wall decorated with Kufi script, a type of Arabic calligraphy characterized by right angles. To the left of the mosque is the *zaouia* (sanctuary), where you can see the ruins of individual cells surrounding a basin and some ancient mosaic work. Beyond the mosque and zaouia are some beautiful, well-maintained walled gardens. Spring water runs through the gardens at one point, and they give Chellah a serenity that's quite extraordinary, considering that it's less than a mile from the center of a nation's capital. There is no place comparable in Morocco. From the walled gardens you can look out over the River Bou Regreg: you'll see cultivated fields below, and cliffs across the river. On the right is a hill with a small white koubba. ■ TIP→ **Tour groups are elsewhere at lunchtime, so try to come then to experience Chellah at its most serene.** ✉ *Chellah* 🎫 *10 DH* ⏲ *Daily 8:30–5:30 (or until sunset if earlier).*

Hassan Tower. At the end of the 12th century, Yaqoub al-Mansour—fourth monarch of the Almohad dynasty and grandson of Abd al-Mu'min, who founded Rabat—planned a great mosque. Intended to be the largest mosque in the Muslim world, the project was abandoned with the death of al-Mansour in 1199. A further blow to the site occurred with the strong tremors of the 1755 Lisbon earthquake, and this tower is the only significant remnant of al-Mansour's dream. A few columns remain in the mosque's great rectangular courtyard, but the great tower was never even completed (which is why it looks too short for its base). Note the quality of the craftsmanship in the carved-stone and mosaic decorations at the top of the tower. From the base there is a fine view over the river. Locals come here at dawn to have their wedding photos taken. ✉ *Hassan* 🎫 *Free.*

★ **Kasbah des Oudayas.** The history of the kasbah is the early history of Rabat. Built on high ground over the mouth of the Bou Regreg river and the Atlantic, the kasbah was originally built here for defensive purposes. Still inhabited, it originally comprised the whole of the city, including the castle of Yaqoub al-Mansour.

Walk up the steps to the huge, imposing ornamental gate, built, like Bab Rouah, by the Almohads. The gate's interior is now used for art exhibits. Enter the kasbah and turn right into Rue Jama (Mosque Street). The **mosque,** which dates from Almohad times (it was built in the mid-12th century), is on the left; it was supposedly reconstructed in the late 18th century by an English Muslim—Ahmed el-Inglizi. Continue to the end of the road past a house called Dar Baraka, and you'll emerge onto a large platform overlooking the Bou Regreg estuary. Here you have a magnificent view across the river to the old quarter of Salé, and you can walk down to the water's edge. Go back along Rue Jama until you come to Rue Bazo on the left; this winds down the kasbah past picturesque houses. Turn left, walk to the bottom of the street, and proceed down to the banks of the Bou Regreg river to see the beautiful **Jardin des Oudayas** (Oudayas Garden), a walled retreat that you can explore at your leisure. The garden was laid out in the early 20th century (and is now wheelchair accessible), but its enclosure dates from the beginning of the present Alaouite dynasty in the 17th century.

At the top of the garden, accessible by a bridge across a pool, is the **Musée des Oudayas** (Oudayas Museum), which holds various objects of traditional Moroccan art. The museum is set in a house built by Moulay Ismail in the traditional style, with rooms arranged around a courtyard. Thanks to fortuitous design, the rooms get sun in winter but not in summer. The two most valuable items are the 12th- or 13th-century Almohad Koran and the medieval astrolabe; other exhibits include Andalusian musical instruments, clothing, jewelry, and pottery from Fez. Leave the garden by the wrought-iron gate at the top and turn left as you come out to exit the kasbah by the lower gate. ■ TIP→ **You may be approached by a potential guide at the entrance, but you won't really need one.** ✉ *Oudayas Museum, 1, bd. Al Marsa, Medina* ☎ *0537/73–15–37* 🎫 *Kasbah free, museum 10 DH* ⏲ *Kasbah freely accessible, museum Wed.–Mon. 8:30–noon and 3–5:30.*

NEED A BREAK?

Oudayas Café. The Oudayas Café is an excellent place to pause for a drink or snack; the shady terrace is decorated with mosaic tilework and looks across the river to Salé. ✉ ***Oudayas Museum, 1, bd. Al Marsa, Medina*** ☎ ***0537/73–15–37.***

Mohammed V Mausoleum. Resting place of King Mohammed V, who died in 1961, the mausoleum is adjacent to the Hassan Tower and, thanks to a commanding position above the river, is similarly visible to anyone approaching Rabat from Salé. The tomb itself is subterranean; the terrace that overlooks it is approached by steps on each side. Looking down, you're likely to see someone ritually reading the Koran. Beyond the central sarcophagus of King Mohammed V are those of his sons Prince Moulay Abdallah and King Hassan II, who was interred here in July 1999 as world leaders stood by for his state funeral. Designed by a Vietnamese architect and built between 1962 and 1966, the tomb is cubical, with a pyramidal green-tile roof, a richly decorated ceiling, and onyx interior walls. A mosque, built at the same time, adjoins the tomb. ✉ *Hassan.*

WORTH NOTING

Bab Rouah (*Gate of the Winds*). Currently an art gallery, this city gate was built by Yaqoub al-Mansour in 1197. To see it, go outside the city walls and look to the right of the modern arches. Originally a fortification, the gate has an elaborately decorated arch topped by two carved shells. The entrance leads into a room with no gate behind it; you have to turn left into another room and then right into a third room to see the door that once led into Rabat. ✉ *1, av. de la Victoire, Centre Ville* 🎫 *Free* ⏲ *Daily 8:30–noon and 2:30–7:30.*

Ensemble Artisanal. Near the River Bou Regreg is a series of small workshops where you can see artisans create Morocco's various handicrafts: everything from traditional mosaic tilework, embroidery, leatherwork, traditional shoes, and painted wood to brass, pottery, and carpets. You can buy the items at fixed prices, which are a little higher than well-negotiated prices in nearby Rue des Consuls but which save you the trouble of bargaining. ✉ *6, Tarik el-Marsa, Espace les Oudayas, Medina* ☎ *0537/73–05–07* 🎫 *Free* ⏲ *Daily 9–12:30 and 2:30–6.*

Royal Palace (*Mechouar*). Built in the early 20th century, Morocco's Royal Palace is a large, cream-color building set back behind lawns. Its large ornamental gate is accented by ceremonial guards dressed in white and red. The complex houses the offices of the cabinet, the prime minister, and other administrative officials. Don't stray from the road down the middle of the complex; the palace is occupied by the royal family and closed to the public. ✉ *Mechouar.*

Sunna Mosque. Rabat's most important mosque was built in the 1960s, but because it was designed in a traditional Maghrebi style, it was sheltered from the architectural anarchy of the time and remains beautiful and dignified today. In their day the French wanted to extend Avenue Mohammed V through this site, but the Moroccans resisted, and thanks to the martyrs of that confrontation, the mosque stands here on the site of an earlier one. Non-Muslims may not enter. ✉ *At the top of Ave. Mohammed V, Centre Ville.*

WHERE TO EAT

$$$$ MOROCCAN ★ ✕ **Dinarjat.** This is a true palatial restaurant that provides traditional Moroccan meals, but the real draw is the beautiful ambience of its setting in a medina house. Live Andalusian music creates a charming background. Start your à la carte meal with a spread of Moroccan salads, and then savor classic dishes like tagines or couscous. You can get here from Boulevard Laalou, not far from the Kasbah des Oudayas; in the evening a man stands at the nearest entrance to the medina with a lantern, ready to guide you to the restaurant. ✉ *6, rue Belgnaoui, Medina* ☎ *0537/70–42–39* 🌐 *www.dinarjat.com.*

$$$$ FRENCH ✕ **Le Goéland.** Located near the flower market on Place Petri, Le Goéland is an elegant restaurant specializing in fresh fish with a warm yet dignified atmosphere. The French cuisine and the service are excellent. The catch of the day is showcased on ice near the entrance and the meats are well prepared. Try the huge and elegantly presented turbot encrusted in salt, and for dessert a delicious café *liégeois* (iced coffee with ice cream and whipped cream). The only drawback is the high prices. ✉ *9, rue Moulay Ali Cherif, Hassan* ☎ *0537/76–88–85* ⏲ *Closed Sun.*

$$$$ FRENCH ✕ **Le Grand Comptoir.** This popular French bistro in the Centre Ville offers tasty food along with live music. It's a nice option for dinner or an after-dinner drink, though prices are relatively high. Because of the music, things can get noisy as the evening progresses. ✉ *279, av. Mohammed V, Centre Ville* ☎ *0537/20–15–14.*

$$ ITALIAN ✕ **La Mamma.** This is the most popular of Rabat's many pizzerias, and with good reason. Pastas, pizzas, and grilled meats are excellent here, as are the pitchers of sangria. From the central brick oven to the garlands of garlic hanging from the rafters, the atmosphere is homey Italian kitchen. Though the place is always bustling, service is fast. ✉ *6, Zankat Tanta, Centre Ville* ☎ *0537/70–73–29.*

$$ JAPANESE ✕ **Matsuri.** This Japanese restaurant chain has restaurants in several Moroccan cities serving the best Japanese food in town. The selection of fish, though limited, is always very fresh, and the staff are helpful.

You can get quick service if you are in a hurry. Alcohol is served. ✉ *Av. Mohammed VI–Route de Zaers, Souissi* ☎ *0537/75–75–72.*

$$ FRENCH ✕ **Paul.** Café, bakery, and distinguished French restaurant all rolled into one, Paul is one of Rabat's most popular spots. In the evening there is a variety of fish, game, and meat dishes, such as *rôti du canard* (roast duck) and *rouget grillé* (grilled red snapper). You can lunch on delicious quiches, sandwiches, and crepes. The kitchen stays open late, the menu changes seasonally, and the dining room is occasionally animated by jazz performers. Sadly, the service doesn't match the food quality. The bakery is a standout in its own right, and makes what may be the best fresh-baked bread in town. ✉ *82, ave. Nations Unies, Agdal* ☎ *0537/67–20–00* 🌐 *www.paul.fr.*

$$$ MOROCCAN ✕ **Le Petit Beurre.** This attractive à la carte restaurant serves standard Moroccan fare such as couscous, brochettes, tagines, and hearty *harira* (bean-based soup with vegetables and meat). Everything is well prepared and flavorful. The lovely tiled walls and painted ceilings give you the impression of dining in richer surroundings than the moderate prices and casual mood suggest. It offers good value for the price, but the restaurant can be a bit noisy. ✉ *8, rue Dumas, Centre Ville* ☎ *0537/73–13–22.*

$$$ MEDITERRANEAN ✕ **Piccolo's.** This friendly restaurant serves Mediterranean cuisine and offers a broad selection of fish, meat, and pasta dishes. The fettuccine with grilled vegetables and fresh Parmesan is divine. The restaurant also has a beautiful airy garden and intimate tables amongst the garden's greenery. ✉ *149, rte. des Zaers, Souissi* ☎ *0537/63–69–69.*

$$$$ SEAFOOD ✕ **Restaurant de la Plage.** Fish takes many forms at this restaurant in the kasbah. You can eat such dishes as *sole meunière* (fillet of sole cooked in butter and almonds) or *filet St. Pierre* (fish cooked in fennel and green onions) served with little boiled potatoes and rice. Wines include the likes of Les Trois Domaines (a Guerrouane red from Meknès) and claret. You dine right next to the Kasbah des Oudayas, overlooking the Atlantic Ocean. The only drawback is service, which is sometimes spotty. ✉ *Plage Oudaya, Medina* ☎ *0537/20–29–28.*

WHERE TO STAY

For expanded hotel reviews, visit Fodors.com.

$$$$ **Le Diwan Rabat.** Built on a busy intersection, this luxury hotel, part of the MGallery-Accor chain, is remarkably quiet inside. **Pros:** beautiful facility; free guarded parking lot. **Cons:** rates are high for the area. ✉ *Pl. de l'Unité Africaine, Hassan* ☎ *0537/26–27–27* 🌐 *www.mgallery.com* *88 rooms, 6 suites* *In-room: a/c, Internet, Wi-Fi. In-hotel: restaurant, bar, spa, parking* *No meals.*

$ **Ibis Moussafir.** The Ibis Moussafir is adjacent to the Rabat-Agdal train station—that is, the first station you come to from Casablanca. **Pros:** good breakfast; near business district. **Cons:** views are not impressive. ✉ *32, rue Abderrahmane el Ghafiki, Agdal* ☎ *0537/77–49–19* *99 rooms* *In-room: a/c, Wi-Fi. In-hotel: restaurant, bar* *Breakfast.*

$ **Mercure Relais Sheherazade.** On a quiet street near the Hassan Tower, this hotel has what must be the city's most unusual dining: an Australian

Rabat's Kasbah des Oudayas is visible behind fishing boats overturned on the banks of the Oued Bou Regreg.

restaurant specializing in grilled meat. **Pros:** unbeatable breakfast buffet; interesting restaurant. **Cons:** exposed plumbing in bathrooms. ✉ *21, rue Tunis, Hassan* ☎ *0537/72–22–26* 🌐 *www.mercure.com* *77 rooms* *In-room: a/c, Internet, Wi-Fi. In-hotel: restaurant, bar, spa* *Breakfast.*

$ **Rabat Yasmine.** This good-value hotel is not far from the Hassan Tower and offers a spacious lobby and a warm welcome. **Pros:** well-maintained facility; soothing decor. **Cons:** no gym. ✉ *Rue Marinyne at Rue Makka, Hassan* ☎ *0537/72–20–18* *55 rooms* *In-room: a/c. In-hotel: restaurant, bar* *Breakfast.*

$$ ★ **Riad Oudaya.** With an intimate feel, this French-run hideaway in the depths of the medina is one of the finest in Rabat. **Pros:** authentic decor; central location. **Cons:** basic rooms; two-night minimum. ✉ *46, rue Sidi Fateh, Medina* ☎ *0537/70–23–92* 🌐 *www.riadoudaya.com* *2 rooms, 2 suites* *In-room: no a/c, no TV. In-hotel: restaurant, bar, parking* *Breakfast* ☞ *2-night min.*

$$$$ ★ **Sofitel Rabat Jardin des Roses.** Completely renovated in 2010, this former Hilton was reopened as part of the Sofitel chain. **Pros:** a true luxury five-star hotel; beautiful grounds. **Cons:** expensive. ✉ *Quartier Aviation, Souissi* ☎ *0537/67–56–56* 🌐 *www.sofitel.com* *202 rooms, 27 suites* *In-room: a/c, Internet, Wi-Fi. In-hotel: restaurant, bar, golf course, pool, tennis court, gym, spa, water sports, laundry facilities, parking* *Multiple meal plans.*

$$$$ **La Tour Hassan.** If you want a luxury hotel that reflects classic Moroccan architecture, stay at the Tour Hassan. **Pros:** located in city center. **Cons:** rooms in north wing are near a nightclub; some furnishings

need updating. ✉ *26, rue Chellah, Hassan* ☎ *0537/23–90–00* 🌐 *www.latourhassan.com* ⇒ *122 rooms, 18 suites* *In-room: a/c, Internet, Wi-Fi. In-hotel: restaurant, bar, pool, gym, spa, parking* 🍴 *Breakfast.*

$$$$ Fodor's Choice ★ **Villa Mandarine.** This gorgeous villa in the residential neighborhood between Agdal and the Royal Palace offers all the comforts of home along with smart hosts, savvy fellow guests, and outstanding French and Moroccan cuisine with contemporary touches. **Pros:** romantic setting; relaxing hammam. **Cons:** no public transportation. ✉ *19, rue Ouled Bou, Souissi* ☎ *0537/75–20–77* 🌐 *www.villamandarine.com* ⇒ *31 rooms, 5 suites* *In-room: a/c, Internet, Wi-Fi. In-hotel: restaurant, bar, pool, tennis court, gym, spa, parking* 🍴 *Breakfast.*

3

SHOPPING

In addition to finding traditional Moroccan furniture, clothing, artwork, and other locally made crafts, Rabat, like other major Moroccan cities, is becoming more and more Europeanized in terms of shopping options and access to clothing and other imported products.

AGDAL

ANTIQUES

The Agdal neighborhood has a high concentration of furniture and antiques stores.

Arabesque. Arabesque carries beautiful old and new carved-wood furnishings, leather-covered chests, iron-framed mirrors, painted screens, and countless other decorative items. You may have to dig deeper into your pocketbook for the high-quality pieces here than you would in the souks. ✉ *61, rue Fal Ould Oumeir, Agdal.*

CRAFTS

Coté Maisons. Coté Maisons is a great place to pick up souvenirs for friends or yourself. Its stock is continuously updated and highlights local artisans' collections, often with a modern touch. ✉ *1, rue Soumaya, Agdal* ☎ *0537/67–07–45.*

CENTRE VILLE

CLOTHING

In addition to Rue des Consuls, the lower part of **Avenue Mohammed V** is a good place to buy traditional Moroccan clothing.

SOUISSI

SHOPPING CENTERS AND MALLS

Mega Mall. If you are feeling homesick or just in the mood for some hassle-free shopping, Rabat's MegaMall will do the trick. Following the design of a typical American mall, it has over 80 mid- to high-end European stores, a food court, bowling alley, and ice-skating rink. ✉ *Rte. de Zaers, Souissi* ☎ *0537/63–18–15* 🌐 *www.megamall.ma.*

MEDINA

CRAFTS

Rue des Consuls. The medina's Rue des Consuls is a great place to shop for handicrafts and souvenirs: it's pedestrian-only, has a pleasant atmosphere, and imposes no real pressure to buy. Here you can find carpets, Berber jewelry, leather goods, wooden items, brass work, traditional clothing, slippers, and more. You can peruse Zemour carpets (striped in white and burgundy) from Khémisset, near Meknès; deep-pile Rabati carpets, in predominantly blue-and-white designs; and orange, black, and white Glaoui carpets. Many of the larger shops take credit cards. ■ **TIP→ Try to visit Rue des Consuls on a Monday or Thursday morning when the entire street turns into a carpet market.** ✉ *Medina.*

NIGHTLIFE

AGDAL

BARS AND CLUBS

5th Avenue. 5th Avenue is Rabat's Manhattan disco scene, complete with Claudia Schiffers waiting to be discovered and DJs spinning torrid tunes. ✉ *4, rue Bin Alaouidan, Agdal* ☎ *0537/77–52–54.*

Pachanga. Pachanga is a good option for drinks, music, food, and people-watching. ✉ *10, pl. des Alaouites, Centre Ville* ☎ *0537/26–29–31.*

Upstairs Bar. Upstairs is one of the hottest places to be at night for both upscale Rabatis and the expat crowd. ✉ *8, av. Michliffen, Agdal* ☎ *0537/67–41–11.*

CENTRE VILLE

BARS AND CLUBS

Le 173. This hip bar/restaurant is one of the newest additions to the Rabat nightlife scene. ✉ *173, av. Mohammed VI, Centre Ville* ☎ *0537/63–09–04.*

SPORTS AND THE OUTDOORS

GOLF

Fodor's Choice ★ **Royal Golf Dar es Salam.** The most famous golf course in Morocco is on the road toward Romani, at the far edge of Souissi on the right. Designed by Robert Trent Jones, it's considered one of the 50 best courses in the world. There are two 18-hole courses and one 9-hole course in 162 verdant acres. ✉ *Av. Mohammed VI–Rte. des Zaers, Km 9, Souissi* ☎ *0537/75–58–64* 🌐 *www.royalgolfdaressalam.com.*

HAMMAMS AND SPAS

Moving Club. On the menu of this popular health club used by modern Moroccans is the Royal and Ancestral hammam with massage. ✉ *33, ave. Mehdi Benbarka, Souissi* ☎ *0537/65–29–60* 🎫 *130 DH with exfoliation* ▭ *No credit cards* ⏲ *Daily 6 am–10 pm.*

La Tour Hassan Hammam. Built in 1914 next to the famous unfinished tower of the Moorish Hassan Mosque, this elegant yet affordable hotel spa offers a hammam, massage, sauna, Jacuzzi, and beauty treatments. ✉ *26, rue Chellah, Hassan* ☎ *0537/70–42–01* 🎫 *250 DH* ⏲ *By appointment.*

EXCURSIONS FROM RABAT

SKHIRAT BEACH

20 km (12 mi) southwest of Rabat.

Southwest of Rabat, towards Casablanca, is the beautiful Skhirat Beach. Perfect for either an afternoon at the beach or a weekend getaway, Skhirat, while just minutes from Rabat, feels worlds away. Home of the luxurious L'Amphitrite Palace, Skhirat is a convenient and lovely place to spend the night if you feel like staying outside of the city. History buffs might be interested to know that the 1971 attempt to overthrow King Hassan II during his birthday gala occurred at the Royal Palace of Skhirat.

3

Skhirat Plage. Long, sandy, surfer-friendly Skhirat Plage is home to the luxurious Amphitrite Palace hotel. It lies just beyond the Royal Palace of Skihirat. ✉ *Skhirat.*

GETTING HERE AND AROUND

Public transportation does not reach Skhirat, so a car is essential.

WHERE TO STAY

For expanded hotel reviews, visit Fodors.com.

$$$ ★ **L'Amphitrite Palace.** This luxury hotel is a great place to get away from it all. **Pros:** modern building; fresh decor; beautiful beach. **Cons:** somewhat remote location. ✉ *Skhirat Plage, Skhirat* ☎ *0537/62–10–00* 🌐 *www.lamphitrite.com* *178 rooms, 14 suites* *In-room: a/c, Internet, Wi-Fi. In-hotel: restaurant, bar, pool, gym, spa, beach, water sports, parking* 🍽 *Breakfast.*

SALÉ

37 km (23 mi) southwest of Kenitra, just 13 km (8 mi) northeast of Rabat across river.

Salé was probably founded around the 11th century. In medieval times it was the most important trading harbor on the Atlantic coast, and at the beginning of the 17th century it joined Rabat in welcoming Muslims expelled from Spain. Rabat and Salé were rival towns for more than 100 years after that, but Rabat eventually gained the upper hand, and today Salé is very much in its shadow. The medina, however, is worth a trip even apart from its monuments, as it's particularly authentic; you're more likely to see people in traditional dress or practicing traditional crafts than you are in most other Moroccan large-city medinas.

GETTING HERE AND AROUND

The new Rabat–Salé tramway provides the ideal option for traveling between the two cities, costing just 7 DH per ride. Buses and taxis are also options.

TIMING AND PRECAUTIONS

Most travelers visit Salé just for the day. Salé is a relatively safe city, with most hassles coming from vendors near the medina. If you feel harassed by them, do not hesitate to summon police.

EXPLORING

Although there are a few things to see on the city's outskirts, most of Salé's most interesting sights are located in the medina. A good place to start a tour of Salé is at the entrance to the medina, near the Great Mosque, which you can access from the road along the southwest city wall. Don't worry if you lose track of where you are in the medina; many a shop will distract you, but you're never far from an entrance gate. Follow the car noise.

★ **Abou el-Hassan Medersa.** Turn left around the corner of the Great Mosque, and you'll see on your right the Abou el-Hassan Medersa, built by the Merenid sultan of that name in the 14th century and a fine example of the traditional Koranic school. Like the Bou Inania in Fez or the Ben Youssef in Marrakesh, this medersa has beautiful intricate plasterwork around its central courtyard, and a fine *mihrab* (prayer niche) with a ceiling carved in an interlocking geometrical pattern representing the cosmos. Upstairs, on the second and third floors, you can visit the little cells where the students used to sleep, and from the roof you can see the entire city. *10 DH Daily 9–noon and 2:30–6.*

Djemaâ Kabir (*Great Mosque*). Just after the tomb of Zanqat Sidi Abdellah ben Hassoun you come to the Djemaâ Kabir, which dates from the 12th-century Almohad dynasty and is the third-largest mosque in Morocco after the Hassan II in Casablanca and the Kairaouine in Fez.

Pottery complex. Salé's pottery complex in the village of Oulja, just off the road toward Fez (to the right after you cross the river from Rabat) is a whole series of pottery stores that sell their own wares. Each store has its own style, and you can walk around and see them all without any pressure to buy. For traditional Berber pottery, try Mohamed El Rhalmi's shop, Poterie El Amal, number 6. Other crafts have been added to this complex, notably bamboo and straw work and mosaic-tile furnishings. The shops inside the large central building carry a variety of handicrafts at rather high prices. ✉ *Oulja.*

Tomb of Zanqat Sidi Abdellah ben Hassoun. You enter Salé's medina on Zanqat Sidi Abdellah ben Hassoun—a street named after the patron saint of Salé, whose tomb you pass on the left.

Zaouia (*spiritual meeting place, or sanctuary*). On the right, before the tomb of Zanqat Sidi Abdellah ben Hassoun, is the zaouia of the Tijani order, a mystical Sufi Islamic sect founded by Shaykh Ahmad al-Tijani (1739–1815).

WHERE TO STAY

$ ★ **The Repose.** This beautifully restored Moroccan-chic riad in the medina offers a pampering environment while mainting an exotic feel. **Pros:** great staff; English spoken; a true feel of traditional Moroccan medina. **Cons:** off the beaten path; difficult to find; no parking at the riad. ✉ *17, rue Zankat Talaâ, Ras Chejra* ☎ *0537/88–29–58* *www.therepose.com* *4 rooms* *In-room: a/c, Internet, Wi-Fi. In-hotel: restaurant, bar, spa* *Breakfast.*

SIDI-BOUKNADEL

18 km (11 mi) northeast of Rabat.

Sidi-Bouknadel (also known as Bouknadel) isn't accessible from the autoroute, but its attractions lie to the north, halfway between Kenitra and Rabat, and are accessible via the coastal road from either of the two.

3

GETTING HERE AND AROUND

Taxis run regularly from Salé to Sidi-Bouknadel in summer. If traveling from Rabat by bus, board Bus 13 at Avenue Moulay Hassan in Rabat. You can take the same bus back to Rabat from Sidi-Bouknadel. Taxis can be chartered to and from Rabat, Salé, and Kenitra throughout the year.

TIMING AND PRECAUTIONS

Most travelers visit Sidi-Bouknadel for the day en route to Rabat or on their way north. Sidi-Bouknadel is generally safe, with minimal hassling of visitors. The beach, however, is rather secluded after sundown, so caution is advised for those desiring an evening walk on the shore.

EXPLORING

Belghazi Museum. In 1991 an entrepreneurial craftsman named Abdelila Belghazi was contracted to carve cedar decorations for the huge sliding domes on the Prophet's Mosque in Medina, Saudi Arabia. Thanks to this windfall, he established a workshop in this building in Bouknadel and founded the Belghazi Museum to exhibit his collection of traditional Moroccan art. Patronized (that is, publicly supported) by Princess Lalla Meriam, it is the first private museum in the country and houses a far larger collection than any state museum. On display are pottery, wood carvings, embroidery, manuscripts, musical instruments, agricultural tools, and weapons. One interesting room is full of Moroccan Jewish art, such as wedding clothes and temple furnishings. ✉ *Rte. de Kenitra, Km 17* ☎ *037/82–21–78* 🎟 *20 DH* ⏲ *Daily 9–6:30.*

Jardins Exotiques (*Exotic Gardens*). South of Bouknadel are the Jardins Exotiques, created in the mid-20th century by a Frenchman named François, who used to play classical music to his plants. Since François's death the gardens have been maintained by the government, and although the landscaper's house has fallen into ruin, the leaves are still swept up daily. The gardens were originally planned to represent different regions, such as Polynesia, China, and Japan. They're a haven for birds and frogs, and the profusion of walkways and bridges makes them a wonderful playground for children. A touching poem by François about his life forms an epitaph at the entrance. 🎟 *5 DH* ⏲ *Daily 9–18:30.*

Plage des Nations. The Plage des Nations is a spectacular, long sandy beach with large Atlantic breakers that is popular with the locals. A heavy undertow makes it hazardous to swim here, which is why you'll see lifeguards patrolling the beach. Caution is advised, lifeguards or not.

WHERE TO STAY

For expanded hotel reviews, visit Fodors.com.

$ **Hotel Firdaous.** This hotel has a spectacular location on the Plage des Nations. **Pros:** peaceful setting; eye-popping location. **Cons:** rooms are small. ✉ *Plage des Nations* ☎ *0537/82–21–31* *17 rooms, 1 suite* *In-room: Wi-Fi. In-hotel: restaurant, bar, pool, beach* *Breakfast.*

MEHDIYA PLAGE

40 km (25 mi) northeast of Rabat.

If you are traveling by car along the coast north of Rabat (toward Moulay Bousselham) and are in the mood for a beach stroll, Mehdiya Plage, which is about 11 km (7 mi) west of Kenitra, will do the trick. Its long, sandy beach is known for good surfing as well as swimming, although the strong undertow along Morocco's Atlantic coast is widely feared and respected. There's a great daily fish market where prawns are among the fresh (and inexpensive) treats on offer, and a handful of beachside cafés.

GETTING HERE AND AROUND

You can take a shuttle train (every 30 minutes) from Rabat to Kenitra, but to reach Mehdiya Plage you must still drive or take a taxi from there. Mehdiya Plage is really best scene as a brief stopover when you are driving north from Rabat.

EXPLORING

Lake Sidi Bourhaba. Slightly inland from Mehdiya is the lovely freshwater Lake Sidi Bourhaba, internationally famous for the number and variety of birds that pass through on their way to the south side of the Sahara desert. Ornithologists flock here nearly as eagerly as the itinerant birds themselves, looking especially for the rare marbled teal along with another 200 species. ✉ *Kenitra.*

MOULAY BOUSSELHAM

46 km (29 mi) southwest of Larache, 82 km (51 mi) northeast of Kenitra, 150 km (93 mi) northeast of Rabat.

The laid-back fishing village of Moulay Bousselham is very popular with Moroccans. It's made up of little more than a single street crowded by cafés and souvenir shops. Moulay Bousselham's lagoon and beach are breathtaking. Its sandbar is somewhat dangerous for swimmers due to a rapid drop-off that causes a continual crash of breaking waves. However, this is one of northern Morocco's prime bird-watching locations, with boat trips organized to see thousands of birds—herons, pink flamingos, sheldrakes, and gannets. The best time for watching birds is just after dawn.

GETTING HERE AND AROUND

Moulay Bousselham has a train station with daily service from Larache and Rabat. There are frequent buses and taxis to Moulay Bousselham from Souk el-Arba du Rharb, which is accessible from Rabat and Larache by grand taxi.

CLOSE UP

The Legend of the Blue Lagoon

The legend of the Blue Lagoon and Moulay Bousselham dates from the 10th century, when the saint Saïd ben Saïd immigrated to the Maghreb from Egypt, following a revelation instructing him to pray where the sun sets over the ocean. He had a disciple called Sidi Abdel Jalil who (according to legend) saw Saïd ben Saïd fishing one day with a hook and asked him why a man with such great powers needed a hook. To show that he needed no such aids himself, Sidi Abdel Jalil put his hands into the water and pulled out fish as numerous as the hairs on his hand. Provoked by this act, Saïd ben Saïd took off his *selham* (cloak), swept it along the ground, called out, "Sea, follow me," and proceeded to walk inland. He did not stop until he had walked 10 km (6 mi). The sea followed him, and so the lagoon was formed. After this, Saïd ben Saïd was called Moulay Bousselham—"Lord, Owner of the Cloak." Both Moulay Bousselham and Sidi Abdel Jalil are buried in the town.

3

TIMING AND PRECAUTIONS

Most travelers stay in Moulay Bousselham for one or two nights. Moulay Bousselham is generally considered safe, with most annoyances stemming from vendors hawking their wares. The village becomes desolate after sundown, so it's wise to take the usual precautions.

Visitor Information **Mansoury el-Boukhary Tourism Office** ☎ *0663/09–37–94.*

EXPLORING

Merdja Zerga (*Blue Lagoon*). Moulay Bousselham is at the head of Merdja Zerga (the Blue Lagoon), which gives its name to the 17,000-acre national park that contains it. This is a major stopover for countless birds migrating from Norway, Sweden, and the United Kingdom to Africa: the birds fly south at the end of summer and stop at Merdja Zerga in September, October, and November before continuing on to West Africa and even as far as South Africa. They stop off again on their way back to Europe in spring, so spring and fall are the times for bird-watching. The pink flamingoes on their way to and from Mauritania are particularly spectacular.

WHERE TO STAY

For expanded hotel reviews, visit Fodors.com.

$ **Driftwood.** With an idylic setting on the lagoon, with spectacular views, Driftwood is great for a weekend of sun and surf, bird-watching, or simple relaxation. **Pros:** beautiful setting; helpful staff; kitchens in apartments. **Cons:** not accessble by public transportation. ☎ *0537/43–21–95* *www.driftwoodmagic.com* *1 1-bedroom apartment, 2 2-bedroom apartments* *In-room: no a/c, kitchen, Internet, Wi-Fi. In-hotel: restaurant, beach, parking* *No meals.*

¢ **Hôtel Le Lagon.** With panoramic views over the inland lagoon and the Atlantic as well, this comfortable hotel on the outskirts of Moulay Bousselham has breezy rooms and a spacious terrace for breakfast or evening cocktails. **Pros:** good views; comfortable rooms. **Cons:** poor access to public transportation. ✉ *Le Lagon, Front de Mer* ☎ *0537/43-26-50* *30 rooms* *In-room: no a/c, Wi-Fi. In-hotel: restaurant* *Breakfast.*

¢ **La Maison des Oiseaux.** This sweet B&B has a beautiful garden, though it's not on the beach. **Pros:** friendly atmosphere; comfortable, clean rooms. **Cons:** very difficult to find; can't be booked online. ☎ *0537/43-25-43* *8 rooms (6 with bath)* *In-room: no a/c* *Breakfast.*

CASABLANCA

91 km (57 mi) southwest of Rabat.

Casablanca is Morocco's most modern city, and various groups of people call it home: hardworking Berbers who came north from the Souss Valley to make their fortune; older folks raised on French customs during the protectorate; pious Muslims; wealthy business executives in the prestigious neighborhoods called California and Anfa; new and poor arrivals from the countryside, living in shantytowns; and thousands of others from all over the kingdom who have found jobs here. The city has its own stock exchange, and working hours tend to transcend the relaxed pace kept by the rest of Morocco.

True to its Spanish name—*casa blanca,* "white house," which, in turn, is Dar el-Beida in Arabic—Casablanca is a conglomeration of white buildings. The present city, known colloquially as Casa or El Beida, was only founded in 1912. It lacks the ancient monuments that resonate in Morocco's other major cities; however, there are still some landmarks, including the famous Hassan II Mosque.

GETTING HERE AND AROUND

BY AIR

From overseas, Casablanca's Mohammed V Airport is the best gateway to Morocco itself: you'll find a well-maintained arrivals hall, relatively efficient and courteous staffers, and a not-so-complicated continuation of your journey by train or car. Trains connect the airport to the national network from 7:35 am to 10:30 pm, and taxis are available to the city of Casablanca at relatively expensive but fixed rates (250 DH–300 DH). *For contact details for international airlines serving Morocco, see Flights in Travel Smart.*

BY BUS

Buses are fine for short trips, such as from Casablanca to El Jadida or Safi, but trips longer than a couple of hours can be interminable, hot, and dusty. Inquire at the station for schedule and fare information. In Casablanca the Compagnie de Transports au Maroc bus station is by far the most convenient, since the other stations are on the outskirts of town.

Contacts CTM Casablanca ✉ *23, rue Léon l'Africain, Centre Ville* ☎ *0522/54-10-10* 🌐 *www.ctm.co.ma.*

BY CAR

You won't want or need a car if you are staying in Casablanca, but it is possible to rent one if you are planning to explore the country on your own. Others may want to move onto their next destination such as Fez or Marrakesh, before renting a car.

Rental Cars **Avis** ✉ *19, ave. des Forces Armées Royales, Centre Ville* ☎ *0522/31–24–24* 🌐 *www.avis.com.*

BY TRAIN

Casablanca has three train stations: Casablanca Port, Casablanca, and Casablanca l'Oasis (the former two both downtown, the latter in the Oasis neighborhood). By train you can travel quickly and pleasantly to Marrakesh, Fez, Rabat, Tangier, and smaller towns like El Jadida and Azemmour. Direct trains from the airport go to both Casa Voyageurs and l'Oasis. Trains to Rabat depart hourly. (The train is by far the best way to move between Casablanca and Rabat.) Casablanca is less than 3 hours by train from Marrakesh (nine trains daily), 3½ hours from Meknès (eight trains daily), and 4½ hours from Fez (nine trains daily). In addition, there are overnight trains from Casablanca to Oujda (three daily, 10 hours) and direct trains daily to Tangier (three daily, 6 hours).

Contacts **Office National des Chemins de Fer, Casa-Port** (*ONCF*). ✉ *Bd. Houphouet Boigny, Medina* ☎ *0890/20–30–40* 🌐 *www.oncf.org.ma.* **Office National des Chemins de Fer, Casa-Voyageurs** (*ONCF*). ✉ *Bd. Mohammed V, Centre Ville* ☎ *0890/20–30–40* 🌐 *www.oncf.org.ma.*

GUIDES AND TOURS

There are numerous travel agencies in downtown Casablanca. Select Travel & Event is particularly good—the staff speaks English and is quite helpful; it's on Boulevard Rachidi not far from Place Mohammed V.

Contacts **Select Travel & Event** ✉ *24, bd. Rachidi, Centre Ville* ☎ *0522/47–59–00.*

TIMING AND PRECAUTIONS

Many visitors spend at least one or two nights in Casablanca, often visiting Rabat on day trips. As in any large city, travelers should be cautious at night when walking in the Casablanca city center and around the old medina. It is best to use a taxi late at night when returning from a restaurant or the nightclubs.

EXPLORING

TOP ATTRACTIONS

★ **Habous.** At the edge of the new medina, the Quartier des Habous is a curiously attractive mixture of French colonial architecture with Moroccan details built by the French at the beginning of the 20th century. Capped by arches, its shops surround a pretty square with trees and flowers. As you enter the Habous, you'll pass a building resembling a castle; this is the Pasha's Mahkama, or court, completed in 1952. The Mahkama formerly housed the reception halls of the Pasha of Casablanca, as well as a Muslim courthouse; it's currently used for district government administration. On the opposite side of the square is the Mohammed V Mosque—although not ancient, this and the 1938 Moulay Youssef Mosque, in the adjacent square, are among the finest examples of traditional Maghrebi (western North African) architecture in Casablanca. Look up at the minarets and you might recognize a style used in Marrakesh's Koutoubia Mosque and Seville's Giralda. Note also the fine wood carving over the door of the Mohammed V. The Habous is well known as a center for Arabic books; most of the other shops here are devoted to rich displays of traditional handicrafts aimed at locals and tourists. ■ TIP→ **This is the best place in Casabalanca to buy Moroccan handicrafts.** You can also buy traditional Moroccan clothes such as kaftans and *djellabas* (long, hooded outer garments). Immediately north of the Habous is Casablanca's Royal Palace. You can't go inside, but the outer walls are pleasing; their sandstone blocks fit neatly together and blend well with the little streets at the edge of the Habous. ✉ *Habous.*

Fodor's Choice ★ **Hassan II Mosque.** Casablanca's skyline is dominated by this massive edifice. No matter where you are, you're bound to see it thanks to its attention-grabbing green-tile roof. The building's foundations lie partly on land and partly in the sea, and at one point you can see the water through a glass floor. The main hall holds an astonishing 25,000 people and has a retractable roof so that it can be turned into a courtyard. The minaret is more than 650 feet high, and the mezzanine floor (which holds the women's section, about 6 feet above the main floor) seems dwarfed by the nearly 200-foot-high ceiling. Still, the ceiling's enormous painted decorations appear small and delicate from below.

Funded through public subscription, designed by a French architect, and built by a team of 35,000, the mosque went up between 1987 and 1993 and is now the third-largest mosque in the world, after the Haramain Mosque in Mecca and the Prophet's Mosque in Medina. It was set in Casablanca primarily so that the largest city in the kingdom would have a monument worthy of its size. Except for Tin Maland, this is the only mosque in Morocco that non-Muslims are allowed to enter. ■ TIP→ **If you fly out of Casablanca, try to get a window seat on the left for a good view of the mosque in relation to the city as a whole.** ✉ *Bd. de la Corniche, Medina* ☎ *0522/48–28–86* 🎟 *120 DH* ⏲ *Guided tours Sat.–Thurs. at 9, 10, 11, and 2 (all visits by guided tour).*

Place Mohammed V. This is Casablanca's version of London's Trafalgar Square: it has an illuminated fountain, lots of pigeons, and a series of impressive buildings facing it. Coming from the port, you'll pass the main post office on your right, and on your left as you enter the square is its most impressive building, the courthouse, built in the 1920s. On the other side of Avenue Hassan II from the post office is the ornate Bank Al Maghrib; the structure opposite, with the clock tower, is the Wilaya, the governor's office. The more modest buildings on the right side of the square house the notorious customs directorate (where importers' appeals against punitive taxes stand little chance). To avoid confusion, note that Place Mohammed V was formerly called Place des Nations Unies and vice versa, and the old names still appear on some maps. ✉ *Centre Ville.*

DID YOU KNOW?
Casablanca's Hassan II Mosque, which was finished in 1993, is the third-largest in the world, behind the massive mosques in Mecca and Medina.

Casablanca

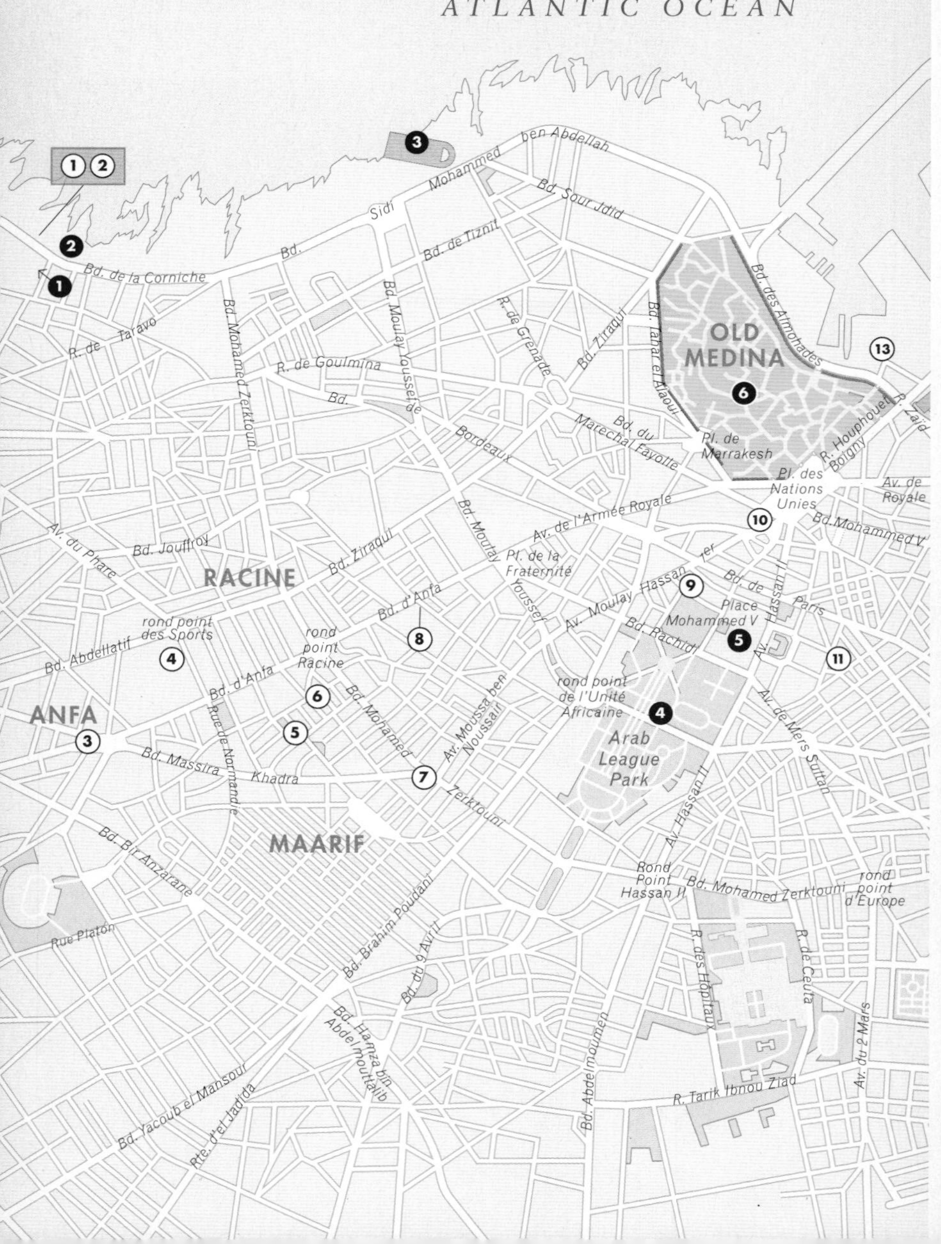

ATLANTIC OCEAN
OLD MEDINA
RACINE
ANFA
MAARIF
Arab League Park
Bd. Sidi Mohammed ben Abdellah
Bd. de la Corniche
Bd. Sour Jdid
Bd. de Tiznit
Bd. des Almohades
Bd. Tahar el Alaoui
Bd. Ziraoui
R. de Grenade
Bd. Moulay Youssef
Bd. Mohamed Zerktouni
R. de Taravo
R. de Goulmina
Bd. de Bordeaux
Bd. du Marechal Fayolle
Pl. de Marrakesh
R. Houphouet Boigny
R. Zaid
Pl. des Nations Unies
Av. de Royale
Bd. Mohammed V
Av. de l'Armée Royale
Av. du Phare
Bd. Jouffroy
Bd. Ziraoui
Pl. de la Fraternité
Av. Moulay Hassan 1er
Bd. de Paris
Place Mohammed V
Av. Hassan II
Bd. Rachidi
Bd. d'Anfa
rond point des Sports
rond point Racine
Bd. Abdellatif
rond point de l'Unité Africaine
Av. de Mers Sultan
Rue de Normande
Av. Moussa ben Noussair
Bd. Massira Khadra
Zerktouni
Bd. Bir Anzarane
Rue Platon
Av. Hassan II
Rond Point Hassan II
Bd. Mohamed Zerktouni
rond point d'Europe
Bd. Brahim Poudani
Bd. du 9 Avril
R. des Hôpitaux
R. de Ceuta
Bd. Hamza bin Abdelmouttalib
Bd. Abdelmoumen
Av. du 2 Mars
R. Tarik Ibnou Ziad
Bd. Yacoub el Mansour
Rte. d'el Jadida

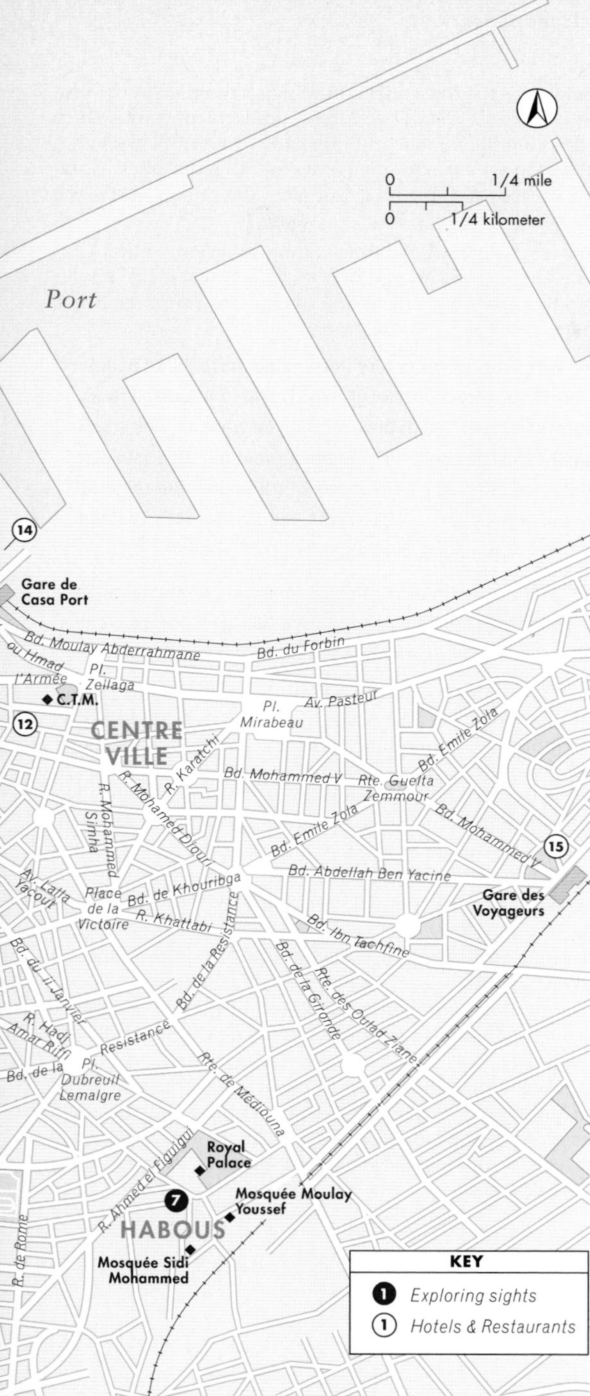

Exploring ▼

Arab League Park 4
Corniche 2
Habous 7
Hassan II Mosque 3
Old Medina 6
Place Mohammed V 5
Sidi Abderrahman 1

Hotels ▼

Barcelo Casablanca 8
Hotel and Spa Le Doge 9
Hôtel Bellerive 1
Hyatt Regency 10
Ibis Moussafir 15
Kenzi Tower 7

Restaurants ▼

Aeropostale 4
Al-Mounia 11
Kaiten 5
La Bodega 12
Le Cabestan 2
Paul 3
Restaurant du Port 13
Taverne du Dauphin 14
Tulik 6

WORTH NOTING

Arab League Park. This is the most substantial patch of green in the center of Casablanca. There is a small children's amusement park, which has seen better days, on the far side of Boulevard Moulay Youssef and, to the right of the amusement park an avenue of tall palm trees. Casablanca's modern cathedral, built in 1930, is at the park's northwest corner. ✉ *Centre Ville.*

La Corniche. Get a feel for Casa's Atlantic setting by stopping at a Corniche café and basking in the sun and breeze. This is where the people of Casablanca go to relax—a seafront line of cafés, restaurants, beach resorts, nightclubs, and hotels. ✉ *Ain Diab.*

NEED A BREAK?

La Sqala. Situated within an 18th-century Portuguese fortress, La Sqala enchants with it beautiful garden, patio, greenery, and fountains. It may serve the best Moroccan breakfast in town, and if you want a quick snack while sightseeing, the pastries and mint tea are a great bet. La Sqala also serves lunch and dinner, offering a perfect mix of traditional but tasteful Moroccan design and atmosphere coupled with yummy Moroccan salads and tagines. ✉ *Bd. des Almohades, Medina* ☎ *0522/26–09–60.*

Venezia Ice. After strolling along the Corniche, take a break and relax on the trendy Venezia's terrace and enjoy one of their 60 flavors of ice creams and sorbets. ✉ *La Corniche, Tahiti, Ain Diab* ☎ *0522/79–83–64.*

Old Medina. The simple whitewashed houses of the medina, particularly those closest to the harbor, form an extraordinary contrast to Morocco's economic and commercial nerve center just a few hundred yards away. European consuls lived here in the 19th century, the early trading days, and there are still a youth hostel and a few very cheap hotels within. The medina has its own personality and charm due in part to the fact that Moroccans living in more affluent areas may never even enter it. Near Place des Nations Unies a large conglomeration of shops sells watches, leather bags and jackets, shoes, crafted wood, and clothes. ✉ *Medina.*

Sidi Abderrahman. If you follow the Corniche to its southwestern edge, you will see the tomb of Sidi Abderrahman, a Sufi saint, just off the coast on a small island. Moroccans come to this shrine if they are sick or if they feel they need to rid themselves of evil spirits. It is accessible only at low tide, at which point you can simply walk to the small conglomeration of white houses, built practically one on top of the other, along the sandy beach. Non-Muslims are allowed to visit the tiny island and have their futures told by an in-resident fortune-teller, although access to the shrine itself is prohibited. **TIP→** On the Corniche, just in front of the tomb, you can enjoy some snails and Moroccan mint tea, along with the locals. ✉ *Ain Diab.*

WHERE TO EAT

$$$ FRENCH **Aéropostale.** In line with its name, the walls of this popular French bistro are covered with antique prints of air-post carriers. The menu is presented on large chalkboards and includes tasty seafood, duck and meat dishes, generous salads, and a perfect fish soup poured into your bowl from a small clay pitcher. A daily three-course menu is available, and there's an impressive Belgian beer list. ✉ *6, rue Molière, Racine* ☎ *0522/36–02–52.*

$$$ MOROCCAN **Al-Mounia.** Come to this large Moroccan restaurant if you want to try the national dishes, such as couscous or tagines, in cosmopolitan Casablanca. The excellent cooking sometimes presents surprising flavors—a carrot salad is perfumed with oranges, and the chicken and almond tagine has a buttery, brown sugar sauce. You can dine in rooms with typically Moroccan decor or on the outdoor terrace under a hundred-year-old tree. ✉ *95, rue Prince Moulay Abdallah, Centre Ville* ☎ *0522/22–26–69* ⊙ *Closed Sun.*

$$$ SPANISH: TAPAS ★ **La Bodega.** Every night is tapas and fiesta night at La Bodega. Opposite the central market, the restaurant offers a warm and colorful atmosphere with a lively Spanish and Latin flavor. There's live music every night by theme—Tuesday is salsa night, with a professional salsa dancer to give tips if you feel like improving your moves. Stop by for Spanish tapas and a drink or stay for a full meal. The menu is typically Spanish; try the jambon Serrano or the fried calamari as a tasty starter, and the paella can't be beat. If you are looking to unwind and enjoy good food, drink, and music, this is your place. ✉ *129, rue Allal ben Abdellah, Centre Ville* ☎ *0522/54–18–42* ⊙ *No lunch Sun.*

$$$$ FRENCH ★ **Le Cabestan.** Recently renovated and offering spectacular views of the Atlantic Ocean in a great location near the Corniche lighthouse, this restaurant offers Mediterranean cuisine at its finest. Look down from a window seat onto blue rock pools as you savor delicious fish dishes. To wind down, you might have *tarte fine caramélisée aux pommes d'oulmès* (caramelized apple tart). ✉ *90, bd. de la Corniche, Phare d'el Hank, Ain Diab* ☎ *0522/39–11–90* ⊙ *Closed Sun.*

$$$$ JAPANESE **Kaiten.** This spot is hands-down the best Japanese restaurant in Casablanca. The menu includes a very large selection of sushi, sashimi, maki, and other specialties served in an elegant and fashionable atmosphere. It's pricey, but worth it. ✉ *18, rue Oumaima Sayeh, Racine* ☎ *0522/39–87–66.*

$$ CAFÉ **Paul.** Paul, an outlet of a French café, bakery, and restaurant chain, is housed in the beautiful Art Deco Villa Zevaco. Whether for breakfast, lunch, or afternoon tea, Paul's terrace, is always packed and for good reason—their pastries are the best in town. Try the Royal, a decadent, chocolate mousselike cake, or the *mille-feuille* (literally translated as "one thousand leaves"), which melts in your mouth. ✉ *Angle Bd. d'Anfa at Bd. Moulay Rachid, Anfa* ☎ *0522/36–60–00.*

$$ SEAFOOD **Restaurant du Port.** Tucked inside the port, this is perhaps Casablanca's best-known fish restaurant, and as such gets rather crowded at lunchtime. The fried fish is particularly good at any time of day. To find the place, enter the port by the gate near the train station and turn left toward the fishing port. If you're arriving on foot, don't let the strong

Casablanca has a lively nightlife and dining scene.

outdoor port odors deter you—the restaurant's interior is clean and fresh. ✉ *Port de Pêche, Medina* ☎ *0522/31–85–61.*

$$ SEAFOOD ✕ **Taverne du Dauphin.** Decorated in a marine style, the popular Dolphin is a good alternative to its pricier counterparts for all fish and seafood dishes. You'll find it on the left side of the boulevard leading to the port station; the entrance is around the back. ✉ *115, bd. Félix Houphouet Boigny, Medina* ☎ *0522/22–12–00* 🌐 *www.taverne-du-dauphin.ma* ⏲ *Closed Sun.*

$ CAFÉ ✕ **Tulik.** Casablanca's first salad bar offers a breath a fresh air for travelers looking for a healthy and fresh lunch option. In addition to a variety of fresh vegetables, yummy toppings, and homemade dressings for the salads, Tulik also offers homemade quiches, soups, muffins, and pies. The location in the city center is convenient, and it's great for vegetarians and nonvegetarians alike. ✉ *Rue Asilm at Rue Yarmouk, Racine* ☎ *0526/92–21–31* ▭ *No credit cards* ⏲ *Closed Sun. No dinner.*

WHERE TO STAY

For expanded hotel reviews, visit Fodors.com.

$$ **Barceló Casablanca.** Ideally located on Casablanca's Boulevard Anfa, this hotel is perfect for business travelers. **Pros:** great location; full business hotel. **Cons:** no gym or pool; chain feel. ✉ *139, bd. Anfa, Racine* ☎ *0522/20–80–00* 🌐 *www.barcelo.com* *83 rooms, 2 suites* *In-room: a/c, Internet, Wi-Fi. In-hotel: restaurant, bar, parking* *Breakfast.*

$$$$ ★ **Hotel & Spa Le Doge.** Le Doge is a charming refuge amidst the cacophony of Casablanca and the first Relais & Chateaux property in

Morocco. **Pros:** staff attentiveness; great restaurant for dinner. **Cons:** difficult to find. ✉ *9, rue du Docteur Veyre* ☎ *0522/46–78–00* 🌐 *www.hotelledoge.com* *3 rooms, 13 suites* *In-room: a/c, Internet, Wi-Fi. In-hotel: restaurant, bar, gym, spa* *Breakfast.*

$ **Hotel Bellerive.** Though nothing exciting, most rooms at the budget hotel have ocean views and are perfectly fine for short stays. **Pros:** easy on the wallet; good for families with young children. **Cons:** bland decor; rooms facing street are noisy. ✉ *Bd. de la Corniche, Ain Diab* ☎ *0522/79–75–04* 🌐 *www.belleriv.com* *37 rooms* *In-room: a/c, Wi-Fi. In-hotel: restaurant, bar, parking* *Breakfast.*

$$$$ **Hyatt Regency.** Casablanca's most conspicuous hotel occupies a large site next to Place des Nations Unies. **Pros:** plenty of shopping nearby; great views. **Cons:** too kitschy for many travelers. ✉ *Pl. des Nations Unies, Centre Ville* ☎ *0522/43–12–34* 🌐 *www.casablanca.hyatt.com* *222 rooms, 33 suites* *In-room: a/c, Internet, Wi-Fi. In-hotel: restaurant, bar, pool, gym, spa, parking* *No meals.*

$ **Ibis Moussafir.** The Ibis is right next to the Casablanca Voyageurs train station, which makes it very convenient for those catching the train to or from the airport. **Pros:** friendly staff; near public transportation. **Cons:** could use updating. ✉ *Ave. Ba Hmad, Pl. de la Gare–Casa Voyageurs, Centre Ville* ☎ *0522/40–19–84* 🌐 *www.ibishotel.com* *106 rooms* *In-room: a/c, Wi-Fi. In-hotel: restaurant, bar* *Breakfast.*

$$$ **Kenzi Tower.** The 28th floor of Casablanca's Twin Center, the modern and elegant Kenzi Tower—one of the city's newest hotels—offers a stunning view of the city, the Atlantic Ocean, the Hassan II Mosque, and the port. **Pros:** fantastic views; excellent location. **Cons:** impersonal service. ✉ *Bd. Zerktouni, Maarif* ☎ *0522/97–80–00* 🌐 *www.kenzi-hotels.com* *190 rooms, 47 suites* *In-room: a/c, Internet, Wi-Fi. In-hotel: restaurant, bar, pool, spa, parking* *No meals.*

SHOPPING

Every year, Casablanca becomes more and more a cosmopolitan city, with a significant selection of European stores. Morocco Mall, one of the 20 largest malls worldwide, opened in December 2011 at the Southern edge of the Corniche. In addition to over 300 stores, the mall will have a skating rink, bowling alley, fun park, aquarium, IMAX theater, and spa.

Casablanca also prides itself on the availability of fashionable Western clothing. The greatest concentration of clothing boutiques by far is found in the Maarif area, on both sides of Boulevard Massira Al Khadra, near Boulevard Zerktouni. Here you'll find the Twin Center shopping mall, European stores like Zara, Mango, and Massimo Dutti, and all manner of specialty stores from Belgian chocolatiers to fashionable shoe stores to Portuguese porcelain warehouses.

CRAFTS

The best place to shop for souvenirs and handicrafts in Casablanca is the **Quartier des Habous**. It offers the best variety and prices, but you should still try to get an idea of the market prices before starting to bargain. In close proximity to Casa's luxury hotels, the shops lining the **Boulevard Houphouet Boigny** offer few bargains, and their business is mostly geared to tourists. They do present a broad sampling of all things Moroccan however, and are convenient for last minute, one-stop shopping. For hassle-free shopping, Coté Maisons has high quality artisanal products, often with a modern flair.

Coté Maisons. Coté Maisons is the in place for souvenirs and upscale artisan products. ✉ *10, rue Molière, Racine* ☎ *0522/39–11–47.*

Thema Maison. Moroccan themes in household paraphernalia are the rule at Thema Maison, a good choice for drapes, pillows, or minor decorative trinkets. ✉ *27, rue Houssine Ben Ali, Centre Ville.*

NIGHTLIFE

Most Casablanca nightlife for the young and wired develops out along the Boulevard de la Corniche, a 30 DH to 35 DH taxi fare from the center of town. Exceptions are the major hotel discos such as the Black House in the Hyatt Regency.

DANCE CLUBS

Le Carré de Casablanca. Underneath the Villa Blanca hotel, this chic, hip, nightclub is where you will find the well-to-do local crowd. ✉ *Villa Blanca Hotel, Bd. de la Corniche* ☎ *0661/61–71–32.*

BARS AND PUBS

La Petite Roche. La Petite Roche, over the restaurant of the same name, has stunning views of the Hassan II Mosque and a young and thoroughly Europeanized Moroccan clientele. Local and international jazz bands are featured on the weekends. ✉ *Bd. de la Corniche, Phare El-Hank, Ain Diab* ☎ *0522/39–57–48.*

Rick's Café. Rick's Café is the place to wax nostalgic about the romantic Casablanca evoked in the Bogey film. The most recent renovation faithfully reconstructed the 1942 movie set. Rick's Café, of course, has its own Sam the pianist, aka Issam, playing jazz nightly. Also, every Sunday night is open jazz night, attracting a host of talented local musicians. The waiters' fedoras and trench coats are de rigueur to complete this exercise in faux-nostalgia. ✉ *248, bd. Sour Jdid, Medina* ☎ *0522/27–42–07.*

Rose Bar. Inside the Cabestan restaurant, the Rose Bar is an elegant choice to end the evening, with spectacular views of the coast and live music nightly. ✉ *Cabestan, 90, bd. de la Corniche* ☎ *0522/39–11–90.*

SPORTS AND THE OUTDOORS

BEACH CLUBS

The Tahiti Beach Club. The Tahiti Beach Club is the best of a series of semi-private clubs along the Corniche in Ain Diab that are also open to the public (250 DH per person during the week and 400 DH on the weekends). Along with sun and sand, the Tahiti offers many recreational activities appealing to adults and children alike. It has 10 pools, four top-notch restaurants with views of the ocean, a spa, a well-equipped gym, playgrounds, a surf school, and other sports options. ✉ *Bd. de la Corniche, Ain Diab* ☎ *0522/79–80–25.*

GOLF

Royal Golf de Mohammedia. The satellite commuter town of Mohammedia (which also happens to be Morocco's oil port) is 25 km (16 mi) northeast of Casablanca. It's also home to a good golf course. The Royal Golf de Mohammedia is laid out between sea pines, eucalyptus trees, acacias, and oleanders. Par is 72 for 18 holes totaling 6,469 yards. To find it, take the Mohammedia exit from the autoroute and inquire when you get to the traffic circle (it's close by). ✉ *Mohammedia* ☎ *0523/32–46–56.*

3

NEED A BREAK?

Restaurant du Port. People come to Restaurant du Port from outside Mohammedia to eat fish and other seafood, but its proximity to the Royal Golf course makes it an ideal spot for a bite after 18 holes. It's worth the trip for the freshest catches, tasty preparations, and attentive service, although cheap it is not. Located right near the port, the restaurant has been completely and beautifully renovated. The *crevettes au gratin* (baked shrimp and cheese) is particularly good. ✉ *1, rue du Port, Mohammedia* ☎ *0523/32-24-66* ⏲ *Closed Mon.*

HAMMAMS AND SPAS

The following hammams are open to all (even nonguests, if in a hotel). *(For more on the hammam experience, see the illustrated feature in Chapter 5, Marrakesh.)*

PUBLIC HAMMAMS

Hammam Le Pacha. Popular with modern Moroccans, this is one of the best private baths in Casablanca; use of the hammam with combo exfoliation/soaping costs 100 DH; massage costs an additional 120 DH; towels are 40 DH. ✉ *484, bd. Gandhi* ☎ *0522/77–42–41* 🎫 *40 DH* ▭ *No credit cards* ⏲ *Daily 8 am–8 pm.*

Hammam Ziani. Opened in 1995, this upscale hammam offers exfoliation for 40 DH, soaping for 80 DH, and a package including massage and an algae wrap for 250 DH. ✉ *5, rue Abou Rakrak* ☎ *0522/31–96–95* 🌐 *www.hammamziani.ma* 🎫 *35 DH* ▭ *No credit cards* ⏲ *Daily 8 am–10 pm.*

HOTEL HAMMAMS

Royal Mansour Meridien. This is a great place to get rid of jet lag, or relax before you return home. The hammam is in a typical Moroccan setting with expert attendants. ✉ *27, ave. des Forces Armées Royales* ☎ *0522/31–30–11* 🌐 *www.lemeridien.com* 🎫 *Hammam 150 DH, 310 DH with exfoliation* ⏲ *Daily, women: 6 am–3 pm; men: 3 pm–10 pm.*

EXCURSIONS FROM CASABLANCA

DAR BOUAZZA

20 km (12.5 mi) southwest of Casablanca.

A small beach town on the outskirts of Casablanca, Dar Bouazza is a great day trip or overnight option. A haven for the Casablanca expat community, the town has a funky mix of traditional locals—fisherman, surfers, rural families—and American and European expats. These expat residents, along with well-off Moroccans looking to relax and get away from the stresses of Casablanca, have spurred an increase in entertainment and leisure activity in this small town. Surfing, jet-skiing, beachside dining with live music (and wine), a water park, and even a high-end spa are all options. If you are just looking for a relaxing day at the beach, Dar Bouazza is an excellent choice. Stop at any of the free public beaches for some fun in the sun.

GETTING HERE AND AROUND

Renting a car is the best option for visiting the area. Head out of Casablanca south on the Route d'Azemmour, and take the first right exit down to Plage Oud Merzeq.

Grands taxis from the southern end of Casablanca, in Hay Hassani, can also take you to Dar Bouazza, but specify that you are going to the beach because some of the taxis don't take the beach road and continue on directly south. The trip costs 10 DH per person.

WHERE TO EAT

$$ DELI ✕ **Natty Natty.** If you are in the mood for a picnic on the beach, or perhaps a gourmet ice cream, Natty Natty is the best bet. Owned by a young Frenchman, this specialty deli is the only place within miles to find a fantastic selection of imported cheeses, Spanish hams, specialty waters, etc. Service is fantastic and the atmosphere relaxed. Bring a bottle of wine from Casablanca since there is no place to buy alcohol in Dar Bouazza. ✉ *Dar Kouch* ☎ *0660/72–03–70* ▭ *No credit cards.*

$$ SEAFOOD ✕ **Sunny Beach.** While the food served here—fresh fish cooked to order—is similar in all these oceanfront establishments in Dar Bouazza, Sunny Beach stands out in that it is the only one open year-round, and for both lunch and dinner. It's the perfect place to put your feet up, sip a local wine, and enjoy the waves. The fried calamari is particularly tasty. ✉ *Tamaris 1* ☎ *0522/33–04–65.*

WHERE TO STAY

For expanded hotel reviews, visit Fodors.com.

$$ **Hotel des Arts.** This hotel, built in 2004, was designed by a resident architect—it's fun, laid-back, and unique. **Pros:** ideal location; interesting design. **Cons:** expensive for the area; service is slack. ✉ *1120, Jack Beach* ☎ *0522/96–54–50* *22 rooms, 28 suites* *In-room: a/c, Internet, Wi-Fi. In-hotel: restaurant, bar, gym, spa* *Breakfast.*

SPORTS AND THE OUTDOORS

Gliss School. If you feel like trying your hand at surfing, Gliss School, on Jack Beach, has excellent instructors—some of whom speak English—and reasonable rates to boot. Plus, it's open year-round. A 1½-hour lesson (with equipment) runs 200 DH. ✉ *Jack Beach* ☎ *0669/79–69–60.*

Tamaris Aquaparc. If the children are looking for some thrills, Morocco's largest water park will do the trick. Open from May to September, it's surprisingly modern and well maintained. ✉ *Rte. d'Azemmour, Km 15* ☎ *0522/96–53–69,* 🌐 *www.tamaris-aquaparc.com* 160 DH ⏲ *May–Sept., daily 10–6:30.*

AZEMMOUR

75 km (46 mi) southwest of Casablanca.

Azemmour, situated on the banks of the Oum Errabi River, is a fantastic weekend or day-trip option from Casablanca. The small town boasts a quaint Portuguese medina, friendly locals, and an artistic influence that gives the charming town a unique flavor. The Portuguese built Azemmour in 1513, and it proudly claims Estavanico, or "Stephan the Black," as a resident. Estavanico, born in 1500 into slavery, is the first North Africa–born person to arrive in what now is the United States. Traveling with Álvar Núñez Cabeza de Vaca, he was one of just four survivors of the Spanish Narvéaz expedition.

GETTING HERE AND AROUND

Train service from Casablanca to Azzemour leaves from the l'Oasis station, with trains running about every two hours. With a car, the drive from Casablanca to Azemmour takes about an hour. Buses also run regularly between the two cities. If you are staying in one of the small riads, take a *petit* taxi from the train or bus station (about 5 DH) to one of the doors of the Azemmour medina. Once at an entrance to the medina, it's best to call the riad where you are staying to have an escort take you from the medina entrance to the riad. The small medina streets and alleys are mazelike and not easy to navigate alone. That being said, most locals are friendly and will try to help if you become lost.

Train Contacts **Office National des Chemins de Fer** ☎ *0890/20–30–40* 🌐 *www.oncf.ma.*

EXPLORING

To fully enjoy the attractions within the medina, it's best to arrange for a guide from your riad. The medina is divided into three parts: the mellah (the ancient Jewish quarter), the kasbah, and the old medina. While the medina retains much of its traditional charm, the artistic influence of local and foreign artists can also be seen. Azemmour's unique lighting has attracted many artists, who have chosen to set up shop in Azemmour. As you wander through the cobblestone streets, murals by artists are a delightful surprise throughout the medina; it's worth stopping into one of the studios to see the artists at work.

Ahmed el-Amine. Ahmed el-Amine, perhaps the most recognized of Azemmour's resident artists, has been painting in and around the Medina for more than a decade. ✉ *6, derb el-Hantati* ☎ *0523/35–89–02.*

WHERE TO STAY

For expanded hotel reviews, visit Fodors.com.

Azemmour's tourism infrastructure is in its infancy, so restaurant and accommodation options are sparse. That being said, Azemmour has two fantastic riads that offer exceptional accommodations and dining. Further, the magnificent Mazagan Beach Resort is just down the road. Staying at one of the smaller, more intimate riads and taking advantage of Mazagan's facilities for dining or daytime use is an economical option.

$ **Dar Wabi.** Dar Wabi, a riad in the medina, offers guests a quiet, hidden, treat. **Pros:** friendly, at-home atmosphere; delightful owners. **Cons:** no Internet service. ✉ *Azemmour Medina* ☎ *0661/15–10–26* 🌐 *www.darwabi.over-blog.com* *5 rooms* *In-room: no a/c, no TV. In-hotel: restaurant* *No credit cards* *Breakfast.*

$$$$ **Mazagan Beach Resort.** Mazagan is a spectacular luxury resort on the outskirts of Azemmour. **Pros:** luxury accommodations; beautiful setting; lots of leisure activities. **Cons:** not accessible to public transportation ✉ *Mazagan Beach Resort* ☎ *0523/38–80–00* 🌐 *www.mazaganbeachresort.com* *468 rooms, 32 suites* *In-room: a/c, Internet, Wi-Fi. In-hotel: restaurant, bar, golf course, pool, tennis court, gym, spa, beach, water sports, children's programs, parking* *Breakfast.*

$ **L'Oum Errabia.** With spectacular views of its namesake river, this riad combines the simple, traditional architectural lines with bold, contemporary art, making it a delightful place to stay. **Pros:** provocative design; delicious meals; spectacular view. **Cons:** difficult to find. ✉ *Azemmour Medina* ☎ *0523/34-70-71* 🌐 *www.azemmour-hotel.com* *7 rooms* *In-room: no a/c, Internet, Wi-Fi. In-hotel: restaurant, spa* *No credit cards* *Breakfast.*

SPORTS AND THE OUTDOORS

In addition to water sports like jet-skiing, surfing, and kayaking, boat trips and fishing excursions along the river can be arranged by the riads. Beaches just south of the city are also beautiful for a stroll or swim.

GOLF

Mazagan Golf Club. The Mazagan Golf Course is a links course, meaning the course literally links the land with the sea. Designed by South African golfer Gary Player, this 72 par, 18-hole golf course follows the natural contours of the dunes and has spectacular panoramic sea views. ✉ *Mazagan Beach Resort* ☎ *0523/38–80–00.*

EL JADIDA

99 km (62 mi) southwest of Casablanca.

El Jadida's new town has a large, sandy bay and a promenade lined with palm trees and cafés. The name El Jadida actually means "the New" and has alternated more than once with the town's original Portuguese name, Mazagan.

GETTING HERE AND AROUND

Train service to El Jadida is limited, and the train station is inconveniently located 4 km (2.5 mi) south of town. Buses are fine for trips from Casablanca to El Jadida. Frequent buses also come from the south from

El Jadida's Portuguese cistern was one of many locations where Orson Welles filmed part of *Othello*.

Safi and Oulidia. In El Jadida, one bus station, Gare Routière, serves all the bus companies and the *grands taxis*.

El Jadida has inexpensive metered *petits taxis*. For local runs, however, it is always advisable to establish an agreed-upon fare before getting in. The going rate for local trips is around 8 DH. The taxi station is next to the bus station. The larger, more-roadworthy *grands taxis* are available for intercity journeys, such as El Jadida to Oulidia (40 DH) or for longer trips to Marrakesh (69 DH) or Essaouira (62 DH).

Bus Information CTM ✉ *Av. Mohammed V, southeast end of El Jadida* ☎ *0522/54–10–10* 🌐 *www.ctm.co.ma.*

Train Information Office National des Chemins de Fer ✉ *4 km [2 mi] south of El Jadida* ☎ *0890/20–30–40* 🌐 *www.oncf.org.ma.*

TIMING AND PRECAUTIONS

Most travelers stay in El Jadida for one night. El Jadida is generally considered safe, however, the Cité Portugaise area is poorly lighted at night. Visitors should exercise caution if visiting the area after sundown.

Visitor and Tour Information El Jadida Délégation de Tourisme ✉ *Av. Jaich el-Malaki* ☎ *0523/34–47–88.*

EXPLORING

Cité Portugaise. To see El Jadida's attractions—about half a day's diversion—drive south along the coastal road until you see a sign pointing to the Cité Portugaise, where you can park opposite the entrance; or take a small white taxi there. The Portuguese city was originally a rectangular island with a bastion on each corner, connected to the mainland by a single causeway. Take the entrance on the right. You'll see that the original Portuguese street names have been retained, the contemporary ones written underneath.

Fortress. At the end of the Rua da Carreira, you can walk up ramps to the walls of the fortress. Looking down from the fortress, you'll see a gate that leads directly onto the sea and, to the right, El Jadida's fishing harbor.

Jewish cemetery. If you walk around the walls to the other side of the fortress, you can look down on the Jewish cemetery.

Mosque. Beyond the Portuguese church, Our Lady of the Assumption, is a fine old mosque with a minaret dating from Portuguese times.

Our Lady of the Assumption. Walk down Rua da Carreira (Rue Mohammed al-Achemi), and you'll see on the left the old Portuguese church, Our Lady of the Assumption, built in 1628 with a roof from the French period.

Portuguese Cistern. Beyond the mosque on Rua da Carreira, you'll see on the left an old Portuguese cistern, where water was stored when El Jadida was the fortress of Mazagan (some say the cistern originally stored arms). A small amount of water remains to reflect the cistern's Gothic arches, a lovely effect. El Jadida's cistern was not rediscovered until 1916, when a Moroccan Jew stumbled on it in the process of enlarging his shop—whereupon water started gushing in. Orson Welles filmed parts of his famously low-budget *Othello* here. ✉ *Rua da Carreira* 🎫 *10 DH* ⏲ *Daily 9–1 and 3–6:30.*

Sidi Bouzid Beach. About 5 km south of El Jadida on the coastal road is the beautiful Sidi Bouzid beach, the perfect place for a stroll or watching the sunset. If you want to make an afternoon of it, the Requin Blue restaurant serves up excellent fish.

NEED A BREAK?

Requin Blue. Stop by this beachside restaurant for fresh fish if you get hungry while sunning at Sidi Bouzid. ✉ ***Centre Balnéaire, Sidi Bouzid*** ☎ ***0523/34–80–67.***

WHERE TO EAT

$$$$ FRENCH

Au Petit Paris. Arguably the best table in El Jadida, this French restaurant is certainly a great choice for a quality meal in an elegant environment. Au Petit Paris is one of the few restaurants in El Jadida where the service, atmosphere, and menu options are all top-notch. Try the house specialty chocolate mousse, the perfect treat for day's end. ✉ *Bd. Mohammed VI, Residence Les Grands Palmiers* ☎ *0523/39–24–64.*

¢ SEAFOOD

Tchikito. For excellent fresh fish, Tchikito is the way to go. This no-frills, no-thrills, easy-on-the-wallet restaurant just outside the medina walls serves up some of the best fish along the coast. ✉ *4, rue Smiha* ☎ *0523/37–18–19* 💳 *No credit cards.*

WHERE TO STAY

For expanded hotel reviews, visit Fodors.com.

¢

Palais Andalous. The Palais Andalous is, in fact, an actual converted palace, and while the rooms aren't as inviting as the building itself, it is remarkable for its elaborate decorations of intricately carved plaster.

Pros: authentic decor; unique furnishings. **Cons:** rooms are dark; lacking in facilities. ✉ *Bd. Docteur de Lanouy* ☎ *0523/34–37–45* *27 rooms, 1 suite* *In-room: a/c. In-hotel: restaurant, parking* *Breakfast.*

$$ **Pullman Mazagan Royal Golf & Spa.** The large, well-appointed rooms of this luxury hotel are brightened by cheery turquoise and yellow linens and blue-striped armchairs. **Pros:** very quiet area; good for golf; excellent spa. **Cons:** no public transportation. ✉ *Rte. de Casablanca, Km 7* ☎ *0523/35–41–41* 🌐 *www.pullmanhotels.com* *117 rooms, 10 suites* *In-room: a/c, Internet, Wi-Fi. In-hotel: restaurant, bar, golf course, pool, tennis court, gym, spa, water sports, parking* *Breakfast.*

3

SPORTS AND THE OUTDOORS

GOLF

Royal Golf El Jadida. Royal Golf El Jadida's 18-hole course next to the Atlantic is still worth a visit, even though it pales in comparison to the new neighboring Mazagan Beach Resort course. Greens fees are 400 DH. ✉ *Rte. de Casablanca Km 7* ☎ *0523/37–91–00.*

To leave El Jadida in the direction of El Oualidia, follow the sign to Jorf Lasfar. Jorf Lasfar itself is the site of a chemical plant responsible for serious pollution in this region. After this, the coastal road becomes more scenic, passing fertile fields and lagoons.

EL OUALIDIA

175 km (109 mi) southwest of Casablanca, 89 km (55 mi) southwest of El Jadida. From El Jadida, follow sign to Jorf Laser.

★ As you enter El Oualidia you'll see salt pans at the end of a lagoon. This town is famous for its oysters, and if you visit the oyster parks, you can sit right down and eat them after learning how they're cultivated. (Oyster Park 7 is best.) Turn right in the center of town to reach the beach. El Oualidia's bay must be one of the most beautiful places on Morocco's entire Atlantic coast. The fine sand is gently lapped by the calm turquoise waters of the lagoon, and in the distance you can see the white breakers of the sea. The beach is surrounded by a promontory to the south, a gap where the sea enters the lagoon, an island, and another promontory to the north. Around the corner is a beach that seems wholly untouched: sandy bays and dunes bearing tufts of grass alternate with little rocky hills. The summer months see a large influx of travelers and beach campers here, and thus far less tranquillity.

There aren't many "sights" in El Oualidia, but if you have a car, it's worth taking a drive south along the coastal road from El Oualidia to Essaouira, which has magnificent views, especially in spring, when the wildflowers are out.

GETTING HERE AND AROUND

Grands taxis and local buses offer services to Essaouira and El Jadida. Both depart from a stop near the post office on the main road. There is also regular bus service north and south. If you are traveling by car from Marrakesh, follow the road to Safi and take the scenic coast road to Oualidia. If you are driving from El Jadida, follow the coast road down to Oualidia and allow extra time for possible congestion.

Bus Information CTM ✉ *El Jadida–Safi Rd.* ☎ *0523/34–26–64* 🌐 *www.ctm.ma.*

TIMING AND PRECAUTIONS

El Oualidia is a great choice for a stopover on the way to or from the north or south or as a destination of its own for a relaxing beach weekend.

WHERE TO STAY

For expanded hotel reviews, visit Fodors.com.

$$ ★ **L'Hippocampe.** This family-run hotel overlooks the lagoon, offering direct access to the beach. **Pros:** easy beach access; friendly staff. **Cons:** few amenities. ✉ *Oualidia Plage* ☎ *0523/36–61–08* *23 rooms, 2 suites* *In-room: a/c, no TV, Wi-Fi. In-hotel: restaurant, bar, pool, beach, water sports, parking* *Multiple meal plans.*

¢ **Motel Restaurant à l'Araignée Gourmande.** This motel has sea views and is a good place to eat even if you aren't staying overnight. **Pros:** tasty restaurant; good value. **Cons:** steps to climb. ✉ *Oualidia Plage* ☎ *0523/36–61–44* *45 rooms* *In-room: no a/c, Internet, Wi-Fi. In-hotel: restaurant* *Breakfast.*

$$$$ Fodor's Choice ★ **La Sultana Oulidia.** Breathtakingly beautiful, this luxurious boutique hotel on a secluded corner of Oulidia's lagoon is worth the price if you are in the mood to be truly pampered. **Pros:** great location; excellent facilities; flawless service. **Cons:** expensive. ✉ *3, Parc à Huîtres, Bled Gaïlla Oualidia* ☎ *0523/36–65–95* *11 suites* *In-room: a/c, Internet, Wi-Fi. In-hotel: restaurant, bar, pool, gym, spa, beach, water sports, children's programs, parking* *Breakfast.*

SPORTS AND THE OUTDOORS

SPAS

La Sultana. La Sultana overlooks the turquoise-blue lagoon of Oualidia, the tiny seaside village on the Atlantic Coast famous for its oysters and spider crabs. It offers a hammam, indoor and outdoor massage, beauty treatments, Jacuzzi, sauna, and an indoor heated pool. ✉ *3, Parc à Huîtres, Bled Gaïlla Oualidia* ☎ *0524/38–80–08* 🌐 *www.lasultanaoualidia.com* *Treatments 330 DH–1000 DH* *By appointment.*

SURFING

Gentle waves make El Oualidia's lagoon a great place to learn how to surf; experienced surfers will find waves to their liking on the straightforward Atlantic beaches south of town, one of the better ones is called Mateisha Plage in the Moroccan dialect, or Tomato Beach.

Surfland. Surfland, a surfing school in El Oualidia, runs surfing holidays, including English-speaking instructors and camping accommodations for both adults and children. Surfers staying elsewhere can join up without a reservation if there's enough space. ✉ *Oualidia, El Jadida* ☎ *0523/36–61–10.*

4

Fez and the Middle Atlas

WITH MEKNÈS, VOLUBILIS, AND MOULAY IDRISS

WORD OF MOUTH

"The [Fez] medina is incredible. Fascinating just to walk around looking at all the sights/sounds. We had a local guide . . . the first day—getting lost is a real option—but felt confident on our own thereafter. Liked this medina much better than Marrakech. Less hawkers/pressure and more authentic feeling."

—stilltravelingat62

WELCOME TO FEZ AND THE MIDDLE ATLAS

TOP REASONS TO GO

★ **Go back in time:** Fez el-Bali is the world's largest active medieval city and promises a sensorial vacation from modern life and technology.

★ **Indulge your senses in the Meknès food souk:** On the Place el-Hedime sample famous olives, aromatic spices, and dried fruit, available in a dizzying array of colors and flavors.

★ **Explore an archaeological gem in Volubilis:** A short trip from Meknès, these well-preserved Roman ruins are considered the most impressive in the country.

★ **Ski the Moroccan Aspen:** Drawing both royalty and the Moroccan elite, the highest peak of the Michlifen ski resort rises to 2,000 meters.

★ **Take an overland adventure:** Two of the most stunning sights in the Middle Atlas are the cascading waterfalls of Ouzoud and the Friouato caves near Taza. Imilchil's September marriage festival, the *moussem*, is a Berber ritual steeped in local tradition.

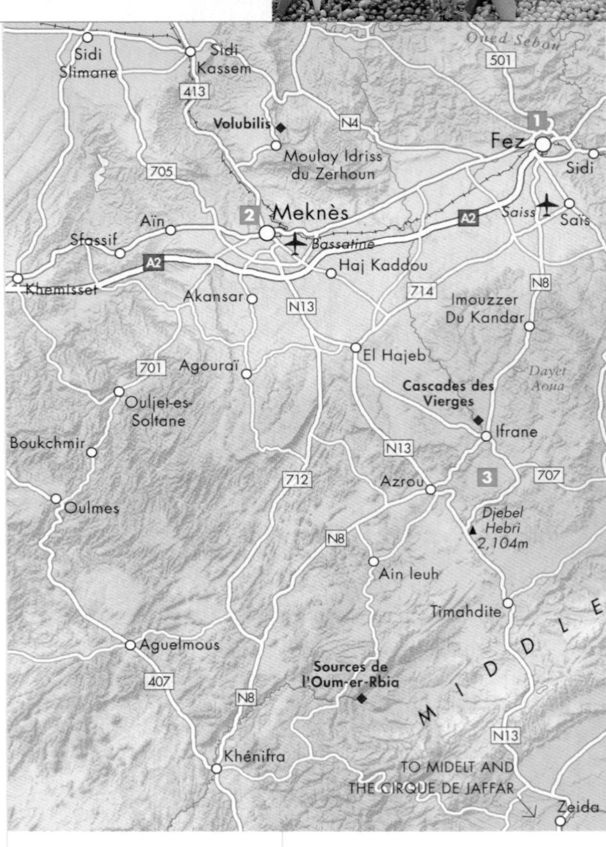

1 Fez. Founded in the 8th century on the banks of the Fez River by Moulay Idriss, Fez remains Morocco's grandest and oldest imperial city. Within the medieval stone walls of the medina there are two distinct historic areas: Fez el-Bali (Old Fez) and Fez el-Djedid (New Fez). Farther south, the Ville Nouvelle (New Town) is a modern district built in 1912, attracting wealthier residents and strong commercial activity. The city's labyrinthine heart is the medina, enclosing historic minarets, souks, mosques, museums, fountains, and squares that get the well-deserved attention of most visitors throughout the year.

GETTING ORIENTED

Situated between the mountainous Middle Atlas and plains of the Rif, Fez and Meknès are rewarding visits with historic monuments, sumptuous palaces, imposing ramparts, and vibrant markets. Fez is by far the more significant destination. Meknès is a calmer city with fewer tourists and hustlers to experience authentic local life. Side trips to the Roman ruins in Volubilis and sacred village of Moulay Idriss are highly recommended if time permits. The Middle Atlas, the most northern part of the three Atlas Mountain chains, is a brief surprise to or from the Sahara. Explore provinces like Ifrane, considered "Morocco's Switzerland," Berber cities of Azrou and Sefrou, beautiful forests, picturesque mountain ranges, and the canyons of the Cirque du Djebel Tazzekais near Taza.

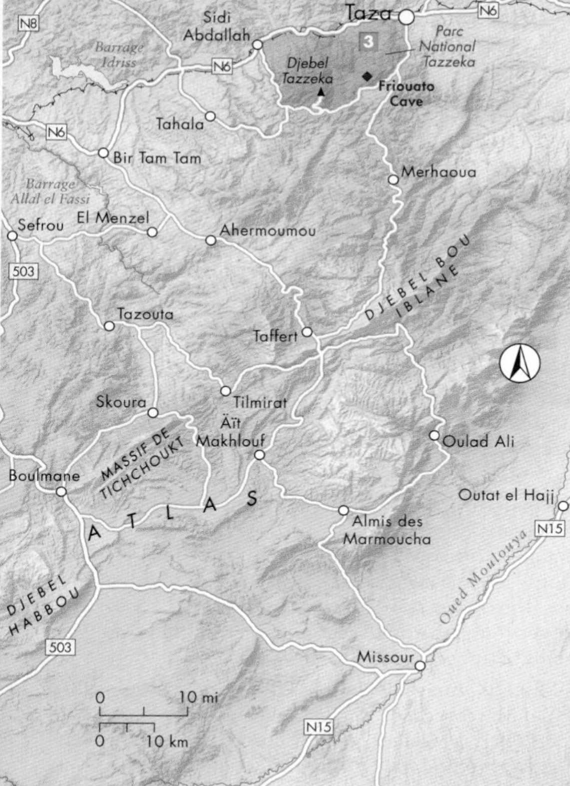

2 Meknès. Founded in the 11th century by the Almoravids, Meknès became an imperial city under the rule of Sultan Moulay Ismail. The city has three distinct areas—the ancient medina with its central Place el-Hadime, the Imperial City that contains the most impressive monuments, and the Ville Nouvelle (New Town).

3 The Mediterranean Middle Atlas. The northern Middle Atlas begins south and east of Fez and stretches southwest. The Azrou Cedar Forest and the Djebel Tazzeka Massif above Taza are the main attractions in this heavily forested northern zone, along with the ski region near Ifrane and the rugged Cirque de Jaffar.

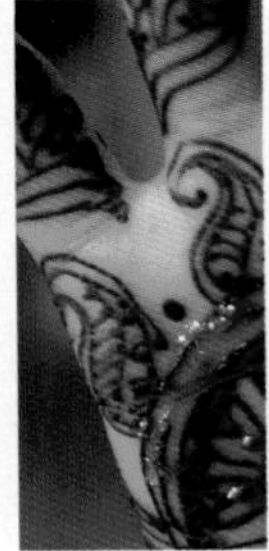

Updated by Victoria Tang

Designated as UNESCO World Heritage Sites, Fez and Meknès are, respectively, the Arab and Berber capitals of Morocco, ancient centers of learning, culture, and craftsmanship. Recognized as Morocco's intellectual and spiritual center, Fez has one of the world's oldest universities as well as the largest intact medieval quarters. It is the country's second-largest city (after Casablanca) with a population of approximately 1 million. Meknès, with nearly 850,000 inhabitants, offers a chance to experience all the sights, sounds, and smells of Fez on a slightly smaller, more manageable scale. Both Fez and Meknès still remain two of Morocco's most authentic and fascinating cities, outstanding for their history and culture and rival Marrakesh as top tourist destinations and hosts of international events and festivals.

In between Fez and Marrakesh, the Middle Atlas is a North African Arcadia, where rivers, woodlands, and valley grasslands show off Morocco's inland beauty. Snowy cedar forests, ski slopes, and trout streams are not images normally associated with the country, yet the Middle Atlas unfolds like an ersatz alpine fantasy less than an hour from medieval Fez. To remind you that this is still North Africa, Barbary monkeys scurry around the roadsides, and the traditional *djellaba* (hooded gown) and veil appear in ski areas.

Most travelers to Morocco can get a glance of the Middle Atlas as they whiz between Fez and Marrakesh, or between Meknès and points south. The central highland's Berber villages, secret valleys, scenic woods, dramatically barren landscapes, and hilly plains blanketed with olive groves lie in stark contrast to the exotic imperial cities. For this reason alone, the region is rewarding to discover for its integrity and authenticity.

PLANNING

WHEN TO GO

Busloads of tourists and intense heat tend to suppress the romance of just about anything. Try to visit Fez and Meknès between October and early March, before the high season or extreme sun makes it unbearable to sightsee, but spring is really the best time to visit any part of Morocco.

The Middle Atlas is relatively cool year-round, and often snowbound in midwinter with temperatures dropping below 0°C (32°F). For skiing or driving through the snow-filled Michlifen mountain region or Azrou Cedar Forest (occasionally snowed in from January to March, but normally well plowed), come between December and April. April–June is the best time to hike. The high tourist season in the mountains runs mid-March through summer. The most popular festival is the September marriage *moussem* (pilgrimage festival) in Imilchil.

GETTING HERE AND AROUND

Most tourists visiting the Middle Atlas set down in Fez, the region's largest city. Traveling within Fez is best done on foot, but taking a petit taxi to points of interest such as the Ville Nouvelle is an inexpensive option. To visit Meknès or Volubilis, take a bus, train or grand taxi (negotiate a price before the journey). To visit the Middle Atlas, you'll need a car or a tour.

BY AIR

Daily flights to Fès-Saïss Airport operate regularly from international and domestic destinations. But you can't fly directly into Fez from the United States. You must connect in Europe or Casablanca. Upon arrival, *petits taxis* wait outside the airport terminal and train station and carry two to four people. *Grands taxis* carry six people. Avoid unofficial drivers who hang around the terminals and charge false rates. Taxis should have their meters running. Most drivers request cash payment.

BY BUS

The CTM is Morocco's best bus company and has service from most major cities to Fez and Meknès. You can reach some destinations in the Middle Atlas by bus, but ultimately, you're going to have to drive or take a taxi.

BY CAR

The easiest way to tour the well-paved regions in and around Fez and the Middle Atlas is by car. The best map to use is the Michelin Map of Morocco 959; if you can't find this map at home, ask your car-rental company to provide one. A map is a necessity if you plan to venture far from the beaten path. Road signs at major intersections in larger cities are well marked to point you in the right direction. Little white pillars alongside routes indicate distance in kilometers to towns. Traveling further afield into the Middle Atlas, many secondary roads are unpaved and require a four-wheel-drive vehicle. Through mountain passages, roads can be dangerously narrow, steep, and curvy.

BY TRAIN

Fez and Meknès are served by the ONCF train station that goes east to Oujda, south to Marrakesh, and west to Tangier, Rabat, and Casablanca. Fez and Meknès are also connected by local trains, a 45-minute trip.

RESTAURANTS

Every Moroccan city has its own way of preparing the national dishes. *Harira,* the spicy bean-based soup filled with vegetables and meat, may be designated as Fassi (from Fez) or Meknessi (from Meknès) and varies slightly in texture and ingredients. Note that few medina restaurants in Fez and Meknès are licensed to serve alcohol. Proprietors generally allow oenophiles to bring their own wine, as long as they enjoy it discreetly. Larger hotels and luxury *riads* (renovated guesthouses and villas) have well-stocked bars that serve wine, beer, and cocktails, as do more-upscale restaurants.

Most of the Middle Atlas hotels we recommend have fair to excellent restaurants, but venture to stop at small town crossroads or souks for a homemade bowl of harira for 5H or less. Brochettes (beef or lamb kebabs) cost about US$1. Note: some Islamic villagers frown upon alcohol of any kind. Be discreet if you carry your own wine or beer.

HOTELS

Hotels in Fez range from the luxurious and the comprehensively comfortable, such as the Sofitel Palais Jamaï, to more personal, atmospheric riads that offer everything from kitschy decor to authentic traditional living, and more upscale, boutique versions such as the trendy Palais Amani. Hotels in or near the Fez el-Bali are best, as the medina is probably what you came to see. In Meknès, there is a more limited choice, with a few gems competing at the top end. In the Middle Atlas, the newly renovated resort of Michlifen Suites and Spa draws local elite for its Anglo-European styling. The Middle Atlas offers a selection of good hotels. Some of the inns and auberges off the beaten path should be thought of as shelter rather than full-service hotels, as lodging tends to be indistinguishable.

WHAT IT COSTS IN DIRHAMS

	¢	$	$$	$$$	$$$$
Restaurants	under 100 DH	100 DH–200 DH	201 DH–300 DH	301 DH–400 DH	over 400 DH
Hotels	under 600 DH	600 DH–1,200 DH	1,201 DH–1,600 DH	1,601 DH–2,000 DH	over 2,000 DH

Restaurant prices are per person for a main course at dinner. Hotel prices are for a high-season standard double room, excluding service and tax.

SAFETY

In general, Fez and Meknès are safe cities. In Fez—less in Meknès—pickpocketing and unwanted hassling from hustlers and false guides will be the biggest concern. Harassment from those offering to be tour guides or drivers is best avoided by smiling and firmly saying "no thank you," preferably in Arabic or French; never become visibly agitated, as it could exacerbate the situation.

You can safely explore the Fez medina during the day, but avoid quieter areas. If you get off-track, turn around and head back to more populated areas. If you are followed, enter a store, hotel, restaurant, or café and ask for help. Avoid any contact with solicitors. At night, barely lit passageways and dark medina alleys are intimidating.

From December through January, heavy snowfall may cover Middle Atlas roads; however, the snow-removal system in places such as the Azrou Cedar Forest are relatively good with cleared driving routes. More remote roads (marked in white on the Michelin map of Morocco) will be difficult to access or completely closed in snowy conditions. Driving off-road or to natural sites such as the Cascades d'Ouzoud in winter when snowfall can be significant is not advised.

FEZ

Fez is one of the world's most spectacular city-museums and exotic medieval labyrinth—mysterious, mesmerizing and sometimes overwhelming. Passing through one of the *babs* (gates) into Fez el-Bali is like entering a time warp, with only the numerous satellite dishes installed on nearly every roof as a reminder you're in the 21st century, not the 8th. As you maneuver your way through crowded passages illuminated by shafts of sunlight streaming through thatched roofs of the *kissaria* (covered markets), the cries of "Balek!" ("Watch out!") from donkey drivers pushing overloaded mules—overlapped with the cacophony of locals bartering, coppersmiths hammering, and citywide call to prayer—blend with the strong odors of aromatic spices, fresh dung, curing leather, and smoking grills for an incredible sensorial experience you will never forget.

GETTING HERE AND AROUND

Fez is an enigmatic, exotic city best explored on foot. Walking beneath one of the imposing arched babs, or gateways, and into the maze of cobbled streets stimulates all the senses. Summer months can be unbearably hot with little air circulation, especially beneath canopied and crowded alleys. The best time to tour is the morning; crowds and temperatures won't be too intense. Nights are cool throughout the year with a refreshing desert breeze. Remember that Friday is a traditional day of prayer, and many establishments are closed.

BY AIR

The main gateway to the region is Fès-Saïss Airport. Driving to downtown Fez takes about 30 minutes. A taxi will cost around 130 DH; a local bus 4 DH.

BY BUS

Hourly CTM buses cover the Fez–Meknès route. The trip takes about one hour and costs 20 DH. The bus to Marrakesh takes about 10 hours and costs 150 to 170 DH. The bus to Casablanca takes five hours and costs 90 DH. Three buses daily connect Fez with Tangier in six hours for 90 DH.

Bus Contacts CTM ✉ *Av. Mohammed V* ☎ *0535/62–20–41, 0522/54–10–10 in-country client services* 🌐 *www.ctm.ma.*

BY CAR

You will not want a car in Fez. Indeed, a car would probably impede your ability to negotiate the city. But if you plan to explore the Middle Atlas region, or if you are beginning a larger trip to Morocco in Fez, then a car may be appropriate and even necessary.

Rental Cars Avis ✉ *50, bd. Chefchaouni* ☎ *0525/62–69–69* 🕓 *Mon.–Sat. 8 am–7, Sun. 8 am–noon* ✉ *Fès-Saïss Airport* ☎ *0525/62–69–69* 🕓 *Daily 8 am–11 pm.* **Budget** ✉ *Fès-Saïss Airport* ☎ *0532/03–09–21* 🕓 *Daily 7 am–10:30 pm.* **Hertz** ✉ *Bd. Lalla Meryem* ☎ *0535/62–28–12* 🕓 *Mon.–Fri. 8 am–6:30 pm, Sat.–Sun. 9–noon.* **Hertz** ✉ *Av. Lalla Meryem* ☎ *0535/62–28–12* ✉ *Fès-Saïss Airport* ☎ *0535/94–32–62.*

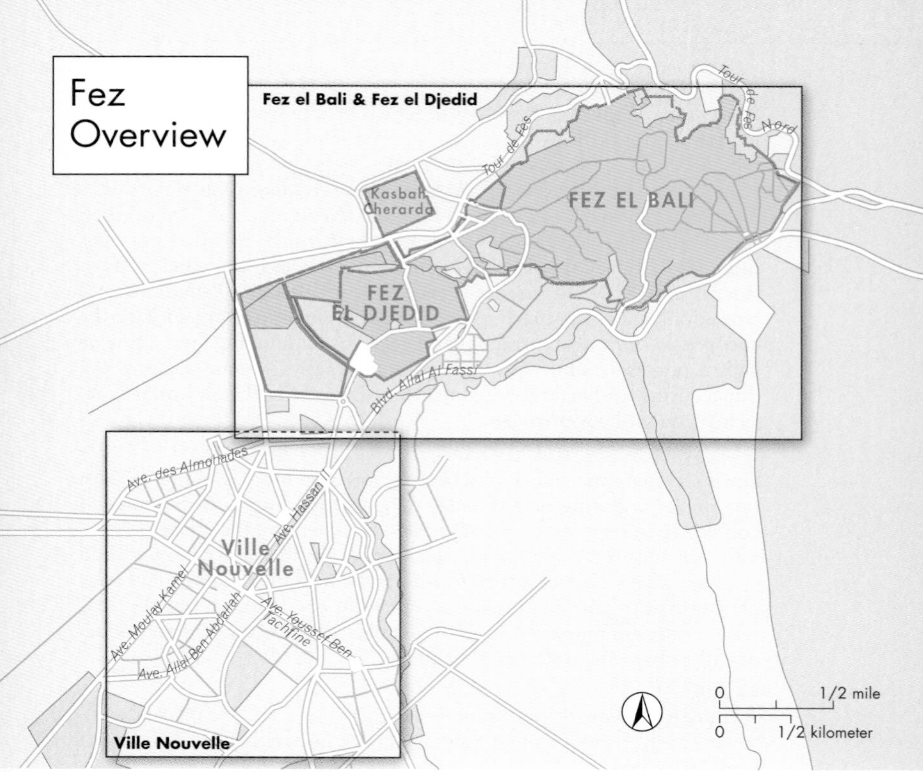

BY TAXI

Grands taxis are large, usually shared taxis (up to six passengers) that make long-distance runs between cities. This can be faster, more comfortable, and better value than bus travel. The local petits taxis are metered, take up to four passengers, and may not leave the city limits. If the driver refuses to turn on the meter or agree to a reasonable price, don't hesitate to get out. There is a 50% surcharge after 8 pm.

BY TRAIN

Trains run between Fez and Meknès each day. They cost 25 DH and take 45 minutes. There are seven daily trains to Casablanca (five hours, 155 DH) via Rabat (four hours, 90 DH). There are five daily trains to Marrakesh (eight hours, 250 DH). The train to Tangier takes five hours and costs 125 DH. The Fez train station is on the north side of the Ville Nouvelle, a 10-minute walk from the center of town.

Train Information **Fez Train Station** ✉ *Av. des Almohads* ☎ *0555/94–09–18.*

GUIDED TOURS

There's much to be said in favor of employing a good guide in Fez; you'll be left alone by faux guides and hustlers, and if your guide is good you'll learn much and be able to see more of your surroundings than when having to read and navigate as you move around. On the other hand, getting lost in Fez el-Bali is one of those great travel experiences.

Maps of the medina really do work, and there are now numerous signs on medina walls pointing you to important sites, eating establishments and hotels.

The tourist office and your hotel are the best sources for qualified guides. An official guide costs around 200–250 DH for a half a day and around 300–350 DH for a full day. Guides can run up to 500–1000 per day if it includes touring regions or special destinations by car.

Local Agent Referral **Carlson Wagonlit** ✉ *Immeuble du Grand Hotel, 5, bd. Mohammed V* ☎ *0535/62–29–58* 🌐 *www.carlsonwagonlit.com.*

Tour-Operator Recommendation **ONMT** ✉ *Pl. Mohammed V* ☎ *0535/62–47–69.*

VISITOR INFORMATION

Contacts **Fez Tourist Office** ✉ *Pl. Mohammed V* ☎ *0535/62–34–60, 0535/94–12–70.*

EXPLORING

FEZ EL-BALI

Fez el-Bali is a living crafts workshop and market that has changed little in the past millennium. With no vehicles allowed and some 1,000 very narrow *debris* (dead-end alleys), it beckons the walker on an endless and absorbing odyssey. Exploring this honeycomb of 9th-century alleys and passageways with occasionally chaotic crowds, steep inclines and pitted cobblestone steps is a challenging adventure. At night, the adventure can become quite intimidating. Fez isn't really yours, however, until you've tackled it on your own, become hopelessly lost a few times, and survived to tell the tale.

TOP ATTRACTIONS

Andalusian Mosque. This mosque was built in AD 859 by Mariam, sister of Fatima al-Fihri, who had erected the Kairaouine Mosque on the river's other side two years earlier with inherited family wealth. The gate was built by the Almohads in the 12th century. The grand carved doors on the north entrance, domed Zenet minaret, and detailed cedarwood carvings in the eaves, which bear a striking resemblance to those in the Fondouk Nejjarine, are the main things to see here, as the mosque itself is set back on a small elevation, making it hard to examine from outside. ✉ *Rue Nekhaline or Bab Ftouh and Rue Sidi Bou Ghaleb* ☞ *Entrance restricted to Muslims.*

★ **Attarine Medersa.** The Attarine Medersa (Koranic school of the Spice Sellers) was named for local spice merchants known as *attar*. Founded by Merinid Sultan Abou Saïd Othman in the 14th century as a students' dormitory attached to the Kairaouine Mosque next door, its graceful proportions, elegant, geometric carved-cedar ornamentation, and excellent state of preservation make it one of the best representations of Moorish architecture in Fez. ✉ *Boutouil Kairaouine* 🕒 *Daily 9–1 and 3–6:30.*

★ **Bab Boujeloud.** Built in 1913 by General Hubert Lyautey, Moroccan commander under the French protectorate, this Moorish-style gate is 1,000

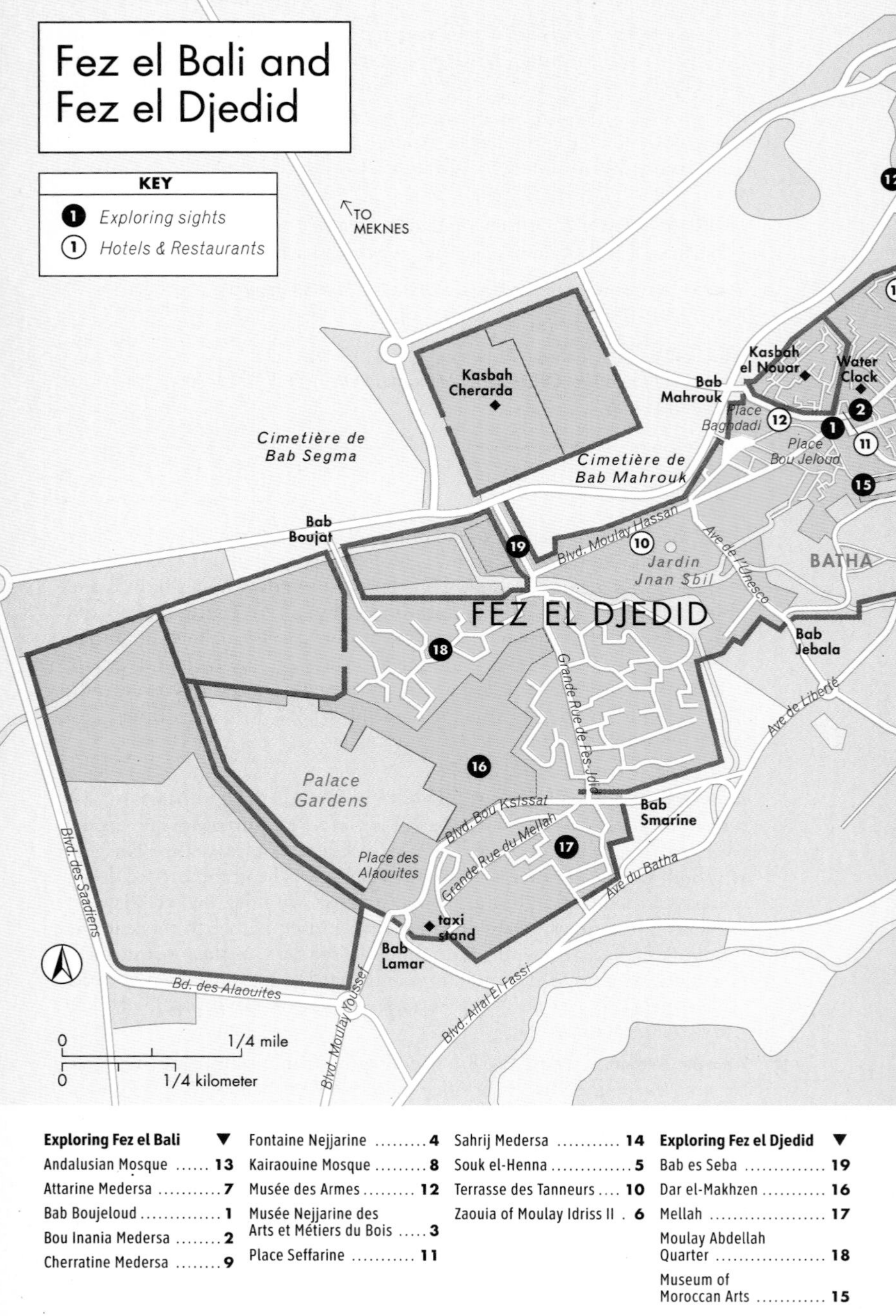

Exploring Fez el Bali ▼

Andalusian Mosque **13**
Attarine Medersa **7**
Bab Boujeloud **1**
Bou Inania Medersa **2**
Cherratine Medersa **9**
Fontaine Nejjarine **4**
Kairaouine Mosque **8**
Musée des Armes **12**
Musée Nejjarine des Arts et Métiers du Bois **3**
Place Seffarine **11**
Sahrij Medersa **14**
Souk el-Henna **5**
Terrasse des Tanneurs **10**
Zaouia of Moulay Idriss II . **6**

Exploring Fez el Djedid ▼

Bab es Seba **19**
Dar el-Makhzen **16**
Mellah **17**
Moulay Abdellah Quarter **18**
Museum of Moroccan Arts **15**

Hotels ▼

Hotel Batha 9
Hotel Les Mérinides 4
Le Jardin des Biehn 6
Palais Amori 3
Riad Fés 7
Palais Shéhérazade 8
Ryad Mabrouka 13
Sofitel Palais Jamaï 2

Restaurants ▼

Al Firdaous 1
Fez Lounge 5
La Mezzanine 10
Le Kasbah 11
Medina Café 12

years younger than the rest of the medina. It's considered the principal and most beautiful point of entry into the Fez el-Bali. The side facing towards the Fez el-Djedid is covered with blue ceramic tiles painted with flowers and calligraphy; the inside is green, the official color of Islam—or of peace, depending on interpretation. ✉ *Pl. Pacha el-Baghdadi.*

★ **Bou Inania Medersa.** From outside Bab Boujeloud you will see this medersa's green-tile tower, generally considered the most beautiful of the Kairaouine University's 14th-century residential colleges. It was built by order of Abou Inan, the first ruler of the Merenid dynasty, which would become the most decisive ruling clan in Fez's development. The main components of the medersa's stunningly intricate decorative artwork are: the green-tile roofing; the cedar eaves and upper patio walls carved in floral and geometrical motifs; the carved-stucco mid-level walls; the ceramic-tile lower walls covered with calligraphy (Kufi script, essentially cursive Arabic) and geometric designs; and, finally, the marble floor. Showing its age, the carved cedar is still dazzling, with each square inch a masterpiece of handcrafted sculpture involving long hours of the kind of concentration required to memorize the Koran. The black belt of ceramic tile around the courtyard bears Arabic script reading "this is a place of learning" and other such exhortatory academic messages. ✉ *Talâa Kebira* 🎫 *10 DH* ⏲ *Daily 9–7.*

Fontaine Nejjarine. This ceramic-tile, cedar-ceiling public fountain is one of the more beautiful and historic of its kind in Fez el-Bali. The first fountain down from Bab Boujeloud, Fontaine Nejjarine seems a miniature version of the Nejjarine *fondouk* (medieval inn), with its geometrically decorated tiles and intricately carved cedar eaves overhead. ✉ *Pl. Nejjarine.*

★ **Kairaouine Mosque.** This is considered one of the most important mosques in the Western Muslim world. One look through the main doorway will give you an idea of its immensity. With about 10,760 square feet, the Kairaouine was Morocco's largest mosque until Casablanca's Hassan II Mosque came along in the early 1990s. Built in AD 857 by Fatima, the daughter of a wealthy Kairaouine refugee, the mosque became the home of the West's first university and the world's foremost center of learning at the beginning of the second millennium. Stand at the entrance door's left side for a peek through the dozen horseshoe arches into the *mihrab* (marked by a hanging light). An east-facing alcove or niche used for leading prayer, the mihrab is rounded and covered with an arch designed to project sound back through the building. Lean in and look up to the brightly painted and intricately carved wood ceiling. If you're lucky enough to visit during the early morning cleaning, two huge wooden doors by the entrance swing open, providing a privileged view of the vast interior. For a good view of the courtyard, also head to the rooftop of the Attarine Medersa. ✉ *Bou Touil* ☎ *0535/64–10–16* ☞ *Entry restricted to Muslims.*

Musee des Armes. Built in 1582 under the command of Saadian sultan Ahmed el-Mansoor, this former fortress perched above the city guarded and controlled the Fez el-Bali. In 1963, a huge collection of weapons originally housed in the Museum Dar el-Batha was brought to the

DID YOU KNOW?

The Moorish-style Bab Boujeloud is commonly considered the most beautiful of Fez el-Bali's entry gates; however, it is 1,000 years younger than the rest of the medina, having been designed and built only in 1913.

The dye vats of the Terrasse des Tanneurs may be pleasing to the eye, but they are not pleasing to the nose.

historic site, creating the interesting display in what is now the Museum of Arms. Sabres, swords, shields, and armor from the 19th century showcase the history of how arms played a social role in tribal hierarchy. Of importance is the arsenal of sultans Moulay Ismail and Moulay Mohammed Beh Abdellah—the elaborate Berber guns encrusted in enamel, ivory, silver, and precious gems date back to the 17th century. ■ **TIP→ Walk up to the crenellated rooftop in late afternoon for a beautiful panoramic view of the city.** ✉ *Borj Nord* ☎ *0535/64–75–66* 🎫 *10 DH* ⏲ *8:30–noon and 2:30–6.*

Musée Nejjarine des Arts et Métiers du Bois (*Nejjarine Museum of Wood Arts and Crafts*). This 14th-century fondouk, or Inn of the Carpenters, is without a doubt the medina's most modern-looking restored monument. The three-story patio displays Morocco's various native woods, 18th- and 19th-century woodworking tools, and a series of antique wooden doors and pieces of furniture. For 10 DH enjoy mint tea on the rooftop *consommation terrasse* with panoramic views over the medina. Don't miss the former jail cell on the ground floor, or the large scales—a reminder of the building's original functions, commerce on the patio floor and lodging on the three levels above. ■ **TIP→ Check out the palatial, cedar-ceiling public bathrooms, certainly the finest of their kind in Fez.** ✉ *Pl. Nejjarine* ☎ *0535/74–05–80* 🎫 *20 DH* ⏲ *Daily 10–5.*

Place Seffarine. This wide, triangular souk of the *dinandiers,* or coppersmiths, is a welcome open space, a comfortable break from tight crags and corners. Donkeys and their masters wait for transport work here, and a couple of trees are reminders this was once a fertile valley alongside the Fez River. Copper and brass bowls, plates, and buckets are wrought and hammered over fires around the market's edge, where the smells of soldering irons and donkey droppings permeate the air. Look towards the Kairaouine Mosque at the top of the square to see the Kairaouine University library, which once housed the world's best collection of Islamic literature. Recently restored, it is open only to Muslim scholars. ✉ *Pl. Seffarine.*

Sahrij Medersa. Built by the Merenids in the 14th century and showing its age, one of the medina's finest medersas is named for the *sahrij (pool)* on which its patio is centered. Rich chocolate-color cedar wall carvings have significantly faded from intense sun exposure and the zellij mosaic tiling, some of the oldest in the country, are crumbling, but the medersa remains active, providing rooms and an open bathing area for mostly Senegalese students of Koranic studies. Head up the narrow steps leading to empty rooms over the central patio—you may hear the chanting of Koranic verses or see numerous birds roosting in the ancient eaves. ✉ *Andalusian Quarter* 🎫 *20 DH* ⏲ *Daily 9–1 and 3–6:30.*

4

Souk el-Henna. This little henna market is one of the medina's most picturesque squares, with a massive, gnarled fig tree in the center and rows of spices, hennas, kohls, and aphrodisiacs for sale in the tiny stalls around the edges. The ceramic shops on the way into the henna souk sell a wide variety of typically blue Fassi pottery. At the square's end is a plaque dedicated to the Maristan Sidi Frej, a medical center and psychiatric and teaching hospital built by the Merenid ruler Youssef Ibn Yakoub in 1286. Used as a model for the world's first mental hospital—founded in Valencia, Spain, in 1410—the Maristan operated until 1944.

Fodor's Choice ★ **Terrasse des Tanneurs.** The medieval tanneries are at once beautiful, for their ancient dyeing vats of reds, yellows, and blues, and unforgettable, for the nauseating, putrid smell of rotting animal flesh on sheep, goat, cow, and camel skins. The terrace overlooking the dyeing vats is high enough to escape the place's full fetid power and get a spectacular view over the multicolor vats. Absorb both the process and the finished product on Chouara Lablida, just past Rue Mechatine (named for the combs made from animals' horns): numerous stores are filled with loads of leather goods, including coats, bags, and *babouches* (traditional slippers). One of the shopkeepers will explain what's going on in the tanneries below—how the skins are placed successively in saline solution, lime, pigeon droppings, and then any of several natural dyes: poppies for red, turmeric for yellow, saffron for orange, indigo for blue, and mint for green. Barefoot workers in shorts pick up skins from the bottoms of the dyeing vats with their feet, then work them manually. Though this may look like the world's least desirable job, the work is relatively well paid and still in demand for a strong export market. ✉ *Chouara Lablida.*

Zaouia of Moulay Idriss II. Originally built by the Idriss dynasty in the 9th century in honor of the city's founder—just 33 at the time of his death—this *zaouia* (sanctuary) was restored by the Merenid dynasty in the 13th century and has become one of the medina's holiest shrines. Particularly known for his *baraka* (divine protection), Moulay Idriss II had an especially strong cult among women seeking fertility and pilgrims hoping for good luck. The wooden beam at the entrance, about 6 feet from the ground, was originally placed there to keep Jews, Christians, and donkeys out of the *horm,* the sacred area surrounding the shrine itself. Inside the horm, Moroccans have historically enjoyed official sanctuary—they cannot be arrested if sought by the law. You may be able to catch a glimpse of the saint's tomb at the far right corner through the doorway; look for the fervently faithful burning candles and incense and tomb's silk-brocade covering. Note the rough wooden doors themselves, worn smooth with hundreds of years of kissing and caressing the wood for *baraka.* ✉ *Rue Bou Touil Kairaouine, on north side of mosque* ⏲ *Daily 24 hrs* ☞ *Entrance restricted to Muslims.*

WORTH NOTING

Cherratine Medersa. Recent restoration against humidity and other natural agressions has kept this important historical site intact. Constructed in 1670 by Moulay Rachid, this is one of Fez's two Alaouite medersas. More austere than the 14th-century medersas of the Merenids, the Cherratine is more functional, designed to hold over 200 students. It's interesting primarily as a contrast to the intricate craftsmanship and decorative intent of the Merenid structures. The entry doors beautifully engraved in bronze lead to the *douiras,* narrow residential blocks consisting of a honeycomb of small rooms. ✉ *Derb Zaouia* 🎫 *20 DH* ⏲ *Daily 9–1 and 3–6:30.*

FEZ EL-DJEDID

TOP ATTRACTIONS

Fez el-Djedid (New Fez) lies southwest of Bab Boujeloud between Fez el-Bali and the Ville Nouvelle. Built after 1273 by the Merenid dynasty as a government seat and stronghold, it remained the administrative center of Morocco until 1912, when Rabat took over this role and diminished this area's visibility and activity. The three distinct segments of Fez el-Djedid consist of the Royal Palace in the west, the Jewish Quarter in the south, and Muslim District in the east.

Bab es Seba. Named for the seven (*seba*) brothers of Moulay Abdellah who reigned during the 18th century, the Gate of Seven connects two open spaces originally designed for military parades and royal ceremonies, the Petit Méchouar and Vieux Méchouar, now known as Moulay Hassan II Square. It was from this gate that Prince Ferdinand, brother of Duarte, king of Portugal, was hanged head-down for four days in 1437 after being captured during a failed Portuguese invasion of Tangier. ✉ *Av. des Français.*

Dar el-Makhzen. Fez's Royal Palace and gardens are strictly closed to the public, but they're an impressive sight even from the outside. From Place des Alaouites, take a close look at the door's giant brass knockers, made by artisans from Fez el-Bali, as well as the brass doors themselves. Inside are various palaces, 200 acres of gardens, and parade grounds, as well as a medersa founded in 1320. One of the palaces inside, Dar el-Qimma, has intricately engraved and painted ceilings. The street running along the palace's southeast side is Rue Bou Khessissat, one side of which is lined with typically ornate residential facades from the mellah's edge. Note: Security in this area is high and should be respected. Guards watch visitors carefully and will warn that photographs of the palace are forbidden; cameras are sometimes confiscated.

Mellah. With its characteristically ornate balconies and forged-iron windows, the mellah was created in the 15th century when the Jews, forced out of the medina in one of Morocco's recurrent pogroms, were removed from their previous ghetto near Bab Guissa and set up as royal financial consultants and buffers between the Merenid rulers and the people. Fez's Jewish community suffered repressive measures until the beginning of the French protectorate in 1912. Faced with an uncertain future after Morocco gained independence in 1956, nearly all of Fez's Jews migrated to Israel, the United States, or Casablanca. ■ TIP→ **Head to the terrace of Danan Synagogue on Rue Der el-Ferah Teati for a panoramic view of the district.** ✣ *Accessible via Place des Alaouites or Bab el-Mellah.*

4

★ **Museum of Moroccan Arts.** Housed in **Dar Batha,** a late-19th-century Andalusian palace built by Moulay el-Hassan, the museum of Moroccan Arts has one of Morocco's finest handicrafts collections. The display of pottery, for which Fez is particularly famous, includes rural earthenware crockery and elaborate plates painted with geometrical patterns. Other displays feature embroidery stitched with real gold, astrolabes from the 11th to the 18th century, illuminated Korans, and Berber carpets and kilims. ✉ *Dar Batha, Pl. de l'Istiqlal, Batha* ☎ *0535/63–41–16* 🎫 *20 DH* ⊙ *Wed.–Mon. 8:30–noon and 2:30–6.*

WORTH NOTING

Moulay Abdellah Quarter. Built by the Merenids as a government seat and a stronghold against their subjects, this area lost its purpose when Rabat became the Moroccan capital under the French protectorate in 1912. Subsequently a red-light district filled with brothels and dance halls, the quarter was closed to foreigners for years. Historic highlights include the vertically green-striped **Moulay Abdellah Mosque** and the **Great Mosque Abu Haq,** built by the Merenid sultan in 1276.

WHERE TO EAT

Culinary pleasures are everywhere in Fez. From simple food stalls and cafés (for grilled meat kebabs, honey-laden pastries, and fresh mint tea) to gourmet restaurants (for succulent tagines, couscous, and mechoui), there is no shortage of outstanding dining options for every budget.

When you're looking for something quick and filling, you can always grab a 35 DH bowl of cumin-laced pea or bean soup at one of the many little stands and stalls near the medina's main food markets just inside Bab Boujeloud. Lamb brochettes marinated in Moroccan spices and cooked over coals are another ubiquitous and delicious specialty costing less than a cup of coffee back home. If pastries are on your mind in the heart of the medina, look for the Pâtisserie Kortouba next to the Attarine Medersa on Talâa Kebira, near the Kairaouine Mosque.

FEZ EL-BALI

$ MOROCCAN ✕ **Al Firdaous.** Moroccan tagines, pastillas, and couscous are just the beginning here: Al Firdaous (Arabic for "paradise") shows off Moroccan art, belly dancing, and Berber Gnaoua and Andalusian music along with award-winning cuisine and attentive service in a historic 15th-century aristocratic house. Attracting large groups of tourists, it succeeds to deliver a complete evening of authentic Moroccan gastronomy and culture. ✉ *10, rue Zenjfor, Bab Guissa* ☎ *0535/63–43–43* ☎🖷 *0535/63–50–74* 🌐 *www.palais-alfirdaous.com.*

¢ MOROCCAN ✕ **Fez Lounge.** On a quiet alleyway off the main Tala Kbira, an unexpectedly urban café and bar lounge serves a limited but cosmopolitan and inexpensive menu of briouates, tabbouleh, meat tagines, Camembert tartines, and even burgers and hot dogs. Finish off with warm brownies or a carpaccio of cinnamon-soaked oranges. The Shisha Lounge welcomes the weary who puff on hookahs, ancient smoking pipes filled with water. ✉ *95, Zkak Roua* ☎ *0535/63–30–97.*

¢ MOROCCAN ✕ **Le Kasbah.** The second-floor tables perched over the street at this handsome spot just below Bab Boujeloud offer an entertaining look down into the street life below. The location is the primary draw, and you're probably better off sticking to an afternoon mint tea with pastries. The food menu is standard tourist fare. ✉ *Rue Serrajine* ☎ *0535/63–34–30.*

$ MOROCCAN ✕ **Medina Café.** Next to the most important gate into the medina, this reliable little winner offers excellent people-watching and simple Moroccan cuisine in a setting distinguished by well-crafted wood and ceramic elements and a lively buzz. Ask for the daily specials. ✉ *6, Derb Mernissi Bab Boujeloud* ☎ *0535/63–34–30.*

FEZ EL-DJEDID

$ MOROCCAN ✕ **La Mezzanine.** A five-minute walk from Fez el-Djedid, this small glass-and-gray-stone restaurant and lounge-bar remains a trendy "in" place for young and fashionable Moroccans and still gets crowded at night. A haven of Fassi cool, you enter the air-conditioned ground and upper floor, passing designer tables and a well-stocked bar, and carefully maneuver up the narrow, open stairway to a rooftop terrace lined with cushions and oversized lanterns overlooking the lush Jnan Sbil garden across the street. Enjoy a casual meal of salads, fusion tapas such as Roquefort-filled *briouates* (spicy dumplings), chicken brochettes, or a tapenade of Moroccan olives with a refreshing cocktail or fresh fruit juice. Round it off with a homemade lemon tart or sorbet. Naturally, this chic oasis managed by an equally hip and friendly staff is outfitted with Wi-Fi and sound system for the latest house music. ✉ *17, Kasbat Chams* ☎ *0535/63–86–68* 🌐 *www.restaurantfez.com.*

VILLE NOUVELLE

The Ville Nouvelle is a modern neighborhood with tree-lined avenues, contemporary hotels, fashionable boutiques, and upscale residences. Considerable commercial development is taking place to attract younger, affluent Fassis. There are no outstanding historical sites, but visit for newer cafés, restaurants, and lodging.

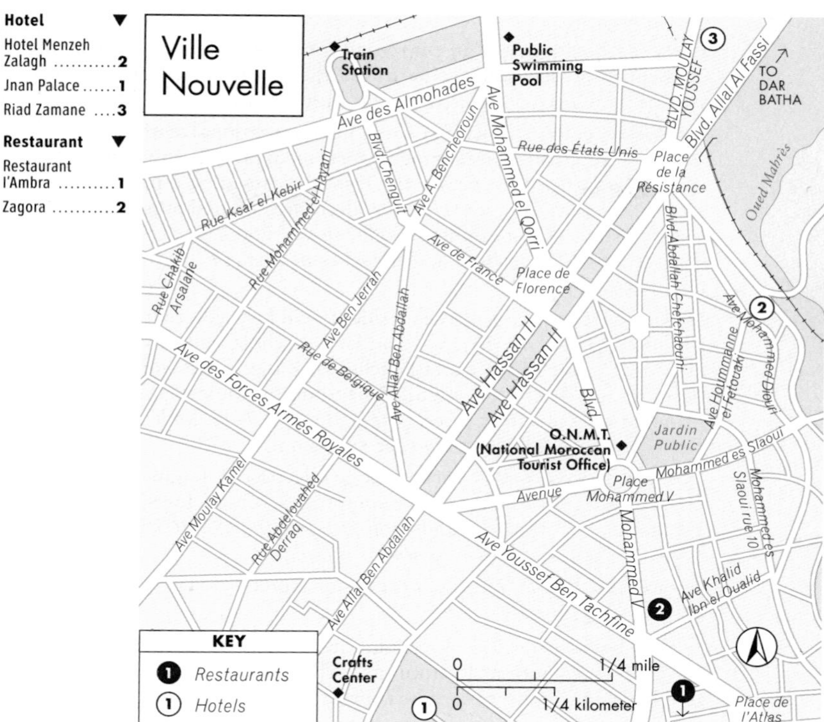

¢ MOROCCAN ✕ **Restaurant L'Ambra.** A private home in the Ville Nouvelle on the road to Imouzzèr and Ifrane (N8), this cozy spot is like dropping by a friend's place for dinner. Decorated with antiques, the house is small but charming. The full range of Fassi gourmet specialties is available here in an intimate and friendly setting. ✉ *47, rte. d'Imouzzèr* ☎ *0535/64–16–87* ✍ *Reservations essential.*

$ MOROCCAN ✕ **Zagora.** This Ville Nouvelle establishment attracts locals as well as tourists and is known for its classic Moroccan and international cuisine. The succulent lamb tagines and grilled fish are especially good, and the briouates (spicy dumplings) are house specialties. The wine list is an anthology of Moroccan vineyards; the service is always friendly. Decorated in a fusion of European and Moroccan motifs, Zagora has a modern, sophisticated atmosphere. ✉ *5, bd. Mohammed V* ☎ *0535/94–06–86* ✍ *Reservations essential.*

WHERE TO STAY

Staying in Fez's medina offers such a unique experience that you're best off choosing a hotel either in or very near medieval Fez el-Bali. Choose an atmospheric *riad* (converted private home) or modern resort. There are also some good hotels in the Ville Nouvelle. There are no hotels in Fez el-Djedid.

RIAD RENTALS

Enjoying the privacy of an entire riad for a few days with your family or friends is a memorable experience. The following agencies can help you arrange a stay in your very own Moroccan palace.

Fez Medina. Founder Lori Wood and her international team have a passion for saving and maintaining historic medina homes to rent. With a strong commitment to preserving historical integrity, a portion of the rental or restoration tour fees she collects are donated to preserve common treasures such as fountain tiling, mosaic floors, and cedar porticos. ☎ *831/724–5835 in the U.S.* ⊕ *www.fesmedina.com* ☞ *Accepts major credit cards online.*

Fez Riads. Helen Ranger, a Fez resident, will help you rent a room in a traditional guesthouse, or you can have a whole riad to yourself with cleaning service and breakfast included. Rates range from 70 DH to more than 120 DH per night, depending on the category of rental. Profits go to renovation projects. ☎ *0535/63–77–13 landline, 0672/51–33–57 mobile number* ⊕ *www.fez-riads.com.*

Splendia. This Web site offers a unique selection of lodgings. The properties range from the simple to sumptuous. Check for special online promotions. ☎ *866/986–5844 toll-free in the U.S., 305/749–2696 in the U.S.* ⊕ *www.splendia.com/morocco.php.*

For expanded hotel reviews, visit Fodors.com.

FEZ EL-BALI

¢ **Hôtel Batha.** Near Bab Boujeloud, just outside the medina entrance, the Batha has a great location as well as comfortable and recently updated air-conditioned rooms. **Pros:** central location; good value; family-friendly pool. **Cons:** street noise; uninspiring décor. ✉ *Pl. de l'Istiqlal, Batha* ☎ *0535/74–10–77* *62 rooms* *In-room: a/c, Wi-Fi. In-hotel: restaurant, bar, pool, laundry facilities, business center, parking* *Breakfast.*

$$$$ **Hôtel Les Mérinides.** Strategically placed to overlook the city, Les Mérinides is popular with those seeking a resort-style hotel with modern amenities. **Pros:** panoramic view; large pool; family-friendly **Cons:** inconvenient location; expensive rates. ✉ *36, Chrablyne Borj Nord* ☎ *0535/64–52–26, 0535/64–62–18* ⊕ *www.lesmerinides.com* *102 rooms, 4 suites* *In-room: a/c, Wi-Fi. In-hotel: restaurant, bar, pool, laundry facilities, business center, parking* *Breakfast.*

$$$$ **Le Jardin des Biehn.** Attracting a European clientele, this *maison d'hôtes* with a French flavor is a serene experience. ✉ *13, Akbat Sbaa Dough* ☎ *0535/74–03–47, 0664/64–76–79* ⊕ *www.jardindesbiehn.com* *9 suites* *In-room: a/c, Wi-Fi. In-hotel: restaurant, spa* *Breakfast.*

$$$ ★ **La Maison Bleue.** Originally the private residence of Sidi Mohammed el-Abaddi, a famous judge and astrologer, this 19th-century family home has been handsomely renovated and expanded, although the years of wear and tear are beginning to show. **Pros:** central location; historic building; private balconies. **Cons:** unreliable service; dull decor. ✉ *33, Derb el-Miter, Ain Asliten* ☎ *0535/63–60–52* ⊕ *www.maisonbleue.com* *1 room, 18 suites* *In-room: a/c, Internet. In-hotel: restaurant, pool, gym, spa* *Breakfast.*

At sunset, Fez begins to come alive with lights.

$$$$ ★ **Palais Amani.** Amid the bustling alleyways near the tanneries and active parking area of Oude Zhoune River, the eco-friendly Palais Amani is an unexpected oasis of tranquillity and elegance that has garnered much attention. **Pros:** personalized service; spacious rooms; elegant design. **Cons:** located near tanneries; no pool. ■ TIP→ **For the best Wi-Fi connectivity, head to the open terrace.** ✉ *12, Derb el-Miter, Hay Blida* ☎ *0535/63–32–09* ☎ *0535/63–32–29* 🌐 *www.palaisamani.com* *13 rooms, 1 apartment* *In-room: a/c, Wi-Fi. In-hotel: restaurant, bar, spa, laundry facilities, parking* 🍴 *Breakfast.*

$$$ **Palais Sheherazade.** The revamped Riad Sheherazade set in the former home of a 19th-century minister is a perfect expression of traditional style, with spectacular woodwork and tranquil views onto the vast courtyard. **Pros:** spacious rooms; central location; terrace. **Con:** very cold pool water. ✉ *23, Arsat Bennis Douh* ☎ *0535/74–16–42* 🌐 *www.sheheraz.com* *2 rooms, 11 suites* *In-room: a/c, Wi-Fi. In-hotel: restaurant, bar, golf course, pool, spa, laundry facilities* 🍴 *Breakfast.*

$$$$ ★ **Riad Fès.** For an architecturally refined interpretation of riad living, head to this well-equipped guesthouse. **Pros:** quiet location; full of charm; luxurious appointments, hammam, and terrace. **Cons:** very expensive; small fountainlike pool. ✉ *5, Derb Ibn Slimane Zerbtana* ☎ *0535/74–12–06* 🌐 *www.riadfes.com* *12 rooms, 14 suites* *In-room: a/c, Wi-Fi. In-hotel: restaurant, bar, pool, spa, laundry facilities, business center, parking* 🍴 *Breakfast.*

$$ ★ **Riad Zamane.** This intimate guesthouse was designed and decorated by Madame Sakina Belcadi, a Fez native who owns and operates a thoroughly relaxing refuge in the middle of the chaotic medina. **Pros:** very personal setting; friendly staff. **Con:** may be too small for some.

TIP→ Ask about private cooking lessons with Madame Belcadi. A class to learn how to make traditional Moroccan dishes and subsequent dinner costs 500 DH. ✉ *12, Derb Skallia Douh, Batha* ☎ *0535/74–04–40* 🌐 *www.riadzamane.com* *2 rooms, 4 suites* *In-room: a/c, Internet, Wi-Fi. In-hotel: restaurant, bar, spa, parking* *Breakfast.*

$$ **Ryad Mabrouka.** This carefully restored Andalusian townhouse in the heart of the medina is consistently a pleasure. **Pros:** central location; elegant rooms; good service; terrace. **Con:** not for families with young children. ✉ *25, Derb el-Miter* ☎ *0535/63–63–45* 🌐 *www.ryadmabrouka.com* *2 rooms, 6 suites* *In-room: Internet, Wi-Fi. In-hotel: restaurant, pool, spa* *Breakfast.*

$$$$ ★ **Sofitel Palais Jamaï.** With an unbeatable location above the medina, plenty of creature comforts, and a gorgeous pool, the family-friendly Palais Jamaï remains a popular choice. **Pros:** peaceful location; historic building; outstanding pool. **Cons:** impersonal service; some rooms need refreshing. ✉ *Bab Guissa* ☎ *0535/63–43–31* 🌐 *www.sofitel.com* *123 rooms, 19 suites* *In-room: a/c, Wi-Fi. In-hotel: restaurant, bar, pool, tennis court, gym, spa, business center* *Multiple meal plans.*

VILLE NOUVELLE

$ **Hôtel Menzeh Zalagh.** Built in 1942, the Hotel Zalagh, near the Andalusian gardens, was one of the original hotels par excellence in Fez. **Pros:** panoramic views; pretty pool area. **Con:** attracts large tour groups; nightclub may be noisy; 4 km (2½ mi) from medina ✉ *10, rue Mohammed Diouri* ☎ *0535/93–22–34, 0535/93–20–33* 🌐 *www.zalagh-palace.ma* *143 rooms, 6 suites* *In-room: a/c, Wi-Fi. In-hotel: restaurant, bar, pool, gym, spa, business center, parking* *Multiple meal plans.*

$$ **Jnan Palace.** For comfort and service, this glass-and-stucco structure is unsurpassed among the Ville Nouvelle's hotels. **Pros:** spacious rooms; tasty buffet breakfast; luxurious pool area. **Cons:** overpriced food; far from the medina. ✉ *Av. Ahmed Chaouki* ☎ *0535/65–22–30* *217 rooms, 17 suites* *In-room: a/c, Internet, Wi-Fi. In-hotel: restaurant, bar, pool, laundry facilities, business center, parking* *Breakfast.*

NIGHTLIFE

The Ville Nouvelle has a more active nightlife in Fez, though many of the best hotel bars are in or near the edge of the medina.

FESTIVALS

Annual Festival of Culinary Arts. The three-day Annual Festival of Culinary Arts has become an important part of October's calendar. Exhibitions, tastings, workshops, lectures, demonstrations, and a gala dinner take place in magnificent palaces and riads, and include award-winning restaurateurs, experienced oenophiles, and experimental cooks from around the world. ✉ *Sidid El Khayat, Batha* ☎ *0535/74–05–35* 🌐 *www.festivalartculinaire.com* *3-day pass 1000 DH,1-day pass 300 DH (Friday or Sunday), 1-day pass 600 DH (Saturday).*

Fodor's Choice ★ **World Sacred Music Festival.** The World Sacred Music Festival is sponsored by the Foundation of Fez, a nonprofit association focused on maintaining the city's cultural heritage. The June festival has become an international favorite, attracting some of the world's finest musicians and intellectual scholars. Concerts are held in such diverse venues as the ruins of Volubilis and the Grand Méchouar parade grounds. ☎ *0535/74–05–35, 0535/74–06–91* 🌐 *www.fesfestival.com.*

FEZ EL-BALI

BARS

Hôtel les Mérinides. The open-air bar and lounge at the Hôtel les Mérinides overlooking the city is a favorite watering hole with live music at night, a wide selection of alcoholic and nonalcoholic beverages, and one of the best panoramic views. ✉ *Rte. Du Tour de Fès, Fez el-Bali* ☎ *0535/64–52–26* ⏲ *Daily 9 am–11 pm.*

Sofitel Palais Jamaï. The English-style lobby bar at the Sofitel Palais Jamaï is a prime spot to relax with live jazz and well-prepared cocktails. ✉ *Bab Guissa, Fez el-Bali* ☎ *0535/63–43–31* ⏲ *Daily 10 pm–1 am.*

FEZ EL-DJEDID

DANCE CLUBS

La Mezzanine. With its surround-sound of imported house music, the small but trendy La Mezzanine attracts a young and hip crowd. The nicest touch is the 3rd floor open-air terrace. ✉ *17, Kasbat Chams, Fez el-Djedid* ☎ *0535/63–86–68.*

VILLE NOUVELLE

BARS

Pub Cala Iris. This second-floor English-style pub is located in the Ville Nouvelle. ✉ *26, ave. Hassan II, Ville Nouvelle* ☎ *0535/74–10–77.*

DANCE CLUBS

Le Phoebus. The bar at the Jnan Palace hotel often has live performances, while the hotel's disco, Le Phoebus, is among Fez's best. ✉ *Jnan Palace, Av. Ahmed Chaouki, Ville Nouvelle* ☎ *0535/65–22–30.*

SHOPPING

FEZ EL-BALI

Fez el-Bali is a gigantic souk. Embroidery, pottery, leather goods, rugs and carpets, copper plates, brass pots, silver jewelry, textiles, babouches, and spices are all of exceptional handmade quality and sold at comparatively low prices, considering the craftsmanship that has remained authentic for nearly 1,000 years.

METAL

L'Art du Bronze. Hundreds of bronze, copper and silver objects, antique and new, are sold at affordable prices. ✉ *35, Talaa Sghira, Fez el-Bali* ☎ *0535/74-02-77.*

Boutique Tafoukt. The Acharki brothers have a wide assortment of inlaid thuya wood crafts and lamp sconces. ✉ *179, Talâa Kebira, Fez el-Bali* ☎ *0662/01–27–79.*

Le Trésor Mirinides. All sorts of jewelry and artisanal Moroccan articles are sold at this friendly shop. ✉ *22, Ain Alou, Fez el-Bali* ☎ *0535/63–44–81, 0663/34–68–11.*

Continued on page 160

THE AUTHENTICITY OF ARTISANSHIP

Traditional Moroccan Crafts

Shopping in Morocco is an experience you will never forget. In cities like Marrakesh and Fez, the souks are both magical and chaotic, their narrow alleyways overflowing with handcrafted products created using centuries-old techniques.

by Victoria Tang

Open bazaars and medieval markets display the bright colors, bold patterns, and natural materials found throughout Morocco's arts and crafts tradition. Items are proudly made in artisan workshops dating back to ancient times.

Handmade Moroccan arts and crafts demonstrate the influence of Berber, Arab, Andalusian, and European traditions. Using natural resources like copper, wool, silver, wood, clay, and indigenous plants, artisans and their apprentices incorporate symbolic motifs, patterns, and color into wood carvings, textiles, ceramics, jewelry, slippers, clothing, and other decorative arts. Traditional processes from the Middle Ages are still used in many cases and can be observed from start to finish. Be prepared to negotiate a good price for anything you would like to buy: bartering here is expected and considered an art form in itself.

(top left) Ceramic tagines (top right) leather slippers (bottom right) perfume bottles

THE BEST OF MOROCCAN GOODS

Visiting Morocco's souks also gives you the opportunity to view the techniques still used to mass-produce a wide assortment of authentic goods by hand. While prices in Morocco may not be as cheap as they once were, hand-crafted goods can be found at any price point. Even the highest-quality pieces are half of what you'd pay back home.

SILVER

The most popular silver jewelry in Morocco is crafted by Berbers and Arabs in the southern High Atlas and in the Anti-Atlas Mountains. Taroudant and Tiznit are the most well-known jewelry-producing areas. Desert nomads—Touaregs and Saharaouia—craft silver items for tribal celebrations. Smaller items include fibulas (ornamental clasps to fasten clothing), Touareg "crosses," delicate filigree bracelets, and hands of Fatima (or *khamsa,* meaning five, for the five fingers) that are said to offer protection from the evil eye. There's also a good variety of Moroccan Judaica that includes silver *yads* (Torah pointers), Torah crowns, and menorahs. Silver teapots, serving trays, and decorative pieces capture the essence of Moroccan metalwork with geometric designs and ornate detail.

LEATHER

Moroccan leather, known as *maroquinerie,* has been sought after worldwide. Fez and Marrakesh have extensive working tanneries, producing large quantities of items for export. Sold inexpensively in local markets are bags, belts, luggage, jackets, vests, and beautifully embroidered goat skin ottomans. Leather and suede *babouches* are the ultimate house slippers; myriad colors and styles are available, and they make an inexpensive gift.

SPICES

Markets overflow with sacks of common spices used extensively in local cuisine and natural healing treatments. To create tajines and couscous back home, look for cayenne, cumin, turmeric, cinnamon, ginger, paprika, and saffron. Ask shopkeepers to blend *ras el hanout,* an essential mixture of ground aromatic spices including cardamon, nutmeg, and anise used for stews and grilling.

TEXTILES

For centuries, weaving in Morocco has been an important artisanal tradition to create beauty and spiritual protection. Looms operate in medina workshops, while groups of tribal nomads can be seen weaving by hand on worn carpets in smaller villages. The best buys are multicolored silk-and-gold thread scarves, shawls, and runners, as well as hand-embroidered fabrics used for tablecloths, decorating, and traditional caftans and djellabas.

WOOD

From the forests of the Rif and Middle Atlas, cedar wood is used to create beautiful *mashrabiyya* latticework often found on decorative household chests, doors, and tables. Essaouira is the source of all thuya-wood crafts. Here, only the gnarled burls that grow out of the rare coniferous tree's trunk are used to carve a vast variety of objects, from tiny boxes and picture frames to trays, games, and even furniture often decorated with marquetry in ebony and walnut.

ARGAN OIL

Much valued by the Berbers, argan oil has been used for centuries as an all-purpose salve, a healthy dip for homemade bread, protection for skin and nails, a treatment for scars and acne, a hair conditioner, a skin moisturizer, and even a general cure for aches and pains. With its strong nutty and toasty flavor, argan oil is popularly sold in the food souks of Essaouira, Marrakesh, and Meknès in its purest form for culinary use. The oil is often mixed with other essential oils for beauty and naturopathic treatments.

The Origins of Argan: The oil from the Argania spinosa, a thorny tree that has been growing wild in Morocco for some 25 million years, is a prized commodity. Today, the tree only grows in the triangular belt along Morocco's Atlantic coast from Essaouira down to Tafraoute in the Anti-Atlas Mountains and eastward as far as Taroudant. It takes about 35 kg (77 pounds) of sun-dried nuts to produce one liter of oil.

(top) Pressing argan oil in a traditional press (bottom) argan oil and its source

MOROCCAN POTTERY

Morocco has earned a reputation as one of the world's best producers of artisanal ceramics. Decorative styles, shapes, and colors vary from city to city, with three major areas producing the best. From platters and cooking vessels to small pots decorated with silver filigree, this authentic craft makes for an inexpensive, high-quality, and practical souvenir.

FEZ

Morocco's most stunning ceramics are the distinctive blue-and-white *Fassi* pieces. Many of the pieces you'll find actually have the word *Fas* (the Arabic pronunciation of Fez) written in Arabic calligraphy and incorporated into geometric designs. Fassi ceramics also come in a beautiful polychrome of teal, yellow, royal blue, and burgundy. Another design unique to Fez is the simple *mataysha* (tomato flower) design. You'll recognize it by the repetition of a small, four-petal flower design. Fez is also at the forefront of experimental glazes—keep your eyes out for solid-color urns of iridescent chartreuse or airy lemon yellow that would look at home next to a modernist piece by Philippe Starck or Charles Eames.

(top) Blue-and-white Fassi ceramics (left) Moroccan teapot

SAFI

Safi's flourishing pottery industry dates to the 12th century. Produced near the phosphate mines known as Jorf el Asfar (*asfar*, like *safran*, means yellow), because of the local yellow clay, the pottery of Safi has a distinctive mustard color. The potters' elaborate designs and colors rival those of Fez but are in black with curving lines of leaves and flowers, with less emphasis on geometric patterns. The pottery is predominantly overglazed with a greenish blue, though brown, green, and dark reds are also used.

SALÉ

In Salé, potters work on the clay banks of the River Bou Regreg estuary to produce glazed and unglazed wares in classic and contemporary styles, from huge garden urns to delicate dinner sets.

(top) Safi ceramic teapots

ASSESSING POTTERY

Look for kiln markings left after the ceramics have been fired. Pottery fired en masse is put in the kiln on its side, so the edges of bowls are often painted after they have been fired. The paint tends to flake off after a while, giving the bowls a more rustic, or antiqued, look.

Another technique for firing en masse is to stack the bowls one on top the other. This allows for the glazing of the entire piece but results in three small marks on both the inside and outside of bowls from the stands on which they were placed. Small touch-ups tend to disrupt the fluidity of the designs, but such blemishes can be used as a bargaining angle to bring down the price.

You can spot an individually fired piece by its lack of any interior faults. Only three small marks can be seen on the underside of the serving dish or bowl, and the designed face should be immaculate. These pieces, often large, intricately glazed serving pieces, are the most expensive that you'll find.

THE ART OF NEGOTIATION

Everywhere in Morocco you will haggle and be hustled by experienced vendors who pounce on you as soon as you blink in their direction. Your best defense is the proper mindset. For your first souk visit, browse rather than buy. Wander the stalls and see what's for sale. Don't enter stores or make eye contact with vendors, or you will certainly be pulled in. You can also visit one of the state-sponsored artisan markets found in most large Moroccan cities, where prices are rather high but fixed.

Once you've found what you want to buy, ask the price (in dirhams). Stick to the price you want to pay. The vendor will claim you are his first customer and never look satisfied. If he won't decrease the price far enough, walk away. Chances are the vendor will run after you, either accepting your best offer or making a reduction.

MOROCCAN RUGS

Moroccan rugs vary tremendously in quality and design. There are basically two types: urban (*citadin*) and rural (Berber); each type has endless varieties of shapes, sizes, and patterns. In general, smaller bazaars in the souks carry rural rugs, while larger bazaars and city stores carry a selection of both.

URBAN RUGS

Urban rugs have been woven in Morocco since the 18th century. They have higher knot counts (they're more "finely" woven) than the rural rugs, which technically makes them of higher quality. Urban rugs typically have seven colors and varied patterns including bands of different colors with geometric and floral designs. They are woven by women in cooperatives, Rabat and Salé being the main centers, but also in Meknès, Fez, and Marrakesh.

RURAL CARPETS

Rural carpets, some of which are known as *kilims* (tapestry weave or flat weave) are identified first by region and then by tribe. They are mostly woven by hand in the Middle Atlas (**Azrou** and **Oulmes**) and on the plains around Marrakesh (**Chichaoua**) by women. They're dark red and made of high-quality wool and have bands of intricate geometric designs. A single rug can take weeks or months to complete. No two rugs are ever alike.

BUYING TIPS

- **Check the color.** If artificially aged, the back will be lighter than the front. Natural dyes are very bright but usually uneven. Artificial dyes can bleed when swiped with a damp cloth.
- **Check the weave's knot count.** Urban carpets should have a high knot count—about 100 per square inch.
- **The age of rugs.** Rugs don't have labels with identification, provenance, or origin date. Rural rugs are rarely more than 50 years old.
- **Carpet Prices.** Good-quality rugs are expensive. Expect to pay 200 DH to 750 DH per square foot. Flat-weave rugs are generally cheaper than pile rugs. Cotton is much less expensive than wool. It's worth taking the time to check comparable prices at one of the fixed-price state-run cooperatives.

OTHER RUG-PRODUCING REGIONS

Middle Atlas rugs are widely available in the town of **Khemisset,** between Meknès and Rabat, where the highly detailed red-striped *zemmour* rugs sell at near wholesale prices. In the mountains north of Fez the women of the **Beni Ouarain** tribe weave rugs with patterns of fine stripes in black and white; they also weave the thick beige pile rugs with cross-hatching that have now become popular with U.S. and European interior designers.

The flat-weave rugs of the High Atlas Mountains (**Aït Ouaourguite,** near Ouarzazate) have a natural background with beige and brown stripes. The wool-pile rugs from this region have alternating soft plush pile with intricate woven motifs—diamonds, zigzags, and tattoo-like motifs in warm tones like mustard-yellow and tomato-red—and are most plentiful in **Taznakht** and the **Tifnout Valley.**

The white, sequined blanket-like rugs displayed on rural roadsides are made in the Middle and High Atlas, and are used both practically and ceremonially, their sequins prized for their reflection of light. Natural dyes are still used for most Berber rugs: orange from henna, blue from indigo, yellow from saffron, and red from the indigenous madder plant.

HAOUZ

The four principal carpet-producing tribes are the **Rehamna, Oulad bou Sbaa, Ahmar** and **Chiadma.** There are two carpet types: reddish-orange monochrome style and the *zarbia*, noted for its enigmatic motifs.

(top left) A modern rug showroom (top right) a rug souk (bottom right) flat-weave kilims

POTTERY

Au Bleu de Fès. Au Bleu de Fès specializes in Fassi pottery and mosaic tables ✉ *4, Tala Kebira Rha Chemse El Fokia, Fez el-Bali* ☎ *0667/25–40–79.*

Mostafa Alman. Traditional Fassian pottery and mosaic tiling are available in all shapes and sizes. ✉ *10, Talaa Kébira, Chrabliyenne, Fez el-Bali* ☎ *0678/34–22–81 GSM.*

★ **Les Poteries de Fès.** Les Poteries de Fès produces the famous blue-and-white Fassi pottery; and here you can see how craftsmen mold, glaze, and paint plates, dishes, bowls, and all things ceramic, as well as piece together mosaics with classic *zellij* tiling. From Bab el-Ftouh a 20-minute walk west or a petit taxi ride will get you to the new potters' quarter. ✉ *32, Aïn Nokbi, Ville Nouvelle* ✣ *Take Rte. N6 (Sidi Hrazem) to Taza* ☎ *0535/76–16–29, 0535/64–97–26* 🌐 *www.poteriefes.ma.*

RUGS

★ **Aux Merveilles du Tapis.** A staple through the years, this rug dealer is probably the most well-known in the medina. Owner Hakim Hamid greets and meets guests with mint tea and carpet conversation, while assistants roll and unroll kélims and rugs galore. The store takes credit cards and ships overseas. ✉ *22, Derb Sebaâ Louyat, Seffarine, Fez el-Bali* ☎ *0535/63–87–35.*

Dar Ibn Khaldoun. Prices of the rugs and carpets at Dar Ibn Khaldoun are determined by the square meter. Major credit cards are accepted. Shipping by DHL is available. ✉ *45, Derb Bem Chakroune Lablida, Fez el-Bali* ☎ *0535/63–33–35.*

TEXTILES

Chez Alibaba. For a huge selection of Berber fabrics, artisanal kaftans, and djellabas, this friendly boutique carries some of the best. ✉ *7, Derb Elmitere, Lablida, Fez el-Bali* ☎ *0535/63–69–32.*

VILLE NOUVELLE

CRAFTS

★ **Ensemble Artisanal.** Ensemble Artisanal is a haul across town on the southeastern edge of the city near the Hôtel Crown Palace, but those who make the trek will have the rare treat of seeing a cooperative of artisans working on everything from leather to copper to pottery and wood. The Ensemble is also useful if you want to comparison shop and to get a sense of how prices here line up with the prices you hear elsewhere in the city. The iron smith's lanterns are of a quality you won't easily find in the medina. ✉ *Av. Allah ben Abdullah, Ville Nouvelle* ☎ *0535/62–27–04, 0535/62–56–62.*

MEKNÈS

60 km (37 mi) west of Fez, 138 km (85 mi) east of Rabat.

Meknès occupies a plateau overlooking the Bouefekrane River, which divides the medina from the Ville Nouvelle. Meknès's three sets of imposing walls, architectural Royal Granaries, symmetrical Bab Mansour, and spectacular palaces are highlights in this well-preserved imperial city. Less inundated with tourists and more provincial than Fez,

Meknès offers a low-key initiation into the Moroccan processes of shopping and bargaining. The pace is slower than Fez and less chaotic. Whether it was post–Moulay Ismail exhaustion or the 1755 earthquake that quieted Meknès down, the result is a pleasant middle ground between the Fez brouhaha and the business-as-usual European ambience of Rabat.

GUIDE OR NO GUIDE?

An official guide from the tourist office costs about 250 DH for a half day or 500 DH for a full day. Private guides are helpful for first-time visits to the medina and the Imperial City, though you'll almost certainly end up haggling over rugs for the last hour of your tour. However, the palaces that house these rug enterprises are usually architectural gems, and the historical background of the rug-weaving craft is fascinating. The problem comes when you attempt to depart without purchasing one; be firm when saying "no thanks."

GETTING HERE AND AROUND

BY AIR

Fès-Saïss Airport serves both Fez and Meknès. The taxi or bus ride from there into Meknès takes about 30 minutes.

BY BUS

Regular CTM buses cover the Fez–Meknès route hourly. There are buses to Casablanca (four hours, 80 DH). Tangier (five hours, 95 DH), and Marrakesh (eight hours, 200 DH).

Bus Contacts **CTM Meknès.** The CTM bus station is situated east of the Ville Nouvelle at the Avenue des Forces Royales and Avenue de Fès. ✉ *43, bd. Mohammed V, Ville Nouvelle* ☎ *0535/52–25–83 Call Center* 🌐 *www.ctm.ma.*

BY CAR

You don't need (and probably don't want) a car if you are just visiting Meknès or just Fez and Meknès; however, if you want to explore the immediate region of the Middle Atlas, a car (or car and driver) will be crucial since these places can be difficult to reach by bus or grand taxi.

Rental Cars **Bab Mansour Car** ✉ *8, av. Idriss II, Ville Nouvelle* ☎ *0535/52–66–31.* **Meknès Car** ✉ *Av. Hassan II, Ville Nouvelle* ☎ *0535/51–20–74, 0535/51–21–65.* **Zeit Wagen** ✉ *4, rue Antisrabé, Ville Nouvelle* ☎ *0535/52–59–18.*

BY TAXI

Grands taxis carry up to six passengers and make long-distance runs between Fez and Meknès. This can be faster, more comfortable, and a better value than bus travel.

Metered petits taxis take up to four passengers, but may not leave the city limits. If the driver refuses to turn on the meter or agree to a reasonable price, do not hesitate to get out. There is usually a 50% surcharge after 8 pm.

BY TRAIN

The most convenient train station in Meknès is the rue el-Amir Abdelkader stop close to the administrative center of the city. If you're coming from Tangier, this will be the first stop; from Fez it will be the second. All trains stop at both stations.

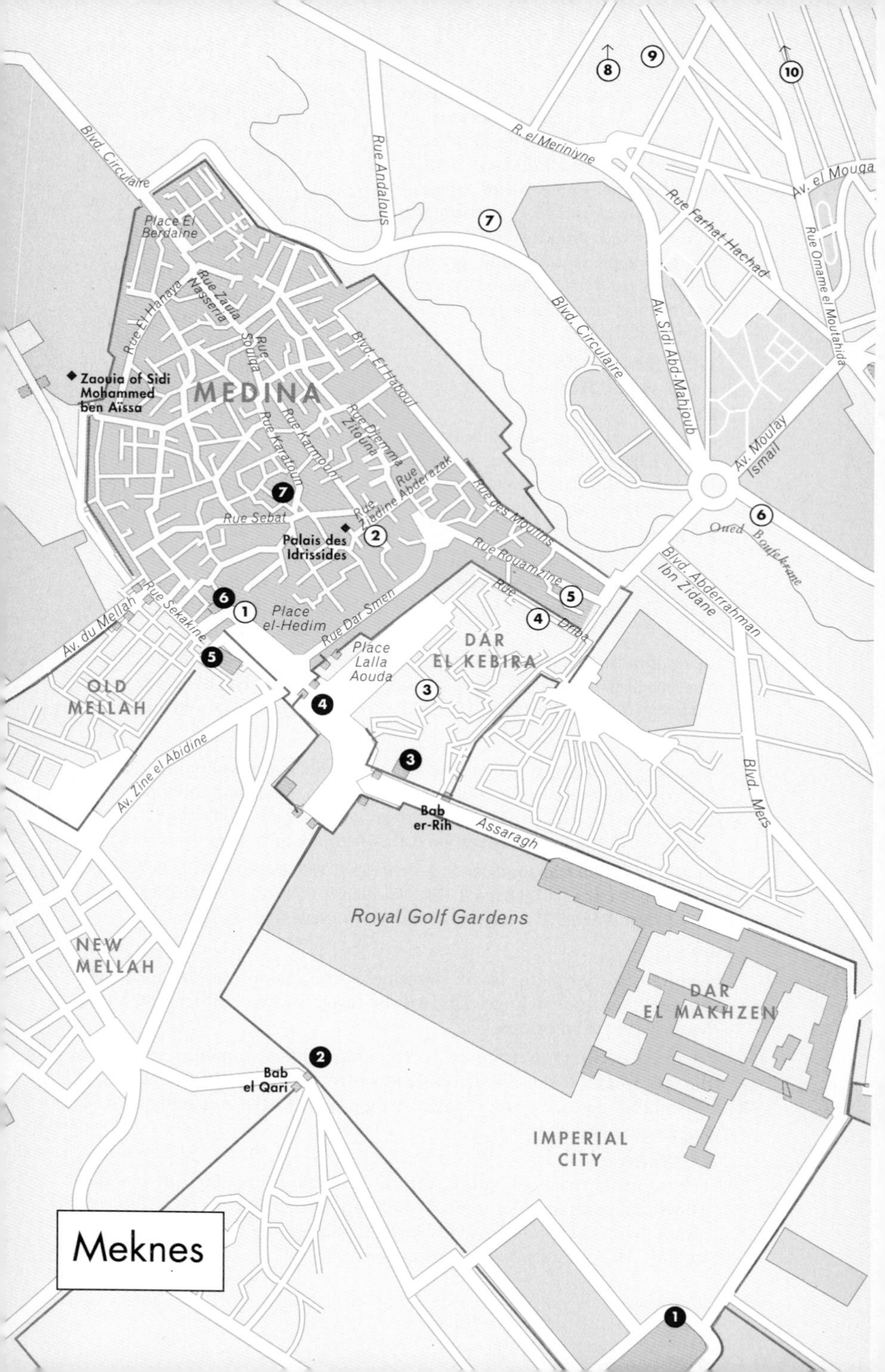
Meknes
MEDINA
Place El Berdaine
Rue El Hanaya
Rue Zaula Nasseria
Rue Souiqa
Blvd. El Haboul
Rue Karmouni
Rue Karatoun
Rue Djemma Zitouna
Rue Ziadine Abderazak
Rue des Moulins
Rue Sebat
Palais des Idrissides
Rue Rouamzine
Rue Driba
Place el-Hedim
Rue Dar Smen
Place Lalla Aouda
DAR EL KEBIRA
Rue Sekakine
Av. du Mellah
OLD MELLAH
Av. Zine el Abidine
Bab er-Rih
Assaragh
Royal Golf Gardens
NEW MELLAH
Bab el Qari
DAR EL MAKHZEN
IMPERIAL CITY
Zaouia of Sidi Mohammed ben Aïssa
Blvd. Circulaire
Rue Andalous
R. el Meriniyne
Rue Farhat Hachad
Av. el Mouqa
Rue Omame el Moutahida
Av. Sidi Abd-Mahjoub
Av. Moulay Ismail
Oued Boufekrane
Blvd. Abderrahman Ibn Zidane
Blvd. Mers

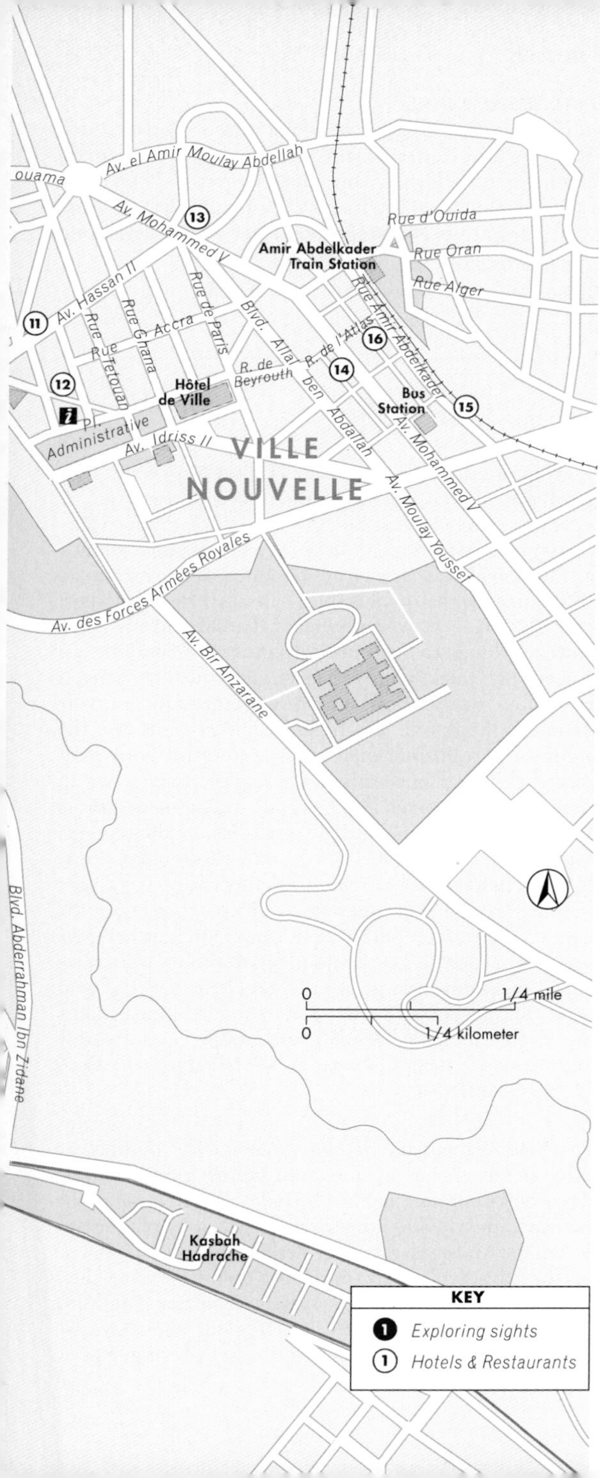

Exploring ▼

Bab Mansour 4
Bou Inania Medersa 7
Dar Jamai 6
Food souk 5
Haras Régional 2
Heri el Souani 1
Moulay Ismail Mausoleum 3

Hotels ▼

Hotel Akouas 15
Hôtel Rif 12
Hotel Transatlantique 8
Hotel Zaki 7
La Relais de Paris 9
Palais Didi 6
Riad d'Or 2
Ryad Bahia 1

Restaurants ▼

Annexe Restaurant Metropole II 10
Collier de la Colombe 4
Le Dauphin 13
Le Tangerois 16
Les Senteurs de la Mer 3
Metropole Restaurant & Brasserie 11
Restaurant Marhaba 14
Restaurant Omnia 5

KEY

❶ *Exploring sights*
① *Hotels & Restaurants*

4

TIMING AND PRECAUTIONS

Meknès is a beautifully intact medieval city worth exploring as a short excursion from Fez. From the central Place el-Hedime you can discover the medina's network of small open and covered streets flanked by shops, artisan studios, and food stalls. To see the Imperial City quarter, take a petit taxi or a more atmospheric *caléche* (horse-drawn carriage).

VISITOR INFORMATION

Meknès Tourist Office ✉ *Pl. Administrative* ☎ *0535/52–44–26, 0535/51–60–22.*

EXPLORING

THE IMPERIAL CITY

TOP ATTRACTIONS

Fodor's Choice ★ **Heri el-Souani** (*Royal Granaries*). Also known as Dar el-Ma (Water Palace) for the Agdal Basin reservoir beneath, the granaries were one of Moulay Ismail's greatest achievements and are the first place any Meknessi will take you to give you an idea of the second Alaouite sultan's grandiose vision. The Royal Granaries were designed to store grain as feed for the 10,000 horses in the royal stables—not just for a few days or weeks but over a 20-year siege if necessary. Ismail and his engineers counted on three things to keep the granaries cool enough that the grain would never rot: thick walls (12 feet), suspended gardens (a cedar forest was planted on the roof), and an underground reservoir with water ducts under the floors. The high-vaulted chamber on the far right as you enter has a 30-foot well in its center and a towpath around it—donkeys circulated constantly, activating the waterwheel in the well, which forced water through the ducts and maintained a stable temperature in the granaries. Out behind the granaries are the remains of the royal stables, roofless after the 1755 Lisbon earthquake. Some 1,200 purebreds, just one-tenth of Moulay Ismail's cavalry, were kept here. Stand just to the left of the door out to the stables—you can see the stunning symmetry of the stable's pillars from three different perspectives. The granaries have such elegance and grace that they were once called the Cathedral of Grain by a group of Franciscan priests, who were so moved that they requested permission to sing religious chants here. Acoustically perfect, the granaries and surrounding park are now often used for summer concerts and receptions. ✉ *Heri el-Souani* 🎫 *20 DH* ⊙ *Daily 9–1 and 3–6:30.*

WORTH NOTING

Haras Régional. Purebred Arabian and Berber horses and fine hybrids are treated like royalty at this 165-acre equestrian breeding and training farm used for Morocco's military until 1947. Under the direction of the Ministry of Agriculture, nearly 300 horses are identified by plaques on their stable walls: red for Arabians; green for Berber stallions and mares; and red and green for hybrids. The ratio of the two colors indicates their exact percentages in the horse's bloodline. Manicured pastures, multiple dressage and jumping quarters, and a 30-acre hippodrome showcase these spectacular "horses of the Maghreb"—the other regional equine

A horse-drawn caleche is a more relaxing and traditional way to tour Meknès.

centers are located in Rabat and Casablanca. ■ **TIP→ Guided horseback outings can be arranged here.** ✉ *El Hajeb Rd.* ☎ *0535/53–97–53* 🌐 *www.dramt-agriculture.com.*

BAB MANSOUR AND THE MEDINA

A walk around Bab Mansour and Place el-Hedime takes in nearly all of Meknès's major sites, including Moulay Ismail's mausoleum and the Prison of the Christian Slaves.

TOP ATTRACTIONS

★ **Bab Mansour.** Widely considered North Africa's most beautiful gate, this huge horseshoe-shape triumphal arch was completed in 1732 by a Christian convert to Islam named Mansour Laalej (whose name means "victorious renegade") and looms over the medina square. The marble Ionic columns supporting the two bastions on either side of the main entry were taken from the Roman ruins at Volubilis, while the taller Corinthian columns came from Marrakesh's El Badi Palace, part of Moulay Ismail's campaign to erase any vestige of the Saadian dynasty that preceded the Alaouites. Ismail's last important construction project, the gate was conceived as an elaborate homage to himself and strong Muslim orthodoxy of the dynasty rather than a defensive stronghold—hence, its intense decoration of green and white tiles and engraved Koranic panels, all faded significantly with age. ✉ *Rue Dar Smen, in front of the Place el-Hedime.*

French novelist Pierre Loti (1850–1923) penned the definitive description of Bab Mansour: ". . . rose-hued, star-shaped, endless sets of broken lines, unimaginable geometric combinations that confuse the eye like a labyrinthine puzzle, always in the most original and masterly taste, have been gathered here in thousands of bits of varnished earth, in relief or recessed, so that from a distance it creates the illusion of a buffed and textured fabric, glimmering, glinting, a priceless tapestry placed over these ancient stones to relieve the monotony of these towering walls."

Bou Inania Medersa. Begun by the Merenid sultan Abou el-Hassan and finished by his son Abou Inan between 1350 and 1358, the Meknès version of Fez's residential college of the same name is arguably more beautiful and better preserved than its better-known twin. Starting with the cupola and the enormous bronze doors on the street, virtually every inch of this building is covered with decorative carving or calligraphy. The central fountain is for ablutions before prayer. Head upstairs to visit the small rooms that overlook the courtyard. These housed the 60 communal *tolba*, or student reciters. **■ TIP→ The rooftop terrace has one of the best panoramic views of Meknès's medina.** ✉ *Rue des Souks es-Sebbat* 🎫 *10 DH* ⏲ *Mon.–Fri., 9–12 and 3–6.*

Dar Jamai. This 19th-century palace just inside the medina was built by the same family of *viziers* (high government officials) responsible for the Palais Jamaï hotel in Fez. The building itself is exquisite, especially the second-floor carved-cedar ceilings, interior Andalusian garden, and *menzah* (pavillion), which now houses the ethnographic **Museum of Moroccan Art** with an important collection of carpets, jewelry, ceramics, needlework, and woodwork. **■ TIP→ Facing away from Bab Mansour, the ceramics stalls on Place el-Hedime's left side sell oversize tagine pots for as little as 15 DH to 20 DH.** ✉ *Pl. el-Hedime* 🎫 *20 DH* ⏲ *Wed.–Mon., 9–1 and 3–6:30.*

★ **Food souk.** On the southern side of the medina square are the food souks. A tour through this gastronomic oasis stuffed with all manner of products heaped in elaborately arranged cones and pyramids—prunes, plums, olives, spices, nuts, dates, meats, fish, and pastries in every conceivable shape, color, aroma, and taste—is a veritable feast for the senses. The variety of olives on display and the painstaking care with which each pyramid of produce has been set out daily is nearly as geometrically enthralling as the decorative designs on the Bab Mansour. Look for the bustling fish stalls for seafood of all sorts straight from the Atlantic an hour's drive away. **■ TIP→ The kissaria (covered market) is a good place to stock up on Moroccan spices and aromatic herbs.** ✉ *South end of Place el-Hedime.*

★ **Moulay Ismail Mausoleum.** One of four sacred sites in Morocco open to non-Muslims (the others are Casablanca's Hassan II, Rabat's Mohammed V Mausoleum, and Rissani's Zaouia of Moulay Ali Sherif), this mausoleum was opened to non-Muslims by King Mohammed V (grandfather of Mohammed VI) in honor of Ismail's ecumenical instincts. An admirer of France's King Louis XIV—who, in turn, considered the sultan an important ally—Moulay Ismail developed close ties with Europe and signed commercial treaties even as he battled to eject the Portuguese from their coastal strongholds at Asilah, Essaouira, and Larache. The mausoleum's site once held Meknès's Palais de Justice (Courthouse), and Moulay Ismail deliberately chose it as his resting place with hopes he would be judged in his own court by his own people. The deep ochre-hue walls inside lead to the sultan's private sanctuary, on the left, heavily decorated with colorful geometric *zellij* tiling. At the end of the larger inner courtyard, you must remove your shoes to enter the sacred chamber with Moulay Ismail's tomb, surrounded by hand-carved cedar-and-stucco walls, intricate mosaics, and a central fountain. ✉ *Rue Sarag, near Bab er-Rih* 🎫 *Free* 🕑 *Sat.–Thurs., 9–noon and 3–6.*

Zaouia of Sidi Mohammed ben Aïssa. Built in 1776 by Sultan Sidi Mohammed ben Abdellah, the Zaouia of Sidi Mohammed ben Aïssa is the focal point of the legendary Aïssaoua cult, known for such voluntary rituals as: swallowing scorpions, broken glass, and poison; eating live sheep; and cutting themselves with knives in prayer-induced trances.

Ben Aïssa was one of Morocco's most famous saints. He was said to have made a pact with the animal world and possessed magical powers, such as the ability to transform the leaves of trees into gold and silver coins. Thought to have been a 17th-century contemporary of Moulay Ismail (1646–1727), Ben Aïssa was known as the protector of Moulay Ismail's 50,000-man workforce, and persuaded hungry laborers that they were able to eat anything at all, even poisonous plants, glass, or scorpions. Ben Aïssa went on to become the general protector of all his followers. It was said that women, for example, could travel safely under his protection.

The cult of Aïssa is still around, and has in fact proliferated throughout North Africa to Algeria and beyond. Every year, during Ben Aïssa's *moussem* (pilgrimage) on the eve of the birth of the prophet Mohammed, members of the Aïssaoua fraternity from all over North Africa gather at the shrine. Processions form and parade through Meknès, snakes are charmed, and the saint's followers perform ecstatic dances, often imitating the behavior of certain animals. Although some of the Aïssaoua's more brutal practices have been outlawed, this moussem remains one of Morocco's most astonishing and mysterious events. ✉ *Bd. Circulaire* 🎫 *20 DH* 🕑 *Daily 9–noon and 3–6.*

WORTH NOTING

Habs Kara (*Prison of the Christian Slaves*). After you pass through Place Lalla Aouda and Bab Filala, the pyramid-shape dome on the right side of the next square is the Koubba al-Khayatine (Tailors' Pavilion), named for the seamsters who sewed military uniforms here. Originally known as the Koubba Essoufara (Ambassadors' Pavilion), this was where Moulay Ismail received ambassadors from abroad. The stairs to the right of the pavilion entrance lead down to storage chambers originally built as a prison by the Portuguese architect Cara, himself a prisoner who earned his freedom by constructing these immense subterranean slave quarters. Go below to see where the 60,000 slaves (of which 40,000 were reportedly Christian prisoners of war) were shackled to the wall, forced to sleep standing up, and ordered to work on the sultan's laborious building projects. Ambassadors visiting Meknès to negotiate the ransoms and release of their captive countrymen were received in the pavilion above, never suspecting that the prisoners were directly under their feet. ✉ *Pl. Habs Qara* 🎫 *10 DH* 🕑 *Daily 9–1 and 3–6.*

The souks of Meknès are smaller and easier to navigate than those of Fez.

WHERE TO EAT

There are only a few culinary gems in Meknès, but chances are you'll want to sample local delicacies, snack on exotic fruits, and savor the ritual sweet pastries and mint tea, purported to be the best in the country. Good cafés and restaurants are scattered in the medina (many near the Place el-Hedime). Avenues Mohammed V and Hassan II in the Ville Nouvelle provide a wide choice of Moroccan and French or Mediterranean dishes.

$ MOROCCAN ★ ✕ **Collier de la Colombe.** A five-minute walk to the left inside Bab Mansour, this graceful medina space with intricate carvings, giant picture windows, and terraces overlooking the Boufekrane River and Ville Nouvelle is an excellent place to enjoy authentic Moroccan specialties. The menu is classic Moroccan, with highly recommended pastilla (a house specialty), tender grilled lamb, spicy beef brochettes, and mouthwatering fish tagines. Local Moroccans regularly line up and wait for choice seating on the panoramic rooftop terrace. Prices are a steal for the experience and quality of cooking. Alcohol is served. ✉ *67, rue Driba, via Bab Mansour and P. Lalla Aouda, Ville Nouvelle* ☎ *0535/55–50–41* 🌐 *www.lecollier.amawebs.com.*

$ FRENCH ✕ **Le Dauphin.** Le Dauphin is well respected for it extensive menu of French and international cuisine, lively ambience, and attentive service. Fresh fish, duck, and foie gras are reliable standards, as are wines from beyond North Africa. Desserts are decadent in a traditional French manner with crepes, tarts, and sorbets. ✉ *5, av. Mohammed V, Ville Nouvelle* ☎ *0535/52–34–23.*

¢ MOROCCAN **Metropole Restaurant and Brasserie.** On the corner near the central food market, this family-friendly, heavily tiled eatery serves a daily menu of traditional Moroccan fare, all at reasonable prices. The menu includes savory lamb tagine and coucous, but the restaurant specializes in freshly grilled chicken brochettes. ✉ *12, av. Hassan II, Ville Nouvelle* ☎ *0535/52–25–76.*

$ FRENCH ★ **Le Relais de Paris.** Need a break from tagine? For some of the best traditional French cuisine in town, Le Relais offers a prix-fixe menu featuring grilled specialties in a simply relaxing atmosphere overlooking Mount Zerhoun and pretty gardens. Owners Sayerh Fatima-Zehra and Mostafa Haffou bring gastronomic pleasures in the form of egglant and goat cheese lasagna, braised lamb, and classic chocolate profiteroles. The restaurant is open every day. ✉ *46, rue Oqba Ibn Nafia, Ville Nouvelle* ☎ *0535/51–54–88.*

¢ MOROCCAN **Restaurant Marhaba.** Fuel up at this canteen-style eatery for oustanding Moroccan cheap eats. Start with freshly made Berber bread and thick harira soup. Share a plate of grilled brochettes and *makoda,* sweet potato fritters. Portions are generous, and a full meal will cost less than a cup of coffee back home. ✉ *23, av. Mohammed V* ☎ *035/52–16–32.*

¢ MOROCCAN **Restaurant Omnia.** Seek out this lovely family restaurant in the heart of the medina serving incredibly delicious cuisine with warm smiles in an authentic traditional atmosphere. The sweet meat pastillas, spicy soup, and beef couscous are part of a set menu that finishes off with mint tea and honey-laden pastries. As an added bonus the prices are happily inexpensive. ✉ *8, Derb Ain el-Fouki, Rouamzine* ☎ *0535/53–39–38.*

$$ SEAFOOD **Les Senteurs de la Mer.** Locals flock to this highly rated, chic restaurant whose menu focuses mostly on fish and crustaceans. Affordable prices in a designer setting add to an impressive à la carte menu with such dishes as grilled Atlas trout, a specialty house salad composed of five types of fish, and a fresh seafood pizza. ■ TIP→ **Ask to sit on the upper floor for a more romantic, intimate ambience.** ✉ *17, rue Badre, El Kobra, Ville Nouvelle* ☎ *0535/52–66–57* *Reservations essential.*

WHERE TO STAY

Unlike Fez, Meknès has yet to attract strong commercial development and active restoration of riads. Staying within the medina in the limited choices available is especially exotic here. For more updated accommodations, there are several decent hotels in the Ville Nouvelle that are reasonably priced and a short walk or taxi ride from the train station.

For expanded hotel reviews, visit Fodors.com.

¢ **Hotel Akouass.** With a friendly staff, the Art Deco–inspired rooms here are adequate and air-conditioned. **Pros:** central location near public transportation; ample breakfast; free Wi-Fi. **Con:** some rooms are noisy. ■ TIP→ **Book a room on the upper floor to escape the noise of the nightclub.** ✉ *27, rue Zenkat el-Emir Abdelkader* ☎ *0535/51–59–69, 0535/51–59–68* 🌐 *www.hotelakouas.com* *52 rooms and suites* *In-room: a/c, Wi-Fi. In-hotel: restaurant, bar, pool* *Breakfast.*

$ **Hôtel Transatlantique.** Across the river from Meknès, the Transatlantique has simple rooms punctuated with beautiful views over an expanse of 14 acres. **Pros:** great views; spacious grounds. **Con:** no full-service restaurant. **TIP→ To see Volubilis from here, head to the bus station and hire a grand taxi, which costs around 400 DH.** ✉ *Rue Zankat al-Meriniyne* ☎ *0535/52–50–50* *120 rooms* *In-room: a/c, Wi-Fi. In-hotel: bar, pool, tennis court, business center, parking* *Breakfast.*

$$ **Hotel Zaki.** Facing the ramparts of the medina and valley of the Oued Boufekrane, this salmon-hued low-rise block conceals a spacious garden with an outdoor pool. **Pros:** good value for money; convenient location to the medina and Volubilis. **Cons:** poor service; needs some refurbishing. ✉ *Bd. al-Massira* ☎ *0535/51–41–46* *www.hotelzaki.ma* *169 rooms, 11 suites* *In-room: a/c, Wi-Fi. In-hotel: restaurant, bar, pool, gym, spa, business center, parking, some pets allowed* *Breakfast.*

$$ **Palais Didi.** Next to Bab Mansour and steps from the Moulay Ismail Mausoleum, this stately 18th-century palace was restored by owner Ismaili Raouf as an homage to his grandfather, who was affectionately known as Didi. **Pros:** medina location; panoramic terrace. **Cons:** some rooms old-fashioned; very expensive. ✉ *7, Dar el-Kbira* ☎ *0535/55–85–90* *www.palaisdidi.com* *7 double rooms, 5 suites* *In-room: a/c, Wi-Fi. In-hotel: restaurant, parking* *Breakfast.*

¢ **Riad d'Or.** Traditional styling in this basic bed-and-breakfast provides the Moroccan home experience. **Pros:** central location near Place el-Hadime; large well-appointed rooms; pool. **Cons:** noise; impersonal service; unreliable air-conditioning. ✉ *17, rue Ain el-Anboub, at Rue Lalla Alcha Adoula, Hammam Jdid-Bab Issy* ☎ *0535/53–38–71* *www.riaddor.com* *10 rooms, 1 suite* *In-room: a/c, Wi-Fi. In-hotel: restaurant, pool, spa, parking* *No credit cards* *Breakfast.*

$ ★ **Ryad Bahia.** Renovated in recent years, this 14th-century family house has been lovingly restored by a couple with years of experience working as Meknès guides and is an impressive anthology of ceramic, rug weaving, and woodworking crafts tucked away on the medina just a few steps from the Dar Jamai museum on the Place el-Hedime. **Pros:** medina location; outstanding service; family-friendly atmosphere. **Cons:** long walk from parking lot; no alcohol allowed on premises. ✉ *Derb Sekkaya, between Pl. el-Hedime and Bouanania Medersa, just behind Dar Jamai museum, Tiberbarine* ☎ *0535/55–45–41, 0662/08–28–64* *www.ryad-bahia.com* *6 rooms, 2 suites* *In-room: Wi-Fi. In-hotel: restaurant, laundry facilities* *Breakfast.*

NIGHTLIFE

A somewhat seedy disco scene thrives in the hotels around the train station in the Ville Nouvelle. More interesting are the bar and live-music scenes in the better hotels, especially the Transatlantique and the Rif, where sometimes you'll hear traditional Gnaoua, sometimes Western folk music.

Summer concerts in the Heri el-Souani are great favorites for Meknès music lovers. Check with the tourist office for dates and dress warmly—the 12-foot walls built to cool oats and barley chill people as well.

Meknès International Animated Film Festival. Meknès's international animated film festival (FICAM) takes place in mid-May. ☎ *0535/51–58–51* 🌐 *www.ficam.ma*.

SHOPPING

The Meknès souk, as with Meknès generally, seems somehow easier to embrace than vast Fez. Getting lost here is difficult; it just isn't that big. Meknès's merchants and craftsmen are as exceptional as those in Fez, and what's more, they're easier to negotiate with. Just be prepared, if you try to tell a rug salesman that you're pressed for time, to hear, "Ah, but a person without time is a dead person."

THE SOUKS

Beginning from the Place el-Hedime, just past the pottery stands brimming with colorful tagine vessels, a narrow corridor leads into the **food souk,** a wonderful display of everything from spices to dried fruit to multicolor olives. The **Souk Nejjarine,** the woodworkers' souk, leads into the rug and carpet souk. Farther on in this direction is the **Souk Bezzarine,** a general flea market along the medina walls. Farther up to the right are basket makers, iron smiths, leather workers, and saddle makers, and, near Bab el-Djedid, makers of odd items like tents and musical instruments. The Souk es-Sebat begins a more formal section, where each small section is devoted to a specific craft, beginning with the babouche (leather-slipper) market. If you are in the market for a carpet, then follow signs to the **Palais des Idrissides,** a wonderful 14th-century palace and carpet emporium.

CRAFTS

Centre Artisanale. The government-run Centre Artisanale is, as always in Moroccan cities, a good place to check for quality handcrafted products and prices before beginning to haggle in the souks. ✉ *Av. Zine el-Abidine Riad* ☎ *0535/53–09–29* ⏲ *Mon.–Sat., 9–1 pm and 3–7.*

Palais de l'Artisan. Palais de l'Artisan is a specialist in damascening (watered steel or silver inlay work) and sells jewelry, souvenirs, and decorated pottery. ✉ *11, Koubt Souk Kissaria Lahrir, Bab Mansour and the Medina* ☎ *0535/53–35–02.*

FOOD

Ben Moussa. Enter the Place el-Hedime's south side across the Bab Mansour and head down the first aisle to the right. On the left, look for the caged chameleons to find the fragrant, colorful stall of Ben Moussa—the perfect place to stock up on aromatic spices, herbs, and oil. ✉ *Food market, Pl. el-Hedime* ☎ *0535/55–73–21.*

RUGS

Palais des Idrissides. Much more than a carpet emporium, this magnificent 14th-century palace built by the cult of the Idrissid dynasty is a treasury of art, artisanship, and architecture not to be missed. The multilingual proprietors deliver a memorable discourse on the house's history and craftsmanship before moving on to an eloquent and entertaining history and ethnographical portrait of Berber kilim and carpet creation.

The unusual carved and inlaid ceilings of olive wood, rather than the customary cedar, are extraordinarily rich and ornate. The sloped floor, built for drainage, is made of Carrara marble, in exchange for which Morocco used to trade sugar. The large grandfather clocks were gifts of Louis XIV, allegedly bestowed on the sultan to ease Ismail's chagrin at the refusal of Louis's daughter, Princesse de Conti, to marry him. This carpet and kilim cooperative displays work from the 45 Berber tribes that have traditionally lived near Meknès, each with its own symbols and techniques. *For tips on buying rugs, see the Shopping feature earlier in this chapter.* ✉ *11, rue Kermouni* ☎ *0535/55–78–92* ⏲ *Daily 8–7.*

SIDE TRIPS FROM FEZ AND MEKNÈS

Volubilis and Moulay Idriss are highly recommended side trips from Fez and Meknès. Volubilis was the Roman Empire's farthest-flung capital, and Moulay Idriss has Morocco's most sacred shrine, the tomb of founding father Moulay Idriss I. Both sites are key to an understanding of Moroccan history. It's possible to see both places in one day, but if you're not independently mobile and need to sign up for a tour from Meknès or Fez, you might not get the chance to do both. If you must choose between trips to Volubilis and Moulay Idriss, go with the former. The Roman ruins at Volubilis are some of the best archaeological treasures in the country.

Another option is to head over to Oulmès (81 km [50 mi] from Meknès) for an excursion further into the countryside.

MOULAY IDRISS

23 km (14 mi) north of Meknès, 3 km (2 mi) southeast of Volubilis, 83 km (50 mi) west of Fez.

Moulay Idriss is Morocco's most sacred town, the final resting place of the nation's religious and secular founder, Moulay Idriss I. It is said that five pilgrimages to Moulay Idriss are the spiritual equivalent of one to Mecca; thus the town's nickname: the poor man's Mecca. A view over the town is a panoramic and informative look at a provincial Moroccan village, but it must be said that Moulay Idriss, for all its importance to Moroccans, is of only marginal interest to visitors compared to other Moroccan sights and scenes. Non-Muslims are not allowed inside the tomb at all, and until recently were not allowed to spend the night in town.

A splash of white against Djebel (Mt.) Zerhoun, Moulay Idriss attracts thousands of pilgrims from all over Morocco to its moussem in late August or early September. *Fantasias* (Berber cavalry charges with blazing muskets), acrobats, dancers, and storytellers fill the town, while hundreds of tents cover the hillsides. Non-Muslims are welcome to attend the secular events.

The moussem in Moulay Idriss draws pilgrims from far and wide in late August or early September.

GETTING HERE AND AROUND

Buses (10 DH) leave Meknès for Moulay Idriss hourly from 8 am until 6 pm. Getting afternoon buses back to Meknès from Moulay Idriss can be difficult, however.

TIMING AND PRECAUTIONS

Moulay Idriss is a holy town and requires utmost respect for sacred rituals and customs. Dress conservatively and avoid taking pictures of people. Try to arrive on a Saturday, since this is the most active time of the week. Friday is a day of prayer, so expect to see many establishments shut down.

EXPLORING

Moulay Idriss Medersa. An outstanding historic site from the Merinids, the Moulay Idriss Medersa was built in the 14th century by sultan Abou el-Hassan. Hidden in the town's steep and twisting streets, the medersa's striking cylindrical minaret constructed in 1939 is the only one of its kind in Morocco, standing as testimony to Turkish and Arab influences. Originally built with materials from Volubilis, the minaret is decorated with green ceramic tiles bearing inscriptions of the 114 *suras* (chapters) of the Koran. ☞ *All sites restricted to Muslims.*

Sidi Abdellah el-Hajjam Terrace. From the Sidi Abdellah el-Hajjam Terrace, in the Khiber quarter, you will have the best vantage point to see the holy village of Moulay Idriss and its sacred sanctuaries. A casual and friendly café on the top level is the perfect place to enjoy Moroccan morsels while sipping a cool beverage and taking in the view. The adjoining quarter across the gorge is called Tasga.

★ **Zaouia of Moulay Idriss I.** This important shrine and zaouia of the Idrissid dynasty's patriarch is off-limits to non-Muslims, marked by a wooden bar to restrict access. For a good view, climb to a vantage point overlooking the religious sanctuary—the hike up one of many hills through the town's surrounding alleys is invigorating and a symbolic bow to Morocco's secular and spiritual history.

WHERE TO EAT

The main street through Moulay Idriss (up to the parking area just in front of the Zaouia) is lined with a series of small, indistinguishable stands and restaurants serving everything from brochettes of spicy meat to harira and boiling-hot mint tea.

VOLUBILIS

28 km (17 mi) northwest of Meknès, 88 km (53 mi) northwest of Fez, 3 km (2 mi) west of Moulay Idriss.

Volubilis was the capital of the Roman province of Mauritania (Land of the Moors), Rome's southwesternmost incursion into North Africa. Favored by the confluence of the Rivers Khoumane and Fertasse and surrounded by some of Morocco's most fertile plains, this site has probably been inhabited since the Neolithic era.

Volubilis's municipal street plan and distribution of public buildings are remarkably coherent examples of Roman urban planning. The floor plans of the individual houses, and especially their well-preserved mosaic floors depicting mythological scenes, provide a rare connection to the sensibilities of the Roman colonists who lived here 2,000 years ago.

If you prefer to see Volubilis on your own without a guide(less informative but more contemplative), proceed through the entrance, and make a clockwise sweep. After crossing the little bridge over the Fertasse River, climb up to the plateau's left edge, and you'll soon come across a Berber skeleton lying beside a sculpture with his head pointed east, a deliberate placement suggesting early Islamization of the Berber populace here.

GETTING HERE AND AROUND

Volubilis is a 30-minute drive north from Meknès, and an hour's drive from Fez. Sometimes marked on road signs as "Oualili," Volubilis is beyond Moulay Idriss on Route N13, which leaves R413 to head northeast 15 km (9 mi) northwest of Meknès. Grand taxis to Volubilis are available from Meknès and Fez, for 350 DH and 400 DH respectively. From Moulay Idriss there are shuttles to Volubilis (6 DH). From Fez, the only regularly scheduled bus connection to Volubilis is via Meknès.

TIMING AND PRECAUTIONS

Volubilis is an expansive site that requires intense walking and sun exposure. Tour earlier in the day, wear a hat, and carry a water bottle.

Visitor Information **Volubilis Tourist Office** ✉ *Main Gate* ☎ *0535/52–44–26* 🌐 *www.tourisme.gov.ma.*

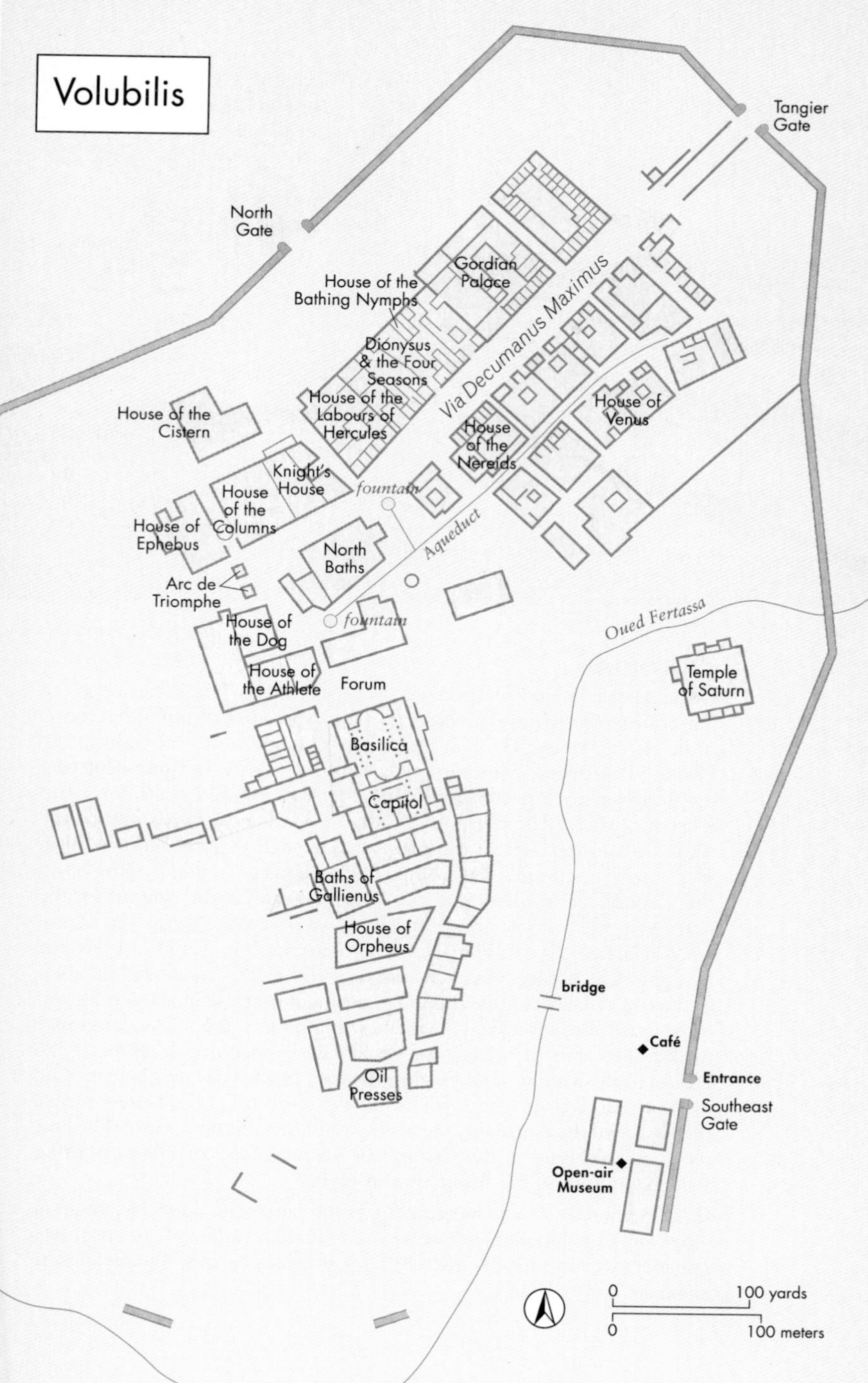
Volubilis
Tangier Gate
North Gate
Gordian Palace
House of the Bathing Nymphs
Via Decumanus Maximus
Dionysus & the Four Seasons
House of the Labours of Hercules
House of the Cistern
House of Venus
House of the Nereids
Knight's House
fountain
House of the Columns
House of Ephebus
Aqueduct
North Baths
Arc de Triomphe
House of the Dog
fountain
Oued Fertassa
Temple of Saturn
House of the Athlete
Forum
Basilica
Capitol
Baths of Gallienus
House of Orpheus
bridge
Café
Oil Presses
Entrance
Southeast Gate
Open-air Museum
0
100 yards
0
100 meters

Volubilis was the Roman capital of Mauritania.

EXPLORING

Remains of **Roman olive presses** can be seen to the left, evidence of the importance of the olive-oil industry that supported 20,000 inhabitants of this 28-acre city. The first important mosaics are to the right in the **House of Orpheus,** consisting of a dolphin mosaic and one depicting the Orpheus myth in the Tablinum, a back room used as a library and receiving room. Past the public **Baths of Gallienus,** in a room to the right, are a dozen sets of footprints raised slightly above floor level in what was a communal bathroom. The wide-paved street leading up to the **Capital,** the **Basilica** and the **Forum** is the **Cardus Maximus,** the main east-west thoroughfare of any Roman town. Across the forum were the market stalls. The **Triumphal Arch,** built in AD 217, destroyed by the 1755 Lisbon earthquake and restored in 1932, is down to the left at the end of **Decumanus Maximus,** the main north-south street. As you look south through the arch, the first building to the left is the **House of the Dog,** named because of unearthed bronze dog sculpture. The **House of the Knight** has an incomplete but beautifully designed mosaic of Dionysus. Beyond the northernmost gate—the **Tangier Gate**—stands the **Palace of the Gordians,** the residence of the administrators. The best mosaics are found in the **Cortege of Venus.** Look for **Diana Bathing with Nymphs** and the **Abduction of Hylas.**

■ TIP→ Volubilis can be hot and dry, as the ruins offer no shade. Wearing a hat and bringing plenty of water are essential. Walking is the best and cheapest way to tour the area. Bring your best pair of walking shoes or sneakers.

Dionysus and the Four Seasons. Along the Decumanus Maximus, the small spaces near the street's edge held shop stalls, while mansions—10 on the left and 8 on the right—lined either side. The house of Dionysus and the Four Seasons is about halfway down the Decumanus Maximus; its scene depicting Dionysus discovering Ariadne asleep is one of the town's most spectacular mosaics.

House of the Bathing Nymphs. The House of the Bathing Nymphs is named for its superb floor mosaics portraying a bevy of frolicking nymphs in a surprisingly contemporary, all but animated, artistic fashion. On the main street's right side, the penultimate house has a marble bas-relief medallion of Bacchus. As you move back south along the next street below and parallel to the Decumanus Maximus, there is a smaller, shorter row of six houses that are worth exploring. 🌐 *whc.unesco.org.*

★ **House of Ephebus.** The ancient town's greatest mansions and mosaics line the Decumanus Maximus from the town brothel north to the Tangier Gate, which leads out of the enclosure on the uphill end. One of the most famous is the House of Ephebus, just west of the triumphal arch, named for the nude ivy-crowned bronze sculpture discovered here (now on display in Rabat). The *cenacula,* or banquet hall, has colorful mosaics with Bacchic themes. Opposite the House of Ephebus is the House of the Dog, where a bronze canine statue was discovered in 1916 in one of the rooms off the *triclinium,* a large dining room.

★ **House of Orpheus.** One of the important houses you will want to visit in the Roman ruins is the House of Orpheus, the largest house in the residential quarter. Three remarkable mosaics depict Orpheus charming animals with his lyre, nine dolphins symbolizing good luck, and Amphitrite in his sea-horse drawn chariot. Head north from here to explore the public Baths of Gallienus and freestanding Corinthian pillars of the Capitol.

Fodor's Choice ★ **House of Venus.** The House of Venus contains Volubilis's best set of mosaics and should not be missed. Intact excavations portray a chariot race, a bathing Diana surprised by the hunter Actaeon, and the abduction of Hylas by nymphs—all are still easily identifiable. The path back down to the entrance passes the site of the Temple of Saturn, across the riverbed on the left.

★ **Triumphal Arch of Volubilis.** Impressively rising in fertile plains and olive groves, the grand stone arch of Volubilis is the centerpoint of the ancient Roman site. Decorated only on the east side, it is supported by marble columns, built by Marcus Aurelius Sebastenus to celebrate the power of Emperor Caracalla.

WHERE TO STAY

$ **Hôtel Volubilis Inn.** Surrounded by olive groves high on a hillside, this comfortable hotel has exceptional views from its pool and terrace over the valley to the southwest. **Pros:** modern rooms; outstanding views. **Cons:** popular with tour groups. ✉ *Rte. de Volubilis (N13), Douar Fartassa Oualili, Moulay Idriss Zerhoun* ☎ *0535/54–44–05, 0661/63–84–22* 🌐 *www.hotelvolubilisinn.com* *53 rooms* *In-room: a/c, Internet. In-hotel: restaurant, bar, pool, business center, parking* *Breakfast.*

THE MEDITERRANEAN MIDDLE ATLAS

Spreading south and east of Fez, the northern Middle Atlas is drained by the River Moulouya en route to the Mediterranean Sea near the Algerian border. The Azrou Cedar Forest and the Djebel Tazzeka Massif above Taza are the main attractions in this heavily forested northern zone, along with Midelt and the Cirque de Jaffar at the more barren southern edge.

GETTING HERE AND AROUND

The Fès–Saïss Airport serves the Middle Atlas as well as Fez and Meknès. Azrou, Ifrane, Sefrou, Imouzzer du Kandar, Beni-Mellal, Azilal, Midelt, Kasba Tadla, and Khénifra are all served by CTM buses, if somewhat sporadically. The bus from Casablanca to Ifrane to Azrou takes six hours from beginning to end; the one from Meknès to Azrou to Midelt takes four to five hours total.

If you have any intention of wandering into the overlands, you must drive a four-wheel-drive vehicle. Ensure your car is equipped with a spare tire and emergency fuel. Depending on where you're coming from, it's best to rent a car in Fez or Meknès. (*For more information, see the Fez and Meknès sections earlier in the chapter.*)

Contacts **Midelt CTM Terminal** ✉ *Av. Mohammed V, Midelt* ☎ *0535/56-06-35* 🌐 *www.ctm.ma.*

The contacts here organize tours beyond their immediate towns, so feel free to check out any of these when planning your trip.

HIKING AND TREKKING

Major treks arise from the Djebel Ayachi Massif, south of Midelt, as well as above Beni-Mellal, Azilal, and Demnate. The Tessaout gorges above Lac des Aït-Aadel, west of Demnate, have some of Morocco's best and most spectacular long-distance trekking.

HORSEBACK RIDING

For the equestrian, several stables offer mountain or rural outings on horseback. Try the Centre Equestre et de Randonnée.

Contacts **Centre Equestre et de Randonnée.** Three kilometers from Fez, this center is affiliated with the Royal Equestrian Federation and can arrange leisurely horse promenades. ✉ *Aïn Amyer, Rte. d'Immouzzer, Fez* ☎ *0535/60-51-16.*

FISHING

Morocco, surprisingly, offers trout fishing in the foothills of the High Atlas and in the Azrou Cedar Forest. European brown trout and rainbows, nearly all stocked fish or descendants of repopulated fisheries, thrive in select highland environments. March through May are the prime angling months. Permits and further orientation are available through the Administration des Eaux et Forêts offices in Rabat.

Permits **Administration des Eaux et Forêts** ✉ *605 Rabat-Chellah, Rabat* ☎ *0537/76-00-38, 0537/76-00-41* 🌐 *www.eauxetforets.gov.ma.*

RAFTING

One of best ways to see Morocco is through the natural beauty of its flowing rivers and dramatic canyons. Moroccan Rafting is a 12-year-old company specializing in rafting tours on the Ahansei, Oum Er Rbia, Ourika and Nifiss rivers. Adventure holidays are available with a range of activities that combine rafting, kayaking, canyoning and tubing.

Contact **Moroccan Rafting.** This company—open since the late 1990s—specializes in white-water rafting tours on the Ahansei, Oum Er Rbia, Ourika, and Nifiss rivers. ✉ *Rue Beni Marine, Marrakesh* ☎ *0672/88–25–29.*

4

TAZA

120 km (72 mi) east of Fez.

An important capital during the Almohad, Merenid, and early Alaouite dynasties (11th to 16th century), Taza was used as a passage into Morocco by the first Moroccan Arabs—the Idrissids—and nearly all successive invaders en route to Fez. Fortified and refortified over the centuries, the city, located in the mountain pass known as the Taza Gap separating the Rif from the Middle Atlas Mountains, is marked by a medina that houses a 14th-century madrassa and four mosques.

ESSENTIALS

Bus Contacts **Taza CTM Terminal** ✉ *Pl. de l'Indépendance* ☎ *055/67–30–37* 🌐 *www.ctm.co.ma.*

Visitor Information **Délégation du Tourisme de Taza** ✉ *Immeuble des Habbous, 30, ave. Mohammed V* ☎ *0555/67–27–37.*

EXPLORING

First constructed in the 12th century, the haunting city walls have been in various states of renovation. Accessing the main entry point, the Bab er-Rih (Gate of the Wind) leads up to a beautiful panoramic view of the Djebel Tazzeka hills. Through the center of town, walk the main street that connects the medina's four principal mosques—the Grande Mosque, the Sidi Azouz mosque, the Mosque du Marché, and the Andalous Mosque.

★ **Grande Mosquée.** With its perforated cupola, the Great Mosque is a historically significant UNESCO World Heritage Site. Dating from the 12th century, the mosque, founded by Sultan Abd el-Moumen, is possibly the oldest Almohad structure in existence and believed to predate the mosque at Tin Mal. Of architectural importance is the mosque's inscribed 3-ton chandelier and intricately designed windows and doorways. ✣ *Walk towards Bab er-Rih past the medina* 🌐 *www.mosquee.taza.free.fr.*

WHERE TO EAT AND STAY

¢ MEDITERRANEAN ✕ **Les Deux Rives.** This small Mediterranean restaurant offers light entrées including salads, soups, and pizzas. ✉ *20, av. Oujda* ☎ *0535/67–12–27* 💳 *No credit cards.*

¢ 🏨 **Grand Hôtel du Dauphiné.** Though the period charm has diminished, this budget hotel offers clean rooms, shuttered balconies, and agreeable service. **Pros:** very close to public transportation. **Cons:** no heat in winter; old-fashioned decor. ✉ *Av. Prince Héritier Sidi Mohammed, Intersection of Place de l'Indépendance and Av. de la Gare, Ville Nouvelle* ☎ *0535/67–35-67* *26 rooms, 9 with bath* *In-room: no a/c. In-hotel: restaurant, parking* *No credit cards* *Breakfast.*

EXCURSIONS FROM TAZA

The 123-km (74-mi) loop around the Cirque du Djebel Tazzeka southwest of Taza is one of the most varied and spectacular day trips in the Middle Atlas. Packing a range of diversions from picnicking by the waterfalls of Ras el-Oued to spelunking in the Gouffre du Friouato (Friouato Cave), reaching the summit of the 6,494-foot Djebel Tazzeka, or navigating the gorges of the Oued Zireg, this tour is geared for the serious adventurer. Without stops, the entire multisurface drive takes approximately five hours. The S311 road south from Taza is narrow and serpentine. The Cascades of Ras-El, 10 km (6 mi) south of Taza is the first stop. The Parc National de Tazzeka has tranquil picnic spots. The right fork on the S311 brings you to the Friouato Caves within the park, while the left path leads out to the lake bed of Daia Chike, most impressive in springtime when subterranean waters keep it filled.

Beyond the caves, the road climbs through a pine forest to the village of Bab Bou Idir, abandoned except in summer when the campground and chalets fill with vacationers. After another 8 km (5 mi), the right-hand fork leads 9 km (5.5 mi) to the crest of Djebel Tazzeka, 6,494 feet, a tough climb by car or on foot. Your reward is the unique view over the Rif and south to the Middle Atlas.

From Djebel Tazzeka there are another 38 km (23 mi) north along the spectacular Zireg river gorges to Sidi Abdallah de Rhiata, where you can get on the N6 back to Taza or Fez. ⚠ **The 7-km (4.5-mi) track to the crest of Djebel Tazzeka is a dangerous drive in bad weather.**

★ **Friouato Cave.** One of the most breathtaking natural sights in the Middle Atlas, the Friouato Cave complex, 26 km (16 mi) from Taza, is North Africa's deepest caverns—they extend steeply down 520 stairs to a depth of 590 feet. Explored by the eminent French speleologist Norbert Casteret in 1930, the caves consist of various large chambers filled with enormous stalagmites in strange and fantastic shapes and colors. Chambers such as the Salle de Lixus, the Salle de Draperies, and the Salle Casteret lead through what has been referred to as an underground palace. This experience is not advised for claustrophobes or the faint of heart. The caves are muddy and wet, the climb down and back is strenuous, and opportunities for minor injuries are many since you must squeeze through narrow crevices and slick passageways. As with many caves, the Friouato Caves are home to a large family of bats. Proper hiking footwear and waterproof warm clothes are recommended, as are powerful flashlights. *Top Gallery 10 DH; three-hour guided tour 120 DH (includes flashlight rental)* *Daily 7 am–8 pm.*

SEFROU

33 km (20 mi) southeast of Fez, 136 km (82 mi) southwest of Taza.

A miniature Fez at an altitude of 2,900 feet, the small town of Sefrou lies in the fertile valley of the notoriously flood-prone River Agdal. A first stop on the caravan routes between the Sahara and the Mediterranean coast, it was originally populated by Berber converts to Judaism, who came north from the Tafilalt date palmery and from Algeria in the 13th century. The town remained a nucleus of Jewish life until 1956, when, upon the country's declaration of independence from France, virtually all of the Jewish community fled Morocco.

EXPLORING

Sefrou is a picturesque ancient walled city whose medina is well preserved and worth a visit. With cooler temperatures than nearby Fez, the town is a pleasant summer day trip. Wander around the mellah quarter and explore the tame souks. The town is most noted for its annual Fête des Cerises, or Cherry Festival, that celebrates the yearly harvest every mid-June with food, music, dance, and cultural activities.

Kef el-Moumen. During the town's famous Cherry Festival, in May or June, a procession ventures across the Aggai River to the Kef el-Moumen cave containing the prophet Daniel's tomb, a pilgrimage venerated by Jews and Muslims alike. According to legend, seven followers of Daniel slept here for centuries before miraculously resuscitating.

Lalla Rekia. West of Sefrou is the ancient fountain of Lalla Rekia, believed to contain miraculous holy water to cure mental illness. Some visitors still bring jugs to the spring to carry away alleged healing benefits from the fount's source. The area is best accessed by rental car or taxi, as public transportation in the area is limited.

Sidi Lahcen Ben Ahmed. The *zaouia* (sanctuary) of Sidi Lahcen Ben Ahmed is the final resting place of this 17th-century saint.

WHERE TO STAY

For expanded hotel reviews, visit Fodors.com.

¢ **Hôtel Sidi Lahcen el-Youssi.** Named for the local saint, this low-key complex with an alpine chalet feel is blessed with a decent restaurant and calm setting on the outskirts of town. **Pros:** clean rooms; quiet location. **Cons:** bathrooms slightly worn; staff don't speak good English. ✉ *Rue Sidi Ali Boussarghine* ☎ *0535/68–34–28* *20 rooms, 3 bungalows* *In-room: no a/c. In-hotel: restaurant, pool, parking* *Breakfast.*

IFRANE

25 km (15 mi) southwest of Imouzzer du Kandar, 63 km (37 mi) southwest of Fez.

Built in 1929 during the French protectorate to create a "poche de France" (pocket of France) for expatriate French diplomats, administrators, and business personnel, Ifrane's alpine chalets, contemporary villas, and modern boulevards have become the place to see and be-seen for local elite, whose wealth is visibly flaunted with Western designer clothing in European-style cafés and a recently renovated luxury resort and spa overlooking the Azrou Cedar Forest. Nicknamed "Morocco's Switzerland," Ifrane sits at an altitude of 5,460 feet (1,700 meters) and is visibly well maintained with manicured gardens, curvy tree-lined streets, and new architecture. As a royal mandate, the Al Akhawayn University, an English-language public university with an American curriculum, opened in the mid-1990s. The modern facility helped to build the town's reputation as a desirable tourist destination for local vacation-goers.

ESSENTIALS

Bus Terminals **Ifrane CTM Terminal** ⊠ *Av. de la Marché Verte* ☎ *0535/56–68–21.*

Taxis **Ifrane Taxi Stand.** The taxi stand is located about a half mile from the village square behind the central market. ⊠ *Ifrane–Meknès Rd.*

Visitor Information **Délégation du Tourisme d'Ifrane** ⊠ *Pl. du Syndicat-Av. Mohammed V* ☎ *0663/77–26–87, 0662/19–08–89* 🌐 *www.tourisme-vert-ifrane.com.*

EXPLORING

Known primarily as an upscale ski-resort town, Ifrane is also famous for its cold-water trout fishing and excellent hiking trails up the **Cascades des Vierges** (Waterfall of the Virgins). Zaoula de Ifrane, a small village just north of the city, is home to local artisans. Near the well-photographed stone lion statue in the center of town, the royal palace of the ruling Alaouite dynasty is still in use by the ruling kingdom and off-limits with extraordinarily high security in the area.

WHERE TO EAT AND STAY

¢ MOROCCAN **La Paix.** Situated on the ground floor of the Appart Hotel (which has 20 suite-style rooms), this airy, modern eatery is a family-friendly restaurant-pizzeria-tea salon popular with visitors. The menu offers a range of international dishes in addition to authentic Moroccan tagines, plus tasty soups, salads, pizzas, and desserts. ⊠ *Av. de la Marche Verte* ☎ *0535/56–61–61* 🌐 *www.lapaixifrane.ma* ▭ *No credit cards.*

$$$$ Fodor's Choice ★ **The Michlifen Ifrane Suites and Spa.** Less than an hour south of the world's largest medieval city at Fez, this newly renovated five-star resort hotel perched atop a hill is a stunningly luxurious retreat near the Michlifen ski slopes and continues to attract wealthy locals. **Pros:** beautiful views; sumptuous rooms and spa; sports center. **Cons:** limited public transportation; very expensive. ⊠ *Av. Hassan II, Ville d'Ifrane* ⊠ *BP 18, Ville d'Ifrane* ☎ *0535/86–40–00, 0535/86–41–00* 🌐 *www.michlifenifrane.com* *70 rooms* *In-room: a/c, Wi-Fi. In-hotel: restaurant, bar, pool, tennis court, gym, spa, laundry facilities, business center, parking* *Breakfast.*

SPORTS AND THE OUTDOORS

HORSEBACK RIDING

Royal Club Equestre de Randonnée d'Ifrane. Group and individual riding tours through scenic mountain wilderness are available from this stable in Ifrane. ⊠ *Dayet Aoua* ☎ *0535/86–26–99* 🌐 *lucyin.walon.org.*

The scenery around Ifrane is almost alpine; it's not uncommon to see woolly sheep grazing on the hillsides.

SKIING

Michlifen and Djebel Hebri are the two ski resorts nearest Ifrane and within day-trip range of Fez. If your expectations are modest, a day on the slopes is a pleasant option to relax—there are four trails that are relatively simple. Skis and sleds can be rented at the resorts.

Contact **Hôtel Aghlias.** Located at an altitude of 2,040 meters and 16 km (10 mi) from the village of Ifrane, this 3-star hotel sits in the middle of the cedar forest. ✉ *Station de Ski de Michlifen* ☎ *0535/56–04–92.*

AZROU

17 km (10 mi) southwest of Ifrane, 67 km (40 mi) southeast of Meknès, 78 km (47 mi) southwest of Fez.

Occupying an important junction of routes between the desert and Meknès and between Fez and Marrakesh, Azrou—from the Berber word for "rock"—is a significant ancient Berber capital named for the city's quarry of black volcanic rocks. It was one of Sultan Moulay Ismail's strongholds after he built an imposing fortress here (now in ruins) in 1684. For centuries Azrou remained unknown, a secret mountain town that invading forces never fully located, thanks in part to a cave system designed for concealment and protection. Enjoy the mellow pace and lifestyle of traditional Berber mountain life. The weekly souk and small medina are pleasant contrasts to the larger, noisier crowds of Fez.

ESSENTIALS

Bus Terminals **Azrou CTM Terminal** ✉ *Bd. Moulay Abdelkader* ☎ *0535/56–20–20.*

EXPLORING

Place Mohammed V, a square lined with numerous cafés, holds an important Tuesday souk that attracts residents from many neighboring towns for its vast selection of local produce.

★ **Azrou Cedar Forest.** The Azrou Cedar Forest is a unique habitat in Morocco, as much a state of mind as a woodland. Moroccans are proud of their cedar forest, always one of the national geography's crown jewels. Even in the Fez medina you can sense a breath of fresh air when the forest is mentioned, usually as the source of some intricate cedar carving. Moroccan cedars, some more than 400 years old, grow to heights of close to 200 feet, and cover some 320,000 acres on the slopes of the Middle Atlas, the High Atlas, and the Rif at altitudes between 3,940 and 9,200 feet. Cedar is much coveted by woodworkers, particularly makers of stringed musical instruments. Living among the enormous cedars to the south of Azrou are troops of Barbary macaques that curiously climb towards visitors, and birdlife ranging from the redheaded Moroccan woodpecker to owls and eagles. Flora include the large-leaf peony, the scarlet dianthus, and the blue germander, all of which attract butterflies, including the cardinal and the colorful sulphur Cleopatra. If you'd like to visit, you should pick up information, guides, and maps of the forest showing trails and hikes at the Ifrane Tourist Office on weekdays, 8:30–12:30 and 2:30–6:30 (*see ⇨ Ifrane, above*).

Collège Berbère. Seeing a Berber nucleus, the French established the Collège Berbère here in an attempt to train an elite Berber opposition to the urban Arab ruling class; both Arabic and Islam were prohibited. After independence, the movement faded. The Berber college became an Arabic school and was renamed the Lycée Tariq Ibn Ziyad Du Azrou. With nearly 400 locals matriculated, it now teaches a progressive curriculum and hosts international exchange students. ✉ *Bd. Prince Heritier* ☎ *0535/56–24–16.*

Maison de l'Artisanat. Azrou's artisan center, the Maison de l'Artisanat, just off the P24 to Khénifra (and a mere five-minute walk from Place Mohammed V), is one of the town's main attractions—it's a trading post for the Beni M'Guild tribes, who are known for their fine carpets, kilims, and cedar carvings.

WHERE TO EAT AND STAY

¢ CAFÉ ✕ **Patisserie Azrou.** This corner café, located near the mosque in the city center, is smoky and dark on the ground floor but more pleasant and spacious upstairs or outdoors. The coffee is flavorful and the service friendly. ✉ *Pl. Hassan II* ☎ *No phone* ▭ *No credit cards.*

¢ **Hôtel Panorama.** Up on a hill near Azrou's center, this rustic hotel has good views over the forest and town as well as a decent restaurant and reliable heating—more than welcome during Azrou's long, snowy winters. **Pros:** helpful staff; quiet location. **Cons:** a bit dated. ✉ *Rue el-Hansali, Azrou Center, Hay Ajelabe* ☎ *0535/56–36–49, 0535/56–20–10, 0535/56–22–42* 🌐 *www.hotelpanorama.ma* *38 rooms* *In-room: no a/c, Internet. In-hotel: restaurant, bar, parking* *Multiple meal plans.*

$ **Palais des Cerisiers.** Situated close to the village center en route to the Azrou Cedar Forest, this pretty hotel is set in a stone mansion on verdant grounds and well-equipped with classic wood furnishings, air-conditioned and centrally heated rooms, serene mountain views, and large pool. **Pros:** tranquil atmosphere; pool. **Cons:** service may be slow. ✉ *Rte. Cèdre Gouraud, Hay Ajelabe* ☎ *0535/56–38–30* 🖷 *0535/56–34–36* 🌐 *www.lepalaisdescerisiers.com* *14 rooms, 4 suites, 2 apartments* *In-room: a/c, Wi-Fi. In-hotel: restaurant, bar, pool, gym, spa, parking* 🍽 *Breakfast.*

SOURCES DE L'OUM-ER-RBIA

57 km (35 mi) southwest of Azrou.

An unexpected natural wonder in the middle of the country, the 40 freshwater and seven saltwater springs that arise from the River Oum-er-Rbia are best approached from Azrou and Aïn Leuh through the cedar forest. Flowing across nearly the entire Moroccan heartland from the Middle Atlas to the Atlantic Ocean (at Azemmour, south of Casablanca), the great Oum-er-Rbia, Morocco's longest river, has been diverted, dammed, and largely destroyed over the years in favor of irrigation and hydroelectric projects. The sources are now impressive for the great volume of crystal clear water bursting from the adjoining mountain's side, part of the Djebel Hebri Massif and the Michlifen ski area's snow runoff. The Aguelmane Azigza (Lake Azigza), another 20 km (12 mi) south of the sources on Route 3211 is equally impressive with stunning red cliffs surrounding undulating blue-green waters.

Kayaking trips are only available during April, possibly March or early May depending on weather conditions. Several tour companies offer memorable itineraries by experienced instructors who provide kayak clinics on the scenic Ahansai.

MIDELT

206 km (124 mi) southeast of Khénifra, 232 km (139 mi) south of Fez, 126 km (76 mi) north of Er-Rachidia.

Midelt itself is flat, nondescript and not worth a special trip, but for the more adventurous, the nearby Cirque de Jaffar and Djebel Ayachi definitely are. Midelt is the logical base camp for these excursions. The town itself has an interesting carpet souk with rugs in original geometric designs and kilims made by Middle Atlas Berber tribes.

ESSENTIALS

Taxis **Midelt Taxi Stand.** In the center of town, the taxi stand is about 300 feet south of the bus station. ✉ *Er Rachidia Rd.*

EXPLORING

Atelier de Tissage–Kasbah Miryem. The Atelier de Tissage–Kasbah Myriem is a workshop run by the Notre Dame d'Atlas convent and monastery since 1925. Off the road to the Cirque de Jaffar, en route to Tattiouine and surrounded by trees, it is a good place to buy local Berber carpets, blankets, and hand-embroidered textiles of all kinds as well as to chat with the benevolent French Franciscan nuns, all of whom are experts on Moroccan weaving. On-site is a small church with an icon of the Seven Sleepers of Ephesus, a legend referenced in both Christianity and Islam. A small community of Trappist monks from Algeria resides on the property. ☎ *055/58–24–43* ⏲ *Mon.–Thurs. and Sat., 8 am–noon and 2–5:30.*

★ **Cirque de Jaffar.** You'll need four-wheel drive to tackle the notoriously rough but spectacular 80-km (48-mi) loop through the Cirque de Jaffar, a verdant cedar forest running around the Ayachi peak's lower slopes. The 12,257-foot **Djebel Ayachi,** the dominant terrain feature in the Atlas Mountains south of Midelt, was long thought to be Morocco's highest peak before Djebel Toubkal, south of Marrakesh, was found to be 13,668 feet. The view of this snowcapped (from December to March) behemoth from the eponymous hotel's roof is inspiring. If you have time for serious exploration, the 130-km (78-mi) loop around Boumia and Tounfite will take you across the immense Plateau de l'Arid, through the gorges of the upper Moulouya river valley, and into the Cirque de Jaffar on your way back into Midelt. Seasoned adventurers with four-wheel drive might be tempted to bivouac in the Cirque de Jaffar and climb Djebel Ayachi. After that, the route over to Tounfite on the right fork of Route 3424 is another exotic journey. Even more rugged still is the left fork, Route 3425, over the 10,749-foot Djebel Masker to Imilchil.

Gorges d'Aouli. Off the beaten track, a digression from Midelt takes you to the silver and lead mines at the Gorges d'Aouli, a 24-km (14-mi) round-trip negotiable by a standard car. Formed by the Oued Moulouya—Morocco's longest river, flowing all the way to the Mediterranean—the gorges are sheer rock walls cut through the steppe.

WHERE TO EAT AND STAY

¢ MOROCCAN ✕ **Restaurant de Fes.** This small restaurant offers delicious Moroccan dishes, including tasty vegetarian tajines and seven different salads. ✉ *2, av. Mohammed V, Midelt* ☎ *No phone.*

¢ **Kasbah Asmaa Midelt.** Mountains and gardens encircle this 19th-century hotel built in the kasbah style a few miles from Midelt center. **Pros:** large pool; convenient stopover; friendly staff. **Cons:** some rooms may be shabby; no phones or Wi-Fi; attracts large bus tour groups. ✉ *Rte. De Er Rachidia* ☎ *0535/58–04–05* 📠 *0535/58–39–45* *30 rooms, 5 junior suites* *In-room: a/c. In-hotel: restaurant, bar, pool, parking* *No credit cards* *Breakfast.*

5

Marrakesh

WORD OF MOUTH

"The square in Marrakesh, the Djemaâ el-Fna, is a sight in and of itself. What is so remarkable is the transformation that takes place in the evening. One must visit in the afternoon as well as nighttime to view this spectacle. It is truly Morocco at its best."

—Lolo12

WELCOME TO MARRAKESH

TO PALMERY (SEE INSET AT RIGHT)
0 1 miles
0 1 kilometers
GUÉLIZ
VILLE NOUVELLE
HIVERNAGE
Blvd. de Safi
Majorelle Garden
Blvd. Allal el Fassi
Ave. Moulay Abdallah
Ave. Mohammed V
Rue des Nations Unies
Place du 16 November
Ave. Hassan II
Rue Cadi Ayad
Rue de Bab Doukkala
Place de la Liberté
El Harti Gardens
Ave. Mohammed VI
Ave. Moulay El Hassan
Blvd. El Yarmouk
Rue Echouada
Rue Hafid Ibrahim
Rue Abou El Abbas Sebti
Jardins de la Koutoubia
Ave. Bab Jdid
Ave. de la Ménara
Place de la Jeunesse
Ave. Gmassa
Route du Barrage

TOP REASONS TO GO

★ **Djemaâ el-Fna:** Wander amid the sizzle and smoke of the world's most exuberant marketplace.

★ **Souk shopping:** Lose yourself (literally) in the alluring lanes of the bizarre bazaars of the souk and the city.

★ **Authentic accommodations:** Stay in a riad and sip mint tea in the airy confines of your bougainvillea-filled courtyard haven.

★ **Historic sights:** Step back in time to the elaborate tombs and palaces of the Saadian sultans, and the calm and beauty of the intricate medersa.

★ **Dance till dawn:** From intimate clubs with belly dancers and sheesha pipes, to full-on techno raves with international DJs, Marrakesh is the hedonistic capital of Morocco.

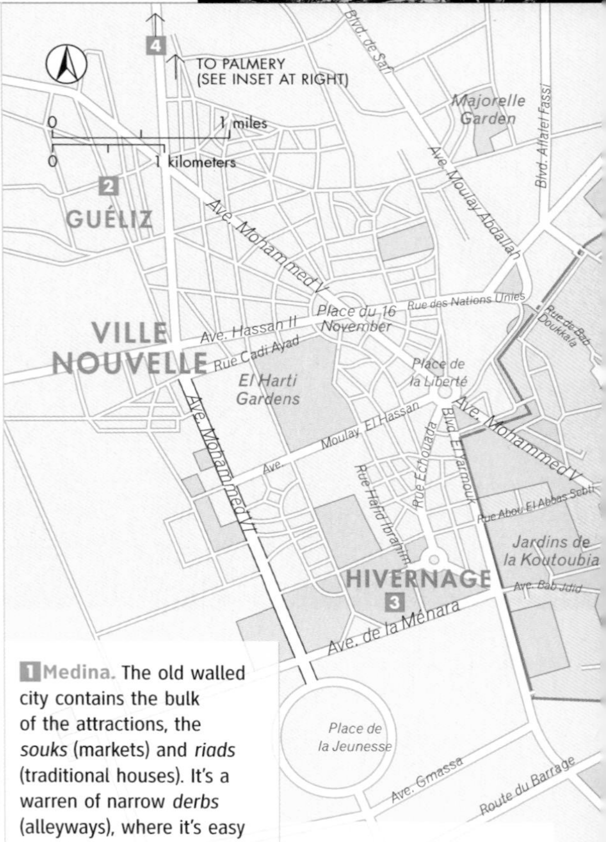

1 Medina. The old walled city contains the bulk of the attractions, the *souks* (markets) and *riads* (traditional houses). It's a warren of narrow *derbs* (alleyways), where it's easy to get lost.

2 Guéliz. Northwest of the medina, Guéliz is the modern administrative center, home to the tourist information office, numerous tour agencies, fashionable boutiques, art galleries, cafés, and restaurants; Avenue Mohammed V runs down its spine.

3 Hivernage. Hivernage is the area to the southwest of the ramparts, south of Avenue Hassan II and Avenue Mohammed V, and is populated largely with upmarket hotels and nightclubs. Its long, tree-lined boulevards stretch out to the Agdal and Menara gardens.

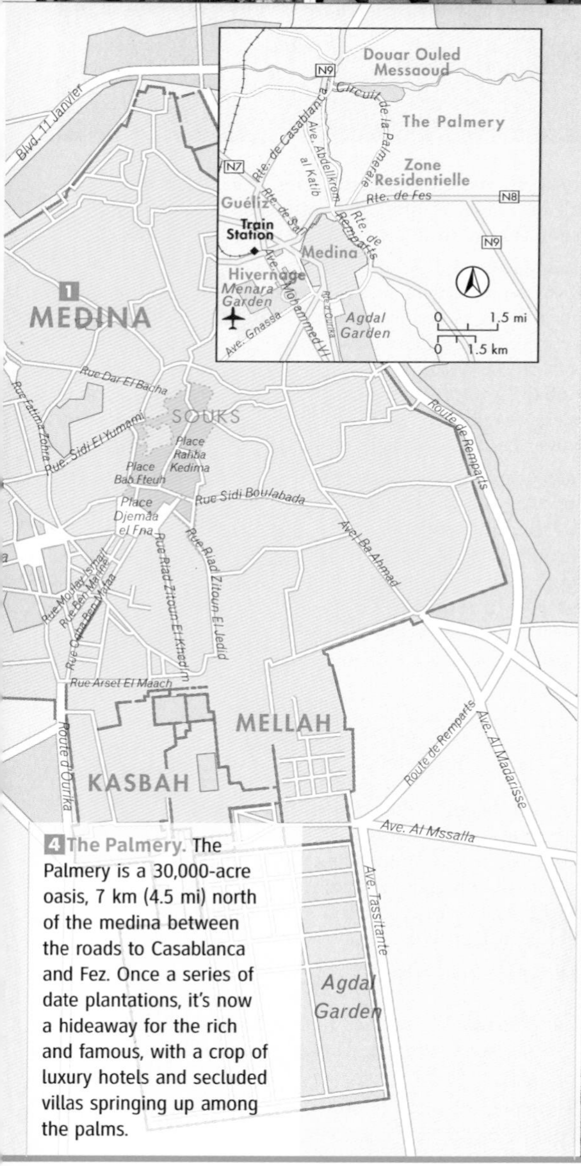

GETTING ORIENTED

Negotiating the twisting and turning alleys deep in the medina is a voyage in itself. If you don't hire a guide, keep a guidebook or at least a map with you at all times. The medina, although not quite as enclosed and intense as the one in Fez, takes some patience—street names are often signposted only in Arabic. A small street is called a *rue* in French or a *zencat* in Arabic; an even smaller alley is called a *derb*. If you get lost, keep walking and you'll eventually end up at one of the 14 original *babs* (arched gates) that lead in and out of this ancient quarter. Guéliz, in comparison, is easy to navigate. The wide streets are signposted in French and lined with orange and jacaranda trees, office buildings, modern stores, and a plethora of sidewalk cafés.

1 MEDINA

4 The Palmery. The Palmery is a 30,000-acre oasis, 7 km (4.5 mi) north of the medina between the roads to Casablanca and Fez. Once a series of date plantations, it's now a hideaway for the rich and famous, with a crop of luxury hotels and secluded villas springing up among the palms.

Updated by Rachel Blech

Marrakesh is Morocco's most intoxicating city. Ever since Morocco's Jewel of the South became a trading and resting place on the ancient caravan routes from Timbuktu, the city has barely paused for breath.

Lying low and dominating the Haouz Plain at the foot of the snow-capped High Atlas Mountains (a marvelous sight on a sunny day), the city was stubbornly defended against marauding tribes by successive sultans. They maintained their powerful dynasties and surveyed their fertile lands from the Menara Garden's tranquil olive groves and lagoon, and the Agdal Gardens' vast orchards. Today, exploring the city has never been easier. A crackdown on hustlers who hassle means that you're freer than ever before to wander and wonder.

The medina is Marrakesh's miracle—a happy clash of old and new, both beguiling and confusing in turn. Virtually unchanged since the Middle Ages, Marrakesh's solid salmon-pink ramparts encircle and protect its mysterious labyrinthine medina, hiding palaces, mansions, and bazaars. Pedestrians struggle to find their balance on the tiny cobbled lanes among an endless run of mopeds, donkey carts, and wheelbarrows selling a mixture of sticky sweets and saucepans. But pick up your jaw, take your time, and take it all in, stewing in the Rose City like a mint leaf in a pewter teapot.

PLANNING

WHEN TO GO

Marrakesh can get surprisingly cold in the winter and after the sun goes down. Although the sun shines almost year-round, the best time to visit is in spring, when the surrounding hills and valleys are an explosion of colorful flowers, and fall, when the temperature is comfortable enough to warrant sunbathing. The only exception in that period is during Easter week, which brings crowds.

GETTING HERE AND AROUND

BY AIR

Menara Airport in Marrakesh receives both domestic flights as well as international connections from the United States, Europe, and the Middle East.

The trip from the airport to town is only 15 minutes by car, taxi, or bus. The No. 19 public bus from the airport stops at the Place Djemaâ el-Fna and continues through to Guéliz serving most of the main hotels along Avenue Mohammed V and Avenue Mohammed VI (cost 20 DH). The standard charge for a run into the medina in *petits taxis* (small taxis that serve the city and its suburbs) starts at about 100 DH during the daytime and 150 DH after dark, but you will have to negotiate.

BY BUS

Intercity buses all leave from Marrakesh. Use the *gare routière* at Bab Doukkala for national public buses, or the Supratours or Compagnie du Transports au Maroc (CTM) bus stations in Guéliz. Buses arrive to the *gare routière* from Casablanca, Rabat, Fez, Agadir, Ouarzazate, and other cities. CTM or Supratours buses have their own terminals, but also stop at the gare routière. They are quicker and more comfortable than public buses to most key destinations. Supratours, which has its office next door to the train station on Avenue Hassan II, links up with Morocco's train network, with bus routes to destinations south and west of Marrakesh.

Within Marrakesh, frequent public buses run all over town; fares are approximately 3 DH.

Bus Contacts Compagnie de Transports au Maroc ✉ *Gare Routière, Bab Doukkala* ☎ *0524/43–42–44* ✉ *Rue Abou Bakr Seddiq, near Theatre Royal, Guéliz* ☎ *0524/44–83–28* 🌐 *www.ctm.ma.* **Supratours** ✉ *Ave. Hassan II, near train station, Guéliz* ☎ *0524/43–55–25* 🌐 *www.supratours.ma.*

BY CALÈCHE

Calèches are green, canopied, horse-drawn carriages that hold four to five people. Even if they do scream "tourist," they're a great way to reach your evening meal, and children love riding up front beside the driver. They're also picture-perfect for trips out to enjoy the Majorelle, Menara, and Agdal gardens. You should always agree on a price beforehand, but keep in mind that rides generally cost a minimum of 150 DH per hour; trips to the Palmery might cost 300 DH, and round-trip excursions (circling the ramparts, say) might cost 200 DH. There are two main pickup stops: one is in the medina, along the left side of the street stretching from the Djemaâ el-Fna to the Koutoubia Mosque; the other is in Guéliz, just south of the Place de la Liberté and west of Bab Nkob. You can also always try flagging one down.

BY CAR

Marrakesh is in Morocco's center, so it connects well by road with all other major destinations. Most of these roads are good, two-lane highways with hard, sandy shoulders for passing. There is a new freeway connecting Marrakesh to Casablanca and Agadir.

Within Marrakesh, driving isn't the best way to get around. Cars can pass through many of the medina's narrow alleys, but not all, and unless you know the lay of the land you risk getting suddenly stuck and being hard-pressed to perform a U-turn.

Rental Cars Amsterdam Cars ✉ *Appt. B, 112, av. Mohammed V, Guéliz* ☎ *0524/43–99–52, 0662/20–00–21* 🌐 *www.amsterdamcar.com.* **Avis** ✉ *137, av. Mohammed V, Guéliz* ☎ *0524/43–37–27.* **Europcar** ✉ *63, bd. Zerktouni, Guéliz* ☎ *0524/43–12–28.* **Hertz** ✉ *154, av. Mohammed V, Guéliz* ☎ *0524/43–13–94.*

Medloc ✉ *75, rue Ibn Aicha, 1st floor, No. 3, Guéliz* ☎ *0524/43–57–57* 🌐 *www.medloc-maroc.com.*

BY TAXI

Petits taxis in Marrakesh are small, beige, metered cabs permitted to transport three passengers. A petit taxi ride from one end of Marrakesh to the other costs around 20 DH. *Grands* taxis are the ubiquitous old Mercedes and other large four-doors and have two uses. Most often they simply take a load of up to six passengers on short hauls to suburbs and nearby towns, forming a reliable, inexpensive network throughout each region of Morocco. They can also be chartered for private hire for excursions and airport transfers.

BY TRAIN

Marrakesh is connected by good train service to Tangier, Rabat, Casablanca, and Fez. The train station is located on Avenue Mohammed VI at the junction with Avenue Hassan II in Guéliz and is Morocco's main southern terminus. Advance reservations can be made for first class only. Trains leave for Tangier five times a day; trains to Casablanca leave nine times a day.

Train Contacts ONCF ✉ *Av. Mohammed VI, at Av. Hassan II, Guéliz* ☎ *0890/20–30–40* 🌐 *www.oncf.ma.*

GUIDES AND TOURS

Guides can be helpful when navigating the medina's serpentine streets. They can point out little-known landmarks and help you understand the city's complicated history. You are best off booking a licensed guide through a tour company, and your hotel's staff will be able to suggest one to suit your interests. Although guides can be very knowledgeable about the city, don't rely on them for shopping. Store owners will inflate prices in order to give the guides kickbacks. The going rate for a city guide is 300 DH for a half day, 500 DH for a full day.

If you want a top-notch private guide for Marrakesh, you can't beat English-speaking Mohammed Lahcen. Having grown up in the valley, his knowledge of the region is unsurpassed. Likewise, the amiable Said el-Fougasse has encyclopedic knowledge of Marrakesh's secret treasures and Moroccan history, and he is a qualified guide for both city and nationwide destinations. Legendes Evasions is a highly respected local agency that runs chauffeured vehicle tours to some of the Berber villages around Marrakesh. Sahara Expedition is a budget agency that runs daily excursions and tours throughout the region, including Ourika Valley and Essaouira day trips as well as three-day sprints to the desert at Zagora and Merzouga. SheherazadVentures is an English-Moroccan company with an ethical conscience; based in Marrakesh, the company organizes tailor-made cultural trips to the Sahara, working in partnership with nomads from the region. The Conseil Regional du Tourisme office near the Koutoubia Mosque has maps, brochures, and general tourist information for Marrakesh and the surrounding area.

Tour Companies and Guides Brigade Touristique (Tourist Police) ✉ *Rue Sidi Mimoune, south of Koutoubia Mosque* ☎ *0524/38–46–01.* **Conseil Régional du Tourisme** ✉ *Place Youssef Ibn Tachfine, opposite Koutoubia*

Gardens, Medina ☎ *0524/38–52–61.* **Legendes Evasions** ✉ *Galerie Elite, 212, av. Mohammed V, 1st Floor, Guéliz* ☎ *0524/33–24–83* 🌐 *www.legendesevasions.com.* **Mohammed Lahcen** ☎ *0661/33–81–02* ✍ *bab_adrar@hotmail.com.* **Office National Marocain du Tourisme** ✉ *Place Abdel Moumen Ben Ali, at Av. Mohammed V, opposite Les Negoçiants café, Guéliz* ☎ *0524/43–61–31.* **Sahara Expedition** ✉ *Corner of Rue el-Mouahidine and Bani Marine, Medina* ☎ *0524/42–97–47* 🌐 *www.saharaexpe.ma.* **Said El Fagousse** ☎ *0662/02–47–04* ✍ *moroccotourguide@gmail.com.* **SheherazadVentures** ✉ *Appt. 55, Residence Ali (C), Av. Mohammed VI, near Café Csar, Guéliz* ☎ *0615/64–79–18* 🌐 *www.sheherazadventures.com.*

BEST MARRAKESH MAP

A highly detailed map is key to finding your way around Marrakesh. The best one is "Marrakesh Evasions," subtitled "La Carte." It's particularly helpful because it marks key riads, hotels, restaurants, and bars, as well as monuments, landmarks, and transportation hubs. It should cost no more than 20 DH, and is widely available at newsstands, bookstores, and tobacco shops.

5

SAFETY

Like other Moroccan cities, Marrakesh is quite safe. While women—particularly those traveling alone or in pairs—are likely to suffer from catcalls and whistles, there is generally little physical risk. The city does have its fair share of pickpockets, especially in markets and other crowded areas; handbags should be zippered and held beneath an arm, and wallets placed in front pockets. The old city shuts down relatively early, so don't wander its dark alleys late at night. The Moroccan Tourist Police take their jobs very seriously, so don't hesitate to call on them.

EXPLORING MARRAKESH

Most of the medina's monuments charge an entry fee of 10 DH to 40 DH and have permanent but unsalaried on-site guides; if you use one, tip him about 30 DH–50 DH.

MEDINA

If you can see the ramparts, you're either just inside or just outside the medina. In some respects not much has changed here since the Middle Ages. The medina is still a maze of narrow cobblestone streets lined with thick-walled, interlocked houses; designed to confuse invaders, the layout now serves much the same purpose for visitors. Donkeys and mules still deliver produce, wood, and wool to their destinations, and age-old crafts workshops still flourish as retail endeavors.

TOP ATTRACTIONS

Fodor's Choice ★ **Ali ben Youssef Medersa.** If you want a little breath taken out of you, don't pass up the chance to see this extraordinarily well-preserved 16th-century Koranic school, North Africa's largest such institution. The delicate intricacy of the *gibs* (stucco plasterwork), carved cedar, and *zellij* (mosaic) on display in the central courtyard makes the building seem to

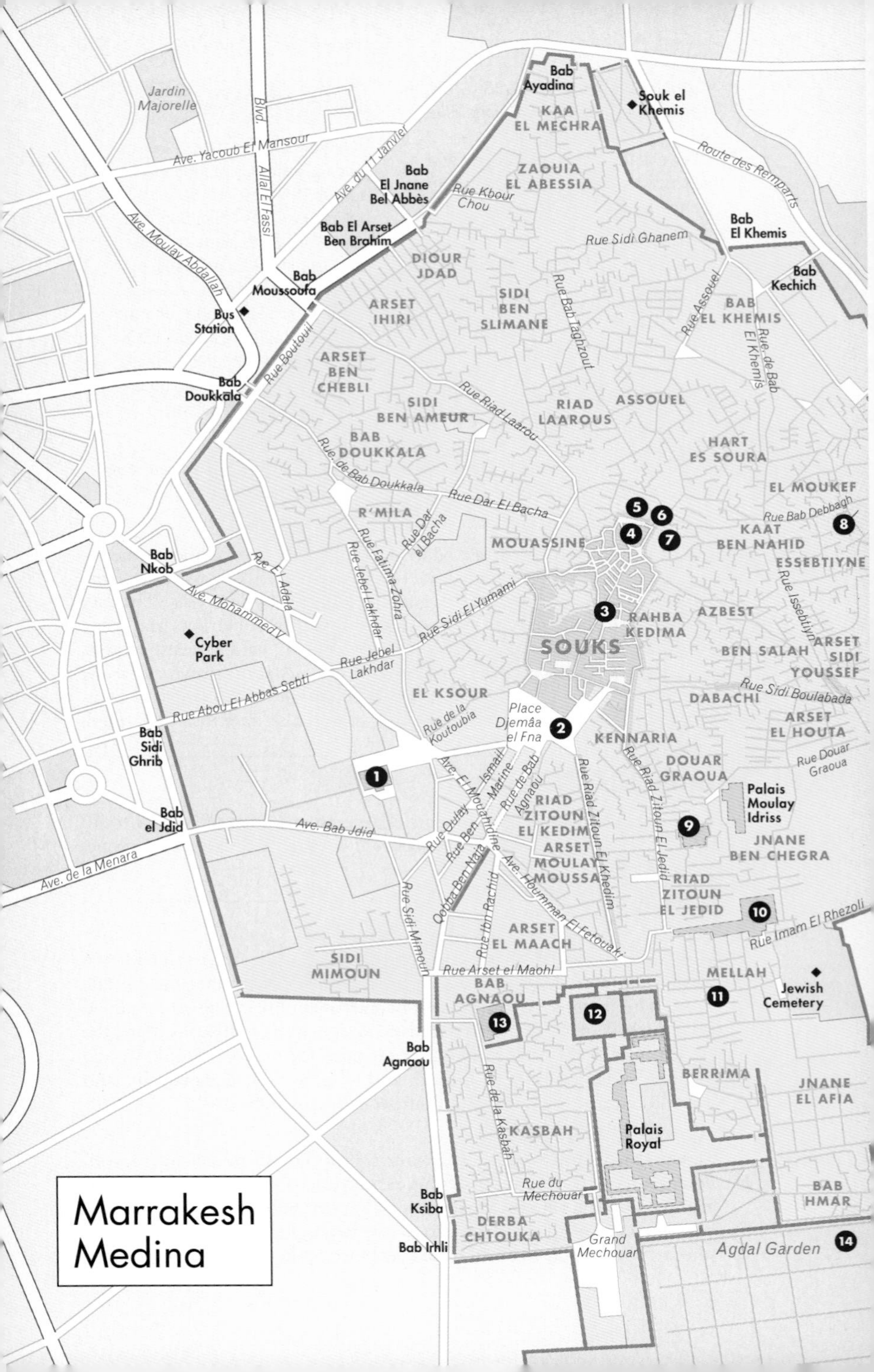
Marrakesh Medina
Jardin Majorelle
Blvd. Allal El Fassi
Ave. Yacoub El Mansour
Ave. du 11 Janvier
Ave. Moulay Abdallah
Bab Ayadina
KAA EL MECHRA
Souk el Khemis
ZAOUIA EL ABESSIA
Route des Remparts
Bab El Jnane Bel Abbès
Rue Kbour Chou
Bab El Arset Ben Brahim
Bab El Khemis
Rue Sidi Ghanem
DIOUR JDAD
Bab Moussoufa
Bab Kechich
Bus Station
ARSET IHIRI
SIDI BEN SLIMANE
Rue Bab Taghzout
Rue Assouel
BAB EL KHEMIS
Rue de Bab El Khemis
Rue Boutouil
ARSET BEN CHEBLI
Bab Doukkala
Rue Riad Laarou
SIDI BEN AMEUR
RIAD LAAROUS
ASSOUEL
BAB DOUKKALA
HART ES SOURA
Rue de Bab Doukkala
Rue Dar El Bacha
EL MOUKEF
R'MILA
Rue Bab Debbagh
Rue Dar el Bacha
KAAT BEN NAHID
MOUASSINE
Bab Nkob
Rue El Adala
Rue Fatima Zohra
Rue Jebel Lakhdar
ESSEBTIYNE
Ave. Mohammed V
Rue Issebtiyn
RAHBA KEDIMA
AZBEST
Rue Sidi El Yumami
Cyber Park
SOUKS
BEN SALAH
ARSET SIDI YOUSSEF
Rue Jebel Lakhdar
Rue Abou El Abbas Sebti
EL KSOUR
DABACHI
Rue Sidi Boulabada
Place Djemâa el Fna
Rue de la Koutoubia
ARSET EL HOUTA
Bab Sidi Ghrib
KENNARIA
Rue Douar Graoua
Rue Riad Zitoun El Khedim
Rue Riad Zitoun El Jedid
DOUAR GRAOUA
Palais Moulay Idriss
Ave. El Mouahidine
Rue Oulay Ismail
Rue Ben Marine
Rue de Bab Agnaou
RIAD ZITOUN EL KEDIM
Bab el Jdid
Ave. Bab Jdid
JNANE BEN CHEGRA
Ave. de la Menara
Rue Ben Naja
ARSET MOULAY MOUSSA
Ave. Houmman El Fetouaki
RIAD ZITOUN EL JEDID
Qobba Ben Naja
Rue Ibn Rachid
Rue Sidi Mimoun
ARSET EL MAACH
Rue Imam El Rhezoli
SIDI MIMOUN
Rue Arset el Maohl
MELLAH
BAB AGNAOU
Jewish Cemetery
Bab Agnaou
BERRIMA
JNANE EL AFIA
Rue de la Kasbah
KASBAH
Palais Royal
Rue du Mechouar
BAB HMAR
Bab Ksiba
DERBA CHTOUKA
Grand Mechouar
Bab Irhli
Agdal Garden
1
2
3
4
5
6
7
8
9
10
11
12
13
14

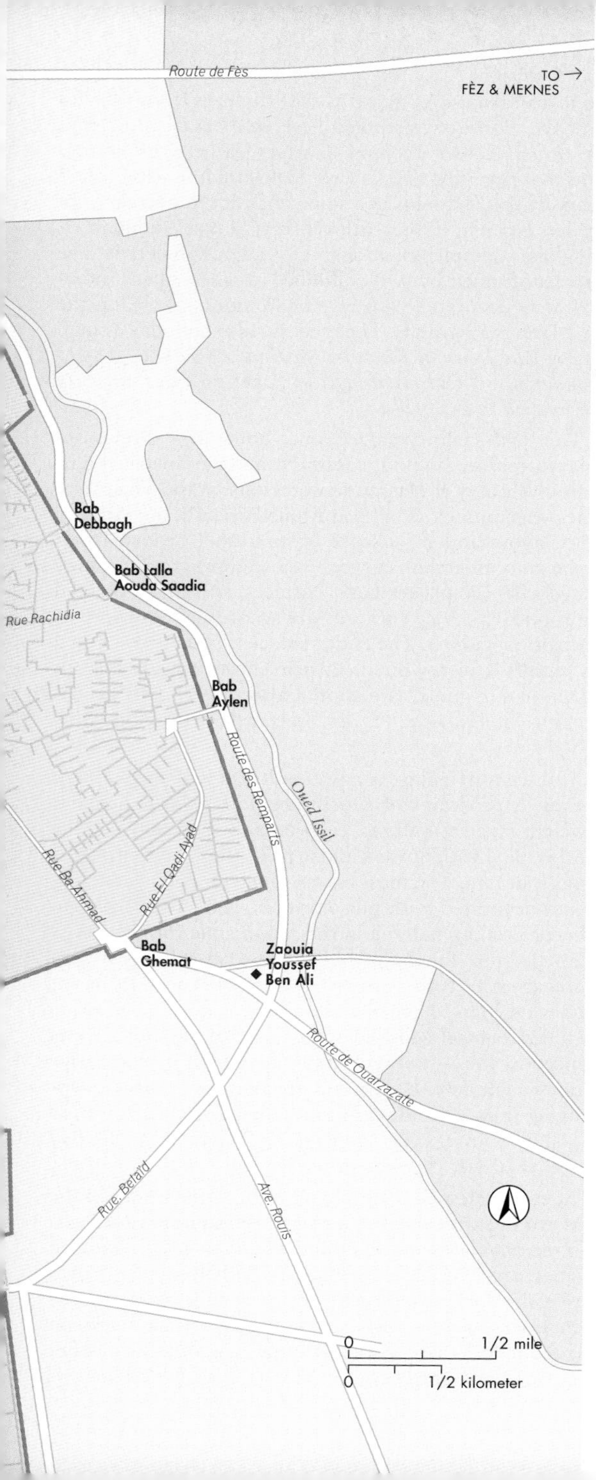

Agdal Garden **14**
Ali ben Youssef Medersa **6**
Ali ben Youssef Mosque **5**
Dar Si Saïd **9**
Djemaâ el Fna **2**
El Badi Palace **12**
Koutoubia Mosque **1**
La Bahia Palace **10**
Mellah **11**
Musée de Marrakesh **7**
Quobba Almoravid **4**
Saadian Tombs **13**
Souks **3**
Tanneries **8**

loom taller than it really does. As many as 900 students from Muslim countries all over the world once studied here, and arranged around the courtyard are their former sleeping quarters—a network of tiny upper-level rooms that resemble monks' cells. The building was erected in the 14th century by the Merenids in a somewhat different style from that of other medersas; later, in the 16th century, Sultan Abdullah el-Ghallib rebuilt it almost completely, adding the Andalusian details. The large main courtyard, framed by two columned arcades, opens into a prayer hall elaborately decorated with rare palm motifs as well as the more-customary Islamic calligraphy. The medersa also contains a small mosque. ✉ *Just off Rue Souk el Khemis, Medina* ☎ *0524/44–18–93* 🎫 *50 DH for medersa, 60 DH combination ticket includes museum and Qoubba Almoravid* ⏲ *Daily 9–6.*

La Bahia Palace. This 19th-century palace, once home to a harem, is a marvelous display of painted wood, ceramics, and symmetrical gardens. Built by Sultan Moulay el-Hassan I's notorious Grand Vizier Bou Ahmed, the palace was ransacked on Bou Ahmed's death, but you can still experience its layout and get a sense of its former beauty. Don't forget to look up at smooth arches, carved-cedar ceilings, *tadlak* (shiny marble) finishes, *gibs* (stucco plasterwork) cornices, and zouak painted ceilings. Fancy a room? Each one varies in size according to the importance of each wife or concubine. The entire palace is sometimes closed when the royal family is in town, since their entourage often stays here. If you use an on-site guide, you should also tip 30 DH–50 DH. ✉ *Av. Houmman el-Fetouki, near Pl. des Ferblantiers, Medina* 🎫 *10 DH* ⏲ *Daily 9–5.*

Dar Si Saïd. This 19th-century palace is now a museum with an excellent collection of antique Moroccan crafts including pottery from Safi and Tamegroute, jewelry, daggers, kaftans, carpets, and leatherwork. The palace's courtyard is filled with flowers and cypress trees, and furnished with a gazebo and fountain. The most extraordinary salon is upstairs; it's a somber room decorated with gibs cornices, zellij walls, and an amazing carved-cedar ceiling painted in the *zouak* style (bright colors in intricate patterns). Look for the prize exhibit, a marble basin with an inscription indicating its 10th-century Córdoban origin. The basin, which is sometimes on loan to other museums, was once given pride of place in the Ali ben Youssef Mosque in the north of the souk. It was brought to Morocco by the Almoravid sultan in spite of its decorative eagles and griffins, which defy the Koran's prohibition of artistic representations of living things. Guides are available on-site. ✉ *Rue Riad Zitoune El Jdid, 1st derb on right just up from La Bahia Palace, Medina* ☎ *0524/38–95–64* 🎫 *10 DH* ⏲ *Wed.–Mon., 9–5.*

Fodor's Choice ★ **Djemaâ el-Fna.** The carnivalesque open square right at the center of the medina is Marrakesh's heartbeat. This centuries-old square was once a meeting point for regional farmers and tradesmen; today it's surrounded by bazaars, mosques, and terraced cafés with perfect balcony views over the action. Transvestite dancers bat their eyelashes; cobras sway to the tones of snake charmers; henna women make their swirling marks on your hands; fortune-tellers reveal mottled futures; apothecaries offer bright powder potions and spices; bush dentists with Berber molars

The Ali ben Youssef Medersa was founded in the 14th century.

piled high on tables extract teeth; and, best of all, men tell stories to each other the old way, on a magic carpet around a gas lamp.

All day (and night) long you can get fresh orange or grapefruit juice from the green gypsy carts that line up round the square, for about 4 DH a glass. You can also buy a shot of cool water from one of the roving water sellers, whose eye-popping costumes carry leather water pouches and polished-brass drinking bowls. Or snack on sweet dates, apricots, bananas, almonds, sugarcoated peanuts, and walnuts from the dried-fruit-and-nut stalls in the northwest corner. Meat and vegetable grills cook into the night, when Marrakshis come out to eat, meet, and be entertained. It might be a fun bazaar today, but once upon a time the Djemaâ's purpose was more gruesome; it accommodated public viewings of the severed heads of sinners, criminals, and Christians. *Djemaâ* actually means "meeting place" and *el-Fna* means "the end" or "death," so as a whole it means something along the lines of "assembly of death" or "meeting place at the end of the world."

Fodor's Choice ★ **El Badi Palace.** This 16th-century palace was once a playground for Saadian princes and visiting diplomats—a mammoth showpiece for opulent entertaining. Today it's a romantic set of sandstone ruins, policed by nesting storks. Sultan Ahmed el-Mansour's lavish creation was ransacked by Moulay Ismail in the 17th century to help him complete his own palace at Meknès. But it's not hard to see why the palace, whose name translates as "The Marvel," was once among the world's most impressive monuments. A huge swimming pool in the center (still there today, but empty) is flanked by four others, along with four sunken orange orchards. The main hall was named the Koubba el Khamsiniyya,

The El Badi Palace, built by the Saadian sultans, is one of the largest structures in Marrakesh's medina.

referring to its 50 grand marble columns. Along the southern wall is a series of belowground corridors and underground dungeons. It's a vast, calm, and mystical place. Also on display is a collection of goods from the Minbar (pulpit from which the Imam gives services) of the Koutoubia Mosque. If you use an on-site guide (otherwise unpaid), who can bring the place to life, you should also tip 30 DH–50 DH. ✉ *Enter ramparts and enormous gateway near Pl. des Ferblantiers, Kasbah* ☎ *0524/37–81–63* 🎫 *10 DH for palace, 20 DH for palace and display of the Koutoubia Mosque Minbar* ⏲ *Daily 9–4:45.*

★ **Saadian Tombs.** This small, beautiful 16th-century burial ground is the permanent resting place of 166 Saadians, including its creator, Sultan Ahmed el-Mansour, the Golden One. True to his name, he did it in style—even those not in the lavish mausoleum have their own colorful zellij graves, laid out for all to see, among the palm trees and flowers. Because the infamous Moulay Ismail chose not to destroy them (he was apparently superstitious about plundering the dead), these tombs are one of the few Saadian relics left. He simply sealed them up, leaving only a small section open for use. The complex was rediscovered only in 1917 by General Hubert Lyautey during the French protectorate. Passionate about every aspect of Morocco's history, the general undertook the restoration of the tombs.

The central mausoleum, the **Hall of Twelve Columns,** contains the tombs of Ahmed el-Mansour and his family. It's dark, lavish, and ornate, with a huge vaulted roof, carved cedar doors and *moucharabia* (carved wooden screens traditionally used to separate the sexes), and gray Italian marble columns. In a smaller inner mausoleum, on the site of an earlier structure containing the decapitated body of the Saadian dynasty's founder, Mohammed esh Sheikh, is the tomb of El Mansour's mother. ■ TIP→ **Get here either early or late to avoid the crowds and to see the monuments swathed in soft golden light of a restful sun.** If you use one of the on-site guides (who are unpaid), you should tip 30 DH to 50 DH. ✉ *Rue de la Kasbah, across small square from mosque, Kasbah* 🎫 *10 DH* ⏲ *Daily 9–4:45.*

Fodor's Choice ★ **Souks.** The vast, labyrinth of narrow streets and derbs at the center of the medina is the souk—Marrakesh's marketplace and a wonder of arts, crafts, and workshops. Every step brings you face-to-face with the colorful handicrafts and bazaars for which Marrakesh is so famous. In the past, every craft had a special zone within the market—a souk within the souk. Today savvy vendors have pushed south to tap trading opportunities as early as possible, and few of the original sections remain. Look for incongruities born of the modern era. Beside handcrafted wooden pots for kohl eye makeup are modern perfume stores; where there is a world of hand-sewn djellabas at one turn, you'll find soccer jerseys after the next; fake Gucci caps sit beside handmade Berber carpets, their age-old tassels fluttering in the breeze.

■ TIP→ **As you wander through the souk, take note of landmarks so you can return to a particular bazaar without too much trouble. Once the bazaars' shutters are closed, they're often unrecognizable.** The farther north you go the more the lanes twist, turn, and entwine. Should you have to retrace your steps, a compass comes in handy, as does a mental count of how many left or right turns you've taken since you left the main drag. But mostly you'll rely on people in the souk to point the way. If you ask a shopkeeper, rather than a loitering local you'll be less likely to be "guided." ✉ *North of Place Djemaâ el-Fna, Medina.*

NEED A BREAK?

Chez Lamine Hadj Mustapha. English TV chef, Jamie Oliver, chose this spit-and-sawdust street restaurant in a filming trip for a gutsy example of Moroccan roast lamb speciality, *mechoui*—and it's not every day you walk past a whole lamb being cooked. Follow a tiny street that leads off the Djemaâ el-Fna (to the left of Les Terrasses de l'Alhambra) and you'll see exactly that. Although the row of upstanding severed lambs' heads set upon tagines may not be everyone's idea of culinary heaven, Marrakshis love Chez Lamine Hadj Mustapha, and you'd be missing out not to try it. Ask to see the oven—a hole in the ground where the entire animal is cooked over hot wood ash. The meat is then hauled up and cut in front of you, served with bread for a cheap 20 DH sandwich, or for larger amounts at 140 DH per kilogram. If you're nervous, ask for a small taste first. However much you have, sprinkle the meat with a delicious cumin-and-salt spice mix and wash it all down with mint tea. Get there before noon. ✉ *Souk Ablouh, 18–26* ☎ *0661/39–84–28.*

WORTH NOTING

Agdal Garden. Some say dull scrub; others, pinnacle of romance. Stretching a full 3 km (2 mi) south of the Royal Palace, the Jardin de l'Aguedal comprises vast orchards, a large lagoon, and other small pools, all fed by an impressive, ancient system of underground irrigation channels from the Ourika Valley in the High Atlas. The entire garden is surrounded by high *pisé* (a mixture of mud and clay) walls, and the olive, fig, citrus, pomegranate, and apricot orchards are still in their original raised-plot form. The largest lagoon, the grandiose Tank of Health, is said to be the 12th-century creation of an Almohad prince, but, as with most Moroccan historic sites, the Agdal was consecutively abandoned and rebuilt—the latest resurrection dates from the 19th century. Until the French protectorate's advent, it was the sultans' retreat of choice for lavish picnics and boating parties. **■TIP→ If you're here on a clear day, don't miss the magic and majesty of a 180-degree turn, from facing the Koutoubia Mosque (northwest) to facing the Atlas Mountains (southeast).** ✉ *Medina* ✣ *Approach via Méchouar; or from outside the ramparts, walk left on Rue Bab Irhli and the garden will be on your right* ⏲ *Fri. and Sun., 9–6.*

Ali ben Youssef Mosque. After the Koutoubia, this is the medina's largest mosque and Marrakesh's oldest. The building was first constructed in the second half of the 12th century by the Almoravid sultan Ali ben Youssef, around the time of the Qoubba Almoravid. In succeeding centuries it was destroyed and rebuilt several times by the Almohads and the Saadians, who changed its size and architecture accordingly; it was last overhauled in the 19th century, in the then-popular Merenid style. Non-Muslims may not enter. ✉ *Just off Rue Souk el-Khemis, next to Ali ben Youssef Medersa, Medina.*

NEED A BREAK?

Café Palais El Badi. One rule of thumb is that every old Marrakshi monument has a café nearby to rest your feet in after all those historical exertions. The Café Palais El Badi is a cheap and popular lunch spot (the 80 DH menu includes *kefta [beef patties]* and tagine). It's a pretty, wrought-iron terrace overlooking both the palace and the Place des Ferblantiers. Look, too, for the gracious storks nesting opposite. ✉ *4, rue Touareg, Bab Berrima, Mellah, Medina* ☎ *0524/38–99–75.*

Koutoubia Mosque. Yacoub el-Mansour built Marrakesh's towering Moorish mosque on the site of the original 11th-century Almoravid mosque. Dating from the early 12th century, it became a model for the Hassan Tower in Rabat and the Giralda in Seville. The mosque takes its name from the Arabic word for book, *koutoub,* because there was once a large booksellers' market nearby. The minaret is topped by three golden orbs, which, according to one local legend, were offered by the mother of the Saadian sultan Ahmed el-Mansour Edhabi in penance for fasting days she missed during Ramadan. The mosque has a large plaza, walkways, and gardens, as well as floodlights to illuminate its curved windows, a band of ceramic inlay, pointed *merlons* (ornamental edgings), and various decorative arches. Although non-Muslims may not enter, anyone within earshot will be moved by the power of the evening muezzin call. ✉ *South end of Ave. Mohammed V, Medina.*

Mellah. As in other Moroccan cities, the mellah is the old Jewish quarter, once a small, walled-off city within the city. Although it was once home to a thriving community of native and Spanish Jews, along with rabbinical schools and scholars, today, it's home to only a few Jewish inhabitants. You can visit the remains of a couple of synagogues with the help of an official guide. The mellah gets it's name from the Arabic word for salt, as many of the Jewish residents here were wealthy salt traders. ✉ *Medina.*

Musée de Marrakesh. The main reason to come to this small but perfectly formed museum next door to the Ali ben Youssef Medersa is not the exhibitions, but rather the stunning central atrium, a tiled courtyard containing a huge lampshade that resembles a UFO descending. This is a perfect place to relax while enjoying Moroccan architecture and gentle strains of guitar music piped through speakers. The temporary exhibitions in the courtyard are often of beautiful artifacts and paintings (some for sale), but they're poorly displayed and lack English translations. The museum also has a good bookstore and a café. ■ TIP→ **The toilets are spotless and worth the admission price if you find yourself far from your hotel.** ✉ *Place ben Youssef, Medina* ☎ *0524/44–18–93* 🎫 *40 DH for museum, 60 DH combination ticket includes Ali ben Youssef Medersa and Qoubba Almoravid* ⏲ *Daily 9–6.*

Qoubba Almoravid. This is the city's oldest monument and the only intact example of Almoravid architecture in all of Morocco (the few other ruins include some walls here in Marrakesh and a minaret in El Jadida). Dating from the 12th century, this masterpiece of mechanical waterworks somehow escaped destruction by the Almohads. It was once used not only for ablutions before prayer in the next-door Ali ben Youssef Mosque (relying on the revolutionary hydraulics of *khatteras*, drainage systems dug down into the water table), and also had a system of toilets, showers, and faucets for drinking water. It was only excavated from the rubble of the original Ali ben Youssef Mosque and Medersa in 1948. You can scramble around at your leisure. 🎫 *60 DH combination ticket includes Musée de Marrakesh and Ali ben Youssef Medersa* ⏲ *Daily 9–6.*

Ramparts. The medina's amazingly well-preserved walls measure about 33 feet high and 7 feet thick, and are 15 km (9 mi) in circumference. Until the early 20th century, before the French protectorate, the gates were closed at night to prevent anyone who didn't live in Marrakesh from entering. Eight of the 14 original *babs* (arched entry gates) leading in and out of the medina are still in use. Bab Agnaou, in the kasbah, is the loveliest and best preserved of the arches. ■ TIP→ **The best time to visit the walls is just before 7 pm, when the swallows that nest in the ramparts' holes come out to take their evening meal.** A leisurely calèche drive around the perimeter takes about an hour.

Tanneries. For a whiff of Marrakesh life the old way, the tanneries are a real eye-waterer, not least because of the smell of acrid pigeon excrement, which provides the ammonia that is vital to the dyeing process. The method relies on natural dyes such as wild mint, saffron, cinnamon, and henna. Six hundred skins sit in a vat at any one time, resting there for up to two months amid constant soaping, scrubbing, and polishing. Goat and sheepskins are popular among Berbers, while Arab dye-masters rely on camels and cows and tend to use more machine processes and chemical dyes.

IN THE KNOW

For the Real McCoy, visit Berber tannery El Guezmiri, a door on the right and the fourth tannery you come across when arriving from the southwest. Soulimane, the kind manager, can guide you around with expertise. There's also a boutique at the end where you can buy the wares more cheaply than in the souk. Look for No. 84, Chez Abdel Jalil.

Thirteen tanneries, mixing both Berber and Arab elements, are still in operation in the Bab Debbagh area in the northeast of the medina. Simply turn up at Rue de Bab Debbagh and look for the tannery signs above several open doorways to both the right and left of the street. To visit one of them, just pop in and the local manager will offer you mint leaves to cover the smell, explain the process, and guide you around the vats of dyes. In return he'll hope for a healthy tip to share with his workers; this is a dying art in a poor dyeing area, so the more you can tip, the better.

■ TIP→ **Finding the Rue de Bab Debbagh can be frustrating; it's easier to approach via taxi from outside the ramparts and be dropped off at Bab Debbagh, or to ask an official guide to include the visit as part of a set itinerary. Once in the vicinity, you'll be inundated with offers from would-be guides to take you to there and who will then ask for money. Solo travelers should exercise caution.**

GUÉLIZ AND HIVERNAGE

In addition to office buildings and contemporary shops—none of which may exceed the nearest mosque's height—Guéliz has plenty of sidewalk cafés, international restaurants, upscale boutiques, and antiques stores.

TOP ATTRACTIONS

Fodor's Choice ★ **Majorelle Garden.** The Jardin Majorelle was created by the French painter Louis Majorelle, who lived in Marrakesh between 1922 and 1962. It then passed into the hands of another Marrakesh lover, the late fashion designer Yves Saint Laurent. If you've just come from the desert, it's a sight for sore eyes, with green-bamboo thickets, little streams, and an electric blue gazebo. There's also a villa housing a small Islamic art museum with regular exhibitions, a nice museum shop, and a delightful café. ✉ *Av. Yacoub el-Mansour, main entrance on side street, Guéliz* ☎ *0524/30–18–52* 🎫 *Garden 40 DH, museum 25 DH additional* ⏲ *Daily 8–6:30.*

The Majorelle Gardens were most famously owned by the French designer Yves Saint Laurent.

WORTH NOTING

Marché Central. The once-thriving Central Market in Guéliz has recently been moved from its old home on Avenue Mohammed V to nearby Rue Ibn Toumert to make way for a massive shopping-mall development. The market can now be found opposite the Gendarmerie Royale behind Marrakesh Plaza. It's much more low-key, but still is a favorite place for locals and expats to shop for meat, fish, fruits, flowers, and vegetables. There's also some interesting craft shops. ✉ *Rue Ibn Toumert, opposite the Gendarmerie Royale, Guéliz.*

Menara Garden. The Menara's lagoon and villa-style pavilion are ensconced in an immense royal olive grove, where pruners and pickers putter and local women fetch water from the nearby stream, said to give *baraka* (good luck). A popular rendezvous for Marrakshis, the garden is a peaceful retreat. The elegant pavilion—or *minzah,* meaning "beautiful view"—was created in the early 19th century by Sultan Abd er-Rahman, but it's believed to occupy the site of a 16th-century Saadian structure. In winter and spring snowcapped Atlas peaks in the background appear closer than they are; and, if you are lucky, you might see green or black olives gathered from the trees from October through January. ✉ *Hivernage* ✣ *From Bab el-Djedid, the garden is about 2 km (1.3 mi) down Av. de la Menara* ⏲ *Daily 8–6.*

WHERE TO EAT

Marrakesh has arguably the best selection of restaurants in Morocco; as a group they serve equal parts Moroccan and international cuisine. Restaurant dining, however, is a relatively new phenomenon for Moroccans, who see eating out as somewhat of a shame on the household. Even the wealthiest Marrakshis would prefer to invite friends over to sample home cooking than to go out for the evening. A treat is to spend an evening at one of Marrakesh's popular riad restaurants in the medina. These will give you an idea (albeit a rather expensive one) of traditional yet sumptuous Moroccan entertaining.

You can also eat well at inexpensive sidewalk cafés in both the medina and Guéliz. Here, don't miss out on a famous local dish called *tangia,* made popular by workers who slow-cook lamb or beef in an earthenware pot left in hot ashes for the whole day.

Restaurants in Marrakesh tend to fall into two categories. They're either fashionable, flashy affairs, mostly in Guéliz and the outlying areas of Marrakesh, which serve à la carte European and Moroccan cuisine, or they're more-traditional places, often tucked inconspicuously into already-out-of-the-way places in the medina. Both types can be fairly pricey, and, to avoid disappointment, are best booked in advance. They also tend to open quite late, usually not before 7:30 in Guéliz and 8 in the medina, although most people don't sit down to eat until 9 or 9:30.

There's no set system for tipping. Your check will indicate that service has been included in the charge; if not, tip 10% or 15% for excellent service.

WHAT IT COSTS IN DIRHAMS

	¢	$	$$	$$$	$$$$
AT DINNER	under 125 DH	125 DH–200 DH	201 DH–350 DH	351 DH–450 DH	over 450 DH

Prices are per person for a main course at dinner.

MEDINA

$$$ MOROCCAN

Al Baraka. It's easy to fancy yourself one of Morocco's 19th-century elite in this grand, white-tile riad, once home to the pasha. Set menus for different budgets feature traditional *briouates* (spicy dumplings) as well as tagines and couscous. You have the choice of dining on brocade divans in the salon or in the enormous courtyard filled with orange trees, musicians, and the odd belly dancer. ✉ *1, Djemaâ el-Fna, next to Commissariat de Police, Medina* ☎ *0524/44–23–41* 🌐 *www.albaraka-marrakech.com* ✥ *E3.*

$ MOROCCAN

Café Arabe. This three-story restaurant in the heart of the medina is a happening place by day and by night. Homemade pastas are on offer at this Italian-owned place, but main courses also include grilled swordfish, lamb, and beef. This is a great choice for both lunch and dinner. The lantern-lighted terrace, complete with a trickling fountain, is a good place to stop for drinks. ✉ *184, rue el Mouassine, Medina* ☎ *0524/42–97–28* 🌐 *www.cafearabe.com* ✣ *E2.*

¢ CAFÉ ✕ **Café des Épices.** In the medina's spice market, this little café is a surprisingly glamorous and modern affair. It teeters over three levels, and has a great rooftop view over the spice square below. Suitably enough, it offers spiced tea and cinnamon coffee along with a good complement of drinks and light meals. For dinner, you may wish to check out new additions to the expanding "Des Épices" label, including "La Terrasse des Épices" and the vegetarian-friendly "Le Jardin des Épices," both in Souk Cherifia to the north of the café. ✉ *75, Rahba Lakdima, Medina* ☎ *0524/39–17–70* 🌐 *www.cafedesepices.net* ▭ *No credit cards* ✣ *F2.*

¢ MOROCCAN ✕ **Chez el Bahia.** It won't win prizes for design, but this cheap joint is perfect for a lunchtime pit stop. Locals and visitors alike frequent this friendly and atmospheric canteen just on the right before the road opens into Djemaâ el-Fna. Tagine pots stand two rows deep on the street stall outside, and a barbecue sizzles away. If you place your order in advance there are much more interesting specialties available, including spiced aubergine tagine and pastillas. ✉ *206, Riad Zitoune el Kdim, Medina* ☎ *0524/37–89–46* ▭ *No credit cards* ✣ *F4.*

$$$$ MOROCCAN Fodor's Choice ★ ✕ **Dar Marjana.** If you can only visit one of Marrakesh's traditional riad restaurants, make it this one. Cocktails featuring *mahia*—fig liqueur—are served on low-slung tables around a delightful courtyard. Then you move to salons (ask for the larger minzah) to recline on brocade divans and enjoy wave after wave of classic Moroccan cuisine. The couscous is impossibly fluffy, and if the lamb tagine came off the bone any easier it would be floating. To round this off, a troupe of lively Gnaoua musicians brings you to your senses before a belly dancer brings you to your feet. The fixed price includes an aperitif, wine with the meal, and an after-dinner drink. ✉ *15, Derb Sidi Tair, Bab Doukkala, opposite Dar el Basha, Medina* ☎ *0524/38–51–10* 🌐 *www.darmarjanamarrakech.com* *Reservations essential* ⏲ *Closed Tues. Closed Jul. No lunch* ✣ *D1.*

$$$$ MOROCCAN ✕ **Dar Moha.** This isn't the most stylish riad, but it has an established reputation for its fixed menu of *nouvelle cuisine marocaine*. Delicious adaptations of traditional dishes include a tiny melt-in-the-mouth *pastilla* (sweet pigeon pie) filled with a vegetable purée, and strawberries wrapped in wafer-thin pastry and rolled in ground almonds. Steer clear of the poky salons; head instead for the outside tables arranged around a small pool and shaded by lush banana palms. With the accompaniment of Andalusian lutes, these are where it's at. The fixed-price lunch is less than half the cost of dinner. ✉ *81, rue Dar el Bacha, Medina* ☎ *0524/38–64–00* 🌐 *www.darmoha.ma* ✣ *F1.*

$ MOROCCAN ✕ **Le Foundouk.** This French-run place hidden at the souk's northern tip is regularly booked with upscale tourists and expats, and is good for an intimate evening for two. The sunny rooftop garden is a good lunch or afternoon tea spot. A lighter terrace adorned with statues and masks from West Africa rounds out the dining-room options. Chic à la carte dishes include foie gras and fig tagine; for a lighter snack at lunchtime try a *croque-monsieur* (hot ham-and-cheese sandwich). The drawback is that it desperately wants you to know how seriously stylish it is. ✉ *55,*

Souk Hal Fassi, Kat Bennahid, near the Medersa Ben Youssef, Medina ☏ *0524/37–81–90* 🌐 *www.foundouk.com* ⏲ *Closed Mon.* ✥ *G1.*

¢ MOROCCAN ✕ **Haj Brik.** In a row of grill cafés on a narrow side street running south off Djemaâ el-Fna, Haj Brik is one of the best. Everything is prepared so well that it has been in business longer than most. The menu focuses on grilled lamb chops, merguez sausages, kefta, and kidneys, each served with bread, olives, tomato salad, and hot sauce. Everything cooks on an indoor grill at the front of the shop, sending billowing smoke and smells over the diners. ✉ *39, rue Bani Marine, through arch just left of post office in Djemaâ el-Fna, Medina* ☏ *No phone* ▭ *No credit cards* ✥ *E4.*

$ MOROCCAN ✕ **Le Marrakchi.** With zellij walls, painted cedar ceilings, and white tile floors, this old palace serves up good Moroccan cuisine with modern flair—and belly dancers thrown in. You can choose from the à la carte menu, or choose one of the set menus that begin at 280 DH. Book a table on the top floor for the panoramic view of the square. Service can be surly, and prices are rather high. ✉ *52, rue des Banques, just off Djemaâ el-Fna, Medina* ☏ *0524/44–33–77* ⏲ *No lunch* ✥ *F3.*

¢ MOROCCAN ✕ **Restaurant el Bahja.** This small, tiled medina café next door to Marrakesh institution Haj Brik is just as popular and has almost the same food at the same prices. You can also get beef and chicken tagines and, in winter, *loubia* (bean stew) or spicy lentils in addition to standard grill fare. ✉ *41, rue Bani Marine* ☏ *0524/44–03–43* ▭ *No credit cards* ✥ *E4.*

¢ MOROCCAN ✕ **Restaurant Tiznit.** Climb the narrow tiled stairway into this tiny little restaurant right at the edge of the Djemaâ el-Fna square and you can find simple, delicious food—most notably the rabbit tagine cooked with raisins. Squeeze yourself into the table at the back by the window and you get one of the best sunset views across the buzzing square below and to the Koutoubia beyond. ✉ *28, Souk el-Kessabine, just past Café France, Medina* ☏ *0524/42–72–04* ▭ *No credit cards* ⏲ *Closed during Ramadan* ✥ *F3.*

$ MOROCCAN ✕ **Le Tanjia.** This swanky restaurant has rose-filled fountains on each of its three floors. By day, dine on elegant arugula salads and other items on the lunch menu on the covered terrace overlooking a busy souk. By night, enjoy dinner and a glass of wine while marveling at the shimmying of belly dancers. ✉ *14, Derb J'did, next to Pl. des Ferblantiers, Medina* ☏ *0524/38–38–36* 🌐 *www.letanjia.com* ✥ *F6.*

¢ MOROCCAN ✕ **La Terrasse des Épices.** Following the success of Café des Épices, this younger rooftop sister was born to fill the demand for atmospheric dining in contemporary and stylish surroundings in the heart of the medina. With great food and a romantic atmosphere, La Terrasse is justifiably popular. One of few open-air medina restuarants with a license to serve alcohol, it also offers a well-priced menu of Moroccan cuisine, *grillades* (grilled meat and kebabs), and vegetarian pasta dishes. ✉ *15, souk Cherifia, Sidi Abdelaziz, Medina* ☏ *0524/37–59–04* 🌐 *www.terrassedesepices.com* ✥ *F1.*

$$$$ MOROCCAN ✕ **Le Tobsil.** The name may be Arabic for "dish," but get ready for several. The traditional Moroccan fixed menu, featuring not one but two tagines (first poultry, then lamb) followed by couscous, not to mention starter and dessert, is wheeled out in serious style. Dine among lanterns and petals in the intimate yellow-ocher courtyard of the small riad

Dar Marjana is the best of Marrakesh's riad-style restaurants.

just inside Bab Laksour. It's stylish and friendly, and the cuisine is very good. A fixed-price menu includes four courses and drinks. ✉ *22, Derb Abdellah ben Hessaien, R'mila Bab Ksour, Medina* ☎ *0524/44–15–23* ⏲ *Closed Tues. and July and Aug. No lunch* ✥ *D3.*

GUÉLIZ

Marrakesh's restaurant scene changes faster than a belly dancer at quitting time, and today's hot tagine can quickly become tomorrow's soggy couscous. This is especially true in trendy, finicky Guéliz. Some of the most celebrated restaurants have built their reputations around stunning decor rather than stunning food, but they're still worth going to as long as you know this. Sound out local opinion, and don't be afraid to take a chance.

¢ MOROCCAN ★ ✕ **Al Fassia Guéliz.** Serving some of the best à la carte Moroccan food in the city, Al Fassia breaks the mold in several ways. It's run by women, avoids the dictates and giant portions of normal set menus, and brings classic cooking to the modern district. This restaurant has long been the most highly recommended dining address in town, and the owners have now expanded, opening a second restaurant, ⇨ *Al Fassia Aguedal,* to cope with demand. ✉ *55, bd. Zerktouni, Guéliz* ☎ *0524/43–40–60* 🌐 *www.alfassia.com* ✍ *Reservations essential* ⏲ *Closed Tues.*

$ LEBANESE ✕ **Azar.** Comprising both a restaurant and a nightclub in the heart of Guéliz, Azar exudes contemporary *orientale* charm both through its Lebanese-Moroccan cuisine and its intriguingly modern take on traditional Moroccan design. The interiors are bedecked with brass

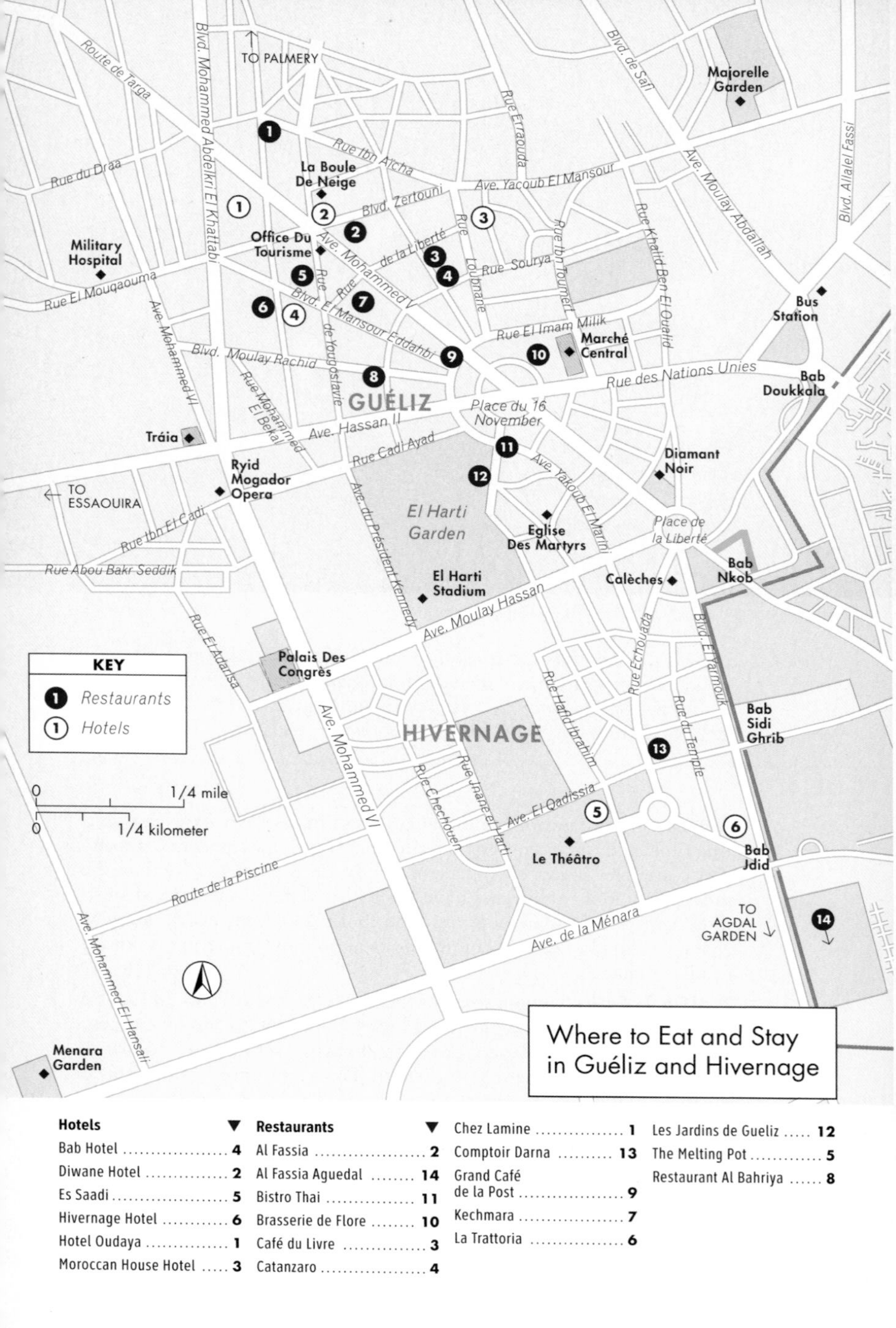

Hotels	▼
Bab Hotel	**4**
Diwane Hotel	**2**
Es Saadi	**5**
Hivernage Hotel	**6**
Hotel Oudaya	**1**
Moroccan House Hotel	**3**

Restaurants	▼
Al Fassia	**2**
Al Fassia Aguedal	**14**
Bistro Thai	**11**
Brasserie de Flore	**10**
Café du Livre	**3**
Catanzaro	**4**
Chez Lamine	**1**
Comptoir Darna	**13**
Grand Café de la Post	**9**
Kechmara	**7**
La Trattoria	**6**
Les Jardins de Gueliz	**12**
The Melting Pot	**5**
Restaurant Al Bahriya	**8**

lanterns, leather pouffes, and satin cushions intermingled with retro plastic-molded chairs and honeycomb-effect sculpted plaster walls. The mezzanine restaurant is a more intimate space, ideal for romantic dinners. The menu offers Lebanese staples such as tabouleh, falafel, and hummus as starters, with marinaded grilled meat kebabs and cutlets for main courses. A selection of nine Lebanese *mezzé du chef* to share with a friend makes a very enjoyable and affordable light meal. The top floor of the restaurant hosts live Oriental music every night in its sultry club and bar. ✉ *Rue de Yougoslavie, at Bd. Hassan II, Guéliz* ☎ *0524/43–09–20* 🌐 *www.azarmarrakech.com.*

$ ASIAN Fodor's Choice ★ ✕ **Bistro Thai.** Thai, Vietnamese, and Japanese specialities are served with pizazz here in stylish surroundings. Following the success of Thai Wok, the restaurant has taken larger premises near place 16 Novembre and can show off its authentic cuisine. Flaming woks are open to view from the kitchen along the back wall, and diners can sit at the counter to watch their meal being prepared while snacking on sushi. There's also an elegant sunken dinner restaurant and a street-fronted terrace decorated with Asian artifacts, including Balinese goddesses and printed silks. The menu offers oodles of noodles, dim sum, and the chef's own witty creation, the "Japanese pizza," which consists of steamed rice with salmon and mozarella topping. The food is all very light and extremely tasty. ✉ *8, av. Oued el-Markhazine, opposite the Royal Tennis Club, Guéliz* ☎ *0524/45–73–11.*

5

$ FRENCH BISTRO ✕ **Brasserie de Flore.** French expat Philippe Duranton's brasserie occupies a prime position on the Marrakesh Plaza at Place du 16 Novembre in Guéliz. With seemingly acres of outdoor seating from which to watch the weary shoppers as well as comfortable indoor seating, you could imagine yourself in early 20th-century Paris. Crystal chandeliers and fans hang from the high ceilings, while the walls are lined with huge mirrors and art nouveau Grecian nymphs. The menu is hearty French rustic cuisine, which means plenty of pork specials, including pig's trotters, paté, smoked ham, and artisanal sausages. ✉ *Place du 16 Novembre, Guéliz* ☎ *0524/45–80–00.*

¢ FRENCH ✕ **Café du Livre.** Peruse a quirky collection of English-language books and log onto the free Wi-Fi while you lunch or an early dinner in this popular café tucked away behind Hotel Toulousaine. Café du Livre closes at 9, rather early by Moroccan standards, and the interior can get very smoky as the day progresses. Enjoy such Continental fare as a delicious entrecôte or American-style dishes like a tasty cheeseburger. For dessert, enjoy the chocolate cake while relaxing on the comfortable velvet seating. The restaurant serves wine and beer. ✉ *44, rue Tarik ben Ziad, Guéliz* ☎ *0524/43–21–49* 🌐 *www.cafedulivre.com* ⏲ *Closed Sun.*

¢ ITALIAN ★ ✕ **Catanzaro.** One of Marrakesh's most popular restaurants, this homey Italian spot offers dining on two floors, brightened by red-chintz tablecloths. The menu has a good selection of basic Italian dishes and pizzas at prices that make them fabulous values. Pizza Royal—that is, with everything on it—is a favorite. ✉ *Rue Tariq Ibn Ziad, Guéliz* ☎ *0524/43–37–31* ✍ *Reservations essential* ⏲ *Closed Sun.*

The Djemâa el Fna really comes alive at sunset, when its many food vendors open their stalls.

¢ MOROCCAN ★ **Chez Lamine.** Slightly more elegant than its hole-in-the-wall branch in the souks, Chez Lamine has a reputation for the best *mechoui* (whole-roasted lamb) in town. It's streetside tables in Guéliz are regularly filled with Moroccan families, especially on Sunday afternoons. You can choose to sit indoors or outdoors in this popular local eatery at tables made from sewing-machine stands. Apart from mouthwatering tajines, try the restaurant's other speciality, *tangia marrakchia* (lamb cooked very slowly for hours in earthenware jars). ✉ *Rue Ibn Aicha, opposite Montecristo, Guéliz* ☎ *0524/43–11–64.*

$ FRENCH **Grand Café de la Poste.** The colonial atmosphere provides a fabulous backdrop for excellent (if pricey) salads, pastas, steaks, and fish specials including oysters from Oualidia. In spring and summer, you can enjoy a cold Casablanca beer on the covered veranda. For an indulgent dessert try the *gâteau chocolat coulant.* Arrive early to enjoy a free tapas buffet nightly from 6:30 to 7:30. ✉ *Bd. el-Mansour Eddahbi at Av. Imam Malik, just off Av. Mohammed V, Guéliz* ☎ *0524/43–30–38* 🌐 *www.grandcafedelaposte.com.*

¢ FRENCH **Les Jardins de Guéliz.** Entering the gateway to Les Jardins de Guéliz feels like discovering a secret garden—which in effect it is. Wooden gates, half-shrouded in foliage, disguise the entrance before you find yourself inside a mini faux-kasbah. Backing directly on to the delightful Harti Gardens, on what was once a basketball court, the restaurant is in a light airy conservatory, perfect for a family lunch. The midday buffet is good value and has lots of vegetarian choices, including tortillas, stuffed vine leaves, cooked salads, and rice and pasta salads. (though sadly there are fewer veggie choices for dinner). For carnivores there are plenty of choices, including beef Stroganoff, steaks, lasagna, and

CLOSE UP

Marrakesh Street Food

Marrakshis have perfected the art of cooked street food, traditionally the province of the working class. There are hundreds of sidewalk grills scattered throughout both the medina and Guéliz. Step up for a tasty, satisfying meal at one of these institutions; it's a priceless experience that costs next to nothing. From midday to midnight, choose from grilled minced beef, sausage, lamb chops, brochettes, Moroccan salads, and french fries, supplemented by bread, olives, and hot sauce. No credit cards, clearly.

DJEMAÂ EL-FNA

For the ultimate grilling experience, there's only one place. By dusk, more than a hundred stalls sizzle and smoke their way through mountains of fresh meat and vegetables. Step up to the stall of your choice and order from the wild array of perfectly done veggies, salads, *kefta* (beef patties), *merguez* sausages, beef brochettes, couscous, and even french fries. In cooler months or during Ramadan, try a bowl of hearty *harira* (chickpea, lentil, and meat soup) or country eggs in homemade bread. The meal starts with free bread (to weigh down your paper place setting) and a hot dipping sauce called *harissa*. The mint tea at the end should be free, too.

There's little continuity of quality, even at the same stall, so it's potluck and instinct all the way for each sitting. However, since leftovers are given to the poor every night, the food is always freshly made. Vendors will do anything to attract your attention, from dragging you to a seat, chasing you down the lanes, and best of all, performing the occasional comic rundown of classic English phrases ("it's bloody marvelous") with matching Cockney accent. ■ TIP→ **Watch the Moroccans: they know what to order, and they really get into their food.**

OTHER MEDINA GRILLS

If the idea of dining at one of the stalls on the square does not appeal to you, there are a lot of casual grill restaurants either on the square or in the streets immediately surrounding it. We can recommend three in particular that are popular with the locals: Haj Brik, Restaurant Tiznit, Restaurant El Bahja *(see ⇨ Medina in Where to Eat)*. Remember that none of these serve alcohol.

5

also some Moroccan dishes. The pretty gardens are child-friendly; there are tables outside on shaded terraces, and there's a couple of turtles patrolling. ✉ *Av. Oued el-Makhazine, next to Royal Tennis Club, Guéliz* ☎ *0524/42–21–22* ⏲ *Closed during Ramadan.*

$ EUROPEAN ✕ **Kechmara.** Marrakesh doesn't get hipper than this. Ice-cool mid-century design and exhibitions by Moroccan and European artists put this on a par with something that might sprout in New York's East Village. Local cognoscenti believe the food could be better—this makes it better as a lunch drop-in than an all-out dinner option. You can always go back in the evening for relaxed drinks on the terrace if you like. There's live music every weekend. ✉ *3, rue de la Liberté, Guéliz* ☎ *0524/42–25–32* 🌐 *www.kechmara.com.*

¢ CAFÉ **The Melting Pot.** A new venture by two young Moroccan entrepreneurs—one a photographer, the other an interior designer—The Melting Pot is more of a café (with free Wi-Fi) than a restaurant. But it's also become a trendy meeting place for artists, students, and creative types. Exhibitions of local painters line the walls, and there's a small library of books, too. The decor is 1970s retro, and the food (tagines, brochettes, panini, and pastas) is only average; however, there are some interesting virgin cocktails on offer, such as a "Crazy Cow" (with coconut, peach, pineapple, and crème fraîche). It's open till late. No alcohol. *Residence al-Andalous V, Rue Yougolsavie, Guéliz 0524/45–77–73.*

¢ SEAFOOD **Restaurant Al Bahriya.** Cheap and cheerful, this restaurant is possibly the best catch in town. The no-frills Moroccan street restaurant in the heart of Guéliz (near La Grande Poste) is packed at night with locals getting their fishy fix. Choose from the sidewalk display of fresh seafood as you walk in, or simply ask for a mixed plate—sole, calamari, monkfish, prawns—all served with wedges of lime and olives. *75 bis, av. Moulay Rachid, Guéliz 0524/84–61–86 No credit cards.*

$ ITALIAN **La Trattoria.** Due partly to the pizzazz of its late owner, Giancarlo, La Trattoria has long held a place among Marrakesh's top restaurants. The current owner, Mohammed Anaflouss, took over in 2000, and with neo-Moorish renovations overseen by Bill Willis, this ornate restaurant still draws a loyal and select clientele. Tapas and predinner drinks can be enjoyed in the lush terrace bar, with jungle foliage in danger of dipping in to your aperitif, or you can sit beside the pool and enjoy a good entrecôte or one of the many seafood pastas. *179, rue Mohammed el-Béqal, Guéliz 0524/43–26–41 www.latrattoriamarrakech.com Reservations essential No lunch.*

HIVERNAGE

Hivernage is known for its large upmarket chain hotels and some very exclusive apartment buildings. Amongst them are also a scattering of decent restaurants and cafés—some independent, some located within hotels, and some even attached to the outlying nightclubs. On Avenue Mohammed VI (opposite the Palais de Congrès) are a number of pizzerias. You'll find a few fine-dining restaurants on Avenue du President Kennedy and out in the commercial zones beyond Agdal Gardens. Towards the Guéliz end of Avenue Moulay el-Hassan, near the old football stadium, is a cluster of international restaurants.

¢ MOROCCAN **Al Fassia Aguedal.** The Al Fassia name has become synonymous for fine Moroccan cuisine in Marrakesh, and with tables hard to come by in Guéliz, the doors have recently opened to the new restaurant within the boutique Hotel Al Fassia near the Agdal Gardens. The high standards set by the older sister restaurant are in no way undermined, and service and style is impeccable. *9 bis, rte. de Ourika, Zone Touristique de l'Aguedal, Hivernage 0524/38–38–39 www.alfassia-aguedal.com Reservations essential No lunch.*

$ MOROCCAN **Comptoir Darna.** Like the dark mahogany beams and panels that give the interior its clubby feel, this restaurant has aged well. À la carte dining blends traditional Moroccan and European cuisines. It remains a nighttime draw for hip Marrakshis and visitors alike; musicians, belly dancers (starting at 9:45), and an upstairs DJ and small dance floor provide added bite. ✉ *Av. Echouhada, Hivernage* ☎ *0524/43–77–02* 🌐 *www.comptoirmarrakech.com* ⏲ *No lunch.*

THE PALMERY

$ INTERNATIONAL Fodor's Choice ★ ✕ **Le Blokk.** Located in the Palmery, outside of town, Le Blokk is well worth the taxi ride. The decor is chic, and dishes like duck with balsamic vinegar and lamb with thyme are reasonably priced. The live music, however, takes center stage. Tap your feet while talented singers perform songs from the last 50 years. ✉ *Circuit de la Palmeraie, next to Mehdi Palace, Palmery* ☎ *0674/33–43–34* 🌐 *www.leblokk.com.*

$$ FRENCH ✕ **Dar Ennassim.** Indulge in top-notch French cuisine prepared by Michelin-starred chef Fabrice Vulin. By day enjoy an artfully arranged salad and other light menu options on the terrace. By night, partake in the stunning restaurant interiors and feel like one of "the beautiful people." It's not cheap, so consider this a special splurge. ✉ *Pavillon du golf, Circuit de la Palmeraie, Palmery* ☎ *0524/33–43–08* 🌐 *www.fabricevulin.com/darennassim.html* ⚠ *Reservations essential* ⏲ *Closed during Ramadan.*

5

WHERE TO STAY

For expanded hotel reviews, visit Fodors.com.

Marrakesh has exceptional hotels. Five stars are dropped at every turn, the spas are superb, and the loving attention to detail is overwhelming. If, however, you'd prefer not to spend a fortune sleeping in the bed where a movie star once slumbered, solid budget and midrange options abound. They're small, clean, and suitably Moroccan in style to satisfy adventurous penny-pinchers.

To take on the historic heart of Marrakesh and live like a pasha of old, head to one of the medina's riads. Riad restorations, many by ultrafashionable European expats, have taken over the city; you'd trip over them, if only you knew where they were. Anonymous doors in the narrow, twisting derbs of the medina, and especially the souks, transport you to hidden worlds of pleasure. There are cheap ones, expensive ones, chic ones, funky ones, plain ones.

Marrakesh is something of a Shangri-la for designers who, intoxicated by the colors, shapes, and patterns of the city, are free to indulge themselves in wildly opulent and ambitious designs. Although it isn't all tasteful, much of the decor and style in Marrakesh hotels and riads is fascinating and easy on the eye.

Most of the larger hotels (classified as three, four, or five stars by the Moroccan government) are in Guéliz, Hivernage, and the surrounding areas of Marrakesh. If you prefer something authentic and inexpensive near the action, choose one of the numerous small and clean hotels in the medina near Djemaâ el-Fna.

Where to Eat and Stay in the Medina
A
B
C
D
1
2
3
4
5
6
Le Yacout
Dar Marjana
Rue de Bab Doukkala
Riad Malika
R'MILA
La Maison Arbe
Rue Fatima Zohra
Rue Dar El Bacha
Rue El Adala
Rue Jebel Lakhdar
BAB NKOB
Ave. Mohammed V
Rue. Sidi El Yumami
Riad el Fenn
Rue Jebel Lakhdar
Rue Abou El Abbas Sebti
Rue. Fatima Zohra
Le Tobsil
Les Jardins de la Koutoubia
BAB SIDI GHRIB
Ave. El Mouahidine
Rue. Ibn Khaldoun
KAUTOUBIA
Jardins de la Koutoubia
CALÈCHES
Rue Moulay Ismail
BAB JDID
Ave. Bab Jdid
La Momounia
Rue Lalla Rikia
Villa des Orangers
Rue Oqba Ben Mafaa
Rue Sidi Mimoun
SIDI MIMOUN
La Suitana
KEY
Restaurants
Hotels
Market street area
Pedestrian plazas & Streets
following dining and lodging reviews indicates a map-grid coordinate

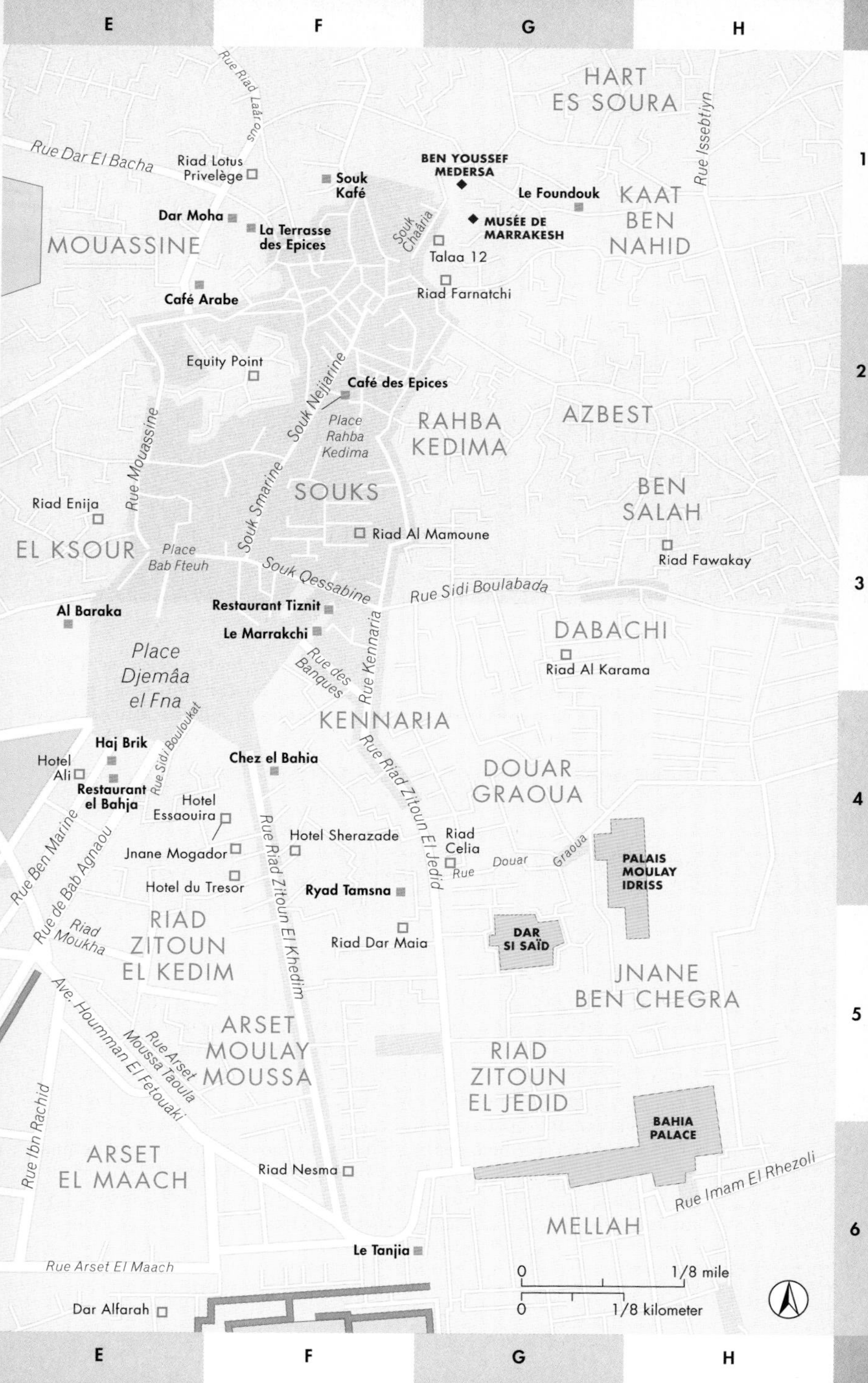

E
F
G
H
1
2
3
4
5
6
HART ES SOURA
Rue Riad Laârous
Rue Dar El Bacha
Riad Lotus Privelège
Souk Kafé
BEN YOUSSEF MEDERSA
Le Foundouk
KAAT BEN NAHID
Rue Issebtiyn
Dar Moha
La Terrasse des Epices
MUSÉE DE MARRAKESH
Souk Chaâria
Talaa 12
MOUASSINE
Café Arabe
Riad Farnatchi
Equity Point
Café des Epices
Souk Nejjarine
Place Rahba Kedima
RAHBA KEDIMA
AZBEST
Rue Mouassine
Souk Smarine
SOUKS
BEN SALAH
Riad Enija
Riad Al Mamoune
EL KSOUR
Place Bab Fteuh
Riad Fawakay
Souk Qessabine
Rue Sidi Boulabada
Al Baraka
Restaurant Tiznit
Le Marrakchi
DABACHI
Rue Kennaria
Rue des Banques
Place Djemâa el Fna
Riad Al Karama
KENNARIA
Rue Sidi Bouloukat
Haj Brik
Hotel Ali
Chez el Bahia
Restaurant el Bahja
DOUAR GRAOUA
Rue Riad Zitoun El Jedid
Hotel Essaouira
Rue Ben Marine
Rue Riad Zitoun El Khedim
Hotel Sherazade
Riad Celia
Jnane Mogador
Rue Douar Graoua
PALAIS MOULAY IDRISS
Rue de Bab Agnaou
Hotel du Tresor
Ryad Tamsna
RIAD ZITOUN EL KEDIM
Riad Moukha
Riad Dar Maia
DAR SI SAÏD
JNANE BEN CHEGRA
Ave. Houmman El Fetouaki
Rue Arset Moussa Taoula
ARSET MOULAY MOUSSA
RIAD ZITOUN EL JEDID
Rue Ibn Rachid
ARSET EL MAACH
BAHIA PALACE
Riad Nesma
Rue Imam El Rhezoli
MELLAH
Le Tanjia
Rue Arset El Maach
0
1/8 mile
0
1/8 kilometer
Dar Alfarah
E
F
G
H

La Mamounia is one of Morocco's grand dame hotels, not to mention one of the finest luxury hotels in Africa.

Hotels and riads vary their prices wildly between high and low season. This means that if you time your trip right you can find some great deals. High season runs from October to May, with spikes at Christmas, New Year's, and Easter.

WHAT IT COSTS IN DIRHAMS					
	¢	$	$$	$$$	$$$$
FOR TWO PEOPLE	under 400 DH	400 DH–1,000 DH	1,000 DH–2,500 DH	2,500 DH–4,000 DH	over 4,000 DH

Prices are for two people in a standard double room in high season, including service and tax.

RENTING A RIAD

Nothing beats taking over a riad for a few days. We mean booking the whole darn thing—not just a room. Staying in a beautifully restored 16th-century palace isn't cheap, but riads in the medina and small villas in the Palmery are geared up for this. Their staffs can help organize meal plans, special itineraries, weddings, birthday parties, and literary salons. There are more than 800 riads in Marrakesh, and at least half of these claim to be the trendiest. The choices may seem overwhelming, but as long as you find one that appeals to you (not hard!), you're set for a special night. In addition to the individual riads listed below, try the following agencies that specialize in Marrakesh:

Boutique Souk ☎ *0661/32–44–75* 🌐 *www.boutiquesouk.com.* **Marrakech Medina** ✉ *102, rue Dar el-Bacha, Souika Sidi Abd al-Aziz, Medina* ☎ *0524/29–07–07* 🌐 *www.marrakech-medina.com.* **Marrakech Riads** ☎ *0524/42–64–63* 🌐 *www.marrakech-riads.com.*

MEDINA

$$ **Dar Alfarah.** This lovely riad is near the Badi Palace in the mellah quarter, tucked down a sidestreet that leads to the kasbah area. **Pros:** good location; plenty of atmosphere. **Cons:** small pool. ✉ *58 Derb Touareg, Ksibat N'Hass, Kasbah* ☎ *0524/38–46–67* 🌐 *www.daralfarah.com* *2 rooms, 7 suites* *In-room: a/c, no TV, Wi-Fi. In-hotel: restaurant, pool, business center* *Some meals* ✣ *E6.*

¢ **Hotel Ali.** Backpackers pile into sparsely furnished rooms or stay on the crowded roof terrace. **Pros:** great place to meet fellow travelers; right on the main square. **Cons:** a little noisy. ✉ *Rue Moulay Ismail, 55 yards from Dejmaâ el-Fna, Medina* ☎ *0524/44–49–79* 🌐 *www.hotel-ali.com* *43 rooms, 2 dorms* *In-room: a/c, Wi-Fi. In-hotel: restaurant, business center* *No credit cards* *Breakfast* ✣ *E4.*

$ ★ **Hotel Sherazade.** A series of gorgeous rooftop terraces, stylish tents, and plant-filled courtyards of two conjoined riads beguile you into thinking this is a much more expensive hotel. **Pros:** good location; restful setting. **Cons:** few amenities; not all rooms have private bathrooms. ✉ *3, Derb Djemaâ, Riad Zitoun Elkedim, Medina* ☎ *0524/42–93–05* 🌐 *www.hotelsherazade.com* *23 rooms, 19 with bath* *In-room: a/c. In-hotel: restaurant, business center* *Multiple meal plans* ✣ *F4.*

$ **Hotel du Tresor.** A haven for artists and design lovers, this beautifully converted hotel has been featured in design magazines. **Pros:** fantastic location; top-notch design; helpful management. **Cons:** pool is tiny and no privacy; cash only. ✉ *77, Sidi Boulokat, Riad Zitoun Kdim, Medina* ☎ *0524/37–51–13* 🌐 *www.hotel-du-tresor.com* *10 rooms, 3 suites* *In-room: a/c, no TV, Wi-Fi. In-hotel: pool, business center* *No credit cards* *Breakfast* ✣ *F4.*

$$$ **Les Jardins de la Koutoubia.** After La Mamounia, this might be the sultan of the medina. **Pros:** plenty of atmosphere; great pool area. **Cons:** expensive. ✉ *26, rue de la Koutoubia, Medina* ☎ *0524/38–88–00* 🌐 *www.lesjardinsdelakoutoubia.com* *68 rooms, 40 suites* *In-room: a/c, Wi-Fi. In-hotel: restaurant, bar, pool, gym, spa, business center, parking, some pets allowed* *Multiple meal plans* ✣ *D3.*

$ **Jnane Mogador.** Run by the same proprietor as the long-standing and nearby backpackers' Hotel Essaouira, this budget option is a cut above the rest. **Pros:** near the main square; very good value. **Cons:** some rooms can be dark; unoriginal decor; books up months in advance. ✉ *116, Riad Zitoun Kedim, Derb Sidi Bouloukate, Medina* ☎ *0524/42–63–23* 🌐 *www.jnanemogador.com* *17 rooms, 1 suite* *In-room: no a/c, Internet. In-hotel: restaurant, spa, business center* *No meals* ✣ *F4.*

$$ ★ **La Maison Arabe.** Owner Fabrizio Ruspoli created this small hotel for those craving old-fashioned charm. **Pros:** lots of little nooks; renowned cooking school; free Wi-Fi. **Cons:** small rooms; a bit pricey. ✉ *1, Derb Assehbe, Bab Doukkala, Medina* ☎ *0524/38–70–10*

www.lamaisonarabe.com 12 rooms, 14 suites In-room: a/c, Wi-Fi. In-hotel: restaurant, bar, pool, spa, laundry facilities, business center Breakfast C1.

$$$$ Fodor's Choice ★ **La Mamounia.** Since 1923, Morocco's most prestigious hotel has achieved legendary status for its opulence, grandeur, celebrity guest list, and hefty price tag. **Pros:** one of the finest hotels in the world; exquisite food; excellent service. **Cons:** the standard rooms are on the small side; ground-floor rooms have no view of garden; exorbitant bar/restaurant prices. *Bab Jdid, Medina 0524/38–86–00 www.mamounia.com 136 rooms, 71 suites, 3 riads In-room: a/c, Wi-Fi. In-hotel: restaurant, bar, pool, tennis court, gym, spa, laundry facilities, business center, parking No meals B5.*

$ **Riad Al Karama.** This inexpensive and delightful riad is within easy walking distance of Place Djemaâ el-Fna and the souks. **Pros:** beautiful style; great personal service. **Cons:** the Coriander Room is very cramped; minimum three-night stay required in high season (between Christmas and New Year's). *119, Derb Jdid, off Rue Dabachi, Medina 0661/42–04–44 www.riadalkarama.com 4 rooms, 1 suite In-room: a/c, no TV, Wi-Fi. In-hotel: business center Breakfast G3.*

$ **Riad Al Mamoune.** This French-owned riad is a peaceful retreat amid the chaos of the souk. **Pros:** local cell phones loaned to guests, piping-hot water at all times. **Cons:** a bit hard to find. *140, Derb Aarjane, Rahba Kédima, east of Rue Semmarine through Souk aux Epices, then follow signs from Rahba Lakdima, Medina 0524/39–19–58 www.riadalmamoune.com 5 rooms, 1 suite In-room: a/c, no TV. In-hotel: business center, some pets allowed Breakfast F3.*

$ **Riad Celia.** This simple riad is a good choice for budget-friendly riad accommodation in the medina. **Pros:** great location; helpful staff; lunch and dinner are available by request. **Cons:** can be noisy; cheapest rooms are small. *1, Douar Graoua, Riad Zitoune Jdid, Medina 0524/42–99–84 www.hotelriadcelia.com 11 rooms, 1 suite In-room: a/c, no TV. In-hotel: laundry facilities, business center, some pets allowed Breakfast G4.*

$ ★ **Riad Dar Maia.** This pretty little riad is perfectly located for easy access to the Bahia Palace and the Place Djemaâ el-Fna. **Pros:** great location; good value. **Cons:** small bathrooms. *31, Derb Zouina, Riad Zitoune Jdid, Medina 0524/37–62–31 www.riad-dar-maia.com 5 rooms In-room: a/c, no TV. In-hotel: business center No credit cards Breakfast F5.*

$$$ **Riad el Fenn.** For high-octane creative types who want real style, Vanessa Branson (sister of the British entrepreneur) has created this riad "adventure." **Pros:** dripping with good taste; an exclusive vibe; accessible to travelers with disabilities. **Cons:** very expensive. *2, Derb Moulay Abdellah ben Hessaien, Bab Ksour, Medina 0524/44–12–10 www.riadelfenn.com 12 rooms, 8 suites In-room: a/c, Wi-Fi. In-hotel: restaurant, bar, pool, spa, laundry facilities, business center Multiple meal plans D3.*

$$ ★ **Riad Enija.** Walking into this unmarked riad at the end of an anonymous derb is like stepping into another world. **Pros:** great central location; high-quality services. **Cons:** expensive. *9, Derb Mesfioui, Rahba*

The elaborately tiled courtyard at Riad Enija is a great place to have tea or an entire meal.

Lakdima, Medina ☎ *0524/44–00–14* 🌐 *www.riadenija.com* *6 rooms, 9 suites* *In-room: a/c, Wi-Fi. In-hotel: restaurant, bar, pool, spa, laundry facilities, business center* 🍽 *Breakfast* ✥ *E3.*

$$$ **Riad Farnatchi.** On the souk's northern tip in the oldest part of Marrakesh is this stylish and traditional riad. **Pros:** excellent service; royal treatment **Cons:** expensive. ✉ *2, Derb el-Farnatchi, Qa'at Benahid, Medina* ☎ *0524/38–49–10* 🌐 *www.riadfarnatchi.com* *9 suites* *In-room: a/c, Wi-Fi. In-hotel: restaurant, pool, spa, laundry facilities, business center* ⏲ *Closed Aug.* 🍽 *Breakfast* ✥ *G2.*

$$$ **Riad Lotus Privilège.** With exquisite decor, this lovely riad will leave you breathless. **Pros:** romantic enough for a honeymoon; decadent decor. **Cons:** smaller rooms are considerably less stylish; tricky to find; very expensive. ✉ *9, Derb Sidi Ali Ben Hamdouch, Rue Dar Bacha, Medina* ☎ *0524/38–73–18, 0524/43–15–37* 🌐 *www.riadslotus.com* *5 rooms* *In-room: a/c, Internet, Wi-Fi. In-hotel: restaurant, pool, spa, laundry facilities, business center* 🍽 *Breakfast* ✥ *F1.*

$$ **Riad Malika.** The rambling, relaxing Malika was one of the first riads to reinvent itself in the 1990s, and owner Jean-Luc Lemée and his English-speaking wife are full of anecdotes about Morocco. **Pros:** plenty of charm; congenial hosts. **Cons:** mixed decor is a bit cluttered; far from main square. ✉ *29, Arsat Aouzal, Bab Doukkala, Medina* ☎ *0524/38–54–51* 🌐 *www.riadmalika.com* *4 rooms, 5 suites* *In-room: a/c, Wi-Fi. In-hotel: pool, spa, business center* 🍽 *Breakfast* ✥ *D1.*

$ **Fodor's Choice** ★ **Riad Nesma.** Riad Nesma is proof that staying in a beautiful riad with elegant rooms does not have to break the bank. **Pros:** excellent value; beautiful rooms; rates include Wi-Fi. **Cons:** often booked; no pool. ✉ *128, Riad Zitouen Lakdim, Medina* ☎ *0524/44–44–42* 🌐 *www.riadnesma.com* ⇨ *7 rooms* ♨ *In-room: a/c, Wi-Fi. In-hotel: laundry facilities, business center* 🍴 *Breakfast* ✥ *F6.*

$$$ **La Sultana.** There's a certain over-the-top charm to this series of five luxurious riads of palatial proportions. **Pros:** fireplaces in every room; impeccable service. **Cons:** decor is a bit pompous; very expensive. ✉ *403, rue de la Kasbah, on a tiny alley heading left just south of Saadian tombs, Kasbah* ☎ *0524/38–80–08* 🌐 *www.lasultanamarrakech.com* ⇨ *28 rooms* ♨ *In-room: a/c, Wi-Fi. In-hotel: restaurant, bar, pool, gym, spa, laundry facilities, business center* ⊙ *Closed Aug. (usually)* 🍴 *Breakfast* ✥ *D6.*

$$ ★ **Talaa 12.** This achingly trendy temple to modernist riad chic is in the middle of the medina. **Pros:** very stylish; friendly staff. **Cons:** some find it overdesigned. ✉ *12, Talaa ben Youssef, on the way to Ali ben Youssef Medersa* ☎ *0524/42–90–45* 🌐 *www.talaa12.com* ⇨ *4 rooms, 4 suites* ♨ *In-room: a/c, Wi-Fi. In-hotel: restaurant, spa, laundry facilities, business center* 🍴 *Multiple meal plans* ✥ *G1.*

$$$ **Villa des Orangers.** This property has all the understated glamour and class you'd expect from a Relais & Chateaux hotel, with unobtrusive service, libraries to hide away in, and bedrooms with enormous bathrooms. **Pros:** unsurpassed luxury; plenty of privacy. **Cons:** very expensive. ✉ *6, rue Sidi Mimoune, Medina* ☎ *0524/38–46–38* 🌐 *www.villadesorangers.com* ⇨ *21 suites, 6 rooms* ♨ *In-room: a/c, Wi-Fi. In-hotel: restaurant, pool, gym, spa, laundry facilities, business center* 🍴 *Some meals* ✥ *D5.*

GUÉLIZ

Unless you're with a family in need of a big hotel to drown out the noise you make, the hotels in Guéliz mostly cater to package holidays. They overflow with facilities but lack the character or service you find elsewhere. Still, we've found a few that buck the trend.

$$ **Bab Hotel.** This upmarket boutique hotel is chic and hypermodern in style, with designer furniture, a space-age lounge bar, and minimalist bedrooms furnished in shades of white. **Pros:** funky interior design; great location. **Cons:** small pool; ugly views from some rooms. ✉ *Rue Mohammed el-Beqqal at Bd. Mansour Eddahbi, Guéliz* ☎ *0524/43–52–50* 🌐 *www.babhotelmarrakech.com* ⇨ *30 rooms, 15 suites* ♨ *In-room: a/c, Wi-Fi. In-hotel: restaurant, bar, pool, gym, spa, laundry facilities, business center* 🍴 *Breakfast.*

$$ **Diwane Hotel.** This upmarket hotel has a huge, riad-style atrium, giving it some sense of charm. **Pros:** great location; good-sized pool. **Cons:** the bars are inelegant; food in the buffet restaurant is inconsistent. ✉ *24, rue de Yougoslavie, corner of Av. Mohammed V, Guéliz* ☎ *0524/43–22–16* 🌐 *www.diwane-hotel.com* ⇨ *115 rooms, 10 suites* ♨ *In-room: a/c. In-hotel: restaurant, bar, pool, gym, spa, laundry facilities, business center, parking* 🍴 *Multiple meal plans.*

$ **Hotel Oudaya.** The unpretentious Oudaya, on a busy tree-lined side street in Guéliz, is popular with young travelers and tour operators. **Pros:** spic-and-span rooms. **Cons:** some rooms are noisy; the food is not good, so take your meals elsewhere. ✉ *147, rue Mohammed el-Bequal, Guéliz* ☎ *0524/44–85–12* 🌐 *www.oudaya.ma* *146 rooms, 15 suites* *In-room: a/c. In-hotel: restaurant, bar, pool, laundry facilities, business center* *Multiple meal plans.*

$ **Moroccan House Hotel.** This Morrocan-run hotel has questionable taste in interior decor, but it's a well-priced option with spacious rooms, lots of character, and a friendly atmosphere. **Pros:** reasonable prices; authentic Moroccan feel. **Cons:** small pool; no bar. ✉ *3, rue Loubnane, Guéliz* ☎ *0524/42–03–05* 🌐 *www.moroccanhousehotels.com* *55 suites, 40 rooms* *In-room: a/c, Wi-Fi. In-hotel: restaurant, pool, spa, laundry facilities, business center* *Multiple meal plans.*

HIVERNAGE

Wide, shaded streets lined with orange and olive trees, a few secluded villas with palm trees towering above the garden walls—all creates a sense of tranquillity and affluence in this neighborhood just to the west of the ramparts. However, Hivernage also houses a number of large hotels that are ideal for families that need plenty of amenities, exotic garden space, swimming pools, and even wheelchair access. It is an ideal location not too far from the old medina. After dark, Hivernage is abuzz as many of the smartest nightclubs are in this area. A calèche ride along the avenues makes for a pleasant afternoon jaunt as part of a city tour.

$$$ **Es Saadi.** This large hotel started as Marrakesh's first casino, and then grew and grew. **Pros:** on-site casino; family-friendly atmosphere. **Cons:** dated design; impersonal; expensive. ✉ *Rue Ibrahim el-Mazini, Hivernage* ☎ *0524/44–88–11* 🌐 *www.essaadi.com* *140 rooms, 9 suites, 10 villas, 84 palace suites* *In-room: a/c, Wi-Fi. In-hotel: restaurant, bar, pool, tennis court, gym, spa, laundry facilities, business center, parking, some pets allowed* *Multiple meal plans.*

$$ ★ **Hivernage Hotel & Spa.** Hip couples with serious pampering needs will enjoy this exclusive pleasure dome nestled among the Hivernage megachain hotels. **Pros:** impressive design; great food. **Cons:** chain-hotel feel. ✉ *Av. Echouhada, at Rue des Temples, Hivernage* ☎ *0524/42–41–00* 🌐 *www.hivernage-hotel.com* *85 rooms, 10 suites* *In-room: a/c, Wi-Fi. In-hotel: restaurant, bar, pool, gym, spa, laundry facilities, business center, parking, some pets allowed* *Multiple meal plans.*

THE PALMERY

Staying in the Palmery is a good choice if you're looking for a relaxing vacation and won't feel guilty about exchanging the medina's action for an idyll in your own private country palace. It's also close to Marrakesh's famous golf courses. The drawback is the 7-km (4½-mi) distance from Marrakesh, which necessitates a car, a taxi, or use of infrequent hotel shuttles.

$$ ★ **Dar Zemora.** The unpretentious charms of this country villa will ease your guilt about staying in the Palmery and possibly seeing less of Marrakesh. **Pros:** regal views; friendly English-speaking staff. **Cons:** minimum stay usually required. ✉ *72, rue el-Aandalib, Ennakhil, just*

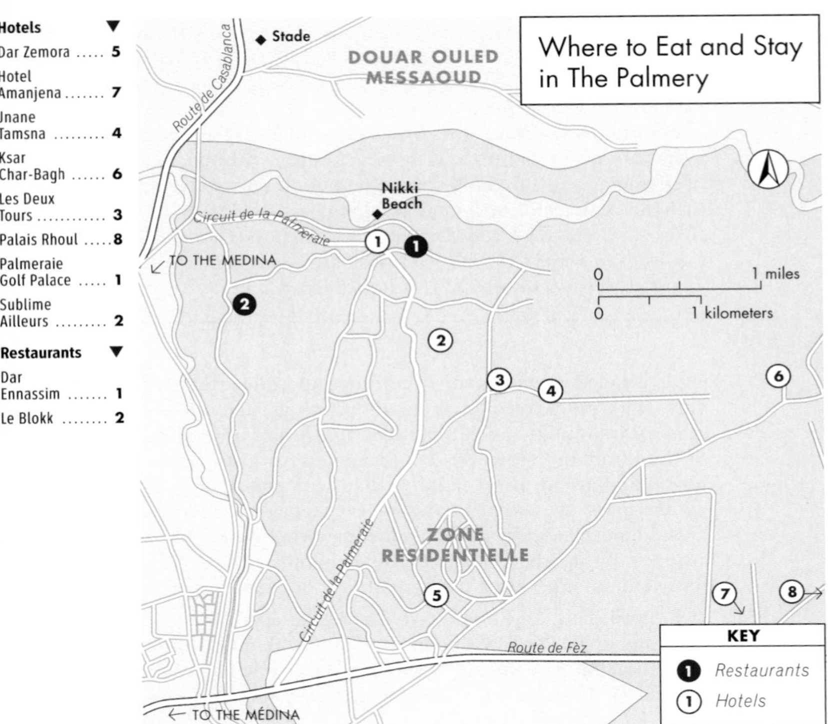

off road to Fez, Palmery ☎ *0524/32–82–00* 🌐 *www.darzemora.com* *3 rooms, 3 suites, 1 pavilion* *In-room: a/c. In-hotel: restaurant, bar, pool, spa, laundry facilities, business center, parking* *Breakfast.*

$$ **Les Deux Tours.** The Two Towers has the advantages of a luxurious garden setting and classic Charles Boccara architecture. **Pros:** lovely common areas; pretty pool. **Cons:** extra 300 DH charge required to heat private pools. ✉ *Douar Abiad, Circuit de la Palmeraie, Palmery* ☎ *0524/32–95–27* 🌐 *www.les-deux-tours.com* *31 suites* *In-room: a/c, Wi-Fi. In-hotel: restaurant, bar, pool, spa, laundry facilities, business center, parking* *Breakfast.*

$$$$ **Hotel Amanjena.** If you saw *Sex & the City* 2 in 2010, then you might just recognize this flashy retreat. **Pros:** Stunning architecture; incredible attention to detail; great Thai restaurant. **Cons:** You will need deep pockets to stay here for even a short time. ✉ *Rte. de Ouarzazate, Km 12, Palmery* ☎ *0524/39–90–00* 🌐 *www.amanresorts.com* *32 pavilions, 7 villas* *In-room: a/c, Wi-Fi. In-hotel: restaurant, bar, pool, tennis court, gym, spa, laundry facilities, business center, parking, some pets allowed* *Multiple meal plans.*

$$$ **Jnane Tamsna.** The word *jnane* means "garden," and this, the third of Meryanne Loum-Martin's jet-set luxury properties, lives up to its name. **Pros:** plenty of pampering; attentive staff. **Cons:** expensive rates; swimming pools not heated year-round. ✉ *Douar Abiad, Circuit de la*

Palmeraie, Palmery ☎ 0524/32–84–84 🌐 www.jnanetamsna.com ↳ 9 rooms, 5 cottages ♿ In-room: a/c. In-hotel: restaurant, bar, pool, tennis court, laundry facilities, business center, parking, some pets allowed 🍴 Multiple meal plans.

$$$$ ★ **Ksar Char-Bagh.** Rising like a Byzantine, 14th-century kasbah from the Palmery and surrounded by its own moat and acres of grounds, this hotel is the last word in sumptuous, escape-it-all luxury. **Pros:** beautiful decor; heated pool. **Cons:** service sometimes falls short. ✉ *Djnan Abiad, Circuit de la Palmeraie, Palmery ☎ 0524/32–92–44 🌐 www.ksarcharbagh.com ↳ 12 suites, 1 apartment ♿ In-room: a/c, Wi-Fi. In-hotel: restaurant, bar, pool, tennis court, spa, laundry facilities, business center, parking ⊗ Usually closed during Ramadan 🍴 Multiple meal plans.*

$$$ **Palais Rhoul.** This flashy, horseshoe-shaped mansion is the height of bohemian boutique chic, if a bit Beverley Hills. **Pros:** the height of luxury. **Cons:** restaurant overrated. ✉ *Rte. de Fès, Circuit de la Palmeraie ☎ 0524/32–94–94 🌐 www.palais-rhoul.com ↳ 5 rooms, 7 suites, 6 luxury garden tents ♿ In-room: a/c, Wi-Fi. In-hotel: restaurant, bar, pool, tennis court, spa, laundry facilities, business center, parking 🍴 Breakfast.*

$$$ **Palmeraie Golf Palace.** Tasteful it isn't, but this giant, gaudy self-contained bubble in the middle of the Palmery offers every kind of distraction, and plenty to keep children amused. **Pros:** great for golfers; plenty of pampering. **Cons:** not much charm; personal service is lost to bureaucracy. ✉ *Les Jardins de la Palmeraie, Circuit de la Palmeraie, Palmery ☎ 0524/36–87–04 🌐 www.pgpmarrakech.com ↳ 286 rooms, 70 suites ♿ In-room: a/c, Wi-Fi. In-hotel: restaurant, bar, golf course, pool, tennis court, gym, spa, children's programs, laundry facilities, business center, parking, some pets allowed 🍴 Multiple meal plans.*

$$$$ **Sublime Ailleurs.** Two villas and a riad stand in 5 acres of gardens, each with its own pool and terrace. **Pros:** lots of privacy. **Cons:** villa rooms must be rented as pairs. ✉ *Circuit de la Palmeraie, Palmery ☎ 0524/32–96–44 🌐 www.sublimeailleurs.com ↳ 4 rooms, 2 villas ♿ In-room: a/c, kitchen, Wi-Fi. In-hotel: restaurant, pool, spa, laundry facilities, business center, parking 🍴 Multiple meal plans.*

NIGHTLIFE

Without doubt, Marrakesh is Morocco's nightlife capital. Options include everything from the free but fascinating goings on at the Djemaâ el-Fna square to the nightly over-the-top show at Chez Ali.

GUÉLIZ

BARS

Night owls in search of something livelier will have to take a taxi over to the trendy hangouts in Guéliz and Hivernage. Late-night drinking is one of the few ways to sample the interiors of Marrakesh's most prestigious hotels.

5

CLOSE UP

Annual Festivals

Marrakesh's annual folklore festival of Moroccan music, theater, and dance—the **Festival National des Arts Populaires**—draws performers from all over Morocco and may even include an equestrian fantasia event. Held in July on the grounds of El Badi Palace, this highly worthwhile festival lasts about a week. Check the Web site for exact dates and times: 🌐 *www.marrakechfestival.com.*

The Marrakesh International Film Festival is held in early December. Since 2000, this high-profile event has attracted the glitterati of the international movie world for screenings of Moroccan and international films throughout the city. Previous special guests have included Susan Sarandon, Leonardo Dicaprio, Martin Scorcese, and Alan Parker. For more information, the festival has a Web site: 🌐 *www.festivalmarrakech.info.*

Aïd el-Arch, or Throne Day, the commemoration of the king's coronation, is always on July 30. Parades and fireworks create a festive ruckus, and throngs of people fill the streets to listen and dance to live music. **Aïd el-Seghrir** celebrates the end of Ramadan and is felt largely as a citywide sigh of relief. **Aïd el-Kebir,** the Day of Sacrifice, has a somber tone; approximately 2½ months after the end of Ramadan, Muslims everywhere observe the last ritual of the pilgrimage to Mecca by slaughtering a sheep. The Youth Festival, **La Fête de Jeunesse,** held on July 9, celebrates children, who generally just run around the streets singing, dancing, and horsing around.

Sky Bar. For a birds-eye view of the red city, climb to the Sky Bar at the top of La Renaissance Hotel in Guéliz. Drinks are expensive, but it's a rum with a view that encompasses everything in the city, from the Koutoubia Mosque to the High Atlas Mountains in the distance. ✉ *La Renaissance Hotel, Av. Mohammed V, corner of Bd. Zerktouni, Guéliz* ☎ *0524/33–77–77.*

NIGHTCLUBS

Le Diamant Noir. In the town center, Le Diamant Noir, a Marrakesh institution, piles on the R&B and has remained popular since the early 1990s. It's known as a gay club, but everybody is welcome, especially on weekends. ✉ *Pl. de la Liberté, behind Hotel Le Marrakech, Guéliz* ☎ *0524/44–63–91.*

Montecristo. The Cuban-theme surrounds and sounds of Montecristo, complete with Che Guevara portraits, has also caught the imagination of the city's groovers and shakers. You can smoke *shisha* (a hookah water pipe) on the roof terrace, dine downstairs, or dance the night away in the discotheque—but be aware of the omnipresent "working girls." ✉ *20, rue Ibn Aicha, Guéliz* ☎ *0524/43–90–31.*

Paradise. Another popular nightclub is Paradise, at the Hotel Mansour Eddahbi. ✉ *Hotel Mansour Eddahbi, Av. Mohammed VI, near Palais de Congrès, Guéliz* ☎ *0524/33–91–00.*

HIVERNAGE

BARS

La Casa Tapas Bar. La Casa Tapas Bar attracts young Marrakshis and tourists alike and plays a selection of Latin and Top 40 hits. ✉ *Hotel el-Andalous, Av. Prsident Kennedy, Hivernage* ☎ *0524/44–82–26.*

Comptoir Darna. A lively crowd gathers regularly at the popular darkened corners of Comptoir Darna to dance to the tunes of the top-floor DJ. ✉ *Av. Echouhada, Hivernage* ☎ *0524/43–77–02.*

CASINOS

Es Saadi. The only other casino of note is the one in the gardens of the Es Saadi hotel, set apart from the main building. The first in Marrakesh, it has undergone a revamp and contains a mixture of one-armed bandits and tables for roulette and blackjack. ✉ *Hotel Es Saadi, Rue Ibrahim el-Mazini, Hivernage* ☎ *0524/44–88–11.*

5

NIGHTCLUBS

Pacha. The supertrendy supper club has been the hottest nightspot in Marrakesh since it opened in 2005 and boasts a reputation as one of the biggest clubs in Africa. There are two restaurants, a swimming pool, bar, boutique, chill-out room with live music, and, of course, a dance floor featuring international DJs. Restaurants Crystal and Jana offer Mediterranean and Moroccan menus, respectively. ✉ *Zone Touristique Aguedal, Av. Mohammed VI, Hivernage* ☎ *0524/38–84–00* 🌐 *www.pachamarrakech.com* 🎫 *From 200 DH.*

Palais Jad Mahal. One of the hippest nightspots is the Indian-tinged Jad Mahal, with its exorbitantly priced drinks and lavish belly-dancing display that manages to soothe your empty wallet. ✉ *10, rue Fontaine de la Mamounia, Bab Jdid, next to the Sofitel, Hivernage* ☎ *0524/43–69–84* 🌐 *ww.jad-mahal.com.*

SO Night Lounge. The latest chic nightclub in Marrakesh can be found within the Sofitel in Hivernage. Live music and resident DJs, floor shows, a Moroccan restaurant, a chill-out space, and cocktail bar draw those looking for a night out. A hefty cover of 200 DH gets you in as well as a free drink. ✉ *Sofitel, Rue Haroun Errachid, Hivernage* ☎ *0524/42–56–00* 🎫 *200 DH.*

Le Théâtro. Le Théâtro is hip, loud, and gregarious. House music and hard-core Dutch house, with resident live DJs, candy girls, and international guest DJs is usually on the menu. ✉ *Hotel Es Saadi, Rue Ibrahim el-Mazini, Hivernage* ☎ *0664/86–03–39* 🌐 *www.theatromarrakech.com.*

MEDINA

BARS

Alcohol was once frowned upon in the medina, and while it's still unthinkable to swig liquor on the streets, there are a few good places to go for a drink within the city walls. However, things tend to wind down early in the medina.

Café Arabe. One of the most beautiful settings is Café Arabe, a galleried, bougainvillea-strewn riad with a sleek rooftop bar and two dance floors. Pastas are homemade, so come for dinner and make an evening of it. ✉ *184, rue el-Mouassine, Medina* ☎ *0524/42–97–28.*

Les Jardins de la Koutoubia. The attractive Art Deco stylings and extensive cigar rack of Les Jardins de la Koutoubia are decadent. ✉ *26, rue de la Koutoubia, Medina* ☎ *0524/38–88–00.*

Kosy Bar. The cuddly sounding Kosy Bar and restaurant has been criticized for poor service in the past, but the sushi and a jazz pianist make it worth a look. Inventive cocktails can be enjoyed on the large roof terrace and the interiors are camera worthy, as well. ✉ *47, pl. des Ferblantiers, Kzadria, Medina* ☎ *0524/38–03–24.*

La Maison Arabe. The intimate surroundings of the African bar at La Maison Arabe provide a less formal environment and tapas for late-night munchies. ✉ *1, Derb Assehbe, Bab Doukkala, Medina* ☎ *0524/38–70–10.*

CAFÉS

Nowhere is café culture busier than on Djemaâ el-Fna, where several terraces compete for the award for best view of the square.

Café de France. Just opposite Les Terrasses, Café de France is much past its prime, but as long as you're only interested in a late-night hot chocolate with a good view (it stays open until 11 pm), it does the trick; go right up to the top terrace corner. ✉ *Place Djemaâ el-Fna, on northeastern corner, Medina* ☎ *0524/44–23–19.*

Grand Balcon du Café Glacier. To catch the sunset and the beginnings of the alluring smoke and sizzle of the grills, the rightly named Grand Balcon du Café Glacier, to the south of the square, is a top choice. It shuts relatively early, though, and you'll have to compete for elbow room with all the amateur photographers who throng the best spot. Service is slow and soft drinks overpriced—but that's not unexpected for this birds-eye view. ✉ *Place Djemaâ el-Fna, south side, Medina.*

Les Terrasses de l'Alhambra. Les Terrasses de l'Alhambra in the square's northeastern corner is the classiest option, with decent pizza and pasta and warm wood panels. It's tucked away at the edge of the square, but still has lovely views. Bag a seat on the top terrace. No credit cards are accepted and no alcohol served. ✉ *Place Djemaâ el-Fna, opposite Café de France* ☎ *0663/18–93–60.*

CASINOS

La Grand Casino de La Mamounia. The casino at La Mamounia has a large room for roulette, poker and blackjack, a slot-machine hall, and is open until 6 am. You'll need to dress up to gain entrance to this exclusive establishment. ✉ *Av. Bab Jdid, Medina* ☎ *0524/44–45–70* 🌐 *www.grandcasinomamounia.com.*

PALMERY

DINNER SHOWS

Chez Ali. Don't leave the city without visiting Chez Ali, a Vegas-meets-Marrakesh experience. After your multicourse dinner in breezy tents, the show begins. Featuring hundreds of performers and dozens of horses, this singing-and-dancing extravaganza is a celebration of traditional culture. It's somewhat cheesy but very enjoyable. Taxis can take you there, or your hotel can organize an all-inclusive price that includes round-trip transportation. ✉ *La Palmeraie* ☎ *0524/30–77–30* 🎟 *450 DH.*

SHOPPING

5

Marrakesh is a shopper's bonanza, full of the very rugs, handicrafts, and clothing you see in the pages of magazines back home. Most bazaars are in the souk, just north of Djemaâ el-Fna and spread through a seemingly never-ending maze of alleys. Together, they sell almost everything imaginable and are highly competitive. Bargaining here is hard, and you can get up to 80% discounts. So on your first exploration, it's often a better idea to simply wander and take in the atmosphere than to buy. You can check guideline prices in some of the more well-to-do parts of town, which display fixed price tags for every object.

There are a number of crafts and souvenir shops on Avenue Mohammed V in Guéliz, as well as some very good Moroccan antiques stores and designer shops that offer a distinctly modern take on Moroccan clothing, footwear, and interior decoration. These allow buyers to browse at their leisure, free of the souk's intense pressures. Many have fixed prices, with only 10% discounts after haggling. Most of these stores are happy to ship your purchases overseas. Bazaars generally open between 8 and 9 am and close between 8 and 9 pm; stores in Guéliz open a bit later and close a bit earlier, some breaking for lunch. Some bazaars in the medina close on Friday, the Muslim holy day. In Guéliz, most shops are closed on Sunday.

BARGAINING

Bargaining is part of the fun of shopping in the medina's souks. Go back and forth with the vendor until you agree on an acceptable price. If you are not sure if the vendor's "lowest price" is really the lowest, slowly leave the store—if the vendor follows you, then you can negotiate further. If bargaining is just not your thing and you don't mind paying a little extra, consider the shops of Guéliz. Although these shops are not as colorful as the souks, a reasonable variety of high-quality goods are on offer.

SHOPPING GUIDES

Many guides have (undeclared) affiliations with certain shops, and taking on a guide may mean you'll be delivered to the boutique of their choice, rather than your own discovery. You should be fine on your own, as long as you keep your eyes peeled for mini-adventures and touts. Small boutique shopkeepers who can't afford to tip guides will thank you for it.

There are also a few personal shopping guides working in Marrakesh (mostly European expats), trying to strike the best deal for the customer and take the pain out of seeking, finding and haggling for those "must-have" items.

FONDOUKS

If you tire of the haggling in the souk but still want to pick up a bargain, try visiting a *fondouk*. These were originally storehouses, workshops, and inns frequented by merchants and artisans on their journeys across the Sahara (known as *caravanserai* in the Middle East), and are still in use today, particularly by Berber merchants bringing carpets and other goods from surrounding villages; others are staffed by artisans at work on goods destined for the market. They're easily recognized by courtyards full of junk, usually with galleries on upper levels. Fondouks always keep their doors open, so feel free to look around. Because you deal with the artisans directly, there's less of a mark-up on prices. There are a couple of fondouks on the Dar el Bacha as you head towards the souk, and on Rue Bab Taghzout by the fountain known as Shrob ou Shouf ("Drink and Look").

Kati Lawrence—personal shopper. Kati Lawrence is a British expat, who charges around €200 per day to be your personal shopping guide both inside and outside the Medina. Kati knows the ropes (and the rogues) and will be able to source the best-quality items. Kati and her husband have lived in Marrakesh for more than 10 years, having moved from London where she was a fashion buyer for luxury retail stores. ☎ *0646/09–20–45* ✉ *katilawrence@gmail.com.*

MEDINA

THE SOUKS

From dried fruit to handbags, carpets to candlesticks, the jumbled labyrinth of merchants and artisan workshops to be found in the souks of the Marrakesh medina is one of the wonders of the city where all manner of curious exotic items can be found. It stretches north from the Place Djemaâ el-Fna to the Medersa ben Youssef. Each souk has a name that defines its specialty and that relates to the crafts guilds that used to control each area.

Heading north from Bab Fteuh square, near the Place Djemaâ el-Fna, the souks are laid out roughly as follows:

Souk Semmarine: textiles and souvenirs; Souk Rahba Kdima: spices, herbs, apothecaries, woolen hats, baskets. Souk el-Kebir: carpets, leather goods and carpenters; Souk Zarbia: carpets; Souk des Bijoutiers/Souk Tagmoutyime: jewelry; Souk el-Attarine: polished copper and brass and mirrors; Souk des Babouches/Souk Smata: leather slippers; Souk des Teinturiers/Souk Sebbaghine: fabric and wool. Several other souks—including Souk Chouari: carpenters; Souk Haddadine: blacksmiths; and Souk Cherratine: leatherworkers—are at the northern end.

Generally, credit cards are not accepted here, except at the more upmarket bazaars and shops. Most places are open daily from 9 to 9, though some places close on Friday.

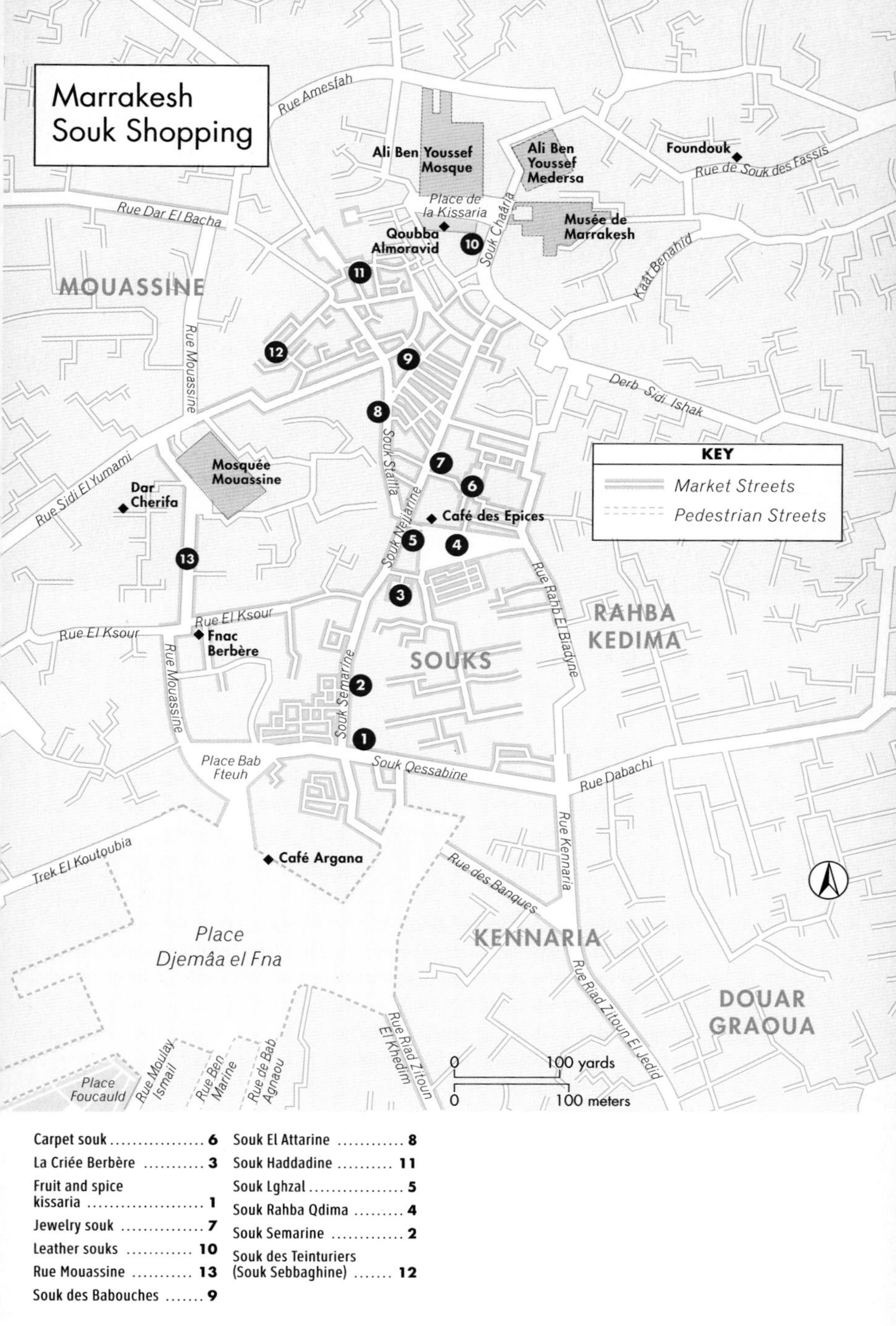

Carpet souk **6**	Souk El Attarine **8**
La Criée Berbère **3**	Souk Haddadine **11**
Fruit and spice kissaria **1**	Souk Lghzal **5**
Jewelry souk **7**	Souk Rahba Qdima **4**
Leather souks **10**	Souk Semarine **2**
Rue Mouassine **13**	Souk des Teinturiers (Souk Sebbaghine) **12**
Souk des Babouches **9**	

Colorful spices are sold in the Marrakesh souks.

Carpet Souk. North on Rue Semmarine and just after the Souk el-Attarine branches off left, the next right turn off the street (which is now more properly named Rue Souk el-Kebir—the Big Souk Street) brings you into the main carpet souk called the Souk Zrabia or *Le Criée Berbère*. This small square was the site of the old slave auctions held up until the French occupied the city in 1912. Thankfully nowadays, it's only carpets that are sold off. The flat, shiny floor in the middle of the surrounding boutiques makes a change from the cobbles, and is used to roll out the rugs to display to potential buyers. The carpet souk can also be reached from a passage in Rahba Qdima's northeast corner (to the right of Le Café des Épices). ■ TIP→ **There are auctions at 5 pm daily (except Friday), when Berbers come down from the mountains to sell their wares to the vendors.** This is strictly for the "trade" only, but it's a marvelous sight. You can also ask a vendor in advance to buy for you, at reduced rates. ✉ *Rahba Qdima, Medina.*

Leather Souks. At the northeastern edges of the souk (just beyond the northern end of the main Rue Souk el-Kebir) are the leatherworkers—busy cutting out templates for babouches, hammering and polishing, and making up bags and satchels from several types of animal skins. Look for signs to the Souk des Sachochiers (bag makers), Souk Chairia, and Souk Cherratine, all leatherworking areas. The tanneries, where the raw hides have been prepared and dyed, are some 20 minutes walk further northeast from Souk Cherratine along Rue Bab Debbagh. Also in the northeast are a range of instruments, especially drums (Souk Moulay aii) and woven baskets (Souk Serrajine). ✉ *Rue Souk Chairia, Medina.*

Rue Mouassine. One of the easiest ways to head back to Djemaâ el-Fna from a day of souk shopping is to find Rue Mouassine, the souk's westernmost main north–south artery (the other main artery is Rue Souk Semmarine, on the eastern side of the souks). Rue Mouassine is quite easy to find, and it's almost impossible to veer away from the correct path once you're on it; the simplest route is to take a counterclockwise loop from behind the Ben Medersa Mosque—when you hit the big mosque, you've hit Rue Mouassine. This is heavy souvenir territory, with the whole gamut of goods on display—lanterns, teapots, scarves, babouches, djellabas. It's an easy trip south. ■ TIP→ **Look for Fnac Berbère, the Berber bookshop, on Rue Mouassine. It's a good landmark.** The street spits you out into the northeast corner of Bab Fteuh square, and from there it's a short hop down to Djemaâ el-Fna. ✉ *Medina*.

NEED A BREAK?

Dar Cherifa. Wind down at Dar Cherifa, an airy riad turned café turned library turned art gallery. It puts on the occasional cultural evening, including poetry readings and storytelling. It also styles itself as a literary café, so you can take a book on Morocco down from the shelves, sit on the low-slung cushions at the foot of the four pillars, and sip mint tea. Alternatively, you can gaze for hours at the outsize modern art (all for sale) hanging on the 16th-century white walls below the stucco and cedar carvings. Magical. ✉ ***8, Derb Cherfa Lakbir, Mouassine, Medina*** ☎ ***0524/42–64–63.***

5

Souk des Babouches. This souk is best approached by taking the main left fork on to Souk el-Attarine where it branches off from Rue Souk el-Kebir and then continuing north for about 150 yards. The Souk Principal des Babouches, which is also called Souk Smata, is on the right-hand side and is filled with the pointed leather slippers so beloved of Moroccans. The small doorway opens up to an enormous emporium with examples in every color imaginable.

It can be hard to judge the proper value of these fairy-tale leather slippers, since price depends on so many things, such as the thickness of the sole, the number of layers, the presence or absence of a stepped heel, and of course the decoration. Use your nose, but be warned that a fair price can vary from 30 DH to 400 DH, depending on quality.

Look for the tiny wool boutique on the left as you come to the arch before the right turn for the babouches market. It's on the way to the Souk des Teinturiers (Dyers' Souk). You can see men rolling out wool to make into fetching striped handbags, and, best of all, into small balls, and looping them up into the most unusual necklaces going. ✉ *Rue Souk Smata, Medina*.

Souk des Bijoutiers. North of the carpet souk on Rue Souk el-Kebir you'll see an overhead sign for the Souk des Bijoutiers (also labeled Souk Tagmoutyime). Follow that just off to the right into a thin mall, full of jewelry stores displaying their wares behind glass. It is by no means the only place in Marrakesh to buy jewelry, however, especially the bulky kind. ✉ *Rue Souk Tagnaoutuyime, Medina*.

Souk des Teinturiers. Using the Mouassine Mosque as a landmark, keep the Mouassine fountain on your right and continue until the street widens out with shops on either side. At the point where it branches into two alleys running either side of a shop selling handmade lamps and textiles, take an immediate sharp left turn. You can follow that derb and look for the helpfully daubed word "teinturies" in spray paint and then head right. Souk des Teinturiers is also called Souk Sebbaghine. The main square for fabric dyeing is hidden down a little shimmy to the right and then immediately left, but anyone can direct you. Here you'll see men dipping fabrics into vats full of hot dye. Don't forget to look up—there are scarves and trains of wool hanging all over, in individual sets of the same bright colors.

For the best view, head into the dyers' square and ask to be led into the boutique. A dyer can show you the powders that the colors come from. A lovely bit of magic involves the fact that green powder dyes fabric red; red powder dyes things blue; and yellow powder dyes things purple. Head up the steep stairs and onto the roof if you are allowed—a spectacular view of industry unfolds, with head scarves and threads of every color hanging up to dry in separate color blocks all over the rooftops. ⌧ *Rue Souk Sebbaghine, Medina.*

Souk el-Attarine. Souk el-Attarine is traditionally the market street for perfumes, essential oils, and spices. This street is one of the main left turns from Souk Semmarine (as you head north), leaving the road at a "10 o'clock" angle. If this is as deep as you wish to explore in the souks, then you can make an interesting loop by walking as far as the entrance to the Souk des Babouches (on the right) and then soon after take a turn off left, passing through the wool dyers souk and heading to the Mouassine mosque. Turning left after the mosque you head back south eventually, down Rue Mouassine to rejoin Bab Fteuh square. ⌧ *Rue Souk el Attarine, Medina.*

Souk Haddadine. From Rue Souk el-Attarine, follow that main souk street as faithfully as possible, and it will take you north, looping clockwise to the east, through the ironmonger's souk, where you'll see blacksmiths at work, hammering out lanterns and wrought-iron chairs. ⌧ *Medina.*

Souk Lghzal. North of Djemaâ el-Fna on Souk Semmarine, you pass a fairly prominent derb that turns off to the left (Rue R'mila Bab Ksour, also called Rue el-Ksour). Take the next right turn and wander down and a few yards (towards the Spice Square or Rahba Qdima) and on the right you will find the small square of "Souk Lghzal," which translates as the Wool Souk. Today women sell secondhand clothes in the square, and the odd djellaba. A real treat can be found in the apothecary stalls leading up to the entrance to the square, and immediately to the right on entering it. There are spices and potions galore, as well as animal skins (zebra, snake, leopard), used by women for magic: mostly in their desire for marriage and pregnancy. ⌧ *La Criée Berbère, Medina.*

Souk Rahba Qdima. Just a quick turn right and then left out of the Souk Lghzal (via Rue Souk Semmarine) is the large square called Souk Rahba Qdima. Pushier and more mass-market than the spice street, this is the souk's main spice center. There are also lots of woven baskets and hats for sale here. If you are feeling peckish or just tired, pause for a pleasant pit stop at the Café des Epices. ✉ *Souk Rahba Qdima, Medina.*

Souk Semmarine. Your first mission is to find Rue Semmarine, one of the two main souk arteries stretching north. From Djemaâ el-Fna take the street just to the left of the Café Argana, which leads into the small Bab Fteuh square and then keep bearing right. To the left there is a *kissaria* (covered market), with dried fruits, herbs and spices, essential oils, and traditional colored eye kohls (expect to pay about 10 DH for a kohl holder and 5 DH for the kohl itself). Veer right into the covered market, past a couple of stands selling teapots and mint-tea glasses, and take a left onto Rue Souk Semmarine. It's signposted and lined with fabrics and inexpensive souvenirs. ✉ *Rue Semmarine, Medina.*

NEED A BREAK?

Souk Kafé. After a hectic few hours in the souks, sampling potions, tasting tea, haggling prices, and nimbly jumping out of the way of mopeds, the Souk Kafé welcomes the frazzled traveler. Just beyond the Souk Cherifa and Souk Semmarine, you can relax in the stylish lounge of this converted old family house and admire your purchases. Colorful textiles, leather pouffes, African artifacts, and old photos adorn the walls; from the small terrace you can gaze over the surrounding rooftops. The menu offers standard Moroccan dishes, or you can just call in for mint tea, coffee, or a fresh fruit smoothie. Open till late, it has plans to serve wine and beer starting sometime in 2012. ✉ ***11, Derb Souk Jdid, Sidi Abdelaziz, Medina*** ☎ ***0662/61–02–29*** ▭ ***No credit cards.***

5

SPECIALTY STORES

ANTIQUES

ETs. Bouchaib Complexe d'Artisanat. ETs. Bouchaib Complexe d'Artisanat is usually either full or empty, depending on whether the latest tour bus has dropped off a load of shoppers. Still, don't let that put you off. Originally a carpet store, it has expanded to three floors of ornate goods ranging from Jewish-Berber handwritten scrolls to man-size Oriental teapots, and each one has an individual price tag. The best thing about it is that the reliable shipping department will wrap fragile items in more rolls of bubble wrap than you thought possible. On large orders, haggle up to 25%. ✉ *7, Derb Baissi, Rue de la Kasbah, Kasbah* ☎ *0524/38–18–53* 🌐 *www.complexeartisanal.com.*

Fodor's Choice ★ **Khalid Art Gallery.** Popular with the international jet set, the reputable Khalid Art Gallery is a gorgeous riad stuffed full of the most sought-after Moroccan antiques. Owner Khalid speaks excellent English, and is an authority on most of the art coming out of Marrakesh. ✉ *14, rue Dar el-Basha, Mouassine, Medina* ☎ *0524/44–24–10.*

Le Trésor des Nomades. The highly respected Le Trésor des Nomades sells antique doors and all kinds of lamps. ✉ *142, rue Bab Doukkala, Medina* ☎ *0524/38–52–40.*

Twizra. Twizra is a general antiques and jewelry store in the kasbah. Prices are high here—so haggle hard! The store can (reliably) organize international shipping and also accepts credit-card payments. ✉ *361, Bab Agnaou, Medina* ☎ *0524/37–65–65.*

ART

Atelier de Marrakech Art et Culture. Atelier de Marrakech Art et Culture puts on exhibitions by local artists and showcases artists at work. You'll find them in the arcades surrounding the 16th-century public fountain next to Bab Doukkala mosque; the building that houses the fountain has been transformed into a gallery. Visitors can buy work they like. ✉ *Fontaine Lalla Aouda, Rue Bab Doukkala, behind mosque Bab Doukkala, Medina* ☎ *0668/32–84–74* ⏲ *Mon.–Sat. 10:30–1.30 pm and 3.30–7:30 pm.*

Light Gallery. Light Gallery has a reliable hip collection of contemporary art and design shown off in an all-white setting. ✉ *2, Derb Chtouka, Kasbah* ☎ *no phone* ⏲ *Tues.–Sat. 2 pm–7pm.*

Maison de la Photographie. A new addition to the Marrakesh cultural scene, this restored riad houses a special collection of original black and white photos depicting life in Moroccan communities between 1862 and 1950. There is also a very pleasant roof terrace café. You can find the Maison de la Photographie just behind the Medersa Ben Youssef. ✉ *Rue Ahel Fes, near Medersa Ben Youssef, Medina* ☎ *0524/38–57–21* 🌐 *www.maisondelaphotographie.ma* 🎫 *40 DH* ⏲ *Daily 9:30 am–7 pm.*

Miloud Art Gallery. Miloud Art Gallery has a very nicely curated collection of upscale Moroccan items for the home. Clothing and bags for women are in the back. ✉ *48, Souk Cheratine, Medina* ☎ *0524/42–67–16.*

Ministero del Gusto. For something a bit more cutting edge, Ministero del Gusto combines boutique and gallery and shows off gorgeous items in both. ✉ *22, Derb Azzouz el-Mouassine, off Rue Sidi el-Yamami, Medina* ☎ *0524/42–64–55* 🌐 *www.ministerodelgusto.com.*

BOOKS

Fnac Berbère. Fnac Berbère has a city-renowned range of books on Berber life and culture. ✉ *Rue Mouassine, Medina* ☎ *No phone.*

Librarie el-Ghazali Ahmed Ben Omar. Librarie el-Ghazali Ahmed Ben Omar has a range of guidebooks, cookery books, volumes on Moroccan history in English, and maps. ✉ *51, Bab Aganou, Mouassine, Medina* ☎ *0524/44–23–43.*

CARPETS

Bazaar Jouti. Bazaar Jouti has a wide selection of rugs and carpets in its spacious two-story shop. They can also arrange for shipping on the spot. ✉ *16–19, Souk des Tapis, Rahba Lakdima, Medina* ☎ *0524/44–32–19.*

Mohamed Taieb Sarmi at Bazaar ben Rahal. No longer in the Medina's Souk des Tapis, but rather in a shop in Guéliz, Mr. Sarmi, of Mohamed Taieb Sarmi at Bazaar ben Rahal, has a magnificent array of Berber tribal rugs and carpets. He can also show you more examples from his stockroom upstairs or from his house in Bab Doukkala, where he will painstakingly explain their origins and value. Sarmi sends rugs and carpets anywhere in the world; for packages to the United States, the import tax is paid in Morocco. ✉ *28, rue de la Liberté, Guéliz* ☎ *0524/43–32–73.*

Palais Saâdiens. Palais Saâdiens has an enormous selection of Berber, Bedouin, and Arab carpets. ✉ *16, rue Moulay Taib, Ksour, Medina* ☎ *0524/44–51–76.*

CLOTHING

Bouriad Karim. Bouriad Karim turns out some of the most fashionable handmade clothes in Marrakesh, and many end up on the hangers of boutique stores in the United States and Europe. His colorful selection of Moroccan-style shirts is perfect for beach or evening wear, while a made-to-measure djellaba will keep out the cold back home. ✉ *Rue Fatima Zahra, near Dar el-Bacha, Medina* ☎ *0524/38–65–17.*

Warda La Mouche. Warda La Mouche stocks reasonably priced clothing for women in great fabrics. The tunics are especially wearable and figure flattering. ✉ *127, rue Kennaria, Medina* ☎ *0524/38–90–63.*

CRAFTS

Antiquités du Sahara. Antiquités du Sahara specializes in handcrafted jewelry from southern Morocco of Berber, Touareg, and Blue Men traditions. ✉ *176, Rahba Lakdima, Medina* ☎ *0524/44–23–73.*

5

Ensemble Artisanal. L'Ensemble Artisanal is a great way to see all the wares of the souk under one hassle-free umbrella. Several boutiques in modern confines display fixed prices (which are high) for handicrafts including babouches, embroidery, lanterns, bags, jewelry, carpets, and paintings. There's even a snack bar. ■ TIP→ **Make a note of prices here and then aim to pay around 25% less in the souks.** ✉ *Av. Mohammed V, Medina* ☎ *0524/38–66–74.*

Najib La Joie. Najib La Joie sells tiny lanterns that are so inexpensive that you'll be tempted to buy a dozen. ✉ *44, pl. des Ferblantiers, Medina* ☎ *No phone.*

Wish Wish Art. This emporium of jewelry and furnishings has a variety of beautiful handicrafts, including magnificently inlaid game tables. ✉ *23, rue el Mouassine, Medina* ☎ *0524/39–09–90.*

HEALTH AND BEAUTY

Aachab Atlas. Aachab Atlas is an apothecary stuffed from floor to ceiling with spices, perfumes, and traditional medicines for ailments such as rheumatism and back pain. The helpful staff speak fluent English, and credit cards are accepted. ✉ *Rue Sidi el-Yamani, Bab Laksour, Medina* ☎ *0524/42–67–28.*

GUÉLIZ

SPECIALTY STORES

ANTIQUES

Marco Polo. Marco Polo has been in Guéliz for years, selling all kinds of antique Moroccan and Asian furniture as well as other artifacts. ✉ *55, bd. Zerktouni, Immeuble Taieb, Guéliz* ☎ *0524/43–53–55* 🌐 *www.ilove-marrakesh.com/marcopolo.*

L'Orientaliste. L'Orientaliste is a charming mixed bag of a place, with old bottles, copper bowls, candlesticks, early-20th-century engravings, Fez pottery, furniture, perfume, and all sorts of antiques. There are two locations on the same street. ✉ *11 and 15, rue de la Liberté, Guéliz* ☎ *0524/43–40–74* ⏲ *Closed Sun.*

La Porte d'Orient. La Porte d'Orient, a sibling of the medina's Porte d'Or, sells Moroccan and Asian antiques. It's geared toward those who prefer to browse before buying. ✉ *9, bd. Mansour Eddahbi, near Hotel Agdal, Guéliz* ☎ *0524/43–89–67* 🌐 *www.ilove-marrakesh.com/portedorient.*

ART

David Bloch Gallery. This small modern gallery showcases up-and-coming contemporary Moroccan artists. ✉ *8 bis, rue des Vieux Marrakchi, Guéliz* ☎ *0524/45–75–95* 🌐 *www.davidblochgallery.com.*

Matisse Gallery. The Matisse gallery has an interesting collection of works by young Moroccan artists, Moroccan masters, and the Orientalists. ✉ *No. 43 Passage Ghandouri, 61, rue de Yougoslavie, Guéliz* ☎ *0524/44–83–26*✉ *43, Passage Ghandouri, off Rue de Yugoslavie, Guéliz* ☎ *0524/44–83–26.*

BOOKS

American Language Center. The American Language Center has a small English-language bookstore. ✉ *3, Impasse du Moulin, Guéliz* ☎ *0524/44–72–59.*

Librairie Papeterie Ahmed Chatr. Greetings cards, artists supplies, schoolbooks in Arabic and French, and some English-language books—including some novels, maps, and books on Moroccan culture—are sold here. ✉ *19–21, av. Mohammed V, Guéliz* ☎ *0524/44–79–97.*

CLOTHING

Atika Boutique. Atika Boutique is best known for its shoes, especially its soft leather moccasins in every shade of the rainbow. ✉ *34, rue de la Liberté, Guéliz* ☎ *0524/43–64–09.*

Intensite Nomade. Intensite Nomade carries chic and rather expensive Moroccan-inspired clothing for men and women. ✉ *139, av. Mohammed V* ☎ *0524/43–13–33.*

Michele Baconnier. Michele Baconnier sells high-end clothing, jewelry, babouches, and bags that offer a hip twist on contemporary design. ✉ *6, rue des Vieux Marrakchis, Guéliz* ☎ *0524/44–91–78.*

Place Vendome. Place Vendome stocks gorgeous leather goods of much better quality than what is offered in the souks. ✉ *141, av. Mohammed V, corner of Rue de la Liberté, Guéliz* ☎ *0524/43–52–63.*

CRAFTS

Al Badii. Al Badii sells artworks, crafts, and antiques in a quiet setting, and the store has furnished some of the most luxurious riads in town. ✉ *54, bd. Moulay Rachid, Guéliz* ☎ *0524/43–16–93.*

JEWELRY

Bazar Atlas. Bazar Atlas sells an enormous selection of jewelry, including the heavy silver *filbules* favored by Berber women to weigh down their dresses; the filbules have become a symbol of the Berber way of life. Owner Said speaks good English and has another store in the medina. ✉ *129, av. Mohammed V, Guéliz* ☎ *0663/62–01–03.*

SPORTS AND THE OUTDOORS

With more than 300 days of sunshine a year, Marrakesh residents pretty much live outdoors. Beat the heat in one of the upscale swanky pool complexes or meander through the public gardens and stop to smell the roses. Whatever you do, don't forget the sunscreen for outdoor activities. But also realize that not all activities take place outdoors. Going to a Moroccan hammam or taking a cooking class can also be a rewarding experience.

COOKING SCHOOLS

With so many chic riads serving up a culinary storm, it's no surprise that cooking schools in Marrakesh have taken off in recent years. Tagines, couscous, and briouates are all on the menu for the Maghrebian master chef in the making.

5

Jnane Tamsna. Cookery classes are offered upon request in the charming cottage compound with a thriving organic garden in the middle of the Palmery. An English-speaking chef gives instruction in the preparation of exquisite Moroccan recipes that are easy to replicate back home. ✉ *Douar Abiad, Circuit de la Palmeraie, Palmery* ☎ *0524/32–94–23* 🌐 *www.jnanetamsna.com* 🎫 *550 DH per person, minimum 2 people.*

Kasbah Agafay. Hidden away in a quiet corner of the kasbah's grounds is the garden in which cooking classes are held. At the start of class you'll pick the herbs and vegetables for the dishes to be prepared, which include various tagines and couscous. Lessons also include bread and pastry making, and you'll use the traditional ovens that give these foods their distinctive flavor. Advice is also given about the excellent variety of Moroccan wines. ✉ *Rte. de Guemassa, Km 20* ☎ *0524/36–86–00* 🌐 *www.kasbahagafay.com* 🎫 *1,500 DH 1-day lesson.*

La Maison Arabe. This boutique hotel began its life as a famous restaurant and, aptly, is now one of the best places for cooking workshops for amateurs and professionals alike. The workshops are conducted by a *dada* (Moroccan cook, traditionally female) and are organized in small groups around easy-to-use modern equipment. A translator (Arabic, English, French) provides detailed preparation and cooking instructions. At the end of each workshop participants dine on the meal they have prepared. Reservations are required. ✉ *1, Derb Assehbe, Bab Doukkala, Medina* ☎ *0524/38–70–10* 🌐 *www.lamaisonarabe.com* 🎫 *800 DH per person for groups of 1–3 persons; 600 DH per person in groups of 4–10 persons.*

GOLF

There are three championship golf courses in and around Marrakesh.

Golf Amelkis Club. With 9 new holes added in 2008, the 27-hole Golf Amelkis Club offers plenty of challenges. The greens fee is 500 DH plus 100DH for caddie. ✉ *Rte. de Ouarzazate, Km 12, Palmery* ☎ *0524/40–44–14.*

Palmeraie Golf Palace. Robert Trent Jones designed the 18-hole course at the Palmeraie Golf Palace, 7 km (4½ mi) north of Marrakesh in the Palmery, and 9 new holes were opened in 2009. Facilities include a clubhouse and restaurant, pro shop, and equipment rental, and greens fees are 500 DH. ✉ *Palmeraie Golf Palace Hotel, Circuit de la Palmeraie, Palmery* ☎ *0524/37–87–66* 🌐 *www.pgpmarrakech.com/golf/golf.html.*

Royal Golf club. The long-established Royal Golf club, founded in 1923, is a tree-filled haven, with a 27-hole course 7 km (4 mi) south of Marrakesh on the old Ouarzazate road. The greens fee is 550 DH, plus 100 DH for a caddie, but save a little extra cash for an open-air lunch at the casual Garden of Eden restaurant. ✉ *Rte. de Ouarazate, Km 7, Palmery* ☎ *0524/40–98–28* 🌐 *www.royalgolfmarrakech.com.*

HORSEBACK RIDING

Les Cavaliers de l'Atlas. Half-day and full-day trekking excursions on horseback are offered from this ranch in the Palmery. Both novices and experienced riders are catered to. ✉ *Rte. de Casablanca, opposite Afriquia gas station, Palmery* ☎ *0672/84–55–79* 🌐 *www.lescavaliersdelatlas.com.*

Royal Club Equestre. The Royal Club Equestre is 5 km (3 mi) southwest of Marrakesh on the Amizmiz road. Guided rides are 150 DH per person per hour. Take the road signed towards Imlil and you'll see see it on the left, opposite Oasiria Water Park. ✉ *Route du Barrage, Km 5, Palmery* ☎ *0524/38–18–49.*

HAMMAMS AND SPAS

The following hammams and spas are open to all (even nonguests, if in a hotel).

PUBLIC HAMMAMS

Hammam el Basha. As far as public hammams go, this is one of the largest and most accessible (it's 10 minutes north of Djemaâ el-Fna). Even in its current rundown condition you get a good sense of how impressive this hammam must have been in its heyday. Instead of the typical series of small low rooms, here you bathe in large, white-tiled chambers that give a pleasant sense of space. After your bath, dry and dress in a huge domed hall skirted with inset stone benches. There are segregated hours for both men and women. ✉ *20, rue Fatima Zohra, Medina* ☎ *No phone* 🎟 *20 DH* 💳 *No credit cards* 🕑 *Daily: men 4 am–noon and 7:30–11 pm; women noon–7:30 pm.*

Hammam Majorelle/Es Salama. This is a clean and modern hammam located 165 yards from the famous Majorelle Garden in Guéliz. ✉ *57, Quartier Rouidate, off Ave. Yacoub el-Mansour, Guéliz* ☎ *No phone* 🎟 *20 DH* 💳 *No credit cards* 🕑 *Daily 6 pm–10 pm.*

Semlalia Hammam. The oldest public hammam in Guéliz opened in 1965 and is still thriving. For the uninitiated, you can ask for somebody to help you through the process and they'll scrub you down with black soap, made from olives. For the basic use of the hammam you'll pay

Continued on page 243

HAMMAM RITUAL
SPREADER OF WARMTH

by Victoria Tang

To escape the bustling souks and crowded cities—or simply to recover from hours of trekking and touring—a hammam is the perfect retreat to soothe both your body and soul in a uniquely Moroccan way.

Essential to Moroccan life, hammams are hydrotherapeutic rooms best described as something between a Turkish bath and a Finnish sauna. Like the tagines used to cook the national dish, hammams provide a mixture of baking and steaming. Water pipes run beneath marble-tiled floors, which are heated by wood fires below ground. For public hammams, at least, these fires are the same ones used for the neighborhood's breadbaking ovens, which is why you'll usually find them in the medina of any Moroccan town. Water arrives through taps and creates a constant, light steam before being removed by drains at the center of the room. Although many hammams are old, all public hammams are relatively clean and subject to constant checks.

Walking into a public hammam for the first time can be daunting or disenchanting if you're imagining a luxurious bathing chamber. It isn't a full-service spa—like those now offered in many upscale riads and hotels—but rather a basic, unadorned public bath, with no signs for the uninitiated. But if you know what to expect, there is nothing like it to make you feel you are truly in Morocco.

The tayeba at a hammam will wash you with a kessel scrubbing glove.

HOW TO USE THE HAMMAM

You need two buckets at a hammam: one for hot and one for cold water.

ORIGINS

Islamic public baths were originally cold, and only men were permitted to use them. When the prophet Mohammed came to believe that hot water could promote fertility, the heated hammam (meaning "spreader of warmth") was inaugurated, and its use was extended to women. It soon became central to Muslim life, with several in each city, town, and village annexed to the mosque, to make hygiene available to everyone in accordance with the laws of Islam. The hammam's popularity also increased because the heat was thought to cure many types of diseases. The price of entry was—and still is—kept low so that even the poorest can afford it. Unlike the Roman baths, which were large, open, and designed for socializing, Moroccan hammams are mostly small, enclosed, and dimly lighted to inspire piety and reflection. In time the hammams drew people to socialize, especially women, whose weekly visits became so important to them—the only time they were allowed to leave the confines of their house—that it eventually was viewed as a right.

CHOOSE A LOCATION

If you're looking for an authentic experience, head to a public hammam. If you're shy, have a higher budget, or seek a more luxurious experience, head to a private one. But realize that all hammams are sex-segregated. When looking for a public hammam, ask at your hotel about public hammam that are welcoming to foreigners. Avoid hammams with seedy reputations. Entry to a public hammam is usually 5–10 DH; private hotel hammams cost 200–500 DH. Upscale spa treatments can add 800–1000 DH.

WHAT TO BRING

In a public hammam, take basic toiletries: soap, shampoo, comb and/ or hairbrush, razor, a towel (women should bring an extra towel to wear as

Public hammams, which are usually found in medinas, are simple places with simple signage.

a turban when you leave, as hair dryers are not permitted), and a spare pair of underwear. You may also want to bring a pair of flip-flops, as the hammam's tiled floors are slippery and hot. Buy a small plastic water jug, scrubbing glove called a kessel (or *kees,* or *kis*), the dark olive soap called *savon noir,* and mineral-laden clay for conditioning hair and skin called *rhassoul* from a local grocer or pharmacy.

Don't bring any valuables; you'll leave your belongings in an open cubby (the attendants watch diligently over these, so bring 3–5 DH for a tip). If you hire a *tayeba,* an assistant, who will basically do everything from start to finish for you, tip 20–50 DH. Private hammams usually provide individual bags containing everything you need.

HAMMAM ETIQUETTE

The hammam is generally relaxed, with the echo of voices and splashing water resounding from each room. As a tourist, you may be stared at, but a big smile will ease anxiety. A warm *salaam* when you arrive will help break the ice. Once you have stripped down to your underwear and stored your bagged belongings in a cubby, take two buckets from the entry room and enter the hammam. Most hammams consist of three interconnected rooms, usually dimly lit from tiny windows in a small, domed roof. The floors are often white marble tiles—both hot and slippery—so tread carefully. The first room is warm, the next hot, and the last is the hottest.

Choose a spot in the hot room first. Then go to the taps and fill your buckets, one with hot water, the other with cold for mixing. Go back and rinse your sitting area, and sit on a mat (which is usually provided). You can either stay here to let your pores open or go to the hottest room for 15 minutes or so.

Apply the olive soap over your body. Sit for a while before rinsing it off, then begin scrubbing your skin with the kessel mitt. Particularly in women's hammams, one of the other bathers may offer to scrub your back; it's polite to allow her to scrub yours and offer to scrub hers in return. Now rinse off with jugs of water mixed from the hot and cold buckets. You may refill your buckets at any time. Apply the rhassoul over your hair, and comb or brush until it's silky smooth, then repeat.

Finally, lather your body with regular soap, followed by a final all-over rinse, including rinsing your sitting area clean before leaving. Wrapped in your towel, you can relax back in the changing room before dressing and going outside. If you hired a tayeba, pay him or her now, and tip the attendant who looks after the belongings. (Moroccan women never leave a hammam with exposed wet hair, and you may want to wrap yours with a towel or scarf as well; this isn't such a big deal for men.)

Private hammams follow the same ritual. Towels are usually supplied or rented. Specialized products are available for purchase. In hotels and upscale spas, you won't need to take anything with you, as attendants, towels, and all products are included in the fee. Tayebas in private hammams should be tipped 40–60 DH.

WHERE TO FIND BLISS

The health and well-being industry is flourishing in Morocco, where luxury resorts and riads offer tantalizing treatments to rejuvenate the most weary traveler.

MARRAKESH

The glow of candles and scent of jasmine leading to private hammam cabins at **Les Bains de Marrakech** (at Riad Mehdi) and **La Sultana Spa & Boutique Hotel** are guaranteed to restore and destress. The **Caravan Serai** has a divine spa. **Hamman Ziani** is a wonderfully modern, private hammam that also offers some spa services.

FEZ AND THE MIDDLE ATLAS

In Fez, the **Riad Fès** has a wonderful, small private hammam. In Ifrane, the newly renovated **Hôtel Mischliffen** on a countryside hilltop, offers the hammam experience with an ultra-chic, contemporary flavor.

NORTHERN ATLANTIC COAST

La Tour Hassan in Rabat has an elegant yet affordable hammam. **Hammam Ziani,** a sister to the one in Marrakesh, is in Casablanca. The **L'Amphitrite Palace** in Skhirat offers a full-service hammam in a large resort setting. **La Sultana** in El Oualidia is a blissful retreat.

SOUTHERN ATLANTIC COAST

The **Atlantic Palace** in Agadir has a full-service hammam in a large resort setting. You can pamper yourself with traditional techniques and natural products in the hammam of the **Sofitel Essaouira Medina & Spa**. Also in Essaouira, **Hammam Mounia** is a nicely renovated old hammam, and the **Villa Maroc** also has a private hammam.

HAMMAN VOCABULARY

Kessel: Scrubbing glove made from coarse natural or synthetic fabric; used for exfoliation.

Savon noir: organic molasses-like paste derived from black olives; used as cleanser.

Rhassoul: natural clay from Middle Atlas rich in mineral salts; used to condition the hair and skin.

Tayeba or ghalassa: attendant who will fill water buckets, wash, and scrub you.

SAFETY TIPS

- Not all public hammams are welcoming to foreigners.
- Avoid going to public hammams on crowded Thursday evenings, and on Friday and Saturday afternoons.
- Drink plenty of water before entering a hammam.
- If you feel hot at any point, exit quickly and head for a cooler room.

Hammams may be simple places (left, above), or they may be more elaborate and upscale (right, above).

10 DH; for the use of the hammam, exfoliation, and soap the cost is 100 DH. ✉ *48, bd. Mohammed el-Khattabi Abdelkrim, Rte. de Casablanca, Guéliz* ☎ *0661/92–99–25* 🎫 *10 DH* ⏲ *Daily 6 am–9 pm.*

PRIVATE HAMMAMS

Hammam Hilton. A short petit-taxi ride (15 DH–20 DH) will bring you to an upscale private hammam in the Targa district of Marrakesh that few tourists know about. In addition to the hammam, it also offers massage (100 DH). ✉ *Rte. de Targa, Guéliz* ☎ *0524/49–31–29* 🎫 *80 DH* ▭ *No credit cards* ⏲ *Daily 7 am–10 pm.*

Fodor's Choice ★ **Hammam Ziani.** Sister to Casablanca's Ziani, this hammam is highly recommended, and is located not far from Bahia Palace in the medina. Both men and women are welcome. It's traditional without being in the slightest bit down-at-the-heels. The full hammam and *gommage* (exfoliation) works cost 120 DH, while packages priced between 250 DH and 300 DH include hammam, scrubbing, massage, and an algae wrap. ✉ *14, Riad Zitoune Jdid, near Bahia Palace, Medina* ☎ *0662/71–55–71* 🌐 *www.hammamziani.ma* 🎫 *100 DH* ▭ *No credit cards* ⏲ *Daily 7 am–10 pm.*

5

HOTEL HAMMAMS

Les Couleurs de l'Orient. This hammam is in a riad near the Djemaâ el-Fna, with affordable prices from 400 DH for massage and hammam. Afterward, you can relax with a mint tea on the terrace. ✉ *22, Derb Lakhdar, Riad Zitoune Lakdim, Medina* ☎ *0524/42–65–13* ▭ *No credit cards.*

La Maison Arabe. This one is worth a try, especially in order to visit this sumptuous hotel. A morning or afternoon spent in this hotel's hammam will make you feel like royalty. The staff may not scrub you quite as hard as you like, but the hammam room is beautiful, and the small pool filled with roses is just for you. It's popular, so call at least two days in advance. ✉ *La Maison Arabe, 1, Derb Assehbe, Bab Doukkala, Medina* ☎ *0524/38–70–10* 🌐 *www.lamaisonarabe.com* 🎫 *650 DH for hammam and massage* ⏲ *By appointment.*

La Mamounia. A day-pass to the Mamounia's hammam, spa, and swimming pool is an extravagance fit for special celebrations and lets you spend some downtime at this famously exclusive establishment. The hammam is open by reservations only, which are required for both hotel guests and nonguests. ✉ *Av. Bab el-Djedid* ☎ *0524/44–44–09* 🌐 *www.mamounia.com* 🎫 *500 DH day pass, 900 DH hammam* ⏲ *Weekdays by reservation only.*

La Sultana Spa & Boutique Hotel. La Sultana is in the kasbah district, close to the Royal Palace, and offers bath therapy, affusion showers (showers with lukewarm water combined with hand massage), hammam, Jacuzzi, and sauna. ✉ *403, rue de la Kasbah, Kasbah* ☎ *0524/38–80–08* 🌐 *www.lasultanamarrakech.com* 🎫 *400 DH for hammam, 900 DH with massage* ⏲ *Daily 10 am–8 pm.*

SPAS

Les Bains de Marrakech. A temple to exotic beauty treatments and therapies, Les Bains de Marrakech will bathe you in milk with orange water and rose petals, massage you with argan oil and and rub you down with mint-steamed towels. Reservations are required. ✉ *2, Derb Sedra, Bab Agnaou, Kasbah* ☎ *0524/38–14–28* 🌐 *www.lesbainsdemarrakech.com* 🎟 *150 DH hammam.*

Riad des Eaux. In the simple elegance of this renovated riad just a few steps south of Djemaâ el-Fna you can relax in an apricot-color tiled hammam and be treated to clay beauty masks and massaged with essential oils from plants gathered in the Ourika Valley. ✉ *24, Derb Lakhdar, Riad Zitoune Lakdim, Medina* ☎ *0524/42–80–72* 🌐 *www.riaddeseaux.com* 🎟 *150 DH hammam, treatments from 250 DH* ⏲ *By appointment.*

QUAD BIKING

Quad bikes and sand buggies are available for hire in the outskirts of Marrakesh, with most of the outfitters taking advantage of the sandy tracks of the Palmery for a half day or so of fun, but some can organize treks that range farther afield.

American Buggies Adventures. Sand buggies and quad bikes are available for guided excursions in the Palmery and in the outlying Agafay desert region. ☎ *0524/02–40–80* 🌐 *www.americanbuggiesadventures.com.*

Dunes & Desert Exploration. Dunes & Desert Exploration is for those who like the more-adrenaline-pumping entertainment of quad bikes. The outfitter can also arrange white-water rafting excursions in the Ourika Valley. ☎ *0661/24–69–48* 🌐 *www.dunesdesert.com.*

SWIMMING

Oasiria. The jewel in Marrakesh's aquapark crown is Oasiria, where children will enjoy a kids' lagoon, a pirate ship, a wave pool, an inner-tube ride, and three twirly waterslides, while parents chill out at the Bellevue restaurant. There's a free shuttle bus from near Koutoubia Mosque and from Harti Gardens in Guéliz during summer months. ✉ *Rte. de Barrage, Km 4* ☎ *0524/38–04–38* 🌐 *www.oasiria.com.*

La Plage Rouge. Just outside the city, La Plage Rouge is one of Marrakesh's collection of stylish and sexy city "beaches." A huge, sunken pool edged with sand is the centerpiece of this pool-restaurant-bar complex. During the day, it's great for families, and at night DJs spin house music. You can enjoy cocktails as you relax on Balinese sunbeds by the pool. The entrance fee is 250 DH (125 Dh for children). A shuttle bus leaves the Koutoubia Mosque every 30 minutes (but is not reliable). ✉ *Rte. de l'Ourik, a Km 10* ☎ *0524/37–80–86.*

6

The High Atlas

WORD OF MOUTH

"I recommend spending one night in the High Atlas Mountains at the Kasbah du Toubkal near Imlil—incredible Berber village and hiking."

—betts123

WELCOME TO THE HIGH ATLAS

TOP REASONS TO GO

★ **The chance to hike North Africa's tallest peak:** Djebel Toubkal, which soars to 13,671 feet, is only a two-day climb. Trekkers can find everything they need at the base of the mountain.

★ **Legendary hospitality:** Many travelers say their favorite experiences involve staying with a traditional Berber family and engaging in simple pleasures such as rambling, horseback riding, and bird-watching.

★ **Adrenaline junkies getting their fix:** From quad biking to skiing to skydiving and hot-air ballooning, outdoor activities in magical surroundings abound.

★ **Magnificent views in high style:** Some truly first-class hotels have opened their doors to travelers in the High Atlas; the best even contribute to the local community.

★ **Some of the most adventurous driving on the African continent:** Stunning passes switchback through mountains with panoramas you have to see to believe.

1 The Central High Atlas. Forested with olive groves and live oaks on their lower slopes, the rugged mountains to the south of El-Ksiba and Beni-Mellal offer memorable trek and jeep excursions and form a striking contrast to Azilal's lush Cascades d'Ouzoud and Demnate's natural bridge at Imi-n-Ifri.

2 Imlil. A village between Marrakesh and Mount Toubkal, Imlil is the center of adventure tourism in Morocco. Trekkers en route to the mountain stop here for rest, relaxation, and to breathe in the fresh mountain air so rarely found elsewhere.

3 Ourika Valley. The verdant Ourika Valley, just south of Marrakesh, is home to a string of charming villages. Visitors to the region marvel at the waterfalls of Setti Fatma and pause for pictures in front of Morocco's only brick mosque at Aghbalou.

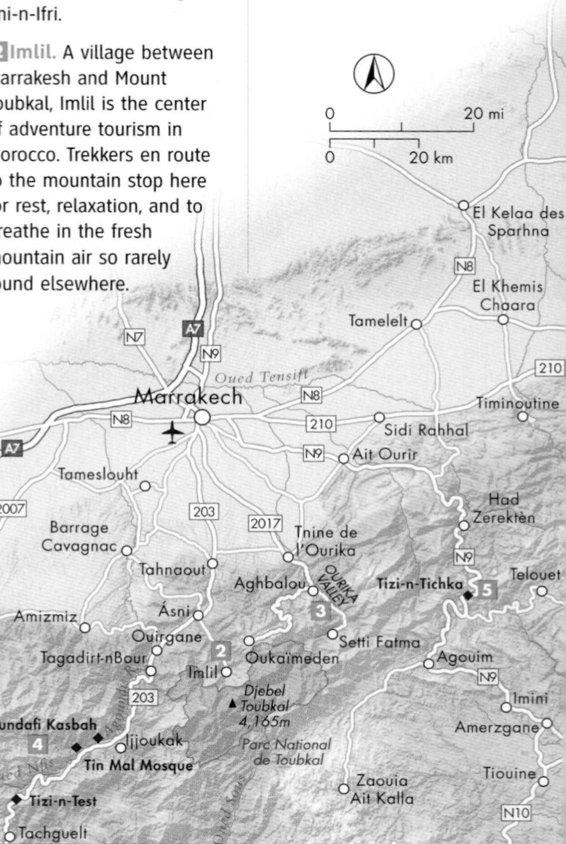

4 To Tizi-n-Test. The pass southwest of Marrakesh leads to the trekking center of Ourigane and on to Taroudant.

5 Tizi-n-Tichka. Completed in 1936, the Tizi-n-Tichka can be a daunting prospect. Though the road is safer and wider than the one over the Tizi-n-Test, it can be a dangerous drive, particularly in winter weather conditions. Still, the views from the pass are like nothing else.

GETTING ORIENTED

The two routes over the Tizi-n-Test (Test Pass) and Tizi-n-Tichka (Tichka Pass) are spectacular. For serious trekking, the area around Imlil is justifiably famous. There are also less strenuous walks along many of the dirt roads in the region, for instance along the Agoundis River. Alternatively, visitors can make the hotels around Ouirgane their bases, exploring the area on muleback or simply lounging by the pool. The Tin Mal Mosque and the Goundafi Kasbah can easily be reached from Ouirgane on a day trip.

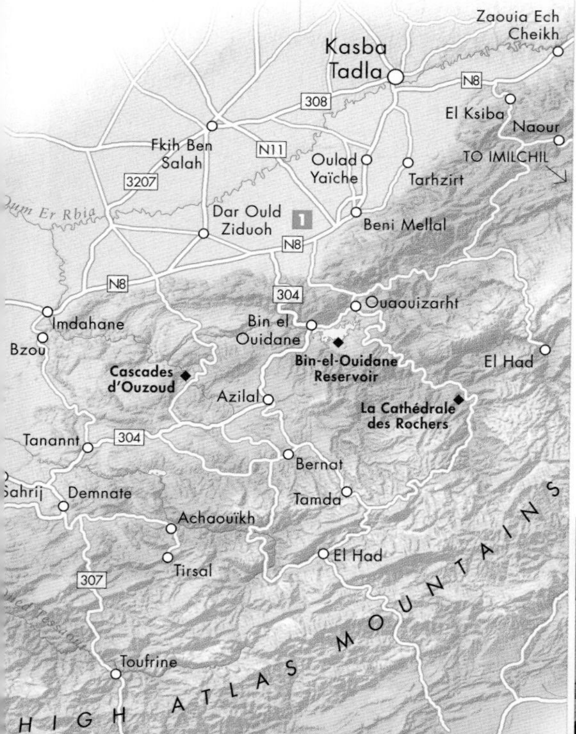

TREKKING IN THE ATLAS

(above) Two trekkers walking along a river in the Central High Atlas (opposite page, bottom) walking in the Tizi-n-Tichka pass (opposite page, top) a terrace restaurant with a view of the snow-covered Atlas peaks

There are few better antidotes to the marvelous mayhem that is Marrakesh than the clear air and amazing vistas offered by the High Atlas Mountains. From gentle strolls through unspoiled Berber villages to full-blown, week-long mountain treks, outfitters can cater to all levels of experience and budget.

Most travelers to the High Atlas associate it with one thing: Djebel Toubkal, North Africa's highest peak, scraping the clouds at 13,761 feet. It is indeed a magnificent sight, and for most of the year is a relatively easy climb. From late April to early October a strong pair of legs will suffice. As the focal point of the range, Djebel Toubkal is very popular in high season, but over its 600-plus-mile length, the High Atlas has over 400 peaks that exceed 10,000 feet, so there are plenty of alternatives. In typical Moroccan style, flexibility is the name of the game. Pretty much any type or length of trek can be organized, from a half-day excursion to a lengthy expedition involving mules and guides. Your level of fitness will determine which you choose!

SAFETY ADVICE

Never walk alone. Always tell someone where you are going, and when you hope to return. Take suitable quantities of food; warm, lightweight clothing; a hat and sunscreen; and a first-aid kit and water purifying tablets (not bottled water). Most important, wear comfortable boots. Litter and general pollution are a growing problem, so please leave no traces of your visit.

It is generally agreed that the launch point for any foray into the High Atlas is the small, albeit largest, Berber village in the region, Imlil. Here, accommodations are both plentiful and cheap, though they can be a little jaded. Moreover, Berber hospitality is included, on which one cannot put a price. If price is indeed not an issue, a short walk (or mule ride) up the hill takes one to the marvelous and calm Kasbah Toubkal, an award-winning eco-hotel.

In the shadow of Djebel Toubkal, Imlil is unprepossessing but has a purposeful bustle, offering all that is necessary for a trek. Everything is for hire: boots (though bring your own if possible), jackets, sleeping bags, crampons, and even a mule, which can carry the loads of four people over most terrain.

What marks out the High Atlas from the rest of Morocco is not only its stunning geography and the Berber tradition that lives on there, but also its relative proximity to lively urban centers such as Marrakesh and Essaouira, a fact that should be exploited.

GUIDES

Detailed maps are scarce, but with a guide you shouldn't need one, and Imlil seems bursting with people willing to lead an expedition. They vary widely in competence and legitimacy. Official guides can be found at the Bureau des Guides et des Accompagnateurs à Imlil, in the main square, but don't completely rule out those attached to local hotels. In terms of cost, expect to pay 350 to 400 DH each for one day. Mules come in at a very reasonable 100 DH. Bargaining is permitted, but make sure you know what you're paying for: food and overnight stays are sometimes not included.

TREKKING ROUTES

The choice of route will depend upon your level of experience, the season, the time available and the budget. The obvious option is to attack Djebel Toubkal—you can be up and down in two days. Head south from Imlil past Sidi Chamarouch and make the easy ascent. Overnight on the mountain in the Neltner hut (a common shelter before the peak) and proceed to the summit in the morning.

Those with more time and stamina may opt for a circular route, east from Imlil. Over five days, you might visit Tacchedirt, Tizi Likemt (at an impressive 11,663 feet), spend the second night at Azib Lkemt, and the third in Amsouzerte. To the west, Lac d'Ifni (a serene mineral-rich lake) awaits, then back to the Neltner hut before descending to Imlil. Those wishing to contrast the trekking experience with a luxurious stay in beautiful surroundings may continue to Ouirgane, where many top hotels await.

6

Updated by Ian Thomas

The High Atlas region is perfect for outdoors adventure and the perfect antidote to the concentration and animation of Marrakesh. You can hang glide, ski, hot-air balloon, quad-bike, and ride mules. Best of all, you can walk. And if trekking in the snowy mountain ranges for days on end with only Berber women and their mules for friends isn't your thing, you can wimp out and drive.

In fact, there's nothing wimpy about it. The roads career around bends for miles on end, carving their way through the rock. You and your fellow passengers will ooh and aah at every vista and every new combination of snow and sun. Stretching from the ocean to the desert, the mountain scenery is utterly compelling.

The High Atlas Mountains rise as a natural fortress between the fertile Haouz Plain around Marrakesh and the deserts of the south. Trapping moisture that blows in from the Atlantic, the mountains pass this bounty along to the land and to the thin rivers that vanish into the southern desert. To reach the mountains, even today's travelers must pass through one of the routes guarded by age-old passes: Tizi-n-Test in the west and Tizi-n-Tichka in the east. They benefit from some glorious spots to stay, and the chance to take a quiet look at some intriguing relics of Moroccan history.

PLANNING

WHEN TO GO

For some the High Atlas is at its best in April, when the trees are flowering and the mountains are still cloaked in white. High-country hiking is safest and easiest in late summer. Winter can be cold but very peaceful, and on sunny days the lower passes just south and north of Imlil and the area around the Agoundis can make for pleasant day hikes. The high passes should be attempted in winter only by serious alpinists with serious gear, and even in summer the higher peaks are worthy of respect.

GETTING HERE AND AROUND

True, there's no air travel directly into the High Atlas, but getting to the region isn't as difficult as it seems.

BY AIR

The closest airport is Marrakesh Menara, both to the Central High Atlas regions east of the city and to the areas south of Marrakesh, including the Ourika Valley. Many of the better hotels can arrange direct airport transfers from Marrakesh on your behalf, though the trip will be at an additional charge.

BY BUS

You can also hop on a bus (a little daunting), but this kind of travel can be time-consuming. If going to Azilal or other areas north and east of Marrakesh, try to avoid the marathon bus that goes from Marrakesh to Fez (via Beni-Mellal); buses run from Beni-Mellal up to Azilal, a common departure point for hiking excursions, departing approximately every three hours between 7 am and 4 pm. Buses also reach destinations in the High Atlas south of Marrakesh.

BY CAR

Unless you are taking a guided excursion, a car is the best way to explore off the beaten path at your own pace. If you have any intention of wandering into the hinterland independently, be sure you're driving a four-wheel-drive vehicle, and consider carrying more than one spare as well as emergency fuel. It's best to rent a car in Marrakesh. *See ⇨ Chapter 5, Marrakesh, for more information on rental cars.*

BY TAXI

You can also take a *grand* taxi, a large Mercedes, which can take up to six passengers, to many of these destinations. Agree on the fare prior to travel.

SAFETY

The High Atlas is no longer the wily region it used to be, but travelers should take precautions. Rural sentiments are quite different from urban ones, so women should dress more conservatively than in larger cities. The biggest safety concern is, of course, for trekkers; beginners should consult a local expert or join a group.

RESTAURANTS

There are a few excellent restaurants in some of the major hotels, but beyond these, fare is limited mostly to what's available in small hotel restaurants and cafés—mostly tagines. Avoid alcohol except in hotels. In general, drinking won't raise any eyebrows as long as you're among other tourists, but the practice of carrying wine and spirits into the backcountry is not appreciated by villagers. Alcohol is *haram* (forbidden by the Koran), but on a more earthly level it's simply not very socially acceptable.

HOTELS

Most of the better hotels in the High Atlas are located in or around Ouirgane, which is quickly becoming a sought-after refuge from the sometimes excessive stimulation of Morocco's cities. There are a couple of stunning kasbahs around Imlil. Most other lodging in the region consists of inexpensive backpackers' refuges (*gîtes*). Heterosexual couples staying in private homes while trekking will be assumed to be married. It's best not to disabuse your hosts of their assumptions.

WHAT IT COSTS IN DIRHAMS					
	¢	$	$$	$$$	$$$$
Restaurants	under 60 DH	60 DH–90 DH	91 DH–120 DH	121 DH–150 DH	over 150 DH
Hotels	under 250 DH	250 DH–400 DH	401 DH–650 DH	651 DH–1,000 DH	over 1,000 DH

Restaurant prices are per person for a main course at dinner. Hotel prices are for a high-season standard double room, excluding service and tax.

FESTIVALS

The most famous of festivals in this region is the Imilchil Marriage Festival, held each year in September. Legend has it that a Romeo and Juliet story happened here ages ago; since then, an annual festival is held for young people to choose their own partner. Though lately the festival has been attracting more and more tourists, it's still a sight to behold. The Setti Fatma Moussem, held in August, still contains the religious elements of a *moussem* (pilgrimage festival). Foreigners are welcome and will be pulled into the games and entertainment.

WHAT TO WEAR

As weather in this region can be unpredictable, it's best to bring layers. Having a wool sweater or fleece pullover is a necessity, as it can get quite frigid at night. Solid footwear, such as boots or sneakers, is important. Although sandals are socially acceptable, they're mostly useless here. Both women and men should dress conservatively: no shorts or sleeveless tops. Women will be better received by locals if they wear longish sleeves and long pants or skirts. And although locals are used to seeing uncovered heads, some travelers report that keeping a scarf handy is a good idea. Women should bear in mind that pants are more practical when mule riding, unless you are accomplished at riding sidesaddle.

IMILCHIL

113 km (70 mi) southwest of Midelt, 150 km (93 mi) northeast of Marrakesh.

The joy of a visit to Imilchil is in the journey; however, if you find yourself in the area during August or September, you'll have an extra reason to visit. The September (sometimes late August) marriage *moussem,* which brings the Aït Haddidou tribe together to marry off eligible—but not always fully consenting—young people, is an event that over time has become more of a tourist attraction than a marriage mart. The surrounding **Plateau des Lacs** (Plateau of the Lakes) includes the lakes of Iseli and Tislit (His and Hers, or Fiancé and Fiancée). Lac Tislit is 5 km (3 mi) from Imilchil, while Iseli is another 10 km (6 mi) east.

GETTING HERE AND AROUND

Some people will approach Imilchil from Midelt (*see ⇨ Chapter 3, Fez and the Middle Atlas*). To reach Imilchil from the west, leave Beni Mellal on Av. 20 Août Ex (N50), and shortly after take Route Principale 24.

CLOSE UP

The Berbers

Berbers, the ancestral people of north Africa west of the Nile (the area known as the Maghreb), live in every part of Morocco and move in every social class, from the poorest rural farms to the wealthiest neighborhoods in Rabat. The word "Berber" is thought by many to derive from "barbarian," used by the Romans to describe foreigners, especially those from the untamed hinterlands of their empire. Berbers themselves are manifold, dividing into three broad groups (Masmouda, Sahanja, and Zénètes). Although there were numerous Berber-speaking Jewish communities until the mid-20th century (when many moved to Israel at its foundation in 1948), the population is now almost entirely Muslim.

LANGUAGE

There are three main divisions of the Berber language: Taririft in the Rif area; Tamazight in the Mid-Atlas; and Tashelhit in the Anti-Atlas and Souss. However, the divisions don't necessarily match the broad groups mentioned above. High Atlas Berbers call themselves Ishelhin, and also speak Tashelhit. The language seems to have arrived with migrants from somewhere in the Middle East at least 3,000 years ago, perhaps in several waves.

THE BERBER WAY

Attention to local sensitivities is much appreciated and often rewarded with the celebrated Amazigh hospitality. Smiling goes further than anything in creating good will. Dress modestly, and wear something on your head if you're female (even a baseball cap). It is always appreciated. Smoking is an urban phenomenon, so everyone (particularly women) should smoke discreetly. Many High Atlas villagers are outraged that their children behave as beggars by demanding money, pens, or sweets from foreigners; the polite way to refuse is to say, *Allah esahel,* which means "God make it easy on you." Always ask permission before you photograph Moroccans.

CLOSE UP

The Imilchil Moussem

Every year hundreds of people get married at the three-day marriage *moussem*, the engagement festival that takes place at Imilchil every August/September, at the northern end of the Todra Gorges. The reason? Long ago Isli and Tislit, a young man and woman from opposing tribes, fell in love. Sound familiar? It's Shakespeare with a twist. The warring tribes were so angered by their love that they separated the pair, whereupon they wept and wept until their tears formed the lake that rests there today. They threw themselves into it and drowned. The villagers were so shocked that they vowed to honor their love henceforward, and started the ceremony in their honor.

Continue on the P3221, After 5 km, take the N8 for 44 km, then take a right onto the R317 and continue for 119 km (74 mi), arriving at Imilchil after a total of about 170 km (105 mi) and three hours driving.

BENI-MELLAL

198 km (148 mi) northeast of Marrakesh, 30 km (18 mi) south of Kasba Tadla, 211 km (127 mi) southwest of Azrou.

Ringed with fortifications built by Moulay Ismail in 1688, this rapidly growing country town nestles in the shadow of 7,373-foot Djebel Tassemit, surrounded by verdant orchards that are well irrigated by the Bin-el-Ouidane reservoir, 59 km (35 mi) to the southwest. Beni-Mellal is largely modern and of little architectural interest, but its Tuesday souk, known especially for its Berber blankets with colorful geometric designs, is an event to catch. ■TIP→ **The 10-km (6-mi) walk up to the Aïn Asserdoun spring and the Kasbah de Ras el-Aïn is well worth the haul for the gardens and waterfalls along the way and the views over the olive groves and the Tadla Plain.**

GETTING THERE AND AROUND

Beni-Mellal can be reached by either bus or car from Marrakesh.

Bus Contacts **Beni-Mellal CTM Station** ✉ *Av. Hassan II* ☎ *0523/48–39–81.*

Visitor and Tour Info **Délégation du Tourisme de Beni-Mellal** ✉ *Av. Hassan II, Immeuble Chichaoua* ☎ *0523/48–86–63.*

WHERE TO EAT AND STAY

For expanded hotel reviews, visit Fodors.com.

$$$ MOROCCAN ✕ **SAT Agadir.** This small restaurant offers light entrées like hearty soups and tagines. The upper dining-room area offers a lovely view of the square. ✉ *155, bd. el-Hansali* ☎ *0523/48–14–48.*

The Imilchil wedding moussem draws more than just happy couples; livestock vendors are also there in full force.

$$ **Hôtel Ouzoud.** Although regarded as Beni Mellel's best hotel it falls short of it's proclaimed four-star status. **Pros:** more amenities than elsewhere available; children under 12 stay free. **Cons:** lacks charm; needs refurbishing; can be noisy at night. ✉ *Rte. de Marrakesh* ☎ *0523/48–37–52, 0523/48-98-22* *56 rooms* *In-room: a/c, Wi-Fi. In-hotel: restaurant, bar, pool, tennis court, gym, laundry facilities, parking* *Breakfast.*

AZILAL

171 km (103 mi) northeast of Marrakesh, 86 km (52 mi) southwest of Beni-Mellal on the S508, off the P24.

Azilal is a small garrison town used as a jumping-off point for routes into the southern highlands, especially toward the M'Goun Massif in the High Atlas, north of Ouarzazate. The pistes south of here become a maze of loops and tracks, great for exploring, but the main route forks 28 km (17 mi) after Aït Mohammed. To the right (southwest), the 1809 road descends into the Aït Bou Guemés valley, passing ksour (villages or tribal enclaves) at El Had and Agouti and looping eventually back to Aït Mohammed after a tough, tremendous 120-km (72-mi) trek that's much more effectively absorbed on foot than from a car.

GETTING THERE AND AROUND

Unless you are driving, the only practical way to get to Azilal is by bus from Beni-Mellal or by grand taxi. Azilal is more important as a jumping-off point for tours through the region.

CLOSE UP

Moroccan Wines

During their occupation of the Maghreb, the Romans exercised their viniculture skills and exploited the climate and the soil, but upon their departure, and with the strengthening of Islam, the grapes literally withered on the vine. Under the French protectorate the vineyards were revived, but fell into state hands once they left in 1956, marking a second decline in production. The French once again took the helm in the 1990s, replaced all the vines and planted them in sand, which maintains the heat and kills phylloxera (the organism that once decimated French vineyards in the 19th century). The harvest is at the end of August and bottling takes place in France. The reds are quite low in tannin and the whites reasonably sharp and benefit from chilling. Wines of note are Médallion and Volubilis (reds and whites), both at the high end of the price range, but don't exclude the bargain and tasty Guerrouane Gris (a slightly orange-colored rosé) or the Président Sémillon Blanc. Look out for Gérard Depardieu Lumiere, a Syrah blend produced from the vineyards of the larger-than-life French actor.

—Ian Thomas

Bus Contacts **Azilal CTM Station** ✉ *Av. Hassan II, Azilal* ☎ *0523/45–87–22.*

Visitor and Tour Info **Délégation du Tourisme d'Azilal** ✉ *Av. Mohammed V, Azilal* ☎ *0523/45–87–22.*

EXPLORING

The left (northeast) fork takes the 1807 road through the Tizi-n-Ilissi Pass to the Zaouia Ahanesal shrine and eventually reaches the 260-foot rock formations known and marked on the Michelin 742 National as **La Cathédrale des Rochers** (Cathedral of Rocks) for its resemblance to the spiky spires of a Gothic cathedral. The road eventually becomes 1803 and passes through a live-oak forest to reach the Bin-el-Ouidane reservoir after 113 km (68 mi) of slow and tedious, though wildly scenic, driving.

CASCADES D'OUZOUD

153 km (95 mi) northeast of Marrakesh, 22 km (14 mi) northwest of Azilal.

No trip to the Atlas would be complete without a stop at these impressive falls, which are approachable from the S508 via the 1811. You will most likely hear the roaring water before you get your first glimpse, especially in late spring when the melting snow swells the rivers. The cascades, which are a popular destination for holidaying Moroccan families, as well as foreigners, are rarely seen without a rainbow halo. Have a snack at one of the jaunty cafés on your way down, take a short boat ride towards the gushing torrent in one of the brightly colored boats, or have a refreshing swim in the basin carved out of the rock at the base of the falls. As dusk falls, look out for the indigenous Barbary apes. At present, say locals, the apes fall into three categories: those liking olives, those liking tourists, and those disliking both and preferring to hide in holiday season. If you are very lucky, you might spot the youngsters swinging on the phone lines.

Downstream, past the Ouzoud falls on the 1811 road, is the Berber hillside village of **Tanaghmelt**. Nicknamed "the Mexican village," the small community is connected by a web of narrow alleyways and semi-underground passages. You may also wish to continue up the 1811 (toward the P24) to see the **river gorges** of the Oued-el-Abid.

GETTING THERE AND AROUND

Around 170 km (105 mi) of reasonably good road separate Marrakesh from the Cascade d'Ouzoud, a journey that takes some two to three hours of driving; however, this is a worthwhile and popular day trip. Leaving Marrakesh, take the Fez road (N8). Continue for around 60 km (37 mi). Turn right toward Azilal (the S508). Approximately 20 km (12 mi) before Azilal, turn left, following signs to "Ouzoud."

6

WHERE TO EAT AND STAY

For expanded hotel reviews, visit Fodors.com.

$$$ MOROCCAN ✕ **Dar Es-Salam.** Located near the parking area for the falls, this small restaurant offers delicious crudités and tagines, best enjoyed with the signature mint tea. ✉ *Cascades d'Ouzoud, Ouzoud* ☎ *0523/45–96–58.*

$$ **Riad Cascades d'Ouzoud.** After the hair-raising, hairpin bends leading up to the Cascades, you may find it hard to leave this stylish yet unspoiled riad. **Pros:** the owner has not simply cashed in on an amazing location; children under five stay free (ages 5–10 stay for half price); the owner is one of the best guides in the Atlas. **Cons:** his approach is no-nonsense, so if you want to be fussed over, go elsewhere; not all rooms have air-conditioning. ✉ *Cascades d'Ouzoud, Ouzoud* ☎ *0523/42–91–73* 🌐 *www.ouzoud.com* *8 rooms, 1 suite* *In-room: a/c, no TV. In-hotel: restaurant, parking* *Some meals.*

DEMNATE

72 km (43 mi) southwest of Azilal, 158 km (95 mi) southwest of Beni-Mellal, 99 km (59 mi) east of Marrakesh.

Demnate is a market center to which Berbers from the neighboring hills and plains bring multifarious produce, especially for the Sunday souk held outside the walls. Once famed for its ceramics artisans, Demnate still has some traditional kilns. The rectangular ramparts are made of an unusual ocher-color pisé (clay) and pierced by two monumental portals; within is a kasbah built by T'hami el-Glaoui. As you approach the town, look out for the government-built dam, towering above the road. The Moroccan star symbol decorating it is captioned: "My God, My Country, My King."

Up a 6-km (4-mi) piste above Demnate is the natural stone bridge **Imi-n-Ifri**, where the diminutive River Mahseur has carved out a tunnel

DID YOU KNOW?

The village of Imlil is a popular jumping-off point for High Atlas treks. With a surplus of cheap rooms and equipment-rental shops, you can find everything you need for a short or long trip into the mountains.

inhabited by hundreds of crows. A path twists down through the boulders and under the "bridge," where stalactites and sculpted hollows dramatize the natural rock formations. Women come to bathe in the stream because it is said to bring them good luck, but the crows are considered harbingers of doom. The legend associated with these birds—a St. George and the Dragon–type saga in which a lovely maiden is saved from an evil genie who, when destroyed by the brave hero, dematerializes into crows—is told in several variations by imaginative guides.

Bus Contacts **Demnate CTM Station** ✉ *Av. Mohammed V* ☎ *0523/45–60–87.*

IMLIL

64 km (40 mi) southeast of Marrakesh.

The village of Imlil is the preeminent jumping-off point for the high country, a vibrant mountain retreat whose existence has been given over to preparing walkers for various climbs around the peaks. It's filled with guides, cheap rooms, and equipment-rental shops. Imlil is a long strip of a village, built up around the main road. The main square is a parking area on the left, often crammed with the camper vans and cars of trek-minded travelers. Simple terraced cafés teem with *accompagnateurs* (guides), people offering you lodging in their homes, and mule owners renting the services of these essential means of mountain transport. ⚠ **Storms may occasionally make the road into town impassable, something to consider if you're heading up in rough weather.**

GETTING HERE AND AROUND

Rental cars are available from numerous international and local agencies in Marrakesh. You can get as far as Asni by bus (20 DH to 30 DH from Marrakesh, heading to Taroudant), and then for 15 DH get a seat in a grand taxi to Imlil. If moving between high-end hotels, ask how much it would cost to hire a private car and driver.

TIMING AND PRECAUTIONS

Depending on how adept you are at trekking, you could enjoy hiking for a day or spend an entire week trekking about the region. The best time to visit is early or late summer, but winter is best avoided except for by the most avid of outdoors enthusiasts.

Bus Contacts **Imlil CTM Station** ✉ *12 Bd. Zerktouni, Bab Doukala* ☎ *0524/44–83–28* 🌐 *www.ctm.co.ma.*

Visitor and Tour Info **Bureau des Guides** ✉ *Village Center* ☎📠 *0524/48–56–26* ⏲ *Daily 9–5.*

EXPLORING

Djebel Toubkal. You can unlock the adventurer inside by scaling this peak, the highest in North Africa. In truth, there are several ways to make the ascent, from hikes lasting several days to gentler—and briefer—options: from Neltner Hut, the summit is achievable in around four hours. Take into consideration the time of year; winter is a season only for experienced climbers, while spring is breathtaking (in every sense), with snowy mountains framed by the fields of fruit blossom and wildflowers below. Ascents start from the small, buzzing village of Imlil, where guides and necessary equipment may be secured. The road to Imlil is a left turn off the S501 (the Tizi-n-Test road that leads south from Marrakesh), just after Asni. The 17-km (11-mi) stretch is a spectacular expanse of scrub and cacti, which reaches out to the very foot of Ouanoukrim Massif. **TIP→ For the best views, try to time your arrival on the peak for late morning.**

WHERE TO EAT

Given that food is pretty basic in Imlil (primarily consisting of cafés that provide skewers and tagines), you may wish to seek out Kasbah du Toubkal, a 10-minute hike through the town. (There is a reception center on the main street.) The kasbah provides excellent Moroccan dishes to nonguests, in magnificent surroundings.

$$ MOROCCAN **Café Aksoual.** A rustic establishment that is popular with locals and hikers out to experience the "real" Morocco, Cafe Aksoual offers traditional dishes: tagines, skewers, bread, and salads, all washed down with eyelid-flickeringly sweet mint tea. Look out for locals texting: it is an intriguing fact that although neighboring villages have only the most basic running water, electricity, and troubled cell reception, Imlil boasts its very own cell tower. *The restaurant is before the main square in Imlil, on right as you approach from Asni 0524/48–56–12 No credit cards.*

WHERE TO STAY

For expanded hotel reviews, visit Fodors.com.

Most of Imlil's hotels are right on the main square as you enter the village. There are a couple of stunning and luxurious places to stay nearby, but in general accommodations are fairly basic; you'll find hot water and sometimes a towel, but don't count on niceties like soap. You can always stay in a private home for about 50 DH a night per person, if invited; this can be a nice way to see something of everyday Moroccan life. If you go this route, pay special attention to our etiquette suggestions and make sure you find out before nightfall what and where the bathroom facilities are. Bring your own toilet paper if you'd rather not go all that local.

$$ **Café Soleil.** This simple yet authentic café/hotel is on the main square of Imlil. **Pros:** great local color; hotel can organize treks and tours and will hold luggage for trekkers. **Cons:** basic accommodations. *On town square 0524/48–56–22 12 rooms In-room: a/c, no TV, Wi-Fi. In-hotel: restaurant, bar, parking No credit cards Some meals.*

$$$$ Fodor's Choice ★ **Kasbah du Toubkal.** Thank your stars that the short trek to this stunning, yet simple kasbah keeps some guests away; it's easy to see why Scorsese filmed part of his film *Kundun* here. **Pros:** freedom to inhale in the crisp air in near-solitude; excellent on-site hammam; hotel can organize tours, including a packed lunch. **Cons:** luxury comes at a price,

The Kasbah de Toubkhal, now a luxury hotel, sits high above the village of Imlal.

even though 5% of room prices goes back to the local community. *Follow main road through Imlil and go right at fork, follow the signs up the hill, and keep going until you reach the top* *0524/48–56–11* *www.kasbahdutoubkal.com* *5 rooms, 6 suites, 1 house, 3 dorms* *In-room: no a/c, Internet. In-hotel: restaurant, bar, spa, parking* *Breakfast* *2-night minimum.*

$$$$ **Kasbah Tamadot.** Should Hollywood-set makers get to work on a super-deluxe Moroccan mountain retreat, they might come up with something like this. **Pros:** heaven on earth; 20% of your breathtaking bill goes to the local Berber community. **Cons:** far removed from real Morocco; children's programs are strictly seasonal. *Rte. d'Imlil* *The kasbah is just after Asni on road to Imlil, on the left* *877/577–8777 U.S. Toll Free, 0524/36–82–00* *www.virgin.com/kasbah* *24 rooms including 6 tented Berber-style suites* *In-room: a/c, Wi-Fi. In-hotel: restaurant, bar, pool, tennis court, gym, spa, children's programs, laundry facilities, parking* *Breakfast.*

¢ **Refuge de Club Alpin Français.** This is one of a series of refuges maintained by an association of French mountaineering buffs and is a good place to pick up a guide or information; you can stay here, too, in one of the basic rooms. **Pros:** a relaxing, no-nonsense place to be; mules, as well as guides, can be arranged through the hotel. **Cons:** very basic rooms. *Across main square from Café Soleil* *0524/48–51–22* *23 rooms* *In-room: no a/c, no TV. In-hotel: parking* *No credit cards* *No meals.*

OURIKA VALLEY

A great day trip from Marrakesh, the Ourika Valley is prime hiking territory in all seasons, especially if you aren't up to hitting the heights of Djebel Toubkal. It's also stunning. Less than 20 minutes out of Marrakesh you can see green gorges, sparkling yellow wheat fields at the foot of snowcapped mountains, and the ferocious flush of the Ourika River, where women wash clothes in the spray of waterfalls at the roadside. Look out, too, for flat Berber homes; they're assembled in stacked villages the same red as the earth they merge into. The only vertical line that breaks the slither of horizontal roofs is that of the village mosque, whose minaret towers above it all. As you leave Marrakesh, the approach to the valley is lined with flat, spiky cactus and eucalyptus trees, before reaching the foothills of the Atlas and hugging the left-hand bank of the fast-flowing River Ourika.

The best and most free-spirited way to enjoy the valley is probably from the window of a rental car (or a hired car with driver), with plenty of pit stops and a couple of days trekking. There are also five daily buses from Marrakesh (6 DH to Ourika) and grand taxis (10 DH to Ourika, 20 DH to Setti Fatma).

OUKAÏMEDEN

20 km (13 mi) from Imlil.

So you probably didn't go to Morocco for the snow. But if Vail's novelty value has worn off—and if you have a day or two to kill—then a bit of powder isn't out of the question. The ski station at Oukaïmeden is also a good place for novices to get in some practice without the stress of jam-packed slopes, and is becoming an increasingly popular retreat. A range of walks is available outside the ski season.

Unless you're Moroccan, or a ridiculously enthusiastic ski bum, it's highly unlikely you'll arrive with any of the right gear. Numerous shops are ready to help out. As in the souk, nothing has a fixed price, so you may need to bargain. As a general rule, expect to pay around 150 DH per day for some warm clothing, boots, skis, and poles. The next step is the ski-lift pass, which is in fact a frustratingly long distance away (particularly in ski boots). To ride on the big lift to the very top of the mountain (known as the *télésiège* in French) a lift pass costs 100 DH per day; access to the six smaller chairlifts (*téléskis*) costs 50 DH per day.

Although Oukaïmeden is small, don't think its 20-odd runs (*pistes*) are basic. Apart from three green (easy) runs and four blue (medium), everything else is either red (advanced) or black (difficult). Only red and black runs go down the télésiège, so go ready for a challenge. The long red run starts to the right of the lift drop-off point—everything else to the left is black, and with names like *Combe du mort* (Vale of Death) they aren't for the faint-hearted. It's currently undergoing massive investment. The ski season lasts from December until late March.

Oukaïmeden is the most popular ski resort in Morocco.

GETTING HERE AND AROUND

Transport can be a problem here as a grand taxi from Marrakesh will drop you off but might prove unreliable for collection. There is no scheduled bus service. In the busy ski season, you should find shared taxis or even minibuses shuttling between the resort and Marrakesh. Otherwise, consider taking a tour of Oukaïmenden with an operator such as the UK-based Do Something Different or call a car and driver from a reliable company such as the excellent El Jarssi Transport.

Guides and Tours **Do Something Different** ☎ *(44) 0208/0903790 in the UK* 🌐 *www.dosomethingdifferent.com.* **El Jarssi Transport** ☎ *0661/32–07–58.*

TIMING AND PRECAUTIONS

For skiers, Oukaïmeden is often a day trip from Marrakesh. There are a few hotels for those wishing to spend the night. Oukaïmeden, being a resort, is extremely safe. Just be sure to bring warm clothes.

WHERE TO STAY

For expanded hotel reviews, visit Fodors.com.

¢ **Club Alpin Français.** Offering a safe place to sleep for trekkers, skiers, and summer ramblers alike, this very simple and basic dormitory-style accommodation is clean and well run. **Pros:** a relaxing, clean and no-nonsense place to be; hotel can organize treks. **Cons:** very basic accommodations. ✥ *On the right as you first enter Oukaimeden* ☎ *0524/31–90–36* 🌐 *www.ffcam.fr* *158 beds (82 dormitory-style and a total of 76 beds in rooms for 4 or 8 people)* *In-room: no a/c. In-hotel: restaurant, bar* *No credit cards* *Multiple meal plans.*

$$$ **Kenzi Louka.** This hotel may look retro from the outside, but the luxurious rooms, public areas, and restaurant are purely modern. **Pros:** luxurious suites; centrally located; hotel arranges outdoor activities. **Cons:** a bit pricey if you're spending the whole day outside anyway. ✉ *Oukaïmeden, on right after Club Alpine Français* ☎ *0524/31–90–80* *101 rooms, 5 suites* *In-room: a/c, Wi-Fi. In-hotel: restaurant, bar, pool, gym, spa, laundry facilities, parking* *Some meals.*

SHOPPING

Small stands line the road from before Ourika to Setti Fatma, at the end of the road, selling crafts, pottery, and the carpets for which the Berbers are so famous. Many of these small stands supply the great boutiques and bazaars of Marrakesh, so if you're in the mood for bargain hunting, you're likely to find a better deal here. Two shops stand out, a couple of kilometers apart and both a few kilometers before the right turn to Oukaïmeden (heading south), as the road starts to climb.

Pottery at Le Kasbah de Tifirte. Pottery at Le Kasbah de Tifirte is a marvelous emporium of tagine pots, plates, and vases. You can watch experts sitting at a clay wheel knock off a tiny tagine pot and lid within minutes, judging everything expertly by eye and experience. Pieces are then fired in a kiln, decorated, and fired again. It's an excellent place to learn the difference between *tadelakt*, a hand-polished finish that takes an entire day, and painted stucco imposters. A half day in the workshop costs 70 DH. ✉ *On Ourika road, 39 km [24 mi] from Marrakesh* ☎ *067/34–49–06.*

La Source de Tapis. La Source de Tapis is a Berber women's cooperative with more than 7,000 carpets on sale. Five-hundred women from villages all over the region bring their carpets down to the enormous three-level shop, and are paid when their own carpet sells. There's a plethora of choices, but it's a particularly good source for embroidered rugs. Expect to be offered an 8-foot by 5-foot rug for 2,500 DH–3,000 DH. The shop also ships. ✉ *Ourika Valley Amassin, 37 km [23 mi] from Marrakesh* ☎ *0524/48–24–58.*

SPORTS AND THE OUTDOORS

Auberge Le Maquis. Auberge Le Maquis is a springboard into the hills and a great place to plan local walks. The company employs Berber guides and has a large selection of hand-drawn maps to take you around the surrounding hills. The night watchman doubles as a daytime guide and can organize walks to a nearby farm and his home village of Tamzerdit, explain the flora and fauna of the valley, and even enable guests to have a go at pottery or tadelakt (70 DH for a half-day, 120 DH for a full day). For more demanding treks, this is also a gateway into the mountains, and a bit of luxury compared to camping and other local lodging options. Working in conjunction with the guides at Setti Fatma, it's possible to organize a two-day hike to the snow station of Oukaïmeden (from 950 DH per person) and a three-day hike, including a night under the stars, to the Yagour Plateau to see ancient rock carvings (from 1,500 DH per person). The hotel also has a good range of drives for four-wheel-drive junkies hankering after some dirt-track action.

✉ To right of the Ourika road heading south, just after Oukaïmeden turnoff, Tnine ☎ 0524/48–45–31 🌐 www.le-maquis.com.

TNINE DE L'OURIKA

35 km (22 mi) south of Marrakesh.

Tnine de l'Ourika is a small village and easily explored on foot. Its Monday souk ranks among the best in the region. Aside from that, the only thing to see is the local *zaouia* (sanctuary) and the ruins of an ancient kasbah. However, there are two must-see sights nearby.

To get to either Nectarome or La Safranière (two magnificent gardens), take the left turn at Ourika for the road that heads for Tnine de l'Ourika and Dr. Caid Ourika. The turn is signposted to both Nectarome and La Safranière, but easy to miss. La Safranière is down one of the first left turns down a small track (signposted); Nectarome is also a left, a little farther up (also signposted); then through a gate on the left after a few minutes' drive. Any local can give directions. If you are looking to take a break in Ourika, have a cool drink on the terrace of the stunning Riad Bab Ourika, which perches above the village; the tourist information center can give you directions.

GETTING HERE AND AROUND

The Tnine de l'Ourika, at the start of the Ourika Valley, is best reached by car or grand taxi, though a few buses stop here on their way to Oukaïmeden.

Visitor and Tour Info Centre d'informations Touristique *✉ Tnine Ourika ☎ 068/96–55–45 ⏲ Mon.–Sat. 8–6.*

EXPLORING

★ **Nectarome.** The absolute pièce de résistance of any visit to the Ourika Valley is a trip to Nectarome, the region's first aromatic garden. It produces essential oils for massages, spas, and hammams in the classiest of hotels and riads back in Marrakesh. Started by two Moroccan brothers (one a biochemist, the other a pharmacist), it grows 50 species of aromatic and medicinal plants, all in 2.5 acres of beautifully maintained and colorful gardens. They pick the plants on-site, then extract, process, and bottle the oil in the top-secret perfume workshop. You can take a guided tour (80 DH to 120 DH depending on number in tour) through the grounds and learn about the healing properties of each plant (lavender for rest; rosemary for blood circulation; thyme for digestion; geraniums for menopause, etc.), or wander on your own (for 15 DH). You can also have an essential-oils open-air pedicure in specially constructed basins dug into the ground (80 DH for 15 minutes) or bake your own Berber bread in one of three types of clay oven to accompany your lunch (100 DH to 150 DH per person). Whatever you do, don't miss the seven-plant tea infusion, taken in a garden gazebo or Berber tent, or the boutique, where you can buy the goods. **■ TIP→ Don't munch on the leaves of the oleander rose; they're pretty on the outside but poisonous on the inside. Two leaves are enough to kill a man.** *✉ Tnine d l'Ourika Haouz ☎ 0524/48–21–49 🌐 www.nectarome.com ⏲ Daily 9–5.*

La Safranière de l'Ourika. La Safranière de l'Ourika, just before the turn to Nectarome, also has guided tours around its gardens of the valuable saffron plant. For the ultimate saffron experience, go between October 30 and May 15, when the plants are in flower and you can even participate in the picking and drying process. ✉ *Ferme Boutouil, Takateret* ☎ *0524/48–44–76* 🌐 *www.safran-ourika.com.*

TO TIZI-N-TEST

To the west of Djebel Toubkal the southern road from Marrakesh through Asni and Ouirgane carves its way through the High Atlas Mountains and offers spectacular views all the way to the Tizi-n-Test pass and beyond. Ouirgane is a great base for trekking and playing in the hills, and has the best lodging options for miles around. South of Ouirgane is best done as a road trip, with stops for occasional sights and breathtaking views.

OUIRGANE

60 km (37 mi) south of Marrakesh.

Ouirgane is the most luxurious base for mountain adventure Morocco has to offer. It doesn't have the highest peaks, but it has a glorious choice of charming hotels and day trips that take in captivating scenery toward the mountainous Tizi-n-Test to the south. You can climb Djebel Toubkal in three days or stay up in the High Atlas for a little longer, safe in the knowledge that you have a snug hotel waiting for you back in Ouirgane. Even if you keep close to town, you can explore the surrounding hills on two "wheels" (foot or bicycle) or four (mule, horse, or quad bike) with ease. In town there's a lively morning souk on Thursday. For many, Ouirgane is just a pleasant stop before tackling Tizi-n-Test. But the charming village has a few auberges that make it a good starting point for treks.

GETTING HERE AND AROUND

If you have your own car, Ouirgane is a fairly short drive from Marrakesh. Failing that, a grand taxi costs 25 DH per person from Marrakesh; taxis from Tnine de l'Ourika are available for about 20 DH. The cheapest way is by bus (15 DH), which leaves Marrakesh's Gare Routière five times daily. However, most visitors make the journey in hired vehicles, often with a hired driver.

EXPLORING

Mouflon Rouge. Although counting sheep isn't everyone's idea of fun, seeking out Morocco's wild Berber sheep (*mouflon* in French; *aoudad* in Tashelhit) at the Mouflon Rouge will by no means put you to sleep. The wooly creatures are famed throughout the region, and can be seen at a lovely viewing area just before Ouirgane. It's worth it to see what all the fuss is about. ✣ *On approach to Ouirgane from the north, look for a right turn signposted to "La Bergerie" near the village of Marigha. Keep going south on main road for about 0.5 km (0.25 mi), then take left turn for the viewing area, which parallels Ouirgane River.*

Salt Mines. It is worth negotiating the pot-holed road to the salt mines just off the Amizmiz road (stop at the turning for the Amizmiz road and walk the last part). For centuries, the Berbers have produced salt here but today's relatively low value of the once highly prized natural commodity has greatly endangered the livelihoods of the salt-mining families. To support them, be sure to flag down a merchant as you see him riding from village to village on his donkey and if you tour the mines, tip the miners. ■ **TIP→ Don't go on a Saturday as that is when they make their way to the souk at Asni.** ✧ *From Ouirgane, take the Amizmiz Rd.*

Shrine of Haïm ben Diourne. Site of one of the few Jewish festivals still held in Morocco, this complex contains the tombs of Rabbi Mordekai ben Hamon, Rabbi Abraham ben Hamon, and others. The shrine, known locally both as the "tigimi n Yehudeen" and "marabout Juif" (House of the Jews in Arabic and French, respectively), is a large white structure. The moussem generally happens in May. Tip the gatekeeper after a tour. ✧ *About 4 km (2.5 mi) outside Ouirgane, the shrine is accessible on foot or by mule in less than an hour, or you can drive right up to gate on a dirt piste. Drive south from Au Sanglier and turn left after about 1 km (0.5 mi) at Ouirgane's souk; follow road as it winds through village until you reach a pink cubic water tank. Turn right and go to the end of road, about 3 km (2 mi).*

6

WHERE TO EAT

$$$$ FRENCH ★ ✕ **La Bergerie.** Delightful restaurant and guesthouse, which combines shaker style with *Little House on the Prairie*. French owners Christian and Françoise have devised a menu with both excellent French and Moroccan dishes and offer a full bar (something of a rarity in these parts). Specialties include wild boar, frog's legs, and the wonderful *souris d'agneau* (a rich dish of slow-cooked lamb shank). The attached inn has 10 standard rooms, five bungalows for two people sharing, and three family suites that accommodate up to four. Be sure to say hello to Mimi, the establishment's sleek ginger cat. ✉ *Marigha, Rte. de Taroudant, Km 59, Par Marrakesh, Asni* ✉ *B.P. 64, Asni, Morocco* ☎ *0524/48–57–17, 0524/48–57–18, 0661/15–99–06* 🌐 *www.labergerie-maroc.com.*

$$$$ MOROCCAN ★ ✕ **Chez Momo.** When the government built a dam and reservoir in the area at the end of 2008, the "old" Chez Momo was in the way and is now 50 feet under water. The owner's friends raised funds to buy him a new piece of land. The result is the Chez Momo of today, nestling higher than its predecessor in the foothills of the mountains, near Ouirgane. Sip a cocktail by the small pool or have a barbecued dinner seated on one of the chairs fashioned from tree trunks. It is well worth sampling their signature dish, lamb Tagine Zahra accompanied by homemade bread and oranges with cinnamon. After such a feast you may find yourself inquiring about one of the six cozy rooms (priced around 1,100 DH), to which a breakfast of morning coffee and *beghrir* (pancakes) is brought to your door. ✉ *Rte. d'Asni, Km 61 from Marrakesh* ✧ *The dirt road to Chez Momo is roughly 1 km (½ mi) south of the bridge over the Ouirgane River. Turn right at the sign and continue about 164 feet downhill. Turn right again and park among the olive trees* ☎ *0524/48–57–04, 061/58–22–95* ✉ *chezmomo@menara.ma* 🌐 *www.aubergemomo.com.*

WHERE TO STAY

For expanded hotel reviews, visit Fodors.com.

$$$ **Auberge Au Sanglier Qui Fume.** Few places stick in the heart as does this loveable hunter's lodge; with its clublike atmosphere and mismatched oddities, it is a blend of ramshackle and historic. **Pros:** few places like this still exist; kids under five stay free; hotel rents bicycles and quads. **Cons:** shabby, although loveable. ✉ *Vallée d'Ouirgane, Km 61 from Marrakesh* ☎ *0524/48–57–07* 🌐 *www.ausanglierquifume.com* *15 rooms, 10 suites* *In-room: no a/c, Wi-Fi. In-hotel: restaurant, bar, pool, spa, laundry facilities, parking* *Some meals.*

$$$ **La Résidence de la Roseraie.** The grande dame of this part of the Atlas, La Roseraie is plush but slightly fading. **Pros:** rooms hidden in private natural parkland; kids under 6 stay free **Cons:** quite costly for faded splendor. ✉ *Rte. de Taroudant, Km 60* *B.P. 769, Marrakesh, Morocco* ☎ *0524/48–56–94, 0524/43–91–28* 🌐 *www.laroseraiehotel.com* *21 rooms, 21 suites* *In-room: a/c, Internet. In-hotel: restaurant, bar, pool, tennis court, gym, spa, water sports, laundry facilities, parking* *Some meals.*

SPORTS AND THE OUTDOORS

"Sights" aside, by far the best thing to look at here is the surrounding countryside with its poppies, yellow wheat, snowcapped mountains, rushing rivers, and glorious, looming hills. You can get out there in so many different ways, and your hotel (or a better-equipped one nearby) is the best way to rent equipment for outdoor activities.

BIKING

You can rent bikes from La Roseraie, Au Sanglier Qui Fume, or, for the cheapest option, La Bergerie (from 20 DH an hour). Quad-biking adventurers can rent the beasts from Au Sanglier Qui Fume for 300 DH an hour (550 DH for half a day).

HORSEBACK RIDING

For horseback riding, La Roseraie is *the* place for the entire region. You can rent horses for local rides or for full-blown tours in the mountains, complete with food and lodging in Atlas villages. Prices start at 200 DH for an hour. As there might be an additional levy elsewhere, it's best to come straight here.

WALKING

Every hotel will be able to fix you up with a walking guide to wander the local hills and rivers, dropping in on the salt mines, the remains of the Jewish settlement, and a Berber house, as you like. It's also only three days on foot (with the help of a mule or two) to the summit of Djebel Toubkal. The route bypasses Imlil altogether, a significant benefit for anyone keen to avoid the trekker base camp.

TIZI-N-TEST

The road to Tizi-n-Test is the most glorious mountain drive in Morocco. The route south from Ouirgane to Tizi-n-Test takes you through the upper Nfis Valley, which was the spiritual heart of the Almohad Empire in the 12th century and later the administrative center of the Goundafi *caids* (local or tribal leaders) in the first half of the 20th century. It's best enjoyed as a day trip by car from Ouirgane, especially as lodging options are seriously basic and few. There are plenty of cafés on the way, however, and a great stop off at Tin Mal Mosque.

The route to Tizi-n-Test clings to the mountainside, sometimes triple-backing on itself to climb the heights in a series of precipitous hairpin bends. It's often only a narrow single lane, with sheer drops, blind corners, and tumbling scree. Expect every bend to reveal a wide and furiously fast Land Rover coming right at you, or worse, a group of children playing soccer. Honk as you round sharp corners, and give way to traffic climbing uphill. There is no need to pick up hitchhikers, as they are most probably just moving from one nearby village to another. However, if asked for water, it is customary to stop and hand over any water bottles you can spare.

GETTING HERE AND AROUND

To drive the stunning mountain road that winds south toward Tizi-n-Test, you'll need transport. You can pick up a bus (a scary option) or a grand taxi (only slightly better) from Ouirgane. Better still to opt for individual transport. It is most advisable to hire a car and driver through one of the better hotels in Marrakesh (or a good hotel around Ouirgane). Otherwise, the member of your party brave enough to volunteer to drive will need all their concentration for the treacherous bends and so miss the splendid scenery.

6

EXPLORING

Goundafi Kasbahs. Most of the massive Goundafi Kasbahs, strongholds of the Aït Lahcen family that governed the region until independence in 1956, have long since crumbled away. But just past the small village of Talat-n-Yacoub, look up. A great hulking red kasbah sits at the top of the hill, amid a scene that is today eerily peaceful, with hawks nesting among the scraps of ornately carved plaster and woodwork still clinging to the massive walls. Built as a counterpart to the original Goundafi redoubt in Tagoundaft, the kasbah is a compelling testament to the concentration of power in an era said to be governed "tribally." Locals say the hands of slack workers were sealed into the kasbah's walls during construction. There's usually not a tourist in sight. Better yet, its future is secure, since it has been bought for conversion into a restaurant, what will surely become one of the best-placed spots to eat in the area. It's a rocky, although fairly easy, walk up to it. From the kasbah you can see the Tin Mal Mosque to the south, across the juncture of the Nfis and Tasaft rivers. Just southeast are the mines of Tasaft. The Ouanoukrim Massif (the group of big mountains at the center of the High Atlas Mountains) dominates the view to the north. ⊠ *Above Talat-n-Yacoub, about 40 km (25 mi) south of Ouirgane.*

★ **Tin Mal Mosque.** One of only two mosques in the country that non-Muslims may enter (the other is Casablanca's enormous Hassan II mosque), Tin Mal sits proudly in the hills and is well worth a visit. Built by Ibn Tumart, the first Almohad, its austere walls in the obscure valley of the Nfis formed the cradle of a formidable superstate and was the birthplace and spiritual capital of the 12th-century Almohad empire. Today the

The Tin Mal Mosque is one of only two mosques in Morocco that non-Muslims may enter.

original walls stand firm, enclosing a serene area with row after row of pale brick arches, on a huge scale built to impress. ■ TIP→ **Admission to the mosque is free, but tip the guardian, who can also show you around and explain a little of the history.** ✉ *Talat-n-Yacoub* ✣ *The signposted turnoff for mosque is about 4 km (2.5 mi) south of Talat-n-Yacoub. Turn right, cross bridge, and follow path up other side of valley.*

Tizi-n-Test. The Tizi-n-Test, at 6,889 feet, provides wonderful views to the north and south. It's the summit of any trip from Ouirgane, and a moment's rest from the hair-raising road trip. ✉ *76 km (47 mi) southwest of Ouirgane.*

WHERE TO EAT AND STAY

For expanded hotel reviews, visit Fodors.com.

¢ CAFÉ ✕ **Café/Restaurant du Col Tizi-n-Test Bellevue.** This small café right at the summit of Tizi-n-Test is the perfect place to take in the astounding view with some Berber biscuits and mint tea on beautiful wrought-iron chairs made by the owner's son. It's also a good spot to stop on the road and wander up the hills. Although the restaurant has a hotel attached, it's best avoided. ✉ *Tizi-n-Test summit, 6,889 feet, Tizi-n-Test* ☎ *066/93–47–65* ▭ *No credit cards.*

¢ **La Belle Vue.** A kilometer down the road from Tizi-n-Test pass, this concrete block of a hotel has a totally different *belle vue* (beautiful view) from the café at the top. **Pros:** breathtaking views; spotless rooms. **Cons:** shared bathrooms; disappointing views from the rooms. ✉ *1 km (½ mi) south of Tizi-n-Test summit, Tizi-n-Test* ☎ *067/59–57–58* 🌐 *boumzough.free.fr/* *12 rooms without bath* *In-room: no a/c. In-hotel: restaurant, parking* ▭ *No credit cards* *Some meals.*

THE TICHKA PASS

The scenery around the Tichka Pass is peaceful and more low-key than that of the rest of the High Atlas. It's soothing and stunning in equal measure, a good bet for stimulating walks and a relaxing hotel stay. If you're just passing through en route to the southern oases, the vista from the Tichka road itself is amazing—especially in spring—and the Glaoui Kasbah at Telouet is worth a look.

TIZI-N-TICHKA

110 km (68 mi) southeast of Marrakesh.

Winding its way southeast toward the desert, the Tichka Pass is another exercise in road-trip drama. Although the road is generally well maintained and wide enough for traffic to pass—and lacks the vertiginous twists of the Tizi-n-Test—it still deserves respect. Especially in winter, take warm clothes with you, as the temperature at the pass itself can seem another latitude entirely from the balmy sun of Marrakesh. ■ TIP→ **Sometimes gas can be difficult to find, particularly unleaded, so fill up before you hit the mountains. There's a station at the town of Aït Ourir, on the main road to Ouarzazate.**

The road out of Marrakesh leads you abruptly into the countryside, to quiet olive groves and desultory villages consisting of little more than a *hanut* (convenience store) and a roadside mechanic. You'll pass the R'mat River, the Oued Zat, and the Hotel Hardi. From here the road begins to rise, winding through fields that are either green with barley and wheat or brown with their stalks. At Km 55 you'll encounter the Hotel Dar Oudar in Touama. In springtime magnificent red poppies dot the surrounding fields.

On the way up into the hills, look for men and boys, often standing in the middle of the road, waving shiny bits of rock. These are magnificent pieces of quartz taken from the mountains that they sell for as little as 5 DH. On your left at Km 124 from Marrakesh you'll see the **Palais-n-Tichka**, a sort of Wal-Mart for these shiny minerals, as well as other souvenirs. It's also a good restroom stop.

The road begins to climb noticeably, winding through forests and some of the region's lusher hillsides. A broad valley opens up to your left, revealing red earth and luminously green gardens. At Km 67 stands Mohammad Noukrati's Auberge Toufliht. From Toufliht there is little between you and the Tichka Pass but dusty villages, shepherds, and rock. You might find a decent orange juice, trinket, or weather-beaten carpet in villages like Taddert, but you'll probably feel pulled toward the pass. The scenery is rather barren, and as the naked rock of the mountains begins to emerge from beneath the flora, the walls of the canyon grow steeper, more enclosing.

Around Km 105 you'll see several waterfalls across the canyon. The trail down is precipitous but easy enough to follow; just park at the forlorn-looking refuge and the Café Tichka at Km 108. The trail winds to the left of the big hill, then cuts to the right and drops down to the falls after a short walk of half an hour or so. The Tichka Pass is farther along, at 7,413 feet above sea level. Depending on the season and the weather, the trip over the pass can take you from African heat to European gloom and back.

NEED A BREAK?

La Maison Berbère. La Maison Berbère has made more of an effort than most of the rest stops on this route, with a high-ceiling, traditionally decorated salon permeated by the unmistakable smell of real coffee. Take a late breakfast or a tagine on the terrace at the back, overlooking a small garden and poppy-dotted fields. ✉ ***5 km [3 mi] before Taddert, Rte. de Ouarzazate*** ☎ ***0524/37–14–67*** ⏲ ***Daily 6–5.***

WHERE TO EAT AND STAY

For expanded hotel reviews, visit Fodors.com.

$ MOROCCAN ✕ **Dar Oudar.** More a restaurant with rooms than an out-and-out hotel, this is a good stop-off point before the climb to the Tichka Pass. The kitchen is justifiably proud of its reputation and makes delicious french fries, as well as tagines and grills. The *kefta* (spiced minced beef) brochettes are outstanding. ✉ *Rte. de Ouarzazate, Km 55* ☎ *0524/48–47–72* ▭ *No credit cards.*

¢ **Auberge Toufliht.** At this basic hotel, as the "Speciale" sign indicates, beer, wine, and cocktails are available, and the place has a pleasantly rowdy feel, particularly on weekends. **Pros:** sweet little touches; charming rooms. **Cons:** can get noisy; sometimes closed without warning. ✉ *P31, Km 67 from Marrakesh (Km 135 from Ouarzazate), Toufliht* ☎ *0524/48–48–61* *9 rooms, with baths* *In-room: no a/c. In-hotel: restaurant, bar* ▭ *No credit cards* *No meals.*

¢ **Le Coq Hotel Hardi.** The riverside Hardi makes a reasonable base for exploring Marrakesh from the relative peace of the countryside. **Pros:** cozy poolside seating; well-manicured gardens. **Cons:** rooms are bare; restaurant is overpriced. ✉ *Rte. d'Ouarzazate, Km 38 from Marrakesh, Pont du Zat, Ait Ouir* *B.P. 18, Marrakesh, Morocco* ☎ *0544/48–00–56* *www.ait-ourir.com/CoqHardi/* *23 rooms, 1 suite* *In-room: no a/c. In-hotel: restaurant, bar, pool, parking* ▭ *No credit cards* *Breakfast.*

$$$ Fodor's Choice ★ **I Rocha.** Hidden on a promontory above Tizirine, a somewhat inhospitable Berber town, is one of the best lodges in the region. **Pros:** lovely terrace; sparkling rooms; hotel can arrange cooking courses, trekking, or stargazing by telescope. **Cons:** wine prices are very inflated. ✉ *Tizirine* *Douar Tisselday, B.P. 7 Igrhrem N'Oudal, Ouarzazate, Morocco* ✣ *Take a signposted left at Tizirine (also called Douar Tisselday), halfway down the main road that runs from Tizi-n-Tichka to Ouarzazate. Follow a steep dirt track for 500 feet* ☎ *067/73–70–02* *www.irocha.com* *7 rooms* *In-room: no a/c, no TV. In-hotel: restaurant, bar, pool, spa* ▭ *No credit cards* *Some meals.*

TELOUET

116 km (72 mi) southeast of Marrakesh, 20 km (12 mi) east of P31.

The main reason for visiting this otherwise unremarkable village is to see the incredible kasbah of the Glaouis (which is sometimes referred to simply as "Telouet"). Built in the 19th century, the kasbah is now in near-ruin, but the interior still hints of the luxury that once was.

It was from Telouet that the powerful Glaoua family controlled the caravan route over the mountains into Marrakesh. Although the Goundafi and Mtougi *caids* (local or tribal leaders) also held important High Atlas passes, by 1901 the Glaoua were on the rise. Having secured artillery from a desperate Sultan Moulay el-Hassan, the Glaoua seized much of the area below the Tichka Pass, and were positioned to bargain when the French arrived on the political scene. The French couldn't have been pleased with the prospect of subduing the vast, wild regions of southern Morocco tribe by tribe. Thus the French-Glaoua alliance benefited both parties, with Mandani el-Glaoui ruling as Grand Vizier and his brother Tuhami serving as pasha of Marrakesh.

GETTING HERE AND AROUND

Getting to Telouet isn't always easy. The best way, aside from with a tour group, is to take a grand taxi from Marrakesh or drive yourself.

TIMING AND PRECAUTIONS

The kasbah itself takes no more than three hours to explore. Take care, as parts of it are beginning to crumble.

EXPLORING

Glaoui Kasbah. About five minutes south of Tizi-n-Tichka is the turnoff for the Glaoui Kasbah at Telouet. The road is paved but narrow, and winds from juniper-studded slopes down through a landscape of low eroding hills and the Assif-n-Tissent (Salt River). In spring, barley fields soften the effect, but for much of the year the scene is rather bleak. Just before the kasbah itself is the sleepy little town of Telouet, where you might find a café open, especially if it's Thursday (souk day).

Parking for the kasbah is down a short dirt road across from the nearby auberge Chez Ahmed. Entry is free, but you should tip the parking attendant and the guardian of the gate. Inside, walking through dusty courtyards that rise to towering mud walls, you'll pass through a series of gates and big doors, many threatening to fall from their hinges. Different parts are open at different times, perhaps according to the whims of the guard. Most of the kasbah looks ravished, as though most of the useful or interesting bits had been carried off when the Glaoui reign came to its abrupt end in 1956. This sense of decay is interrupted, however, when you get upstairs: here, from painted wood shutters and delicately carved plaster arabesques, exquisitely set tile and broad marble floors, you get a taste of the sumptuousness the Glaoui once enjoyed. Because it was built in the 20th century, ancient motifs are combined with kitschy contemporary elements, such as traditionally carved plaster shades for the electric lights. The roof has expansive views.

NEED A BREAK?

Chez Ahmed. A small but clean café is located next door to the Glaoui Kasbah parking lot. Owner Ahmed is highly knowledgeable of Glaoui history, and he can organize tours of the surrounding area. He is also happy to sit and chat as well as feed you well for around 70Dh. ■ TIP→ Should you not wish to take a tour, politely make this plain toward the beginning of the conversation. ☎ *0524/89–07–17*.

WHERE TO STAY

For expanded hotel reviews, visit Fodors.com.

$$$$ **Domaine Malika.** This small boutique hotel would not be out of place in one of the world's hippest capitals: how wonderful, then, that it is here in the High Atlas. **Pros:** light-hearted, tasteful, unique decor; hotel will organize tours, airport transfers, and cooking lessons. **Cons:** the place is very small, so book ahead. ✉ *Ouirgane* ✣ *From Marrakesh, take the Taroudant road in the direction "Tahanaoute." Before Ouirgane, in Douar of Maghira, turn right toward Amizmiz. The hotel is 500 meters ahead on left* ☎ *0661/49–35–41* 🌐 *www.domaine-malika.com* *7 rooms* *In-room: a/c, Wi-Fi. In-hotel: restaurant, bar, pool, spa, laundry facilities, parking* *Breakfast.*

$$$$ Fodor's Choice ★ **Kasbah Bab Ourika.** This luxurious retreat is a delightful example of how to build a near-perfect romantic getaway that's eco-friendly to boot. **Pros:** an ambience hard to top; staff can arrange activities and treks in the area. **Cons:** the road to the kasbah is bumpy. ✉ *Kasbah Bab Ourika, Ourika Valley Atlas Mountains, Oukaïmeden* ☎ *0524/38–97–97, 0668/74–95–47* 🌐 *www.kasbahbabourika.com* *14 rooms, 1 suite* *In-room: a/c, Wi-Fi. In-hotel: restaurant, bar, pool, spa, laundry facilities, parking* *Breakfast.*

$$$$ **Widiane Suites and Spa.** This hotel offers a level of luxury unusual in Morocco's mountains. **Pros:** the place to go to treat yourself; the hotel can arrange a wide variety of activities in the area. **Cons:** opulence on this scale jars somewhat with the rural simplicity of surroundings. ✉ *Chemin du Lac de Ben el-Ouidane, Bin el-Ouidane* ☎ *0523/44–27–76* 🌐 *www.widiane.net* *30 rooms* *In-room: a/c, Wi-Fi. In-hotel: restaurant, bar, pool, gym, spa, water sports, laundry facilities, parking* *Some meals.*

7

The Great Oasis Valleys

WORD OF MOUTH

"After Fez, we traveled over the Middle Atlas Mountains to Erfoud where we learned of the Blue Men of the Sahara. . . . One of the highlights of staying at this remote location was the opportunity to awaken before dawn and see the sun rise over the Saharan dunes. It was a sight to behold."

—Lolo12

WELCOME TO THE GREAT OASIS VALLEYS

TOP REASONS TO GO

★ **Desert dreams:** Live out those Lawrence of Arabia fantasies by sleeping on dunes under the stars.

★ **Dadès Gorge:** Follow mountain trails in some of Morocco's most beautiful scenery.

★ **Kasbah trail:** Marvel at and stay in ancient strongholds that dot the landscape.

★ **Morocco's Hollywood:** Spot celebs in Ouarzazate, home to visiting film crews.

★ **Flower power:** Spring is perfect for a visit to the Valley of Roses to see endless specimens in the wild.

1 Ouarzazate. Ouarzazate (pronounced wah-zaz-zatt) is a natural crossroads for exploring southern Morocco. The town has a wide range of accommodations as well as a few sights that can fill up a day of exploring. Most important, Ouarzazate has excellent road connections, making the entire south of Morocco within reach.

2 The Dadès and Todra Gorges. These sister canyons, located within about two hours' drive from each other northeast of Ouarzazate, have been carved into the rocks over millennia by the snowmelt waters of the High Atlas. Trekking, mountain biking and rock climbing are favorite activities for tourists.

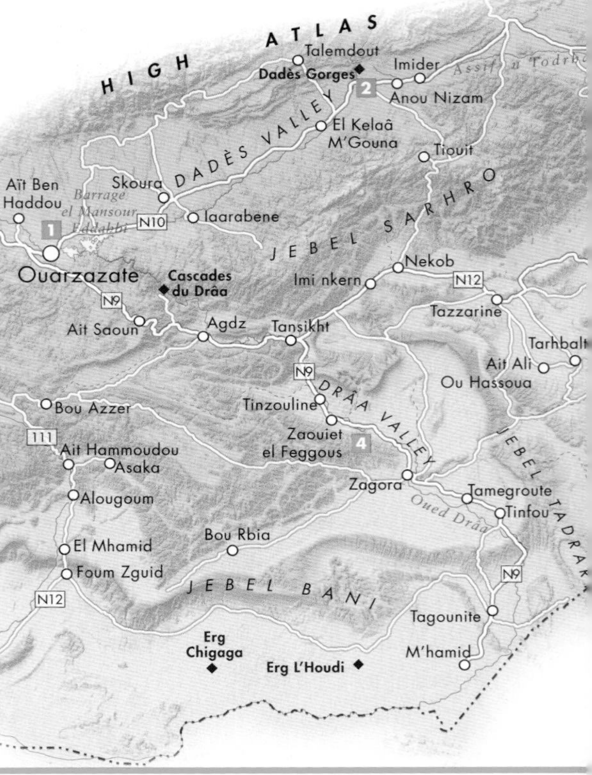

3 Merzouga and the Dunes. If you opt to visit the south of Morocco, then it's almost criminal not to at least spend a night in the Sahara. The village of Merzouga is easily accessible by road, and the dunes of Erg Chebbi are within reach on foot or by camel.

4 The Draâ Valley. The fertile Draâ Valley extends along the shores of Morocco's longest river from Agdz, through Zagora as far as M'Hamid, and offers arguably one of the most beautiful, colorful, and diverse landscapes in the kingdom. For those heading into the Sahara for the dunes at Erg Chigaga, Zagora is your last contact with modern services such as banks, pharmacies, and gas stations.

GETTING ORIENTED

The Great Oasis Valleys cover a huge area, in a sort of lopsided horseshoe from Ouarzazate, the largest town in the northwest corner, east past the magnificent Dadès and Todra gorges on the northern road, south to the dunes at Merzouga, and looping back west on the southern road, farther south, through the Draâ Valley to Zagora, M'Hamid, and the great expanse of desert that reaches all the way across Erg Chegaga to Foum Zguid. To miss any of these roads would be to miss some of Morocco's most characteristic immensity—wide-open spaces and tundralike desolation.

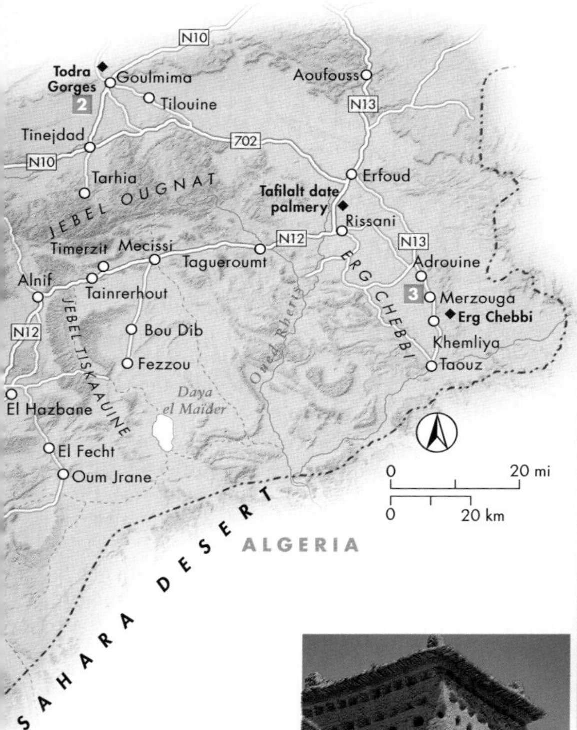

By Rachel Blech

Morocco without the Sahara is like Switzerland without the Alps, and a trip to the desert is fundamental to an understanding of the country. After you've seen the Atlas Mountains, followed by gorges, oases, palmeries, and kasbahs, a trip down to the desert may seem a long way to go to reach nothing, and some Moroccans and travelers will warn you against it. Don't listen to them. The void you encounter in the Sahara will remind you why prophets and sages sought the desert to purge and purify themselves.

Once, the caravan routes from the Sudan, Timbuktu, and Niger to Marrakesh and Fez passed through Morocco's Great Oasis Valleys and were fundamental to the region's history. From the Draâ Valley came the Saadian royal dynasty that ruled from the mid-12th to mid-17th century, and from the Ziz Valley and the Tafilalt oasis rose the Alaouite dynasty, which relieved the Saadians in 1669 and which still rules (in the person of King Mohammed VI) in 21st-century Morocco.

A trip through the oasis valleys doesn't just get you sand for your trouble. The asphalt might end and the desert begin at Merzouga and M'Hamid, but in between are the oases flanked by the High Atlas Mountains and the Todra and Dadès gorges—sister grand canyons separating the High Atlas from the Djebel Sarhro Massif.

Doing the entire circuit in the Great Oasis Valleys is a serious undertaking, and you might easily miss the best parts for all the whirlwind traveling. Walking in the Dadès or Todra gorge could easily take three days, and you should stay in at least one for a few days. Whichever gateway you choose, you should allot two days and a night at the very minimum for a trip to the desert. Unless you have oodles of time you'll have to choose between the dunes of Erg Chebbi at Merzouga and Erg Chegaga beyond M'Hamid, which are separated by 450 km (279 mi) of long, hard driving.

PLANNING

WHEN TO GO

For off-season rates, better temperatures, and fewer convoys of travelers, try to travel the oasis routes between October and April. The high season begins in early March but doesn't kick in until April. Summer is extremely hot in the desert, and the oases and gorges are crowded. ■ TIP→ **Keep yourself stocked up on bottles of water: it's very hot.**

GETTING HERE AND AROUND

The most convenient arrival and departure points for touring this vast region is via the towns of Ouarzazate (if you're traveling from Marrakesh and the Atlantic coast) or Er-Rachidia (if you're traveling from Fez, Meknès, or the Mediterranean coast). Given a choice, opt for Ouarzazate, as it is an interesting town in its own right. Ouarzazate is a key transport hub for exploring the Dadès and Todra gorges, Draâ valley, and the desert regions beyond Zagora. Er-Rachidia, aside from being a stop for those en route to Erfoud, Rissani, and Merzouga, is itself of little interest to travelers.

BY AIR

Ouarzazate's Taourirt International Airport, 1 km (½ mi) north of town, receives direct flights from Paris and domestic connections to Casablanca and Agadir on Royal Air Maroc. Er-Rachidia also has an airport for domestic flights. *Petits* taxis (local taxis) are available for the 10-minute ride into town. If you need to catch an early flight, it's best to arrange transportation through your hotel the night before.

BY BUS

There are no train connections south of Marrakesh. Compagnie du Transports au Maroc (locally known as CTM) and Supratours buses run to Ouarzazate, through the Draâ Valley, and down to Zagora and M'Hamid, but busing around southern Morocco is not recommended unless you don't mind assuming a full-time study of transport logistics.

BY CAR

The only practical way to tour the Great Oasis Valleys is to drive. Being surrounded by gorgeous and largely unexplored hinterlands like the Todra or Dadès gorges without being able to explore safely and comfortably defeats the purpose of coming down here. Driving the oasis roads requires full attention and certain safety precautions: slow down when cresting hills, expect everything from camels to herds of sheep to appear in the road, expect oncoming traffic to come down the middle of the road, and be prepared to come to a full stop if forced to the right and faced with a pothole or other obstacle. If you haven't rented a car someplace else, you can rent one on arrival in Ouarzazate.

Rental Cars **Amzrou Transport** ✉ *41, av. Mohammed V, Ouarzazate* ☎ *0524/88–23–23* 🌐 *www.amzroutrans.com.* **Hertz** ✉ *33, av. Mohammed V, Ouarzazate* ☎ *0524/88–20–84* 🌐 *www.hertz.com.* **Tafoukt Cars** ✉ *88, rue Er-Rachidia, Ouarzazate* ☎ *0667/35–87–99* 🌐 *www.tafouktcars.com.*

WHAT TO DO

Hikes, treks, and even camel safaris can be the highlight of any trip through the southern oases, dunes, or gorges. The main roads through the region are all paved, making most places accessible in a rental car or in a taxi. For venturing across country between the two gorges—or into the desert on any road marked as a *piste* (an unpaved backcountry road)—then a 4x4 will be necessary. In both the Dadès and Todra gorges it is well worth giving yourself time to hike in the area and

Rose petals are offered along the roadside at a rose moussem.

employ the services of a local guide who will take you on tracks giving you much more spectacular perspectives on the canyons and local life. North of Msemrir, a trekker with a fly rod in his backpack might even find a trout or two. Serious trekking adventures through the M'Goun Massif (above the Dadès Valley) or around Djebel Sarhro, south of Tinerhir, are by far the best way to see this largely untouched Moroccan backcountry. For exploring the desert either at Merzouga or M'Hamid it is best to travel by camel, or if budget allows by 4x4. Wonderful multiday camel treks can take you through the lower reaches of the Draâ Valley oasis and into the dunes.

SAFETY

You shouldn't have problems traveling this part of Morocco, but always exercise caution if going into remote areas. Don't stop for hitchhikers or for people whose car has broken down, as there are still some dishonest individuals wanting to take advantage of tourists.

Be prepared to be followed by local kids who may want to engage you in conversation. Rather than money, give them items such as pens or pencils. If they are selling homemade handicrafts, then of course give them a few dirhams for their efforts.

■ TIP→ **Where possible, make sure you engage a qualified guide through one of the official Bureaus de Guides—this is especially important when trekking in the desert or mountains.**

RESTAURANTS

Far from the set-menu Moroccan cuisine of the urban palaces, the fare along the southern oasis routes leans to hearty tagines and couscous. Harira is more than welcome as night sets in and temperatures plunge.

Mechoui (roast lamb) is a standard feast—if you can order it far enough in advance. Some of the best lamb and vegetable tagines in Morocco are simmered over tiny camp stoves in random corners and campsites down here. You may want to keep a bottle of wine in the car or in a day pack, as many restaurants don't serve alcohol but have no problem with customers bringing their own. Always ask first, though, as some places object.

HOTELS

Hotels on the southern oasis routes generally range from mediocre to primitive, with several charming spots and a few luxury establishments thrown in. Come here with the idea that running water and a warm place to sleep are all you really need, and accept anything above that as icing on the cake. Sleeping outdoors on hotel terraces is common (and cheap) in summer, as are accommodations in *khaimas* (Berber nomad tents). The stars and the sky are so stunning here that failing to sleep at least one night *à la belle étoile* (under the stars) seems almost criminal.

WHAT IT COSTS IN DIRHAMS

	¢	$	$$	$$$	$$$$
Restaurants	under 40 DH	40 DH–70 DH	71 DH–100 DH	101 DH–150 DH	over 150 DH
Hotels	under 200 DH	200 DH–350 DH	351 DH–500 DH	501 DH–700 DH	over 700 DH

Restaurant prices are per person for a main course at dinner. Hotel prices are for a high-season standard double room, excluding service and tax.

OUARZAZATE

204 km (122 mi) southeast of Marrakesh, 300 km (180 mi) west of Erfoud.

Ouarzazate is Morocco's Hollywood, and the industry can regularly be found setting up shop in this sprawling desert crossroads with wide, palm-fringed boulevards. Brad Pitt, Penélope Cruz, Angelina Jolie, Samuel L. Jackson, Cate Blanchett, and many more have graced the suites and streets. Despite the Tinseltown vibe and huge, publicly accessible film sets, Ouarzazate remains at its heart a dusty ghost town. Its main recommendation is the dramatic surrounding terrain that makes it a mainstay for filmmakers: the red-glowing kasbah at Aït Ben Haddou; the snowcapped High Atlas and the Sahara, with tremendous canyons, gorges, and lunarlike steppes in between.

Ouarzazate, which means "no noise" in the Berber Tamazigh language, was once a very quiet place. An isolated military outpost during the years of the French protectorate, it now benefits from increased tourism and economic development thanks to the Moroccan film industry. The movie business provides casual work for almost half of the local population and there is now a film school providing training in the cinema arts for Moroccan and international students. But the town retains its

CLOSE UP

Camel or Jeep?

Those cash-rich and time-poor are likely to plump for travel by 4x4, especially to the desert south of M'Hamid that stretches west to Foum Zguid. Getting to Erg Chegaga, for example, takes two hours by four-wheel drive and at least two days by camel. There are also great off-road routes around Zagora, M'Hamid, and Foum Zguid for those who love four-wheel-drive adventure. Some even prefer to go by quad bikes, which are also readily available.

But spare a thought for the poor desert, which thrives on being alone and slowly buckles under the weight of car fumes, carelessly discarded rubbish, and intrusive revving and whooping in an otherwise noiseless environment. Camels may take longer, but they're quieter, more authentic, and fit with the nomadic way of life.

laid-back atmosphere, making it a great place to sit at a sidewalk café, sip a café noir, and spot visiting celebrities.

GETTING HERE AND AROUND

BY AIR

There are daily flights to Ourzazate's Taourirt Airport from Casablanca and flights twice weekly to Paris. There are also connecting shuttle flights to Agadir and Casablanca three times per week with Royal Air Maroc. The airport is 2 km (1 mi) from the town center and can be reached by petits taxis.

BY BUS

Oaurzazate is well served by buses from Marrakesh (4 hours), Agadir (8½ hours), Casablanca (8½ hours), Taliouine (3½ hours), Taroudant (5 hours), Tinerhir (5 hours), Er-Rachidia (6 hours), Erfoud (7 hours), Zagora (4½ hours), and M'Hamid (7 hours). CTM buses run from the eastern end of Avenue Mohammed V. Supratours buses run from the western end of Avenue Mohammed V. Other public buses run from the gare routière (bus station) about 2 km (1 mi) from the town center just off the N9 route to Marrakesh (a petit taxi will get you here for about 10 DH). Shared *grands* taxis (long-distance taxis) also bring you here from Marrakesh, Er-Rachidia, Agadir, and Zagora and can be hired to take you privately for day excursions, too.

Bus Contacts **CTM Ouarzazate** ✉ *Av. Mohammed V, next to main Post Office at east end of Av. Mohammed V* ☎ *0524/88–24–27* 🌐 *www.ctm.ma.*

GUIDES AND TOURS

There are many travel agents and tour companies in Ouarzazate that offer day excursions and longer trips to include nights in the Dadès and Todra gorges, Sahara desert camps, and camel trekking. You'll find them along Avenue Mohammed V, in the Place el-Mouahidine, and frequently attached to hotels, so shop around and ensure you know exactly what is being included in price (e.g., 4x4, driver, guide, meals, hotels, camel trip, etc.). If you book a desert tour in Ouarzazate, you'll avoid being hassled by touts when you reach Merzouga or M'Hamid.

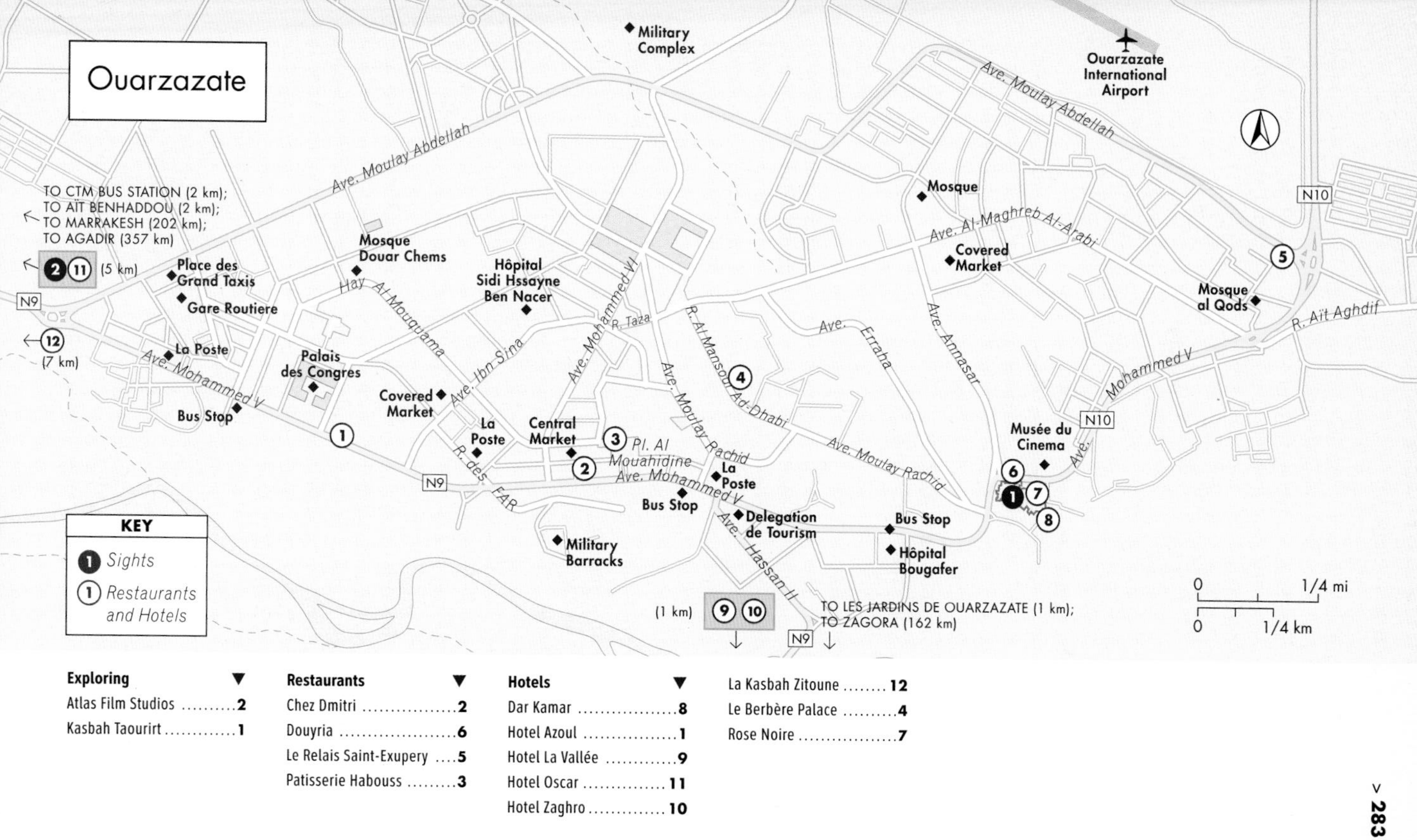

Exploring ▼

Atlas Film Studios 2

Kasbah Taourirt 1

Restaurants ▼

Chez Dmitri 2

Douyria 6

Le Relais Saint-Exupery 5

Patisserie Habouss 3

Hotels ▼

Dar Kamar 8

Hotel Azoul 1

Hotel La Vallée 9

Hotel Oscar 11

Hotel Zaghro 10

La Kasbah Zitoune 12

Le Berbère Palace 4

Rose Noire 7

Zbar Travel is a well-regarded company with English-speaking local guides who have an in-depth knowledge of the region. Cherg Expeditions, Iriqui Excursions, and Ksour Voyages are also good choices. If you want to drive yourself, there are many car rental agencies along Avenue Mohammed V.

Contacts **Cherg Expeditions** ✉ *2, pl. el-Mouahidine* ☎ *0524/88–79–08, 0661/24–31–47* 🌐 *www.cherg.com.* **Iriqui Excursions** ✉ *Pl. du 3 Mars at Av. Mohammed V* ☎ *0524/88–57–99* 🌐 *www.iriqui.com.* **Ksour Voyages** ✉ *11, pl. du 3 Mars* ☎ *0524/88–29–97* 🌐 *www.ksour-voyages.* **Zbar Travel** ✉ *12, pl. el-Mouahidine* ☎ *0524/88–56–10, 0668/51–72–80* 🌐 *www.zbartravel.com.*

TIMING AND PRECAUTIONS

For those traveling to the desert, this is an important town for stocking up on cash. It's also a good place to purchase essentials like map, batteries, and other supplies. It is the last town where you will find a supermarket selling wine, beer, and liquor.

VISITOR INFORMATION

Contacts **Ouarzazate Delegation de Tourisme** ✉ *Av. Mohammed V* ☎ *0524/88–24–85.*

EXPLORING

Atlas Studios. If you're looking for things to do in Ouarzazate, visit Atlas Studios, next to the Hotel Oscar. Flanked with beautiful impropriety by two giant Egyptian statues, these are Morocco's most famous studios. Guided tours start every 45 minutes, and the price is discounted if you're a guest of the hotel. It isn't Disney World, but you do get a sense of just how many productions have rolled through town including such Hollywood blockbusters as *The Mummy, Kingdom of Heaven,* and *Gladiator,* and such classics as *Cleopatra* and *Lawrence of Arabia.*

For another angle on the Ouarzazate film industry, check out the rather grand-looking kasbah off to the right just out of town on the way to Skoura. One enterprising local producer, frustrated by the increasingly expensive charges being levied on film crews wanting to film around real kasbahs, decided to build his own and undercut the competition. ✉ *Tamassint, Rte. de Marrakesh, Km. 5, next to Hotel Oscar* ☎ *0524/88–22–12* 🌐 *www.hotel-oscar-ouarzazate.com* 🎫 *50 DH* ⏲ *Daily 8:30 am–7:15 pm.*

Kasbah Taourirt. Known for its fine artisan traditions in ceramics and carpet making, the Kasbah Taourirt, once a Glaoui palace, is the oldest and finest building in Ouarzazate, a rambling *pisé* (a sun-dried mixture of mud and clay) castle built by those so-called Lords of the Atlas in the late 19th century. You can hire a guide at the entrance to take you around. 🎫 *20 DH* ⏲ *Daily 8–4:30.*

WHERE TO EAT

$$ MOROCCAN ★ ✕ **Chez Dimitri.** If Ouarzazate is the crossroads of the southern oasis routes, Chez Dimitri is at the heart of it. Founded in 1928 as the first store, gas station, post office, telephone booth, dance hall, and restaurant in Ouarzazate, Chez Dimitri may look unimpressive on an initial sweep down the town's banal main drag, but the food, whether Greek or Moroccan, is invariably excellent. The owners are friendly

The busy Atlas Studios is one of the top attractions in Ouarzazate.

and helpful, and the signed photographs of legendary movie stars on the walls are sometimes enhanced by real stars at the next table. ✉ *22, av. Mohammed V* ☎ *0524/88–73–46.*

$$ MOROCCAN Fodor's Choice ★ ✕ **Douyria.** This *douyria,* or "small house," was opened in 2008 by French-Moroccan couple Alexandra and Driss. Building up from the base of an old *pisé* (mud-built) family house alongside the Kasbah Touarirt, Douyria marries tradition with contemporary flair. There are two Moroccan salon-style restaurants, with bold color schemes of lilac and lime and the menu is creative and adventurous, offering interesting selection of starters and mains. If you are willing to go with something more exotic and Moroccan, try goat cooked in argan oil and sesame, or camel tagine with figs and almonds. The small terrace restaurant has wonderful views towards the lake at Ouarzazate. Actor Sir Ben Kinglsey is a fan, as the guestbook will testify. Alcohol is served. ✉ *Taourirt, next to Kasbah Touarirt* ☎ *0524/88–52–88* 🌐 *www.restaurant-ouarzazate.net.*

¢ CAFÉ ✕ **Patisserie Habouss.** If you've time to relax in Ouarzazate, there's no place better for people-watching than the terrace of Patisserie Habouss. Locals and visitors can be found indulging in its famous homemade *gâteaux* or honey-soaked Moroccan pastries accompanied by cinnamon coffee or freshly squeezed fruit juice. As the sun sinks, witness the sleepy Place el-Mouahidine transform into a busy evening marketplace. ✉ *Pl. Al Mouahidine* ☎ *0524/88–26–99* ▭ *No credit cards.*

$$$$ MOROCCAN ✕ **Le Relais Saint-Exupéry.** In a town not renowned for its dining scene, this French-run restaurant is a glorious exception. Owner Jean-Pierre is also an active subscriber to the slow-food quality ethic. Checkered floor tiles and red tablecloths give it the air of a French bistro, but

the cuisine is high Moroccan, with French panache. House specialties include *pastilla* (salty-sweet pigeon in puff pastry) and camel meat with pureed potato, served in a gingery Mali sauce. There are several four-course set menus available. ✉ *13, Moulay Abdellah, Quartier el-Qods* ☎ *0524/88–77–79* 🌐 *www.relaissaintexupery.com.*

WHERE TO STAY

For expanded hotel reviews, visit Fodors.com.

$$$$ **Le Berbère Palace.** Movie stars and magnates tend to stay at this ultra-expensive hotel when on location in Ouarzazate. **Pros:** Plenty of creature comforts; top-notch service. **Cons:** Rooms feel a bit charmless; air-conditioners too close to the bed for comfort. ✉ *Ave. Elmansour Eddahbi* ☎ *0524/88–31–05* 🌐 *www.hotel-berberepalace.com* *160 rooms, 89 suites* *In-room: a/c, Wi-Fi. In-hotel: restaurant, bar, pool, tennis court, gym, spa, laundry facilities, business center, parking, some pets allowed* *Multiple meal plans.*

$$$$ ★ **Dar Kamar.** For anyone seduced by tales of Glaoui wealth and influence, this 17th-century pasha's courthouse has magisterial appeal. **Pros:** beautiful interiors; doting service. **Cons:** cheaper rooms (3rd category) get little daylight. ✉ *45, Kasbah Taourirt* ☎ *0524/88–87–33* *www.darkamar.com* *12 rooms, 2 suites* *In-room: a/c, no TV. In-hotel: restaurant, bar, spa, laundry facilities, business center, parking, some pets allowed* *Closed in Jul. (sometimes)* *Breakfast.*

$$ **Hotel Azoul.** Opened in 2010, this small hotel on the main strip has been built by a local family in the style of an old kasbah. **Pros:** central location; interesting design. **Cons:** bedrooms are cramped. ✉ *Av. Mohammed V, 100 meters on left after Pl. du 3 Mars* ☎ *0524/88–30–15* 🌐 *www.hotelazoul.com* *8 rooms, 4 suites* *In-room: a/c, Wi-Fi. In-hotel: restaurant, spa, business center, parking* *Multiple meal plans.*

$$$ **Hotel Oscar.** For its proximity to one of Ouarzazate's biggest silver-screen attractions, Atlas Studios, this is the movie buff's hotel of choice. **Pros:** ideal for families with children; good restaurant. **Cons:** far from town center. ✉ *Tamassint, Rte. de Marrakesh, Km 5* ☎ *0524/88–22–12* 🌐 *www.hotel-oscar-ouarzazate.com* *57 rooms, 8 suites* *In-room: a/c, Wi-Fi. In-hotel: restaurant, bar, pool, laundry facilities, business center, parking, some pets allowed* *Multiple meal plans.*

$ **Hotel La Vallée.** Across the river from Ouarzazate on the road to Zagora, this friendly, English-speaking hotel is popular with tour groups. **Pros:** well-run hotel; friendly service. **Cons:** bathrooms need renovating. ✉ *Tabount, Rte. de Zagora, Km 1* ☎ *0524/85–40–34* 🌐 *www.hotellavalleemaroc.com* *51 rooms* *In-room: a/c, Wi-Fi. In-hotel: restaurant, pool, business center, parking* *Multiple meal plans.*

$ ★ **Hotel Zaghro.** You really can't beat this budget hotel. **Pros:** friendly staff; easy on the wallet. **Cons:** not all rooms have air-conditioning; some rooms share bathrooms. ✉ *Tabount, Rte. de Zagora, KM 1.5* ✣ *1.5 km (0.75 mi) on route to Zagora, south of town over bridge* ☎ *0524/85–41–35* 🌐 *www.hotel-zaghro.com* *55 rooms* *In-room: a/c, no TV, Wi-Fi. In-hotel: restaurant, pool, business center, parking* *Multiple meal plans.*

$$$ **La Kasbah Zitoune.** This hotel sits proud on the site of an ancient olive grove, hence the name, Arabic for "olive." **Pros:** peaceful and

spacious surroundings; cooking classes. **Cons:** pool still under construction; need a car to get around. ✉ *Zone Touristique de Tiffoultoute* ✣ *From Marrakesh, take turn to Tiffoultoute/Agdz, pass the kasbah on left, and it's the first right turn after bridge* ☏ *0524/88–70–14* 🌐 *www.kasbahzitoune.com* *10 rooms, 3 suites* *In-room: a/c, no TV. In-hotel: restaurant, bar, laundry facilities, business center, parking, some pets allowed* 🍽 *Breakfast.*

$$$$ **Rose Noire.** Jmiaa and Bernard Rose lovingly restored a 300-year-old riad in the kasbah, with rooms arranged around a courtyard open to the sky. **Pros:** beautiful building; welcoming hosts; tasty meals. **Cons:** hard to find; not for those with mobility issues. ✉ *Quartier de la Mosquée, Kasbah Taourirt* ☏ *0524/88–20–16* 🌐 *www.maisondhote-rosenoire.com* *4 rooms, 3 suites* *In-room: a/c, no TV, Wi-Fi. In-hotel: restaurant, business center, parking, some pets allowed* 🍽 *Breakfast.*

SPORTS AND THE OUTDOORS

FOUR-WHEELING

Quads Aventures. You can rent quad bikes from Quads Aventures, just outside town at the entrance to Atlas Studios, on the main Marrakesh road. They're good for day trips to the natural and historic wonders that have become backdrops to blockbuster films, including the kasbah at Aït Ben Haddou and a plateau used in *Gladiator.* The outfitter also rents canoes, great for the sparkling lake just southeast of town. Two hours of quad biking costs 450 DH per person with reductions for groups. ✉ *Rte. de Marrakesh, Km. 5, next to entrance to Atlas Film Studios* ☏ *0524/88–40–24* 🌐 *www.quadsaventures.com.*

7

HAMMAMS AND SPAS

The following hammams and spas are open to all (even nonguests, if in a hotel).

Le Berbere Palace. A common destination for movie stars filming in the nearby studios, this kasbah-style hotel has a deluxe hammam "Oasis," sauna, and Jacuzzi that are open to nonguests. ✉ *Av. Elmansour Eddahbias* ☏ *0524/88–31–05* *Hammam 150 DH, 250DH with exfoliation (30 mins)* ⏲ *Daily 10 am–8 pm.*

Hammam. There is a good public hammam five minutes from town center, two minutes from Kasbah Taourirt, in the Erac *quartier.* ✉ *Bd. Mohammed V* ☏ *No phone* *10 DH* *No credit cards.*

AÏT BEN HADDOU

32 km (20 mi) northeast of Ouarzazate.

The *ksar* (fortified village) at Aït Ben Haddou is something of a celebrity itself. This group of earth-built kasbahs and homes hidden behind defensive high walls has come to fame (and fortune) as a backdrop for many films, including David Lean's *Lawrence of Arabia,* Ridley Scott's *Gladiator,* and Oliver Stone's *Alexander.* Of course, it hasn't always been a film set. It got going in the 11th century as a stop-off on the old caravan routes, with salt heading one way and ivory and gold heading back the other. Strewn across the hillside and surrounded by flowering almond trees in early spring, the red-pisé towers of the village fortress resemble a sprawling, dark-red sand castle. Crenellated and topped with an ancient granary store, it's one of the most sumptuous sights in the Atlas. The ksar is a UNESCO World Heritage Site.

When it's not seething with camera crews, it can get inundated with visitors desperate to capture the postcard-perfect snap. You can usually manage a moment or two alone with the ksar to take in its beauty, no matter how many people are there. You can get here in a standard car from Ouarzazate, or take a superb four-wheel-drive outing from Telouet to Ouarzazate, detouring to the village and ksar.

GETTING HERE AND AROUND

The village of Aït Ben Haddou, 29 km (18 mi) northwest of Ouarzazate, is easily reached by road. There are very few buses to Aït Ben Haddou, so if you don't have a car the best and cheapest option is to charter a grand taxi in Ouarzazate. On arriving in the village, there are two main entrances to the kasbah. The first entrance, by the Hotel-Restaurant Le Kasbah, has ample safe parking and you can cross the riverbed via stepping-stones. Farther down the road is the second entry point opposite the Riad Maktoub. Here you can leave your car at the side of the road and then take a short stroll to a footbridge across the river to the kasbah.

TIMING AND PRECAUTIONS

The narrow road to Aït Ben Haddou is filled with vehicles traveling faster than they should. Proceed with caution and keep well over to the right, giving way to anything bigger than you. To reach the kasbah itself involves crossing a river, the Oued Mellah; however, a footbridge and new pathways up through the kasbah have been built by locals and have made exploration much easier and safer than ever before.

WHERE TO STAY

For expanded hotel reviews, visit Fodors.com.

$$ **Auberge Kasbah du Jardin.** This is a friendly and low-key outpost at the far edge of town, where rooms are basic yet cheerful. **Pros:** kitchen uses produce from its own garden; friendly staff; there's a pool. **Cons:** rooms on ground floor are dark and depressing. ✉ *At far end of Aït Ben Haddou* ☎ *0524/88–80–19* 🌐 *www.kasbahdujardin.com* *15 rooms* *In-room: no a/c, no TV. In-hotel: restaurant, pool, business center, parking* *No credit cards* *Some meals.*

$$ **La Kasbah.** Despite being a favorite of tour groups, this is a good choice because it has stunning views of the kasbah. **Pros:** gorgeous pool, excellent restaurant; stunning views. **Cons:** lacks a personal touch. ✉ *Complexe Touristique, Aït Ben Haddou* ☎ *0524/89–03–08* 🌐 *www.hotel-lakasbah.com* *110 rooms* *In-room: a/c, Wi-Fi. In-hotel: restaurant, pool, spa, parking, some pets allowed* *Some meals.*

$$$$ **Ksar Ighnda.** The most upmarket accommodation in the village, Ksar Ighnda has been built in the grounds of an old mud-built *ksar*—though only the original olive trees remain in the garden near the pool. **Pros:** great service; spacious gardens. **Cons:** standard rooms are small; expensive. ✉ *Douar Asfalou, 2 km (1 mi) east of Aït Ben Haddou* ☎ *0524/88–76–44* 🌐 *www.ksar.ighnda.net* *13 rooms, 14 suites* *In-room: a/c.*

In-hotel: restaurant, bar, pool, gym, spa, laundry facilities, business center, parking 🍽 *Breakfast.*

$$$ **Riad Maktoub.** Former photographer Abdellah Hassoun stumbled upon his *maktoub*, or "destiny," when he found himself searching for a spot to open a small restaurant back in 2000. **Pros:** family-run business; attention to detail. **Cons:** remote location. ☎ *0524/88–86–94* 🌐 *www.riadmaktoub.com* *7 rooms, 12 suites* *In-room: a/c, no TV, Wi-Fi. In-hotel: restaurant, pool, business center, parking, some pets allowed* 🍽 *Multiple meal plans.*

SKOURA

50 km (30 mi) southwest of El Kelaâ M'Gouna, 42 km (25 mi) northeast of Ouarzazate.

★ Surprisingly lush and abrupt as it springs from the tawny landscape, Skoura deserves a lingering look for its kasbahs and its rich concentration of date palms and olive, fig, and almond trees. Pathways tunnel through the vegetation from one kasbah to another within this fertile island—a true oasis, perhaps the most intensely verdant in Morocco. **■ TIP→ Skoura is such a pleasant and magical place to hole up that if you're on a grand tour of the Great Oasis Valleys it's well worth considering staying here rather than in often lackluster Ouarzazate.**

With so many grand deep orange–hue and majestic kasbahs in Skoura, a tour of the palmery is compulsory. The main kasbah route through Skoura is approached from a point just over 2 km (1 mi) past the town center toward Ouarzazate. The 17th-century **Kasbah Aït Ben Moro** is the first fortress on the right (now restored and converted to a hotel); you can leave your car at the hotel, which will happily arrange for a local guide to take you through the Palmery, past the Sidi Aïssa *marabout* (shrine to a learned holy man). By the Amerhidil River is the tremendous **Kasbah Amerhidil,** the largest kasbah in Skoura and one of the largest in Morocco.

Down the (usually bone-dry) river is another kasbah, **Dar Aït Sidi el-Mati,** while back near the Ouarzazate road is the **Kasbah el-Kabbaba,** the last of the four fortresses on this loop. North of Skoura, on Route 6829 through Aït-Souss, are two other kasbahs: **Dar Lahsoune,** a former Glaoui residence, and, a few minutes farther north, the **Kasbah Aït Ben Abou,** the second largest in Skoura after the Amerhidil.

WHERE TO STAY

For expanded hotel reviews, visit Fodors.com.

$$$ **Auberge Chez Talout.** Run by one of Morocco's friendliest hoteliers, this farmhouse is worth the trek for Talout's warm welcome, his wife's wonderful cooking, and the roof-terrace views across the Palmery to Skoura's kasbahs. **Pros:** excellent cuisine; lovely pool. **Cons:** well off the beaten track. ✉ *Oulad Aarbia, Skoura* ✥ *7 km (4.5 mi) before Skoura if coming from Ouarzazate, turn left off main road just after Idelssane* ☎ *0524/85–26–66 or* ☎ *0662/49–82–83* 🌐 *www.talout.com* *14 rooms* *In-room: a/c, no TV. In-hotel: restaurant, pool, business center, parking, some pets allowed* *No credit cards* 🍽 *Multiple meal plans.*

The Kasbah Amerhidil is the largest in Skoura.

$$$$ ★ **Dar Ahlam.** If money is no object, then consider a stay in this restored kasbah, Morocco's most exclusive and sumptuous hideaway. **Pros:** heavenly accommodations; pampering beyond your wildest dreams. **Cons:** it's well beyond the reach of most mortals. ✉ *Kasbah Madihi, Skoura Palmery* ☎ *0524/85–22–39* 🌐 *www.darahlam.com* *9 suites, 3 villas* *In-room: a/c, no TV, Wi-Fi. In-hotel: restaurant, bar, pool, spa, laundry facilities, business center, parking* *All-inclusive.*

$$$$ Fodor's Choice ★ **Les Jardins de Skoura.** Styling itself as a "*maison de repos,*" this restored farmhouse throws such a charm over guests that many of them find it difficult to leave, staying on for days in its warm, lazy embrace. **Pros:** idyllic surroundings, excellent facilities. **Cons:** may be too isolated for some. ✉ *Skoura Palmery* ✣ *2 km (1 mi) before Skoura (from direction of Ouarzazate), and after passing Kasbah Aït Ben Moro follow yellow arrow signs for left turn, additional 4 km (2.5 mi) of track to get to house* ☎ *0524/85–23–24* 🌐 *www.lesjardinsdeskoura.com* *5 rooms, 3 suites* *In-room: a/c, no TV. In-hotel: restaurant, pool, laundry facilities, business center, parking* *No credit cards* *Closed Jul. for 2 weeks* *Breakfast.*

$$$$ **Kasbah Aït Ben Moro.** This stunning pisé kasbah is a 17th-century desert castle that overlooks the Palmery, the Kasbah Amerhidil, and the High Atlas Mountains. **Pros:** splendid terraces; rooms are in a kasbah. **Cons:** no pool, though one planned for 2012. ✉ *Douar Taskoukamte, Rte. P32, 38 km (23 mi) east of Ouarzazate* ☎ *0524/85–21–16* 🌐 *www.aitbenmoro.com* *16 rooms, 4 suites* *In-room: no a/c, no TV. In-hotel: restaurant, bar, business center, parking, some pets allowed* *Some meals.*

SPORTS AND THE OUTDOORS

FOUR-WHEELING

X.trem Explorer. On the way into Skoura, about 35 km (22 mi) from Ouarzazate and before Kasbah Aït Ben Moro, look out for signs on your left to X.trem Explorer. Here, at the guest house Dar Ikram, you can rent buggies from 300 DH an hour and drive them around the sands, palms, and kasbahs. ✉ *Dar Ikram* ☎ *0666/43–53–77* 🌐 *www.darikram.net.*

HORSEBACK RIDING

Skoura Equestrian Centre. This very-well-run riding center is located near Skoura. Professional English-speaking instruction and trekking amongst the kasbahs of Skoura oasis is offered from two hours (for 250 DH) to full day with picnic (for 450 DH). The center is managed by Sport-Travel Maroc in Marrakesh. Book in advance. ✉ *2 km (1 mi) from Skoura on Road to Toundout* ☎ *0661/43–21–63.*

THE DADÈS AND TODRA GORGES

The drive through Morocco's smaller versions of the Grand Canyon is stunning, and the area merits several days' exploration. The Dadès Gorge is frequented more by independent travelers than tours, while the Todra is much more about mass-organized tourism. So many buses stop at the most beautiful point that you almost forget it's supposed to be beautiful. If you avoid lunchtime (when all the tour buses disgorge), however, and venture on, there are some great walks and lovely spots where you can feel much more alone.

7

THE DADÈS GORGE

Boumalne du Dadès is 53 km (31 mi) southwest of Tinerhir, 116 km (70 mi) northeast of Ouarzazate.

GETTING HERE AND AROUND

The easiest access point for the Dadès Gorge is the town of Boumalne du Dadès. The N10 brings you here from Ouarzazate in the west or Er-Rachidia in the east. Buses frequent this route, and although there is no longer a CTM bus office in Boumalne du Dadès, tickets can be purchased from outlets along the main street displaying the yellow sign reading "Espace Service." The CTM and Supratours buses will not get you to the gorge; rather, they provide transportation only to and from Boumalne du Dadès. The road through the gorge itself is paved as far as Msemrir. Traveling beyond Msemrir requires a four-wheel-drive vehicle, and even then only if conditions are right. The piste routes can be treacherous, especially during the rainy season between December and February. If you do not have your own transport, grands taxis from Boulmane du Dadès will take you on the scenic drive.

TIMING AND PRECAUTIONS

The Dadès Gorge is beautiful all year. In summer the steep canyon walls and rushing rivers are refreshing after the heat of the desert. In winter, however, the region gets considerable rainfall that makes the pistes impassable. Always ensure you have a full tank of gas, a spare tire, and plenty of water if embarking on cross-country routes. **■ TIP→ There are very few shops or cafés along the Dadès Gorge; when planning your day, make sure you have either packed a picnic or scheduled to stop at one of the hotels where they will be almost certainly serving lunch for passing tour groups, such as Hotel La Kasbah de La Vallée.**

VISITOR INFORMATION

Contacts **Bureau des Guides a Boumalne Dadès.** A small office at the bottom of the main street is manned by local official mountain guides who can organize and accompany treks for you according to your abilities. If nobody is in the office, then ring the published telephone number (French-speaking only). ✉ *West end of Av. Mohammed V, just after the bridge, Boumalne du Dadès* ☎ *0667/59–32–92.*

EXPLORING

The town of **Boumalne du Dadès** marks the southern entrance to the Dadès Gorge, which is even more beautiful—longer, wider, and more varied—than its sister, the Todra Gorge. The 63 km (38 mi) of the Dadès Gorge, from Boumalne through Aït Ali and on to Msemrir, are paved and approachable in any kind of vehicle. Beyond that are some great rocky mountain roads for four-wheel-drive vehicles with good clearance. Boumalne itself is only of moderate interest, though the central market square is a good vantage point for a perusal of local life. The shops Artisanale de Boumalne and Maison Aït Atta merit a browse for their local products at local prices, particularly rosewood carvings and rosewater.

The lower Dadès Gorge and the Dadès River, which flows through it, are lined with thick vegetation. While the Todra has its lush date palmery, the Dadès has figs, almonds, Atlas pistachio, and carob trees. A series of kasbahs and ksour (plural of *ksar,* a fortified house) give way to Berber villages such as Aït Youl, Aït Arbi, Aït Ali, Aït Oudinar, and Aït Toukhsine—*Aït* meaning "of the family" in the Tamazight Berber language.

Two kilometers (1 mi) up the road from Boumalne is the **Glaoui Kasbah,** once part of the empire of the infamous pasha of Marrakesh, T'hami el-Glaoui. The ksour at **Aït Arbi** are tucked neatly into the surrounding volcanic rock 3 km (2 mi) farther on from Glaoui Kasbah.

Ten kilometers (6 mi) from Aït Arbi is the village of Aït Sidi Boubker in the **Tamlalt Valley,** mostly known for the bizarre red rock formations called "Les Doigts de Singes" (or "Monkey's Fingers") after their curiously organic shapes carved by water and wind. A little further beyond "Monkey Fingers" are more sculpted rocks known as the "Valley of Human Bodies," where local legend says that lost travelers died of hunger and were transformed into rocks. A few minutes' north is the Auberge Gorges du Dadès, another option for a temporary halt, an exploration of the river, or an overnight stay.

After Aït Oudinar, where most of the lodging options are clustered, the road crosses a bridge and gets substantially more exciting and empty, and the valley narrows dramatically, opening up around the corner into some of the most dramatic views in the Dadès. Six kilometers (4 mi) north of the bridge are three little inns, the best of which is the **Kasbah de la Vallée,** offering different levels of comfort ranging from tent to terrace to rooms with bath.

Aït Hammou is the next village, 5 km (3 mi) past the Kasbah de la Vallée. It makes a good base camp for walking and climbing north to vantage points over the Dadès River or, to the east, to a well-known cave with stalactites (ask the Hotel la Kasbah de la Vallée for directions). At the top of the gorges is **Msemrir,** a village of red-clay pisé ksour that has a café with guest rooms. To go farther from Msemrir, you'll need four-wheel drive to follow the road (R704) that leads north over the High Atlas through Tilmi, the Tizi-n-Ouano Pass, and Agoudal to Imilchil and eventually up to Route P24 (N8), the Marrakesh–Fez road. The road east climbs the difficult Route 3444, always bearing right, to another gorge-top town, Tamtattouchte. It makes for a great off-road drive.

WHERE TO EAT

$$$ MOROCCAN ★ **Chez Pierre.** This Belgian-run operation is the best choice in the Dadès Gorge, but is only open about six months of the year. This French-Moroccan restaurant serves some of the best food in the area (there's a reasonably priced prix-fixe menu) as well as such delicacies as cheese grilled with honey and apples and *briouates* (spicy dumplings) with mint leaves. *Douar Aït Oufi, Dadès Gorge, Km 27, Boumalne du Dadès 0524/83–02–67 No credit cards Closed June–Aug. and Jan.–Mar.*

WHERE TO STAY

For expanded hotel reviews, visit Fodors.com.

$ **Auberge des Gorges de Dadès.** The Berber designs that adorn the walls give this spacious hotel an Andean feel well suited to the surrounding scenery. **Pros:** ideal for trekkers. **Cons:** lacks the charm of smaller auberges. *Dadès Gorge, Km 24, Aït Oudinar, Boumalne du Dadès 24 km (16 mi) north of Boumalne 0524/83–01–53 www.aubergeaitoudinar.com 30 rooms In-room: a/c, no TV. In-hotel: restaurant, business center, parking, some pets allowed No credit cards Some meals.*

$ **Auberge des Peupliers.** Rooms at this destination for anyone craving some traditional Berber touches are cozy, with distinctive clay sinks. **Pros:** friendly and helpful service. **Cons:** older rooms look shabby. *Km 27 from Boumalne du Dadès 0524/83–17–48 www.hoteldespeupliers.com 12 rooms In-room: no a/c, no TV. In-hotel: restaurant, parking, some pets allowed Some meals.*

$$ **Auberge Tissadrine.** Run by brothers Daoud and Youssef, this pleasant Berber-style auberge is tucked away from view of passersby. **Pros:** family-run vibe. **Cons:** rooms are basic; no English-speaking staff. *27 km (16 mi) from Boumalne 0524/83–17–45 www.auberge-tissadrine.com 14 rooms In-room: no a/c, no TV. In-hotel: restaurant, business center, parking No credit cards Some meals.*

$$$ **Hôtel La Kasbah de la Vallée.** Halfway between Boumalne and Msemrir, the hotel overlooks one of the most dramatic parts of the canyon. **Pros:** owners have in-depth knowledge of area; plenty of activities. **Cons:** lots of tour groups. *Aït Oufi 27 km (16 mi) north of Boumalne 0524/83–17–17 www.kasbah-vallee-dades.com 40 rooms, 2 suites In-room: no a/c, no TV. In-hotel: restaurant, bar, business center, parking, some pets allowed No credit cards Multiple meal plans.*

Continued on page 303

SEEING THE

Life's truly picture-perfect moments come few and far between: a sea of sand dunes, shimmering gray, yellow, orange, and red throughout the day, is one of them. The Sahara is the most beautiful, enigmatic, and awe-inspiring natural wonder that you can experience in Morocco—but if at all possible, don't rush through the experience.

SAHARA

by Rachel Blech

The Touareg freedom fighter Mano Dayek once wrote, "The desert will not tell you about itself—it is a way of life". The nomadic tribes of "Blue Men" who have lived for generations in the Moroccan Sahara understand this better than most. The desert is partly a state of mind that requires you to bow to nature in the search for humility, so prepare yourself for enlightenment here amongst the billowing *ergs* (dunes), stark stony *hamada* (plains), and scattered oases.

Should you have time for it, an expedition into the deeper desert provides a glimpse into a forgotten world. You may enter the desert by camel or jeep, but you will be able to sleep in a traditional bedouin tent or something even more comfortable and luxurious. You may even have the opportunity to snowboard down the dunes.

DID YOU KNOW?

Merzouga is best known for the magnificent, undulating dunes at Erg Chebbi, but nearby there is also a seasonal salt lake, Dayet Sjiri, the largest natural body of water in Morocco.

POINTS OF ENTRY

The two main desert destinations in Morocco are very different—Merzouga lies 9 hours' drive due east of Ouarzazate via the Dadès and Ziz valleys; M'Hamid is 5 hours' drive south of Ouarzazate via the Drâa Valley.

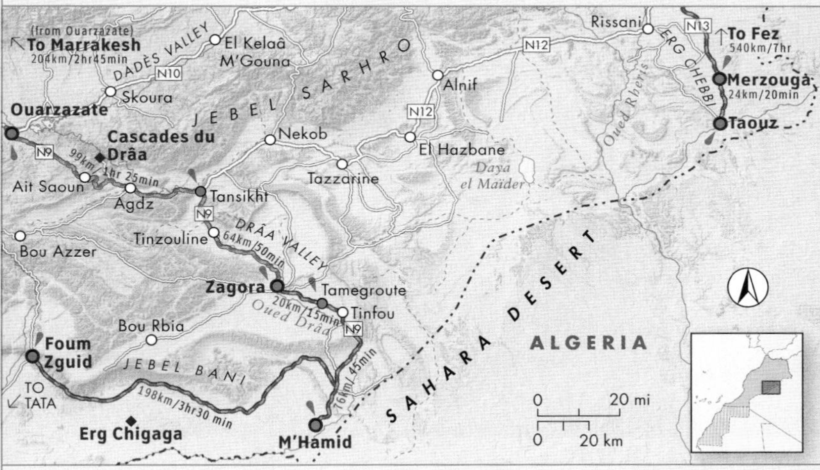

MERZOUGA

From Fez, Merzouga is the most convenient overnight desert stop. The onward route then takes you through the Todra and Dadès gorges before reaching Ouarzazate, or alternatively via the southern oasis route through the Drâa Valley to Zagora and then M'Hamid. The dunes near Merzouga, called Erg Chebbi, have sand piled high like a fancy hairdo, and you can dip your toe in as you like. The desert is easily accessible by road right to the edge of the golden sands. Here you can spend a night very happily in an oasis bivouac camp, sleeping under the stars, and another back in Merzouga at an auberge or luxury hotel with majestic dune views. **TIP→ To escape from other travelers seeking solitude, head for the northernmost or southernmost tip of the dunes—away from the village of Merzouga.**

M'HAMID

M'Hamid is the best entry point for the more adventurous and is the easiest place to reach if you are coming from Marrakesh. The paved road ends in the village, and beyond there's nothing but desert scrub, stony hamada, and soft dunes. Erg Chigaga is the star attraction, some 50 kms distant from the village. The sands go on for miles, and excursions by 4x4, camel, or a combination of both can be for as long or short as you like. Typically, a one-night trip by camel from M'Hamid gets you to nearby Erg L'Houdi (The Dunes of the Jews); four days round-trip gets you to Erg Ezahaar (The Screaming Dunes), and five days gets you to the highest dunes in the region, Erg Chigaga.

OTHER HIGHLIGHTS

ERG CHIGAGA

Erg Chigaga can be reached by desert *piste* (unsealed dirt road) in a 4x4 in around three hours, so an overnight getaway is possible. Alternatively, a two-day camel trek from M'Hamid will get you to Erg Chigaga, and you can book a 4x4 vehicle to bring you back the next day. Bivouacs in Erg Chigaga range from simple, nomad-style shared camps to super-deluxe private encampments.

OUARZAZATE

There are no dunes in Ouarzazate, but it's a great place to pick up a rental vehicle, bus, or taxi to take you to either Merzouga or M'Hamid. You can book a private tour with one of the many agencies in town. Tight on time? Fly to Ouarzazate airport from Casablanca.

ZAGORA

The desert vibe really kicks in at Zagora, which is itself an interesting town to visit. Unfortunately, the small sand dunes nearby give only a tiny taste of the desert; M'Hamid is where the Sahara truly begins. Take the extra two-hour drive to the end of the road if you possibly can. In Zagora you can arrange any kind of extended desert tour that will combine the desert at M'Hamid, the dunes of Erg Chigaga, the dried Lake Iriki, and a return via Foum Zguid. Or you can take a quick camel trek down through the Drâa Valley.

(top) A kasbah in Ouarzazate (top right) Merzouga dunes (center) a camel caravan (bottom right) riding motorcycles on the dunes

TINFOU

Less than an hour south of Zagora, there is little to see in Tinfou other than an isolated sand dune with a few bivouac camps and camel rides. Nearby is the Kasbah Hotel Sahara Sky, which has a state-of-the-art observatory for astronomy enthusiasts.

TAOUZ

This tiny village at the very end of the paved road after Merzouga is where the desert closes in. Here you can visit the gnaoua musicians at nearby Khamlia, and from Taouz you can take off-road excursions on complicated desert pistes heading southwest to eventually reach the village of Tagounite (just north of M'Hamid) on the N9/P31. This is at least a 9-hour drive and not recommended without a professional local driver/guide.

FOUM ZGUID

If you are traveling from Ouarzazate or Marrakesh, the dunes of Erg Chigaga can be reached more quickly by entering the desert at Foum Zguid rather than traveling the length of the Drâa Valley to M'Hamid, though most guided trips still leave from M'Hamid. The trip from Ouarzazate to Foum Zguid takes three hours by road and off-road piste to Erg Chigaga, skirting Jbel Bani on the old Paris–Dakar rally trail for another three hours.

TATA

Although it does not serve as a portal to the desert dune regions, Tata is a good base for excursions to the Akka oasis and the prehistoric rock-carvings at Oum el-Alek, Tircht, and Aït Herbil. You can pick up a local guide in Tata to show you the best archeological sites.

WILL I FRY? (AND OTHER QUESTIONS)

A typical desert bivouac camp in the Sahara

WILL I FRY?

Temperatures can reach 55°C (131°F) in June, July, and August. If you must go in summer, take sunset camel rides into the dunes, spend the night, and head back at dawn. The best (and busiest) time is between March and early May. October to February is nice, too, although it can be very cold at night from December through February.

WHAT SHOULD I WEAR?

Cover up with light layers. Loose-fitting clothes (e.g. knee-length shorts or baggy cotton pants and trekking sandals) are best for summer. In winter, lightweight walking boots or sneakers, long pants, T-shirts, long-sleeve tops, and a thick fleece should suffice, but bring something warmer for the night.

WHAT ABOUT MY HEAD?

It's essential to have a head covering to protect you from both sun and sand at any time of year. Donning the *sheish* (turban), beloved of Saharoui and Berbers, is really fun. Knot the end of a lightweight dyed fabric (most often blue), and put it on your head. Wrap the rest around your head and take the end across your nose and tuck it in.

WHAT IF I PREFER SKIING?

Believe it or not, you're in the right place. If camels, four-wheel drives, and long walks don't interest you, think of the sands as a miraculous cross between snow and sea. Most of the desert tour companies in Merzouga or M'Hamid have skis, sand-boards, and bodyboards for hire. Make sure you ask an expert if the sand is suitable. Be warned though... there are no lifts to get you back up the dunes!

DO I EVEN NEED A GUIDE?

The desert is unforgiving, and the inexperienced can easily become the expired. You should never attempt to visit the desert without an experienced guide. If you arrive in Merzouga or M'Hamid without having pre-booked a guided tour, make sure your guide is legitimate. While guiding visitors around the desert has kept hard-up locals in cash for years, you should be on the look-out for people on buses whose "uncle" has a place you can stay in for cheap. These people are almost always touts working on commission. Likewise, some may try to convince you that there is a "better" alternative to the auberge you pre-booked. The best way to avoid hassles is to make all arrangements in advance and arrange pick-up if you don't have your own transportion, or a roadside meeting if you do.

WHICH DUNES SHOULD I VISIT?

The impressive Erg Chebbi, near Merzouga, are more amenable to a quick in/out overnight, but they are a full 10-hour drive from Fez or two full days hard driving from Marrakesh. Erg Chebbi is very impressive, and solitary spots can be found on the fringes, with a good range of basic to deluxe accommodations. Southwest of M'Hamid, however, you have eye-popping dunes that stretch for miles, including the Erg Chigaga. Ideally, allow at least two days (by camel) to get there from M'Hamid, but a round-trip from Marrakesh is possible in three days with a 4x4.

WHAT ESSENTIAL ITEMS SHOULD I BRING?

Bring enough cash to see you through several days; sunscreen; sun glasses or a visor; eco-friendly toiletries; toilet paper; bottled water (at least three liters per day per person); zip-up plastic bags for keeping sensitive items free of sand; a flashlight with spare batteries; a basic first-aid kit; and a road map or GPS if you are driving to your starting point on your own. A sense of humor comes in handy too.

Gazing out on the desert

WHERE SHOULD I STAY?

In the desert, of course! Most tour operators, hotels, and auberges have their own permanent tented camps (*bivouacs*) hidden among the oases and dunes. Tents are usually good for between 2 and 4 people, but you can generally have a tent to yourself if traveling alone. If you want to keep the stars within eyeshot all night, you can also just sleep on a blanket over the sands. Most fixed camps have a restaurant tent (some serving alcohol), separate toilets, and washing facilities of some kind. In Merzouga and M'Hamid, at the edge of the desert, there are also traditional auberges and plusher hotels of varying grades of luxury (some even have swimming pools).

WILL I BE SAFE?

Yes, if you use your common sense. Do not stray far from your group or your guide: it is very easy to get disorientated in the dunes as they all look alike; you can quickly lose sight of your camp or your vehicle.

WHAT IS THERE TO DO IN THE DESERT?

You might think there's not much to do in the desert, but when there are no shops, no electricity, and no running water, just getting by becomes wonderfully time-consuming. You can cook bread in the sand; count stars until the sky caves in; climb to the crest of the dunes at sunset; and listen to hypnotic Berber drumming deep into the night.

Camel trips are de rigueur and in Erg Chebbi, near Merzouga, they rarely last more than three hours, with dinner generally waiting for you at your chosen bivouac camp. Beyond M'Hamid, farther south, there's a much greater range of desert terrain to explore. Away from the fixed camps, the experience of camping *sauvage,* with just a nomad guide and camel for company, gives a much better understanding of the real desert way of life.

For thrill-seekers there are quad bikes and buggies for desert safaris, or you can try your skills at boarding down the high dunes. Alternatively, just take it easy and watch the changing moods, colors, and textures of the dunes all day long.

SPECIAL-INTEREST TOUR OPERATORS

There are dozens of full-service tour operators offering packages that include a visit to the Sahara. In Morocco, there are also hundreds of smaller desert agencies. Prices for a basic 3-day/2-night tour from Marrakesh, virtually all-inclusive, can be less than $400 per person, but luxury trips can cost several times more.

A modern-day camel caravan

Best of Morocco (🌐 www.morocco-travel.com). These UK-based Morocco specialists can package flights, hotels, and general tours, with special-interest add-ons including camel treks and 4x4 safaris.

Desert Majesty (🌐 www.desertmajesty.com). Based in Ouarzazate and with expert local knowledge and guides who know the region inside and out, this company offers a variety of 4x4 tours and a camel/4x4 "Sahara Adventure" combination.

Desert Ways (🌐 www.desertways.co.uk). This UK-based operator offers desert survival training expeditions including instruction in signaling, navigation, emergency vehicle repairs, and water procurement.

Epic Morocco (🌐 www.epicmorocco.co.uk). The UK-based specialist adventure-holiday company offers a trekking and mountain-biking holiday in Merzouga.

Explore! (🌐 www.explore.co.uk). The UK's biggest adventure-travel company operates worldwide, offering some interesting Moroccan itineraries including a cycling/driving tour to the Drâa Valley and Merzouga.

Hidden Trails (🌐 www.hiddentrails.com). This American operator offers a number of different horseback-riding holidays in the Moroccan Sahara.

Morocco by Prior Arrangement (🌐 www.moroccobypriorarrangement.com). An upmarket Australian-Moroccan tour operator offers bespoke 4x4 tours and deluxe itineraries staying in some of the region's most exclusive hotels and selected luxury desert camps.

Red Tread Morocco (🌐 www.redtreadmorocco.com). Located in Ouarzazate, the English-run company has a fleet of Honda CRFX motorbikes for hire and organizes professionally guided off-road motorcycle tours across Southern Morocco.

Sahara Expeditions (wwww.saharaexpe.ma). This no-frills operation offers group desert excursions for 1 to 3 nights with guaranteed daily departures from Marrakesh.

Sheherazadventures (🌐 www.sheherazadventures.com). The Moroccan-English company offers special-interest tours with a community focus to the desert at M'Hamid (e.g. volunteer trips, pottery-making, photography, team incentives, desert expeditions).

SportTravel Maroc (🌐 www.sporttravel-maroc.com). This French-Moroccan specialist offers organized horseback riding, hiking, and camping trips into desert at M'Hamid and Merzouga.

Waypoint Tours (🌐 www.waypoint-tours.com). The company offers self-drive 4x4 off-road tours across Morocco (starting in southern Spain), including traversing western Sahara regions.

Your Morocco Tour (🌐 www.your-morocco-tour.com). This American-Moroccan partnership has a range of ready-made desert itineraries traveling in 4x4 starting from Agadir, Marrakesh, or Fez.

Zbar Travel (🌐 www.zbartravel.com). This company is owned by the Saharoui family, specialists in 4x4 desert safaris and camel-trips including a four-day trek to the remote "Screaming" dunes. There are offices in Ouarzazate and M'Hamid, and a deluxe bivouac camp at Erg Chigaga.

$$ **Hotel Source de Dadès.** Situated at exactly the point where the gorge narrows dramatically, this tiny place has one of the best locations in the valley. **Pros:** great location; helpful staff. **Cons:** rooms are a bit cramped. ✉ *Km 33 from Boumalne* ☎ *0524/83–12–58* *4 rooms* *In-room: no a/c, no TV. In-hotel: restaurant, parking* *No credit cards* *Some meals.*

$$$$ **Hotel Xaluca Dadès.** Part of the Spanish Xaluca chain, this vast hotel complex was built in the 1960s by the Moroccan state-owned hotel company. **Pros:** spacious, airy lounges; plenty of family amenities. **Cons:** far from the gorge; ugly architecture; expensive. ✉ *Rte. de Er-Rachidia, Boumalne du Dadès* ☎ *0524/83–00–60* *www.xaluca.com* *110 rooms* *In-room: a/c. In-hotel: restaurant, bar, pool, tennis court, gym, spa, laundry facilities, business center, parking* *Multiple meal plans.*

$$ **Kasbah de Victor.** Sitting perched on the cliff top, Kasbah de Victor has stunning views of the Dadès Gorge. **Pros:** swimming pool; heating in winter. **Cons:** remote location. ✉ *31 km (19 mi) from Boumalne* ☎ *0622/29–02–68* *www.lakasbahdevictor.com* *4 rooms* *In-room: no a/c, no TV. In-hotel: restaurant, pool, parking, some pets allowed* *No credit cards* *Some meals.*

SPORTS AND THE OUTDOORS

Mohamed Amgom. Mohamed Amgom is an experienced local Berber guide who can organize treks throughout the Dadès Valley for 400 DH per day. He can also organize four-wheel-drive vehicles for excursions throughout the Dadès and Todra gorges and works with his brother at the Hotel la Kasbah de la Vallée. ☎ *0666/59–41–42.*

7

THE TODRA GORGE

194 km (107 mi) northwest of Rissani, 184 km (101 mi) northeast of Ouarzazate.

GETTING HERE AND AROUND

The town of Tinerhir (also spelled "Tinghir") is the most convenient access point for visiting the Todra Gorge. It sits on the main N10 route from Ouarzazate and Er-Rachidia. To reach the gorge, take route R703 (3445) north toward Tamtattouchte, and follow the riverbed upwards for about 15 km (9 mi). The lush date palmery and rugged landscape change dramatically when steep walls of the gorge and glacial waters begin to tower above and block out the sunshine.

Long-distance buses travel here from Agadir, Casablanca, Marrakesh, Fez, Meknès, and Rabat. Buses also arrive from Ouarzazate (5 hours), Er-Rachidia (3 hours), and Erfoud (4 hours). Most buses stop on Avenue Mohammed V, on the northern side of the main square. The **CTM office** is on the southwestern corner of the square on the corner of Avenue Hassan II. If you don't have your own vehicle, you can catch a grand taxi to take you up through the Todra Palmery as far as the Todra Gorge. The drive takes about 30 minutes and should cost about 20 DH per person. There are also minibuses that transport locals to the villages above the Todra Gorge. You can ask to be dropped off at the gorge.

TIMING AND PRECAUTIONS

The steep sides of the gorge can often mean that the route through the gorge itself is in shade, but the effect of angled sunlight shifting across the rock face during the day creates a spectacular sublime canvas of red and orange. Mid- to late afternoon is deemed the best time to visit.

Poste Maroc ✉ *Ave. Hassan II, Tinerhir.*

EXPLORING

The 15-km (9-mi) drive up from Tinerhir to the beginning of the Todra Gorge will take you through lush but slender palmeries, sometimes no wider than 100 feet from cliff to cliff. An inn and a café await near the spring, but you're better off not stopping, as the site itself isn't remarkable, and the concentration of hustlers and over-helpful children is dense.

The 66-foot-wide entrance to the Todra Gorge, with its roaring clear stream and its 1,000-foot-high rock walls stretching 325 feet back on either side, is the most stunning feature of the whole canyon, though the upper reaches aren't far behind. The farther off the beaten path you get, the more rewarding the scenery; a walk or drive up through the gorge on paved roads to Tamtattouchte is particularly recommended.

From the thin palmery along the bottom, the walls of the Todra Gorge remain close and high for some 18 km (11 mi), dappled only with occasional families of nomads and their black *khaimas* (tents) tending sheep, goats, or camels (dromedaries) up on the rocks. Colorfully attired young Berber shepherdesses may appear from nowhere; sometimes you can hear them singing Berber melodies from high in the crags, their sounds echoed and amplified by the rock walls of the canyon. Eagles nest in the Todra, along with choughs (red-beaked rooks), rock doves, and blue rock thrushes.

La Source des Poissons Sacrés (Springs of the Sacred Fish), about halfway to the beginning of the gorge, is so named for the miracle performed by a sage, said to have struck a rock once to produce a gushing spring, and twice to produce fish. Today the sacred source is frequented by young Berber women who are experiencing difficulties in conceiving children. It is rumored that bathing in the water has about 80% success rate. Failing that, you can stop here to camp and have a refreshing drink.

WHERE TO STAY

For expanded hotel reviews, visit Fodors.com.

$$ **Auberge Baddou.** This small hotel is a worthy choice for budget accommodations at the far northern end of the Todra Gorge. **Pros:** spotless rooms; friendly service. **Cons:** rather isolated in unattractive village; few amenities. ✉ *Aït Hani, Tamtatouchtte* ☎ *0672/52–13–89* 🌐 *www.aubergebaddou.com* *11 rooms (6 with bath), 1 suite* *In-room: a/c, no TV. In-hotel: restaurant, parking, some pets allowed* ▭ *No credit cards* *Some meals.*

$$$ Fodor's Choice ★ **Dar Ayour.** Tucked down an alley just before the Todra Gorge is this pretty guesthouse, recently expanded due to its growing popularity. **Pros:** peaceful setting; lovely garden. **Cons:** some rooms very small. ✉ *Rte. des Gorges de Todra, Tinerhir* ☎ *0524/89–52–71, 0672/52–12–51* 🌐 *www.*

darayour.com ⇆ *8 rooms, 4 suites* ♨ *In-room: a/c, no TV, Wi-Fi. In-hotel: restaurant, laundry facilities, business center, parking, some pets allowed* 🍴 *Some meals.*

$$ **Le Festival.** Made from the same mountain rock that surrounds it, this hotel is owned and run by the charming Addi Sror, who speaks excellent English. **Pros:** hotel made of gorgeous stone; great meals. **Cons:** few in-house amenities; three rooms in main house share a bathroom. ✉ *5 km (3 mi) north of the Todra Gorge, 12 km (7 mi) south of Tamtattouchte, Tinerhir* ☎ *0661/26–72–51* 🌐 *www.aubergelefestival-todragorge.com* ⇆ *15 rooms, 3 with shared bath* ♨ *In-room: no a/c, no TV. In-hotel: restaurant, parking, some pets allowed* ▭ *No credit cards* 🍴 *Some meals.*

TO MERZOUGA AND THE DUNES

This particular southeastern corner holds some of Morocco's greatest sights, principally the Sahara's picture-perfect undulating dunes near Merzouga, and the Tafilalt date palmery. It's best to avoid Er-Rachidia, a colonial town with little to offer, and even Erfoud, too, if possible, as it's full of touts. Now that the road to Merzouga is completely paved, you can drive straight there without stopping. ■ **TIP→ For traveling anywhere in the desert, ensure you have enough cash, charged batteries, bottled water, and toiletries to see you through for several days until you get to a major town.**

EN ROUTE

You cannot fail to notice hundreds of holes along the roadside about 25 km before you reach Erfoud (from Tinejdad). The holes that look like giant molehills are actually an ancient irrigation system designed in Persia more than 3,000 years ago, which was first brought to Morocco by the Arabs in the 12th century. The wells are called *khettara,* and access water from the natural water table, channeling it through underground canals to different palm groves. On the left-hand side of the road as sand dunes begin to pile up—and 27 kms (17 mi) before reaching Erfoud (from the direction of Tinejdad)—look out for the ancient wells dating back to 11th century. Local guide, **Said Ouatou,** can be found in a Bedouin tent at the side of the road and will explain the science and history. ■ **TIP→ Be careful if you have young children, the edges of the wells can crumble.**

ERFOUD

81 km (49 mi) south of Er-Rachidia, 300 km (180 mi) northeast of Ouarzazate.

GETTING HERE AND AROUND

Erfoud sits at the southern end of the Ziz Oasis. From the north, the only way here is the N13 via Er-Rachidia. From Ouarzazate, take the N10 and turn onto the R702 just after the village of Tinejdad, and onto the R702. This direct route avoids Er-Rachidia.

Buses to Erfoud depart from Er-Rachidia (1½ hours), Fez (11 hours), Rissani (1½ hours), and Tinerhir (3½ hours). From Er-Rachidia you can take buses to Ouarzazate, Marrakesh, Midelt, and Meknès. The CTM bus station in Erfoud is located on Avenue Mohammed V.

Bus Contacts **CTM Erfoud** ✉ *Av. Mohammed V* ☎ *0535/57–68–86.*

TIMING AND PRECAUTIONS

The biggest event of the year is the annual Erfoud Date Festival, coinciding with the date harvest in October.

EXPLORING

A French administrative outpost and Foreign Legion stronghold, this frontier town on the Algerian border has a definite Wild West (in this case, Wild South) feel to it. The military fortress at Borj-Est, just across the Ziz to the east, provides the best possible view over the date palmery, the desert, and Erfoud from its altitude of 3,067 feet above sea level. Near the Borj-Est are quarries famous for their black marble, one of Erfoud's principal products; interestingly, this luxurious solid is rich in petrified marine fossils.

Erfoud itself is not without its peculiar charm, though this dusty, fly-bitten border post is best known as a traveler's jumping-off point for the Merzouga Dunes. Its finest architectural feature is the main gate into the medina, designed in the typical Almohad style with flanking crenellated bastions and an intricately carved stucco portal.

WHERE TO STAY

For expanded hotel reviews, visit Fodors.com.

$$$ **Hotel Kasbah Tizimi.** This faux kasbah built in the 1960s is popular with European package tour operators, but it is also a decent midrange hotel if you are passing through for a night or two in the desert. **Pros:** reasonable prices; nice pool area **Cons:** filled with tour groups; poor bathrooms. ✉ *Route de Jorf* ☎ *0535/57–61–79* 🌐 *www.kasbahtizimi.com* *65 rooms, 8 suites* *In-room: a/c. In-hotel: restaurant, pool, laundry facilities, business center, parking* *Breakfast.*

$$$$ **Kasbah Xaluca.** Constructed using authentic methods, this hotel is much beloved for its rustic charm. **Pros:** pretty pool area; attentive service. **Cons:** distance from dunes. ✉ *5 km (3 mi) out of Erfoud on road to Er-Rachidia, Maadid* ☎ *0535/57–84–50* 🌐 *www.xaluca.com* *110 rooms, 24 suites, 8 bungalows* *In-room: a/c, kitchen, Wi-Fi. In-hotel: restaurant, bar, pool, tennis court, spa, laundry facilities, business center, parking* *Multiple meal plans.*

SHOPPING

No trip to Erfoud is complete without a visit to one of the many marble and fossil workshops. This region of desert was once a rich seabed with many types of marine creatures that no longer exist today. Trilobytes, urchins, ammonites, and other fossils are abundant in the local stone, and huge slabs are quarried, dissected, polished, and shaped here to create all manner of household object from tabletops to pendants. Most of the workshops can give demonstrations as well as exhibit the finished articles.

Fossiles d'Erfoud. This fossil showroom, workshop, and factory all open to the public, with English-speaking owners who are happy to show individuals and groups around the facilities. The showroom has just about every object you might imagine could be made from fossils, and there are plenty of un-"improved" fossils to go around as well. ✉ *Town Center, 500 meters from Ziz gas station* ☎ *0535/57–60–20* 🌐 *www.fossilesderfoud.com.*

RISSANI

17 km (11 mi) south of Erfoud, 40 km (24 mi) northwest of Merzouga.

Rissani stands on the site of the ancient city of Sijilmassa, Morocco's first independent southern kingdom, which thrived here from the 8th to the 14th century. Founded in 757 by dissident Berbers, who had committed the heresy of translating the Koran to the Berber language (Islamic orthodoxy forbids translation from the Arabic of the direct revelations of God), Sijilmassa and the Filalis, as they were known, prospered from the natural wealth of the Tafilalt oasis and the Tafilalt's key role on the Salt Road to West Africa. Sijilmassa was almost completely destroyed in civil strife in 1393; archaeological excavations are now attempting to determine the city's size and configuration. All that remains of Sijilmassa today is the excellent 13th-century gate Bab Errih, notable for the green ceramic-tile frieze over its three horseshoe arches.

GETTING HERE AND AROUND

There are two main routes into Rissani, the N12 from Tazzarine (west) or the N13 from Erfoud (north). Buses arrive from Erfoud (1½ hours), Er-Rachidia (3 hours), Meknès (8 hours), Tinejdad (3½ hours), Tinerhir (4 hours), and Zagora (10 hours). Grands taxis run to Erfoud and Merzouga. CTM buses operate from the main square, while other companies use the new station just outside the arched entrance to the town.

TIMING AND PRECAUTIONS

Rissani hosts a souk on Sunday, Tuesday, and Thursday.

EXPLORING

Modern Rissani is known as the cradle of the Alaouite dynasty, of which King Mohammed VI is the still-reigning sultan. The well-marked Circuit Touristique guides you through the main remnants of the Alaouite presence here. The **Zaouia of Moulay Ali Sherif,** the mausoleum of the dynasty's founder, is 2 km (1 mi) southeast of the center of Rissani. Next to the zaouia is the **Ksar Akbar,** to which rebellious Alaouite family members and the wives of deceased sultans were exiled. Moulay Ismail had two of his sons sent here to put some distance between his heirs and his power base at Meknès. The **Ksar Oualad Abdelhalim,** the largest and most impressive of these Alaouite structures, is 1 km (½ mi) beyond Ksar Akbar; it was built in 1900 for Sultan Moulay el-Hassan's older brother, who had been named governor of Tafilalt. After Ksar Oualad Abdelhalim, loop around past the remaining ksour and climb the high ground at **Tinrheras,** correctly marked on the Michelin 959 map as an excellent lookout point over the Tafilalt.

The drive back north from Merzouga through Rissani brings you to the **Tafilalt date palmery.** The presence of a million-plus date palms here seems doubly miraculous after you have seen the desert. The palmery is a phenomenon created by the parallel Ziz and Rheris rivers, which flow within 3 km–5 km (2 mi–3 mi) of each other for 26 km (16 mi).

Here's how to navigate Rissani without resorting to outside assistance. On the approach to Rissani from Erfoud is the first of two gates. Just after the first gate, follow the road as it curves left; don't take a right-hand fork for the "Circuit Touristique." You'll quickly reach town, at which point you'll go under a second arch. Ahead are the walls of the kasbah. Turn right so that they are on your left, and follow them until the road ends in a T-junction. Turn left, keep left at the next fork, and you should be on the road that winds through the palmery and leads, eventually, to the dunes.

WHERE TO STAY

For expanded hotel reviews, visit Fodors.com.

$$$$ **Kasbah Ennasra.** Constructed using traditional materials and designs, the Kasbah Ennasra has a laid-back charm. **Pros:** friendly English-speaking staff. **Cons:** far from the dunes. ✉ *Ksar Labtarni, Rte. de Rissani, 2 km (1 mi) north of Rissani, Er-Rachidia* ☎ *0535/77–44–03* 🌐 *www.kasbahennasra.it* *13 rooms, 4 suites* *In-room: a/c, no TV, Wi-Fi. In-hotel: restaurant, bar, pool, spa, business center, parking* *Multiple meal plans.*

MERZOUGA

53 km (32 mi) southeast of Erfoud, 134 km (83 mi) southeast of Er-Rachidia.

A sunrise trip to Erg Chebbi has become a classic Moroccan adventure. A series of café-restaurant-hotels overlooks the dunes, and most run camel excursions out to the top of the dunes, a 45-minute walk on foot, and to oases where you can camp for the night in permanent bivouacs.

GETTING HERE AND AROUND

The N13 from Erfoud can now be driven in an ordinary car. Minibuses and grands taxis bring tourists from Rissani and Erfoud.

GUIDES AND TOURS

Adventures with Ali, run by Ali Mouni, has all-inclusive tours into the desert. Blue Men of Morocco runs tours from an auberge called Haven La Chance near the Merzouga Dunes in Hassi Labied.

Contacts **Adventures with Ali** ✉ *Nomad Palace Hotel* ☎ *0661/56–36–11* 🌐 *www.adventureswithali.com.* **Blue Men of Morocco Company** ✉ *Haven La Chance Desert Hotel, Hassi Labied* ☎ *0535/57–72–89* 🌐 *www.bluemenofmorocco.com.*

TIMING AND PRECAUTIONS

Temperatures can soar in summer, so always have plenty of bottled water, sunglasses, and sunblock. In winter the nights can be viciously cold, so be prepared with extra layers if camping out. ■ TIP→ **The fine sand of the Sahara will find its way into everything. Carry zip-top plastic bags for keeping items sand-free, especially electronic equipment and cosmetics.**

The magnificent dunes at Erg Chebbi are just outside of Merzouga.

EXPLORING

The village of Merzouga itself has little to recommend it other than a few not-too-compelling but survivable hotels. Between Erg Chebbi and the town, have a look at the underground aqueduct, Merzouga's main water supply. It's flowing (oozing) proof that sand dunes form as a result of moisture, which causes the sand to stick and agglomerate. The dune at Merzouga towers at more than 815 feet over the surrounding desert.

Dayet Sjri. Near the dunes, the seasonal salt lake Dayet Sjri is a surprising sight and is filled in early spring with pink flamingos.

Fodor's Choice ★ **Erg Chebbi.** In most cases your hotel is your best bet for an organized tour of Erg Chebbi. Every auberge near the dunes is there because it's the best jumping-off point for a sunrise or sunset journey into the dunes, either on foot or by camel. Most auberges have their own permanent bivouac in the dunes, often not far from others but generally fairly well concealed, so you can pretend no one else is around even if they are. Most bivouac areas are organized into series of small tents for couples and larger groups, so you don't have to share with everyone. If you want to be utterly private, make sure your auberge doesn't share a tented site with any other, or ask to camp in the dunes on your own.

For anything more than camel riding and staying in a desert oasis, such as quad biking, you'll need to go to the right hotel (Tombuctou rents quads) or a local rental agent. Most auberges can get their hands on a four-wheel drive, even if they don't always have them on-site.

WHERE TO STAY

There are few decent options in Merzouga. The best places are north of Merzouga in the desert village Hassi Labied; these also benefit from being closest to the towering sands.

For expanded hotel reviews, visit Fodors.com.

$$ **Auberge Atlas du Sable/Ali "El Cojo."** Auberge Atlas du Sable/Ali "El Cojo." **Pros:** reasonably priced; all the necessary comforts. **Cons:** not all rooms have air-conditioning; not much English spoken. *Hassi Labied 0535/57–70–37 www.alielcojo.com 40 rooms In-room: no a/c, no TV. In-hotel: restaurant, pool, parking, some pets allowed No credit cards Some meals.*

$$ **Kasbah Erg Chebbi.** Appropriately named after the sand dunes everyone is here to see, this lodging is one of the closest auberges to Erg Chebbi, and it's pretty isolated to boot. **Pros:** great staff; close to dunes. **Cons:** air-conditioning not in all rooms. *North of Hassi Labied 0670/77–83–15 w www.kasbahergchebbi.com 20 rooms In-room: a/c, no TV. In-hotel: restaurant, pool, parking, some pets allowed No credit cards Some meals.*

$$$ ★ **Kasbah Mohayut.** There are arches, fountains, and lanterns all over this sweet and sultry auberge. **Pros:** proximity to dunes; pretty pool. **Cons:** this part of dunes is often busy with other tourists. *Hassi Labied 0666/03–91–85 www.mohayut.com 17 rooms, 4 suites In-room: a/c, no TV. In-hotel: restaurant, bar, pool, business center, parking, some pets allowed Some meals.*

$$$$ ★ **Kasbah Tombuctou.** This magnificent camp gets a lot of complaints for being big and noisy, but the fact is that the facilities here are excellent. **Pros:** magnificent view of the dunes; luxurious lodging. **Cons:** lights in rooms are very dim. *Hassi Labied 0535/57–70–91 www.xaluca.com 72 rooms, 2 suites In-room: a/c. In-hotel: restaurant, bar, pool, spa, laundry facilities, business center, parking, some pets allowed Multiple meal plans.*

$$$ **Nomad Palace.** Owner Ali Mouni arranges all manner of desert and mountain outings from this superior and comfortable auberge. **Pros:** full range of desert activities; removed from the crowds. **Cons:** not all rooms are air-conditioned. *6 km south of Merzouga on road to Taoz 0535/88–20–89 www.hotelnomadplace.com 27 rooms In-room: a/c, no TV. In-hotel: restaurant, pool, business center, parking No credit cards Some meals.*

$$$$ **Sahara Garden.** Not a hotel but rather a deluxe eco-bivouac, Sahara Garden is situated far from the madding crowd at the northern tip of Erg Chebbi, outside Hassi Labied. **Pros:** stunning location; deluxe camping. **Cons:** difficult to find. *17 km before Merzouga (19 km from Rissani), follow signs to Hotel Yasmina 0535/77–44–03 www.sahara-garden.com 14 deluxe tents In-room: no a/c, no TV. In-hotel: restaurant, parking No credit cards Some meals.*

SPORTS AND THE OUTDOORS

Les Petales de Merzouga. Les Petales de Merzouga rents bikes and four-wheel-drive vehicles and arranges camel treks. *0610/63–72–45 www.quadmaroc.net.*

DJEBEL SARHRO AND NEKOB

95 km (57 mi) east of Agdz, 165 km (99 mi) southwest of Rissani.

★ If you pick the southern oasis route, don't miss the chance to stay in Nekob, Morocco's most kasbah-filled village. Locals have come up with all sorts of reasons for why there are 45 of them. The amusing and believable theory is that members of a rich extended family settled here in the 18th and 19th centuries and quickly set to work trying to out-build and out-impress each other. There's little in the way of showing off in the village today. The children are wild and the place a little untouched for the moment.

Just when you thought there's nothing to do here but pass through, you find out that the trekking potential to the north of town stretches as far as Boumalne du Dadès, 150 km (93 mi) away and on the northern oasis route. It's a five-day trek to Tagdift or Iknioun to the north. You can pick up handmade carpets and head scarves made by local women at the weekly Sunday souk. Or you can do very little; simply sit back, stare over the palmery, and enjoy. ■ **TIP→ At the moment, Nekob is a nature-lover's dream; it may not be like this in 10 years' time, so get here soon.**

GETTING HERE AND AROUND

Nekob lies on the southern oasis route between Agdz and Rissani, skirting the southern slopes of the Djebel Sarhro. Minibuses and grands taxis travel here from Rissani, Zagora, and Ouarzazate.

Exploring the mountain ranges and peaks of Djebel Sarhro requires a four-wheel-drive vehicle. An official Bureau des Guides, run by Mohamed YaaQoub, in the center of town, can organize hiking trips in the Djebel Sarhro for an afternoon or several days.

Contacts **Bureau des Guides** ✉ *Town Center* ☎ *0667/48–75–09* 🌐 *www.moroccotrek.net.*

EXPLORING

Djebel Sarhro Massif. The wonderfully panoramic oasis Route 6956/R108 (which becomes 3454/N12 after Tazzarine) still appears as a desert piste on some Moroccan road maps, but it has been paved. Indeed, it's one of the safest, fastest, and least crowded roads in Morocco, and it offers unparalleled views up into the Djebel Sarhro Massif and all the way over to the Tafilalt date palmery. Count on four hours for the 233-km (140-mi) trip from Route P31/N9 (the Ouarzazate–Zagora road) to Rissani, in the date palmery.

NEED A BREAK?

Auberge Kasbah Meteorites. Morocco is a magnet for fossil fans, and much of the activity centers around the town of Alnif, on Route 3454/N12 between Rissani and Tazzarine. About 13 km (9 mi) west of Alnif is Auberge Kasbah Meteorites where you can enjoy a simple lunch, a dip in the immaculate pool, and a two- to three-hour excursion with a guide who'll show you the best place to hunt for fossils and ancient stone carvings. There are also 16 bright new bedrooms should you decide to stay over so you can explore the region in greater detail. ✉ ***Ksar Tiguima, 13 km (8 mi) from Alnif*** ☎ ***0535/78–38–09*** 🌐 ***www.kasbahmeteorites.com.***

WHERE TO STAY

For expanded hotel reviews, visit Fodors.com.

$ **Auberge Ennakhile Saghro.** This charming auberge has an entrancing view of the palmery below. **Pros:** great views; plenty of activities. **Cons:** not all rooms have private bathrooms. ✉ *N'kob, at Erfoud end of town* ☎ *0524/83–97–19, 0672/64–15–11* 🌐 *www.kasbah-nkob.com* *15 rooms, 5 with bath* *In-room: a/c, no TV. In-hotel: restaurant, business center, parking, some pets allowed* *No credit cards* *Some meals.*

$$$ **Kasbah Imdoukal.** This lovely Moroccan-owned kasbah sits in the heart of the town. **Pros:** in the center of Nekob; plenty of atmosphere. **Cons:** prices are a bit high; not all rooms have air-conditioning. ✉ *Douar N'Kob* ☎ *0524/83–97–98* 🌐 *www.kasbahimdoukal.com* *18 rooms, 2 suites* *In-room: a/c, no TV. In-hotel: restaurant, pool, business center, parking, some pets allowed* *No credit cards* *Some meals.*

$$$ Fodor's Choice ★ **Ksar Jenna.** This beautiful and calm villa-style lodging could have been plucked from Marrakesh. **Pros:** cool gardens; stunning architecture. **Cons:** no pool; remote location; lack of staff on hand. ✉ *2 km (1 mi) after village, heading west* ☎ *0524/83–97–90* 🌐 *www.ksarjenna.com* *5 rooms, 1 suite* *In-room: a/c, no TV. In-hotel: restaurant, bar, business center, parking* *Some meals.*

THE DRAÂ VALLEY

Morocco's longest river, the Draâ once flowed all the way to the Atlantic Ocean just north of Tan-Tan, some 960 km (600 mi) from its source above Ouarzazate. With the sole exception of a fluke flood in 1989—the only time in recent memory that the Draâ completed its course—the river now disappears in the Sahara southwest of M'Hamid, some 240 km (150 mi) from its headwaters. The Draâ Valley and its palmery continue nearly unbroken from Agdz through Zagora to M'Hamid, forming one of Morocco's most memorable tours.

As wild as you may have found certain parts of Morocco thus far, the trip down to the Sahara will seem more so, something like steady progress into a biblical epic. The plains south of Ouarzazate give way to 120 km (75 mi) of date palmeries and oases along the Draâ River, and between Agdz and Zagora more than two-dozen kasbahs and ksour line both sides of the river. The occasional market town offers a chance to mingle with the diverse peoples you'll see walking along the road in black shawls. Though most of the inhabitants are in fact Berbers, the Draâ Valley also contains Arab villages, small communities of Jews or the mellahs they once inhabited, and numerous Haratin, descendants of Sudanese slaves brought into Morocco along the caravan routes that facilitated salt, gold, and slave-trading until late in the 19th century.

After Zagora and Tamegroute, the road narrows as the Tinfou Dunes rise to the east and, farther south, a maze of jeep tracks leads out to Erg L'Houdi (Dune of the Jew). Finally, in M'Hamid el Ghizlane (Plain of the Gazelles), with sand drifting across the road and the Draâ long since gone underground, there is a definite sense of closure, the end of the road.

AGDZ

69 km (41 mi) southeast of Ouarzazate.

Agdz, at the junction of the Draâ and Tamsift rivers, marks the beginning of the Draâ palmery. A sleepy market town and administrative center, Agdz (pronounced *ah*-ga-dez) has little to offer other than the 5,022-foot peak Djebel Kissane, and the Kasbah Dar el-Glaoui. From Agdz south to M'Hamid, the P31/N9 road follows the river closely except for a 30-km (18-mi) section between the Tinfou Dunes and Tagounite, where the Draâ again draws close before temporarily looping east again.

GETTING HERE AND AROUND

Agdz is served by buses and grands taxis traveling between Ouarzazate and Zagora. The trip is approximately two hours from either town.

TIMING AND PRECAUTIONS

A great time to visit is in October when the date harvest is in full swing. The market is stacked with boxes of the most delicious and succulent varieties. ■ TIP→ **Schistosomiasis, a parasite, has been reported in the Draâ River, so don't be tempted to swim or even wade across.**

EXPLORING

Kasbah Timidarte. Kasbah Timidarte, 8 km (5 mi) south of Tamnougalt on the left side of the road (P31/N9) as you head south, was built in 17th century by the local population and has recently been restored and revived as a community-development centre and guesthouse. ■ TIP→ **For an informed guide to the history of the region and the kasbahs, contact Hussein Achabak, who leads this eco-tourism initative.** ☎ *0668/68–00–47 for Hussein Achabak.*

Ksar Igdâoun. The truncated pyramidal towers and bastions of the Ksar Igdâoun are visible 15 km (9 mi) past the turnoff onto Route 6956/R108 to Tazzarine. There used to be three gates for the ksar: one for Jews; one for other people who lived nearby; and one for the local governor. 🎫 *10 DH.*

Tamnougalt. Lining virtually the entire Draâ Valley from Agdz to Zagora are some two-dozen ksour and kasbahs on both sides of the river. Perhaps the most amazing ksour in this region are at Tamnougalt, 6 km (4 mi) south of Agdz—the second group of red-pisé fortifications on the left. The resident Berber tribe, the Mezguita, governed its own independent republic from here until the late 18th century; the crenellated battlements and bastions were a necessary defense against nomadic desert tribes.

OFF THE BEATEN PATH

Cascades du Draâ. Look for the turnoff to the Cascades du Draâ (also know as the Cascades de Tizgui) on the left, 30 km (19 mi) south of Ouarzazate and 10 km (6 mi) before Agdz. The 10-km (6-mi) track down to the waterfalls is steep, rough, and all but impassable in bad weather (you'll need a 4x4 and good boots), but the falls are magnificent and have carved out natural pools ideal for swimming. With palm trees and oleander flowers springing from the rocks, this is well worth a detour, but make sure you allow enough time for the rough terrain.

WHERE TO STAY

For expanded hotel reviews, visit Fodors.com.

$$$ **Chez Yacob.** Wander through the heavy wooden door into this old house at midday, and its tiny central courtyard will be packed to the rafters with lunching tour groups—a big thumb's-up for the kitchen, with added bonus that you can bring your own wine/beer. **Pros:** full of charm; great views over palmery. **Cons:** very little parking space. ✉ *Tamnougalt* ✥ *4 km (½ mi) from Agdz on route to Zagora* ☎ *0524/84–33–94* 🌐 *www.lavalleedudraa.com* *8 rooms* *In-room: a/c, no TV. In-hotel: restaurant, business center, parking* ▭ *No credit cards* 🍽 *Some meals.*

$$$$ Fodor's Choice ★ **Kasbah Azul.** Kasbah Azul, the "House of Peace," is aptly named; built using traditional methods, this 21st-century kasbah is tucked away in the palm groves about 2½ km (1 mi) outside Agdz. **Pros:** beautiful setting; great for kids **Cons:** expensive. ✉ *Douar Asslim* ☎ *0524/84–39–31* 🌐 *www.kasbahazul.com* *7 rooms* *In-room: a/c, no TV, Wi-Fi. In-hotel: restaurant, pool, business center, parking, some pets allowed, some age restrictions* ⏲ *Closed during Ramadan (call ahead)* 🍽 *Some meals.*

TINZOULINE

59 km (35 mi) southeast of Agdz, 130 km (81 mi) southeast of Ouarzazate.

Tinzouline holds an important weekly souk. If you're here on a Monday, take this opportunity to shop and make contact with the many peoples of this southern Moroccan region where communities of Berbers, Arabs, Jews, and Haratin (descendants of Sudanese slaves) have coexisted for centuries. The Tinzouline ksour are clustered around a majestic kasbah in the middle of an oasis that includes several villages. Tinzouline is also one of the most important prehistoric sites in pre-Saharan North Africa: from the ksour a 7-km (4.5-mi) gravel path leads west of town to cave engravings depicting mounted hunters. These drawings are attributed to Iron Age Libyo-Berbers, lending further substance to the theory that Morocco's first inhabitants, the Berbers, may have originally come from Central Asia via central and eastern Africa.

ZAGORA

95 km (57 mi) southeast of Agdz, 170 km (102 mi) southeast of Ouarzazate.

Zagora is—and does feel like—the boundary between the Sahara and what some writers and travelers have referred to as "reality." After Zagora, time and distance are measured in camel days: a famous painted sign at the end of town (near the impressive new Zagora Province offices) features a camel and reads, "Tombouctu 52 Days"—that is, "52 days by camel." The town of M'Hamid, 98 km (65 mi) farther south, marks the actual end of the paved road and the beginning of the open desert, but Zagora is where the sensation of being in the desert kicks in.

Zagora is the last major town before the Sahara really begins at M'Hamid.

On your way out of Zagora, heading across the bridge signposted toward M'Hamid, you'll find the town of Amezrou and in it, the fascinating **Kasbah des Juifs** (Kasbah of the Jews).

GETTING HERE AND AROUND

Zagora is easily reached by the main road from M'Hamid and Ouarzazate. Buses and grands taxis navigate this route. The CTM bus station in Zagora is on the main street, as is the main bus station.

Zagora is easy to explore on foot or by inexpensive petit taxi. There are numerous tour agencies in town offering everything from camel trips to desert camping. Caravane du Sud is a well-respected local organization based just outside the center of Zagora in the town of Amezrou, just off the main road to M'Hamid. Reima Voyages Croq'Nature is a local tour operator with a conscience. Tombouctour has a great range of circuits through the desert. You stay in bivouacs and travel on foot and by camel and four-wheel drive as you please.

Bus Contacts **CTM Zagora** ✉ *Bd. Mohammed V* ☎ *0524/84–73–27* 🌐 *www.ctm.ma.*

Guided Tour Contacts **Caravane du Sud** ✉ *Amezrou* ☎ *0524/84–75–69, 0661/87–68–74* 🌐 *www.caravanesud.com.* **Reima Voyages Croq'Nature** ✉ *Av. Mohammed V* ☎ *0524/84–70–61* 📠 *0524/84–79–22* ✉ *smazizi@yahoo.fr* 🌐 *www.croqnature.com.* **Tombouctour** ✉ *79 Av. Mohammed V* ☎ *0524/84–82–07* 🌐 *www.tombouctour.com.*

EXPLORING

Amezrou. Pass Amezrou is 3 km (2 mi) south of Zagora. It's famous for its Jewish silversmiths, who made famous jewelry here until the creation of the Israeli State in 1948, when all but 30,000 of Morocco's 300,000 Jews left for Israel. Berber craftsmen continue the tradition in the mellah here, an interesting stop if you don't mind the clamor of children eager to be hired as your guide.

Djebel Zagora. Djebel Zagora, reached via the first left turn south of the Kasbah Asmaa hotel, is worth a stop. (There's also a twisting footpath up the 3,195-foot mountain from the hotel itself.) The town's promontory, with its 11th-century Almoravid fortress, is an excellent sunset vantage point, overlooking the Draâ palmery and the distant Djebel Sarhro Massif to the north and the Tinfou Dunes to the south.

WHERE TO EAT

$ MOROCCAN ★ **Le Dromadaire Gourmand.** Having hung up his *sheshe* (turban) after years of guiding tourists through the desert, Mustapha el-Mekki has established what has rapidly become one of the most popular eateries in Zagora. Little by little the restaurant was built and today serves regional specialities such as *tagine de mariage* (a slow-cooked casserole of beef with apricots, prunes, and almonds) and a Draâ Valley vegetable soup. There's a sidewalk terrace café and spacious, cool interior with Berber motifs carved into the walls. You can bring your own wine or beer. ✉ *Av. Mohammed V, near TOTAL gas station* ☎ *0661/34–83–94* ▭ *No credit cards.*

WHERE TO STAY

For expanded hotel reviews, visit Fodors.com.

$$ ★ **Dar Raha.** This quirkily restored kasbah is in a residential area in Amzrou, just outside Zagora, and allows guests to see a bit more of everyday Moroccan life. **Pros:** feels like living with the locals. **Cons:** shared bathrooms. ✉ *Rue el-Ghzaoui, Hay Amazraou* 📫 *B.P. 142, Zagora* ✣ *2 km (1 mi) from Zagora on road to M'Hamid* ☎ *0524/84–69–93* 🌐 *www.darraha.com* *9 rooms* *In-room: no a/c, no TV. In-hotel: restaurant, business center, parking, some pets allowed* ⏲ *Closed July and Aug.* 🍽 *Multiple meal plans.*

$$$ **Kasbah Sirocco.** A bit like a rambling French country hotel, this is one of Zagora's favorite destinations. **Pros:** excellent reputation; full range of services. **Cons:** can be noisy. ✉ *Amezrou* ☎ *0524/84–61–25* 🌐 *www.kasbah-sirocco.com* *20 rooms* *In-room: a/c, no TV. In-hotel: restaurant, bar, pool, laundry facilities, business center, parking, some pets allowed* 🍽 *Breakfast.*

$$$ **Kasbah Ziwana.** If you're fed up with faux kasbahs, then here's the real deal. **Pros:** comfortable rooms in an authentic kasbah; modern bathrooms. **Cons:** lack of natural light; few amenities. ✉ *Ksar Tissergate, 8 km from Zagora on the road to Ouarzazate* ☎ *0524/84–74–39* 🌐 *www.kasbahziwana.com* *15 rooms* *In-room: a/c, no TV. In-hotel: restaurant, business center, parking, some pets allowed* ▭ *No credit cards* 🍽 *Some meals.*

$$$$ **Palais Asmaa.** Everything is on a grand scale at Zagora's most prestigious address: the impressively lofty lobby leads to a restaurant, bar,

and gardens all filled with Brobdingnagian-size copper kettles and zellij tiles. **Pros:** good range of facilities. **Cons:** full of tour groups; dull room decor. ✉ *Route de M'Hamid* ☎ *0524/84–75–55* 🌐 *www.palais.asmaa-zagora.com* *80 rooms, 5 suites* *In-room: a/c. In-hotel: restaurant, bar, pool, laundry facilities, business center, parking, some pets allowed* *Breakfast.*

$$$$ **Riad Lamane.** You can't go wrong with this for a little bit of Marrakesh living at the edge of the desert. **Pros:** the shaded gardens and pool are a paradise. **Cons:** service can be sluggish. ✉ *Amazraou, at end of town headed towards M'Hamid* ☎ *0524/84–83–88* 🌐 *www.riadlamane.com* *7 rooms, 8 bungalows, 5 deluxe tents* *In-room: a/c, Wi-Fi. In-hotel: restaurant, bar, pool, laundry facilities, business center, parking, some pets allowed* *Some meals.*

Fodor's Choice ★

$$ **Zagour.** Friendly and unpretentious, this is an instantly likable budget hotel. **Pros:** peaceful surroundings; pretty terrace. **Cons:** rooms lack storage space. ✉ *Amezrou* ☎ *0524/84–61–78* 🌐 *www.zagour.ma* *18 rooms* *In-room: a/c, no TV. In-hotel: restaurant, pool, business center, parking, some pets allowed* *Breakfast.*

TAMEGROUTE

18 km (11 mi) southeast of Zagora.

Tamegroute (literally "the last town before the border," an accurate toponym when the Algerian border was closer than it is now) is the home of the **Zaouia of Sidi Mohammed Ben Naceur,** a sanctuary devoted to this extraordinary *marabout* (sage). Closed to non-Muslims, the sanctuary itself can be admired from the outside—the door bears an intricately decorated archway of carved cedar and stucco. The surrounding courtyard is perennially filled with dozens of mental patients hoping for miraculous cures or just for charity from the Naciri brotherhood. Outside to the left are onetime slave quarters still inhabited by descendants of Sudanese slaves.

GETTING HERE AND AROUND

Buses en route from Zagora to M'Hamid stop at Tamegroute but depart in the evening, so for a day trip to Tamegroute it is best to hire a grand taxi or drive yourself.

TIMING AND PRECAUTIONS

A visit to Tamegroute will take no more than two hours.

EXPLORING

Ceramics Cooperative. Don't miss Tamegroute's ceramics cooperative at the south end of the library, medersa, and slave quarters. The characteristic green-glazed pottery sold here is all handmade.

★ **Medersa.** Just north of the Zaouia of Sidi Mohammed Ben Naceur is a 17th-century medersa that still lodges 400 students preparing for university studies. The accompanying Koranic library was once the largest such collection in Morocco, with 40,000 volumes on everything from mathematics, philosophy, medicine, and astronomy to linguistics and Berber poetry. The remaining volumes are plenty impressive: a genealogy of the prophet Mohammed, manuscripts adorned with gold leaf, a

KSOUR AND KASBAHS

Ksour (plural for *ksar*) and kasbahs are fortified villages, houses, and granaries built of *pisé*, a sun-dried mixture of mud and clay. Ksour were originally tribal settlements or villages, while kasbahs were single-family fortresses. The Erfoud–Ouarzazate road through the Dadès Valley is billed as the "Route of the Thousand Kasbahs," with village after village of fortified pisé structures, many decorated with intricate painted and carved geometrical patterns. The Draâ Valley is also lined with kasbahs and ksour for the length of the Agdz–Zagora road. Highlights of the Dadès route are the Kasbah Amerhidil, at the Skoura oasis, and the Tifoultoute and Aït Ben Haddou kasbahs near Ouarzazate; the Draâ valley highlights are Tamnougalt and Ouled Othmane kasbahs, just south of Agdz, the 17th-century Tissergate ksar just north of Zagora, the underground kasbah at Tamegroute, and the kasbah in Ouled Driss, just outside M'Hamid. Increasingly, the kasbahs are being restored and converted into guesthouses. While it may be good for preserving the ancient structures and providing local jobs, fitting one out with modern bathrooms and a swimming pool is hardly in keeping with tradition. It's a delicate balance, and we can only hope that they stay open to the public.

medical book with afflictions written in red and remedies in black, and hand-illuminated manuscripts written in mint (green), saffron (yellow), and henna (red) on gazelle hide. Ask for a look at the 13th-century algebra primer with Western Arabic numerals, which, though subsequently abandoned in the Arab world, provided the basis for Western numbers. Although there is no official admission charge, a small donation is expected.

M'HAMID

162 km (97 mi) south of Zagora, 260 km (157 mi) southeast of Ouarzazate, 395 km (237 mi) southwest of Rissani.

Properly known as M'Hamid el-Ghizlane, or Plain of the Gazelles, M'Hamid neatly marks the end of Morocco's Great Oasis Valleys and the end of the asphalt road. The modern village of M'Hamid is not particularly attractive as a destination in itself—a one-street town with overeager desert tour companies hustling for business. However, it is a vital arrival and departure point for forays into the Sahara, which awaits at the end of the main street. It is from M'Hamid that the doorway opens for visiting Morocco's other great desert destination—Erg Chegaga—the highest dunes in Morocco, towering at 300 meters.

The outlying small villages of Ouled Driss and Bounou in the palm groves just before M'Hamid, have interesting kasbahs that can be visited, and a short hop across the dried river bed of the Draâ, next to the mosque in M'Hamid, takes you toward the site of the original village, some 2 km (1 mi) away, where there is a 17th-century Jewish-built kasbah that is still inhabited by the local Haratin population.

The sand drifting like snow across the road (despite the placement of palm-frond sand breaks and fences), the immensity of the horizon, and the patient gait of camels combine to produce a palpable change in the sense of time and space at this final Draâ oasis.

The town has a famous Monday souk notable for the occasional appearance of nomadic and trans-Saharan traders of the Saharan Reguibat tribe. Much chronicled by writer Paul Bowles, these ebony-skinned fellows habitually wear the indigo *sheish,* a linen cloth wrapped around the head and face for protection from the cold and from sandstorms. The dye from the fabric runs, tinging the men's faces blue and leading to their nickname, the Blue Men. Don't expect too much in the way of merchandise; the souk has lost much of its exotic appeal in recent years.

M'Hamid was once an outpost for the camel corps of the French Foreign Legion. Looking at it now, it's difficult to imagine what's there was worth defending, but the training would have been harsh enough to make a soldier out of any man. Today a large military barracks reminds visitors that the Algerian border is not far away.

The ocean of dunes 7 km (4½ mi) beyond M'Hamid will satisfy any craving for some real Saharan scenery.

GETTING HERE AND AROUND

M'Hamid is the last village before the pavement ends. Buses arrive here twice-daily from Marrakesh via Zagora and Ouarzazate. Grand taxis and minibuses also make the journey to and from Zagora.

Arriving in M'Hamid without reserved accommodations or excursions already booked can be intimidating due to fiercely competing touts. That said, there are several agencies trying to use a community-based approach to making such arrangements. Nomadic Life and Bivouac L'Erg are both committed to this approach. Other recommended companies are Bivouac Mille & Une Nuits, M'hamid Travel, and Sahara Services.

Contacts **Bivouac L'Erg** ✉ *M'Hamid town center, opposite the mosque* ☎ *0661/87–16–30.* **Bivouac Mille & Une Nuit** ✉ *Ouled Driss, 5 km before M'Hamid* ☎ *0524/84–86–85* 🌐 *www.croqnature.com/ouleddriss.htm.* **M'hamid Travel** ✉ *M'Hamid town center* ☎ *0524/88–59–49* 🌐 *www.mhamid-travel.com.* **Nomadic Life** ✉ *M'Hamid town center, next to Hotel El Ghizlane* ☎ *0662/84–26–76* 🌐 *www.nomadiclife.info.* **Sahara Services** ✉ *M'Hamid town center* ☎ *0661/77–67–66* 🌐 *www.saharaservicestravels.com.*

TIMING AND PRECAUTIONS

The International Nomads Festival takes place around mid-March. The event is run by local volunteers aiming to promote understanding of the nomadic traditions of the Moroccan Sahara.

EXPLORING

Ksebt el-Allouj. The ruins of the ksar Ksebt el-Allouj, dating to the Saadien dynasty, is across the Draâ riverbed on the other side from the village from M'Hamid, about 2 km (1 mi) from the town center. The ksar is uninhabited and is interesting to poke around in.

7

WHERE TO STAY

For expanded hotel reviews, visit Fodors.com.

$$ **Auberge El Khaima.** For travelers who want some traditional-style accommodations, this option at the edge of town offers basic comfort and a quiet garden. **Pros:** clean accommodations; eco-friendly. **Cons:** absolutely no frills. *Turn left at town square and cross river* *0667/41–45–02* *www.aubergeelkhaima.com* *13 rooms, 10 tents* *In-room: a/c, no a/c, kitchen, no TV. In-hotel: restaurant, pool, business center, parking* *No credit cards* *Some meals.*

$$$$ ★ **Chez Le Pacha.** Chez le Pacha is constantly evolving to suit the times. **Pros:** stylish accommodations; helpful staff. **Cons:** African huts and mini-kasbahs still under construction at time of writing; half board compulsory. *Bounou, near Ouled Driss* *0524/84–86–96* *www.chezlepacha.com* *16 rooms, 4 suites, 10 African huts, 16 mini-kasbahs* *In-room: a/c, no TV. In-hotel: restaurant, bar, pool, business center, parking, some pets allowed* *Some meals.*

$$$$ ★ **Dar Azawad.** One of the finest addresses in southern Morocco awaits dusty arrivals who want a few better-than-home comforts with their desert adventures. **Pros:** luxury at the edge of the desert. **Cons:** very expensive. *Douar Ouled Driss* *0524/84–87–30* *www.darazawad.com* *9 rooms, 6 suites* *In-room: a/c, Wi-Fi. In-hotel: restaurant, bar, pool, spa, laundry facilities, business center, parking, some pets allowed* *Closed mid-Jun.–mid-Jul.* *Some meals.*

$$$ **Le Drom' Blanc.** Hidden in the palm groves of Bounou (about 5 km/3 mi before reaching M'Hamid village), this simple guesthouse that has been rebuilt on the site of an old family home is reached by way of a sandy track. **Pros:** secluded location in palm groves; wheelchair-accessible room. **Cons:** rooms are very dark. *Bounou* *0524/84–68–52* *www.ledromblanc.com* *4 rooms* *In-room: no a/c, no TV. In-hotel: restaurant, parking, some pets allowed* *No credit cards* *Some meals.*

¢ **Hotel El Ghizlane.** This small, family-run hotel offers very basic rooms geared toward backpackers and those headed further into the desert. **Pros:** budget-priced; friendly staff. **Cons:** few amenities. *Town Center* *0668/51–72–80* *www.zbartravel.com* *7 rooms* *In-room: no a/c, no TV. In-hotel: restaurant, parking, some pets allowed* *No credit cards* *Breakfast.*

$$$$ ★ **Kasbah Azalay.** The only luxurious lodging actually in the village of M'Hamid is this Spanish-owned kasbah hotel at the edge of the palmery. **Pros:** plenty of creature comforts; magnificent pool and spa; at the edge of the desert. **Cons:** lack of communal terraces or salons for socializing. *M'Hamid El Ghizlane* *0524/84–80–96* *www.azalay.com* *38 rooms, 5 suites* *In-room: a/c, Wi-Fi. In-hotel: restaurant, bar, pool, spa, laundry facilities, business center, parking, some pets allowed* *Some meals.*

8

The Southern Atlantic Coast

ESSAOUIRA, AGADIR, AND THE ANTI-ATLAS

WORD OF MOUTH

". . . [We] loved this gem on the ocean! It is the type of place that you can shop (with better prices than Marrakesh); [it] has reasonable hammans, . . . fabulous restaurants, and cute riads . . . an unbelievable coastal area, a beautiful square for great people-watching, and a coastal drive to see the infamous goats in the trees . . ."

—dutyfree

WELCOME TO THE SOUTHERN ATLANTIC COAST

TOP REASONS TO GO

★ **Catch a wave:** From Agadir to Essaouira, the magnificent Atlantic coastline draws hundreds of surfers every year to ride its huge breaks.

★ **Satisfying seafood:** Whether you are haggling down by the port for your own fish or enjoying calamari on a rooftop terrace, both Essaouira and Agadir are a seafood-lover's paradise.

★ **Family fun:** Donkey rides, playgrounds, and ice-cream stalls make Agadir heaven for children, while stylish resort hotels serve up every luxury Mom and Dad could possibly want.

★ **Walking in the Anti-Atlas:** spectacular scenery around Tafraoute and the pretty villages of the Ameln Valley, without another tourist in sight.

★ **Taroudant:** a beautiful walled city with a strong crafts tradition, fascinating souks, and some lovely boutique hotels.

1 Agadir. The resort town of Agadir has long been popular with European sun worshipers. It's also a good base for sampling regional beaches and the Souss Massa Bird Estuary. South of town is "the tourist area," which runs alongside the beach.

2 Essaouira. Essaouira is quieter and more emblematically Moroccan than Agadir, though it's becoming more popular with bus tours coming up for the day. The beach stretches for miles in a curving bay, but most visitors are attracted by the car-free medina and the busy port with its fresh fish restaurants.

3 The Souss Valley and Anti-Atlas. The region around the Anti-Atlas Mountains, comprising Taroudant, Tafraoute, and Tiznit, is relatively compact, and most easily reached from family-friendly Agadir, providing a completely different kind of travel experience.

GETTING ORIENTED

Morocco's southern coastal towns might be just a few hours from bustling Marrakesh, but their laid-back vibe makes you feel you're a world away. Everyone flocks to this region in summer for the sandy beaches, the luxurious resorts, or the numerous festivals that ensure that there's always music in the air.

THUYA: BURIED TREASURE OF THE ATLAS

Coveted since Roman times, Morocco's rare and beautiful thuya wood is particular to the western foothills of the Atlas Mountains. In modern times, this material remains synonymous with wealth, being the first burled wood used for luxury dashboards in the Rolls Royce.

(above) Thuya wood boxes may be carved and polished or inlaid (opposite page, bottom) a carved thuya wood cup (opposite page, top) the seed cones of the thuya tree, a relative of the cedar

At first glance, the thuya tree, a rather unassuming Atlas conifer, is underwhelming. The tree's foliage is rather scrubby while its trunk has unknotted, bland wood. However, the roots hold a treasure trove of beauty—this is from where thuya wood's natural burled grain and complex markings come. Incidentally, these roots are remarkably resilient, surviving constant coppicing with little or no distress. For the Berbers of the Middle Atlas, the thuya industry is a vital aspect of the local economy. Fathers hand down the skills necessary to select, harvest, and work the wood. Theirs is the delicate job of measuring and cutting the root pieces into a variety of shapes and sizes. So precious is it—and so brittle—that any slip of the hand spells catastrophe.

SPOTTING REAL THUYA WOOD

Genuine thuya is a reddish brown color and has myriad darker, knotty whorls: closely resembling burr walnut and bird's-eye maple. Beware of traders offering larger pieces such as dining tables and storage chests, which may not be genuine. Carved pieces (other than antiques) tend to be small. The most popular items found in souks and stores are boxes, bowls, placemats, and penholders.

THE SCENT

Thuya's scent, nature's guard against parasitic attack, once made it a prized ingredient of ancient lore. The Greeks named the tree *thuya* (pronounced *twee-ya*), which means "sacrifice." They used its distilled essence to produce incense for religious ceremonies. As with cedar, its close relative, thuya's distinctive aroma remains decades after the wood is cut. Today, the scent is more likely to feature in aromatherapy rather than ritual. But the Romans commissioned immense carved works, such as doorways and statement pieces of furniture.

SUSTAINABLE HARVESTING

With the substantial part of the tree securing so many livelihoods, its sustainability is of great importance. Not long ago, tourism, a demand from collectors overseas, and a national desire for impressive furnishings had endangered the supply of thuya; many apprentices downed tools and searched for alternative careers. Since the 1990s, the government has been working on a program to protect the future of the precious Atlas forests and establish a replanting program. Today, the thuya industry is closely controlled. Artisans are encouraged to turn their attentions to small, delicate pieces and inlays, thus leaving the majority of trees in the forests to grow to maturity, which can take 70 years. Massive pieces, such as the doorways and carved furnishings favored by the ancient Romans, are extremely rare.

THE CRAFT OF CARVING

The majority of Berber woodworkers now operate in cooperatives, ensuring that the bulk of profits pass directly to the artisans themselves. They, in turn, hand their skills on to their teenage apprentices, while educating them in the environmental issues so key to their future. Tradition dictates that men perform the artistically skilled part of the production process, including both carving and decoration. Women and children polish and feed the intricate grain. These cooperatives are also turning their attentions to maximizing sustainable by-products of the thuya. A pine-scented oil, for example, is extracted from the resin and is valued in both aromatherapy and homeopathy. The sap also yields a lacquer and varnish, used widely by local craftsmen.

BUYING THUYA

Although you can find thuya wood products everywhere in Morocco, those wishing to buy articles fashioned from this beautiful wood are most likely to find reasonably priced items on Morocco's Atlantic coast, such as in Essaouira and Agadir. Check prices prior to purchase at one of the many outlets available online. These are a useful source of style and guide price.

Updated by Rachel Blech

They're both on the coast, and they both have beaches that people rave about, but Essaouira and Agadir couldn't be more dissimilar. A hippie hangout whose secret travelers refused to tell for years, Essaouira is only now coming into the limelight as a mainstream destination, but it nevertheless retains its slightly "other" feel. Windy beaches attract water-sports enthusiasts rather than sunseekers, and riad-hotels cater to independent travelers. Agadir, on the other hand, was made for mass tourism. It's a modern resort city with every kind of singing, dancing, and casino-betting distraction on hand and long stretches of hot, sandy beaches, and calm seas perfect for sunbathing families. Both, however, have lively ports worth seeing in action and superb fresh fish and seafood. In between are less-frequented spots good for diving, surfing, windsurfing, kayaking, and bodyboarding, or, for the less active, sunbathing and hiding out from the world a little.

For those wanting to get closer to nature, head inland to the southeast of Agadir, and you'll find fruit orchards, argan trees, crocus fields, pretty painted villages, and kasbahs. The plains of the Souss Valley and the jagged Anti-Atlas Mountains provide stunning vistas with plenty of scope for adventure. The picturesque walled town of Taroudant has historic sights and markets that attract day-trippers from Agadir, but it is also a great base for exploring and trekking into the Anti-Atlas or Western High Atlas mountains. A very worthwhile circuit from Taroudant will include the towns of Tafraoute and Tiznit. Tafraoute is famed for its scenic backdrop of towering granite boulders, almond blossoms, blue-painted rocks, and nearby rock carvings, while the 19th-century walled town of Tiznit is famed for its silversmiths and jewelry souk.

Whatever your interest, whether holing up in luxury or diving into the surf, this coastal area has a great deal to offer. For nature lovers and culture vultures there are ancient medinas, kasbahs, pretty villages, and wilderness all within easy reach.

PLANNING

WHEN TO GO

Unlike inland destinations that get too hot in summer, high season for the coast is August, with peaks at Christmas, New Year's Day, and June. The best months for visiting may be October and November, when it's off-season but still warm. Summer tends to be busy with vacationing Moroccan families; spring in Agadir is the main season for vacationers and families from abroad. Surfers and divers come year-round, although early spring is by far the best time for surf.

In the Souss Valley, spring is the most spectacular time to visit, when almond trees and wildflowers are in bloom, the harvest is near, and the weather is sunny but not too hot. Fall temperatures are moderate, but landscapes are a bit more drab after the summer harvest. As long as rains don't wash out the roads, winter is pleasant as well—coastal areas are warm, although inland temperatures can be cold and heated rooms hard to find. If you must come in summer, stick to the coast: even an hour inland, in Taroudant, the July and August heat is unbearable in all but the nighttime hours.

GETTING HERE AND AROUND

BY AIR

The key international air hub in the region is Agadir. Agadir's Al Massira Airport is 35 km (21 mi) east of town. *Grands* taxis (large shared taxis) to downtown Agadir cost 150 DH during the day, 200 DH at night and will take you directly to your hotel. There is also a shuttle bus every 30 minutes from the airport to nearby Inezghane (13 km/ 8 mi southeast of Agadir) where several bus services and grands taxis provide connections to other southern destinations as well as to the main bus station in Agadir.

BY BUS

There is frequent bus service offered by both CTM and Supratours connecting to Marrakesh and Casablanca as well as grand taxis that travel between cities.

BY CAR

A freeway now connects Marrakesh and Agadir and has cut travel times considerably; the journey takes approximately three hours. Explorations of the area around Taroudant and Tafraoute can be done as side trips from Agadir. If you don't want to drive yourself, one of the most enjoyable ways to cover this broad area is to organize a tour through one of several agencies based in Agadir. You'll be able to rent a car in either Agadir or Essaouira if you want to explore the region.

SAFETY

Essaouira and Agadir are quite safe, with almost no violent crime. Lone female travelers will feel more comfortable in these towns than in the rest of Morocco. Travelers should keep an eye on their personal belongings, however, as pickpockets are common, especially during festival time when the streets are jam-packed.

RESTAURANTS

All along the coast you can get great grilled and battered fresh fish and seafood. It's inexpensive and tasty at any time of day. For a better fish experience, go to a restaurant and try fish tagine or skewered and marinaded fish brochettes. International cuisine is also available in both Agadir and Essaouira.

WHAT IT COSTS IN DIRHAMS					
	¢	$	$$	$$$	$$$$
Restaurants	under 40 DH	40 DH–70 DH	71 DH–90 DH	91 DH–w110 DH	over 110 DH
Hotels	under 250 DH	251 DH–450 DH	451 DH–700 DH	701 DH–1,000 DH	over 1,000 DH

Restaurant prices are per person for a main course at dinner. Hotel prices are for a high-season standard double room, excluding service and tax.

HOTELS

You'll find a full range of options, from small budget hotels to Agadir's five-star behemoths. In Essaouira, many old traditional family homes, or *riads*, have been restored and converted to beautiful guesthouses. In summer it's best to reserve rooms in advance, and for the more upscale riad options you may have to book several months in advance whatever the time of year. There's also an increasing number of rental apartments in Essaouira and "apartment hotels" in Agadir; both offer self-catering options.

The Souss has some choice small hotels ranging from simple auberges (inns) and restored riads to former palaces and one luxury hotel that's among the best in Morocco.

FESTIVALS

Agadir and Essaouira are music hot spots, so it is no surprise that both cities host popular music festivals. Held in July, Agadir's Festival Timitar celebrates native Berber music, while Essaouira's world-famous Festival of Gnaoua, held each June, hosts international musicians as well as native ones.

ESSAOUIRA

171 km (102 mi) west of Marrakesh, 351 km (211 mi) southwest of Casablanca.

Once famed as a hippie hangout for surfers and expat artists, these days Essaouira offers its cool breezes and relaxed atmosphere to a broader range of visitors. The windy city remains a favorite destination for its picturesque fishing harbor, medina walls, blue shutters, twisting *derbs* (alleyways), and sea, sand, and surf.

Essaouira pretty much has a nine-month high season, from mid-March until early November, with extra peaks around Christmas, New Year's, and the hugely popular Gnaoua Music Festival at the end of June. More hotels and guesthouses have opened in recent years, but the town remains peaceful in its laid-back bustle—an enticing blend of fishing port and seaside haven.

GETTING HERE AND AROUND

The easiest and cheapest way to get to Essaouira is by grand taxi or bus. There is no train service and very little parking space for private cars, but road connections are good, and buses can get you efficiently and easily to Agadir, Casablanca, and Marrakesh. The drive from Marrakesh, Casablanca, or Agadir to Essaouira takes about three hours with bus companies Supratours and CTM operating several daily services. The medina of Essaouira is compact and easily walkable. The local *petits* taxis are blue and metered and can take you to the edge of the city limits if required. You can pick them up outside the medina at Bab Sbâa and should cost no more than 5 DH for any journey.

A'V Voyages is a reliable local travel agent who can arrange a number of day trips and longer tours in minibus or 4x4.

Bus Contacts **CTM Essaouira** ✉ *Av. de Caire, Medina* ☎ *0524/78–47–64.* **Supratours** ✉ *South Bastion, Medina* ☎ *0524/47–53–17.*

Rental Cars **Araucariacar** ☎ *0524/47–22–25* 🌐 *www.araucariacar.com.* **Avis Mogador** ✉ *28, rue Oued el-Makhazine* ☎ *0524/47–52–70.* **El Ghazwa Car** ✉ *Lot 4, Av. al-Aqaba, No.501* ☎ *0524/78–48–41* 🌐 *www.essaouira-location-cars.com.*

Travel Agency Contacts **A'V Voyages** ✉ *1–2, Immeuble Habous, Quartier des Dunes* ☎ *0666/32–90–97* 🌐 *www.essaouiravoyage.com.*

Visitor Information **Delegation Provincial de Tourisme** ✉ *10, rue du Caire, Medina* ☎ *0524/78–35–32* ⏲ *Closed Sat.–Sun.*

TIMING AND PRECAUTIONS

Weekend visitors to Essaouira often leave wishing they had more time. If you can, plan to spend several days in this relaxing seaside town. The best (and most popular) time to visit is summer. Although the temperature is tolerable year-round, this is a windy city, so don't expect to swim before May or after August.

Fodor'sChoice ★ **Gnaoua and World Music Festival.** Essaouira is always packed at the end of June, as 400,000 people from all over the world come to enjoy the annual four-day Gnaoua and World Music Festival. It's one of the best times to listen to traditional Gnaoua musicians. These descendants of African slaves established brotherhoods across Morocco and are healers and mystics as well as musicians. Among their troupes of metal castanet (*krakab*) players, bass lute (*gimbri*) players, and drummers, they have mediums and clairvoyants who perform wild, spellbinding acts. ■ **TIP→ If you plan to visit the festival, make sure you reserve accommodations at least three months in advance, as hotels and guesthouses will be full.** 🌐 *www.festival-gnaoua.net.*

EXPLORING ESSAOUIRA

Medina. This isn't so much a sight as the very essence of Essaouira, where you are most likely to stay, eat, shop, and wander. Brown volcanic stone is the characteristic building material of Portuguese architecture in Morocco, and its best examples (outside El Jadida) are Essaouira's medina and main portal. Unlike the rust-colored earth used for southern Moroccan buildings, this stone is a light brown. Essaouira is benefiting from preservationists' attention while its walls, ramparts, and Portuguese church are being carefully restored. Painted walls, such as those around the main square and near the port, have been restored from a light pink to their former natural beige.

There are two other sections within the city walls: the kasbah, used to house urban aristocrats and governing authorities and thus double-secured with additional walls; and the mellah, the old Jewish quarter, which once housed merchants who benefited from preferential tax and commercial laws designed to establish Essaouira as a market center.

North Bastion. The distinctive outlines of the bastion's corner tubular moldings frame the waves dramatically at sunset. The bastion once held emergency supplies of freshwater, and the large circle of stones in the center marks what was a call point, or alarm system, to warn of approaching invaders. Guards would warn of danger by stomping on the resonant circle. ■ **TIP→ If you stand in the middle of the circle and stomp your foot or yell, you'll hear the echo ring far.**

Fodor's Choice ★ **Port.** Built in 1769 in the reign of Sidi Mohammed Ben Abdellah by an Englishman who had converted to Islam, Essaouira's port is still going strong in the southwest corner of town, and it's the one must-see sight for any traveler coming here. Trawlers and other boats bob along the quay, and middlemen and independent sailors sell the daily catch of sardines, calamari, and skate from small dockside tables. You'll be selling yourself short if you don't have a meal of the freshest fish imaginable at one of the shoreside grill restaurants. As Moroccan ports go, it's also one of the most beautiful, not to mention accessible and tourist-friendly.

Sidi Mohammed Ben Abdellah Ethnological Museum. The stunning former French-colonial town hall holds this smartly arranged collection of items from everyday and ritual life in and around the Essaouira area. Ground-floor displays of musical instruments distinguish between Gnaoua and Sufi sects; upstairs, exhibits survey regional carpet styles, woodcarving techniques and motifs, and Muslim, Jewish, and rural Ishelhin Berber dress. ✉ *7, rue Laalouj, Medina* ☎ *0524/47–53–00* 🎫 *10 DH* 🕒 *Wed.–Mon. 8:30–6.*

NEED A BREAK?

Gelateria Dolcefreddo. Pick up an ice cream from Gelateria Dolcefreddo, which has shiny scoops of flavors such as After 8, tiramisu, and hazelnut, and off you go. ✉ ***25 bis, pl. Moulay Hassan, right on the main square.*** ☎ ***0663/57–19–28.***

Sqala. Essaouira has three *sqala* (bastions), with fabulous cannons: the kasbah sqala (also known as the medina sqala), the port sqala, and the sqala currently housing the Ensemble Artisanal, on Rue Modhem el-Qorry near Bab Marrakesh. Each was a strategic maritime defense point. Unlike the straight-edged Moorish constructions in other Moroccan cities, the ramparts in Essaouira are triangular, so the insider looking out has a broader field of vision than the enemy peering in. Check out the cannon engravings: the second and third to the right are signed "Carlos III, Barcelona 1780," and a Dutch cannon dated 1743 is inscribed with a lion and the Latin phrase "Vigilante Deo Confidentes" ("Those who trust in God are under his protection"). Orson Welles filmed scenes of his film *Othello* from the tower of the port sqala, picking up a magnificent panorama of town, port, and bay all in one. ✉ *Medina.*

Essaouira's medina is one of the country's finest examples of Portuguese architecture.

BEACHES

ESSAOUIRA BAY

Essaouira Bay. Essaouira's beach is a sweeping bay that curves from the sheltered north through the east to the south. You nearly always feel warm when you're bathed in sunlight, but as the wind and treacherous riptides are consistently strong, sunbathers and swimmers won't have much fun. A deck-chair or sun-bed rental is relatively inexpensive.

The wind comes from the north and creates three main areas. The most northerly part, tucked up into the armpit of the port, has wind that comes in gusts. Just south of this the wind strengthens, with fewer gusts. Farther south are the steady, strong winds the town is known for, and that make it a mecca for wind- and kite-surfers. This range of areas makes the bay perfect for every level of water-sportsman and -woman.

The surrounding islets, the Iles de Mogador, are home to nine bird species, including the endangered Eleanora falcon. They are closed to visitors during breeding season (April–October), but otherwise you can get a boat trip from the port, with boats leaving morning and afternoon depending on weather conditions.

DIABAT

Diabat. Essaouira's beach is fine for an early-morning jog or a late-afternoon game of soccer, but serious sunbathers typically head south to quiet Diabat. A few miles south of town, nestled in eucalyptus fields, are some ruins. Opinions differ on whether the ruins are of Portuguese or more-recent French vintage. On a windy day the only escape is a two-story rock that affords a nice resting spot at low tide. ✣ *The Number*

2 bus leaves from Bab Marrakesh in Essaouira for Diabat and Sidi Kaouki. If you're driving, the turnoff for Diabat is 7 km (4.5 mi) south of Essaouira, and 3 km (2 mi) west of the Agadir road.

SIDI KAOUKI

Sidi Kaouki. For the Essaouira ascetic who really wants to concentrate on sand and sea, the tranquil, wind-blasted beach village of Sidi Kaouki is the destination of choice. "Town" consists of an abnormally high number of guesthouses, a few shops and small restaurants, and very little else, apart from pristine stretches of sandy beach. Unlike Essaouira Bay, which is protected by the city, there's nothing to stop the fearsome winds here in summer, making this a top spot for surfing and windsurfing. It's also easy to rent mountain bikes or take a ride on ponies or camels. ✣ *Sidi Kaouki is 27 km (17 mi) southwest of Diabat. The turnoff is 15 km (9 mi) south of Diabat on the Agadir road. The same Number 2 bus that gets you to Diabat continues on to Sidi Kaouki.*

FARTHER AFIELD

Numerous paved roads jut off the road to Agadir heading toward the beaches along the coast, including the fishing and camping site at Plage Tafadna, 37 km (23 mi) south of the Sidi Kaouki turnoff. Accessibility to beaches and the locals' enthusiasm for foreign visitors lessen as you move south until you leave Haha territory (the land of the Ishelhin Berbers) behind and move into Cap Rhir.

WHERE TO EAT

There are some great restaurants in Essaouira. From port catches grilled in front of you to inventive and expensive fish dishes in the swankiest restaurants, seafood tends to headline menus when the surf permits. A must-do experience is lunch or dinner in one of the seafood grills along the port: feast on charcoal-grilled sardines, calamari, red snapper, sea bass, whiting, and shrimp (crab is usually too dry) from among the array of stalls, and experience the color and bustle of the port. You choose your fish then establish a price based on weight. The later in the day, the lower you'll be able to negotiate the price, but as Essaouira can be very windy, enjoying lunch alfresco in the sun makes much more sense than a breezy dinner. This is a great place to go if you are tiring of tagine. You could also take a stroll along Avenue L'Istiqlal, or better still Avenue Mohammed el-Quori. Here you'll be able to pack a bizarre picnic of fresh crab, salty battered fish in fresh Moroccan bread, almonds and peanuts, fruit, and sticky Maghrebian sweets.

However, there are also lots of traditional Moroccan options and excellent examples of French, Italian, and even Mexican food. ■ **TIP→ Most of the local places fill up quickly, but if you can hang on for the second sitting, the crowds thin out again by 9.**

$$$$
FRENCH
Fodor's Choice ★

✕ **After 5.** After 5 is a stylish lounge-bar-restaurant decorated with huge ceiling lamps, modern art, and exposed brickwork, which lends the space a decided contemporary style. Priding itself on authentic French cuisine, intermingled with Moroccan dishes and a reguarly updated menu, the restaurant offers a delicious crab-au-gratin. For dessert, indulge yourself with a zesty lemon tart or an upside-down tarte tatin. There are many vegetarian options, too, and on chilly winter days there's a welcoming fireplace. Very reasonable fixed-price menus are available for lunch. ✉ *7, rue Youssef el Fassi* ☎ *0524/47–33–49.*

$ FRENCH ✕ **Chez Françoise.** There's a daily range of delights, including quiches, salads, tarts, and the occasional crêpe, at this nice little lunch place. With only two rows of four small tables, it makes a perfect stop for afternoon tea. ✉ *1, rue Houmane el Fetouaki* ☎ *0668/16–40–87* ▭ *No credit cards* ⏲ *Closed Sun.*

$ ITALIAN ★ ✕ **Dar Baba.** A night with Orianna and Vicentini Gianfranco's cooking is not to be missed. This family-run Italian restaurant with only five tables on the first floor of their riad and home is affordable and charming. All the pastas and the cheeses are made in-house, and the menu is written in Italian. Tables are surrounded by fish and pasta charts, plants, a tarnished saxophone, a map of the world, and crooning Italian music. ✉ *2, rue de Marrakech* ☎ *0524/47–68–09* ▭ *No credit cards* ⏲ *Closed Sun.*

$$$ SEAFOOD ✕ **Dar Loubane.** Here you can sit among cascading plants in the airy courtyard of an 18th-century riad and dine on fish to your heart's content. It's decorated with 1920s photos and Oriental-style bric-a-brac collected by Jean-Claude and Evelyne Dulac, the aging French couple that runs the restaurant. There's a daily lunch menu, but you can order à la carte anytime. The menu includes *pastilla* (sweet pigeon pie), *briouates* (spicy dumplings), ray with capers, grills, and tagines. There's a full wine list, and local Gnaoua musicians on Saturday night. ✉ *24, rue de Rif* ☎ *0524/47–62–96.*

8

$ MOROCCAN ✕ **Dar Mounia.** Easy to find in the heart of the medina, this unpretentious Moroccan restaurant is spacious and cool. Hidden amongst the extensive menu of couscous, tajine, and pastilla variations are a few refreshing surprises. Try the grilled zucchini short-crust tart or a melt-in-the mouth marinated fish kebab, and wash it down with a zingy freshly squeezed lemon juice with ginger. Along with great food and good prices, there's also a kid's menu. However, there's no alcohol. ✉ *2, rue Laalouj, Medina* ☎ *0524/47–29–88.*

$ MOROCCAN ★ ✕ **Ferdaous.** One of our favorites for authentic homey Moroccan cuisine, the formidable chef, Madame Souad, formerly of the Villa Maroc, cooks up excellent starters and mains. Tagines bubble and boil deliciously, as does the lively banter from the kitchen downstairs. Inventive twists include *briq au poisson* (a fried spring roll of ultra-crispy pastry and Chinese noodles) and *malfouf* (stuffed cabbage with thick tomato sauce). The restaurant is upstairs in what was a private apartment with no fancy furnishings, but it appeals to locals and tourists alike. There are also three-course set menus. ✉ *27, rue Abdesslam Lebadi* ☎ *0524/47–36–55* ▭ *No credit cards* ⏲ *Sundays.*

$ MOROCCAN ✕ **Laayoune.** This is the best of several salon-style Moroccan restaurants in the area. The food is simple but tasty. No alcohol is served, but the restaurant does offer great traditional cooking in a lovely atmosphere made better in the evening, when lights and candles bring the small space to life. ✉ *4 bis, rue El Hajjali* ☎ *0524/47–46–43* ▭ *No credit cards.*

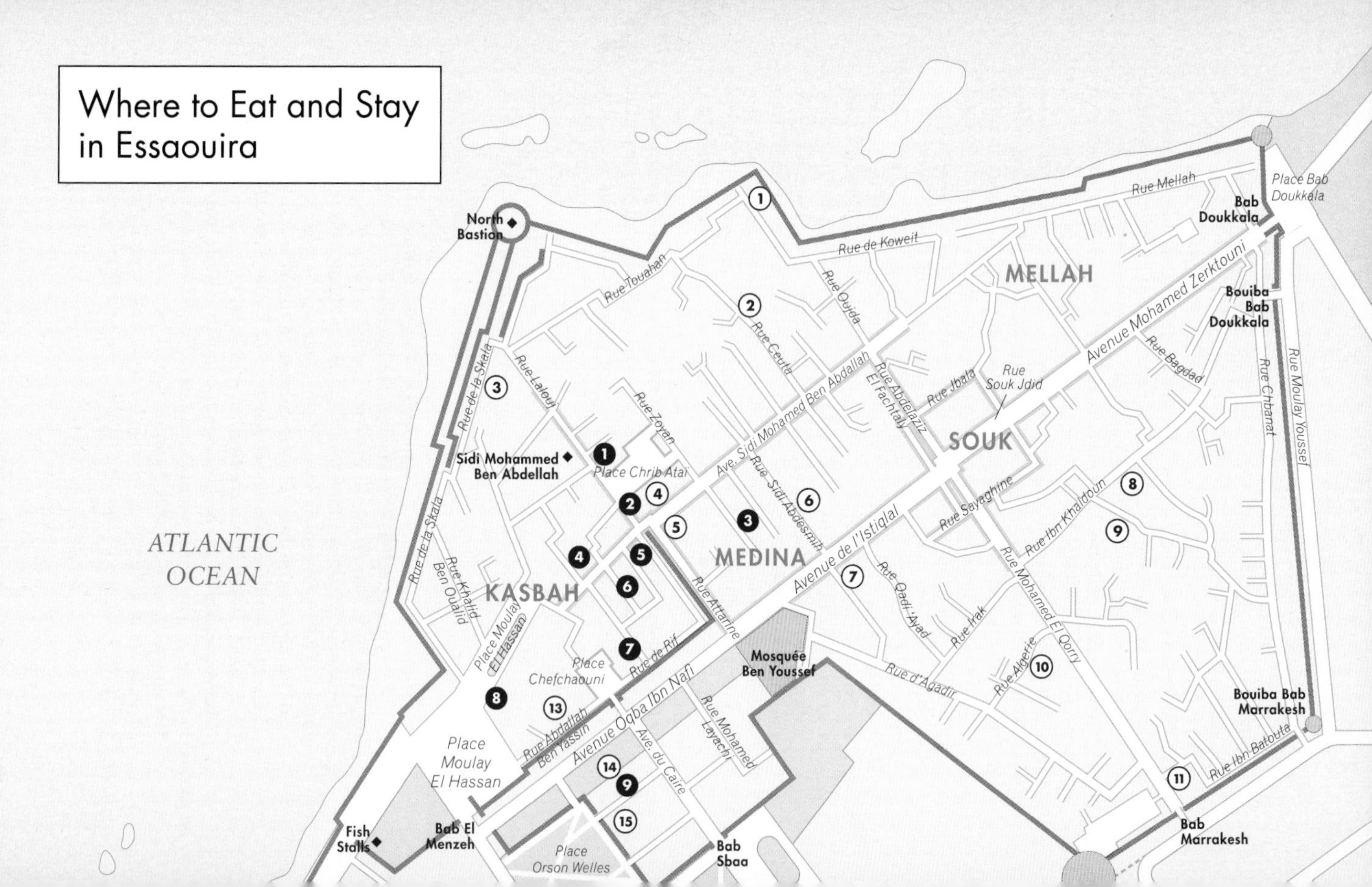
Where to Eat and Stay in Essaouira
ATLANTIC OCEAN
North Bastion
Place Bab Doukkala
Bab Doukkala
Bouiba Bab Doukkala
Rue Mellah
Rue de Koweit
MELLAH
Avenue Mohamed Zerktouni
Rue Touahan
Rue Oujda
Rue Ceuta
Rue de la Skala
Rue Laloui
Rue Zoyan
Ave. Sidi Mohamed Ben Abdallah
Rue Abdelaziz El Fachtaly
Rue Jbala
Rue Souk Jdid
SOUK
Rue Bagdad
Rue Chbanat
Rue Moulay Youssef
Sidi Mohammed Ben Abdellah
Place Chrib Ataï
Rue Sidi Abdesmih
Rue Sayaghine
Rue Ibn Khaldoun
MEDINA
Avenue de l'Istiqlal
Rue Khalid Ben Oualid
KASBAH
Place Moulay El Hassan
Rue Attarine
Rue Qadi 'Ayad
Rue Irak
Rue Mohamed El Qorry
Rue Algerie
Rue de Rif
Place Chefchaouni
Mosquée Ben Youssef
Rue d'Agadir
Bouiba Bab Marrakesh
Rue Abdallah Ben Yassin
Avenue Oqba Ibn Nafi
Rue Mohamed Layachi
Ave. du Caire
Rue Ibn Batouta
Place Moulay El Hassan
Fish Stalls
Bab El Menzeh
Place Orson Welles
Bab Sbaa
Bab Marrakesh

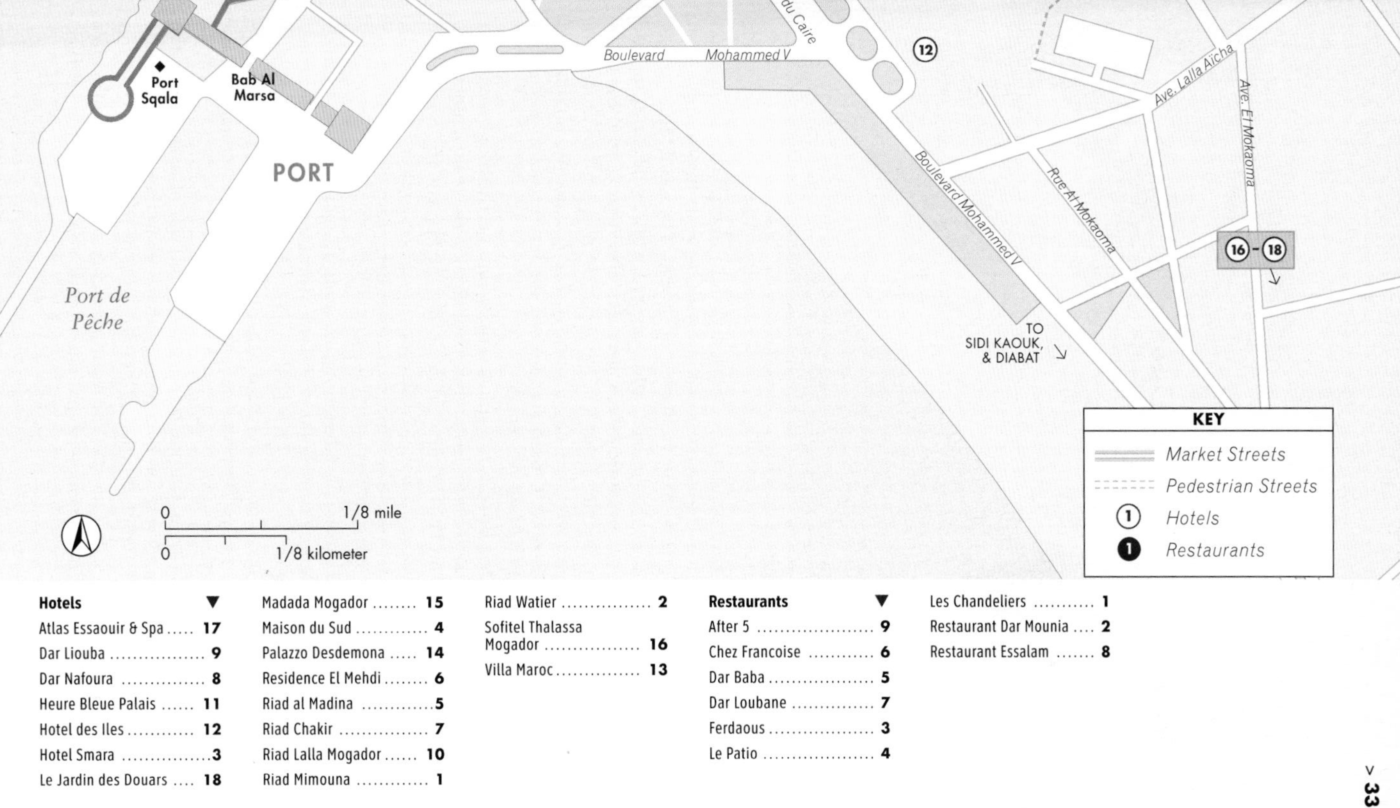

Hotels ▼

Atlas Essaouir & Spa **17**
Dar Liouba **9**
Dar Nafoura **8**
Heure Bleue Palais **11**
Hotel des Iles **12**
Hotel Smara **3**
Le Jardin des Douars **18**
Madada Mogador **15**
Maison du Sud **4**
Palazzo Desdemona **14**
Residence El Mehdi **6**
Riad al Madina **5**
Riad Chakir **7**
Riad Lalla Mogador **10**
Riad Mimouna **1**
Riad Watier **2**
Sofitel Thalassa Mogador **16**
Villa Maroc **13**

Restaurants ▼

After 5 ..... **9**
Chez Francoise **6**
Dar Baba **5**
Dar Loubane **7**
Ferdaous **3**
Le Patio **4**
Les Chandeliers **1**
Restaurant Dar Mounia **2**
Restaurant Essalam **8**

8

The Essaouira medina is a UNESCO World Heritage Site.

$$$$ MOROCCAN ★ ✕ **Le Patio.** A sure winner for "most stylish in town," this French-run restaurant offers Moroccan cooking with a twist, for example, fish tagines are made with pears, apples, or prunes. The small tables are set around a large starry lantern, and deep-red walls, white muslin, and candles create a romantic atmosphere. It's also a great spot for tapas and posing by the bar. There's a house punch, too, with so much rum in it you can see why they call it punch. ✉ *28 bis, rue Moulay Rachid* ☎ *0524/47–41–66* ⊙ *Closed Sun. Closed 1st 3 wks of Dec., last 3 wks of Jan., and all of July. No lunch.*

¢ CAFÉ ✕ **Patisserie Chez Driss.** For a quick, sticky bite on the move you can't beat Chez Driss. This long-standing patisserie on the main square dates back to 1929 and has become an Essaouira institution. The French and Moroccan pastries are baked fresh every day. Prices are very reasonable, so you can start your day with great coffee here from 7 am. ✉ *9, rue el Hajjali* ☎ *0524/47–57–93* ▭ *No credit cards.*

$ MOROCCAN ✕ **Restaurant Essalam.** Situated along Essaouira's main square, this no-frills local place delivers good, standard Moroccan fare, such as couscous and tagines, as well as fried fish and pastilla. Seven set menus offer cheap meals. It's opposite the main strip of cafés, with seats indoors and out, so you're poised for prime people-watching. ✉ *Pl. Moulay Hassan* ☎ *0524/47–55–48* ▭ *No credit cards.*

$$$$ MOROCCAN ★ ✕ **Restaurant le Km 8.** Despite being 8 km (5 mi) out of town, this is the preferred destination for Essaouira's expats when they need a little R and R. French couple Marlène and Bernard staff the kitchen. As a top chef, she looks after most of the menu; as a cheese maker, he looks after the delicious homemade chèvre. The overall effect, with food served

either inside a plush Moroccan salon or on a leafy terrace, is lovely. ✉ *Rte. d'Agadir, Km 8* ☎ *0666/25–21–23* ⊙ *Closed Mon.*

$$$$ SEAFOOD Fodor's Choice ★ **Taros.** Beloved of expats, fun-loving locals, and tourists alike, Taros is restaurant, bar, boutique, art gallery, and library all in one. It's named after the wind that blows off the sea, and you can sip cocktails on a terrific rooftop terrace with views of the port. For starters, try the shrimp salad with argan oil. The crème brûlée is a must for dessert. The café offers drinks and snacks to an international crowd, which gathers to browse the library, sample the impressive CD collection, and play Scrabble. But be sure to dress smart—guests have been turned away for sporting ripped jeans. ✉ *Pl. Moulay Hassan, at Rue de la Skala* ☎ *0524/47–64–07* 🌐 *www.taroscafe.com.*

WHERE TO STAY

The riad mania that has taken over Marrakesh has spread to Essaouira in recent years. Rooms are still less opulent and less expensive than those in Marrakesh, but you'll find plenty of charm and elegance. There are also plenty of even less expensive hotels, but fewer of the seriously budget hippie hangouts of yesteryear.

For hotels with swimming pools you'll have only one expensive option within the medina: L'Heure Bleue Palais. Other beachfront hotels with pools are fine if you have a large family, but they aren't necessary even if you plan to devote a lot of time to water sports; the beach really isn't that far away on foot and, besides, medina lodging puts you right in the heart of the action and is a far more romantic option.

Another option is to rent an apartment, by the night or by the week. There's a wide range of options, from spartan bedrooms with showers that don't work, to an entire super-styled riad. Renting is often a better deal than staying in a hotel, especially if you're with a group. Rooms book up quickly, especially in summer, so reserve (sometimes months) ahead. ■ TIP→ **You can only take a car as far as a medina gate, so you'll have to heave your luggage to that dear little out-of-the-way spot down 10 twisting derbs yourself. The best option? Pick up a charette (a small cart on wheels) from the parking lot outside Bab Sbâa and pay the owner and cart wheeler 10 DH for his trouble.**

APARTMENT RENTAL AGENCIES

Arriving in the city's New Town, you'll see men dangling keys by the side of the road, hoping to rent you an apartment. It's best to go through official agents, however.

Castles in the Sand. Castles in the Sand rents out two villas by London-based interior designer Emma Wilson. Dar Beida, the "White Room," is one of Essaouira's most sumptuous addresses. The villa is filled with a hip furnishings and decor from the 1950s and 1960s. Cool 21st-century perks include iPod speakers and wireless Internet. The other villa, Dar Emma, has a more-traditional feel. ☎ *0667/96–53–86* 🌐 *www.castlesinthesand.com.*

Jack's Apartments. Jack's Apartments own and manage several beautiful old medina studios, apartments, riads, and penthouses. Each is serviced daily, and all are equipped with Moroccan-style kitchens, bedrooms, bathrooms, and salons. Many have great sea views, too. ✉ *1, pl. Moulay Hassan* ☎ *0524/47–44–38* 🌐 *www.jackapartments.com.*

Karimo Immobilier. Karimo Immobilier can locate self-catering apartments or riads all over the medina for pretty much any budget. ✉ *Pl. Moulay Hassan* ☎ *0524/47–45–00* 🌐 *www.karimo.net.*

For expanded hotel reviews, visit Fodors.com.

MEDINA

$$$ Fodor's Choice ★ **Dar Liouba.** Designed in a much more open style than many other Essaouira riads, Dar Liouba contains a central atrium that lets in plenty of light. **Pros:** amazing rooftop views; airy central atrium. **Cons:** some of the rooms can feel damp. ✉ *28, Impasse Moulay Ismail, Medina* ☎ *0524/47–62–97* 🌐 *www.darliouba.eu* *8 rooms* *In-room: no a/c, Wi-Fi. In-hotel: restaurant, laundry facilities, business center, some pets allowed* *Breakfast.*

$$ **Dar Nafoura Mogador.** A kitchen that seems constantly on the go and a warm welcome from husband and wife Sylvie and Jackie make for a homier take on chic riad living. **Pros:** a short walk to the beach; delicious made-to-order meals. **Cons:** bathrooms are particularly small; some rooms lack windows. ✉ *30, rue Ibn Khaldoun, Medina* ☎ *0524/47–28–55* 🌐 *www.darnafoura-essaouira.com* *5 rooms, 4 suites* *In-room: no a/c, no TV, Wi-Fi. In-hotel: laundry facilities, business center, some pets allowed* *Breakfast.*

$$$$ Fodor's Choice ★ **Heure Bleue Palais.** On paper at least, this Relais & Chateaux property is Essaouira's most prestigious lodging, but it doesn't have a lot of Moroccan style. **Pros:** in-house cinema; relaxing hammam; pretty pool. **Cons:** more British than Moroccan. ✉ *2, rue Ibn Batouta, Medina* ☎ *0524/78–34–34* 🌐 *www.heure-bleue.com* *14 rooms, 19 suites* *In-room: a/c, no TV, Wi-Fi. In-hotel: restaurant, bar, pool, spa, laundry facilities, business center, parking* *Breakfast.*

$$$$ **Madada Mogador.** Stylized, elegant, and designed to perfection, the Madada Mogador is perfectly poised within the medina walls to get great ocean views. **Pros:** marvelous massage treatments; cool lounge spaces. **Cons:** no meals served in hotel, just light snacks; expensive rates. ✉ *4, rue Youssef el Fassi, Medina* ☎ *0524/47–55–12* 🌐 *www.madada.com* *5 rooms, 2 suites* *In-room: a/c, no TV, Wi-Fi. In-hotel: bar, spa, laundry facilities, business center* *Breakfast.*

$$ **Maison du Sud.** Enter through a traditional heavy stone arch of Maison du Sud off a busy medina street, and you'll find a friendly, English-speaking management team and comfortable areas for relaxing. **Pros:** delicious evening meals available on request; cozy lounges. **Cons:** interior decor is outdated and some rooms rather drab. ✉ *29, av. Sidi Mohammed Ben Abdellah, Medina* ☎ *0524/47–41–41* 🌐 *www.riad-maisondusud.com* *18 rooms, 6 suites* *In-room: no a/c, no TV. In-hotel: restaurant, bar, laundry facilities, business center, some pets allowed* *Breakfast.*

$$ **Palazzo Desdemona.** This classy small hotel has rooms with sophisticated decor: white woolen blankets, low divans, and delicate accents of selectively placed Moroccan antiques. **Pros:** Large rooms; relaxed atmosphere. **Cons:** Lack of English-speaking staff on hand. ✉ *12–14, rue Youssef el-Fassi, Medina* ☎ *0524/47–22–27* *13 rooms, 2 suites*

The Heure Bleue Palais is one of only six Relais & Chateaux properties in Morocco.

In-room: no a/c, no TV. In-hotel: business center *No credit cards* *Breakfast.*

$$$ **Riad Al Madina.** This beautiful 18th-century riad is wrapped around
★ a stone courtyard where you'll find a trickling fountain. **Pros:** sun-filled rooms; plenty of pampering; in-house hammam. **Cons:** can feel very crowded. *9, rue Attarine, Medina* *0524/47–59–07, 0524/47–57–27* *www.riadalmadina.com* *39 rooms, 16 suites* *In-room: no a/c. In-hotel: restaurant, bar, spa, laundry facilities, business center, some pets allowed* *Breakfast.*

$ **Riad Chakir.** This colorful and friendly budget riad is actually made up of two neighboring houses off a tiny alley. **Pros:** great location; good price. **Cons:** some rooms very small. *13, rue Malek Ben Morhal, off Av. Istiqlal, Medina* *0524/47–33–09* *www.riadchakir.com* *20 rooms* *In-room: a/c, Wi-Fi. In-hotel: restaurant, laundry facilities, business center, some pets allowed* *Breakfast.*

$ **Riad Lalla Mogador.** There's a kind of dollhouse charm to this tiny riad. **Pros:** Unique rooms; filled with tiny treasures. **Cons:** Family rooms are small. *12, rue de l'Iraq, Medina* *0524/47–67–44* *www.riadlallamogador.com* *3 rooms, 5 suites* *In-room: no TV, Wi-Fi. In-hotel: business center* *Breakfast.*

$$$ **Riad Mimouna.** Tight against the northern side of the medina walls,
★ this riad sits over the water's edge, letting you have the raging sea all to yourself. **Pros:** beautiful views; central heating in winter. **Cons:** some rooms rather too weather-beaten. *62, rue d'Oujda, Sandillon, Medina* *0524/78–57–53* *www.riad-mimouna.com* *24 rooms, 9 suites* *In-room: no a/c. In-hotel: restaurant, spa, laundry facilities, business center, some pets allowed* *Breakfast.*

$$$ ★ **Riad Watier.** Ryad Watier is a classy affair, with rooms far more spacious than those in most other riad hotels. **Pros:** some rooms big enough for four people; friendly-family vibe. **Cons:** no sea views from terrace. *16, rue Ceuta, Medina 0524/47–62–04 www.ryad-watier-maroc.com 10 suites Breakfast.*

$$$ ★ **Villa Maroc.** Embodying much of what international travelers seek in a Moroccan hotel, the intimate Villa Maroc is delightfully decorated to epitomize a "traditional" Moroccan style that never really was. **Pros:** delicious breakfasts; sizable rooms. **Cons:** can get booked up; no lunch. *10, rue Abdellah Ben Yassine, Medina 0524/47–61–47 www.villa-maroc.com 21 rooms In-room: no a/c, no TV, Wi-Fi. In-hotel: restaurant, bar, spa, laundry facilities, business center, some pets allowed Multiple meal plans.*

ON THE BEACH

$$$$ **Hotel Atlas Essaouira and Spa.** Opened in 2008, the Hotel Atlas is a superior beachfront hotel that sets out to impress. **Pros:** private beach; restaurant. **Cons:** corporate feel; lacks quality and charm. *Av. Mohammed V, Quartier des Dunes 0524/47–99–99 www.hotelsatlas.com 149 rooms, 7 suites In-room: a/c, Wi-Fi. In-hotel: restaurant, bar, pool, gym, spa, beach, laundry facilities, business center, parking Breakfast.*

$$$$ Fodor's Choice ★ **Sofitel Essaouira Medina & Spa.** Looming over the beach, this five-star hotel has little of the magic that is Essaouira. **Pros:** large pool; plenty of activities. **Cons:** lacks character; quite expensive. *Bd. Mohammed V, Quartier des Dunes 0524/47–90–00 www.sofitel.com 117 rooms, 8 suites In-room: a/c. In-hotel: restaurant, bar, golf course, pool, gym, spa, beach, children's programs, laundry facilities, business center, parking, some pets allowed Breakfast.*

SHOPPING

Essaouira is Morocco's best shopping destination south of Marrakesh, and its stores offer a vast range of high-quality products and very few hustlers. If you've gotten used to haggling in Marrakesh or Fez, you can relax here, as starting prices are often reasonable.

Essaouira is famed as an artisanal center expert in marquetry and inlay. Boxes, platters, and picture frames made of local thuya wood make excellent gifts, and the wood-carvers' souk below the sqala is the best place to purchase them. A hard local wood that shines up to almost plastic perfection, thuya is sculpted for both artistic and practical use. Almost-life-size statues and sculptures sit alongside boxes, bowls, and chess sets. Scan a number of stores to see whether you prefer the even-toned thuya branch inlaid with mother-of-pearl or walnut or one with swirling root designs. To get a bulk price, buy a bunch of picture frames from a craftsman who specializes in them.

Carpets, goatskin lamps, and metal candlesticks are sold in the square next to the clock tower; compare their prices with those in the shops on side streets off Avenue de l'Istiqlal. Rue el-Mahdi is delightful for browsing. Running away from the Cap Sim hotel, this small derb has endless little boutiques, but hasn't yet been overrun with tourists. The goatskin lamps are etched with henna and are highly fashionable at the moment.

There's a veritable warehouse of carpets and carpet-scrap pillow covers down Route de Marrakesh, off Avenue de l'Istiqlal; tell the store owners that you're looking for a bigger selection than they offer, and they'll lead you to the warehouse.

Colorful, square woven baskets hang from herbalists' stores in the medina. New and old silver jewelry is sold in the extensive silver souk between the medina's inner gates and in the shops starting from the BMCE Bank, heading off Place Moulay Hassan down Avenue de l'Istiqlal.

If you packed too light to brave the chilly Atlantic wind, buy a handwoven sweater in Place Moulay Hassan or the square off Rue Laalouj.

ANTIQUES

Galérie Aida. For tasteful used pewter platters and goblets and ceramic teapots, as well as new and used English and French books, check the Galérie Aida, underneath the ramparts. There's also a large selection of antique daggers. The gallery's owner, Joseph Sebag, a Jewish multimedia artist, and his staff are knowledgeable about remnants of the city's Jewish history. ✉ *2, rue de la Skala, next to Cafe Taros, Medina* ☎ *0524/47–62–90.*

Galerie Jama. Galerie Jama seems more museum than shop, and as such is a good bet for specialists. You can browse among wooden doors, mosaic vases, and all sorts of wonderful odds and ends. Prices aren't marked, so get ready to negotiate if you see something you like. ✉ *22, rue Ibn Rochd, Medina* ☎ *0661/77–52–47.*

8

ARGAN OIL

Argan d'Or. Argan d'Or is a little boutique with a great selection of argan-oil products from women's cooperatives all over the country. There are also more-expensive cosmetic oils for the face, hands, and body. ✉ *5, rue Ibn Rocha, Medina* ☎ *No phone.*

ART GALLERIES

Many galleries clustered in one quarter of the medina display contemporary Moroccan and expatriate mixed-media productions.

Espace Othello Gallerie d'Art. Part of Orson Welles's *Othello* was shot at this standout gallery. It's open daily 9–1 and 3–8 (except Sundays). ✉ *9, rue Mohammed Layachi, Medina* ☎ *0524/47–50–95* ⏲ *Closed Sun.*

★ **Galerie d'Art Damgaard.** The Galerie d'Art Damgaard, across from the clock tower, has well-curated displays of work by Essaouira painters and sculptors with biographies of individual exhibitors; the gallery also sells books on regional art and culture and has an annex studio just off the Place Chefchaouni. Both are open all week 10–1 and 3–7. ✉ *Av. Oqba Ibn Nafiaa, Medina* ☎ *0524/78–44–46.*

Slimane Drissi/La Petite Galerie. The quirky, lunar figures in the monochrome paintings of Slimane Drissi are a humourous delight with plenty of take-home potential. La Petite Galerie is open daily from 9 to 1 and 3 to 9. ✉ *Rue Ibn Rochd, Medina* ☎ *0524/47–64–31, 0665/66–06–30* 🌐 *www.artmajeur.com/soulaiman.*

DID YOU KNOW?

Essaouira (originally called Mogador) is one of Morocco's best port towns to visit. A walk along the ramparts and a grilled seafood dinner at one of the quayside restaurants are two must-dos of any visit.

HOUSEWARES

KifKif. KifKif has funky textiles, accessories, and desirable objects for the home, all made using local artisanal techniques. ✉ *204, Marché aux Grains, Medina* ☎ *0661/08–20–41* 🌐 *www.kifkifbystef.com.*

JEWELRY

La Fibule Berbère. La Fibule Berbère has stunning ethnic jewelry, such as huge silver pendants and bulky necklaces made in the Berber and Touareg styles. ✉ *51–53, rue Attarine, Medina* ☎ *0524/47–62–55, 0666/64–19–89.*

Poupa Litza. Delve into an astounding array of brightly colored fabric handbags at Poupa Litza boutique. Goods from this atelier also sell in Europe, but prices are much cheaper here, plus you have the joy of seeing where it's all made. They also have a selection of jewelry. ✉ *135 bis, rue Mohamed el-Kory, Medina* ☎ *0524/47–69–28* 🌐 *www.poupalitza.com* ⏲ *Sundays.*

WOODWORK

Thuya wood furniture is as unavoidable on the streets of Essaouira as in-line skaters in Malibu Beach, and just as painful if you bump into it. If you want to find some untouristy workshops off the main streets, take a right onto Rue Khalid Ibn el-Walid, just off Place Moulay Hassan.

Chez Hassan. Chez Hassan turns out lovely boxes and trinkets ideal for taking home from as little as 20 DH. ✉ *15, rue Khalid Ibn el-Walid, Medina* ☎ *0524/78–40–63.*

Coopérative Artisanale des Marqueteurs. Coopérative Artisanale des Marqueteurs turns out finely decorated tables and larger furniture. Everything has a price tag, and prices are highly reasonable. ✉ *Rue Khalid Ibn el-Walid, off Place Moulay Hassan, Medina* ☎ *0524/47–56–76.*

SPORTS AND THE OUTDOORS

CYCLING

Velo Location Chez Youssef. You can hire bikes from Velo Location Chez Youssef. Their bicycles go for 80 DH a day, or 120 DH with a guide who can point out good local trails depending on interest, distance, and time. ✉ *Hotel Arboussas, 24, rue Laalouj, Medina* ☎ *0668/25–46–02.*

HAMMAMS AND SPAS

The following hammams and spas are open to all (even nonguests, if in a hotel).

PUBLIC HAMMAMS

Hammam Bagdad. This basic but user-friendly hammam for men is located in the medina—ask for directions at any kiosk on Rue Bagdad. ✉ *Rue Bagdad, Medina* ☎ *No phone* 🎟 *10 DH* 💳 *No credit cards* ⏲ *Daily.*

Hammam Pabst. Located in the mellah, this is one of the oldest hammams in Essaouira. Now brightly painted, it has a plaque indicating that Orson Welles once used it as a location during the filming of *Hamlet.* ✉ *Rue Annasr, Medina* ☎ *No phone* 🎟 *10 DH* 💳 *No credit cards* ⏲ *Daily.*

PRIVATE HAMMAM

Hammam Mounia. In addition to hammam, this nicely renovated old spa offers an Arab-Berber 2-hour treatment with hammam, black-soap exfoliation, foot spa, seaweed wrap and argan-oil massage. Be prepared for crowds, as it's very popular. ✉ *17, rue Oum Errabia, Medina* ☎ *0667/23–65–05* 💵 *50 DH, 70 DH with exfoliation* 💳 *No credit cards* 🕒 *Daily: Men 5:30 pm–8.30 pm, Women 3:00 pm–8:30.*

HOTEL HAMMAMS

Hotel Riad Al Madina. This famous riad near the Maison du Sud has a rather good hammam that nonguests can use. ✉ *9, rue Attarine, Medina* ☎ *0524/47–59–07, 024/47–57–27* 🌐 *www.riadalmadina.com* 💵 *Treatments 70 DH–400 DH.*

Lalla Mira Hotel. This small "bio-hotel" in the medina has nicely renovated the oldest hammam in Essaouira, located next door. It's heated by thermo-solar power instead of wood. You need an appointment. ✉ *14, rue d'Algerie, Medina* ☎ *0524/47–50–46* 💵 *Treatments 85DH–180 DH* 💳 *No credit cards* 🕒 *Daily: Women 2 pm–7 pm; Men: 7 pm–10 pm.*

Villa Maroc. The first riad guesthouse in Essaouira has a private "Oriental Spa" hammam open to nonguests and offers a range of treatment packages, including massage for children. ✉ *10, rue Abdellah Ben Yassine, Medina* ☎ *0524/47–31–47* 🌐 *www.villa-maroc.com.*

SPAS

L'Heure Bleue Palais. Located in a busy alley in the medina, this palatial riad hotel has a hammam, massage room, and swimming pool open to nonresidents who book in advance (book either 1 or 2 days ahead). ✉ *2, rue Ibn Batouta, Bab Marrakesh, Medina* ☎ *0524/78–34–34* 💵 *330 DH traditional hammam with exfoliation* 🕒 *By reservation only.*

Hotel Sofitel Thalassa Medina & Spa. Situated on the seafront, this hotel specializes in thalassotherapy, water jet showers, hydrating baths, massages, and aqua gym workouts. There's also a heated outdoor pool and solarium. ✉ *Bd. Mohammed V, Medina* ☎ *0524/47–90–00* 💵 *750 DH with exfoliation and massage* 🕒 *By reservation only.*

HORSEBACK AND CAMEL RIDING

Ranch de Diabat. A long-standing family-run business that organizes camel trips and horse-riding from their ranch in the village of Diabat, at the southern end of Essaouria beach. A camel trip costs from 180 DH per hour; horseback riding lessons and trail rides of several days can be organized for groups. ✉ *Diabat, Quartier des Dunes* ☎ *0662/29–72–03* 🌐 *www.ranchdediabat.com.*

Zouina Cheval. This company organizes horseback riding excursions on Diabat beach and in the countryside around Essaouira, with treks from one hour to a full day for beginners and experienced riders alike. Longer multiday treks with camping for groups and camel trips are also possible. Prices start from around 200 DH per hour and 600 DH for a full day with a picnic lunch. ✉ *Diabat, Quartier des Dunes* ☎ *0669/80–71–01* 🌐 *www.zouina-cheval.com.*

8

The beaches south of Essaouira are one of Morocco's top surfing spots.

FOUR-WHEELING

Sahara Quad. This company organizes quad-bike excursions including pickup from your hotel to their starting point. A two-hour dunes and beach trip costs 500 DH, and riders must have their own insurance. Longer day trips go toward Cap Sim and return through the cedar forests. ✉ *355 Lot Eraounak* ☎ *0673/44–95–41* 🌐 *www.saharaquad.net.*

WATER SPORTS

★ **Club Mistral and Skyriders Centre.** Club Mistral and Skyriders Centre is the biggest outfit in town. It prides itself on the quality of its equipment and its multidisciplinary and multilingual instruction. Factor this into the cost of courses, which are pricier than elsewhere along the bay: two hours of surfing instruction cost 440 DH, while a 10-hour windsurfing starter course costs 2,530 DH. ✉ *Bd. Mohammed V, at the southern end of the beach, Medina* ☎ *0524/78–39–34* 🌐 *www.club-mistral.com* ⏲ *Daily 9–6.*

Fodor's Choice ★ **Explora.** A professional Moroccan-English company offers a wide range of water sports with qualified instruction at prices considerably cheaper than the nearest competition. The company also arranges horseback riding, quad biking, camel treks, desert trips, and mountain biking. Surfing lessons start at 300 DH for two hours. The company has its activity base at the southern end of the beach (on the beach at Av. Mohammed V near junction with Rte. de Agadir) and also a supplies shop in the medina. ✉ *2, Place Chrib Atay, Rue Laalouj, Medina* ☎ *0611/47–51–88* 🌐 *www.exploramorocco.com.*

AGADIR

172 km (103 mi) south of Essaouira.

Agadir is a holiday resort. Don't hope for a medina, a souk, or a kasbah (although it does have all three, after a fashion). Think sun, sea, and sand. These are what it does best, as hundreds of thousands of visitors each year can testify.

There's no reason to begrudge the city its tourist aspirations. Razed by an earthquake in 1960 that killed 15,000 people in 13 seconds, Agadir had to be entirely rebuilt. Today it's a thoroughly modern city where travelers don't think twice about showing considerable skin, and Moroccans benefit from the growing number of jobs.

There's a reason why this popular European package vacation destination is overrun with enormous, characterless beachfront hotels. The beach, all 10 km (6 mi) of it, is dreamy. A 450-yard-wide strip, it bends in an elegant crescent along the bay, and is covered with fine-grain sand. The beach is sheltered and safe for swimming, making it perfect for families. Farther north, where small villages stand behind some of the best waves in the world, is a surfers' paradise.

Even if you have no interest in surfing, diving, jet skiing, golf, tennis, or horseback riding down the beach, you can treat Agadir as a modern bubble in which to kick back. It's equipped with familiar pleasurable pursuits—eating, drinking, and relaxing next to the ocean—and modern amenities such as car-rental agencies and ATMs. It isn't quite Europe, but neither is it quite Morocco.

EN ROUTE

The coastal stretch between Sidi Ifni and Essaouira presents the most spectacular anywhere in Morocco. The northern half of the trip from Agadir on the P8/N1 road to Essaouira is particularly stunning. A drive is pleasant in itself, but you can stop and relax at several turnoffs from the main road both north and south of Agadir. Unspoiled beaches lie just 10 km (6 mi) north of Sidi Ifni; the only travelers who find the unmarked dirt road come in campers during the summer months.

8

GETTING HERE AND AROUND

Most travelers fly directly into Agadir's Al Massira airport. Although there are no direct flights from North America, connections from Casablanca and European airports are easy. Inexpensive buses are easy ways to get here from Essaouira, Marrakesh, and beyond. If all else fails, grands taxis can take you just about anywhere for the right price.

Once in Agadir, you'll find that the city is easily navigable on foot. The city's orange petits taxis are easy to flag down. Agadir also has many car-rental agencies, including Hertz and Avis.

Bus Contacts CTM ✉ *Av. Abderrahim Bouabid, next to the Gare Routiere* ☎ *0528/22–55–96.* **Supratours** ✉ *Av. Abderrahim Bouabid, next to the Gare Routiere* ☎ *0528/22–40–10* 🌐 *www.supratours.ma.*

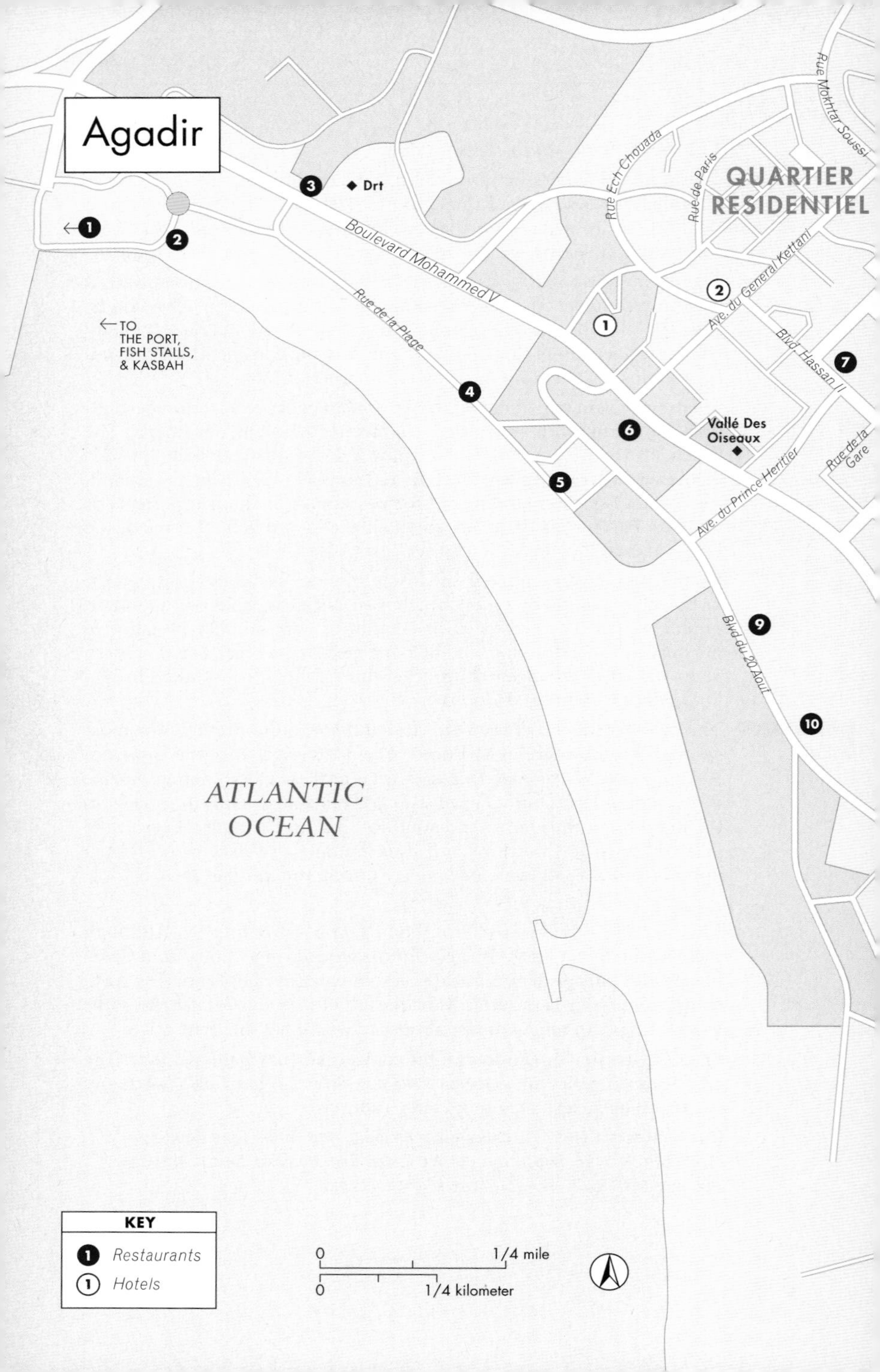

Agadir
QUARTIER RESIDENTIEL
Drt
Boulevard Mohammed V
Rue de la Plage
Rue Ech Chouada
Rue de Paris
Rue Mokhtar Soussi
Ave. du General Kettani
Blvd. Hassan II
Vallé Des Oiseaux
Rue de la Gare
Ave. du Prince Heritier
Blvd du 20 Aout
TO THE PORT, FISH STALLS, & KASBAH
ATLANTIC OCEAN
KEY
Restaurants
Hotels
0
1/4 mile
0
1/4 kilometer

Hotels ▼

Al Madina Palace 5
Atlantic Palace 10
ClubHotel Riu Tikida Dunas 11
Hotel El Bahia 3
Hôtel Marhaba 1
Hotel Solman 6
La Petite Suede 2
Le Tivoli 7
Residence Yamina 4
Riad Villa Blanche 8
Sofitel 9

Restaurants ▼

Cafe les Arcades 8
Camels 5
Chez Mimi La Brochette 4
English Pub 9
Jean Cocteau 6
Johara 10
La Siciliana 7
Le Miramar 3
Les Blancs 2
Yacht Club 1

Rental Car Contacts Avis ⊠ *Av. Mohammed V* ☎ *0528/82–14–14.* **Dan Car** ⊠ *Av. Mohammed V* ☎ *0528/84–82–22, 0528/84–46–00 airport.* **Europcar** ⊠ *Av. Mohammed V* ☎ *028/84–02–03* 🌐 *www.europcar.com.* **Exotik Cars** ⊠ *5 Ave. Général Kettani* ☎ *0528/84–11–42* 🌐 *www.exotikcars.net.* **Hertz** ⊠ *Av. Mohammed V* ☎ *0528/84–09–39, 0528/83–90–71 airport.*

GUIDES AND TOURS

Complete Tours is an English-run operation based in Agadir that can put together your whole trip, including hotels, excursions, and meals—everything but the flight. Massira Travel has a great range of trips to Essaouira, Marrakesh, Imouzzer, Tafraoute, Tiznit, and farther south.

Contacts Complete Tours ⊠ *No. 26, Immeuble Oumlil, Av. Hassan II* ☎ *0528/82–34–01* 🌐 *www.complete-tours.com.* **Massira Travel** ⊠ *25, bd. du 20 Août, next to L'Orange Bleue restaurant* ☎ *0528/84–77–13.* **Conseil Regional du Tourisme** ⊠ *Av. Hassan II, (next to Chamber of Commerce)* ☎ *0528/84–26–96.*

TIMING AND PRECAUTIONS

Many first-time travelers to Morocco never leave Agadir, but that would be a mistake; a great idea for first-timers is to make Agadir home base and take day trips to other towns in the area. Agadir is on the whole fairly safe, though it's a good idea to keep an eye on your wallet, as pickpockets are a problem.

VISITOR INFORMATION

You can pick up good local and regional maps at the Conseil Régionale du Tourisme as well as brochures and seasonal guides to events around town. It's open weekdays only from 9 to 4.

EXPLORING

For those looking for a more comprehensive tour of town, a ridiculous yet amusing way to see the town is with the Petit Train, a small white tram with three carriages pulled by a motorcar at the front. It leaves every 35 minutes (9:15 am until nightfall) from the kiosk south of the Vallée des Oiseaux. It's as touristy as a Hawaiian shirt, but kids love it and it's a great way to get off your feet. Tickets cost 18 DH, and the ride lasts half an hour.

Kasbah. High up on the hill to the northwest that looks over Agadir is the old kasbah. It's in need of restoration, but still worth the exertion to make it to the top and back down to the port for a hearty fish lunch.

Emblazoned on the side of the hill below the kasbah are three Arabic words that keep guard over Agadir at all times. Their meaning? God, country, and the king. By day they're a patchwork of huge white stones against the green grass. By night they're lighted up powerfully against the dark. The huge hill is really a burial mound, covering the old medina and the impromptu graves of those who died in the earthquake.

Fodor's Choice ★ **La Medina d'Agadir.** In Ben Sergao, a few miles south of Agadir on the Inezgane road, is a remarkable 13-acre project orchestrated by Moroccan-born Italian decorator-architect Coco Polizzi. He dreamed of replacing the medina Agadir lost to the 1960 earthquake with a

Agadir is Morocco's top resort destination, with more all-inclusive beach resorts than any other place in the country.

new medina on his own land. This combination of living ethnological museum and high-quality bazaar was finally completed in 2007 by hundreds of Moroccan craftsmen following centuries-old techniques. Each stone is laid by hand, and the buildings are made of earth, rock from the Souss, slate from the High Atlas, and local woods such as thuya and eucalyptus. Decorations follow both Berber and Saharan motifs. Mosaic craftsmen, painters, jewelers, a henna artist, metalworkers, and carpenters welcome spectators as they practice their crafts (and welcome customers for the results) in workshop nooks throughout the medina. The medina also houses restaurants, shops, and even an amphitheater. ✉ *Bensergao* ☎ *0528/28–02–53* 🌐 *www.medinapolizzi.com* 🎫 *40 DH* ⏲ *Daily 9–6.*

8

★ **Musée Municipale du Patrimoine Amazighe.** Agadir's municipal museum celebrates the Berber Amazigh heritage of the region and features exhibitions of photography, jewelry, artifacts, and local handicrafts. ✉ *Passage At Souss, Av. Hassan II* ☎ *0528/82–16–32* 🎫 *20 DH* ⏲ *Mon.–Sat., 9:30–5:30.*

Souk Al Had. In the northeastern corner of the city is a daily bazaar selling both souvenirs and household goods. You'll need to bargain hard. ⏲ *Tues.–Sun.*

Vallée des Oiseaux (*Valley of the Birds*). It's not so much a valley as a pleasure garden connecting Avenue Hassan II to the beach. It not only has birds, but also monkeys, fountains, and lovely green surroundings. ✉ *Bd. Mohammed V* 🎫 *Free* ⏲ *Daily 9:30–12:30 and 2:30–6:30.*

BEACHES

AGADIR

Agadir Beach. Agadir beach swings around a crescent from southeast to northwest. You're more likely to find a quiet spot if you wander south. The most crowded areas, frequented year-round by families and locals, are to the north. Along the flanking thoroughfare, known as the Corniche (promenade), you'll find inexpensive cafés, bars, and restaurants. At the very northern end is the swanky new marina development where private yachts are moored. The promenade can be a little sketchy at night, but it's still a good spot to stop and watch the world go by. The northern tip is also the place to rent a catamaran or surf equipment.

NORTH OF AGADIR

Taghazoute. In late summer the beaches north of Agadir on the Essaouira road—especially those in rapidly expanding Taghazoute area—are crammed with Moroccan families (who often camp there), but it empties out in winter. The Number 14 bus runs from Agadir to Taghazoute and takes about 30 minutes. ✉ *Taghazoute.*

CAP RHIR

Cap Rhir. During most of the year, a few stray Western surfers seek out waves around the bend from the lighthouse at Cap Rhir, but otherwise the neighboring village of Aghroud is, like Taghazoute, quiet—a pretty detour, with empty sands and calm waters. You may come across a bald ibis, as their preserve is south of Agadir at the Souss Massa National Park and Estuary. ✉ *Cap Rhir.*

OFF THE BEATEN PATH

Imouzzer. If you are looking for a more isolated and less developed excursion away from the beach, from Aourir (12 km [7 mi] north of Agadir), take the paved road 50 km (31 mi) up into the Ida Outanane Mountains to the waterfalls here, near Isk. Check with locals—the waterfalls are often dry when the region is experiencing drought. Dry hills closer to the coast give way to the palm gorge of Paradise Valley, where the rocky riverbank welcomes picnicking Moroccan families and foreigners alike. ■ TIP→ **This makes for an ideal day excursion from Agadir or Taroudant.**

WHERE TO EAT

Neon signs throughout Agadir lure you in to sample not so much the delights of Moroccan cuisine as the woes of fast food and international menus. Nevertheless, many of these restaurants have good locations along the beachfront or in the town center.

The main joy of eating in Agadir is the chance to dine in fish restaurants, which also tend to be the least brash and pretentious. Agadir's lively deep-sea fishing port is Morocco's busiest. And best of all, you can eat there, too. Frequented by locals and travelers alike, it's a great bet for cheap and fun eats. Each stall offers nearly identical food, including squid, prawns, sole, lobster, and whiting, and for nearly identical prices. So walk around and pick what you'd like; the better-organized stalls have chalkboards listing the catch of the day and the price. Eating at the stalls is a better choice for lunch (after visiting the hilltop kasbah, say), since at night the area is unlighted and stall owners can be a little aggressive.

All major hotels have both Moroccan and Continental restaurants, and there are many sophisticated new eateries springing up around the new marina. Downtown there is a good selection of Italian, French, Thai, and even Indian restaurants. ■ TIP→ **For some of the town's best seafood and a refreshing change of scenery, head to the warehouses and wharves of the port.**

$$$$ SPANISH Fodor's Choice ★ ✕ **Les Blancs.** At the edge of Agadir's trendy new marina district and sitting right on the northern end of the beach, Les Blancs is a shiny, white, modernist retreat. There's an informal bar-cum-restaurant with boardwalk-style flooring and huge windows overlooking the bay; there are also an outdoor terrace with woven seagrass umbrellas and a contemporary indoor dining room. You can sit at the bar and snack on tapas or choose from house specialities such as colorful Spanish paellas including black squid ink rice, green rice with veggies, and red king prawns. Reservations are recommended in high season. ✉ *Marina* ☎ *0528/82–83–68.*

¢ CAFÉ ✕ **Boulangerie Pâtisserie Yacout.** For breakfast have a buttery *pain au chocolat* (chocolate croissant) and strong coffee at the Boulangerie Pâtisserie Yacout. A full Moroccan breakfast of *m'smen* pancakes or croissants, *harira* soup, orange juice and coffee is also available. ✉ *Corner of Rue de L'Entraide and Bd. Mohammed VI* ☎ *0528/84–65–88.*

$$ STEAKHOUSE ✕ **Camel's.** On the main thoroughfare of beachfront restaurants, Camel's is, as you would expect, one of the few places serving camel meat. Tuck in to a camel tagine or a grilled camel kebab, and forget about ethics for a moment—this is a steak house and not the place for vegetarians. But you don't have to eat camel. Homesick Americans may also smile to see the Grand Texas Burger, Jerk Chicken, Jambalaya Chicken, and Surf n' Turf combos on the menu. Glance upwards inside the restaurant, and don't be surprised to see live fish swimming overhead. ✉ *Rue de la Plage* ☎ *0673/17–79–09* 🌐 *www.restaurant-camels.com* ▭ *No credit cards.*

$$$ SEAFOOD ★ ✕ **Chez Mimi la Brochette.** Run by Mimi and her husband since 1981, this seaside institution brings a little style to the chain of cheapos at the northern end of the beach. Everything is grilled over a wood fire, and you can get great fish, including lobster and prawns. Don't miss the fig-based digestif, Mahia, or the chance to have hot prawns or smoked eel salad. The house specialty is, of course, brochettes of any kind; there's plenty of meat on the menu, too. The only downside is that you can't eat here Friday night. ✉ *Rue de la Plage* ☎ *0528/84–03–87* ⏲ *No dinner Fri. No lunch Sat.*

$$ BRITISH ✕ **English Pub.** Just when you thought you couldn't get Yorkshire pudding in Morocco, you come across this street-side bar, café, and restaurant that prides itself on comfort food such as burgers and fries. You can also get a full English breakfast of sausage, bacon, eggs, and beans. For homesick Brits there are also steak and kidney pies, Cornish pasties, and, of course, fish and chips, all to be washed down with pints of beer. ✉ *Bd. du 20 Août* ☎ *0528/84–73–90* ⏲ *No lunch.*

$$$$ FRENCH ✕ **Jean Cocteau.** You might not expect to find a good restaurant on top of one of Agadir's most happening casinos, but Jean Cocteau is a cut

8

The ClubHotel Riu Tikida Dunas is one of the country's best all-inclusive resorts.

above it all. Choose from a sumptuous international menu with predominantly French selections and Moroccan tagines served as a starter. ✉ *Bd. Mohammed V, 1st fl., above Shem's Casino* ☎ *0528/82–11-11.*

$$$ MOROCCAN ✕ **Johara.** It's right in the middle of tourist central, and owned by the Ryad Mogador Al Madina Hotel to boot, but this restaurant is one of the best options for Moroccan cuisine in the area. Lanterns, low seats, and painted tables are de rigueur, as are pigeon pastillas, tagines, and pastries. With 24 hours' notice you can order such specialties as *mechoui* (roasted lamb) and stuffed royal sea bream. ✉ *Al Madina Center, Bd. du 20 Août, near English Pub* ☎ *0528/84–56–56.*

$$$$ SEAFOOD ✕ **Le Miramar.** Sumptuous fish and pasta dishes are served at small tables in one of Agadir's longest-established restaurants. It's particularly popular with Western expats, but the pressure of newer and slicker competition threatens to overtake this rather old-fashioned restaurant. ■ TIP→ **The chef's night off is Sunday, so it's best to sample the tasty delights on a different night of the week.** ✉ *Hotel Miramar, Bd. Mohammed V, near the Marina* ☎ *0528/84–07–70.*

$ CAFÉ ✕ **Pâtisserie La Fontaine.** For a light meal or coffee at any time of day, go straight to the open-air Pâtisserie La Fontaine, which serves outstanding individual pastillas and spicy shrimp rolls as an alternative to plain old toast. ✉ *Passage Aït Souss, Av. Hassan II* ☎ *0528/84–83–40.*

$ PIZZA ✕ **La Siciliana.** Recently expanded and with a more diverse menu including homemade pasta, this Moroccan-run Italian eatery has really good wood-fired pizza. Run by husband-and-wife team Jalila and Rachid, it's a favourite among locals amid the string of Italian restaurants that line Avenue Hassan II. It also delivers, should you crave a quiet night in. Unfortunately, it does not serve alcohol. Credits cards accepted, but only for meals over 250DH. ✉ *65–67 Av. Hassan II, near Vallée des Oiseaux* ☎ *0528/82–09–73* ⊗ *Closed during Ramadan.*

$$ SEAFOOD ✕ **Yacht Club.** You can't beat fresh-caught fish eaten beside the port. This lively family-run restaurant grills, batters, and fries the catch of the day to simple perfection. Watch the swing of the kitchen doors and enjoy the clatter. At the entry to the port, ask the police customs checkpoint to allow you through for the restaurant, which is second turn on the right. ✉ *Agadir port* ☎ *0528/84–37–08.*

WHERE TO STAY

For the most part, you can forget riad-style intimacy in Agadir; your choices are mainly executive-style functionality or giant beachfront complexes that cater primarily to European package tours. As a general rule the luxury (and price) increases as you move down from the northern tip of the beach. A room with beach views and access right off the property often costs a supplement of about 300 DH.

The hotels along Boulevard du 20 Août have so many amenities and restaurants that you'll feel no need to leave their beachside complexes. Indeed, more and more hotels are becoming all-inclusive. Be wary of these, however, as they don't guarantee fine dining and many local experts think they will lead to a slip in standards. If you just need a bed while passing through Agadir, there are less-expensive, basic hotels in the center of town, north of the beach. There's also a lively trade in "résidences," self-catering apartments which you can rent by the night. These even have communal hotel facilities such as swimming pools and are an affordable bet for families.

For expanded hotel reviews, visit Fodors.com.

$$$$ **Atlantic Palace.** Owned by a Moroccan royal cousin, this ornate affair is the king's choice when he's in town. **Pros:** relaxing spa and great facilities. **Cons:** staff not always very courteous. ✉ *Chemin des Dunes, Secteur Touristique* ☎ *0528/82–41–46* ⊕ *www.atlanticpalaceresort.com* *277 rooms, 52 suites* *In-room: a/c, Wi-Fi. In-hotel: restaurant, bar, golf course, pool, tennis court, gym, spa, children's programs, laundry facilities, business center, parking, some pets allowed* *Breakfast.*

$$$$ Fodor's Choice ★ **ClubHotel Riu Tikida Dunas.** As all-inclusive options go (drinks also incuded!), this one gives you value for your money. **Pros:** pretty pools; lovely gardens. **Cons:** very busy with package tour groups; staff pressurized. ✉ *Chemin des Dunes* ☎ *0528/84–90–90* ⊕ *www.riu.com* *400 rooms, 6 suites* *In-room: a/c. In-hotel: restaurant, bar, pool, tennis court, gym, spa, beach, children's programs, laundry facilities, business center, parking* *All-inclusive.*

$ **Hotel Marhaba.** Tucked behind a street a little way back from the beach, this resort hotel has very reasonable prices. **Pros:** great value; very clean rooms. **Cons:** pool could use a scrubbing; often busy with package tours. ✉ *Av. Hassan II* ☎ *0528/84–06–70* *69 rooms, 6 suites* *In-room: a/c, Wi-Fi. In-hotel: restaurant, bar, pool, spa, laundry facilities, parking* *Multiple meal plans.*

$ **Hotel Solman.** Behind a charming, old-school entrance is a well-worn, good-value hotel with a street-side bar, zellij-tiled reception area and

8

pool at the back. **Pros:** clean rooms; nice swimming pool. **Cons:** street noise; bar is smoky; no meals; 20 mins from beach ✉ *Av. Hassan II* ☎ *0528/84–45–65* *55 rooms* *In-room: no a/c. In-hotel: restaurant, bar, pool, business center* *Breakfast.*

$ **La Petite Suède.** It's one of the few decent options for an inexpensive hotel in town, and the staff is friendly, but rooms here are simple and rather characterless, with tiny en suite bathrooms. **Pros:** very affordable, spic-and-span rooms, close to beach. **Cons:** the hotel itself is drab and old-fashioned. Few facilities. ✉ *Corner of Av. Hassan II and Av. General Kittani* ☎ *0528/84–07–79* *www.petitesuede.com* *20 rooms* *In-room: no a/c. In-hotel: business center, parking, some pets allowed* *Breakfast.*

$$ **Résidence Yasmina.** Common areas at this self-catering complex have impressive hand-painted tiles and trickling fountains, but the older apartments are outdated and shabby. **Pros:** large pools; balconies with great views. **Cons:** shabby decor in old wing; not much character. ✉ *Rue de la Jeunesse, off Ave. Hassan II* ☎ *0528/84–26–60* *www.residence-yasmina.com* *104 apartments, 12 suites* *In-room: a/c, kitchen. In-hotel: pool, business center, parking* *No meals.*

$$$$ Fodor's Choice ★ **Riad Villa Blanche.** An elegant boutique hotel—the first of its kind in Agadir—Riad Villa Blanche feels as though it has been plucked from the chicest Marrakesh address and dropped at the edge of the ocean. **Pros:** beautiful decor; intimate scale; excellent service. **Cons:** beyond the garden wall are major hotel sites; far from main tourist beach or downtown. ✉ *50, Cité Founty, Baie des Palmiers, just past Sofitel on the right, Sonaba* ☎ *0528/21–13–13* *www.riadvillablanche.com* *3 suites, 25 rooms* *In-room: a/c, Wi-Fi. In-hotel: restaurant, bar, pool, gym, spa, laundry facilities, business center, parking, some pets allowed* *Multiple meal plans.*

$$$$ **Ryad Mogador Al Madina.** Formerly a five-star hotel, this resort has been demoted to four-star as it no longer serves alcohol. **Pros:** lovely pool; close to beach. **Cons:** overpriced; tacky decor; no real views. ✉ *Bd. du 20 Août* ☎ *0528/29–80–00* *www.ryadmogador.com* *180 rooms, 26 suites* *In-room: a/c. In-hotel: restaurant, pool, gym, spa, laundry facilities, business center, parking, some pets allowed* *Breakfast.*

$$$$ **Sofitel Agadir Royal Bay Resort.** This is the beach strip's most glamorous and sophisticated option, and it manages to provide both privacy and intimacy on a grand scale. **Pros:** luxury to the extreme; excellent amenities. **Cons:** lacks Moroccan feel; very expensive. ✉ *P4, Cité Founty, Baie des Palmiers, Bensergao* ☎ *0528/82–00–88* *www.sofitel.com* *248 rooms, 25 suites* *In-room: a/c, Wi-Fi. In-hotel: restaurant, bar, pool, tennis court, gym, spa, beach, children's programs, laundry facilities, business center, parking, some pets allowed* *Breakfast.*

$$$ **Le Tivoli.** This is a less expensive option than many of the Agadir behemoths, but the beach is a third of a mile away. **Pros:** wide range of activities available. **Cons:** twin beds in standard rooms; noisy pool area; poor customer service. ✉ *Bd. du 20 Août, Secteur Touristique* ☎ *0528/84–76–40* *www.hoteltivoli.com* *256 rooms, 24 suites* *In-room: a/c. In-hotel: restaurant, bar, pool, tennis court, gym, spa, children's programs, laundry facilities, business center, parking, some pets allowed* *Multiple meal plans.*

NIGHTLIFE

With its relaxed mores, Agadir is a clubbing hot spot, particularly for young people looking to cut loose. Many places don't get going until 3 or 4 am, but the beachfront is always busy earlier on, with diners and drinkers making the most of the beach environment. Although Agadir lacks the class of Marrakesh, a number of places, mostly based in the resort hotels, are putting up some decent competition.

Note: Nighttime also attracts many prostitutes, some underage, who throng the cheap bars. The authorities aren't afraid to imprison foreigners who patronize them.

BARS AND CLUBS

Papagayo. A long-standing favorite is Papagayo, which has an easy, laid-back feel and pumps out fairly mainstream tunes. ✉ *Hotel Riu Tikida Beach, Chemin des Dunes* ☎ *0528/83–27–27* 🎫 *200 DH* ⏲ *Daily midnight–dawn.*

SO Night Lounge. The chicest and best nightclub is without doubt SO, which charges a hefty admission price for nonguests of the Sofitel (300 DH each, including a small drink). There's live music every night, a chic restaurant, two levels, and three bars. It's so trendy you could scream, or simply dance the night—and morning—away. ✉ *Sofitel Agadir Royal Bay Resort Hotel, Baie des Palmiers* ☎ *0528/82–00–88.*

Zanzibar. Those looking for post-dinner, pre-club drinks with a touch of East African colonial elegance should stop by Zanzibar. ✉ *Hotel Riu Tikida Beach, Chemin des Dunes* ☎ *0528/84–54–00* ⏲ *Daily 7 pm–1 am.*

CASINOS

Casino Atlantic. Part of the Atlantic Palace Hotel, Casino Atlantic is the long player of the bunch, with blackjack, roulette, poker, and 70 slot machines going all afternoon, night, and early morning. ✉ *Atlantic Palace Hotel, Secteur Balnéaireet Touristique* ☎ *0528/84–33–66* ⏲ *Daily 2 pm–8 am.*

Casino Le Mirage. Casino Le Mirage is part of the Hotel Valtur and has blackjack, poker, roulette, and slot machines. ✉ *Village Valtur, Chemin des Dunes* ☎ *0528/84–87–77* ⏲ *Daily 6 pm–5 am.*

Casino Shem's. Casino Shem's is a good option for people staying in town offering poker, black jack, and slot machines. ✉ *Bd. Mohammed V, near McDonald's* ☎ *0528/82–11–11* ⏲ *Daily 4 pm–6 am.*

SHOPPING

La Fabrique. You'll have to bargain hard for any of the leather goods and designer labels for sale at La Fabrique. ✉ *91, av. Hassan II, near the turn-off for Pl. Prince Heriter Sidi Mohammed* ☎ *0528/84–61–76.*

Madd. Madd is a boutique jewelry store that entices you with 18-carat gold from behind a warm wooden exterior. There's another branch in the new Marina development at the north end of Agadir beach. ✉ *38–40, av. Hassan II* ☎ *0528/84–05–92.*

Palais du Sud. For an emporium of carpets, ceramics, leather, lanterns, and ornate boxes, visit Palais du Sud. Behind the golden doors, all goods have price tags, which makes buying hassle-free. The store is closed on Sunday. ✉ *Rue de la Foire, north of Av. Hassan II* ☎ *0528/84–35–00* 🌐 *www.palaisdusud.com.*

Scarlette Idées K-do. Scarlette Idées K-do is a lovely boutique selling everything you could possibly want for the home, from candles and lanterns to mirrors, fabrics, and small chests of drawers. ✉ *Imm. I'Yazid, Av. Hassan II, next to La Fabrique* ☎ *0528/82–32–93.*

Tawarguit. Focusing on stylish crockery, Tawarguit also sells lamps, stools, coffee tables, gifts, and artisanal work. The owners have also recently added an art gallery at the same address. ✉ *Lotissement Faiz, 1, rue 206, 1 block north of Rue d'Oujda* ☎ *0528/84–82–25.*

SPORTS AND THE OUTDOORS

GOLF

There are three 27-hole courses within 15 minutes of Agadir.

Golf Club Med Les Dunes. These 27 holes were designed by Cabell Robinson. The Golf Club Med Les Dunes is an American-style course 5 km from the Club Med village in Agadir. The greens fees are 690 DH, including caddie. ✉ *Rte. d'Inezgane* ☎ *0528/82–95–00.*

Golf de L'Océan. The newest of the golf courses along Agadir's coast, the Golf de L'Océan is part of the Atlantic Palace Hotel resort and is open to both resort guests and nonresidents. Designed by Belt Collins and opened in 2009, the course has 27 holes, and the greens fees start at 350 DH for 9 holes incuding caddy. Regular minibus shuttles run from the Atlantic Palace Hotel. ✉ *Atlantic Palace Hotel, Bensergao* ☎ *0528/27–35–42* 🌐 *www.golfdelocean.com.*

Golf du Soleil. Golf du Soleil is American-style, with three courses of 9 holes each. It has Tifway grass across 110 acres. The greens fees for 9 holes are 470 DH, including caddie. There is a regular, free shuttle bus that picks up at some of the big hotels throughout the day. ✉ *Chemin des Dunes, Bensergao* ☎ *0528/33–73–30* 🌐 *www.golfdusoleil.com.*

Royal Golf Club. One of the smaller courses in Agadir, Royal Golf Club is 12 km (7 mi) from Agadir on the road to Aït Melloul. It has 9 holes over 30 acres, with English-style Bermuda 419 and Cucuyo grass. Greens fees are 250 DH for 9 holes including caddie. ✉ *Rte. At Melloul, Km 12* ☎ *0528/24–85–51.*

JET-SKIING

Club Royal de Jet-Ski. At the north end of Agadir beach, next to Ecole de Nautisme, you'll find Jet Skis for hire. ☎ *No phone.*

SPAS

Argane-Spa. The Argane-Spa offers the gamut of baths and scrubbing. A fragrant hot bath followed by a massage costs 400 DH and lasts an hour. Or try "erg-therapy," an active sand wrap at the beach for 150 DH (30 minutes). ✉ *Caribbean Village Agador, Bd. du 20 Août* ☎ *0528/84–71–02.*

Les Bains de la Villa Blanche. Seven kinds of exotic massage with essential oils are offered in the sumptuous, candlelit spa of Riad Villa Blanche. You can choose from a Sahara hot-sand massage, an "apres-souk" massage, or an energizing massage with argan oil and lemon for 350 DH. ✉ *Riad Villa Blanche, Baie des Palmiers Secteur N, Cité Founty, Sonaba* ☎ *0528/21–13–13.*

Diar Argan. Diar Argan offers two hours of Berber massage with argan oil for 300 DH. ✉ *104, Immeuble Iguenouane, at Bd. Mohammed V, next to Délegation du Tourisme* ☎ *0528/84–82–33* ⊕ *www.diarargan.net.*

SURFING

Surf dudes the world over rate Morocco's southern Atlantic coast one of the world's best places to catch waves. There has recently been something of a surfer boom in the region. Today there are about 25 surf schools, many run by foreigners who came to surf and then simply couldn't tear themselves away. Board rentals tend to cost about 200 DH. An hour's training generally costs 300 DH, and a week's worth of lessons can go for between 2,500 DH and 4,000 DH. Here's a rundown of some of the top spots:

At the small village of Taghazoute, 22 km (14 mi) north of Agadir, is the famed Anchor Point (*Les pointes des ancres*). This pleasant bay among the rocky peaks attracts pro surfers from around the world for its point breaks of more than a kilometer. British surfers in the 1970s named it Anchor Point after the nearby row of anchors that used to secure an enormous fishing net to catch tuna. The best surf here is October through February.

Cap Rhir, jutting out into the ocean 40 km (25 mi) north of Agadir, is well known for its large waves. Farther north still, the divers' favorite, Imesouane, is also great for surfers. Beginners especially can benefit from the long portal wave.

South of Agadir, experienced surfers can try to catch the Cathedral and Rif waves, while farther south still, Sidi Ifni and Massa are quieter spots with lovely beach breaks. Mirleft has a beautiful beach, with great surf spots; it's a reminder of how hippie and empty Essaouira once was.

SURFING SCHOOLS

Aftas Trip. In Mirleft, south of Agadir, Aftas Trip is a surf school and guesthouse that can also arrange diving. ☎ *0666/02–65–37* ⊕ *www.aftastrip.com.*

École de Nautisme. Situated at the north end of Agadir beach, look for the white tent on the beach. This company offers a wide range of water sports and instruction, including for windsurfing, kite surfing, beach kayaking, catamaran sailing, and surfing. ☎ *0666/24–52–66.*

Surf Town Morocco. This surf school and guesthouse is 14 km (9 mi) north of Agadir in Tamraght. Instructors can take you to surfer favorites like Boiler, Killer Point, and Devil's Rock. Half-day surfing instruction begins at 300 DH per person. Inexpensive accommodations are also available with half board. ☎ *0664/47–81–76* ⊕ *www.surftownmorocco.com.*

THE SOUSS VALLEY AND ANTI-ATLAS

Few travelers venture this far south in Morocco, but those who do are rewarded with a slice of life in the great Sahara. The Moroccan southwest combines glorious beaches and arid mountains flanked by lush palm, olive, and orange groves. The region's character is strongly flavored by its Tashelhit-speaking Berbers, who inhabited these mountains and plains before Arabs ever set foot in Morocco: there are no imperial cities anywhere in the south, and the feel is distinctively rural.

East and south of Agadir you leave the world of beach vacations and enter Berber country. Scenic drives take you past hills covered with barley and almond trees, palm groves, kasbahs, and the Anti-Atlas Mountains themselves. In town, poke around the monuments and souks of Taroudant or shop for Morocco's finest silver in Tiznit.

TAROUDANT

85 km (51 mi) east of Agadir, 223 km (134 mi) southwest of Marrakesh.

Imagine a mini-Marrakesh, with much of the hectic hustle removed, and you've pretty much got Taroudant. It's a historic market town where people, customs, and the Arabic and Tashelhit Berber languages mix. The town's relaxed feel, the easy interaction with locals, and inexpensive dining make Taroudant an ideal base for exploring the Souss Valley and the western High Atlas.

After a few glory days in the 16th century as a center of the Saadian empire, Taroudant retained allegiance to the sultan even when the Souss Valley plains and Anti-Atlas Mountains revolted. Its population held steady between 5,000 and 10,000 until the 1970s, when rural emigrants to Europe returned to the region, built houses, and opened businesses and the population boomed to 60,000. Nevertheless, the place retains a small-town feel, with narrow streets and active markets.

GETTING HERE AND AROUND

The principal road routes to Taroudant are easily navigable and well signposted. The N10 runs east from Agadir and leads eventually to Taliouine, Tazenakht, and Ouarzazate. There are also scheduled buses from Agadir (1½ hours), Ouarzazate (5 hours), Casablanca (10 hours), Rabat (13hours), and Marrakesh (6½ hours). Efficient and comfortable CTM buses leave from the gare routière outside Bab Zorgane on the southern side of the medina.

Once you arrive in the city, everything is within walking distance. For a treat you could hop aboard a calèche (horse-drawn carriage) and tour the ramparts for about 30 DH per hour.

Bus Contacts **CTM** ✉ *Bab Zorgane, just inside city walls* ☎ *0528/85–38–58* 🌐 *www.ctm.ma.*

Rental Cars **Malja Cars** ✉ *Complexe Ouled Lourzal, Gas Station Afriquia, 2 km from Taroudant* ☎ *0528/55–17–42.*

Some of Taroudant's fortified walls are some 900 years old.

GUIDES AND TOURS

For a guided tour of the city, Moulay Brahim Bouchra, has encyclopedic knowledge and speaks very good English. For traveling further afield and exploring the region, Via Terra offers a number of ready-made excursions and will pick up from your hotel.

Contacts **Moulay Brahim Bouchra** ☎ *0662/19–24–63.* **Via Terra** ☎ *0662/12–24–71* 🌐 *www.viaterra-maroc.com.*

8

TIMING AND PRECAUTIONS

Taroudant attracts visitors all year round thanks to its favorable climate. Most visitors stay a day or two.

EXPLORING

Whatever you do in the late afternoon, don't miss the sight of colorfully dressed Roudani (Taroudant native) women lined up against the ramparts near the hospital like birds on a ledge, socializing in the cool hours before sunset.

Bab el-Kasbah. The main entrance to the old city is the triple-arched Bab el-Kasbah (now called Bab Essalsla) on Avenue Moulay Rachid, one of half a dozen major doors that locked residents in every night after curfew during the French protectorate.

Bab Sedra. On Avenue Moulay Rachid, with the main gate (Bab el-Kasbah) behind you, you'll see a small gate on the right (for pedestrian access only), which is the old entrance into the kasbah quarter. The kasbah was a fortress built by Alouite leader Moulay Ismail in the 17th century and is now in ruins, though some of the pasha's palace remains intact and has been converted into a hotel (Hotel Palais Salam). ✉ *Kasbah.*

Dar Baroud. Diagonally across from Bab Sedra, across the Avenue Moulay Rachid and with the hospital on your right, is the Dar Baroud, once a French ammunition-storage facility. This high-walled building is closed to the public—and is locally rumored to be haunted—but stand back on the sidewalk opposite and you can admire its delicate carved stone walls from the exterior.

Farq Lehbab. The entrance to the neighborhood known as Farq Lehbab, the "loved ones' parting place," is marked by a mosque. In the 16th century, it is said, five holy men reached this spot after years of religious study in Baghdad; each threw a stone, and each settled where his rock landed. The best loved of these saints are Sidi Beni Yaqoub, of the province of Tata; Sidi ou Sidi, who stayed in Taroudant; and Sidi Ahmed ou Moussa, who went on to Tazeroualt (in the province of Tiznit). The mosque is two minutes' walk from Dar Baroud and is found at the edge of a small square near the eastern end of Av. du 20 Août, where it joins Rue Brahim Roudani.

Sidi bu Sbaa. The tomb of holy man Sidi bu Sbaa is hard to spot and has been neglected in recent years. Look upward for the green-painted ornaments and a domed roof above a nondescript wall opposite the French Catholic church on Avenue 20 Août.

Talborjst. Talborjst is an old lookout post, also known locally as Oumensour. It is so-called after the family name of the pasha who lived here in the 19th century; it was used by the French during the years of the protectorate. These days, the buildings of Taroudant have grown tall all around what once was open land.

Tomb of Sidi u Sidi. The tomb of Sidi u Sidi, patron saint of Taroudant, is on the northern edge of the Arab Market and attracts locals hoping for healing and cures. Located just off Avenue Bir Zaran—a street lined with fish vendors, produce carts, and men selling corander from their bike baskets—it's a place where you can take a peek from a respectful distance, but cannot enter.

WHERE TO EAT

$ MOROCCAN ★ ✕ **L'Agence.** An addition to Taroudant's rather sketchy restaurant scene, L'Agence shares street-level premises with a real estate office under the same ownership. Both businesses are run by French-Moroccan couple Maria and Yann, and they have created a charming and eclectic rustic eatery. With only six tables, whitewashed walls, hand-painted wooden beams, Berber textiles, and quirky metal sculptures, it has plenty of character. The food is distinctly Moroccan—salads, tagines, and couscous—but the menu is constantly changing to offer variety. Try *safa*, couscous with minced chicken and sprinkled with almonds and cinnamon. It's fine to bring your own wine and beer (discreetly). ✉ *Av. Sidi Mohammed* ☎ *0528/55–02–70* ▭ *No credit cards* ⏲ *Closed Sun. and during Ramadan.*

$$ MOROCCAN ✕ **Chez Nada.** If you want to stick within the city walls for some no-hassle Moroccan food, you can't go wrong at this father-and-son joint. While the decor is nothing special, the views over the medina are sublime, and dishes such as hearty couscous, harira, and pigeon *pastilla*

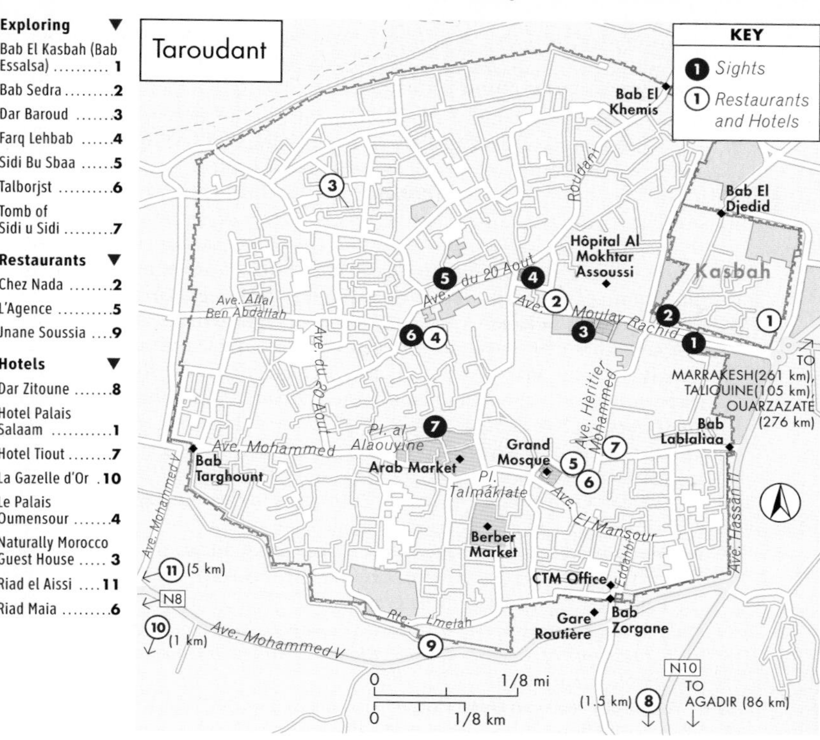

(sweet pigeon pie; order in advance) are part of a top-value set menu. ✉ *Rue Moulay el-Rachid* ☎ *0528/85–17–26* ▭ *No credit cards.*

$$ MOROCCAN

✕ **Restaurant Jnane Soussia.** This outdoor restaurant is a long-standing favorite for Moroccan families, offering great food and lots of space. Traditional cuisine is served under a *caidal* (white canvas) tent around two small swimming pools, in a garden full of orange, fig, and papaya trees and flowers. Weekending Moroccan families are drawn to the excellent specialties of the house, such as the *briouates* (spicy dumplings) and *mechoui* (roasted shoulder of lamb, best ordered in advance). No alcohol is served. ■ **TIP→ Non-Moroccan families with children should be advised that only girls under 12 are allowed to enjoy the swimming pool with the boys.** ✉ *Just outside Bab Zorgan, on right side of road as you head west* ☎ *0528/85–49–80.*

WHERE TO STAY

For expanded hotel reviews, visit Fodors.com.

$$$$ Fodor's Choice ★

Dar Zitoune. Rooms at this countryside retreat are spaced out in a fragrant garden of roses and orange trees, with outdoor patios ideal for breakfast. **Pros:** delightful gardens; English-speaking staff. **Cons:** 2 km from old city. ✉ *Boutarialt el Barrania, on road to Agadir Airport, 2 km (1 mi) from town* ☎ *0528/55–11–41* ⊕ *www.darzitoune.*

com 12 *bungalows, 8 suites* *In-room: a/c. In-hotel: restaurant, bar, pool, gym, spa, laundry facilities, business center, parking, some pets allowed* *Multiple meal plans.*

$$$$ ★ **La Gazelle d'Or.** One of the most exclusive and expensive hotels in Morocco, the Gazelle d'Or has secluded bungalows with airy, exquisitely tasteful rooms and terraces. **Pros:** exclusive feel; first-rate service. **Cons:** very expensive. *2 km (1 mi) outside Taroudant on Amskroud–Agadir road* *0528/85–20–39* *www.gazelledor.com* *20 rooms, 9 suites* *In-room: a/c, no TV, Wi-Fi. In-hotel: restaurant, bar, pool, tennis court, gym, spa, laundry facilities, business center, parking, some pets allowed* *Closed mid-July–mid-Sept.* *Some meals.*

$$$ **Hôtel Palais Salaam.** Any hotel that manages to accommodate the ambassadors of France and the United States must have pretty wide-ranging appeal. **Pro:** lovely gardens and terraces. **Cons:** rooms are disappointing; staff can seem disinterested. *Bd. Moulay Ismail, outside the ramparts* *0528/85–25–01* *88 rooms, 48 suites, 4 apartments* *In-room: a/c, Wi-Fi. In-hotel: restaurant, bar, pool, gym, spa, laundry facilities, business center, parking, some pets allowed* *Breakfast.*

$$ Fodor's Choice ★ **Le Palais Oumensour.** Opened in 2008, this luxurious, Belgian-owned boutique hotel in the heart of Taroudant's medina has been beautifully renovated from an old riad. **Pros:** great location; good price; beautiful architecture. **Cons:** often fully booked; no credit cards accepted. *Al Mansour, Borj Oumensour* *0528/55–02–15* *www.palaisoumensour.com* *4 suites, 2 rooms* *In-room: a/c, no TV. In-hotel: restaurant, bar, pool, spa, laundry facilities, business center, parking* *No credit cards* *Breakfast.*

$$ ★ **Naturally Morocco Guest House.** Also known as "La Maison Anglaise," this family-friendly guesthouse doubles as a cultural center with rooms arranged over four floors. **Pros:** lots of activities; good location. **Cons:** not all rooms air-conditioned; not all rooms have en suite bath; often booked up in advance. *422, Derb Aferdou* *44/1239–710814 in the UK, 0528/55–16–28* *www.naturallymorocco.co.uk* *9 rooms* *In-room: no a/c, kitchen, no TV, Wi-Fi. In-hotel: restaurant, laundry facilities, business center* *Some meals.*

$ ★ **Riad El-Aissi.** Don't be deceived by the riad tag—there's no overdone decor here; rather, you'll find a lot of country-style charm and a wonderful atmosphere amid the 72 acres of this Moroccan-run fruit farm just outside Taroudant. **Pros:** huge rooms; excellent food; great value. **Cons:** not really that close to Taroudant. *Village Nouayl* *3 km (1.8 mi) from Taroudant off N8 Amskroud–Agadir Rd.* *0528/55–02–25* *www.riadelaissi.com* *3 suites, 6 rooms, 1 bungalow* *In-room: a/c. In-hotel: restaurant, pool, business center, parking, some pets allowed* *No credit cards* *Breakfast.*

$$ **Riad Maïa.** There's a sense of history as you approach the wooden door of Riad Maïa in a very old part of the medina. **Pros:** in the heart of the medina; spacious bedrooms. **Cons:** garden patio is very small. *12, Tassoukt Ighezifen, off Av. Sidi Mohammed, near L'Agence Restaurant* *0528/55–01–28* *www.riad-maia-taroudant.com* *3 rooms* *In-room: a/c, Wi-Fi. In-hotel: business center* *Breakfast.*

SHOPPING

Colorful round-toe Berber slippers, some with sequins and fanciful pom-poms, are a favorite with both locals and travelers. There are 200 shops in Taroudant dedicated to sandals alone. A walk down even the quietest of streets will feature the incessant tap-tapping of cordwainers at work. Other local products include saffron and lavender, sold by the ounce in herbal stores. The locally pressed olive oil is nationally renowned; ask the herbalists if they can get you a liter.

Antiquaire Haut Atlas. For serious collectors, Antiquaire Haut Atlas has one of the best collections of Berber jewelry in southern Morocco, some of it dating from the 17th and 18th centuries. Even if you're not in the market for a trinket, wandering around the dusty rooms of carpets, candlesticks, and charms makes for a diverting half hour. And if you *are* in the market, Mr. Houssaine accepts all major credit cards. ✉ *61, Souk el-Kabir* ☎ *0528/85–21–45.*

Sculpteur De Pierre. Sculpteur De Pierre is the best place to go for sculpture, both for quality and range of workmanship. Craftsman Larbi El Hare uses marble, limestone, and alabaster. Small stone masks start at 80 DH. He also makes some of the best mint tea in town, brewed by his erstwhile team of draftsmen polishers. ✉ *Fondouk el-Hare, Rahra Kedima* ☎ *0668/80–78–35.*

EAST OF TAROUDANT: THE SOUSS PLAINS

8

A loop drive east of Taroudant will take you through the agriculturally rich Souss Valley plains and on a tour of colonial-era *caids'* (local dignitaries') former homes. From the main circle outside Taroudant's Bab Kasbah, take the road toward Tata/Ouarzazate to Aït Iazza; then turn right toward Igherm/Tata, crossing the Souss River (provided it's not flooded, as it sometimes is in winter) into Freija. Back on pavement, look on your right for a decorated mud house, the **Kasbah de Freija.** It's now largely deserted, but you can usually find someone to show you around. Continue on until a sign marks the turnoff to Tioute. The **Tioute palmery,** about a 45-minute drive from Taroudant, was the base used by merciless colonial caid El Tiouti, whose French-armed forces broke some of the last pockets of mountain resistance to French rule. From the kasbah or a short hike up the hillside, you have superb views over the palmery and verdant fields of mint.

From here you can continue the scenic loop northeast to Aouluz, then turn back west toward the Tizi-n-Test pass until argan trees give way to olive groves and you reach **Ouled Berhil,** which houses the unique and delightful hotel Riad Hida. As an alternative, if you're pressed for time, simply return to Aït Iazza and take the Ouarzazate road straight to Ouled Berhil.

TAFRAOUTE

152 km (94 mi) southeast of Agadir.

Tafraoute is a pretty and quiet regional market and administrative center, nestled at the bottom of a valley. Usually overlooked by groups, it's a great base for exploring an area rich in natural beauty and overflowing with walks, many of which can be undertaken without bumping into another tourist. Although the dizzying mountains around Tafraoute may prove forbidding to cyclists or light hikers, half-day excursions can take you to prehistoric rock carvings, the Ammeln Valley, or the villages off the main road to Tiznit. It's also worth planning a day's excursion to the Aït Mansour gorges to the south of town.

Tafraoute is a great place to visit some spectacular *agadirs*—hilltop granaries perched at the top of sheer cliffs. They include Amtoudi, Tasguint, and Ikouka.

GETTING HERE AND AROUND

The R105 runs from Agadir to Tafroute via Aït Baha. There are buses from Aït Baha (two hours), Agadir via Tiznit (five hours), Marrakesh (10 hours), and Casablanca (14 hours). There are also grands taxis from Tiznit. Once in Tafraoute, your best bet is to travel on foot or by bicycle. For trekking in the region and into the mountains, Brahim Bahou comes highly recommended as a qualified, local English-speaking guide

Visitor and Tour Info **Tafraout Aventure** ✉ *Pl. Mohammed V* ☎ *0528/80–13–68* 🌐 *www.tafraout-aventure.com.* **Brahim Bahou (Mountain Guide)** ☎ *0661/82–26–77.*

TIMING AND PRECAUTIONS

Travelers report being harangued by persistent fake guides. Your best bet is to hire a guide from Tafraout Aventure in the town center, or if you want to include Tafraoute as part of a longer Souss Valley tour, then it's worth going through one of the many agencies based in Agadir.

EXPLORING

Ammeln Valley. A walk in the Ammeln Valley might start at the village of Oumesmat, where for once the ubiquitous **Maison Berbère** is worth a trip. Here the gentle, blind Si Abdessalem will take you through his traditional Anti-Atlas home, introducing you to domestic implements, and with agility will cloak women visitors in the local gold-laminated black wrap, the *tamelheft*. Express your appreciation for the tour by tipping generously. From Oumesmat you can follow paths to the neighboring villages. **Taghdicte** makes a good base for ambitious Anti-Atlas climbers.

Fodor's Choice ★ **Gazelle Rock Carving.** The prehistoric gazelle rock carving just 2 km (1 mi) south of Tafraoute is an easy walk or bike ride from town. The sparse etching has been retouched, but it's still interesting and gives you an idea about how long these desolate mountains have sustained human cultures. To get here, follow signs to "Tazka" from behind Hôtel Les Amandiers; go through the village to the palm and argan fields beyond. You may find offers to guide you from local children: if you accept, then be sure to thank them with a small gift, such as a pen or toy, but avoid giving money. Although everyone calls it a gazelle, locals in the know will tell you that the celebrated rock carving just out of town is in fact of a mouflon (wild sheep). Those energetic enough can visit more cave paintings at Ukas, south of the town of Souk Had Issi, 50 km (31 mi) southeast of Tafraoute.

Tafraoute, in a quiet valley, is often overlooked by the larger tour groups.

Painted Rocks. A trip to the Painted Rocks outside Tafraoute (follow signs) is most dramatically experienced in late afternoon, when the hillsides stacked with massive round boulders turn a rich mustard hue before sunset. Belgian artist Jean Veran painted a cluster of these natural curiosities in varying shades of blue in 1984; checking out amateur copies is as much fun as looking at the originals.

★ **Palm Groves.** The palm groves southeast of Tafraoute deserve a full day's excursion, and the former piste circuit through them is increasingly paved.

From the rotary take the road in the opposite direction from the Agadir sign. Follow the signs toward Tiznit, and after 2 km (1 mi) you'll see the so-called Napoleon's cap of massive boulders on your right. Occasionally you'll see foreign climbers here, with their incongruously high-tech rock-climbing gear. Follow signs toward Agard Oudad. When the road forks, the right one going to the Painted Rocks, take the left branch. A winding paved road takes you higher into the Anti-Atlas Mountains, with views over the Ammeln Valley below; 20 km (12 mi) out of Tafraoute, turn right toward Aït Mansour, which you'll reach after another 14 km (9 mi) of winding down into the palm groves. Five kilometers (3 mi) farther on is the village of Zawia; another 5 km (3 mi) brings you to Afella-n-Ighir. Along the paved road you'll pass shrouded women, either transporting on their backs palm-frond baskets of dates supported by ropes around their foreheads or walking to Timguilcht to visit its important saint's shrine. Continue on the piste to Souk Lhad, whose busy market is held on Sunday. From there the piste loops back to Tafraoute.

WHERE TO EAT

$ MOROCCAN ✕ **Restaurant L'Etoile du Sud.** Since 1968 the "Star of the South" has been serving delicious couscous and tagines in a red-velvet dining room or under a huge red-and-green velvet caidal tent. The harira is hearty and satisfying after a long day's drive, and the salads are surprisingly fresh. The staff is friendly, and the atmosphere is cheery, with many tour agencies choosing this spot for their clients No one would bat an eye if you kicked off your shoes and rested your weary feet on the couches. The restaurant also serves alcohol. ✉ *Av. Hassan II, next to the Post Office* ☎ *0528/80–00–38* ▭ *No credit cards.*

$ MOROCCAN ✕ **Restaurant Marrakech.** The tagines here are deliciously fresh, and a three-course meal is also remarkably cheap. Cool, fresh-squeezed juices make this a nice spot to catch your breath and get out of the sun. ✉ *Av. Hassan II, in the center of town* ☎ *0663/22–92–50* ▭ *No credit cards.*

WHERE TO STAY

For expanded hotel reviews, visit Fodors.com.

$$ ★ **Hôtel Les Amandiers.** Designed in a mock-kasbah style, this hotel dominates the town, providing panoramic views of the mountains that surround it. **Pros:** great views; pretty pool. **Cons:** decor needs updating. ✉ *Town Center* ☎ *0528/80–00–88* 🌐 *www.hotel-lesamandiers.com* *53 rooms, 7 suites* *In-room: a/c. In-hotel: restaurant, bar, pool, laundry facilities, business center, parking, some pets allowed* *Multiple meal plans.*

$ **Hotel Salama.** Staffed by a helpful team of English speakers, the recently refurbished Salama offers cool rooms with excellent showers. **Pros:** English-speaking staff; nice views. **Cons:** rooms overlooking market can be noisy. ✉ *Town Center* ☎ *0528/80–00–26* 🌐 *www.hotelsalama.com* *31 rooms, 4 suites* *In-room: a/c, Wi-Fi. In-hotel: restaurant, business center, parking, some pets allowed* ▭ *No credit cards* *Multiple meal plans.*

SHOPPING

Tafraoute's central market has a good selection of woven palm-frond baskets, argan oil, and *amalou* (almond and argan paste). Tafraoute is the place to come for mountain *babouches* (slippers). These are different from the slip-on varieties found in the souks of Marrakesh and Fez, as they are specially made with a heel to aid mountain walking. The local market is full of examples at reasonable prices. Take note of Berber babouche color coding: yellow for men, red for women, and spangled designs only for special occasions.

Maison Touareg. The obligatory Maison Touareg is difficult to miss, carries a good selection of regional Berber carpets, and accepts credit cards. ✉ *Rte. de l'Hotel Les Amandiers, Av. Mohammed V* ☎ *0528/80–02–10* 🌐 *www.maisontouareg.com.*

EN ROUTE

The newer road from Tafraoute to Tiznit (follow signs out the back of Tafraoute, beyond the post office) is flat and bike-accessible for about the first 15 km (9 mi), after which it begins an incline into the mountains.

Col du Kerdous. As the road winds over the Anti-Atlas peaks and through the valleys, you'll enjoy many panoramic views. The former kasbah site at Col du Kerdous (1,203 in altitude) is almost exactly halfway between Tafraoute and Tiznit (54 km [34 mi] and 53 km [33 mi] respectively), and is now a 4-star hotel, Hotel Kerdous. You can stop here for lunch or tea and enjoy the view.

TIZNIT

100 km (62 mi) west of Tafraoute, 98 km (61 mi) south of Agadir.

Tiznit suffers from its uncomfortable location on a flat, hot plain, which makes it look ugly in comparison to the picturesque towns of the mountains or the laid-back beach hangouts of the coast. Yet markets in Tiznit's medina offer a great selection of silver jewelry, and the ambience, especially in the evening, is more relaxed than that of Marrakesh or Fez.

Park your car in the main square, the Méchouar, and walk or rent a bike from the bike shop just inside the square's southern entrance.

GETTING HERE AND AROUND

Tiznit is well signposted if traveling by road, with the N1 bringing you from Agadir, or the R104 from Tafraoute. Several daily buses arrive from Sidi Ifni (1½ hours), Agadir (2 hours), and Tafraoute (2 hours). The bus station is a 15-minute walk along Avenue Hassan II from the medina entrance at Bab Jdid. The CTM office is located inside the medina at the end of Avenue du 20 Août. There are also grands taxis from Agadir.

TIMING AND PRECAUTIONS

With shops, restaurants, and a historic souk, Tiznit makes for a pleasant and relaxed day trip from Agadir.

EXPLORING

Grande Mosquée (*Great Mosque*). From the Méchouar, take the Rue Bain Maure. Follow it as it winds through neighborhood markets, and you'll emerge on a main medina street at a slim minaret (visible from the Méchouar). Cross the street and turn right along the arcade; then follow the cemetery walls around to the Grande Mosquée—unusual in Morocco for its sub-Saharan–style minaret, with sticks poking out from all sides that make it look like someone forgot to take out the scaffolding after it was completed.

Lalla Zninia Spring. Facing the *pisé* (sun-dried mud) wall of the prison housed in the old kasbah, continue to the left until you reach the Lalla Zninia Spring (also known as the *Source Bleue*) on your left, which honors the saint after whom Tiznit is named. Legend has it that this shepherd girl brought her flocks to this spot and smelled the then-undiscovered spring below; her sheep dug (if you can imagine sheep digging) until they found the water, and the town was born. To catch a glimpse of her tomb on afternoons when devotees visit, follow the prison wall and turn left on the first narrow neighborhood street; the tomb is behind a green-painted door on your left.

Méchouar. The main square, the méchouar, is the heart of town and was once a military parade ground. Nowadays there are small gatherings of musicians and entertainers as well as a clutch of cheap and cheerful hotels and cafés. Down a side street off the main square (heading in the direction of the ramparts) you'll find a smaller square lined with orange trees, where locals buy from the mint, date, and dried-thyme vendors whose carts are parked between the rows of clothing and housewares. The square then gives way to the main souk, with jewelry and silver at the northern end, and an open-air market at the southern end. You'll also find a larger concentration of tourists (and hasslers).

WHERE TO STAY

For expanded hotel reviews, visit Fodors.com.

$$$$ **Hotel Idou Tiznit.** It may cater primarily to the business market, but this is the best hotel in town, and, for women travelers, the one place that won't feel too intimidating, particularly at night. **Pros:** full range of services. **Cons:** little local color. ✉ *Av. Hassan II* ☎ *0528/60–03–33* 🌐 *www.idoutiznit.com* *87 rooms, 6 suites* *In-room: a/c. In-hotel: restaurant, bar, pool, laundry facilities, business center, parking, some pets allowed* *Some meals.*

SHOPPING

Tiznit has earned a reputation as *the* place to buy silver jewelry in Morocco, and the local market has responded accordingly. The silver markets of Tiznit sell more—and better—silver per square foot than any other market in Morocco. Some vendors also sell handwoven cream-color blankets, traded by local women for a few pieces of new silver. Merchants cater increasingly to Western tastes and wallets. Many shops around the main square are owned by profiteers who ask inflated prices; to find unusual pieces for reasonable amounts, scour the backstreets for older men haggling with local women.

Bijouterie Aziz. The low-pressure Bijouterie sells Saharan and Berber silver jewelry and tasteful, handwoven cream-color blankets made by local women. ✉ *5, Souk Joutia* ☎ *No phone.*

Trésor du Sud. Away from the souk, Trésor du Sud has an enormus showroom of high-quality handcrafted Berber jewelry. In addition, the workshops allow you to see the silversmiths in action. This is not the cheapest jewelry showroom in town, but you can pay with credit card. ✉ *27, Bab al-Khemis* ☎ *0524/86–28–85* 🌐 *www.tresordusud.com.*

MOROCCAN ARABIC VOCABULARY

Most Moroccans are multilingual. The country's official languages are modern standard Arabic and French; most Moroccans speak Moroccan Arabic dialect, with many city dwellers also speaking French. Since the time of the French protectorate, French has been taught to schoolchildren (not all children) starting in the first grade, resulting in several French-language newspapers, magazines, and TV shows. Spanish enters the mix in northern Morocco, and several Berber tongues are spoken in the south as well as the north. In the medinas and souks of big cities, you may find merchants who can bargain in just about any language, including English, German, Japanese, and Swedish.

A rudimentary knowledge of French and, especially, Arabic will get you far in Morocco. If you're more comfortable with French, by all means use it in the major cities; in smaller cities, villages, and the mountains, it's best to attempt some Moroccan Arabic. Arabic is always a good choice, as Moroccans will go out of their way to accommodate the foreigner who attempts to learn their national language. Some letters in Arabic do not have English equivalents. When you see "gh" at the start of a word in this vocabulary, pronounce it like a French "r," lightly gargled at the back of the throat. If unsure, stick to a "g" sound.

GREETINGS & BASICS

ENGLISH	ARABIC TRANSLITERATION	PRONUNCIATION
Hello/Peace upon you.	salaam ou alaikum	sa-**lahm** oo allah-ee-**koom**
(Reply:) Hello/And peace upon you.	wa alaikum salaam	wa allay-koom sa-**lahm**
Goodbye	bislamma	bess-**lah**-ma
Mr./Sir	si	see
Mrs./Madam/Miss	lalla	lah-la
How are you? Fine, thank you.	labass, alhamdul'Illah	la-**bahs**, al-**hahm**-doo-lee-**lah**
(No harm?) (No harm, praise be to God.)	labass	la-**bahs**
Pleased to meet you.	mitsharafin	mitsh-arra-**fayn**
Yes/No	namm/la	nahm/lah
Please	afek	**ah**-feck
Thank you	baraka Allahu fik	**ba**-ra-kah **la**-hoo **feek**
You're welcome.	Allah yubarak fik	ahl-lah yoo-**bah**-rak feek
God willing	insh'Allah	in-**shah**-ahl-lah

Excuse me./I'm sorry (from a man).	smahali	**sma**-hah-li
Excuse me./I'm sorry (from a woman).	smahailia	sma-high-**lee**-ah

DAYS

Today	el yum	el yom
Yesterday	imbarah	im-ber-ah
Tomorrow	ghadaa	gha-dah
Sunday	el had	el had
Monday	tneen	t'neen
Tuesday	thlat	tlet
Wednesday	larbaa	lar-bah
Thursday	el khamis	el kha-mees
Friday	el jemaa	el j'mah
Saturday	sebt	es-sebt

NUMBERS

1	wahad	**wa**-hed
2	jouj	jewj
3	thlata	**tlet**-ta
4	rbaa	ar-**bah**
5	khamsa	**khem**-sah
6	sta	stah
7	sbaa	se-**bah**
8	taminia	ta-**min**-ee-ya
9	tseud	tsood
10	aachra	**ah**-she-ra
11	hadash	ha-**dahsh**
12	tanash	ta-**nahsh**
20	aacherine	ah-**chreen**
50	khamsine	khum-**seen**
100	milla	**mee**-yah
200	millatein	mee-ya **tayn**

USEFUL PHRASES

Do you speak English?	ouesh tat tkelem belinglisia	**wesh** tet te-**kel**-lem **blin**-gliz-**ee**-yah?
I don't understand.	ma fahemtsh	ma-**f'emtch**
I don't know.	ma naarf	ma-**nahr**-ef
I'm lost.	ana tilift	ahna t'-lift
I am American (for man).	ana amriqui	ahna am-ree-kee
I am American (for woman).	ana amriqiya	ahna am-**ree**-kee-yah
I am British.	ana inglisi	anna in-ge-**lee**-zee
What is this?	shnou hada	**shnoo** ha-da
Where is . . . ?	Fein?	fayn?
the train station	mahatat el tren	ma-ha-**tat** eh-tren
the city bus station	mahatat tobis	**ma-ha**-tat **toh**-beese
the intracity bus station	mahatat al cairan	**ma**-ha-tat al-kah-ee-rahn
the airport	el l'aéroport	el lehr-oh-por
the hotel	el l'hôtel	el l'oh-**teel**
the café	l'khaoua	al-kah-**hou**-wah
the restaurant	el restaurant	el rest-oh-**rahn**
the telephone	tilifoon	**til-lee**-foon
the hospital	el l'hôpital	el l'oh-bee-tahl
the post office	l'bosta	**al**-bost-**a**
the restroom	w.c.	**vay**-say
the pharmacy	pharmacien	far-**ma-cienn**
the bank	l'banca	**al** bann-**ka**
the embassy	sifara	**see**-far-**ra**
I would like a room.	bghit bit	**bgheet**-beet
I would like to buy . . .	bghit nechri	bgheet-nesh-**ree**
cigarettes	garro	**gahr**-oh

a city map	kharretta del medina	kha-**ray**-ta del m'**dee**-nah
a road map	kharretta del bled	kha-**ray**-ta del blad
How much is it?	bi sha hal hada	**bshal hah**-da?
It's expensive.	ghaliya	**gha**-lee-ya
A little	shwiya	**shwee**-ya
A lot	bizzaf	bzzef
Enough	baraka	**ba**-rah-ka
I am ill. (a man)	ana marid	ah-na ma-**reed**
I am ill. (a woman)	ana marida	**ah**-na ma-**reed**-ah
I need a doctor.	bghit doctor	bgheet dok-**tohr**
I have a problem.	aandi mouchkila	**ahn**-dee moosh-**kee**-la
left	lessar	**lis**-sar
right	leemen	**lee**-men
Help!	awni!	**aow**-nee
Fire!	laafiya!	**lah**-fee-ya
Caution!/Look out!	aindek!	**aann**-deck

DINING

I would like . . .	bghit	bgheet
water	l'ma	l'mah
bread	l'khobz	l'khobz
vegetables	khoudra	**khu**-dra
meat	l'hamm	l'hahm
fruits	l'fawakeh	el fah-**weh**-kee
cakes	l'haloua	el **hahl**-oo-wa
tea	atay	**ah**-tay
coffee	kahoua	**kah**-wa
a fork	forchette	for-**shet**
a spoon	maalka	**mahl**-ka
a knife	mousse	moose

Travel Smart Morocco

WORD OF MOUTH

"[I] would tell you that the best bank to use esp[ecially] for every visitor to Morocco—[and] the one that you'll never face any troubles with—is BMCE Bank."

–imortaltravels

www.fodors.com/community

GETTING HERE AND AROUND

BY AIR

Morocco is serviced by major airlines to and from North America and Europe. Consider flying if traveling long distances within Morocco. If, for instance, you want to concentrate on the southern oasis valleys, land in Casablanca, fly directly to Ouarzazate, and rent a car there. Domestic carriers may require reconfirmation to hold your seat. Remember to place this call ahead of time, or ask your hotel to do it for you. A call to the airline will also suffice to reconfirm your outbound seat. The national airline, Royal Air Maroc, flies internationally to 74 cities in 22 countries and between 12 cities within Morocco. Look for promotions, including exceptional deals every Thursday, on the "Booking & Special Offers" category on the airline Web site.

AIRPORTS

Casablanca's Mohammed V Airport (CMN) is the main entry point for nonstop flights from the United States, and U.S. travelers can easily connect to other destinations throughout the country on frequent domestic flights. But U.S. travelers can also reach Morocco through Europe; hubs such as London, Paris, Amsterdam, Madrid, and Frankfurt have excellent connections. A number of airlines from Europe offer regularly scheduled direct flights into Marrakesh, Agadir, Fez, Ouarzazate, Rabat, and Tangier. Agadir (AGA), Al Hoceima (AHU), Dakhla (VIL), Essaouira (ESU), Fez (FEZ), Ifrane (GMFI), Laayoune (EUN), Marrakesh (RAK), Ouarzazate (OZZ), Oujda (OUD), Nador (NDR), Rabat (RBA), Tangier (TNG), and Tetouan (TTU) are the other primary airports in Morocco that have regularly scheduled domestic or international service. You can often arrange connecting flights to these cities from Casablanca if you are flying from the United States. Another popular way is to enter Morocco by connecting through a major European hub such as London, Paris, Amsterdam, or Madrid, from where you can get good connecting service to several other airports in Morocco.

Airport Information **Casablanca Mohammed V Airport** ✉ *Office National des Aéroports* ☎ *0522/53–90–40* 🌐 *www.onda.org.ma.* **Moroccan Airport Authority** ☎ *0522/53–90–40* 🌐 *www.onda.ma/onda/an.*

GROUND TRANSPORTATION

Office National des Chemins de Fer, the national rail company, has a station directly under Casablanca's Mohammed V Airport. Trains come and go between 6:30 am and 11 pm and make travel to and from the airport very easy and hassle-free. The ride to the city takes 30 minutes. Taxis are always available outside arrivals at the Casablanca airport; fares to the city are approximately 250 DH. There's also a shuttle bus to Casablanca.

Contacts **Office National des Chemins de Fer** ☎ *0890/20–30–40* 🌐 *www.oncf.ma.*

FLIGHTS

Royal Air Maroc, which has a codeshare partnership with Delta and Air France, offers nonstop flights from New York City to Casablanca every morning and evening (as well as daily service from Montréal); these flights are convenient and dependable, and connect with domestic flights to other Moroccan destinations. Many other airlines, including American and British Airways (partnered with Iberia), KLM, and Lufthansa, offer flights that connect in Europe; it's worth shopping around for deals if you don't mind stopping along the way.

Royal Air Maroc and other major airlines offer daily direct or one-stop flights to Agadir, Casablanca, Fez, Marrakesh, Rabat, and Tangier from nearly all western European countries. In addition, discount airlines Easy Jet and Ryan Air fly to

Marrakesh, Casablanca, Fez, and Tangier from many European cities, including London and Paris.

Airline Contacts **Air France** ☎ *800/237-2747* 🌐 *www.airfrance.com.* **British Midland International (bmi).** London Heathrow's second largest airline has flights to Casablanca and Marrakesh. ☎ *44/1332/64-8181 International, open 24 hours Mon.-Sun., 800/788-0555 in the U.S.* 🌐 *www.flybmi.com.* **Brussels Airlines.** Brussels Airlines is a new low-cost airline operating from Brussels, Belgium, with direct flights to Agadir and Marrakesh. ✉ *Brussels Airlines General Aviation zone, b.house, Building 26, Brussels Airport, Diegem, Belgium* ☎ *322/723-23-45 Reservations, 322/723-23-62 After-sales service or Web helpdesk* 🌐 *www.brusselsairlines.com.* **Delta** ☎ *800/221-1212 for U.S. reservations, 800/241-4141 for international reservations* 🌐 *www.delta.com.* **Easy Jet** ☎ *(44) 0871/244-2366 in the U.S., 0871/244-2366 in the UK* 🌐 *www.easyjet.com.* **Iberia.** Iberia partners with Royal Air Maroc to offer numerous flights via Spain. Frequent-flier programs are also linked. ☎ *800/722-4642 in the U.S.* 🌐 *www.iberia.com.* **KLM.** KLM flies to Rabat and Casablanca. ☎ *800/618-0104 General reservations in the U.S., 866/434-0320 Service Center for online reservations in the U.S.* 🌐 *www.klm.com.* **Royal Air Maroc** ☎ *(212) 0522/48-97-97 in Morocco, 800/344-6726 in the U.S., 0207/43-94-361 in the UK* 🌐 *www.royalairmaroc.com.*

BY BOAT

If you're traveling from Spain, you'll need to take a ferry across the Strait of Gibraltar. The most popular crossing is from Algeciras, Spain, to Tangier. Algeciras to Ceuta (Spain inside mainland Morocco) is a popular and shorter route. High-speed ferries make the trip in about 30 to 40 minutes. Unfortunately, disembarking in Tangier can be a traumatic way to arrive in Morocco. You're likely to be greeted by unpleasant characters who won't cease to harass you until you've parted company with some money, or at best suffered some verbal abuse. Never admit to the hoodlums that you're visiting Morocco for the first time.

Information **Comarit Ferry** ☎ *0522/29-33-29, 0522/29-33-81 in Morocco* 🌐 *www.comarit.com.* **Southern Ferries Ltd** ☎ *0844/815-7785 in the UK* 🌐 *www.southernferries.co.uk/.* **Trasmediterránia** ☎ *902/45-46-45 in Spain* 🌐 *www.trasmediterranea.es.*

BY BUS

For cities not served by trains (mainly those in the south), buses are a good alternative. They're relatively frequent, and seats are usually available.

Compagnie de Transports Marocains (CTM), the national bus company, runs trips to most areas in the country and guarantees your seat and luggage service. No-smoking rules are enforced (the exception is the driver who sometimes smokes out his side window). These buses stop occasionally for bathroom and smoking breaks, but be sure to stay near the bus, as they have been known to leave quickly, stranding people without their luggage in unfamiliar places.

Another major bus company, Supratours, is connected to Morocco's national rail service. It offers comfortable service to major cities. Supratours has ticket counters at each train station and allows travelers to extend their trip past places where the train service ends. Departure times are designed to coordinate with the arrival of trains.

There are a number of smaller bus companies, called "souk buses." They're the only way to get to really rural areas not served by larger companies. They are neither comfortable nor clean. You're much better off shelling out a few extra dirhams for the punctual and pleasant CTM or Supratours buses unless you're going to out-of-the-way places only served by small companies.

In each city the bus station—known as the *gare routière*—is generally near the edge of town. Some larger cities have separate CTM stations. Ignore the posted departure times on the walls—they're never updated. Ask at the ticket booth when the next bus leaves to your chosen destination. There's nothing wrong with checking out a bus before you buy your ticket, as some are dilapidated and uncomfortable. The *greeson* will sell you a ticket, take you to the bus, and put your luggage underneath (you should tip a few dirhams for this).

Buy tickets at the bus station prior to departure (ideally a day ahead of time when you can); payment is by cash only. Tickets are only sold for the seats available, so once you have a ticket you have a seat. Other than tickets, there are no reservations. Often, tickets only go on sale an hour before departure. Inquire at the bus station for departure times; there are no printed schedules and the displayed schedules are not accurate. Children up to age four travel free. Car seats and bassinets are not usually available for children.

FARES

Fares are very cheap (currently around 20 DH for a one-hour journey to 250 DH for daylong trips). Luggage is usually charged by weight. Expect to pay no more than 10 DH per piece. Additionally, most CTM stations have inexpensive luggage storage facilities.

Bus Information **CTM** (*Compagnie de Transports Marocains*). ✉ *Km 13.5, Rte. de Casa-RabatSidi Bernoussi, Casablanca* ☎ *0522/75–36–58* 🌐 *www.ctm.co.ma.*
Supratours ☎ *0524/43–55–25 Marrakesh, Av. Hassan II, 0524/42–17–69 Marrakesh, Nouvelle Gare, 0535/65–26–22 Fez, 0522/40–98–27 Casablanca, 0537/77–93–27 Rabat, 0524/47–53–17 Essaouira, 0535/52– 72–85 Meknès* 🌐 *www.supratours.ma.*

BY CAR

A car is not necessary if your trip is confined to major cities, but sometimes it's the best and only way to explore Morocco's mountainous areas, small coastal towns, and rural areas such as the Middle or High Atlas.

Driving in Morocco is relatively easy and a fantastic way to see the country. Roads are generally in good shape, and mile markers and road signs are easy to read (they're always written in Arabic and French). Remember that small mountain villages are still only reached by *piste* (gravel path), and that these rough roads can damage a smaller car. Watch for children selling herbs, fruit, oil, and honey on the side of the road—trying to make a sale, they literally dart into traffic if they see a foreigner in a car.

Hiring a car and driver is an excellent but more expensive way to really get into the crevices of the country. Drivers also serve as protectors from potential faux guides and tourist scams. Be warned, however, that they themselves will often be looking for commissions and might steer you toward particular carpet sellers and tourist shops. Be sure to negotiate an acceptable price before you take off. Expect to pay at minimum between 1,000 DH to 1,500 DH for a private tour, with prices higher depending on itinerary. Drivers must be licensed and official, so be sure to ask for credentials to avoid any unpleasantness down the road.

BOOKING YOUR TRIP

The cars most commonly available in Morocco are small European sedans, such as Renaults, Peugeots, and Fiats. Expect to pay at least 350 DH a day for these. Many companies also rent four-wheel-drive vehicles, a boon for touring the Atlas Mountains and oasis valleys; expect to pay around 2,500 DH a day for a new Land Cruiser. A 20% VAT (value-added tax) is levied on rental rates. Companies will often let you rent for the day or by the kilometer.

Note that you can negotiate the rental of a taxi with driver just about anywhere in Morocco for no more than the cost of a rental car from a major agency. Normally you negotiate an inclusive price for a given itinerary. The advantage is that you don't have to navigate; the disadvantage is that the driver may have his own ideas about where you should go and will probably not speak English. For less haggling, local tour operators can furnish vehicles with multilingual drivers at a fairly high daily package rate.

The best place to rent a car is Casablanca's airport, as the rental market is very competitive here—most of the cars are new, and you can often negotiate a discount. Local companies will give you a much better price for the same car than the international agencies (even after the latter have offered "discounts"). Most of the agencies we recommend have offices at Casablanca's airport; most have other branches in Casablanca itself, as well as in Rabat and Marrakesh or Fez. To get the best deal, book through a travel agent, who will shop around.

Rental Agencies **Europ Car** ☎ *0522/53-91-61 Casablanca-Mohammed V Airport, 0535/62-65-45 Fez-Saiss Airport, 0524/43-77-18 Marrakesh-Menara Airport, 0537/724141 Rabat-Sale Airport, 0539/941938 Tangier Ibn Battouta Airport, 0539/930108 Tangier Maritime Port* ⊕ *www.europcar.com.* **National Car Rental** ☎ *0522/53-97-16 Casablanca airport, 0524/43-77-18 Marrakesh airport, 0535/62-65-45 Fez airport* ⊕ *www.nationalcar.com.* **Sixt Car** ☎ *0522/53-80-99 Casablanca airport* ⊕ *www.sixt.com.* **Thrifty Car** ☎ *0522/53-20-01 Casablanca airport* ⊕ *www.thrifty.com.*

GASOLINE

Gas is readily available, if relatively expensive. The gas that most cars use is known as *super*, the lower-octane variety as *essence*. Unleaded fuel (*sans plomb*) is widely available but not currently necessary for local cars; it costs around 9.5 DH a liter. Diesel fuel (*diesel*) is significantly cheaper. Most gas stations provide full service; tipping is optional. Some stations take credit cards.

PARKING

When parking in the city, make sure that you're in a parking zone or the authorities will put a locking device on one of your wheels. In parking lots, give the *gardien* a small tip upon leaving. Some cities have introduced the European system of prepaid tickets from a machine, valid for a certain duration.

ROAD CONDITIONS

Road conditions are generally very good. A network of toll highways (*autoroutes*) runs from Casablanca to Larache (near Tangier) and east from Rabat to Meknès and Fez, and from Casablanca to Settat (south toward Marrakesh). These autoroutes are much safer than the lesser roads. There are periodic tollbooths with tolls ranging from 5 DH to 20 DH.

On rural roads expect the occasional flock of sheep or goats to cross the road at inopportune times. In the south you'll see road signs warning of periodic camel crossings as well. In the mountains, side-pointing arrows designate curves in the road. However, be aware that some dangerous curves come unannounced. Also, in the countryside you're much more likely to encounter potholes, narrow roads, and speeding taxi drivers.

Night driving outside city centers requires extreme caution. Many roads are not lit. Beware of inadequate or unfamiliar lighting at night, particularly on trucks—it's not uncommon for trucks to have red lights in the front or white lights in the rear. Ubiquitous ancient mopeds rarely have working lights or reflectors.

ROADSIDE EMERGENCIES

In case of an accident on the road, dial 177 outside cities and 19 in urban areas for police. For firemen and emergency medical services, dial 15. As emergency numbers in Morocco may not be answered quickly, it's wise to hail help from street police if possible. When available, it's also more effective to summon a taxi to reach medical help instead of relying on ambulance service.

RULES OF THE ROAD

Traffic moves on the right side of the road, as in the United States and Europe. There are two main rules in Morocco; the first is "priority to the right," an old French rule meaning that in traffic circles you must yield to traffic entering from the right. The second is "every man for himself."

You must carry your car registration and insurance certificate at all times (these documents are always supplied with rental cars). Morocco's speed limits, enforced by radar, are 100 kph (63 mph) on autoroutes and 40 or 60 kph (25 or 37 mph) in towns. The penalty for speeding is a 400 DH fine payable to the issuing officer or confiscation of your driver's license.

It is mandatory to wear seat belts for both drivers and passengers. Failure to do so will result in a hefty fine. Talking on cell phones while driving is also illegal.

BY TAXI

Moroccan taxis take two forms: *petit* taxis, small taxis that travel within city limits, and *grand* taxis, large taxis that travel between cities. Drivers usually wait until the taxi is full before departing.

Petits taxis are color-coded according to city—in Casablanca and Fez they're red, in Rabat they're blue, in Marrakesh they're beige, and so on. These can be hailed anywhere but can take a maximum of three passengers. The fare is metered and not expensive: usually 5 DH to 30 DH for a short- or medium-length trip. Taxis often pick up additional passengers en route, so if you can't find an empty cab, try hailing a taxi with one or two passengers.

Grand taxis travel fixed routes between cities and in the country. One person can sit in front with the driver, and four sit, very cramped, in the back. Don't expect air-conditioning, luxurious interior, or even fully functioning windows. Fares for these shared rides are inexpensive, sometimes as little as 5 DH per person for a short trip. You can also charter a grand taxi for trips between cities, but you need to negotiate a price in advance.

BY TRAIN

If you're sticking mainly to the four imperial cities—Fez, Meknès, Rabat, and Marrakesh—you're best off taking the train and using petits taxis in the cities. Morocco's punctual rail system, Office National des Chemins de Fer, serves mostly the north. From Casablanca and Rabat the network runs east via Meknès and Fez to Oujda, north to Tangier, and south to Marrakesh. Bus connections link trains with Tetouan, Nador, and Agadir, and you can buy through tickets covering both segments before you leave.

Trains are divided into first-class (*première classe*) and second-class (*deuxième classe*). First-class is a very good buy compared to its counterpart in Europe, but second-class is comfortable, too. Long-distance trains seat six people to a compartment in first-class, eight to a compartment in second-class.

Fares are relatively inexpensive compared to those in Europe. A first-class ticket from Casablanca to Fez costs 160 DH. You can buy train tickets at any station up to six days in advance. Purchasing your ticket on the train is pricier and can only be done in cash. Kids travel at half price on Moroccan trains.

Smoking is prohibited by law on public transport, but in practice people smoke in the corridors or in the areas between coaches.

Information **Office National des Chemins de Fer** ☎ *0890/20–30–40* 🌐 *www.oncf.ma.*

ESSENTIALS

ACCOMMODATIONS

Accommodations in Morocco range from opulent to extremely spare, with everything in between. Hotels can be on a par with those of Europe and the United States, but the farther you venture off the beaten path, the farther you might feel from five-star comforts. Particularly in some of the smaller towns and villages, hotels lack amenities. Take a closer look, though—these hotels often make up for a lack of luxury with genuine charm, character, and, most of all, location.

RIADS

Book a room in or rent an entire well-furnished *riad* (a traditional house) in the medinas of the most-visited cities, such as Fez, Marrakesh, and Essaouira, as well as in smaller seaside towns such as Asilah and Oualidia. This is a unique opportunity to experience traditional Moroccan architecture and live like royalty of old.

Riad Rentals **Marrakech Medina** ✉ *102, Rue Dar el Bacha, Souika sidi abd al Aziz, Medina, Marrakesh* ☎ *0526/10–04–93* 🌐 *www.marrakech-medina.com* ⏲ *09h00* ⏲ *22h00.* **Moroccan Villas** ☎ *0871/711–33–72 in the UK only, 0033/467–360–554 from outside the UK* 🌐 *www.moroccovillas.com* ⏲ *9 am Mon.–Fri.* ⏲ *6 pm Mon.–Fri.* **Riad Selection** ☎ *(39) 0421/33–74–38 in Italy* 🌐 *www.riadselection.com.* **Splendia** ☎ *866/986–5844* 🌐 *www.splendia.com/morocco.php.*

HOTELS

Hotels are classified by the Moroccan government with one to five stars, plus an added category for five-star luxury hotels. In hotels with three or more stars, all rooms have private bathrooms, and there is an on-site bar. Air-conditioning is common in three-star hotels in Fez and Marrakesh and in all five-star hotels. Standards do vary, though; it's possible to find a nice two-star hotel or, occasionally, a four-star hotel without hot water. In the same vein, hotels that are beneath the star system altogether—"unclassified"—can also be satisfactory.

High season in Morocco is generally from mid-December to mid-January and mid-March to mid-April. Early June, before intense summer heat, is also considered high season. In the Atlas region, January and February attract many visitors for winter sports. In the Sahara, September through November are the most popular months. Many properties charge peak-season rates for your entire stay even if your travel dates straddle peak and nonpeak seasons. As with everything in Morocco, hotel rates may be negotiable; always ask if there are any specials.

Most hotels in Morocco now accept email requests for reservations. A few smaller establishments and family-owned riads may still require a fax confirmation. Check with your hotel directly upon booking to verify which method is accepted.

COMMUNICATIONS

INTERNET

Internet use has exploded in Morocco, and you'll find cybercafés everywhere, even in the smaller towns. On average they charge 10 DH to 20 DH an hour. Wi-Fi is becoming increasingly available in hotels and upscale cafés, so it's even easier to keep in touch with friends and family if you bring your laptop, tablet computer, or smart phone.

Take the same security precautions you would anywhere with your electronics, and always use a surge protector.

PHONES

The country code for Morocco is 212. The area codes are as follows: Agadir, 0528; Casablanca, 0522; Settat and El Jadida, 0523; Marrakesh, 0524; Fez and Meknès, 0535; Oujda, 0536; Rabat, 0537; Tangier, 0539; Taroudant, 0528; Tetouan, 0539.

When dialing a Moroccan number from overseas, drop the initial 0 from the area code. To call locally, within the area code, just dial the number (local numbers are six digits).

For international calls from Morocco, dial 00 followed by the country code. Country codes: United States and Canada, 1; United Kingdom, 44; Australia, 61; New Zealand, 64. There are nine digits in local numbers, starting with "0." Note that when calling from out-of-country into Morocco you always drop the "0," and the number becomes nine digits. After the zero there is a two-number area code. Numbers that start with 01, 04, 05, 06 or 07 are mobile phones.

CALLING WITHIN MOROCCO

Public phones are located on the street, and you must purchase a telecarte, or phone card, to use them. They come in denominations from 10 DH to 100 DH. You insert the card and then place your local or international call.

Téléboutiques are everywhere in Morocco. These little shops have individual coin-operated phones. You feed the machine with dirhams and make local calls. You can also make international calls by calling directory assistance or calling directly.

Access directory assistance by dialing 160 from anywhere in the country. Many operators speak English, and they all speak French.

CALLING OUTSIDE MOROCCO

To call the United States directly from Morocco, call 001, then the area code and phone number. Calls from Morocco are expensive, but rates are cut by 20% if you call after midnight. The cheapest option in direct international dialing is to call from a public phone, using a telecarte.

Both AT&T and MCI have local access numbers for making international calls. These are especially useful if you already have calling cards with these companies.

Contacts **AT&T Direct Access** ☎ *00/211-0011 in Morocco.* **MCI** ☎ *00/211-0012 in Morocco.*

CALLING CARDS

Phone cards for use in public phones can be purchased at any téléboutique, librarie, photocopy shop, tobacco shop, or small convenience store. Maroc Telecom and Meditel phone cards, to be used with mobile phones, can also be purchased in these places in denominations of 20, 30, 50, 100, 200, and 600 DH.

MOBILE PHONES

GSM mobile phones with international roaming capability work well in the cities and along major communication routes. Roaming fees can be steep, however: 99¢ a minute is considered reasonable. It's almost always cheaper to send a text message than to make a call, since text messages have a very low set fee (often less than 25¢).

Alternatively, if you just want to make local calls, you can buy a new SIM card in Morocco with a prepaid service plan (note that your provider will have to unlock your phone for you to use a different SIM card). You'll then have a local number and can make local calls at local rates. Morocco currently has two major mobile-phone companies, Maroc Telecom and Meditel. Both offer prepaid calling cards and phone sales. You can even buy a simple phone for as little as 100 DH. If you're spending more than a few weeks in the country or traveling in remote spots, these are indispensable.

Contacts **Cellular Abroad.** Cellular Abroad rents and sells GMS phones and sells SIM cards that work in individual or multiple countries. ☎ *800/287-5072 within the U.S., 310/862-7100 outside the U.S.* 🌐 *www.cellularabroad.com.* **Mobal.** Mobal rents mobiles and sells GSM phones (starting at $29) that will operate in 190 countries. Per-call rates vary throughout the world. ☎ *888/888-9162* 🌐 *www.mobalrental.com* ⏲ *Open 24/7.* **Planet Fone.** Planet Fone rents cell phones and international mobile broadband data keys, but it has expensive per-minute rates for usage. ☎ *888/988-4777* 🌐 *www.planetfone.com.*

CUSTOMS AND DUTIES

Customs duties are very high in Morocco, and many items are subject to various taxes that can total 80%. The following may be imported without customs duty: 5 grams of perfume, 1 liter of wine, 200 cigarettes or 50 cigars or 400 grams of tobacco. Large electronic items will be taxed. (It's possible to import large electronics—such as laptop computers—temporarily without tax, but this will be marked in your passport, and the next time you leave the country you must take the equipment with you.) It's always easier to take things in person instead of having them sent to you and cleared through customs at the post office, where even the smallest items will be taxed.

The importation and exportation of Moroccan dirhams is strictly forbidden. There is no limit for how much foreign currency you import; however, when leaving Morocco, you are limited to changing back only 50% of the amount you exchanged at the beginning of your vacation. This transaction will be questioned at the Bureau de Change in airports, hotels, and banks, often with the specific demand to see verification of any currency transactions made during your stay. Keep all currency exchange receipts on hand, or you may bring home more dirhams than you would like as an unwanted souvenir.

Information **Government of Morocco Customs** ☎ *080/100–7000* 🌐 *www.douane.gov.ma* ⏲ *Mon.–Thurs., 8:30–4:30.* **U.S. Customs and Border Protection** ☎ *877/227–5511 for general inquiries, 703/525–4200 for international callers* 🌐 *www.cbp.gov.*

EATING OUT

Moroccan cuisine is delectable. Dining establishments range from outdoor food stalls to elegant restaurants, the latter disproportionately expensive, with prices approaching those in Europe. Simpler, much cheaper restaurants abound. Between cities, roadside restaurants commonly offer delicious tagines, couscous, or grilled kebabs with bread and salad; on the coast, fried fish is an excellent buy, and you can often choose your meal from the daily catch. Marrakesh and Fez are the places for wonderful Moroccan feasts in fairy-tale surroundings, and Casablanca has a lively and diverse dining scene. The restaurants we list are the cream of the crop in each price range and cuisine type.

MEALS AND MEALTIMES

Moroccan hotels normally serve a Continental breakfast (*petit déjeuner continental*), often included in the room rate. If it is not, you can buy an equivalent meal at any of numerous cafés at a much lower price. The more-expensive hotels have elaborate buffets. Hotel breakfasts are usually served from about 7 am to 10 or 10:30. Lunch, typically the most leisurely meal of the day, is served between noon and 2:30. Hotels and restaurants begin dinner service at 7:30, though crowds are on the thin side until 8:30 or 9. In a Moroccan home you probably won't sit down to eat until 9 or 10 pm. Restaurants stay open later in the more cosmopolitan city centers.

Lunch (*déjeuner*) in Morocco tends to be a large meal, as in France. A typical lunch menu consists of salad, a main course with meat and vegetables, and fruit. In restaurants this is generally available à la carte. On Friday the traditional lunch meal is a heaping bowl of couscous topped with meats and vegetables.

At home, people tend to have afternoon mint tea, then a light supper, often with soup. Dinner (*diner*) in French and international restaurants is generally à la carte; you may select as light or heavy a meal as you like. Many of the fancier Moroccan restaurants serve fixed-price feasts, with at least three courses and sometimes upwards of five. If you're a vegetarian, or have other dietary concerns, state this when you make a reservation; many restaurants will prepare special dishes with advance notice.

Lunch and dinner are served communal style, on one big platter. Moroccans use their right hands to sop up the juices in these dishes with bread. Bread is used as an all-purpose utensil to pull up little pieces of vegetables and meat. In restaurants bread will always be offered in a basket. Utensils will be offered to foreigners. All restaurants, no matter how basic, have sinks for washing hands before and after your meal.

Unless otherwise noted, the restaurants listed in this guide are open daily for lunch and dinner.

Sunday is the most common day for restaurant closings.

During Ramadan, everything changes. All cafés and nearly all restaurants are closed during the day; the *ftir,* or "break fast," is served precisely at sunset, and most people take their main meal of the night, the *souk hour,* at about 2 am. The main hotels, however, continue to serve meals to non-Muslim guests as usual.

PAYING

For price charts deciphering the price categories of restaurants and hotels, see "Planning" at the beginning of each chapter. Only the pricier restaurants take credit cards; MasterCard and Visa are the most widely accepted. Outside the largest cities you'll rarely be able to use your credit card.

RESERVATIONS AND DRESS

Reservations are always a good idea: we mention them only when they're essential or not accepted. Book as far ahead as you can, and reconfirm as soon as you arrive. Jacket and tie are never required.

WINES, BEER, AND SPIRITS

Although alcohol is forbidden by Islam, it is produced in the country. The more-expensive restaurants and hotels are licensed to serve alcohol. Morocco produces some red wines in the vicinity of Meknès, and the national beer is Flag Special. Heineken is produced under license in Casablanca. Apart from restaurants, drinks are available at the bars of hotels and lounges classified by the government with three stars or more. Supermarkets like Marjane, Label Vie, and Acima sell alcohol to foreigners with proper identification (except during Ramadan, when liquor shelves are restocked with tasteful displays of chocolates and dates). Little shops in small towns also sell beer and spirits.

ELECTRICITY

To use electric-powered equipment purchased in the United States or Canada, bring a converter and adapter, though many electronics these days are dual-voltage; check your AC adapter to see if yours is. The electrical current in Morocco is 220 volts, 50 cycles alternating current (AC); wall outlets take the two-pin plug found in Continental Europe. Power surges do occur.

Contacts **Global Electric & Phone Directory.** A comprehensive Web site for global electrical and phone information. 🌐 *www.kropla.com.* **Walkabout Travel Gear.** Walkabout Travel Gear has a good coverage of electricity under "adapters." ☎ *800/852–7085* 🌐 *www.walkabouttravelgear.com.*

EMERGENCIES

Although pharmacies maintain normal hours, a system is in place that ensures that one is always open. You'll find a schedule of late-closing pharmacies posted on the pharmacy door or the adjacent wall. Pharmacies are easy to spot, just look for the neon green crescent-moon symbol.

HEALTH

Although Moroccan water is generally safe to drink (in cities at least), to be on the safe side, it's better to drink only bottled water and canned or bottled soft drinks. Look for the blue-and-white labels of Morocco's most popular bottled mineral water called Sidi Ali. Try to resist the temptation to add ice to room-temperature beverages. Use reasonable precautions and eat only fully cooked foods, but if you have problems, mild cases of traveler's diarrhea may respond to Imodium (known generically as loperamide) or Pepto-Bismol. Be sure to drink plenty of fluids; if you can't keep fluids down, seek medical help immediately.

In summer, heatstroke and dehydration are big risks to travelers and Moroccans alike. Be sure to drink plenty of water and rest in the shade any chance you get. If you do get dehydrated, pharmacies sell rehydration salts called Biosel. **TIP→ Sunscreen is widely available in pharmacies and specialty cosmetic stores but is outrageously expensive. Pack your own.**

Note that scorpions, snakes, and biting insects live in the desert regions. These rarely pose a problem, but it wouldn't hurt to shake out your shoes in the morning. Dog bites pose the risk of rabies; always get a rabies vaccination at the earliest possible opportunity if you are bitten. Fez has seen an inordinate amount of stray cats within the medina. Avoid petting these cute critters that weave in and out of narrow passageways, feeding on refuse.

Medical care is available but varies in quality. The larger cities have excellent private clinics. The rest of the county depends on government-run smaller clinics and dispensaires. The cost of medical care is low—an office consultation and exam will cost 250 DH. Seeing a specialist can cost up to 500 DH. While medical facilities can be quite adequate in urban areas, English-speaking medical help is rare.

OVER-THE-COUNTER REMEDIES

Nearly all medicines, including antibiotics and painkillers, are available over the counter at Moroccan pharmacies. Aspirin is sold as Aspro; ibuprofen is sold as Analgyl, Algantyl, or Tabalon. Acetaminophen, the generic equivalent of Tylenol, is sold as Doliprane and is widely available.

HOURS OF OPERATION

Moroccan banks are open Monday to Thursday 8:30 to noon and 2 to 4. On Friday, the day of prayer, they close slightly earlier in the morning and open a little later in the afternoon. Post offices are open Monday to Thursday 8:30 to noon and 2:30 to 6:30, Friday from 8:30 to 11:30 and 3 to 6:30. Government offices have similar schedules.

Museums are generally open 9 to noon and 2:30 to 6. Standard pharmacy hours are 8:30–12:30 and 3–9:30. Your hotel can help you locate which pharmacies are open around the clock. Shops are open every day except Sunday from about 9 to 1 and from 3 or 4 to 7.

Remember that during Ramadan the above schedules change, often with the midday closing omitted. On Friday many businesses close down for the day or for the noon prayer.

HOLIDAYS

The two most important religious holidays in Morocco are Aïd el-Fitr, which marks the end of the monthlong Ramadan fast, and Aïd el-Adha or Aïd el-Kebir, the sheep-sacrifice feast commemorating the prophet Ibrahim's absolution from the obligation to sacrifice his son. Both are two-day festivals during which all offices, banks, and museums are closed. The other religious holiday is the one-day Aïd el-Mouloud, commemorating the birthday of the prophet Mohammed. The dates change each year, so check ahead.

Ramadan (which lasts for 30 days, beginning on July 20 in 2012, and becomes progressively earlier in the year as the decade progresses) is not a holiday per se, but it does change the pace of life. Because the Muslim calendar is lunar, the dates for Ramadan and other religious holidays shift each year.

The most important political holiday is Aïd el-Arch, or Throne Day (July 30), which commemorates the coronation of

King Mohammed VI. Morocco's other holidays are as follows: January 1, New Year's Day; January 11, anniversary of the proclamation of Moroccan independence; May 1, Labor Day; May 23, National Day; August 14, Oued ed-Dahab, otherwise known as Allegiance Day; August 20, anniversary of the revolution of the king and the people (against the French); August 21, Youth Day; November 6, commemoration of the Green March, Morocco's claim on the Western Sahara in 1975; November 18, Independence Day.

MAIL

Post offices are available everywhere and are visible by their yellow signs. Outgoing airmail is reliable. Note that if you mail letters at the main sorting office of any city (usually situated on Avenue Mohammed V), they will arrive several days sooner than if you mail them from elsewhere, sometimes in as little as three days to Europe. Airmail letters to North America take between five and 14 days; to Europe between three and 10 days; and to Australasia about two weeks.

For a 20-gram airmail letter or postcard, rates are 10 DH to the United States or Canada, 8 DH to the United Kingdom, and 14 DH to Australia or New Zealand.

SHIPPING PACKAGES

Within Morocco, the Express Mail Service (EMS, or Poste Rapide) offers overnight delivery from main post offices to major cities. There is also same-day service between Rabat and Casablanca. The international EMS takes three to five days from Morocco to Europe. DHL is quicker but more than double the price. UPS operates only in Casablanca. FedEx has locations in Agadir, Casablanca, Fez, Marrakesh, Rabat, and Tangier.

Sending packages out of the country is easy enough. Go to the Colis Postaux (parcel post office; one in each town), where you can also buy boxes. You'll need to fill in some forms and show the package to customs officials before wrapping it. Airmail parcels reach North America in about two weeks, Europe in about 10 days. DHL offers a special rate for handicraft items shipped overseas, and some carpet stores can arrange shipping, though some scams have been reported whereby a substandard carpet is shipped to your home, so proceed with caution.

Express Services **DHL** ✉ *40, Av. de France, Rabat* ☎ *0537/77–99–34, 0537/77–99–35* 🌐 *www.dhl.com* ✉ *52, Bd. Abdelmoumen, Casablanca* ☎ *0522/97–20–20 DHL Express Service Center* 🌐 *www.dhl-ma.com.* **FedEx** ✉ *313, Bd. Mohammed V, Casablanca* ☎ *0522/45–80–00 Globex Customer Service, 0522/45–80–41 Globex Customer Service* 🌐 *www.fedex.com/ma.* **UPS** ✉ *210, Bd. Mohammed Zerktouni, Casablanca* ☎ *0522/48–36–36* 📠 *0522/48–35–56* 🌐 *www.ups.com.*

MONEY

Most costs in Morocco are low compared to those in both North America and Europe. Fruit and vegetables, public transportation, and labor are very cheap. (Cars, gasoline, and electronic goods, on the other hand, are relatively pricey.) Sample costs are in U.S. dollars:

Meal in cheap restaurant, $5 to $8; meal in expensive restaurant, $25 to $50; liter of bottled water, 65¢; cup of coffee, 70¢; museum admission, $1.50; liter of gasoline, $1.20; short taxi ride, $1 to $3. Prices throughout this guide are given for adults; reduced fees are usually available for children and large groups, but not students or senior citizens.

Because the dirham's value experiences some flux, some of the more upscale hotels, tour operators, and activity specialists geared towards tourists publish their prices in euros, pounds, and sometimes even dollars, but accept dirhams (these places also usually take credit cards).

ATMS AND BANKS

You'll usually get a better rate of exchange at an ATM than you will at a currency-exchange office, hotel, or even international bank, even accounting for the fees your bank may charge. Reliable ATMs are attached to banks in major cities, and there's one in the arrivals hall at Casablanca's airport. BMCE and Wafabank belong to the Cirrus and Plus networks.

CREDIT CARDS

Inform your credit-card company before you travel, especially if you're going abroad and don't travel internationally very often. Otherwise, the credit-card company might put a hold on your card owing to unusual activity—not a fun thing halfway through your trip. Record all your credit-card numbers and keep them in a safe place, so you're prepared should something go wrong.

Although it's usually cheaper (and safer) to use a credit card abroad for large purchases (so you can cancel payments or be reimbursed if there's a problem), note that some credit-card companies and the banks that issue them add substantial percentages to all foreign transactions, whether they're in a foreign currency or not.

Credit cards are accepted at the pricier hotels, restaurants, and souvenir shops. In all but the top hotels, however, the vendor occasionally has problems obtaining authorization or forms, so it's prudent to have an alternative form of payment available at all times.

CURRENCY AND EXCHANGE

The national currency is the dirham (DH), which is divided into 100 centimes. There are bills for 20, 50, 100, and 200 DH, and coins for 1, 5, and 10 DH and 5, 10, and 20 centimes. You might hear some people refer to centimes as francs; others count money in rials, which are equivalent to 5 centimes each. A million is a million centimes, or 10,000 DH.

The exchange rate for the U.S. dollar is the same at all banks, including those at the airport; wait until you get to Morocco to get your dirhams as they are not widely available anywhere else. You can change dirhams back into U.S. dollars or euros at the airport upon departure, as long as you've kept the exchange receipts from your time of entry. The limit for this transaction is 50% of what you converted over the duration of your stay.

Currency Conversion **Google** 🌐 *www.google.com.* **XE.com** 🌐 *www.xe.com.*

PACKING

The average temperature in Morocco is 63°F (17°C), with minimums around 45°F (7°C) in winter to above 80°F (27°C) in summer (and significantly hotter in the desert). Unless you visit in the sweltering heat of August or the biting cold snap in January, you will most likely need to pack for a range of temperatures. It's especially important not to underestimate how incredibly cold it gets in the mountains, where indoor heating is scarce. If you expect to hike and camp, pack all your gear, including a zero-degree sleeping bag.

Crucial items to bring to Morocco include sunscreen, walking shoes, and for women a large shawl or scarf (that can be wrapped around your head or arms for respect or your shoulders for warmth), a French and/or Moroccan Arabic phrase book (in the countryside many people will not speak French).

Don't expect to find soap, washcloths, or towels in budget hotels. And do not expect toilet paper in most bathrooms; it's smart to pack your own, including tissues, hand sanitizer, and pocket-sized baby wipes for convenient hygiene. Tampons are rarely found in Morocco, so it is best to pack those, too.

Casual clothes are fine in Morocco; there's no need to bring formal apparel. Everywhere but the beach, however, you'll need to wear trousers or long skirts rather than shorts; tank tops, short skirts, and midriff-baring shirts should not be worn.

PASSPORTS

U.S. citizens with a valid passport can enter Morocco and stay up to 90 days without a visa.

RESTROOMS

It's customary to tip the attendant in a public toilet 1 or 2 DH. And be warned that many public toilets are Turkish-style squatters. It's prudent to carry hand sanitizer, a small bar of soap, and a cotton bandana for drying your hands when traveling around the country. **TIP→ Always carry your own toilet paper or tissues—while easy to find in stores, only hotels are reliable to have well-maintained bathrooms.**

SAFETY

Morocco is a relatively safe destination. Violent crime is rare. People who pester you to hire them as guides in places like Marrakesh and Fez are a nuisance but not a threat to your safety. Pickpocketing, however, can be a problem. In souks, open markets, and other crowded areas, carry your backpacks and purses in front of you. Cell phones, cameras, and other portable electronics are big sellers on the black market and should be kept out of sight whenever possible. Keep an eye on your belongings at the crowded beaches, as it is not unheard of for a roving gangs to make off with your stuff while you are swimming.

Female travelers—and especially single female travelers—sometimes worry about the treatment they'll receive on the streets of Morocco. There really isn't anything to worry about; you'll most likely be leered at, spoken to, and maybe even sometimes followed for about a block. Women walking alone are targeted by vendors hoping to make a sale. This attention, however, while irritating, isn't threatening. Don't take it personally; Moroccan women endure it, as well. The best way to handle it is to walk purposefully, avoid eye contact, and completely ignore men pestering you. If they don't let up, a firm reprimand with the Arabic "hashuma" (shame), or the French "laissez-moi tranquille" (leave me alone) should do the trick. If this still doesn't work, look for a local police officer or head into a restaurant or museum.

THE FODORS.COM CONNECTION

Before your trip, be sure to check out what other travelers are saying in Travel Talk forums at *www.fodors.com.*

Contacts **U.S. Consulate.** Check for travel alerts and other important current events direct from the U.S. Department of State. ✉ *2, Av. de Mohamed El Fassi, Rabat* ☎ *0537/76–22–65 Rabat, 0537/76–96–39 Rabat (after hours), 0522/26–45–50 Casablanca* *morocco.usembassy.gov* *Mon.–Fri., 8–5.* **U.S. Department of State** ☎ *888/407–4747 from within the U.S., 202/501–4444 from outside the U.S.* *www.travel.state.gov.* **U.S. Transportation Security Administration** *(TSA).* ☎ *866/289–9673* *www.tsa.gov.*

TAXES

City, local, government, and tourism taxes range between 10 DH and 40 DH at all lodgings. There are no airport taxes above those originally levied on the ticket price. The VAT (called TVA in Morocco) is generally 20%. It is not refundable.

TIME

Morocco observes Greenwich Mean Time year-round (five hours ahead of Eastern Standard Time), so most of the year it's on the same clock as the United Kingdom: five hours ahead of New York and one hour behind Continental Europe. During daylight saving time, Morocco is four hours ahead of New York, and two hours behind Continental Europe.

TIPPING

Tipping is done in Morocco but not as commonly as in the United States. There are no hard-and-fast rules concerning how much and when you do it. Waiters in proper restaurants are always tipped up to 10% of the bill. In taxis, round up to the nearest 5 DH (for example, if the meter says 12 DH, pay 15 DH). At informal cafés the tip is normally 1 DH or 2 DH per person in the dining party. Porters, hotel or otherwise, will appreciate 5 DH or 10 DH. It's customary to give small tips of 1 DH or 2 DH to people such as parking and restroom attendants. When in doubt, you can't go wrong by tipping.

VISITOR INFORMATION

The Moroccan National Tourist Office maintains a site in eight languages, including English.

Contacts **Moroccan National Tourist Office** ✉ *Angle Rue Oued Al Makhazine/Rue Zalaga-BP, Agdal, Rabat* ☎ *0537/67–40–13 in Morocco, 0537/67–39–18 in Morocco, 212/221–1583 in New York* ✉ *info@mnto-usa.org* 🌐 *www.visitmorocco.com.*

INDEX

D

E

PHOTO CREDITS

1, Simon Russell. 3, Lorna Piche/iStockphoto. Chapter 1: Experience Morocco:. 6-7, Simon Russell. 8, Ingenui/iStockphoto. 9 (left), mr.brightside/Shutterstock. 9 (right), Boris Stroujko/Shutterstock. 10, alex saberi/Shutterstock. 11, Alistair Laming / age fotostock. 12 (left), Tomkeene/Wikimedia Commons. 12 (top center), Peky/Shutterstock. 12 (bottom right), Carles Fortuny/Shutterstock. 12 (top right), nikolpetr/Shutterstock. 13 (top left), Rechitan Sorin/Shutterstock. 13 (bottom left), Boris Stroujko/Shutterstock. 13 (top center), Giorgio Fochesato/iStockphoto. 13 (right), posztos (colorlab. hu)/Shutterstock. 14, Jordi Ramisa/iStockphoto. 15 (left), Rechitan Sorin/Shutterstock. 15 (right), La Mamounia. 16, Holger Mette/iStockphoto. 17 (left), Cs˘rf˘ly D/Wikimedia Commons. 17 (right), Rechitan Sorin/Shutterstock. 18, bond girl/Shutterstock. 19 (left), Anne-Mette Jensenhttp://www.flickr.com/photos/annimetti/5085988953/ Attribution-ShareAlike License. 19 (right), Kishnel/Shutterstock. 20, bezikus/Shutterstock. 21 (left), Mlenny Photography/iStockphoto. 21 (right) and 22, La Sultana Hotels. 23, R.V. Bulck/iStockphoto. 24, www.hiddentrails.com. 25 (left), ClubHotel Riu Tikida Dunas. 25 (right), ClubHotel Riu Tikida Dunas. 26, Dar Liouba. 27 (left), Riad Villa Blanche Agadir. 27 (right), Dar Liouba. 28, Tomasz Parys/Shutterstock. 29 (left), Tadej Zupancic/iStockphoto. 29 (right), dp Photography/Shutterstock. 36, Terrance Klassen / age fotostock. 37 (top), JD Dallet / age fotostock. 37 (bottom), Vladimir Melnik/iStockphoto. 38 (left), Ray Hems/iStockphoto. 38 (top right), Attila JANDI/Shutterstock. 38 (bottom right), Uploadalt/Wikimedia Commons. 39 (top left), WitR/Shutterstock. 39 (bottom left), Graham Lawrence / age fotostock. 39 (right), John Copland/Shutterstock. 40 (left), Philippe Michel / age fotostock. 40 (top right), Jerzy Strzelecki/Wikimedia Commons. 40 (bottom right), Anthon Jackson/Shutterstock. 41 (left), Public domain. 41 (top right), Courtyard and Gardens of the Batha Museum by Henry Zbyszynski http://www.flickr.com/photos/hankzby/4317469580/ Attribution License. 41 (bottom right), Holger Mette/iStockphoto. 42 (left), Wendy Connett / age fotostock. 42 (right), Jaroslaw Grudzinski/Shutterstock. 43 (left), Juan Monino/iStockphoto. 43 (right), OPIS/Shutterstock. Chapter 2: Tangier and the Mediterranean:. 45, Alvaro Leiva / age fotostock. 46 (top), Rechitan Sorin/Shutterstock. 46 (bottom), Dans/Wikimedia Commons. 47 (top), Chefchaouen by Jean-François Gornet http://www.flickr.com/photos/ jfgornet/3250649760/ Attribution-ShareAlike License. 47 (bottom), amorrosta/Shutterstock. 48, Koutoubia Mosque by Doug Knuth http://www.flickr.com/photos/94535251@N00/859433565/ Attribution-ShareAlike License. 49 (top), Siham Benchekroun. 49 (bottom), Tahar Ben Jelloun wins Argana poetry award by http://www.flickr.com/photos/magharebia/5276923421/ Attribution License. 50, Holger Mette/iStockphoto. 57, Simon Russell. 58, Peter Erik Forsberg / age fotostock. 62, Gonzalo Azumendi / age fotostock. 67, Aguaviva/Shutterstock. 75 and 82, Alvaro Leiva / age fotostock. Chapter 3: The Northern Atlantic Coast:. 85, Ian Cumming / age fotostock. 86, Boris Stroujko/Shutterstock. 87 (left), Attila JANDI/Shutterstock. 87 (right), OPIS/Shutterstock. 88, Ray Hems/iStockphoto. 89 (top), AISPIX/Shutterstock. 89 (bottom), Basilica--Storks and Schoolchildren, Volubilis, Morocco by Chris Martin http://www.flickr.com/photos/chrismartin76/2379053582/ Attribution-ShareAlike License. 90, Witold Ryka/iStockphoto. 95, Graham Lawrence / age fotostock. 102, JD Dallet/age fotostock. 113, Javier Gil / age fotostock. 118, Graham Lawrence / age fotostock. 125, Vladimir Melnik/Shutterstock. Chapter 4: Fez and the Middle Atlas:. 129, Javier Larrea / age fotostock. 130, Thomas Saupe/iStockphoto. 131 (top left), Cindy Hughes/Shutterstock. 131 (top right), Frank van den Bergh/iStockphoto. 131 (bottom), Jordi Ramisa/iStockphoto. 132, Dallas Events Inc/Shutterstock. 141, Javier Larrea / age fotostock. 142, Mlenny Photography/iStockphoto. 149, Simon Russell. 152 (top), Lorna Piche/iStockphoto. 152 (bottom), Rechitan Sorin/Shutterstock. 153 (top), Gautier Willaume/Shutterstock. 153 (center), Walter Bibikow/age fotostock. 153 (bottom), chiakto/Shutterstock. 154 (left), stefano pensotti/age fotostock. 154 (top right), ventdusud/Shutterstock. 154 (bottom right), Philip Lange/Shutterstock. 155 (top left), David Ooms http://www.flickr.com/photos/davidooms/4251850025/ Attribution License. 155 (bottom left), David Romero Corral/iStockphoto. 155 (top right), Tom Fakler/iStockphoto. 155 (bottom right), Luisa Puccini/Shutterstock. 156 (top), Juan Carlos Muñoz / age fotostock. 156 (center), Philip Lange/Shutterstock. 156 (bottom), chiakto/Shutterstock. 157, Walter Bibikow / age fotostock. 158 (top), Jon Purcell / age fotostock. 158 (bottom), robert van beets/iStockphoto. 159 (top), Philip Lange / Shutterstock.com. 159 (bottom), narvikk/iStockphoto. 165, Bjanka Kadic / age fotostock. 168, JD Dallet/age fotostock. 173, Christophe Boisvieux / age fotostock. 176, Ray Hems/iStockphoto. 183, Peky/Shutterstock. Chapter 5: Marrakesh:. 187, BILDGENTUR-ONLINE / age fotostock. 188 (top), Giuseppe Masci/iStockphoto. 188 (bottom), La Mamounia. 189 (top left), Koutoubia Mosque by Adam Axon http://www.flickr.com/photos/ statto7/4282402445/ Attribution License. 189 (top right), Oleg Seleznev/iStockphoto. 189 (bottom), Karen Pritchett/iStockphoto. 190, Boris Buschardt/iStockphoto. 197, Peky/Shutterstock. 198, Mashaku/Shutterstock. 203, PetePhippTravelshots / age fotostock. 207, Yadid Levy / Alamy. 210, Ugurhan Betin/iStockphoto. 216,

La Mamounia. 219, Simon Russell. 230, jean-pierre lescourre / age fotostock. 239, RABOUAN Jean-Baptiste/age fotostock. 240, HUGHES Hervé/age fotostock. 241, Alvaro Leiva/age fotostock. 242 (left), Alan Keohane /www. kasbahdutoubkal.com. 242 (right), Philip Lange/Shutterstock. Chapter 6: The High Atlas: 245, Kay Maeritz / age fotostock. 246, Martin Maun/Shutterstock. 247 (top), towards Mecca by Rosino http://www.flickr.com/photos/ rosino/3463040837/ Attribution-ShareAlike License. 247 (bottom left), Kasbah in Telouet by Jon Blathwayt http://www.flickr.com/photos/ jonblathwayt/2491072721/ Attribution License. 247 (bottom right), Alan Keohane/www. kasbahdutoubkal.com. 248, Ronald Naar / age fotostock. 249 (top), Alan Keohane/www.kasbahdutoubkal.com. 249 (bottom), DAVID HOLT http://www.flickr.com/photos/zongo/2449822085/ Attribution-ShareAlike License. 250, Alan Keohane/www.kasbahdutoubkal.com. 253, Simon Russell. 255, SUETONE Emilio / age fotostock. 258, PATRICK FORGET/age fotostock. 261, Alan Keohane/www.kasbahdutoubkal.com. 263, Christian Kober / age fotostock. 270, Agostinho Gonçalves/Shutterstock. Chapter 7: The Great Oasis Valleys:. 275, Simon Russell. 276 (top), apdesign/Shutterstock. 276 (bottom), Vladimir Wrangel/Shutterstock. 277 (left), Oleg Seleznev/iStockphoto. 277 (right), Waypoint Tours/www.waypoint-tours.com. 278, Sander Huiberts/iStockphoto. 280, FRILET Patrick / age fotostock. 285, Heeb Christian / age fotostock. 290, FRILET Patrick / age fotostock. 294-95, Postl / age fotostock. 294 (bottom), Walter G Allgöwer / age fotostock. 296, Simon Russell. 297, Styve Reineck/Shutterstock. 298, Philippe Michel / age fotostock. 299 (top), Simon Russell. 299 (bottom left), Erg Chebbi camel trip by Urville Djasim http://www.flickr.com/photos/urville_djasim/5888505097/ Attribution-ShareAlike License. 299 (bottom right), Stefan Auth / age fotostock. 300, www.hiddentrails.com. 301, Rechitan Sorin/Shutterstock. 302, Ingenui/iStockphoto. 309, Carles Fortuny/Shutterstock. 315, Simon Russell. Chapter 8: The Southern Atlantic Coast:. 321, Egmont Strigl / age fotostock. 322, Manuel Cacciatori http://www.flickr.com/photos/ manueluna/2971502670/ Attribution License. 323 (top left), Rechitan Sorin/Shutterstock. 323 (top right), Styve Reineck/Shutterstock. 323 (bottom), Theodoros Stamatiadis/iStockphoto. 324, Nico Tondini / age fotostock. 325 (top), Kokopelado/Wikimedia Commons. 325 (bottom), Wikimedia Commons. 326, AlexandrDmitri/Wikimedia Commons. 331, Philippe Michel / age fotostock. 336, Egmont Strigl /age fotostock. 339, Heure Bleue Palais. 342-43, Egmont Strigl / age fotostock. 346, Explora Essaouira. 351, Grant Rooney / age fotostock. 354, ClubHotel Riu Tikida Dunas. 361, Witold Ryka/iStockphoto. 367, Peter Adams / age fotostock.

ABOUT OUR WRITERS

Rachel Blech is a music broadcaster for RTÉ (Ireland's national radio and television network) with a weekly show called *The Magic Carpet*. Her love of world music first took her to Morocco in 2006 to make a documentary of the Gnaoua Music Festival in Essaouira. Since then she has spent much time traveling in the desert and the Draâ and Souss valley regions reporting for Irish radio, writing articles, and developing community-based desert-tourism projects. She has made programs for BBC Radio and RTÉ and has written for *Songlines* magazine, *TravelSpeak*, *easyJet Inflight* magazine, and other publications. Rachel lives part of the year in Morocco running her travel company, SheherazadVentures, and one day hopes to write a novel set in the Sahara.

Patricia Gorman is a native New Yorker and public policy lawyer. Having traded the hustle and bustle of New York life for the sand and waves on the other side of the Atlantic, she currently lives in a small town on the Atlantic coast just south of Casablanca. No longer practicing law, she now divides her time between writing, teaching, and parenting her three young children.

Tangier and the Mediterranean updater, **Simona Schneider** is a teacher, freelance writer, and artist who has lived in Tangier since 2005. She originally went to Morocco to help found the Cinémathèque de Tanger, a nonprofit cinema in downtown Tangier. She has written travel articles for *Condé Nast Traveler* and the *Sun-Sentinel* and writes the monthly destination guide to Tangier for *easyJet Inflight* magazine. Her writing, translations, and photographs have been published in numerous publications in the United States and in Europe.

Although photographer and writer **Victoria Tang** currently calls Paris home, she has lived and traveled internationally since childhood. She's the author of two guidebooks translated into Dutch, Spanish, and Estonian and has written for numerous publications. Her visits to Morocco throughout the years have left an indelible impression that fuels a love affair with the country, its culture, history, and cuisine. With a passion for authenticity, extensive multicultural experience, and a knowledge of French, German, and basic Arabic, Victoria updated the Fez and the Middle Atlas and Travel Smart chapters.

Ian Thomas is a journalist of many years' experience who has worked for, among others, the BBC, Sky TV, and the Associated Press. He has a passion for photography, having worked for London's prestigious National Portrait Gallery, and is a lover of fine food (he owned a deli in London's East End for 10 years). Having escaped the British weather, he now lives with his wife and children in Casablanca, where he continues to work as a writer and photographer.